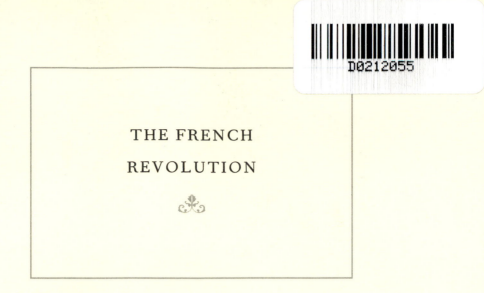

THE FRENCH

REVOLUTION

THE FRENCH

REVOLUTION
(1878 - 1884)

Hippolyte Taine
(1828 - 1893)

Translated by
John Durand

Volume III

Liberty Fund
Indianapolis

This book is published by Liberty Fund, Inc., a foundation established
to encourage study of the ideal of a society of free
and responsible individuals.

𒀀𒈪

The cuneiform inscription that serves as our logo and as the design motif
for our endpapers is the earliest-known written appearance of the word "freedom"
(*amagi*), or "liberty." It is taken from a clay document written about 2300 B.C.
in the Sumerian city-state of Lagash.

The French Revolution is a translation of *La Révolution,* which is the second part of
Taine's *Origines de la France contemporaine.*

Printed in the United States of America
02 03 04 05 06 C 5 4 3 2 1
02 03 04 05 06 P 5 4 3 2 1

Library of Congress Cataloging-in-Publication Data

Taine, Hippolyte, 1828–1893.
[Origines de la France contemporaine. English. Selections]
The French Revolution / Hippolyte Taine; translated by John Durand.
p.   cm.
"The French Revolution is a translation of La Révolution, which is
the second part of Taine's Origines de la France contemporaine"—T.p. verso.
Includes bibliographical references and index.
ISBN 0-86597-126-9 (alk. paper)   ISBN 0-86597-127-7 (pbk. : alk. paper)
1. France—History—Revolution, 1789–1799.   I. Title.

DC148.T35 2002
944.04—dc21   2002016023

ISBN 0-86597-126-9 (set: hc.)   ISBN 0-86597-127-7 (set: pb.)
ISBN 0-86597-363-6 (v. 1: hc.)   ISBN 0-86597-366-0 (v. 1: pb.)
ISBN 0-86597-364-4 (v. 2: hc.)   ISBN 0-86597-367-9 (v. 2: pb.)
ISBN 0-86597-365-2 (v. 3: hc.)   ISBN 0-86597-368-7 (v. 3: pb.)

Liberty Fund, Inc.
8335 Allison Pointe Trail, Suite 300
Indianapolis, Indiana 46250-1684

CONTENTS

I. Weakness of Former Governments—Energy of the new government—
The despotic creed and instincts of the Jacobin— II. Contrast between his
words and his acts—How he dissimulates his change of front—The Constitution of June, 1793—Its promises of freedom— III. Primary Assemblies—Proportion of Absentees—Number of Primary Assemblies—Unanimity of the voters—Their motives for accepting the Constitution—
Pressure brought to bear on voters—Choice of Delegates— IV. They
reach Paris—Precautions taken against them—Constraints and Seductions— V. They make their profession of Jacobin faith—Their part in the
Fête of August 10th—Their enthusiasm— VI. Manoeuvres of the "Mountain"—The Jacobin Club on the eve of August 11th—Session of the Convention on the 11th of August—The Delegates initiate Terror—Popular
consecration of the Jacobin dictatorship— VII. Effect of this manoeuvre—
Extent and Manifesto of the departmental insurrection—Its fundamental
weakness—The mass of the population inert and distrustful—The small
number of Girondists—Their lukewarm adherents—Scruples of fugitive
deputies and insurgent administrators—They form no central government—They leave military authority in the hands of the Convention—
Fatal progress of their concessions —Withdrawal of the departments one
by one—Palinode of the compromised authorities—Effect of administrative habits—Failings and illusions of the Moderates—Opposite character
of the Jacobins— VIII. The last local resistances—Political orthodoxy of
the insurgent towns—They stipulate but one condition—Reasons of State
for granting this—Party arguments against it— IX. The rebel cities

BOOK SIXTH. *The Jacobin Programme*

Chapter I / 901

cal, professional and family spirit— VIII. Formation of soul and intellect—
Civil religion—National education—Measures for equality—Obligatory
civism—The recasting and reduction of human nature to the Jacobin type.

Chapter II / 946

I. Retrograde conception of the State—Analogy between this idea of the
State and that of antiquity—Difference between antique and modern society—Difference in circumstances— II. Difference between men's
souls—Conscience and its Christian origin—Honor and its feudal origin—
The individual of today refuses to surrender himself entirely—His motives—Additional motives in modern democracy—Character of the elective process and nature of the mandatory— III. Origin and nature of the
modern State—Its functions, rights and limits— IV. Temptation to encroachments—Precedents and reasons for its pretensions— V. Direct common interest—This consists in the absence of constraint—Two reasons in
favor of freedom of action—Character, in general, of the individual man—
Modern complications— VI. Indirect common interest—This consists in
the most economical and most productive employment of spontaneous
forces—Difference between voluntary labor and forced labor—Sources of
man's spontaneous action—Conditions of their energy, work and products—Motives for leaving them under personal control—Extent of the
private domain—Individuals voluntarily extend it—What they leave to
the State—Obligatory functions of the State—Optional functions of the
State— VII. Fabrication of social instrumentalities—Application of this
principle—How all kinds of useful laborers are formed—Respect for spontaneous sources, the essential and adequate condition—Obligation of the
State to respect these—They dry up when it monopolises them—The aim
of Patriotism—The aim of other liberal dispositions—Impoverishment of
all the productive faculties—Destructive effect of the Jacobin system—
VIII. Comparison between despotisms—Philip II. and Louis XIV.—
Cromwell and Frederic the Great—Peter the Great and the Sultans—
Proportions of the weight they sustain and the forces they control—Disproportion between the Jacobins' attempt to raise this weight and their
forces—Folly of their undertaking—Physical force the only governmental
force they possess—They are compelled to exercise it—They are compelled to abuse it—Character of their government—Character requisite in
their leaders.

in Alsace—Collot d'Herbois at Lyons—Pressure exercised by the Representatives on the tribunals—Pleasure caused by death and suffering—Monestier, Fouché, Collot d'Herbois, Lebon and Carrier.

Chapter III / 1097

The Rulers (*continued*)— The administrative body at Paris—Composition of the group out of which it was recruited—Deterioration of this group—Weeding-out of the Section Assemblies—Weeding-out of the popular clubs—Pressure of the government— II. Quality of the subaltern leaders—How they rule in the section assemblies—How they seize and hold office— III. A Minister of Foreign Affairs—A General in command—The Paris Commune—A Revolutionary Committee— IV. The administrative staff in the provinces—Jacobinism less in the departmental towns than in Paris—Less in the country than in the towns—The Revolutionary Committees in the small communes—Municipal bodies lukewarm in the villages—Jacobins too numerous in bourgs and small towns—Unreliable or hampered as agents when belonging to the administrative bodies of large or moderately-sized towns—Local rulers recruited on the spot inadequate— V. Importation of a foreign staff—Paris Jacobins sent into the provinces—Jacobins of enthusiastic towns transported to moderate ones—The Jacobins of a *chef-lieu* spread through the district—Resistance of public opinion—Distribution and small number of really Jacobin agents— VI. Quality of the staff thus formed—Social state of the agents—Their unfitness and bad conduct—The administrators in Seine-et-Marne—Drunkenness and feastings—Committees and Municipalities in the Côte d'Or—Waste and extortions—Traffickers in favors at Bordeaux—Seal-breakers at Lyons—Monopolisers of national possessions—Sales of personal property—Embezzlements and Frauds—A *procès-verbal* in the office of the mayor of Strasbourg—Sales of real estate—Commissioners on declarations at Toulouse—The administrative staff and clubs of buyers at Provence—The Revolutionary Committee of Nantes— VII. The Armed Force—National Guard and Gendarmerie—Its composition and operations—The Revolutionary armies in Paris and in the departments—Quality of the recruits—Their employment—Their expeditions into the country towns—Their exploits in the vicinity of Paris and Lyons—The company of Maratists, the American Hussars and the German Legion at Nantes—General character of the revolutionary government and of the administrative staff of the Reign of Terror.

Book Eighth. *The Governed*

taxes, suppression of special organs of labor on a large scale—Fresh measures against small proprietorship—The *Maximum,* requisitions for food and labor—Situation of the shopkeeper, cultivator and laborer—Effect of the measures on labor on a small scale—Stoppage of selling— IV. Famine—In the provinces—At Paris—People standing in lines under the revolutionary government to obtain food—Its quality—Distress and chagrin— V. Revolutionary remedies—Rigor against the refractory—Decrees and orders rendering the State the only depositary and distributor of food—Efforts made to establish a conscription of labor—Discouragement of the Peasant—He refuses to cultivate—Decrees and orders compelling him to harvest—His stubbornness—Cultivators imprisoned by thousands—The Convention is obliged to set them at liberty—Fortunate circumstances which save France from extreme famine— VI. Relaxation of the revolutionary system after Thermidor—Repeal of the *Maximum*— New situation of the peasant—He begins cultivation again—Requisition of grain by the State—The cultivator indemnifies himself at the expense of private persons—Multiplication and increasing decline of *Assignats*— The classes who have to bear the burden—Famine and misery during year III. and the first half of year IV.—In the country—In the small towns— In large towns and cities— VII. Famine and misery at Paris—Steps taken by the government to feed the capital—Monthly cost to the Treasury— Cold and hunger in the winter of 1794–1795—Quality of the bread—Daily rations diminished—Suffering, especially of the populace—Excessive physical suffering, despair, suicides and deaths from exhaustion in 1795— Government dinners and suppers—Number of lives lost through want and war—Socialism as applied, and its effects on comforts, well-being and mortality.

démiaire— III. The Directory chosen among the regicides—It selects agents of its own species—Leading Jacobins are deprived of their civic rights—The Terrorists are set free and restored to their civic rights—Example at Blois of these releases and of the new administrative staff—IV. Resistance of public opinion—Elections, year IV., at Paris and in the provinces—The Directory threatened by ultra Jacobins—Forced amelioration of the Jacobin administration— V. Elections of year V.—Character and sentiments of the elected—The new majority in the Corps Législatif—Its principles and programme—Danger and anxiety of the Jacobin minority—Indecision, division, scruples and weakness of the moderate party—Decision, want of scruples, force and mode of procedure of the Jacobin faction—The 18th of Fructidor— VI. Dictatorship of the Directory—Its new prerogatives—Purgation of the Corps Législatif—Purification of the administrative and judicial authorities—Military commissions in the provinces—Suppression of newspapers—The right of voting reserved to Jacobins alone—Despotism of the Directory—Revival of Terror—Transportation substituted for the guillotine—Treatment of the transported—Restoration of Jacobin feudalism— VII. Application and aggravation of the laws of the reign of Terror—Measures taken to impose civic religion—Arrest, transportation and execution of Priests—Ostracism proposed against the entire anti-Jacobin class—The nobles, or the ennobled, not *émigrés,* are declared foreigners—Decrees against *émigrés* of every class—Other steps taken against remaining proprietors—Bankruptcy, forced loan, hostages— VIII. Propagandism and foreign conquests—Proximity and advantages of peace—Fructidoreans' motives for breaking off peace negotiations and abandoning foreign invasions—How they found new republics—How governed—Estimate of foreign rapine—Number of French lives sacrificed— IX. National antipathy to the established order of things—Paralysis of the State—Intestinal discords of the Jacobin—*Coup de état* of Floréal 22, year VI.—*Coup de état* of Prairial 30, year VII.—Impossibility of establishing a practicable government—Plans of Barras and Sièyes— X. Antisocial character of the sect and the faction—Contrast between civil and military France—Elements of reorganisation—Character of the régime instituted on the 18th of Brumaire, year VIII.

"Iɴ Eɢʏᴘᴛ," says Clement of Alexandria, "the sanctuaries of the temples are shaded by curtains of golden tissue. But on going further into the interior in quest of the statue, a priest of grave aspect, advancing to meet you and chanting a hymn in the Egyptian tongue, slightly raises a veil to show you the god. And what do you behold? A crocodile, or some indigenous serpent, or other dangerous animal, the Egyptian god being a brute rolling about on a purple carpet."

We need not visit Egypt or go so far back in history to encounter crocodile worship, as this can be readily found in France at the end of the last century. Unfortunately, a hundred years is too long an interval, too far away, for an imaginative retrospect of the past. At the present time, standing where we do and regarding the horizon behind us, we see only forms which the intervening atmosphere embellishes, shimmering contours which each spectator may interpret in his own fashion; no distinct, animated figure, but merely a mass of moving points, forming and dissolving in the midst of picturesque architecture. I was anxious to have a nearer view of these vague points, and, accordingly, transported myself back to the last half of the eighteenth century, where I have been living with them for twelve years, and, like Clement of Alexandria, examining, first, the temple, and next the god. A passing glance at these is not sufficient; a step further must be taken to comprehend the theology on which this cult is founded. This one, explained by a very specious theology, like most others, is composed of dogmas called the principles of 1789; they were proclaimed, indeed, at that date, having been previously formulated by Jean-Jacques Rousseau, the well-known sovereignty of the people, the rights of man, and the social contract. Once adopted, their practical results unfolded themselves naturally; in three years, the crocodile brought by these dogmas into the sanctuary installed himself there on the purple carpet behind the golden veil; in effect, he was intended for the place on account of the energy of his jaws and the capacity of his stomach; he became a god through his qualities as a destructive brute and man-eater. Comprehending this, the rites which consecrate him and the pomp which surrounds him need not give us any further concern. We can observe him, like any ordinary animal, and study his various attitudes, as he lies in wait for his prey, springs upon it, tears it to pieces, swallows it, and digests it. I have studied the details of his structure, the play of his organs, his habits, his mode of living, his instincts, his faculties, and his appetites. Specimens abounded. I have handled thousands of them, and have dissected hundreds of every species and variety, always preserving the most valuable and characteristic examples, but for lack of room I have been compelled to let many of them go because my collection was too large. Those that I was able to bring back with me will be found here, and, among others, about twenty individuals of different dimensions, which—a difficult undertaking—I have kept alive with great pains. At all events, they are intact and perfect, and particularly the three largest. These seem to me, of their kind, truly remarkable, and those in which the divinity of the day might well incarnate himself. The bills of butchers, as well as housekeeping accounts, authentic and regularly kept, throw sufficient light on the cost of this cult. We can estimate about how much the sacred crocodiles consumed in ten years; we know their bills of fare daily, their favorite morsels. Naturally, the god selected the fattest victims, but his voracity was so great that he likewise bolted down, and blindly, the lean ones, and in much greater number than the fattest. Moreover, by virtue of his instincts, and an unfailing effect of the situation, he ate his equals once or twice a year, except when they succeeded in eating him. This cult certainly is instructive, at least to historians and men of pure science. If any believers in it still remain I do not aim to convert them; one cannot argue with a devotee on matters of faith. This volume, accordingly, like the others that have gone before it, is written solely for amateurs of moral zoology, for naturalists of the understanding, for seekers of truth, of texts, and of proofs—for these alone and not for the public, whose mind is made up and which has its own opinion on the Revolution. This opinion began to be formed between 1825 and 1830, after the retirement or withdrawal of eye witnesses. When they disappeared it was easy to convince a credulous public that crocodiles were philanthropists; that many possessed genius; that they scarcely ate others than the guilty, and that if they sometimes ate too many it was unconsciously and in spite of themselves, or through devotion and self-sacrifice for the common good.

Menthon Saint Bernard,
July, 1884.

BOOK FIFTH

❧

Establishment of the
Revolutionary Government

CHAPTER I

I. *Weakness of former governments—Energy of the new government—The despotic creed and instincts of the Jacobin—* II. *Contrast between his words and his acts—How he dissimulates his change of front—The Constitution of June, 1793—Its promises of Freedom—* III. *Primary Assemblies—Proportion of Absentees—Number of Primary Assemblies—Unanimity of the voters—Their motives for accepting the Constitution—Pressure brought to bear on voters—Choice of Delegates—* IV. *They reach Paris—Precautions taken against them—Constraints and Seductions—* V. *They make their profession of Jacobin faith—Their part in the Fête of August 10th—Their enthusiasm—* VI. *Manoeuvres of the "Mountain"—The Jacobin Club on the eve of August 11th—Session of the Convention on the 11th of August—The Delegates initiate Terror—Popular consecration of the Jacobin dictatorship—* VII. *Effect of this manoeuvre—Extent and Manifesto of the departmental insurrection—Its fundamental weakness—The mass of the population inert and distrustful—The small number of Girondists—Their lukewarm adherents—Scruples of fugitive deputies and insurgent administrators—They form no central government—They leave military authority in the hands of the Convention—Fatal progress of their concessions—Withdrawal of the departments one by one—Palinode of the compromised authorities—Effect of administrative habits—Failings and illusions of the Moderates—Opposite character of the Jacobins—* VIII. *The last local resistances—Political orthodoxy of the insurgent towns—They stipulate but one condition—Reasons of State for granting this—Party arguments against it—* IX. *The rebel cities crushed—Bordeaux—Marseilles—Lyons—Toulon—* X. *Destruction of the Girondist party—Proscription of the Deputies of the "Right"—Imprisonment of the 73—Execution of the 21—Execution, suicide, or flight of the rest—* XI. *Institutions of the Revolutionary Government—Its principle, object, proceedings, tools, and structure—The Committee of Public Safety—Subordination of the Convention*

841

and ministry—The use of the Committee of General Security and the Revolu-
tionary Tribunal—Administrative centralization—Representatives on Mission,
National Agents and Revolutionary Committees.—Law of Lèse-majesty—Res-
toration and Aggravation of the institutions of the old monarchy.

I

SO FAR, the weakness of the legal government is extreme. For four
years, whatever its kind, everywhere and constantly, it has been
disobeyed; for four years, whatever its kind, it has never dared
enforce obedience. Recruited among the cultivated and refined class,
the rulers of the country have brought with them into power the
prejudices and sensibilities of the epoch; under the empire of the
prevailing dogma they have deferred to the will of the multitude
and, with too much faith in the rights of man, they have had too
little in the rights of the magistrate; moreover, through humanity,
they have abhorred bloodshed and, unwilling to repress, they have
allowed themselves to be repressed. Thus, from the 1st of May, 1789,
to June 2, 1793, they have carried on the administration, or legislated, athwart innumerable insurrections, almost all of them going
unpunished; while their constitutions, so many unhealthy products
of theory and fear, have done no more than transform spontaneous
anarchy into legal anarchy. Wilfully and through distrust of authority they have undermined the principle of command, reduced
the King to the post of a decorative puppet, and almost annihilated
the central power: from the top to the bottom of the hierarchy the
superior has lost his hold on the inferior, the minister on the departments, the departments on the districts, and the districts on the
communes; throughout all branches of the service, the chief, elected
on the spot and by his subordinates, has come to depend on them.
Thenceforth, each post in which authority is vested is found isolated,
dismantled and preyed upon, while, to crown all, the Declaration
of Rights, proclaiming "the jurisdiction of constituents over their
clerks,"[1] has invited the assailants to make the assault. On the

---

1. The words of Marat.

strength of this a faction arises which ends in becoming an organized band: under its clamorings, its menaces and its pikes, at Paris and in the provinces, at the polls and in the parliament, the majorities are all silenced, while the minorities vote, decree and govern; the Legislative Assembly is purged, the King is dethroned, and the Convention is mutilated. Of all the garrisons of the central citadel, whether royalists, constitutionalists, or Girondists, not one has been able to defend itself, to refashion the executive instrument, to draw the sword and use it in the streets: on the first attack, often at the first summons, all have surrendered, and now the citadel, with every other public fortress, is in the hands of the Jacobins.

This time, its occupants are of a different stamp. Aside from the great mass of well-disposed people fond of a quiet life, the Revolution has sifted out and separated from the rest all who are fanatical, brutal or perverse enough to have lost respect for others; these form the new garrison—sectarians blinded by their creed, the roughs (*assommeurs*) who are hardened by their calling, and those who make all they can out of their offices. None of this class are scrupulous concerning human life or property; for, as we have seen, they have shaped the theory to suit themselves, and reduced popular sovereignty to their sovereignty. The commonwealth, according to the Jacobin, is his; with him, the commonwealth comprises all private possessions, bodies, estates, souls and consciences; everything belongs to him; the fact of being a Jacobin makes him legitimately czar and pope. Little does he care about the wills of actually living Frenchmen; his mandate does not emanate from a vote; it descends to him from aloft, conferred on him by Truth, by Reason, by Virtue. As he alone is enlightened, and the only patriot, he alone is worthy to take command, while resistance, according to his imperious pride, is criminal. If the majority protests it is because the majority is imbecile or corrupt; in either case, it merits a check, and a check it shall have. Accordingly, the Jacobin does nothing else from the outset; insurrections, usurpations, pillagings, murders, assaults on individuals, on magistrates, on assemblies, violations of law, attacks on the State, on communities—there is no outrage not committed by him. He has always acted as sovereign instinctively; he was so as a private individual and clubbist; he is not to cease being so, now that he possesses legal authority, and all the more because if he hesitates he knows he is lost; to save himself from the scaffold he has no refuge but in a dictatorship. Such a man, unlike his predecessors, will not allow himself to be turned out; on the contrary, he will exact obedience at any cost. He will not hesitate to restore the central power; he will put back the local wheels that have been detached; he will repair the old forcing-gear; he will set it agoing so as to work more rudely and arbitrarily than ever, with greater contempt for private rights and public liberties than either a Louis XIV. or a Napoleon.

II

In the mean time, he has to harmonize his coming acts with his recent declarations, which, at the first glance, seems a difficult operation: for, in the speeches he has made he has already condemned the actions he meditates. Yesterday he exaggerated the rights of the governed, even to a suppression of those of the governors; tomorrow he is to exaggerate the rights of governors, even to suppressing those of the governed. The people, as he puts it, is the sole sovereign, and he is going to treat the people as slaves; the government, as he puts it, is a valet, and he is going to endow the government with the prerogatives of a sultan. He has just denounced the slightest exercise of public authority as a crime; he is now going to punish as a crime the slightest resistance to public authority. What will justify such a summerset, and with what face can he repudiate the principles on which he has founded his own usurpation? He takes good care not to repudiate them; it would drive the already rebellious provinces to extremities; on the contrary, he proclaims them with renewed vigor, through which manoeuvre, the ignorant crowd, seeing the same flask always presented to it, imagines that it is always served with the same liquor, and is thus forced to drink tyranny under the label of freedom. Whatever the charlatan can do with his labels, signboards, shoutings and lies for the next six months, will be done to disguise the new nostrum; so much the worse for the public if, later on, it discovers that the draught is bitter; sooner or later it must swallow it, willingly or by compulsion: for, in the interval, the instruments are being got ready to force it down the public throat.[2]

As a beginning, the Constitution, so long anticipated and so often promised, is hastily fabricated:[3] declarations of rights in thirty-five articles, the Constitutional bill in one hundred and twenty-four articles, political principles and institutions of every sort, electoral, legislative, executive, administrative, judicial, financial and military;[4] in three weeks, all is drawn up and passed with race-horse speed. Of course, the new constitutionalists do not propose to produce an effective and serviceable instrument; that is the least of their anxieties. Hérault Séchelles, the reporter of the bill, writes on the 7th of June, "to have procured for him at once the laws of Minos, of which he has urgent need"; very urgent need, as he must hand in the Constitution that week.[5] Such a circumstance is sufficiently charac-

2. After the Constitution is completed, said Legendre, in the Jacobin club, we will make the federalists dance.

3. Archives Nationales, F. I. C., 56. (Circular of Gohier, Minister of Justice, to the French people, July 6, 1793). "Certain persons are disposed to pervert the events of May 31 and June 2, by atrocious exaggerations and the grossest fables, and prevent the fortunate results they present from being seen. They are absolutely determined to see nothing but violations of the liberty of the people's representatives in a *step* which was specially designed to hasten on the Constitutional Act on which the liberty of all is established. Of what consequence is it who are the authors of the Constitution presented to you? What does it matter whether it issues from a mountain amidst lightnings and the rolling thunder, like the Tables of the Law given to the Hebrews, or whether it comes, like the laws given to the early Romans, inspired in the tranquil asylum of a divinity jealous of his religious surroundings? Is this Constitution worthy of a free people? That is the only question which citizens who wear the livery of no party need examine!"

4. Buchez et Roux, xxviii., 177. (Report by Hérault Séchelles, June 10, 1793). *Ibid*, xxxi., 400. (Text of the Constitution submitted to discussion June 11th, and passed June 24th.)

5. De Sybel, II., 331. (According to the fac-simile published in the Quarterly Review). "Hérault says that he and four of his colleagues are ordered to furnish the draft of a constitution by Monday."

teristic of both the workmen and the work. All is mere show and pretence. Some of the workmen are shrewd politicians whose sole object is to furnish the public with words instead of things; others, ordinary scribblers of abstractions, or even ignoramuses, and unable to distinguish words from things, imagine that they are framing laws by stringing together a lot of phrases. It is not a difficult job; the phrases are ready-made to hand. "Let the plotters of antipopular systems," says the reporter, "painfully elaborate their projects! Frenchmen . . . have only to consult their hearts to read the Republic there!"[6] Drafted in accordance with the *Contrat-Social*, filled with Greek and Latin reminiscences, it is a summary "in lapidary style" of the manual of current aphorisms then in vogue. Rousseau's mathematical formulas and prescriptions, "the axioms of truth and the consequences flowing from these axioms," in short, a rectilinear constitution which any school-boy may spout on leaving college. Like a handbill posted on the door of a new shop, it promises to customers every imaginable article that is handsome and desirable. Would you have rights and liberties? You will find them all here. Never has the statement been so clearly made, that the government is the servant, creature and tool of the governed; it is instituted solely "to guarantee to them their natural, imprescriptible rights."[7] Never has its mandate been more strictly limited: "The right of expressing one's thoughts and opinions, either through the press or in any other way; the right of peaceably assembling, the free exercise of worship, cannot be interdicted." Never have citizens been more carefully guarded against the encroachments and excesses of public authority: "The law should protect public and private liberties against the oppression of those who govern . . . offences committed by the people's mandatories and agents must never go unpunished. Let free men instantly put to death every individual usurping sovereignty. . . . Every act against a man outside of the cases and forms which the

6. Report by Hérault Séchelles. (Buchez et Roux, xxviii., 178.)

7. Buchez et Roux, xxxi., 400. (Articles of the Declaration of Rights, 1, 7, 9, 11, 27, 31, 35.)

law determines is arbitrary and tyrannical; whoever is subjected to violence in the execution of this act has the right to repel it by force. ... When the government violates the people's rights insurrection is, for the people and for *each portion of the people,* the most sacred of rights and the most indispensable of duties."

To civil rights the generous legislator has added political rights, and multiplied every precaution for maintaining the dependence of rulers on the people. In the first place, rulers are appointed by the people and through a direct choice or nearly direct choice: in primary meetings the people elect deputies, city officers, justices of the peace, and electors of the second degree; the latter, in their turn, elect in the secondary meetings, district and department administrators, civil arbitrators, criminal judges, judges of appeal and the eighty candidates from amongst which the legislative body is to select its executive council. In the second place, all powers of whatever kind are never conferred except for a very limited term: one year for deputies, for electors of the second degree, for civil arbitrators, and for judges of every kind and class; as to municipalities and also department and district administrations, these are one-half renewable annually. Every first of May the fountain-head of authority flows afresh, the people in its primary assemblies, spontaneously formed, manifesting or changing at will its staff of clerks. In the third place, even when installed and at work, the people may, if it pleases, become their collaborator: means are provided for "deliberating" with its deputies. The latter, on incidental questions, those of slight importance, on the ordinary business of the year, may enact laws; but on matters of general, considerable and permanent interest, they are simply to propose the laws, while, especially as regards a declaration of war, the people alone must decide. The people have a suspensive veto and, finally, a definitive veto, which they may exercise when they please. To this end, they may assemble in extraordinary session; one-fifth of the citizens who have the right to vote suffice for their convocation. Once convoked, the vote is determined by a Yes or a No on the act proposed by the legislative body. If, at the expiration of forty days, one-tenth of the primary assemblies in one-half of the departments vote No, there is a sus-pensive veto. In that event all the primary assemblies of the Republic must be convoked and if the majority still decides in the negative, that is a definitive veto. The same formalities govern a revision of the established constitution. In all this, the plan of the *Montagnards* is a further advance on that of the Girondists; never was so insig-nificant a part assigned to governors nor so extensive a part to the governed. The Jacobins profess a respect for the popular initiative which amounts to a scruple.[8] According to them the sovereign peo-ple should be sovereign *de facto,* permanently, and without inter-regnum, allowed to interfere in all serious affairs, and not only possess the right, but the faculty, of imposing its will on its man-datories. All the stronger is the reason for referring to it the insti-tutions now being prepared for it. Hence, after the parade is over, the convocation by the Convention on the 24th of June, also the primary assemblies, and the submission to them of the ratification of the Constitutional bill which it has drawn up.

III

That the ratification will be given admits of no doubt. Everything has been combined beforehand to secure it, also to secure it as wanted, apparently spontaneously, and almost unanimously. The pri-mary assemblies, indeed, are by no means fully attended; only one-half, or a quarter, or a third of the electors in the cities deposit their votes, while in the rural districts there is only a quarter, and less;[9]

8. Buchez et Roux, xxviii., 178. Report by Hérault Séchelles. "Each of us had the same desire, that of attaining to the greatest democratic result. The sovereignty of the people and the dignity of man were constantly in our minds. . . . A secret sentiment tells us that our work is perhaps the most popular that ever existed."

9. Archives Nationales, B. II., 23. (Table of votes by the commission ap-pointed to collect the *procès-verbaux* of the adoption of the Constitution, August 20, 1793.) Number of primary assemblies sending in their *procès-verbaux,* 6,589 (516 cantons have not yet sent theirs in). Number of voters on call, 1,795,908; Yes, 1,784,377; Noes, 11,531. Number of primary assemblies voting Yes unani-mously, not on call of names, 297. At Paris 40,990 voters, at Troyes 2,491, at

repelled by their experience with previous convocations they know too well the nature of these assemblies; how the Jacobin faction rules them, how it manages the electoral comedy, with what violence and menaces it reduces all dissidents to voting either as *figurants* or *claqueurs.* From four to five millions of electors prefer to hold aloof and stay at home as usual. Nevertheless the organization of most of the assemblies takes place, amounting to some six or seven thousand. This is accounted for by the fact that each canton contains its small group of Jacobins. Next to these come the simple-minded who still believe in official declarations; in their eyes a constitution which guarantees private rights and institutes public liberties must be accepted, no matter what hand may present it to them. And all the more readily because the usurpers offer to resign; in effect, the Convention has just solemnly declared that once the Constitution is adopted, the people shall again be convoked to elect "a new national assembly . . . a new representative body invested with a later and more immediate trust,"[10] which will allow electors, if they are so disposed, to return honest deputies and exclude the knaves who now rule. Thereupon, even in the insurgent departments, the mass of the Girondist population, after a good deal of hesitation, resign themselves at last to voting for it.[11] This is done at Lyons and in the

---

Limoges, 2,137. Cf. for details and motives of abstention, Sauzay iv., pp. 157–161. Albert Babeau, ii., pp. 83 and 84. *Moniteur,* xvii., 375 (speech by the representative Des Wars).

10. *Ibid., Moniteur,* xvii., 20. (Report by Barrère on the convocation of the primary assemblies, June 27, 1793.) *Ibid.,* 102 (Report of Cambon, July 11). "It is now a fortnight since you demanded a Constitution. Very well, here it is. . . . Respect for persons and property is amply secured in it. Yes, more definitely than in any other constitution. Does it provide for its own revision? Yes, for in six weeks, we can convoke the primary assemblies and express our desire for the reform that may appear necessary. Will the popular wish be respected? Yes, the people then will make definitive laws."

11. Guillon de Montléon, i., 282, 309.—Buchez et Roux, xxviii., 356, 357. (Journal de Lyon Nos. 223 and 224.) "The acceptance of the Constitution was neither entire nor very sincere; people took credit to themselves for accepting a vicious and sketchy production." Meillan, "*Mémoires,*" 120. (In July he leaves Caen for Quimper). "Although we were assured that we should pass only

department of Calvados only on the 30th of July. A number of constitutionalists or neutrals have done the same thing, some through a horror of civil war and a spirit of conciliation, and others through fear of persecution and of being taxed with royalism;[12] one conception more: through docility they may perhaps succeed in depriving the "Mountain" of all pretext for violence.

In this they greatly deceive themselves, and, from the first, they are able to see once more how the Jacobins understand electoral liberty. At first, all the registered,[13] and especially the "suspects," are compelled to vote, and to vote Yes; otherwise, says a Jacobin journal,[14] "they themselves will give the just measure of the opinion one ought to entertain of their sentiments, and no longer have reason to complain of suspicions that are found to be so well grounded." They come accordingly, "very humble and very penitent." Nevertheless they meet with a rebuff, and a cold shoulder is turned on them; they are consigned to a corner of the room, or near the doors, and are openly insulted. Thus received, it is clear that they will keep quiet

---

through Maratist towns, we had the satisfaction of finding nearly all the inhabitants regarding Marat with horror. They had indeed accepted the Constitution offered by the Committee of Public Safety, but solely to end the matter and on conditions which would speak well for them; for, everywhere the renewal of the Convention was exacted and the punishment of assaults made on it." This desire, and others analogous to it, are given in the *procès-verbaux* of many of the primary assemblies (Archives Nationales, B.II., 23); for example, in those of the thirteen cantons of Ain. A demand is made, furthermore, for the reintegration of the Twenty-two, the abolition of the revolutionary Tribunal, the suppression of absolute proconsulates, the organization of a department guard for securing the future of the Convention, the discharge of the revolutionary army, etc.

12. *Moniteur,* xvii., 20. Report of Barère: "The Constitutional Act is going to draw the line between republicans and royalists."

13. Archives Nationales, F.I.C., 54. (Circular of the Minister, Gohier, July 6, 1793.) "It is today that, summoned to the altar of the country, those who desire the Republic *will be known by name,* and those who do not desire it, whether they speak or *keep silent,* will be equally known."

14. Sauzay, iv., 160, 161. (Article by the *Vidette.*) Consequently, "all the unconstitutionalist nobles and priests considered it a duty to go to the assemblies and joyfully accept a constitution which guaranteed liberty and property to everybody."

and not risk the slightest objection. At Macon, "a few aristocrats muttered to themselves, but not one dared say No."[15] It would, indeed, be extremely imprudent. At Montbrison, "six individuals who decline to vote," are denounced in the *procès-verbal* of the Canton, while a deputy in the Convention demands "severe measures" against them. At Nogent-sur-Seine, three administrators, guilty of the same offence, are to be turned out of office;[16] a few months later, the offence becomes a capital crime, and people are to be guillotined "for having voted against the Constitution of 1793."[17] Almost all the wrong-thinkers foresaw this danger; hence, in nearly all the primary assemblies, the adoption is unanimous, or nearly unanimous;[18] at Rouen, there are but twenty-six adverse votes; at Caen, the centre of the Girondist protestants, fourteen; at Rheims, there are only two; at Troyes, Besançon, Limoges and Paris, there are none at all; in fifteen departments the number of negatives varies from five to one; not one is found in Var. Could there be a more edifying concert of action? The commune of St. Donau, the only one in France, in a remote district of Cotês-du-Nord, dares demand the restoration of the clergy and the son of Capet for king. The rest vote as directed; they have got at the secret of the *plebiscite;* an honest vote is not wanted; the object is to impose on them a Jacobin manifestation.[19]

15. "Journal des Débats de la Société des Jacobins," No. for July 27, 1793 (correspondence, No. 122).

16. *Moniteur,* xvii., 163, 156.

17. Sauzay, iv., 158: "The motives for judgments were thus stated by judges themselves."

18. *Moniteur,* xvii., 40, 48, 72, 140, 175, 194, 263. (Cf. Speeches by Chaumette, July 14, and Report by Gossoin, August 9).—Archives Nationales, B.II., 23. Negative votes in Ardèche 5, in Aude 5, Moselle 5, Saone-et-Loire 5, Côte d'Or 4, Creuse 4, Haut-Rhin 4, Gers 4, Haute-Garonne 3, Aube 2, Bouches-du-Rhone 2, Cantal 2, Basses-Alpes 1, Haute-Marne 1, Haute-Vienne 1, Var 0, Seine 0. The details and circumstances of voting are curious. In the department of Aube, at Troyes, the second section in agreement with the third, excluded "suspects" from the vote. At Paris, the section "Gardes Francaise, Fourcroy president, announces 1,714 voters, of which 1,678 are citizens and 36 *citoyennes.* In the "Mont Blanc" section, the secretary signs as follows: *Trone segretaire general de la semblé.*

19. *Moniteur,* xvii., 375. (Session of the Convention, August 11, 1793). Cha-

In effect, the Club carries out the job it has undertaken. It beats to arms around the ballot-box; it arrives in force; it alone speaks with authority; it animates officers; it moves all the resolutions and draws up the report of proceedings, while the representatives on mission add to the weight of the local authority that of the central authority. In the Macon assembly "they address the people on each article; this speech is followed by immense applause and redoubled shoutings of *Vive la République! Vive la Constitution! Vive le Peuple Français!*" Beware, ye lukewarm, who do not join in the chorus! They are forced to vote "in a loud, intelligible voice." They are required to shout in unison, to sign the grandiloquent address in which the leaders testify their gratitude to the Convention, and give their adhesion to the eminent patriots delegated by the primary assembly to bear its report to Paris.[20]

IV

The first act of the comedy is over and the second act now begins. It is not without an object that the faction has convoked the delegates of the primary assemblies at Paris. Like the primary assemblies, they are to serve as its instruments for governing; they are to form the props of dictatorship, and the object now is to reduce them to that

---

bot: "I demand a law requiring every man who does not appear at a primary meeting to give good reason for his absence; also, that any man who has not favored the Constitution, be declared ineligible to all constitutional franchises." *Ibid.*, 50. (Meeting of the Commune, July 4th). Leonard Bourdon demands, in the name of his section, the Gravilliers, a register on which to inscribe those who accept the Constitution, "in order that those who do not vote for it may be known."—Sauzay, iv., 159. M. Boillon, of Belleherbe, is arrested "for being present at the primary assembly of the canton of Vaucluse, and when called upon to accept the Constitutional Act, leaving without voting."

20. *Moniteur,* xvii., 11. (Instructions on the mode of accepting the Constitution).—Sauzay iv., 158.—*Moniteur,* xvii., 302. (Speech by Garat, August 2.) "I have dispatched commissioners to push the Constitutional Act through the primary assemblies."—Durand-Maillane. 150. "The envoys of the departments were taken from the *sans-culotterie* then in fashion, because they ruled in the Convention."

rôle. Indeed, it is not certain that all will lend themselves to it. For, among the eight thousand commissioners, some, appointed by refractory assemblies, bring a refusal instead of an adhesion;[21] others, more numerous, are instructed to present objections and point out omissions:[22] it is very certain that the envoys of the Girondist departments will insist on the release or return of their excluded representatives; in fine, a good many delegates who have accepted the Constitution in good faith desire its application as soon as possible, and that the Convention should fulfil its promise of abdication, so as to give way to a new Assembly. It is important to suppress at once all these independent fancies and the formation of an opposition party: to this end, a decree of the Convention "authorises the Committee of General Security to order the arrest of 'suspect' commissioners"; it is especially to look after those who, "charged with a special mission, would hold meetings to win over their colleagues, . . . and engage them in proceedings contrary to their mandate."[23] In the first place, and before they are admitted into Paris, their Jacobinism is to be verified, like a bale in the custom-house, by the special agents of the executive council, and especially by Stanislas Maillard, the famous September judge, and his sixty-eight bearded ruffians, each receiving pay at five francs a day. "On all the roads, within a circuit of fifteen or twenty leagues of the capital," the

21. Sauzay, iv., 158.

22. *Moniteur,* xvii., 363. (Report of Gossuin to the Convention, August 9). "There are primary assemblies which have extended their deliberations beyond the acceptance of the Constitution. This acceptance being almost unanimous, all other objects form matter for petitions to be intrusted to competent committees."—*Ibid.,* 333. (Speech of Delacroix). "The antirevolutionary delegates sent by the conspirators we had in the Convention must be punished." (August 6.)—Durand-Maillane.

23. *Moniteur, ibid.,* 333. Speech and motions of Bazire, August 8.—xix., 116. Report of Vouland, January 2, 1794. The pay of Maillard and his acolytes amounted to twenty-two thousand livres.—xviii., 324. (Session of August 5. Speeches of Gossuin, Thibault, and Lacroix.)—*Ibid.,* xxiv., 90. (Session of Germinal 8, year III.) Speech by Bourdon de l'Oise: "We have been obliged to pick men out of the envoys in order to find those disposed for rigorous measures."

delegates are searched; their trunks are opened, and their letters read. At the barriers in Paris they find "inspectors" posted by the Commune, under the pretext of protecting them against prostitutes and swindlers. There, they are taken possession of, and conducted to the mayoralty, where they receive lodging tickets, while a picket of gendarmerie escorts them to their allotted domiciles.[24]—Behold them in pens like sheep, each in his numbered stall; there is no fear of the dissidents trying to escape and form a band apart: one of them, who comes to the Convention and asks for a separate hall for himself and his adherents, is snubbed in the most outrageous manner; they denounce him as an intriguer, and accuse him of a desire to defend the traitor Castries; they take his name and credentials, and threaten him with an investigation.[25] The unfortunate orator hears the Abbaye alluded to, and evidently thinks himself fortunate to escape sleeping there that night. After this, it is certain that he will not again demand the privilege of speaking, and that his colleagues will remain quiet; and all this is the more likely because the revolutionary tribunal holds permanent sessions under their eyes, because the guillotine is set up and in operation on the "Place de la Révolution"; because a recent act of the Commune enjoins on the police "the most active surveillance" and "constant patrols" by the armed force; because, from the first to the fourth of August, the

24. *Moniteur*, xvii., 330. Ordinance of the Commune, August 6.

25. *Moniteur*, xvii., 332. (Session of the Convention, August 6.)—Cf. the "Diurnal" of Beaulieu, August 6. Beaulieu mentions several deputations and motions of the same order, and states the alarm of the "Mountain."—Durand-Maillane, "Mémoires," 151. "Among the envoys from the departments were sensible men who, far from approving of all the steps taken by their brethren, entertained and manifested very contrary sentiments. These were molested and imprisoned."—"Archives des Affaires Etrangères," vol. 1411. (Report of the agents of August 10 and 11.) The department commissioners . . . seemed to us in the best disposition. There are some intriguers among them, however; we are following up some of them, and striving by fraternising with them to prevent them from being seduced or led away by the perfidious suggestions of certain scoundrels, the friends of federalism, amongst them. . . . A few patriotic commissioners have already denounced several of their brethren accused of loving royalty and federalism."

barriers are closed; because, on the 2d of August, a raid into three of the theatres puts five hundred young men in the lock-up:[26] the discontented soon discover, if there are any, that this is not the time or the place to protest.

As to the others, already Jacobin, the faction takes it upon itself to render them still more so. Lost in the immensity of Paris, all these provincialists require moral as well as physical guides; it agrees to exercise toward them "hospitality in all its plenitude, the sweetest of Republican virtues."[27] Hence, ninety-six *sans-culottes*, selected from among the sections, wait on them at the Mayoralty to serve as their correspondents, and perhaps as their guarantees, and certainly as pilots to give them lodging-tickets, to escort and install them, to indoctrinate them, as formerly with the federates of July, 1792, to prevent their getting into bad company, to introduce them into all the exciting meetings, to see that their ardent patriotism quickly rises to the proper temperature of Parisian Jacobinism.[28] The theatres must not offend their eyes or ears with pieces "opposed to the spirit of the Revolution."[29] An order is issued for the performance three times a week of "republican tragedies, such as 'Brutus,' 'William Tell,' 'Caius Gracchus,' and other dramas suitable for the maintenance of the principles of equality and liberty." Once a week the theatres must be free, when Chéniér's alexandrines are spouted on the stage to the edification of the delegates, crowded into the boxes at the expense of the State. The following morning, led by flocks

26. Buchez et Roux, xxviii., 408.

27. *Moniteur*, xvii., 330. (Act passed by the Commune, August 6.)

28. Archives des Affaires Etrangères, vol. 1411. (Reports of agents, Aug. 10 and 11). "Citizens are, today, eager to see who shall have a commissioner at his table; who shall treat him the best. . . . The Commissioners of the primary assemblies come and fraternise with them in the Jacobin club. They adopt their maxims, and are carried away by the energy of the good and true republican *sans-culottes* in the clubs."

29. *Moniteur*, xvii., 307, 308. (Report of Couthon to the Convention, Aug. 2.) "You would wound, you would outrage these Republicans, were you to allow the performance before them of an infinity of pieces filled with insulting allusions to liberty."

into the tribunes of the Convention,[30] they there find the same, classic, simple, declamatory, sanguinary tragedy, except that the latter is not feigned but real, and the tirades are in prose instead of in verse. Surrounded by paid vociferators, as on the previous evening by the Romans "of the lamp," our provincials applaud, cheer and get excited, the same as on the previous evening at the signal given by the *claqueurs* and other frequenters of the house. Another day, the *procureur-syndic* Lhullier summons them to attend the "Evéché," to "fraternise with the authorities of the Paris department";[31] the "Fraternité" section invites them to its daily meetings; the Jacobin club lends them its vast hall in the morning and admits them to its sessions in the evening. Thus taken possession of and kept, as in a diving bell, they breathe in Paris nothing but a Jacobin atmosphere; from one Jacobin den to another, as they are led about in this heated atmosphere, their pulse beats more rapidly. Many of them, who, on their arrival, were "plain, quiet people,"[32] but out of their element, subjected to contagion without any antidote, quickly catch the revolutionary fever. The same as at an American revival, under the constant pressure of preaching and singing, of shouts and nervous spasms, the lukewarm and even the indifferent have not long to wait before the delirium puts them in harmony with the converted.

V

On the 7th of August things come to a head. Led by the department and the municipality, a number of delegates march to the bar of the Convention, and make a confession of Jacobin faith. "Soon," they exclaim, "will search be made on the banks of the Seine for the foul marsh intended to engulf us. Were the royalists and intriguers to die of spite, we will live and die *Montagnards*."[33] Applause and embraces.

30. *Ibid.*, 124. (Session of Aug. 5.)

31. *Ibid.*, 314; (Letter of Lhullier, Aug. 4.)—322, Session of the Commune, Aug. 4th; 332, (Session of the Convention, Aug. 6).—Buchez et Roux, xxviii., 409. (Meeting of the Jacobin Club, Aug. 5th).

32. Buchez et Roux, 411. (Article in the *Journal de la Montagne*.)

33. *Moniteur*, xvii., 348.

From thence they betake themselves to the Jacobin Club, where one of them proposes an address prepared beforehand: the object of this is to justify the 31st of May, and the 2d of June, "to open the eyes" of provincial France, to declare "war against the federalists." "Down with the infamous libelers who have calumniated Paris! . . . We cherish but one sentiment, our souls are all melted into one. . . . We form here but one vast, terrible mountain, about to vomit forth its fires on the royalists and supporters of tyranny." Applause and cheers. Robespierre declares that they are there to save the country.[34] On the following day, August 8th,[35] this address is presented to the Convention and Robespierre has a resolution adopted, ordering it to be sent to the armies, to foreign powers and all the Communes. More applause, more embracings, and more cheers. On the 9th of August,[36] by order of the Convention, the delegates meet in the Tuileries garden, where, divided into as many groups as there are departments, they study the programme drawn up by David, in order to familiarise themselves with the parts they are to play in the festival of the following day.

What an odd festival and how well it expresses the spirit of the time! It is a sort of opera played in the streets by the public authorities, with triumphant chariots, altars, censers, an Ark of the Covenant, funeral urns, classic banners and other trappings! Its divinities consist of plaster statues representing Nature, Liberty, the People, and Hercules, all of which are personified abstractions, like those painted on the ceiling of a theatre. In all this there is no spontaneity nor sincerity; the actors, whose consciences tell them that they are only actors, render homage to symbols which they know to be nothing but symbols, while the mechanical procession,[37]

---

34. Buchez et Roux, xviii., 415 and following pages.

35. *Moniteur,* xvii., 342.

36. *Ibid.,* 352.—Cf. Beaulieu, "Diurnal," Aug. 9.

37. On the mechanical character of the festivals of the Revolution read the programme of "The civic fête in honor of Valor and Morals," ordered by Fouché at Nevers, on the 1st day of the 1st decade of the 2nd month of the year II, (De Martel, "Etude sur Fouché," 202); also, the programme of the "Fête de

the invocations, the apostrophes, the postures, the gestures are reg-
ulated beforehand, the same as by a ballet-manager. To any truth-
loving mind all this must seem like a charade performed by puppets.
But the festival is colossal, well calculated to stimulate the imagination and excite pride through physical excitement.[38] On this gran-
diose stage the delegates become quite intoxicated with their part;
for, evidently, theirs is the leading part; they represent twenty-six
millions of Frenchmen, and the sole object of this ceremony is to
glorify the national will of which they are the bearers. On the Place
de la Bastille[39] where the gigantic effigy of Nature pours forth from
its two breasts "the regenerating water," Hérault, the president, after
offering libations and saluting the new goddess, passes the cup to
the eighty-seven elders (*les doyens*) of the eighty-seven departments,
each "summoned by sound of drum and trumpet" to step forward
and drink in his turn, while cannon belch forth their thunders as if
for a monarch. After the eighty-seven have passed the cup around,
the artillery roars. The procession then moves on, and the delegates
again are assigned the place of honor. The elders, holding an olive-
branch in one hand, and a pike in the other, with a streamer on the
end of it bearing the name of their department, "bound to each other
by a small tricolor ribbon," surround the Convention as if to convey
the idea that the nation maintains and conducts its legal representatives. Behind them march the rest of the eight thousand delegates,
likewise holding olive-branches and forming a second distinct body,
the largest of all, and on which all eyes are centred. For, in their
wake, "there is no longer any distinction between persons and functionaries," all being confounded together, marching pell-mell, executive council, city officials, judges scattered about haphazard and,
by virtue of equality, lost in the crowd. At each station, thanks to

---

l'Etre Supréme," at Sceaux, organized by the patriot Palloy, Presidial 20, year
II. (Dauban, "Paris en 1794," p. 187).

38. It cost one million two hundred thousand francs, besides the travelling
expenses of eight thousand delegates.

39. Buchez et Roux, xxviii., 439, and following pages. *Procès-verbal* of the
National Festival of the 10th of August.—Dauban "La Demagogie en 1791."
(Extract from the Republican Ritual.)

their insignia, the delegates form the most conspicuous element. On reaching the last one, that of the Champ de Mars, they alone with the Convention, ascend the steps leading to the altar of the country; on the highest platform stands the eldest of all alongside of the president of the Convention, also standing; thus graded above each other, the seven thousand, who envelope the seven hundred and fifty, form "the veritable Sacred Mountain." Now, the president, on the highest platform, turns toward the eighty-seven elders; he confides to them the Ark containing the Constitutional Act and the list of those who voted for it; they, on their part, then advance and hand him their pikes, which he gathers together into one bundle as an emblem of national unity and indivisibility. At this, shouts arise from every point of the immense enclosure; salvos of artillery follow again and again; "one would say that heaven and earth answered each other" in honor "of the greatest epoch of humanity." Certainly, the delegates are beside themselves; the nervous machine, strained to the utmost, vibrates too powerfully; the millennium discloses itself before their eyes. Already, many among them on the Place de la Bastille, had addressed the universe; others, "seized with a prophetic spirit," promise eternity to the Constitution. They feel themselves "reborn again, along with the human species"; they regard themselves as beings of a new world. History is consummated in them; the future is in their hands; they believe themselves gods on earth. In this critical state, their reason, like a pair of ill-balanced scales, yields to the slightest touch; under the pressure of the manufacturers of enthusiasm, a sudden reaction will carry them away. They consider the Constitution as a panacea, and they are going to consign it, like some dangerous drug, to this coffer which they call an ark. They have just proclaimed the liberty of the people, and are going to perpetuate the dictatorship of the Convention.

VI

This summerset must, of course, seem spontaneous and the hand of the titular rulers remain invisible: the Convention, as usual with usurpers, is to simulate reserve and disinterestedness. Consequently, the following morning, August 11, on the opening of the session, it simply declares that "its mission is fulfilled":[40] on motion of Lacroix, a confederate of Danton's, it passes a law that a new census of the population and of electors shall be made with as little delay as possible, in order to convoke the primary assemblies at once; it welcomes with transport the delegates who bring to it the Constitutional Ark; the entire Assembly rises in the presence of this sacred receptacle, and allows the delegates to exhort it and instruct it concerning its duties.[41] But in the evening, at the Jacobin Club, Robespierre, after a long and vague discourse on public dangers, conspiracies, and traitors, suddenly utters the decisive words: "*The most important of my reflections was about to escape me.*[42] . . . The proposition made that morning tends to put in the place of the suitable members of the actual Convention the *envoys of Pitt and Cobourg.*" Words of terrible import in the mouth of a man of principles! They are at once understood by the leaders, great and small, also by the selected fifteen hundred Jacobins then filling the hall. "No! no! shouts the entire club." The delegates are carried away: "I demand," exclaims one of them, "that the dissolution of the Convention be postponed until the end of the war." At last, the precious motion, so long desired and anticipated, is made: the calumnies of the Girondists now fall to the ground; it is demonstrated that the Convention does not desire to perpetuate itself and that it has no ambition; if it remains in power it is because it is kept there; the delegates of the people compel it to stay.

And better still, they are going to mark out its course of action. The next day, the 12th of August, with the zeal of new converts,

40. *Moniteur,* xvii., 366. (Session of Aug. 11. Speech by Lacroix and decree in conformity therewith.)

41. *Ibid.,* 374. "Remember that you are accountable to the nation and the universe for this sacred Ark. Remember that it is your duty to die rather than suffer a sacrilegious hand. . . ."

42. Buchez et Roux, xxviii., 458. It is evident from the context of the speech that Robespierre and the Jacobins were desirous of maintaining the Convention because they foresaw Girondist elections.

they spread themselves through the hall in such numbers that the Assembly, no longer able to carry on its deliberations, crowds toward the left and yields the whole of the space on the right that they may occupy and "purify" it.[43] All the combustible material in their minds, accumulated during the past fortnight, takes fire and explodes; they are more furious than the most ultra Jacobins; they repeat at the bar of the house the extravagancies of Rose Lacombe, and of the lowest clubs; they even transcend the programme drawn up by the "Mountain." "The time for deliberation is past," exclaims their spokesman, "we must act[44] . . . Let the people rouse themselves in a mass . . . it alone can annihilate its enemies. . . . We demand that all 'suspects' be put in arrest; that they be despatched to the frontiers, followed by the terrible mass of *sans-culottes*. There, in the front ranks, they will be obliged to fight for that liberty which they have outraged for the past four years, or be immolated on the tyrants' cannon. . . . Women, children, old men and the infirm shall be kept as hostages by the women and children of *sans-culottes*." Danton seizes the opportunity. With his usual perspicacity he finds the expression which defines the situation: "The deputies of the primary assemblies," he says, "have just taken amongst us *the initiative of terror*." He moreover reduces the absurd notions of the fanatics to a practical bearing: "An uprisal *en masse*, yes, but with order" by at once calling out the first class of conscripts, all men from eighteen to twenty-five years of age; the arrest of all 'suspects,' yes, but not to lead them against the enemy; "they would be more dangerous than useful in our armies; let us shut them up; they will be our hostages." In fine, he imagines employment for the delegates who are now in the way in Paris and of use in the provinces. Let us make of them "various kinds of representatives charged with

43. *Moniteur*, xvii., 382. (Session of Aug. 12. Speech by Lacroix).

44. *Ibid.*, 387.—Cf. *Ibid.*, 410, session of August 16. The delegates return there to insist on a levy, *en masse*, the levy of the first class not appearing sufficient to them.—Buchez et Roux, xxviii., 464. Delegate Royer, Curé of Chalons-aur-Saone, demands that aristocrats "chained together in sixes" be put in the front rank in battle "to avoid the risks of *sauve qui peut*."

animating citizens. . . . Let them, along with all good citizens and the constituted authorities, take charge of the inventories of grain and arms, and make requisitions for men, and let the Committee of Public Safety direct this sublime movement. . . . All will swear that, on returning to their firesides, they will give this impulse to their fellow citizens." Universal applause; the delegates exclaim in one voice, "We swear!" Everybody springs to his feet; the men in the tribunes wave their hats and likewise shout the same oath. The scheme is successful; a semblance of popular will has authorised the staff of officials, the policy, the principles and the very name of Terror. As to the tools employed, they are fit only to be sent back to the places they came from. The delegates, of whose demands and interference the "Mountain" is still in dread, are consigned to their departmental holes, where they serve as agents and missionaries.[45] There is no further mention of putting the Constitution into operation; this was simply a bait, a decoy, contrived for fishing in turbid waters: the fishing ended, the Constitution is now placed in a conspicuous place in the hall, in a small monument for which David furnished the design.[46] "The Convention, now," says Danton,"will rise to a sense of its dignity, for it is now invested with the full power of the nation." In other words, astuteness completes what violence had begun. Through the outrages committed in May and June, the Convention had lost its legitimacy; through the manoeuvres of July and August it recovered the semblance of it. The *Montagnards* still hold their slave by his leash, but they have restored his prestige so as to make the most of him to their own profit.

VII

With the same blow, and wearing the same mask, they have disarmed their adversaries. On learning the events of May 31 and June 2, a loud cry of indignation arose among Republicans of the cultivated class in this generation, who, educated by the philosophers, sincerely

45. Decrees of August 14 and 16.
46. *Moniteur,* xvii., 375.

believed in the rights of man;[47] sixty-nine department administrations had protested,[48] and, in almost all the towns of the west, the south, the east and the centre of France, at Caen, Alençon, Evreux, Rennes, Brest, Lorient, Nantes and Limoges, at Bordeaux, Toulouse, Montpellier, Nismes and Marseilles, at Grenoble, Lyons, Clermont, Lons-le-Saulnier, Besançon, Macon and Dijon,[49] the citizens, assembled in their sections, had provoked, or maintained by cheering them on, the acts of their administrators. Rulers and citizens, all declared that, the Convention not being free, its decrees after the 31st of May, no longer had the force of law; that the troops of the departments should march on Paris to deliver that city from its oppressors, and that their substitutes should be called out and assemble at Bourges. In many places words were converted into acts. Already before the end of May, Marseilles and Lyons had taken up arms and checkmated their local Jacobins. After the 2d of June, Normandy, Brittany, Gard, Jura, Toulouse and Bordeaux, had also raised troops. At Marseilles, Bordeaux and Caen the representatives on mission, arrested or under

47. Riouffe, "Mémoires," 19: "An entire generation, the real disciples of Jean-Jacques, Voltaire, and Diderot, could be, and was annihilated, to a large extent under the pretext of federalism."

48. *Moniteur*, xvii., 102. (Speech by Cambon, July 11, 1793). Archives Nationales, AF. II., 46. (Speech of General Wimpfen to the "Société des amis de la Liberté et de l'Egalité," in session at Cherbourg, June 25, 1793). "Sixty-four departments have already revoked the powers conferred on their representatives." Meillan, "Mémoires," 72: "The archives of Bordeaux once contained the acts passed by seventy-two departments, all of which adhered to measures nearly the same as those indicated in our document."

49. Buchez et Roux, xviii., 148. Meillan, 70, 71. Guillon de Montléon, i., 300 (on Lyons) and i., 280 (on Bordeaux). Archives Nationales, AF.II., 46. (Deliberations of the Nantes section July 5). Letter of Merlin and Gillet, representatives on mission, Lorient, June 12. Dissatisfaction at the outrages of May 31 and June 2, was so manifest that the representatives on mission, Merlin, Gillet, Savestre, and Cavaignac, print on the 14th of June a resolution authorising one of their body to go to the Convention and protest "in their name" against the weakness shown by it and against the usurpations of the Paris commune. Sauzay, iv., 260, at Besançon, in a general assembly of all the administrative, judicial, and municipal bodies of the department joined to the commissioners of the section, protest "unanimously" on the 15th of June.

guard, were retained as hostages.[50] At Nantes, the National Guard and popular magistrates who, a week before, had so bravely repulsed the great Vendéan army, dared do more than this; they limited the powers of the Convention and condemned all intermeddling; according to them, the sending of representatives on mission was "an usurpation, an attack on national sovereignty"; representatives had been elected "to make and not to execute laws, to prepare a constitution and regulate all public powers, and not to confound these together and exercise them all at once; to protect and maintain intermediary powers which the people have delegated, and not to encroach upon and annihilate them."[51] With still greater boldness, Montpellier enjoined all representatives everywhere to meet at the headquarters of their respective departments, and await the verdict of a national jury. In short, by virtue even of the democratic creed, "nothing was visible amid the ruins of the Convention," mutilated and degraded, but interloping "attorneys"; "the people's workmen" are summoned "to return to obedience and do justice to the reproaches addressed to them by their legitimate master";[52] the nation

50. Archives Nationales, *ibid.* (Letter of Romme and Prieur, Caen, June 10th, to the Committee of Public Safety). The insurgents are so evidently in the right that Romme and Prieur approve of their own arrest. "Citizens, our colleagues, this arrest may be of great importance, serve the cause of liberty, maintain the unity of the Republic and revive confidence if, *as we hasten to demand it of you,* you confirm it by a decree which declares us hostages. . . . We have noticed that among the people of Caen, there is a love of liberty, as well as of justice and docility."

51. Archives Nationales, A.F.II., 46. (Printed July 5). Result of the deliberations of the Nantes sections. The act is signed by the three administrative bodies of Nantes, by the district rulers of Clisson, Anceries, and Machecoul, who had fled to Nantes, and by both the deputies of the districts of Paimboeuf and Chateaubriand, in all, eighty-six signatures.

52. Archives Nationales, *ibid.,* (letter of General Wimpfen to the "Société des Amis de l'Egalité et de la Liberté" in session at Cherbourg, June 25, 1793).—Mortimer-Ternaux, viii. 126.—On the opinion of the departments cf. Paul Thibaud ("Etudes sur l'histoire de Grenoble et du Department de l'Isére").—Louis Guibert ("Le Parti Girondin dans le Haute Vienne").—Jarrin ("Bourg et Bellay pendant la Révolution").

cancelled the pay of its clerks at the capital, withdrew the mandate they had misused, and declared them usurpers if they persisted in not yielding up their borrowed sovereignty "to its inalienable sovereignty." To this stroke, which strikes deep, the "Mountain" replies by a similar stroke; it also renders homage to principles and falls back on the popular will. Through the sudden manufacture of an ultrademocratic constitution, through a convocation of the primary assemblies, and a ratification of its work by the people in these assemblies, through the summoning of delegates to Paris, through the assent of these converted, fascinated, or constrained delegates, it exonerates and justifies itself, and thus deprives the Girondists of the grievances to which they had given currency, of the axioms they had displayed on their standards, and of the popularity they thought they had acquired.[53] Henceforth, the ground their opponents had built on sinks under their feet; the materials collected by them disintegrate in their hands; their league dissolves before it is completed, and the incurable weakness of the party appears in full daylight.

And in the first place, in the departments, as at Paris,[54] the party is without roots. For the past three years, all the sensible and orderly people occupied with their own affairs, who are not politicians, ninetenths of the electors, either through taste or interest, stay away from the polls, and in this large mass the Girondists have no adherents. As they themselves admit,[55] this class remains attached to the institutions of 1791, which they have overthrown; if it has any esteem for them, it is as "extremely honest madmen." Again, this esteem is mingled with aversion: it reproaches them with the violent

53. Albert Babeau, ii., 83. (Pamphlet by the *curé* of Cleray). "Every primary assembly that acepts the Constitution strikes the factions a blow on the head with the club of Hercules."

54. Cf. "The Revolution," Vol. ii., ch. xi.

55. Buzot.—Archives Nationales, AF. II., 157. Reports by Baudot and Ysabeau to the Convention. The 19th of Aug. at the Hôtel-de-Ville of Bordeaux, they eulogise the 21st of January: "There was then a roar as frightful as it was general. A city official coolly replied to us: What would you have? To oppose anarchy we have been forced to join the aristocrats, and they rule." Another says ironically to Ysabeau: "We did not anticipate that—they are *our tribunes.*"

decrees they have passed in concert with the "Mountain"; with persecutions, confiscations, every species of injustice and cruelty; it
always sees the King's blood on their hands; they, too, are regicides,
anti-Catholics, anti-Christians, destructionists and levellers.[56] Undoubtedly they are less so than the "Mountain"; hence, when the
provincial insurrection breaks out, many Feuillants and even Royalists follow them to the section assemblies and join in their protests.
But the majority goes no further, and soon falls back into its accustomed inertia. It is not in harmony with its leaders:[57] its latent preferences are opposed to their avowed programme; it does not wholly
trust them; it has only a half-way affection for them; its recent
sympathies are deadened by old animosities: everywhere, instead of
firmness there is only caprice. All this affords no assurance of steadfast loyalty and practical adhesion. The Girondist deputies scattered
through the provinces relied upon each department arousing itself
at their summons and forming a republican Vendée against the
"Mountain": nowhere do they find anything beyond mild approval
and speculative hopes.

There remains to support them the élite of the republican party,
the scholars and lovers of literature, who are honest and sincere
thinkers, who, worked upon by the current dogmas, have accepted
the philosophical catechism literally and seriously. Elected judges,
or department, district, and city administrators, commanders and
officers of the National Guard, presidents and secretaries of sections,

---

56. Jarrin, "Bourg et Belley pendant la Révolution" ("Annales de la Société
d'Emulation de l'Ain, 1878, Nos. for January, February, and March, p. 16).

57. Louvet, 103, 108.—Guillon de Montléon, i., 305 and following pages.—
Buchez et Roux, xxviii., 151. (Report of the delegates of the district of Andelys).
"One of the members observed that there would be a good deal of trouble in
raising an armed force of one thousand men." An administrator (a commissioner
of Calvados) replied: "We shall have all the aristocrats on our side." The
principal military leaders at Caen and at Lyons, Wimpfen, Précy, Puisaye, are
Feuillants and form only a provisional alliance with the Girondists properly so
called. Hence constant contentions and reciprocal mistrust. Birotteau and
Chapet leave Lyons because they do not find the spirit of the place sufficiently
republican.

they occupy most of the places conferred by local authority, and hence their almost unanimous protest seems at first to be the voice of all France. In reality, it is only the despairing cry of a group of staff-officers without an army. Chosen under the electoral pressure with which we are familiar, they possess rank, office and titles, but no credit or influence; they are supported only by those whom they really represent, that is to say, those who elected them, a tenth of the population, and forming a sectarian minority. Again, in this minority there are a good many who are lukewarm; with most men the distance is great between conviction and action; the interval is filled up with acquired habits, indolence, fear and egoism. One's belief in the abstractions of the *Contrat-Social* is of little account; no one readily bestirs oneself for an abstract end. Uncertainties beset one at the outset; the road one has to follow is found to be perilous and obscure, and one hesitates and postpones; one feels himself a home-body and is afraid of engaging too deeply and of going too far. Having expended one's breath in words one is less willing to give one's money; another may open his purse but he may not be disposed to give himself, which is as true of the Girondists as it is of the Feuillants. "At Marseilles, at Bordeaux," says a deputy,[58] "in nearly all the principal towns, the proprietor, slow, indifferent and timid, could not make up his mind to leave home for a moment; it was to mercenaries that he entrusted his cause and his arms." Only the federates of Mayenne, Ile-et-Vilaine, and especially of Finisterre, were "young men well brought up and well informed about the cause they were going to support." In Normandy, the Central Committee, unable to do better, has to recruit its soldiers, and especially artillerymen, from the band of *Carabots*, former Jacobins, a lot of ruffians ready for anything, pillagers and runaways at the first cannon-shot. At Caen, Wimpfen, having ordered the eight battalions of the National Guard to assemble in the court, demands volunteers

58. Louvet, 124, 129.—Vaultier et Mancel, "L'Insurrection Normande." Buchez et Roux, xxviii., 360. (Notice by Genl. Wimpfen), July 7. Puisaye, "Memoires."

and finds that only seventeen step forth; on the following day a formal requisition brings out only one hundred and thirty combatants; other towns, except Vire, which furnishes about twenty, refuse their contingent. In short, a marching army cannot be formed, or, if it does march, it halts at the first station, that of Evreux before reaching Vernon, and that of Marseilles at the walls of Avignon.

On the other hand, by virtue of being sincere and logical, those who have rebelled entertain scruples and themselves define the limits of their insurrection. The fugitive deputies at their head would believe themselves guilty of usurpation had they, like the "Mountain" at Paris, constituted themselves at Caen a sovereign assembly:[59] according to them, their right and their duty is reduced to giving testimony concerning the 31st of May and the 1st of June, and to exhorting the people and to being eloquent. They are not legally qualified to take executive power; it is for the local magistrates, the *élus* of the sections, and better still, the department committees, to command in the departments. Lodged as they are in official quarters, they are merely to print formal statements, write letters, and, behaving properly, wait until the sovereign people, their employer, reinstates them. It has been outraged in their persons; it must avenge itself for this outrage; since it approves of its mandatories, it is bound to restore them to office; it being the master of the house, it is bound to have its own way in the house. As to the department committees, it is true that, in the heat of the first excitement, they thought of forming a new Convention at Bourges, either through a muster of substitute deputies, or through the convocation of a national commission of one hundred and seventy members.[60] But time is wanting, also the means, to carry out the plan; it remains suspended in the air like vain menace; at the end of a fortnight it vanishes in smoke;

59. Mortimer-Ternaux, viii., 471. Letter of Barbaroux, Caen, June 18.—*Ibid.*, 133. Letter of Madame Roland to Buzot, July 7. "You are not the one to march at the head of battalions (departmental). It would have the appearance of gratifying personal vengeance."

60. Buchez et Roux, xxviii., 153. (Deliberations of the constituted authorities of Marseilles, June 7.)

the departments succeed in federating only in scattered groups; they desist from the formation of a central government, and thus, through this fact alone, condemn themselves to succumb, one after the other, in detail, and each at home. What is worse, through conscientiousness and patriotism, they prepare their own defeat: they refrain from calling upon the armies and from stripping the frontiers; they do not contest the right of the Convention to provide as it pleases for the national defence. Lyons allows the passage of convoys of cannonballs which are to be subsequently used in cannonading its defenders.[61] The authorities of Puy-de-Dome aid by sending to Vendée the battalion that they had organised against the "Mountain." Bordeaux is to surrender Chateau-Trompette, its munitions of war and supplies, to the representatives on mission; and, without a word, with exemplary docility, both the Bordelais battalions which guard Blaye suffer themselves to be dislodged by two Jacobin battalions.[62] Comprehending the insurrection in this way, defeat is certain beforehand.

The insurgents are thus conscious of their false position; they have a vague sort of feeling that, in recognising the military authority of the Convention, they admit its authority in full; insensibly they glide down this slope, from concession to concession, until they reach complete submission. From the 16th of June, at Lyons,[63] "peo-

---

61. Guillon de Montléon, ii., 40. The contrast between the two parties is well shown in the following extract from the letter of a citizen of Lyons to Kellerman's soldiers. "They tell you that we want to destroy the unity of the Republic, while they themselves abandon the frontiers to the enemy in order to come here and cut their brethren's throats."

62. Guillon de Montléon, i., 288.—Marcelin Boudet, "Les Conventionnels d'Auvergne," p. 181.—Louvet, 193.—*Moniteur*, xvii., 101. (Speech of Cambon, July 11). "We have preferred to expose these funds (one hundred and five millions destined for the army) to being intercepted, rather than to retard this dispatch. The first thing the Committee of Public Safety have had to care for was to save the Republic and make the administrations fully responsible for it. They were fully sensible of this, and accordingly have allowed the circulation of these funds. . . . They have been forced, through the wise management of the Committee, to contribute themselves to the safety of the Republic."

63. Archives Nationales, Letter of Robert Lindet, June 16, AF. II., 43. The

ple begin to feel that it will not answer to break with the Convention." Five weeks later, the authorities of Lyons "solemnly recognise that the Convention is the sole central rallying point of all French citizens and republicans," and decree that "all acts emanating from it concerning the general interests of the Republic are to be executed."[64] Consequently, at Lyons and in other departments, the administrations convoke the primary assemblies as the Convention has prescribed; consequently, the primary assemblies accept the Constitution which it has proposed; consequently, the delegates of the primary assemblies betake themselves to Paris according to its orders. Henceforth, the Girondist cause is lost; the discharge of a few cannon at Vernon and Avignon disperse the only two columns of soldiery that have set out on their march. In each department, the Jacobins, encouraged by the representatives on mission, raise their heads; everywhere the local club enjoins the local government to submit,[65] everywhere the local governments report the acts they pass, make excuses and ask forgiveness. Proportionately to the retraction of one department, the rest, feeling themselves abandoned, are more disposed to retract. On the 9th of July forty-nine departments are enumerated as having given in their adhesion. Several of them

---

correspondence of Lindet, which is very interesting, well shows the sentiments of the Lyonnese and the policy of the "Mountain." "However agitated Lyons may be, order prevails; nobody wants either king or tyrant; all use the same language: the words *republic, union,* are in everybody's mouth." (Eight letters.) He always gives the same advice to the Committee of Public Safety: "Publish a constitution, publish the motives of the bills of arrest," which are indispensable to rally everybody to the Convention (June 15).

64. Guillon de Montléon, i., 309 (July 24).

65. Sauzay, iv., 268.—Paul Thibaud, 50.—Marcelin Boudet, 185.—Archives Nationales AF. II., 46. Extract from the registers of the Council of the department of Loire-Inferieure, July 14. The department protests that its decree of July 5 was not "a rupture with the Convention, an open rebellion against the laws of the State, an idea very remote from the sentiments and intentions of the citizens present." Now, "the plan of a Constitution is offered to the acceptance of the sovereign. This fortunate circumstance should bring people to one mind, and, with hope thus renewed, let us at once seize on the means of salvation thus presented to us."—*Moniteur,* xvii., 102. (Speech of Cambon, July 11.)

declare that the scales have dropped from their eyes, that they approve of the acts of May 31 and June 2, and thus ensure their safety by manifesting their zeal. The administration of Calvados notifies the Breton *fédérés* that "having accepted the Constitution it can no longer tolerate their presence in Caen"; it sends them home, and secretly makes peace with the "Mountain"; and only informs the deputies, who are its guests, of this proceeding, three days afterwards, by posting on their door the decree that declares them outlaws.

Disguised as soldiers, the latter depart along with the Breton *fédérés;* on the way, they are able to ascertain the veritable sentiments of this people whom they believe imbued with their rights and capable of taking a political initiative.[66] The pretended citizens and republicans they have to do with are, in sum, the former subjects of Louis XVI. and the future subjects of Napoleon I., that is to say, the rulers and the ruled, trained to feel all one way and instinctively subordinate, requiring a government just as sheep require a shepherd and a watch-dog, accepting or submitting to shepherd and dog, provided these look and act the part, even if the shepherd be a butcher and the dog a wolf. To avoid isolation, to rejoin the most numerous herd as soon as possible, to always form masses and bodies and thus follow the impulsion which comes from above, and gather together scattered individuals, such is the instinct of the flock. In

---

66. Louvet, 119, 128, 150, 193.—Meillan, 130, 141. (On the disposition and sentiments of the provinces and of the public in general, the reader will find ample and authentic details in the narratives of the fugitives who scattered themselves in all directions, and especially in those of Louvet, Meillan, Dulaure, and Vaublanc.) Cf. the "Memoires de Hua" and "Un Séjour en France in 1792 and 1795."—Mallet-Dupan already states this disposition before 1789 (MS. journal). "June, 1785: The French live simply in a crowd; they must all cling together. On the promenades they huddle together and jostle each other in one alley; the same when there is more space." "Aug., 1787, (after the first riots): I have remarked in general more curiosity than excitement in the multitude. . . . One can judge, at this moment, the national character; a good deal of bravado and nonsense; neither reason, rule, nor method; rebellious in crowds, and not a soul that does not tremble in the presence of a corporal."

the battalion of federates, they begin by saying that, as the Constitution is now accepted and the Convention recognised, it is no longer allowable to protect deputies whom it has declared outlaws: "that would be creating a faction." Thereupon, the deputies withdraw from the battalion, and, in a little squad by themselves, march along separately. As they are nineteen in number, resolute and well armed, the authorities of the market-towns through which they pass make no opposition by force; it would be offering battle, and that surpasses a functionary's zeal; moreover, the population is either indifferent toward them or sympathetic. Nevertheless, efforts are made to stop them, sometimes to surround them and take them by surprise; for, a warrant of arrest is out against them, transmitted through the hierarchical channel, and every local magistrate feels bound to do his duty as gendarme. Under this administrative network, the meshes of which they encounter everywhere, the proscribed deputies can do naught else but hide in caves or escape by sea. On reaching Bordeaux, they find other sheep getting ready and preparing their companions for the slaughter-house. Saige, the mayor, preaches conciliation and patience: he declines the aid of four or five thousand young men, three thousand grenadiers of the National Guard, and two or three hundred volunteers who had formed themselves into a club against the Jacobin club; he persuades them to disband; he sends a deputation to Paris to entreat the Convention to overlook "a moment of error" and pardon "brethren that had gone astray." "They flattered themselves," says a deputy, an eye-witness,[67] "that prompt submission would appease the resentment of tyrants and that these would be, or pretend to be, generous enough to spare a town that had signalised itself more than any other during the Revolution." Up to the last, they are to entertain the same illusions and manifest the same docility. When Tallien, with his eighteen hundred peasants and brigands, enters Bordeaux, twelve thousand National Guards, equipped, armed and in uniform,

---

67. Meillan, 143.—Mortimer-Ternaux, viii., 203. (Session of August 30). Mallet-Dupan, ii., 9.

receive him wearing oak-leaf crowns; they listen in silence to "his astounding and outrageous discourse"; they suffer him to tear off their crowns, cockades and epaulettes; the battalions allow themselves to be disbanded on the spot; on returning to their quarters they listen with downcast eyes to the proclamation which "orders all inhabitants without distinction to bring their arms within thirty-six hours, under penalty of death, to the *glacis* of the Chateau-Trompette; before the time elapses thirty thousand guns, swords, pistols and even pocketknives are given up." Here, as at Paris, on the 20th of June, 10th of August, 2d of September, 3d of May and 2d of June, as at every critical moment of the Revolution in Paris and the provinces, habits of subordination and of amiability, stamped on a people by a provident monarchy and a time-honored civilisation, mollify in man the foresight of danger, the militant instinct, the faculty of self-dependence, of taking his own part, of looking out for his own salvation. Inevitably, when anarchy brings a nation back to the state of nature, the tame animals will be eaten by the savage ones—these are now let loose and immediately they show their natural disposition.

VIII

If the men of the "Mountain" had been statesmen, or even sensible men, they would have shown themselves humane, if not for the sake of humanity, at least through calculation; for in this France, so little republican, all the republican strength is not too great for the founding of the Republic, while, through their principles, their culture, their social position and their number, the Girondists form the élite and the force, the flower and the sap of the party. The death-cry of the "Mountain" against the insurgents of Lozére[68] and Vendèe is intelligible: they had raised the white flag; they accepted leaders and instructions from Coblentz and London. But neither Bordeaux, Marseilles nor Lyons are royalist, or in alliance with the foreigner. "We,

68. Ernest Daudet, "His. des Conspirations royalistes dans le midi." (books ii. and iii.)

rebels!" write the Lyonnese;[69] "Why we see no other than the tricolor flag waving; the white cockade, the symbol of rebellion, has
never been raised within our walls. We, royalists! Why, shouts of
'Long live the Republic' are heard on all sides, and, spontaneously
(in the session of July 2nd) we have all sworn to fall upon whoever
should propose a king. . . . Your representatives tell you that we are
antirevolutionists, when we have accepted the Constitution. They
tell you that we protect *emigrés* when we have offered to surrender
all those that you might indicate. They tell you that our streets are
filled with refractory priests, when we have not even opened the
doors of Pierre-en-Cize (prison) to thirty-two priests confined there
by the old municipality, without indictment, without any charge
whatever against them, solely because they were priests." Thus, at
Lyons, the pretended aristocrats were, then, not only republicans but
democrats and radicals, loyal to the established régime, and submissive to the worst of the revolutionary laws, while the same state
of things prevailed at Bordeaux, at Marseilles and even at Toulon.[70]
And better still, they accepted the outrages of May 31 and June 2;[71]

69. Guillon de Montléon, i., 313. (Address to the National Guards demanded
against Lyons, July 30., ii., 40. Address of a *Lyonais* to the patriot soldiers under
Kellermann.)

70. Mortimer-Ternaux, viii., 222. The insurrection of Toulon, Girondist at
the start, dates July 1st.—Letter of the new administrators of Toulon to the
Convention. "We desire the Republic, one and indivisible; there is no sign of
rebellion with us. . . . Representatives Barras and Fréron lie shamefully in de-
picting us as antirevolutionists, on good terms with the English and the families
of Vendéc." The Toulon administrators continue furnishing the Italian army
with supplies. July 19, an English boat, sent to parley, had to lower the white
flag and hoist the tricolor flag. The entry of the English into Toulon did not
take place before the 29th of August.

71. Guillon de Montléon, ii., 67. (Letter of the Lyonnese to the representatives of the people, Sep. 20): "The people of Lyons have constantly respected
the laws, and if, as in some departments, that of Rhone-et-Loire was for a
moment mistaken in the events of May 31, they hastened, as soon as they
believed that the Convention was not oppressed, to recognise and execute its
decrees. Every day, now that these reach it, they are published and observed
within its walls."

they stopped contesting the usurpations of Paris; they no longer insisted on the return of the excluded deputies. On the 2nd of August at Bordeaux, and the 30th of July at Lyons, the Committee-Extraordinary of Public Safety resigned; there no longer existed any rival assembly opposed to the Convention. After the 24th of July,[72] Lyons solemnly recognised the supreme and central authority, reserving nothing but its municipal franchises. Better still, in striking testimony of political orthodoxy, the Council-General of the department prescribed a civic festival for the 10th of August analogous to that of Paris; already blockaded, the Lyonnese indulged in no hostile manifestation; on the 7th of August, they marched out of their advanced positions to fraternise with the first body of troops sent against them.[73] They conceded everything, save on one point, which they could not yield without destruction, namely, the assurance that they should not be given up defenceless to the arbitrary judgment of their local tyrants, to the spoliations, proscriptions, and revenge of their Jacobin rabble. In sum, at Marseilles and Bordeaux, especially at Lyons and Toulon, the sections had revolted only on that account; acting promptly and spontaneously, the people had thrust aside the knife which a few ruffians aimed at their throats; they had not been, and were not now, willing to be "Septemberised," and that was their sole concern; provided they were not handed over to the butchers bound hand and foot, they would open their gates. On these minimum terms the "Mountain" could terminate the civil war before the end of July; it had only to follow the example of Robert Lindet who, at Evreux the home of Buzot, at Caen the home of Charlotte Corday and central seat of the fugitive Girondists,

72. *Moniteur*, xvii., 269. (Session of July 28). (Letter of the administrators of the department of Rhone-et-Loire to the Convention, Lyons, July 24). "We present to the Convention our individual recantation and declaration; in conforming to the law we are entitled to its protection. We petition the court to decide on our declaration, and to repeal the acts which relate to us or to make an exception in our favor. . . . We have always professed ourselves to be true republicans."

73. Guillon de Montléon, i., 309, 311, 315, 335. Mortimer-Ternaux, viii., 197.

established permanent obedience through the moderation he had shown and the promises he had kept.[74] The measures that had pacified the most compromised province would have brought back the others, and through this policy, Paris, without striking a blow, would have secured the three largest cities in France, the capital of the South-west, that of the South, and the capital of the Centre.

On the contrary, should the Paris faction persist in imposing on them the domination of its Maratists there was a risk of their being thrown into the arms of the enemy. Rather than fall back into the hands of the bandits who had ransomed and decimated them, Toulon, starved out, was about to receive the English within its walls and surrender to them the great arsenal of the South. Not less famished, Bordeaux might be tempted to demand aid from another English fleet; a few marches would bring the Piedmontese army to Lyons; France would then be cut in two, while the plan of stirring up the South against the North was proposed to the allies by the most clear-sighted of their councillors.[75] Had this plan been carried out it is probable that the country would have been lost. In any event, there was danger in driving the insurgents to despair: for, between the unbridled dictatorship of their victorious assassins and the musketry of the besieging army, there could be no hesitation by men of any feeling; it was better to be beaten on the ramparts than allow themselves to be bound for the guillotine; brought to a stand under the scaffold, their sole resource was to depend on themselves to the last. Thus, through its unreasonableness, the "Mountain" condemns itself to a number of sieges or blockades which lasted several months,[76] to leaving Var and Savoy unprotected, to exhausting the

74. Mortimer-Ternaux viii., 141.

75. Mallet-Dupan, i., 379 and following pages; i., 408; ii., 10.

76. Entry of the Republican troops into Lyons, October 9th, into Toulon, December 19th. Bordeaux had submitted on the 2d of August. Exasperated by the decree of the 6th, which proscribed all the abettors of the insurrection, the city drives out, on the 19th, the representatives Baudot and Ysabeau. It submits again on the 19th of September. But so great is the indignation of the citizens, Tallien and his three colleagues dare not enter before the 16 of October. (Mortimer-Ternaux, viii., 197 and following pages.)

arsenals, to employing against Frenchmen[77] men and munitions needed against foreigners, and all this at the moment the foreigner was taking Valenciennes[78] and Mayence, when thirty thousand royalists were organising in Lozére, when the great Vendean army was laying siege to Nantes, when each new focus of incendiarism was threatening to connect the flaming frontier with the conflagration in the Catholic countries.[79] With a jet of cold water aptly directed, the "Mountain" could extinguish the fires it had kindled in the great republican towns; otherwise, nothing remained but to let them increase at the risk of consuming the whole country, with no other hope than that they might at last die out under a mass of ruins, and with no other object but to rule over captives and the dead.

But this is precisely the Jacobin aim; for, he is not satisfied with less than absolute submission; he must rule at any cost, just as he pleases, no matter how, no matter over what ruins. A despot by instinct and installation, his dogma has consecrated him King; he is King by natural and divine right, in the name of eternal verity, the same as Philip II., enthroned by his religious system and blessed by his Holy Office. Hence he can abandon no jot or tittle of his authority without a sacrifice of principle, nor treat with rebels, unless they surrender at discretion; simply for having risen against legitimate authority, they are traitors and malefactors. And who are greater malefactors than the backsliders who, after three years of patient effort, just as the sect finally reaches its goal, oppose its accession to power![80] At Nismes, Toulouse, Bordeaux, Toulon, and

77. Seventy thousand men were required to reduce Lyons (Guillon de Montléon, ii., 226), and sixty thousand men to reduce Toulon.

78. Archives des Affaires Etrangères, vol. cccxxix. (Letter of Chépy, political agent, Grenoble, July 26, 1793). "I say it unhesitatingly, I had rather reduce Lyons than save Valenciennes."

79. *Ibid.*, vol. cccxxix. (Letter of Chépy, Grenoble, August 24, 1793): "The Piedmontese are masters of Cluse. A large body of mountaineers have joined them. At Annecy the women have cut down the liberty pole and burnt the archives of the club and commune. At Chambéry, the people wanted to do the same, but they forced the sick in the hospitals to take arms and kept them under."

80. *Moniteur*, xviii, 474. (Report of Billaud-Varennes, October 18, 1793).

Lyons, not only have they interfered with or arrested the blow which Paris struck, but they have put down the aggressors, closed the club, disarmed the fanatical, and imprisoned the leading Maratists; and worse still, at Lyons and at Toulon, five or six *massacreurs*, or promoters of massacre, Châlier and Riard, Jassaud, Sylvestre, and Lemaille, brought before the courts, have been condemned and executed after a trial in which all the forms were strictly adhered to. That is the inexpiable crime; for, in this trial, the "Mountain" is involved; the principles of Sylvestre and Châlier are its principles; what it accomplished in Paris, they have attempted in the provinces; if they are guilty, it is also guilty; it cannot tolerate their punishment without assenting to its own punishment. Accordingly, it must proclaim them heroes and martyrs, it must canonise their memory,[81] it must avenge their tortures, it must resume and complete their assaults, it must restore their accomplices to their places, it must render them omnipotent, it must fetch each rebel city under the yoke of its populace and malefactors. It matters little whether the Jacobins be a minority, whether at Bordeaux, they have but four out of twenty-eight sections on their side, at Marseilles five out of thirty-two, whether at Lyons they can count up only fifteen hundred devoted adherents.[82] Suffrages are not reckoned, but weighed, for legality is

"The combined efforts of all the powers of Europe have not compromised liberty and the country so much as the federalist factions; the assassin the most to be dreaded is the one that lives in the house."

81. The convention purposely reinstates incendiaries and assassins. (*Moniteur*, xviii., 483. Session of Brumaire 28, year II.): xvii., 176. (Session of July 19, 1793). Rehabilitation of Bordier and Jourdain, hung in August, 1789. Cancelling of the proceedings begun against the authors of the massacre of Melun (September, 1792) and release of the accused.—Cf. Albert Babeau, (i., 277.) Rehabilitation, with indemnities distributed in Messidor, year II, to the rioters and assassins condemned for the riot of September 9, 1789, at Troyes, or to their relatives.—"Archives des Affaires Etrangères," vol. 331. (Letter of Chépy, Grenoble, Frimaire 8, year II). "The criminal court and jury of the department have just risen to the height of the situation; they have acquitted the *castle-burners*."

82. Mortimer-Ternaux, viii., 593. (Deputation of twenty-four sections sent from Bordeaux to the Convention, August 30).—Buchez et Roux, xxviii., 494.

founded, not on numbers, but on patriotism, the sovereign people being composed wholly of *sans-culottes*. So much the worse for towns where the antirevolutionary majority is so great; they are only the more dangerous; under their republican demonstrations is concealed the hostility of old parties and of the "suspect" classes, the Moderates, the Feuillants and Royalists, merchants, men of the legal profession, property-holders, and *muscadins*.[83] These form nests of reptiles and there is nothing to be done but to crush them out.

IX

In effect, whether brought under subjection or not, they are crushed out. Those are declared traitors to the country, not merely members of the departmental committees, but, at Bordeaux, all who have "aided or abetted the Committee of Public Safety"; at Lyons, all administrators, functionaries, military or civil officers who "convoked or tolerated the Rhone-et-Loire congress," and furthermore, "every individual whose son, clerk, servant, or even day-laborer, may have borne arms, or contributed to the means of resistance," that is to say, the entire National Guard who took up arms, and nearly all the population which gave its money or voted in the sections.[84] By virtue of this decree, all are "outlaws," or, in other words, subject to the guillotine on the mere declaration of identity, and their property is confiscated. Consequently, at Bordeaux, where not a gun had been fired, the mayor Saige, and principal author of

---

(Report of the representatives on mission in Bouches-du-Rhone, September 2d).—*Ibid.*, xxx., 386. (Letter of Rousin, commandant of the revolutionary army at Lyons. "A population of one hundred twenty thousand souls. . . . There are not amongst all these, one thousand five hundred patriots, even one thousand five hundred persons that one could spare.—Guillon de Montléon, i., 355, 374. (Signatures of twenty thousand Lyonnese of all classes, August 17th).

83. Guillon de Montléon, i., 394. (Letter of Dubois-Crancé to the Lyonnese, August 10th.)

84. Mortimer-Ternaux, viii., 198. (Decree of Aug. 6.)—Buchez et Roux, xxviii., 297, (Decree of July 12.).—Guillon de Montléon, i., 342. Summons of Dubois-Crancé, Aug. 8.)

the submission, is at once led to the scaffold without any form of trial,[85] while eight hundred and eighty-one others succeed him amidst the solemn silence of a dismayed population.[86] Two hundred prominent merchants are arrested in one night; more than fifteen hundred persons are imprisoned; all who are well off are ransomed, even those against whom no political charge could be made; nine millions of fines are levied against "rich egoists." One of these,[87] accused of "indifference and moderatism," pays twenty thousand francs "not to be harnessed to the car of the Revolution"; another, "convicted of having manifested contempt for his section and for the poor by giving thirty livres per month," is taxed at one million two hundred thousand livres, while the new authorities, a swindling mayor and twelve knaves composing the Revolutionary Committee, traffic in lives and property.[88] At Marseilles, says Danton,[89] the object

85. Meillan, 142.—"Archives des Affaires Etrangéres," vol. cccxxxii. (Letter of Desgranges, Bordeaux, Brumaire 8, year II.): "The execution of Mayor Saige, who was much loved by the people for his benefactions, caused much sorrow; but no guilty murmur was heard."

86. Archives Nationales, AF. II., 46. (Letter of Julien to the Committee of Public Safety, Messidor 11, year II.) "Some time ago a solemn silence prevailed at the sessions of the military commission, the people's response to the death-verdicts against conspirators; the same silence attended them to the scaffold; the whole commune seemed to sob in secret at their fate."

87. Berryat Saint-Prix, "La Justice Révolutionaire," pp. 277–299.—Archives Nationales, AF. II., 46. (Registers of the Com. of Surveillance, Bordeaux). The number of prisoners, between Prairial 21 and 28, varies from 1504 to 1529. Number of the guillotined, 882. (Memoirs of Sénart).

88. Archives Nationales, AF. II., 46. Letter of Julien, Messidor 12, year II. "A good deal has been stolen here; the mayor, now in prison, is charged with defalcations to a considerable amount. The former Committee of Surveillance was gravely compromised; many folks that were outlawed only got back by paying; the fact is verified. . . . Of the number of those who have thus purchased their lives there are some who did not deserve to die and who, nevertheless, were threatened with death."—Buchez et Roux, xxxii., 428. (Extracts from the Memoirs of Sénart). "The president of the military commission was a man named Lacombe, already banished from the city on account of a judgment against him for robbery. The other individuals employed by Tallien comprised a lot of valets, bankrupts, and sharpers."

89. Buchez et Roux, xxviii., 493. (Speech by Danton, August 31, and decree in conformity therewith by the Convention).

is "to give the commercial aristocracy an important lesson"; we must "show ourselves as terrible to traders as to nobles and priests"; consequently, twelve thousand of them are proscribed and their possessions sold.[90] From the first day the guillotine works as fast as possible; nevertheless, it does not work fast enough for Representative Fréron who finds the means for making it work faster. "The military commission we have established in place of the revolutionary Tribunal," he writes, "works frightfully fast against the conspirators. . . . They fall like hail under the sword of the law. Fourteen have already paid for their infamous treachery with their heads. Tomorrow, sixteen more are to be guillotined, all chiefs of the legion, notaries, sectionists, members of the popular tribunal; tomorrow, also, three merchants will dance the *carmagnole, and they are the ones we are after.*"[91] Men and things, all must perish; he wishes to demolish the city and proposes to fill up the harbor. Restrained with great difficulty, he contents himself with a destruction of "the haunts" of the aristocracy, two churches, the concert-hall, the houses around it, and twenty-three buildings in which the rebel sections had held their meetings.

90. Mallet-Dupan, ii., 17. "Thousands of traders in Marseilles and Bordeaux, here the respectable Gradis and there the Tarteron, have been assassinated and their goods sold. I have seen the thirty-second list only of the Marseilles *emigres,* whose property has been confiscated. . . . There are twelve thousand of them and the lists are not yet complete." (Feb. 1, 1794.)—Anne Plumptre. "A Narrative of Three Years' Residence in France, from 1802 to 1805." "During this period the streets of Marseilles were almost those of a deserted town. One could go from one end of the town to the other without meeting any one he could call an inhabitant. The great terrorists, of whom scarcely one was a Marseillaise, the soldiers and roughs as they called themselves, were almost the only persons encountered." The latter, to the number of fifty or sixty, in jackets with leather straps, fell upon all whom they did not like, and especially on anybody with a clean shirt and white cravate. Many persons on the "Cours" were thus whipped to death. No woman went out-doors without a basket, while every man wore a jacket, without which they were taken for aristocrats. (ii., 94.)

91. "Mémoires de Fréron." (Collection Barriére and Berville). Letters of Fréron to Moise Bayle, Brumaire 23, Pluviose 5 and 11, Nivose 16, II, published by Moise Bayle, also details furnished by Huard, pp. 350–365.—Archives Nationales, AF. II., 144. (Order of representatives Fréron, Barras, Salicetti, and Ricard, Nivose 17, year II.)

At Lyons, to increase the booty, the representatives had taken pains to encourage the manufacturers and merchants with vague promises; these opened their shops and brought their valuable goods, books, and papers out of their hiding-places.[92] No time is lost in seizing the plunder; "a list of all property belonging to the rich and to antirevolutionists" is drawn up, which is "confiscated for the benefit of the patriots of the city"; in addition to this a tax of six millions is imposed, payable in eight days, by those whom the confiscation may have still spared;[93] it is proclaimed, according to principle, that the surplus of each individual belongs by right to the *sansculottes*, and whatever may have been retained beyond the strictly necessary, is a robbery by the individual to the detriment of the nation.[94] In conformity with this rule there is an universal swoop, prolonged for ten months, which places the fortunes of a city of one hundred and twenty thousand souls in the hands of its rowdies. Thirty-two revolutionary committees "whose members stick like lice" choose "thousands of keepers devoted to them."[95] In confiscated dwellings and warehouses, they affix seals without an inventory; they drive out women and children "so that there shall be no witnesses"; they keep the keys; they enter and steal when they please, or install themselves for a revel with prostitutes. Meanwhile, the guillotine is kept going, and people are fired at and shot down with grape-shot. The Revolutionary Committee officially avow one thousand six hundred and eighty-two acts of murder committed in five months, while a confederate of Robespierre's privately declares that there were six thousand.[96]

Blacksmiths are condemned to death for having shod the Lyon-

92. Mallet-Dupan, ii., 17.—Guillon de Montléon, ii., 259.

93. Mallet-Dupan, ii., 17.—Guillon de Montléon, ii., 259.

94. *Ibid.*, ii., 281. (Decree of the Convention, Oct. 12); ii., 312. (Orders of Couthon and his colleagues, Oct. 25); ii., 361, 372. (Instructions for the temporary commission, Brumaire 26.)

95. *Ibid.*, iii., 153–156. Letter of Laporte to Couthon, April 13, 1794.

96. *Ibid.*, ii., 135–137. (Resolutions of the Revolutionary Commission, Germinal 17.) and Letters of Cadillot to Robespierre, Floréal, year II). iii., 63.

nese cavalry, firemen for having extinguished fires kindled by republican bombshells, a widow for having paid a war-tax during the
siege, market women for "having shown disrespect to patriots." It
is an organized "*Septembrisade*" made legal and lasting; its authors
are so well aware of the fact as to use the word itself in their public
correspondence.[97] At Toulon it is worse; people are slaughtered in
heaps, almost haphazard. Notwithstanding that the inhabitants the
most compromised, to the number of four thousand, take refuge on
board English vessels, the whole city, say the representatives, is
guilty. Four hundred workmen in the navy-yard having marched
out to meet Fréron, he reminds them that they kept on working
during the English occupation of the town, and he has them put to
death on the spot. An order is issued to all "good citizens to assemble
in the Champ de Mars on penalty of death." They come there to
the number of three thousand; Fréron, on horseback, surrounded
by cannon and troops, arrives with about a hundred Maratists, the
former accomplices of Lemaille, Sylvestre, and other well-known
assassins, who form a body of local auxiliaries and counsellors; he
tells them to select out of the crowd at pleasure according to their
grudge, fancy, or caprice; all who are designated are ranged along
a wall and shot.[98] The next morning, and on the following days, the
operation is renewed: Fréron writes on the 16th of Nivose that "eight
hundred Toulonese have already been shot." . . . "A volley of musketry," says he, in another letter, and after that, volley after volley,
until "the traitors are all gone." Then, for three months after this,
the guillotine despatches eighteen hundred persons; eleven young
women have to mount the scaffold together, in honor of a republican
festival; an old woman of ninety-four is borne to it in an armchair;

97. Guillon de Montléon, ii., 399. (Letter of Perrotin, member of the temporary commission to the revolutionary committee of Moulin.) "The work
before the new commission may be considered as an *organisation of the Septembrisade:* the process will be the same, but legalised by an act passed."
98. "Mémoires de Fréron." (Coll. Barriére et Berville) 350–360. Letters of
Fréron; evidence of surviving Toulonese and eye-witnesses.—Lauvergne, "Histoire du Département du Var."

a population of twenty-eight thousand falls down to six thousand or seven thousand.

All this is not enough; the two cities that dared maintain a siege must disappear from the French soil. The Convention decrees that "the city of Lyons shall be destroyed; every house occupied by a rich man shall be demolished; only the dwellings of the poor shall remain, with edifices specially devoted to industry, and monuments consecrated to humanity and public education."[99] The same at Toulon: "the houses within the town shall be demolished; only the buildings that are essential for army and navy purposes, for stores and munitions, shall be preserved."[100] Consequently, a requisition is made in Var and the neighboring departments for twelve thousand masons to level Toulon to the ground. At Lyons, fourteen thousand laborers pull down the Chateau Pierre-Encize; also the superb houses on Place Bellecour, those of the Quai St. Clair, those of the Rues de Flandre and de Bourgneuf, and many others; the cost of all this amounts to four hundred thousand livres per decade; in six months the Republic expends fifteen millions in destroying property valued at three or four hundred millions, belonging to the Republic.[101] Since the Mongols of the fifth and thirteenth centuries, no such vast and irrational waste had been seen—such frenzy against the most profitable fruits of industry and human civilisation. Again, one can understand how the Mongols, who were nomads, desired to convert the soil into one vast steppe. But, to demolish a town whose arsenal and harbor is maintained by it, to destroy the leaders of manufacturing interests and their dwellings in a city where its workmen and factories are preserved, to keep up a fountain and stop the stream which flows from it, or the stream without the fountain, is so absurd that the idea could only enter the head of a Jacobin. His contracted mind is so worked up that he is no longer aware of

99. Buchez et Roux, xxix., 192. (Decree of October 12).

100. *Ibid.*, xxx., 457. (Decree of November 23).

101. "Mémoires de Fréron." (Letter of Fréron, Nivose 6).—Guillon de Montléon, ii., 391.

contradictions; the ferocious stupidity of the barbarian and the fixed idea of the inquisitor meet on common ground; the earth is not big enough for any but himself and the orthodox of his species. Employing absurd, inflated and sinister terms he decrees the extermination of heretics: not only shall their monuments, dwellings and persons be destroyed, but every vestige of them shall be eradicated and their names lost to the memory of man. "The name of Toulon shall be abolished; that commune shall henceforth bear the name of Port-la-Montagne. . . . The name of Lyons shall be stricken off the list of towns belonging to the Republic; the remaining collection of houses shall henceforth bear the name of Ville-Affranchie. A column shall be erected on the ruins of Lyons bearing this inscription: '*Lyons made war on Liberty! Lyons is no more!*'"[102]

X

In all this there is no idea of sparing the chiefs of the insurrection or of the party, either deputies or ministers; on the contrary, the object is to complete the subjection of the Convention, to stifle the murmurs of the "Right," to impose silence on Ducos, Fonfrède, Vernier, and Couhey, who still speak and protest.[103] Hence the decrees of arrest or death, launched weekly from the top of the "Mountain," fall on the majority like guns fired into a crowd. Decrees of accusation follow: on the 15th of June, against Duchatel, on the 17th against Barbaroux, on the 23d against Brissot, on the 8th of July

---

102. Decrees of October 12 and December 24.—Archives Nationales, AF. II., 44. The representatives on mission wanted to do the same thing with Marseilles. (Orders of Fréron, Barras, Saliceti, and Ricard, Nivose 17, year II.) "The name of Marseilles, still borne by this criminal city, shall be changed. The National Convention shall be requested to give it another name. Meanwhile it shall remain nameless and be thus known." In effect, in several subsequent documents, Marseilles is called the *nameless commune*.

103. Buchez et Roux, xxviii., 204. (Session of June 24: "Strong expressions of dissent are heard on the right." Legendre. "I demand that the first rebel, the first man there (pointing to the "Right" party) who interrupts the speaker, be sent to the Abbaye." Couhey, indeed, was sent to the Abbaye for applauding a Federalist speech.—Cf. on these three months.—Mortimer-Ternaux, vol. viii.

against Devérité and Condorcet, on the 14th against Duperret and Fauchet, on the 30th against Duprat Jr., Vallée, and Mainvielle, on the 2d of August against Roulhier, Brunel, and Carra; Carra, Duperret, and Fauchet, present during the session, are seized on the spot, which is plain physical warning: none is more efficacious, to checkmate the unruly. Decrees are passed on the 18th of July accusing Coustard, on the 28th of July against Gensonné, Lasource, Vergniaud, Mollevault, Gardien, Grangeneuve, Fauchet, Boileau, Valazé, Cussy, and Meillan, each being aware that the tribunal before which he must appear is the antechamber to the guillotine. Decrees of condemnation are passed on the 12th of July against Birotteau, on the 28th of July against Buzot, Barbaroux, Gorsas, Lanjuniais, Salles, Louvet, Bergoeing, Pétion, Guadet, Chasset, Chambon, Lidon, Valady, Fermon, Kervelégen, Larivière, Rabaut St. Etienne, and Lesage; pronounced outlaws and traitors, they are to be led to the scaffold without trial as soon as they can be got hold of. Finally, on the 3d of October, a great haul of the net in the Assembly itself sweeps off the benches all the deputies that still seem capable of any independence: the first thing is to close the doors of the hall, which is done by Amar, reporter of the Committee of General Security;[104] then, after a declamatory and calumnious speech, which lasts two hours, he reads off names on two lists of proscriptions: forty-five deputies, more or less prominent among the Girondists, are to be at once summoned before the revolutionary Tribunal; seventy-three others, who have signed secret protests against the 31st of May and 2d of June, are to be put in jail. No debate, the majority not being allowed even to express an opinion. Some of the proscribed attempt to exculpate themselves, but they are not allowed to be heard; none but the *Montagnards* have the floor, and they do no more than add to the lists, each according to personal enmity; Levasseur has Vigée put down, and Duroi adds the name of Richon. On their names being called, all the poor creatures who happen to be inscribed,

104. Buchez et Roux, xxix., 175.—Dauban: "La Démagogie à Paris en 1793," 436. (Narrative by Dulaure, an eye-witness).

quietly advance and "huddle together within the bar of the house, like lambs destined to slaughter," and here they are separated into two flocks; on the one hand, the seventy-three, and on the other, the ten or twelve who, with the Girondists already kept under lock and key, are to furnish the sacramental and popular number, the twenty-two traitors whose punishment is a requirement of the Jacobin imagination;[105] on the left, the batch for the prison; on the right, the batch for the guillotine.

To those who might be tempted to imitate them or defend them this is a sufficient lesson. Subject to the hootings and foul insults of the hags posted along the street, the seventy-three[106] are conducted to the prisoners' room in the mayoralty, already full; they pass the night standing on benches, scarcely able to breathe. The next day they are crammed into the prison for assassins and robbers, "la Force," on the sixth story, under the roof; in this narrow garret their beds touch each other, while two of the deputies are obliged to sleep on the floor for lack of room. Under the skylights, which serve for windows, and at the foot of the staircase are two pig-pens; at the end of the apartment are the privies, and in one corner a night-tub, which completes the poisoning of the atmosphere already vitiated by this crowded mass of human beings; the beds consist of sacks of straw swarming with vermin; they are compelled to endure the discipline,[107] rations, and mess of convicts. And they are lucky to escape at this rate: for Amar takes advantage of their silent deportment to tax them with conspiracy; other *Montagnards* likewise want to arraign them at the revolutionary Tribunal: at all events, it is agreed

105. There were really only twenty-one brought before the revolutionary Tribunal.

106. Dauban, xxvi., p. 440. (Narrative of Blanqui, one of the seventy-three.)

107. Buchez et Roux, xxix., 178, 179. Osselin: "I demand the decree of accusation against them all."—Amar: "The apparently negative conduct of the minority of the Convention since the 2d of June, was a new complot devised by Barbaroux." Robespierre: "If there are other criminals among those you have placed under arrest the Committee of General Security will present to you the nomenclature of them and you will always be at liberty to strike."

that the Committee of General Security shall examine their records and maintain the right of designating new culprits amongst them. For ten months they thus remain under the knife, in daily expectation of joining the twenty-two on the Place de la Révolution. With respect to the latter, the object is not to try them but to kill them, and the semblance of a trial is simply judicial assassination; the bill of indictment against them consists of club gossip; they are accused of having desired the restoration of the monarchy, of being in correspondence with Pitt and Cobourg;[108] of having excited Vendée to insurrection. The betrayal of Dumouriez is imputed to them, also the murder of Lepelletier, and the assassination of Marat; while pretended witnesses, selected from amongst their personal enemies, come and repeat, like a theme agreed upon, the same ill-contrived fable: nothing but vague allegations and manifest falsehoods, not one definite fact, not one convincing document; the lack of proof is such that the trial has to be stopped as soon as possible. "You brave b—— forming the court," writes Hébert, "don't trifle away your time. Why so much ceremony in shortening the days of wretches whom the people have already condemned?" Care is especially taken not to let them have a chance to speak. The eloquence of Vergniaud and logic of Guadet might turn the tables at the last moment. Consequently, a prompt decree authorises the tribunal to stop proceedings as soon as the jury becomes sufficiently enlightened, which is the case after the seventh session of the court, the record of death suddenly greeting the accused, who are not allowed to defend them-

108. *Ibid.*, xxix., 437, 432, 447.—Report by Amar. (This report served as the bill of indictment against them, "cowardly satellites of royal despotism, vile agents of foreign tyrants."—Wallon, ii., 407, 409. (Letter of Fouquier-Tinville to the Convention). "After the special debates, will not each of the accused demand a general prosecution? The trial, accordingly, will be interminable. Besides, one may ask why should there be witnesses? The Convention, all France, accuses those on trial. The evidence of their crimes is plain; everybody is convinced of their guilt. . . . It is the Convention which must remove all formalities that interfere with the course pursued by the tribunal."—*Moniteur*, xvii. (Session of October 28), 291. The decree provoked by a petition of Jacobins, is passed on motion of Osselin, aggravated by Robespierre.

selves. One of them, Valazé, stabs himself in open court, and the next day the national head-chopper strikes off the remaining twenty heads in thirty-eight minutes. Still more expeditious are the proceedings against the accused who avoid a trial. Gorsas, seized in Paris on the 8th of October, is guillotined the same day. Birotteau, seized at Bordeaux, on the 24th of October, mounts the scaffold within twenty-four hours. The others, tracked like wolves, wandering in disguise from one hiding-place to another, and most of them arrested in turn, have only the choice of several kinds of death. Cambon is killed in defending himself. Lidon, after having defended himself, blows out his brains. Condorcet takes poison in the guardroom of Bourg-la-Reine. Roland kills himself with his sword on the highway. Clavière stabs himself in prison. Rebecqui is found drowned in the harbor of Marseilles, and Pétion and Buzot half eaten by wolves on the moor of St. Emilion. Valady is executed at Perigueux, Duchézeau at Rochefort, Grangeneuve, Guadet, Salles, and Barbaroux at Bordeaux, Coustard, Cussy, Rabaut St. Etienne, Bernard, Mazuyer, and Lebrun at Paris. Even those who resigned in January, 1793, Kersaint and Manuel, atone with their lives for the crime of having sided with the "Right" and, of course, Madame Roland, who pays as the leader of the party, is one of the first to be guillotined.[109] Of the one hundred and eighty Girondists who led the Convention, one hundred and forty have perished or are in prison, or fled under sentence of death. After such a curtailment and such an example the remaining deputies cannot be otherwise than docile;[110] neither in the central nor in the local government will the

109. Louvet, "Mémoires," 321. (List of the Girondists who perished or who were proscribed. Twenty-four fugitives survived.)

110. Mortimer-Ternaux, viii., 395, 416, 435. The terror and disgust of the majority is seen in the small number of voters. The abstaining from voting is the more significant in relation to the election of the dictators. The members of the Committee of Public Safety, elected on the 16th of July, obtain from one hundred to one hundred and ninety-two votes. The members of the Committee of Security obtain from twenty-two to one hundred and thirteen votes. The members of the same committee, renewed on the 11th of September, obtain from fifty-two to one hundred and eight votes. The judges of the revolutionary

"Mountain" encounter resistance; its despotism is practically established, and all that remains is to proclaim this in legal form.

XI

After the 2d of August, on motion of Bazire, the Convention decrees "that France is in revolution until its independence is recognised," which means[111] that the period of hypocritical phrases has come to an end, that the Constitution was merely a signboard for a fair, that the charlatans who had made use of it no longer need it, that it is to be put away in the receptacle of other advertising lumber, that individual, local, and parliamentary liberties are abolished, that the government is arbitrary and absolute, that no institution, law, dogma, or precedent affords any guarantee for it against the rights of the people, that property and lives are wholly at its mercy, that there are no longer any rights of man. Six weeks later, when, through the protest of the forty-five and the arrest of the seventy-three, obedience to the Convention is assured, all this is boldly and officially announced in the tribune. "Under the present circumstances of the Republic," says Saint-Just, "the Constitution cannot

---

Tribunal, completed on the 3d of August, obtain from forty-seven to sixty-five votes.—Meillan, 85. (In relation to the institution of the revolutionary government, on motion of Bazire, Aug. 28.) "Sixty or eighty deputies passed this decree . . . it was preceded by another passed by a plurality of thirty against ten. . . . For two months the session, the best attended, contains but one hundred deputies. The *Montagnards* overran the departments to deceive or intimidate the people. The rest, discouraged, keep away from the meetings or take no part in the proceedings."

111. The meaning and motives of this declaration are clearly indicated in Bazire's speech. "Since the adoption of the Constitution," he says, "Feuillantism has raised its head; a struggle has arisen between energetic and moderate patriots. At the end of the Constituent Assembly, the Feuillants possessed themselves of the words *law, order, public, peace, security,* to enchain the zeal of the friends of freedom; the same manoeuvres are practiced today. You must shatter the weapon in your enemies' hands, which they use against you."—Durand-Maillane, 154. "The simple execution of constitutional laws," said Bazire, "made for peaceable times, would be impotent among the conspiracies that surround you."—Meillan, 108.

be established; it would be self-immolated; it would become the guarantee of attacks on liberty, because it would lack the violence which is necessary to repress these." To govern "according to maxims of natural peace and justice" is no longer an object; "these maxims will do among the friends of liberty"; but, between patriots and the malevolent, they are not applicable. The latter are not of the country, "they do not belong to its sovereignty," they are outside the law, excluded from the social pact, rebellious slaves, fit for chastisement or constraint, and, amongst these, must be placed "the indifferents." "You are to punish whoever is passive in the Republic and does nothing for it";[112] for his inertia is a betrayal and ranks him among public enemies. Now, between the people and its enemies, there is nothing in common but the sword; steel must control those who cannot be ruled "by justice"; the monarchical and the neutral majority must be "kept down"; the Republic will be founded only when the *sans-culottes,* the sole representatives of the nation, the only citizens, *"shall rule by right of conquest."*[113] That is intelligible, and more besides. The régime of which Saint-Just presents the plan, is that by which every oligarchy of invaders installs and maintains itself over a subjugated nation. Through this régime, in Greece, ten thousand Spartans, after the Dorian invasion, mastered

112. *Moniteur,* xviii., 106. (Report of Saint-Just on the organisation of the revolutionary government, October 10th, and the decree in conformity therewith.) *Ibid.,* 473.—Report of Billaud-Varennes on a mode of provisional and revolutionary government, Novem. 18, and decree in conformity therewith.)— *Ibid.,* xviii., 479. (Convention, Session of November 22d, 1793.—Speech of Hébrard, spokesman of a deputation from Cantal). "A central committee of surveillance, a revolutionary army, has been established in our department. Aristocrats, suspects, the doubtful, moderates, *egoists, all gentlemen without distinguishing those who have done nothing for the revolution* from those who have acted against it, await in retirement the ulterior measures required by the interests of the Republic. I have said without distinction of *the indifferent from the suspects;* for we hold to these words of Solon's: *"He who is not with us is against us."* (Honorable mention in the *procès-verbal.*)

113. *Moniteur,* (Speech by Danton, March 26, 1794.) "In creating revolutionary committees the desire was to establish a species of dictatorship of citizens the most devoted to liberty over those who rendered themselves suspects."

three hundred thousand helots and *périocques;* through this régime, in England, sixty thousand Normans, after the battle of Hastings, mastered two million Saxons; through this régime in Ireland, since the battle of the Boyne, two hundred thousand English Protestants have mastered a million of Catholic Irish; through this régime, the three hundred thousand Jacobins of France will master the seven or eight millions of Girondists, Feuillants, Royalists, or Indifferents.

It is a very simple one and consists in maintaining the subject population in a state of extreme helplessness and of extreme terror. To this end, it is disarmed;[114] it is kept under surveillance; all action in common is prohibited; its eyes are always directed to the up-lifted axe and to the prison doors always open; it is ruined and decimated. For the past six months all these rigors are decreed and applied, disarmament of "suspects," taxes on the rich, the *maximum* against traders, requisitions on land-owners, wholesale arrests, rapid executions of sentences, arbitrary penalties of death, and ostentatious, multiplied tortures. For the past six months, all sorts of executive instruments are manufactured and put in operation—the Committee of Public Safety, the Committee of General Security, ambulating proconsuls with full power, local committees authorised to tax and imprison at will, a revolutionary army, a revolutionary tribunal. But, for lack of internal harmony and of central impulsion, the machine

---

114. Mallet-Dupan, ii., 8. (February, 1794). "At this moment the entire people is disarmed. Not a gun can be found either in town or country. If anything attests the supernatural power which the leaders of the Convention enjoy, it is to see, in one instant, through one act of the will and nobody offering any resistance, or complaining of it, the nation from Perpignan to Lille, deprived of every means of defence against oppression, with a facility still more unprecedented than that which attended the universal arming of the nation in 1789."— "A Residence in France," ii., 409. "The National Guard as a regular institution was in great part suppressed after the summer of 1793, those who composed it being gradually disarmed. Guard-mounting was continued, but the citizens performing this service were, with very few exceptions, armed with pikes, and these again were not fully entrusted to them; each man, on quitting his post, gave up his arms more punctually than if he had been bound to do so through capitulation with a victorious enemy."

only half works, the power not being sufficient and its action not sufficiently sweeping and universal. "You are too remote from assaults on you," says Saint-Just";[115] "it is essential that the sword of the law should everywhere be rapidly brandished and your arm be everywhere present to arrest crime. . . . The ministers confess that, beyond their first and second subordinates, they find nothing but inertia and indifference." "The like apathy prevails among all the government agents," says Billaud-Varennes;[116] "the secondary authorities forming the props of the Revolution serve only to impede it." Decrees, transmitted through administrative channels, arrive slowly and are indolently applied. "You are wanting in that coactive force which is the principle of being, of action, of execution. . . . Every good government should possess a centre of volition and levers connected with it. . . . Every emanation of public force should be exclusively derived from its source." "In ordinary governments," says Couthon, finally,[117] "the right of electing belongs to the people; you cannot take it away from them. In extraordinary governments all impulsion must proceed from the centrality; it is from the Convention that elections must issue. . . . You would injure the people by confiding the election of public officers to them, because you would expose them to electing men that would betray them." The result is that the constitutional maxims of 1789 give way to contrary maxims; instead of subjecting the government to the people, the people is made subject to the government. The hierarchy of the ancient régime is reestablished under revolutionary terms, and henceforth all powers, much more formidable than those of the ancient régime, cease to be delegated from below upward that they may be delegated from above downward.

At the summit, a committee of twelve members, similar to the former royal council, exercises collective royalty; nominally, au-

---

115. *Moniteur,* xviii., 106. (Report by Saint-Just, Oct. 10th).

116. *Ibid.,* 473. (Report of Billaud-Varennes, Nov. 13th).

117. *Ibid.,* xviii., 591. (Speech by Couthon, December 4th). *Ibid.,* Barère: "Electoral assemblies are monarchical institutions, they attach to royalism, they must be specially avoided in revolutionary times."

thority is divided amongst the twelve; really, it is concentrated in a
few hands. Several occupy only a subaltern position, and amongst
these, Barère, who, official secretary and mouthpiece, is always ready
to make a speech and indite an editorial; others, with special functions, Jean Bon St. André, Lindet, and above all, Prieur de la Côte
d'Or and Carnot, confine themselves each to his particular department, navy, war, supplies, with blank signatures, for which they
give in return their signatures to the political leaders; the latter,
called "the statesmen," Robespierre, Couthon, Saint-Just, Collot
d'Herbois, Billaud-Varennes, are the real monarchs, and they direct
things generally. It is true that their mandate has to be renewed
monthly; but this is a certainty, for, in the present state of the Convention, its vote, required beforehand, becomes an almost vain formality. More submissive than the parliament of Louis XIV., the
Convention adopts, without discussion, the decrees which the Committee of Public Safety present to it ready made; it is no more than
a registry-office, and scarcely that, for it has relinquished its right
of appointing its own committees, that office being assigned to the
Committee of Public Safety; it votes in a lump all lists of names
which the Committee send in. Naturally, none but the creatures of
the latter and the faithful are inscribed;[118] thus, the whole legislative
and parliamentary power belongs to it. As to executive and administrative power, the ministers have become mere clerks of the Committee of Public Safety; "they come every day at specified hours to
receive its orders and acts";[119] they submit to it "the list with explanations, of all the agents" sent into the departments and abroad; they
refer to it every minute detail; they are its scribes, merely its puppets,
so insignificant that they finally lose their title, and for the "Com-

118. Mortimer-Ternaux, viii., 40. (Decree passed on the proposition of Danton, session of September 13th). The motive alleged by Danton is that "members
are still found on the committees whose opinions, at least, approach federalism."
Consequently the committees are purified, and particularly the Committee of
General Security. Six of its members are stricken off (Sept. 14), and the list sent
in by the Committee of Public Safety passes without discussion.

119. *Moniteur*, xviii., 592. (Session of December 4, speech by Robespierre.)

missioner on External Relations" a former school-master is taken, an inept clubbist, the pander of a billiard-room and liquor-saloon, scarcely able to read the documents brought to him to sign in the café where he passes his days.[120] Thus is the second power in the State converted by the Committee into a squad of domestics, while the foremost one is converted into an auditory of *claqueurs.*

To maintain them true to their obligations it has two hands. One, the right, which seizes people unawares by the collar, is the Committee of General Security, composed of twelve extreme, *Montagnards,* such as Panis, Vadier, Lebas, Geoffroy, David, Amar, Lavicomterie, Lebon, and Ruhl, all nominated, that is to say, appointed by it, being its confederates and subalterns. They are its lieutenants of police, and once a week they come and take part in its labors, as formerly the D'Argengons, the Sartines, and the Lenoirs assisted the Comptroller-general. A man whom the conventicle deems a "suspect," suddenly arrested, no matter who, whether representative, minister, or general, finds himself the next morning under bolt and bar in one of the ten new Bastilles. There, the other hand seizes him by the throat; this is the revolutionary Tribunal, an exceptional court like the extraordinary commissions of the ancient régime, only far more terrible. Aided by its police gang, the Committee of Public Safety itself selects the sixteen judges and sixty jurymen[121] from among the most servile, the most furious, or the most brutal of the fanatics:[122] Fouquier-Tinville, Hermann, Dumas, Payan, Coffinhal,

---

120. Miot de Melito, "Mémoires," i., 47.

121. Buchez et Roux, xxviii., 153. Mortimer-Ternaux, viii., 443. (Decree of September 28th).—Wallon, "Histoire du Tribunal Révolutionaire de Paris," iv., 112.

122. Buchez et Roux, xxxiv., 300. (Trial of Fouquier-Tinville and associates). Bill of indictment. "One of these publicly boasted of always having voted death. Others state that they were content to see people to give their judgment; physical inspection alone determined them to vote death. Another said, that when there was no offence committed it was necessary to imagine one. Another is a regular sot and has never sat in judgment but in a state of intoxication. Others come to the bench only to fire their volleys." (Supporting evidence.) "Observe, moreover, that judges and juries are bound to kill under penalty of

Fleuriot-Lescot, and, lower down on the scale, apostate priests, renegade nobles, disappointed artists, infatuated studio-apprentices, journeymen scarcely able to write their names, shoe-makers, joiners, carpenters, tailors, barbers, former lackeys, an idiot like Ganney, a deaf man like Leroy-Dix-Aout, whose names and professions indicate all that is necessary to be told; these men are licensed and paid murderers; the jurymen themselves are allowed eighteen francs a day, so that they may attend to their business more leisurely. This business consists in condemning without proof, without any pleadings, and scarcely any examination, in a hurry, in batches, whoever the Committee of Public Safety might send to them, even the most confirmed *Montagnards:* Danton, who contrived the tribunal, will soon find all this out. Through these two government engines the Committee of Public Safety keeps every head under the cleaver and each head, to avoid being struck off, bows down,[123] in the provinces as well as at Paris.

Owing to the mutilation of the local hierarchy, in the provinces as well as at Paris, and the introduction of new authorities, the omnipotent will of the Committee becomes everywhere present. Directly or indirectly, "for all government measures or measures of

---

death (*Ibid.*, 30)." Fouquier-Tinville states that on the 22d of Prairial he took the same step (to resign) with Chatelet, Brochet, and Lerry, when they met Robespierre, returning to the National Convention arm-in-arm with Barère. Fouquier adds, that they were treated as aristocrats and antirevolutionists, and threatened with death if they refused to remain on their posts." Analogoes declarations by Pigeot, Ganne, Girard, Dupley, Foucault, Nollin, and Madre. "Sellier adds, that the tribunal having remonstrated against the law of Prairial 22, he was threatened with arrest by Dumas. Had we resigned, he says, Dumas would have guillotined us."

123. *Moniteur*, xxiv., 12. (Session of Ventose 29, year III., speech by Bailleul.) "Terror subdued all minds, suppressed all emotions; it was the force of the government, while such was this government that the numerous inhabitants of a vast territory seemed to have lost the qualities which distinguish man from a domestic animal. They seemed even to have no life except what the government accorded to them. Human personality no longer existed; each individual was simply a machine, going, coming, thinking, or not thinking as he was impelled or stimulated by tyranny."

public safety, all that relates to persons and the general and internal police," "all constituted bodies and all public functionaries, are placed under its inspection,"[124] I leave it to be supposed whether they expose themselves to its guillotine. To suppress in advance any tendency to administrative inertia, it has had withdrawn from the too powerful, too much respected, department governments, "too inclined to federalism," their departmental preëminence and their "political influence";[125] it reduces these to the levying of taxes and the supervision of roads and canals; it winnows them out through its agents; it even winnows out the governments of municipalities and districts. To suppress beforehand all probability of popular opposition, it has had the sessions of the sections reduced to two per week; it installs in them for about forty sous a day a majority of *sans-culottes;* it directs the suspension "until further orders" of the municipal elections.[126] Finally, to have full control on the spot, it appoints its own men, first, the commissioners and the representatives on missions, a sort of temporary corps of directors sent into each department with unlimited powers;[127] next, a body of national agents, a sort of permanent body of subdelegates, through whom in each district and municipality it replaces the *procureurs-syndics.*[128] To

124. Decree of Frimaire 14, year II., Dec. 4, 1793.

125. *Moniteur,* xviii., 473, 474, 478. (Speech by Billaud-Varennes.) "The sword of Damocles must henceforth be brandished over the entire surface." This expression of Billaud sums up the spirit of every new institution.

126. *Moniteur,* xviii., 275. (Session of Oct. 26, 1793, speech by Barère.) "This is the most revolutionary step you can take." (Applause.)

127. *Ibid.* 520. (Report of Barère and decree in conformity). "The representatives sent on mission are required to conform strictly to the acts of the Committee of Public Safety. Generals and other agents of the executive power will, under no pretext, obey any special order, that they may refuse to carry out the said acts."—*Moniteur,* xviii., 291. (Report by Barère, Oct. 29, 1793.) At this date one hundred and forty representatives are on mission.

128. Archives Nationales, AF. II., 22. (Papers of the Committee of Public Safety. Note on the results of the revolution government). "The law of Frimaire 14 created two centres of influence from which action spread, in the sense of the Committee, and which affected the authorities. These two pivots of revolutionary rule outside the Committee were the representatives of the people on

this army of functionaries is added in each town, bourg, or large village, a revolutionary committee, paid three francs a day per member, charged with the application of its decrees, and required to make reports thereon. Never before was such a vast and closely-woven network cast from above to envelope and keep captive twenty-six millions of men. Such is the real constitution which the Jacobins substitute for the constitution they have prepared for show. In the arsenal of the monarchy which they destroyed they took the most despotic institutions—centralisation, Royal Council, lieutenants of police, special tribunals, intendants, and subdelegates; they disinterred the antique Roman law of lèse-majesty, refurbished old blades which civilisation had dulled, aiming them at every throat and now wielded at random against liberties, property and lives. It is called the "revolutionary government"; according to official statements it is to last until peace is secured; in the minds of genuine Jacobins it is to last until, as declared in its formula, all Frenchmen are "regenerated."

---

missions and the national agents controlling the district committees. The words *revolutionary government* alone exercised an incalculable magical influence."— Mallet-Dupan, "Mémoires," ii., p. 2, and following pages.

BOOK SIXTH

The Jacobin Programme

≈ CHAPTER I ≈

I. *Programme of the Jacobin party—Abstract principle and spontaneous development of the theory—* II. *The Jacobin conception of Society—The* Contrat-Social*—Total surrender of the Individual to the Community—Everything belongs to the State—Confiscations and Sequestrations—Preemption and requisitions of produce and merchandise—Individuals belong to the State—Drafts of persons for Military service—Drafts of persons for the Civil service—Personal sentiments and ideas subject to the State, at once philanthropist, pedagogue, theologian, censor, moralist and director—* III. *The object of the State is the regeneration of man—Two branches of this work—Restoration of the Natural man—Formation of the Social man—Grandeur of the undertaking—Force a right and duty in carrying it out—* IV. *The two distortions of the natural man—Positive religion—Proscription of the orthodox cult—Measures against unsworn priests—Measures against the loyal orthodox—Destruction of the constitutional cult—Pressure on the sworn priests—Churches closed and ceremonies suppressed—Prolongation of these persecutions until the Consulate—* V. *Social inequality—Evil doings of the upper aristocracy—Measures against the King and Nobles—Evil doings of the aristocracy of wealth—Measures against landowners, capitalists and people with incomes—Destruction of large fortunes—Measures taken to prevent large fortunes—* VI. *Conditions requisite for making a citizen—Plans for suppressing poverty—Measures in favor of the poor—* VII. *Repression of Egoism—Measures against agriculturists, manufacturers and merchants—Socialistic projects—Repression of Federalism—Measures against the local, professional and family spirit—* VIII. *Formation of soul and intellect—Civil religion—National education—Measures for equality—Obligatory civism—The recasting and reduction of human nature to the Jacobin type.*

I

NOTHING is more dangerous than a general idea in narrow and empty minds: as they are empty, it finds no knowledge there to interfere with it; as they are narrow it is not long before it occupies the place entirely. Henceforth they no longer belong to themselves but are mastered by it; it works in them and through them, the man, in the true sense of the word, being possessed. Something which is not himself, a monstrous parasite, a foreign and disproportionate conception, lives within him, developing and giving birth to the evil purposes with which it is pregnant. He did not foresee that he would have them; he did not know what his dogma contained, what venomous and murderous consequences were to issue from it. They issue from it fatally, each in its turn, and under the pressure of circumstances, at first anarchical consequences and now despotic consequences. Having obtained power, the Jacobin brings his fixed idea along with him; whether at the head of the government or in opposition to it, this idea is fruitful, and the all-powerful dogma projects over a new domain the innumerable links of its endless chain.

II

Let us trace this inward development and go back, along with the Jacobin, to first principles, to the original pact, to the first organisation of society. There is but one legitimate society, that founded on the "contrat-social," and "the clauses of this contract fully understood, reduce themselves to one, the total alienation of each individual, with all his rights, to the community, . . . each surrendering himself up absolutely, just as he actually stands, he and all his forces, of which the property he possesses forms a part."[1] There must be no exception or reservation. Nothing of what he previously was, or had, now belongs to him in his own right; henceforth, what he is,

1. This and the following text are taken from the "Contrat-Social" by Rousseau. Cf. "The Ancient Régime," book iii., ch. iv.

or has, devolves upon him only through delegation. His property and his person now form a portion of the commonwealth. If he is in possession of these, his ownership is at second hand; if he derives any benefit therefrom, it is as a concession. He is their depository, trustee, and administrator, and nothing more.[2] In other words, with respect to these he is simply a managing director, that is to say a functionary like others, with a precarious appointment and always revocable by the State which has commissioned him. "As nature gives to every man absolute power over the members of his body the social pact gives the social body absolute power over all its members." The State, as omnipotent sovereign and universal proprietor, exercises at discretion, its boundless rights over persons and things; consequently we, its representatives, take all things and persons into our hands; as they belong to it, so do they belong to us.

We have confiscated the possessions of the clergy, amounting to about four billion livres; we confiscate the property of the *emigrés*, amounting to three billion livres;[3] we confiscate the property of the guillotined and transported: all this amounts to some hundreds of millions; later on, the count will be made, because the list remains open and is being daily added to. We sequestrate the property of "suspects," which gives us its usufruct: here are many hundred millions more; after the war and the banishment of "suspects," we shall seize the property along with its usufruct: here, again, are millions of capital.[4] Meanwhile, we take the property of hospitals and of other benevolent institutions, about eight hundred million livres; we take

2. This idea, so universally prevalent and precocious, is uttered by Mirabeau in the session of the 10th of August, 1789. (Buchez et Roux, ii., 257.) "I know of but three ways of maintaining one's existence in society, and these are to be either a *beggar, a robber, or a hireling*. The proprietor is himself only the first of hirelings. What we commonly call his property is nothing more than the pay society awards him for distributing amongst others that which is entrusted to him to distribute through his expenses and through what he consumes; *proprietors are the agents, the stewards of the social body.*"

3. Report by Roland, January 6, 1793, and by Cambon, February 1, 1793.

4. Buchez et Roux, xxxi., 311. Report by Saint-Just, Ventose 8, year II., and decree in conformity therewith.

the property of factories, of endowments, of educational institutions, and of literary and scientific associations: another lot of millions.[5] We take back the domains rented or alienated by the State for the past three centuries and more, which gives again about a couple of billions.[6] We take the possessions of the communes up to the amount of their indebtedness. We have already received as an inheritance the ancient domains of the crown, also the later domain of the civil list. More than three-fifths[7] of the soil thus falls into our hands, which three-fifths are much the best stocked; they comprise almost all the large and fine edifices, châteaux, abbeys, mansions, houses of superintendents; and nearly all the royal, episcopal, seignorial, and bourgeois stock of rich and elegant furniture; all plate, libraries, pictures and artistic objects accumulated for centuries. Remark, again, the seizure of specie and all other articles of gold and silver; in the months alone of November and December, 1793, this swoop puts into our coffers three or four hundred millions,[8] not assignats, but ringing coin. In short, whatever the form of established capital may be we take all we can get hold of, probably more than three-fourths of it. There remains the portion which is not fixed capital, that which disappears in use, namely, all that is consumed, all the fruits of the soil, every description of provision, all the products of

5. Decree of 13 Brumaire, year II.—Report by Cambon, Feb. 1, 1793. Cambon estimates the property alone of the order of Malta and of the colleges at four hundred million livres.

6. *Moniteur,* xviii., 419 and 486. Reports by Cambon, 1 Frimaire and Brumaire 22, year II. "Let us begin with taking possession of the leased domains, notwithstanding preceding laws."

7. Cf. "The Ancient Régime," p. 14.

8. Mallet-Dupan, "Mémoires," ii., 19. *Moniteur,* xviii., 565. (Report by Cambon, 11 Frimaire, year II.) Requested to do so by a popular club of Toulouse, the department of Haute-Garonne has ordered all possessors of articles in gold or silver to bring them to the treasuries of their districts to be exchanged for assignats. This order has thus far brought into the Toulouse treasury about one million five hundred thousand or one million six hundred thousand livres in gold and silver. The same at Montauban and other places. "Several of our colleagues have even decreed the death penalty against whoever did not bring their gold and silver within a given time."

human art and labor which contribute to the maintenance of existence. Through "the right of preemption" and through the right of "requisition," "the Republic becomes temporary proprietor of whatever commerce, manufacture, and agriculture have produced and added to the soil of France": all food and merchandise[9] is ours before being owned by their holder. We carry out of his house whatever suits us; we pay him for this with worthless paper; we frequently do not pay him at all. For greater convenience, we seize objects directly and wherever we find them, grain in the farmer's barn, hay in the reaper's shed, cattle in the fold, wine in the vats, hides at the butcher's, leather in the tanneries, soap, tallow, sugar, brandy, cloths, linens, and the rest, in stores, depots, and ware-houses. We stop vehicles and horses in the street. We enter the premises of mail or coach contractors and empty their stables. We carry away kitchen utensils to obtain the copper; we turn people out of their rooms to get their beds; we strip them of their coats and shirts; in one day, we make ten thousand individuals in one town go barefoot.[10] "When public needs require it," says representative Isoré, "all belongs to the people and nothing to individuals."

9. *Moniteur*, xviii., 320. (Session of Brumaire 11, year II.), the words of Barère, reporter of the law.

10. Archives Nationales, AF.II., 106. (Orders by representative Beauchamp, l'Isle Jourdain, Pluviose 2, year II.) "All blue and green cloaks in the departments of Haute-Garonne, as well as of the Landes, Gers, and others, are put in requisition from the present day. Every citizen possessing blue or green cloaks is required to declare them at the depot of the municipality or other locality where he may chance to be." Simon, "suspect" is treated as such. *Ibid.*, AF.II., 92. (Order issued by Taillefer, Brumaire 3, year II., at Villefranche-l'Aveyron.)—De Martel, "Etude sur Fouché," 368. (Order by Fouché, Collot d' Herbois and Delaporte: Lyons, Brumaire 21, year II.) *Moniteur*, xv., 384. (Session of 19th Brumaire. Letter of Barras and Fréron, dated at Marseilles.)— *Moniteur*, xviii., 513. (Orders by Lebon and Saint-Just, at Strasbourg, Brumaire 24 and 25, year II.) Letter of Isoré to the minister Bouchotte, November 4, 1793. (Legros, "La Revolution telle qu'elle est.") The principle of these measures was laid down by Robespierre in his speech on property (April 24, 1793), and in his declaration of rights unanimously adopted by the Jacobin Club (Buchez et Roux, xxvi., 93 and 130).

By virtue of the same right we dispose of persons as we do of things. We decree a general uprising of the people, and, stranger still, we carry it out, at least in many parts of the country, and we keep it up for months: in Vendée, and in the northern and eastern departments, the entire male, able-bodied population, all up to fifty years of age, are driven in flocks against the enemy.[11] We afterwards muster in an entire generation, all young men between eighteen and twenty-five, almost a million of men:[12] whoever fails to appear is put in irons for ten years; he is regarded as a deserter; his property is confiscated, and his relations are punished along with him; later, he is assimilated with the emigrants, condemned to death, and his father, mother, and progenitors, treated as "suspects," are imprisoned and their possessions taken. To clothe, shoe, and equip our recruits, we must have workmen: we summon to head-quarters all gunsmiths, blacksmiths, and locksmiths, all the tailors and shoemakers of the district, "foremen, apprentices, and boys";[13] we imprison those who do not come; we install the rest in squads in public buildings and assign them their tasks; they are forbidden to furnish anything to private individuals; henceforth, French shoemakers must work only for us, and each must deliver to us, under penalty, so many pairs of shoes per decade. But, the civil service is no less important than the military service, and to feed the people is as urgent as it is to defend them. Hence we put "in requisition all who have anything to do with handling, transporting or selling provisions and articles of prime necessity,"[14] especially combustibles and

11. Rousset, "Les Volontaires," p. 234 and 254.

12. Report by Cambon, Pluviose 3, year III., p. 3. "One-fifth of the active population is employed in the common defence."—Decrees of May 12 and Aug. 23, 1793.—Decree of November 22, 1793.—Order of the Directory, October 18, 1798.

13. *Moniteur*, xix., 631. Decree of Ventose 14, year II. Archives Nationales, D.SI., 10. (Orders by representatives Delacroix, Louchet, and Legendre; Pont-Audemer, Frimaire 14, year II.) *Moniteur*, xviii., 622.—(Decree of Frimaire 18, year II.)

14. Decree of 15—Floréal 18, year II. Decree of September 29, 1793, (in which forty objects of prime necessity are enumerated).—Article 9 decrees three days imprisonment against workmen and manufacturers who "without legiti-

food—wood-choppers, carters, raftsmen, millers, reapers, threshers, wine-growers, mowers, field-hands, "country people" of every kind and degree. Their hands belong to us: we make them bestir themselves and work under the penalty of fine and imprisonment. There shall be no idlers, especially in crop time: we take the entire population of a commune or canton into the fields, comprising "the lazy of both sexes";[15] willingly or not, they shall do the harvesting under our eyes, banded together in fields belonging to others as well as in their own, and they shall put the sheaves indiscriminately into the public granary.

But in labor all hangs together, from the initial undertaking to the final result, from the raw material to the most finished production, from the great manufacturer down to the pettiest jobber; grasping the first link of the chain involves grasping the last one. The requisition here again answers the purpose: we apply it to all pursuits; each is bound to continue his own; the manufacturer to manufacture, the trader to trade, even to his own detriment, because, if a loser by this, the public gains, and every good citizen ought to prefer public profit to his own profit.[16] In effect, let his office be what it will, he is an employee of the community; therefore, the community may not only prescribe task-work to him, but select his task; it need not consult him in the matter, for he has no right to refuse. Hence it is that we appoint or maintain people in spite of themselves, in the magistracy, in the army and in every other species of employment; in vain may they excuse themselves or get out of the way; they must remain, or become generals, judges, mayors, national agents, town councillors, commissioners of charity or of the government, in self-defence.[17] So much the worse for them if the

---

mate reason, shall refuse to do their ordinary task."—Decrees of September 16 and 20, 1793, and that of September 11, articles 16, 19, 20, and 21.

15. Archives Nationales, AF.II., iii. Order of the representative Ferry; Bourges, 23 Messidor, year II. *Ibid.*, AF.II., 106. Order of the representative Dartigoyte, Auch, Prairial 18, year II.

16. Decree of Brumaire 11, year II., article 7.

17. Gouvion Saint Cyr, "Mémoires sur les campagnes de 1792 à la paix de Campo-For mio," i., 91–109. "Promotion, which every one feared at this time."

duty be onerous or dangerous, if they cannot afford the time, if they do not feel themselves qualified for it, if the rank or service seems to them to be a step in the direction of a prison or the guillotine; on their alleging that the office is a burdensome tax we reply that they are taxable property of the State. Such is, henceforth, the condition of all Frenchmen, and likewise of all French women. We force mothers to take their daughters to the meetings of popular clubs. We oblige women to parade in companies, and march in procession at republican festivals; we invade the family and select the most beautiful to be draped as antique goddesses, and publicly promenaded on a car; we often designate those among the rich who must wed patriots:[18] there is no reason why marriage, which is the most important of all services, should not be put in requisition like the others. Accordingly, we enter families, we carry off the child, we subject him to a civic education. We are schoolmasters, philanthro-

---

... *Ibid.*, 229. "Men who had any resources obstinately held aloof from any kind of advancement." Archives Nationales, D. SI., 5. Mission of representative Albert in L'Aube and La Marne, and especially the order issued by Albert, Chalons, Germinal 7, year III., with the numerous petitions of judges and town officers soliciting their removal.—Letter of the painter Gosse (published in *Le Temps*, May 31, 1872), which is very curious, showing the trials of those in private life during the Revolution. "My father was appointed charity commissioner and quartermaster for the troops; at the time of the Reign of Terror it would have been imprudent to have refused any office."—Archives Nationales, F[7], 3,485. The case of Girard Toussaint, notary at Paris, who "fell under the sword of the law, Thermidor 9, year II." This Girard, who was very liberal early in the revolution, was president of his section in 1789, but, after the 10th of August, he had kept quiet. The committee of the section of the "Amis de la Patrie," "considering that citizen Girard ... came forward only at the time when the court and Lafayette prevailed against the *sans-culottes*"; that, "since equality was established by the Revolution *he has deprived his fellow citizens of his knowledge, which, in a revolution, is criminal,* unanimously agree that the said citizen is "suspect" and order "him to be sent to the Luxembourg."

18. Ludovic Sciout, "Histoire de la Constitution civile du clergé," iv., 131, 135, (orders issued by Dartigoyte and de Pinet).—"Recueil de pieces authentiques serrant à l'histoire de la révolution à Strasbourg," vol. i., p. 230. (Speech by Schneider at Barr, for marrying the patriot Funck.) Schneider, it appears, did still better on his own account. (*Ibid.*, 317).

pists, theologians, and moralists. We impose by force our religion and our ritual, our morality and our social customs. We lord it over private lives and consciences; we dictate ideas, we scrutinise and punish secret inclinations, we tax, imprison and guillotine not only the evil-disposed, but again "the indifferent, the moderate and the egotistical."[19] Over and above his visible acts we dictate to the individual his ideas and his deepest feelings; we prescribe to him his affections as well as his beliefs, and, according to a preconceived type, we refashion his intellect, his conscience and his sensibilities.

III

There is nothing arbitrary in this operation; for the ideal model is traced beforehand. If the State is omnipotent, it is for the purpose of regenerating man, and the theory which confers rights on it, at the same time assigns to it its object.

In what does this regeneration of man consist? Consider an animal in a domestic state, the dog or the horse. Emaciated, flogged, tied or chained, a thousand are strained and overworked against one which has an easy time and dies of good living; and with all of them, whether fat or lean, the soul is still more abused than the body. A superstitious respect keeps them cowed under the load they carry, or makes them cringe before their master. Servile, slothful, gluttonous, feeble, incapable of resisting changes in the weather, if they have learned to adapt themselves to slavery they have also contracted its infirmities, necessities, and vices. A crust of absurd habits and perverse inclinations, a sort of artificial and supplementary existence, has covered over their original nature. Again, on the other hand, the better side of their original nature has had no chance to develop itself, for lack of use. Each separated from the other, they have not acquired the sentiment of community; they do not know, like their brethren of the prairies, how to help each other and sub-

---

19. Buchez et Roux, xxix., 160. (Report of Saint-Just, October 20, 1793.) "You have to punish not only traitors, but even the *indifferent;* you must punish all in the Republic who are *passive* and do nothing for it."

ordinate private interests to the interests of the flock. Each pulls his own way, nobody cares for others, all are egoists; social interests have miscarried. Such is man nowadays, a disfigured being that has to be made over, an imperfect creature that has to be completed. Our task, accordingly, is two-fold; we have to demolish and we have to construct; we must first set free the natural man that we may afterward build up the social man.

It is a vast enterprise and we are conscious of its vastness. "It is necessary," says Billaud-Varennes,[20] "that the people to which one desires to restore their freedom should in some way be *created anew*, since old prejudices must be destroyed, old habits changed, depraved affections improved, superfluous wants restricted, and inveterate vices extirpated." How sublime the undertaking, for the object is "to fulfil the desires of nature,[21] accomplish the destinies of humanity, and fulfil the promises of philosophy." "Our purpose," says Robespierre,[22] "is to substitute morality for egoism, honesty for honor, principles for usages, duties for proprieties, the empire of reason for the tyranny of fashion, contempt of vice for indifference to misfortune, dignity for insolence, nobleness for vanity, love of glory for the love of lucre, good people for good society, merit for intrigue, genius for intellectual brilliancy, the charm of contentment for the satiety of pleasure, the majesty of man for the high-breeding of the

20. Buchez et Roux, xxxii., 338. Report of the Convention on the theory of democratic government, by Billaud-Varennes (April 20, 1794).

21. Buchez et Roux, xxxi., 270. Report by Robespierre, on the principles which should guide the National Convention in the internal administration of the Republic, February 5, 1794.—Cf. "The Ancient Régime," 227–230, the ideas of Rousseau, of which those of Robespierre are simply a recast.

22. *Ibid.*, 270. The pretension of reforming men's sentiments is found in all the programmes. *Ibid.*, 305. (Report of Saint-Just, February 26, 1794.) "Our object is to create an order of things *such as a universal tendency toward the good establishes,* and to have factions immediately hurled upon the scaffold."—*Ibid.*, 337. (Report of Saint-Just, March 13, 1794.) "We see but one way of arresting the evil, and that is to convert the revolution into a civil power and *wage war on every species of perversity,* as designedly created amongst us for the enervation of the republic."

great, a magnanimous, powerful, and happy people, for an amiable, frivolous and wretched people, that is to say, every virtue and miracle of the Republic in the place of the vices and absurdities of the monarchy." We will do this, the whole of it, cost what it will. Little do we care for the present generation; we are working for generations to come. "Man, forced to isolate himself from society, anchors himself in the future and presses to his heart a posterity innocent of existing evils."[23] He sacrifices to this work his own and the lives of others. "On the day that I am satisfied," writes Saint-Just, "that it is impossible to render the French people kind, energetic, tender, and inexorable against tyranny and injustice, I will stab myself." "What I have done in the South I will do in the North," says Baudot; "I will convert them into patriots; either they or I must die." "We will make France a cemetery," says Carrier, "rather than not regenerate it our own way." In vain may the ignorant or the vicious protest; they protest because they are ignorant or vicious. In vain may the individual plead his personal rights; he has none, for, through the social contract, which is obligatory and solely valid, he has surrendered his entire being; having made no reservation, "he has nothing to claim." Undoubtedly, some will kick, because, with them, the old wrinkle remains and artificial habits still cover over the original instinct. Untie the mill-horse, and he will still go round in the same track; let the mountebank's dog be turned loose, and he will still raise himself on his hind-legs; if we would bring them back to their natural gait we must handle them roughly. In like manner, to restore man to his normal attitude, you must handle him roughly. But, in this respect, have no scruples,[24] for we do not bow him down,

---

23. *Ibid.*, xxxv., 276. (Institutions, by Saint-Just.—*Ibid.*, 287.)—*Moniteur*, xviii., 343. Meeting of the Jacobin Club, Brumaire 13, year II., speech by Baudot.

24. Buchez et Roux, xxix., 142. (Speech by Jean Bon St. André in the Convention, Sep. 25, 1793.) "We are said to exercise arbitrary power, we are charged with being despots. We, despots! . . . Ah, no doubt, if despotism is to secure the triumph of liberty, such a despotism is political regeneration." (Applause.) *Ibid.*, xxxi., 276. (Report by Robespierre, Pluviose 17, year II.) "It has been said that terror is the mainspring of despotic government. Does yours, then,

we raise him up; as Rousseau says, "we compel him to be free"; we confer on him the greatest boon a human being can receive; we bring him back to nature and to justice. For this reason, now that he is warned, if he persists in his resistance, he is criminal and merits every kind of chastisement,[25] for, he declares himself a rebel and a perjurer, inimical to humanity, and a traitor to the social compact.

IV

Let us begin by figuring to ourselves the natural man; certainly we of today have some difficulty in recognising him; he bears but little resemblance to the artificial being who stands in his shoes, the creature which an antiquated system of constraint and fraud has deformed, held fast in his hereditary harness of thraldom and superstition, blinded by his religion and held in check by prestige, speculated on by his government and trained by blows, always with a halter on, always made to work in a counter sense and against nature, whatever stall he may occupy, high or low, however full or empty his crib may be, now in menial service like the blinded hackhorse which turns a mill-wheel, and now on parade like the learned dog which, decked with flags, shows off its antics before the public.[26]

---

resemble despotism? Yes, as the sword which flashes in the hands of the heroes of liberty resembles that with which the satellites of tyranny are armed. . . . The government of the Revolution is the despotism of freedom against tyranny."

25. *Ibid.*, xxxii, 253. Decree of April, 1791. "The Convention declares, that, supported by the virtues of the French people, it will insure the triumph of the democratic revolution and *show no pity in punishing its enemies.*"

26. The bombast and credulity of the day, in this portrayal of the ancient régime, overflows in the most extravagant exaggeration. (Buchez et Roux, xxxi., 300, Report, by Saint-Just, February 26, 1794.) "In 1788, Louis XVI. caused eight thousand persons of both sexes and of every age to be sacrificed in the rue Meslay and on the Pont-Neuf. These scenes were repeated by the court on the Champs de Mars; the court had hangings in the prisons, and the bodies of the drowned found in the Seine were its victims. There were four hundred thousand prisoners in confinement; fifteen thousand smugglers were hung in a year, and three thousand men were broken on the wheel; there were more prisoners in Paris than there are now. . . . Look at Europe. There are four

But imagine all these out of the way, the flags and the bands, the trammels and compartments in the social stable, and you will see a new man appearing, the original man, intact and healthy in mind, soul, and body.

In this condition, he is free of prejudice, he has not been circumvented by falsities, he is neither Jew, Protestant, nor Catholic; if he tries to form an idea of the universe and of the origin of things he will not allow himself to be duped by a pretended revelation; he will listen only to his own reason; he may chance, now and then, to become an atheist, but, generally, he will settle down into a deist. In this condition of things he is not fettered by a hierarchy; he is neither noble nor commoner, land-owner nor tenant, inferior nor superior. Independent of the others, all are equal, and, if all agree in the forming of an association, their common-sense will stipulate that its first article shall secure the maintenance of this primordial equality. Such is man, as nature made him, as history has unmade him, and as the Revolution is to remake him.[27] One cannot batter away too vigorously against the two casings that hold him tight, one the positive religion which narrows and perverts his intellect, and the other the social inequality which perverts and weakens his will;[28]

---

millions of people shut up in Europe whose shrieks are never heard."—*Ibid.*, xxiv., 132. (Speech by Robespierre, May 10, 1793). "Up to this time the art of governing has simply consisted in the art of stripping and subduing the masses for the benefit of the few, and legislation, the mode of reducing these outrages to a system."

27. Buchez et Roux, xxxii., 353. (Report by Robespierre to the Convention, May 7, 1794.) "Nature tells us that man is born for freedom while the experience of man for centuries shows him a slave. His rights are written in his heart and history records his humiliation."

28. *Ibid.*, 372. "Priests are to morality what charlatans are to medical practice. How different is the God of nature from the God of the priests! I know of nothing which is so much like atheism as the religions they have manufactured!" Already, in the Constituent Assembly, Robespierre wanted to prevent the father from endowing a child. "You have done nothing for liberty if your laws do not tend to diminish by mild and efficacious means the inequality of fortunes." (Hamel, i., 403.)

for, at every effort, some band is loosened, and, as each band gives way, the paralysed limbs recover their action.

Let us trace the progress of this liberating operation. Always timid and at loggerheads with the ecclesiastical organisation, the Constituent Assembly could take only half-measures; it cut into the bark without daring to drive the axe into the solid trunk. Its work reduced itself down to the confiscation of clerical property, to a dissolution of the religious orders, and to a check upon the authority of the pope; its object was to establish a new church and transform priests into sworn functionaries of the State, and this was all. As if Catholicism, even administrative, would cease to be Catholicism! As if the noxious tree, once stamped with the public seal, would cease to be noxious! Instead of the old laboratory of falsehoods being destroyed another is patented alongside of it, so that there are now two instead of one. With or without the official label it operates in every commune in France and, as in the past, it supplies the public with its nostrum with impunity. This is precisely what we cannot tolerate. We must, indeed, keep up appearances, and, as far as words go, we will decree anew freedom of worship.[29] But, in fact and in practice, we will demolish the laboratory and prevent the nostrum from being sold; there shall no longer be any Catholic worship in France, no baptism, no confession, no marriage, no extreme unction, no mass: nobody shall preach or listen to a sermon; nobody shall administer or receive a sacrament, save in concealment, and with the prospect before him of imprisonment or the scaffold. To this end, we will take things in their order. There is no difficulty in regard to the self-styled orthodox Church: its members having re-

29. Decree of Frimaire 18, year II. Note the restrictions. "The Convention, in the foregoing arrangement, has no idea of derogating from any law or precaution for public safety against refractory or turbulent priests, or against those who might attempt to abuse the pretext of religion in order to compromise the cause of liberty. Nor does it mean to disapprove of what has thus far been done by virtue of the ordinances of the representatives of the people, nor to furnish anybody with a pretext for unsettling patriotism and relaxing the energy of public spirit."

fused to take the oath are outlaws; one excludes oneself from an association when one repudiates the pact; they have lost their qualifications as citizens and have become ordinary foreigners under the surveillance of the police; and, as they propagate around them discontent and disobedience, they are not only foreigners but seditious persons, enemies in disguise, the authors of a secret and widespread Vendée; it is not necessary for us to prosecute them as charlatans, it is sufficient to strike them down as rebels. As such, we have already banished from France all unsworn ecclesiastics, about forty thousand priests, and we are transporting those who did not cross the frontier within the allotted time: we allow only sexagenarians and the infirm to remain on French soil, and, again, as prisoners and in seclusion; they incur the penalty of death if they do not of their own accord crowd to the prisons of their county town; the banished who return home incur the penalty of death, and there is penalty of death against those who harbor priests.[30] Consequently, in default of an orthodox clergy, there must no longer be an orthodox worship; the most dangerous of the two manufactories of superstition is shut up. That the sale of this poisonous food may be more surely stopped we punish

30. Decrees of May 27 and August 26, 1792, March 18, April 20, and October 20, 1793, April 11, and May 11, 1794.—Add (*Moniteur,* xix., 697) the decree providing for the confiscation of the possessions of ecclesiastics "who have voluntarily left or been so reported, who are retired as old or infirm, or who have preferred transportation to retirement."—*Ibid.,* xviii., 492, (session of Frimaire 2). A speech by Forester. "As to the priesthood, its continuation has become a disgrace and even a crime."—Archives Nationales, AF. II., 36. (An order by Lequinio, representative of the people in Charante-Inférieur, la Vendée and Deux-Sévres, Saintes, Nivose 1, year ii.) "In order that freedom of worship may exist in full plenitude it is forbidden to all whom it may concern to preach or write in favor of any form of worship or religious opinion whatsoever," and especially "it is expressly forbidden to any former minister, belonging to any religious sect whatever, to preach, write, or teach morality under penalty of being regarded as a suspect and, as such, immediately put under arrest. ... Every man who undertakes to preach any religious precepts whatsoever is, by that fact, culpable before the people. He violates ... social equality, which does not permit the individual to publicly raise his ideal pretensions above those of his neighbor."

those who ask for it the same as those who provide it, and we prosecute not only the pastors, but, again, the fanatics of the flock; if these are not the authors of the ecclesiastical rebellion they are its promoters and accomplices. Now, thanks to the schism among them, we already know who they are, and, in each commune, the list is made out. We style as fanatics all who reject the ministry of the sworn priests, the bourgeois who calls him an interloper, all the nuns who confess to him, all the peasants who stay away from his mass, all the old women who do not kiss his paten, all the relations of an infant who do not wish him to baptise it. All these people and those who associate with them, whether nearly related, kinsmen, friends, guests, or visitors, of whatever class, either men or women, are seditious at heart, and, therefore, "suspects." We deprive them of their electoral rights, we withdraw their pensions, we impose on them special taxation, we confine them to their dwellings, we imprison them by thousands, and guillotine them by hundreds; the rest will gradually become discouraged and abandon an impracticable cult.[31] The lukewarm remain, the sheep-like crowd which holds on to its rites: the Constituent Assembly will seize them wherever it finds them, and, as they are the same in the authorised as in the refractory church, instead of seeking them with the priest who does not submit, it will seek them with the one who does. But it will proceed without zeal, without confidence, often even with distrust, questioning itself whether these rites, being administered by one who is excommunicated, are not base metal. Such a church is not substantial, and we have only to give it a push to knock it down. We will do all we can to discredit constitutional priests: we will prohibit them from wearing the ecclesiastical costume, and force them by law to bestow the nuptial benediction on their apostate brethren; we will employ terror and imprisonment to constrain them to marry; we will give them no respite until they return to civil life, some

31. Ludovic Sciout, "Histoire de la Constitution Civile du clergé," vols. iii. and iv., *passim*.—Jules Sauzay, "Histoire de la persécution révolutionaire dans le Doubs," vols. iii., iv., v., and vi., particularly the list, at the end of the work, of those transported, guillotined, sent into the interior and imprisoned.

admitting themselves to be impostors, many by surrendering their priestly credentials, and most of them by resigning their places.[32] Deprived of leaders by these voluntary or forced desertions, the Catholic flock will allow itself to be easily led out of the fold, while, to remove all temptation to go back, we will tear the enclosure down.

32. Order of the day of the Convention September 17, 1792; circular of the Executive Council, January 22, 1793; decrees of the Convention, July 19, August 12, September 17, November 15, 1793.—Ludovic Sciout, iii., ch. xv., and the following chapters; iv., chapters i. to vii.—*Moniteur,* October and November, 1793, *passim.* (November 23, Order of the Paris Commune, closing the churches.)—In relation to the terror the constitutional priests were under, I merely give the two following extracts (Archives Nationales, F[7], 3,116[7]); "Citizen Pontard, bishop of the department of Dordogne, lodging in the house of citizen Bourbon, No. 66 Faubourg St. Honoré, on being informed that there was an article in a newspaper called "le Republicain" stating that a meeting of priests had been held in the said house, declares that he had no knowledge of it; that all the officers in charge of the apartments are in harmony with the Revolution; that, if he had had occasion to suspect such a circumstance, he would have moved out immediately, and that if any motive can possibly be detected in such a report it is his proposed marriage with the niece of citizen Caminade, an excellent patriot and captain of the 9th company of the Champs-Elysées section, a marriage which puts an end to fanaticism in his department, unless this be done by the ordination of a priest *à la sans-culotte* which he had done yesterday in the chapel, another act in harmony with the Revolution. It is well to add, perhaps, that one of his *curés* now in Paris has called on him, and that he came to request him to second his marriage. The name of the said curé is Greffier Sauvage; he is still in Paris, and is preparing to be married the same time as himself. Aside from these motives, which may have given rise to some talk, citizen Pontard sees no cause whatever for suspicion. Besides, so thoroughly patriotic is he, he asks nothing better than to know the truth, in order to march along unhesitatingly in the revolutionary path. He signs his declaration, promising to support the Revolution on all occasions, by his writings as well as by his conduct. He presents the two numbers of his journal which he has had printed in Paris in support of the principles he adheres to. At Paris, September 7, 1793, year II. of the Republic, one and indivisible. F. Pontard, bishop of the Republic in the department of Dordogne."—Dauban *La Demagogie en* 1793, p. 557. Arrest of representative Osselin, letter of his brother, *curé* of St. Aubin, to the committee of section Mutius Scaevola, Brumaire 20, year II., "Like Brutus and Mutius Scaevola, I trample on the feelings with which I idolised my brother! O, truth, thou divinity of republicans, thou knowest the incorruptibility of my intentions!" (and so on for fifty-three lines). "These are my sentiments. I am fraternally, Osselin, minister of worship at St. Aubin."—P.S. "It was just as I

In the communes in which we are masters we will make the Jacobins of the place demand the abolition of worship, while, in other communes, we will get rid of this authoritatively through our missionary representatives. We will close the churches, demolish the steeples, melt down the bells, send all sacred vessels to the Mint, smash the images of the saints, desecrate relics, prohibit religious burials, impose the civil burial, prescribe rest during the *décadi*,[33] and labor on Sundays. No exception whatever. Since all positive religions maintain error, we will proscribe every form of worship: we will exact from Protestant clergymen a public abjuration; we will not let the Jews practise their ceremonies; we will have "an '*auto-da-fé*,' of all the books and symbols of the faith of Moses."[34] But, of all these various juggling machines, the worst is the Catholic, the most hostile to nature in the celibacy of its priesthood, the most opposed to reason in the absurdity of its dogmas, the most opposed to democracy, since its powers are delegated from above downwards, the best protected from civil authority because its head is outside of France. Accordingly, we must be most furious against it; even after Thermidor, we will keep up constant persecution, great and small; up to the Consulate, we will transport and shoot down priests, we will revive against fanatics the laws of the Reign of Terror, we will hamper their movements, we will exhaust their patience; we will keep them anxious during the day and restless at night; we will not give them a moment's repose.[35] We will restrict the population to the decadal cult; we will pursue it with our propagandism even to the dinner-table; we will change the market-days, so that no believer shall be able to buy fish on a fast-day.[36] We have nothing more at

---

was going to answer a call of nature that I learned this afflicting news." (He keeps up this fustian until words fail him, and finally, frightened to death, and his brain exhausted, he gives this postscript to show that he was not an accomplice.)

33. A term denoting the substitution of *ten* instead of seven days as a division of time in the calendar, and forced into use during the Revolution.

34. "Recueil de pieces authentiques servant à l'histoire de la revolution à Strasbourg," ii., 299. (A district order.)

35. Ludovic Sciout, iv., 426. (Instructions sent by the Directory to the National Commissions, Frimaire, year II.)—*Ibid.*, ch. x. to xviii.

36. *Ibid.*, iv., 688. An order of the Directory, Germinal 14, year VI. "The

heart than this war against Catholicism; no article on our programme will be carried out with more determination and perseverance. The question involved is truth. We are its guardians, its champions, its ministers, and never did the servants of truth apply force with such minute detail and such effect to the extirpation of error.

V

Alongside of superstition there is another monster to be destroyed, and, on this side also, the Constituent Assembly began its attack. But on this side also, through lack of courage or of logic, it stopped, after two or three feeble blows. All that it did to restore natural equality consisted in this—an interdiction of heraldic insignia, titles of nobility and territorial names; the abolition, without indemnity, of all the dues belonging to the seigneur by right of his former proprietorship over persons; the permission to purchase other feudal rights at a price agreed upon, and the limitation of royal power. This was little enough; when it concerns usurpers and tyrants they must be treated in another fashion; for their privilege is, of itself, an outrage on the rights of man. Consequently, we have dethroned the King and cut off his head;[37] we have suppressed, without indemnity, the entire feudal debt, comprising the rights vested in the seig-

---

municipal governments will designate special days in each decade for market days in their respective districts, and not allow, in any case, their ordinance to be set aside on the plea that the said market days would fall on a holiday. *They will specially strive to break up all connection between the sales of fish and the days of fasting designated on the old calendar.* Every person exposing food or wares on sale in the markets on days other than those fixed by the municipal government will be prosecuted in the police court for obstructing a public thoroughfare."—The Thermidorians remain equally as anti-Catholic as their predecessors; only, they disavow open persecution and rely on slow pressure. (*Moniteur*, xiii., 523. Speech by Boissy d'Anglas, Ventose 3, year II.) "Superintend what you cannot hinder; regulate what you cannot prohibit.... It will not be long before these absurd dogmas, the offspring of fear and error, whose influence on the human mind has been so steadily destructive, will be known only to be despised.... It will not be long before the religion of Socrates, of Marcus Aurelius and Cicero will be the religion of the whole world."

37. *Moniteur*, xiv., 646. (The King's trial.) Speech by Robespierre: "The right of punishing the tyrant and of dethroning him is one and the same

neurs by virtue of their being owners of real-estate, and merely lessors; we have abandoned their persons and possessions to the claims and rancor of local jacqueries; we have reduced them to emigration; we imprison them if they stay at home; we guillotine them if they return. Reared in habits of supremacy, and convinced that they are of a different species from other men, the prejudices of race are incorrigible; they are incapable of companionship with their social equals; we cannot too carefully crush them out, or, at the very least, hold them firmly down.[38] Besides, they are guilty from the fact of having existed; for, they have taken both the lead and the command without any right to do so, and, in violation of all right, they have misused mankind; having enjoyed their rank, it is but just that they should pay for it. Privileged the wrong way, they must be treated the same as vagabonds were treated under their reign, stopped by the police and sent off with their families into the interior, crowded into prisons, executed in a mass, or, at least, ex-pelled from Paris, the seaports and fortified towns, put on the limits, compelled to present themselves daily at the municipality, deprived of their political rights, excluded from public offices, "popular clubs, committees of supervision and from communal and section assem-blages."[39] Even this is indulgence; branded with infamy, we ought to class them with galley-slaves, and set them to work on the public highways.[40] "Justice condemns the people's enemies and the parti-sans of tyranny to eternal slavery."[41]

---

thing."—Speech by Saint-Just: "Royalty is an eternal crime, against which every man has the right of taking up arms. . . . To reign innocently is impos-sible!"

38. Epigraph of Marat's journal: *Ut redeat miseris, abeat fortuna superbis.*

39. Buchez et Roux, xxxii., 323. (Report of Saint-Just, Germinal 21, year II., and a decree of Germinal 26–29, Art. 4, 13, 15.)—*Ibid.,* 315.

40. Buchez et Roux, xxix., 166. (Report of Saint-Just, October 10, 1793.) "That would be the only good they could do their country. . . . It would be no more than just for the people to reign over its oppressors in its turn, and that their pride should be bathed in the sweat of their brows."

41. *Ibid.,* xxxi., 309. (Report of Saint-Just, Ventose 8, year II.)

But that does not suffice; for, apart from the aristocracy of rank, there are other aristocracies which the Constituent Assembly has left untouched,[42] especially the aristocracy of wealth. Of all the sovereignties, that of the rich man over the poor one is the most burdensome. In effect, not only, in contempt of equality, does he consume more than his share of the common products of labor, and without producing anything himself, but again, in contempt of liberty, he may fix wages as he pleases, and, in contempt of humanity, he always fixes them at the lowest point. Between himself and the necessitous he never makes other than the most iniquitous contracts. Sole possessor of land, capital and the necessaries of life, he imposes conditions which others, deprived of means, are forced to accept at the risk of starvation; he speculates at his discretion on wants which cannot be put off, and makes the most of his monopoly by maintaining the indigent in their indigent situations. "Hence," writes Saint-Just,[43] "opulence is infamous; it consists in feeding fewer natural or adopted children according to every thousand *livres* of in-

---

42. *Ibid.*, xxvi., 435. (Speech by Robespierre on the Constitution, May 10, 1793.) "What were our usages and pretended laws other than a code of impertinence and baseness, where contempt of men was subject to a sort of tariff, and graduated according to regulations as odd as they were numerous? To despise and be despised, to cringe in order to rule, slaves and tyrants in turn, now kneeling before a master, now trampling the people under foot—such was the ambition of all of us, so long as we were *men of birth or well-educated men, whether common folks or fashionable folks, lawyers or financiers, pettifoggers or wearing swords.*"—Archives Nationales, F[7], 3,116[7]. (Report of the *observateur* Charmont, Nivose 10, year II.)—"Boileau's effigy, placed in the college of Lisieux, has been lowered to the statues of the saints, the latter being taken out of their niches. There is now no kind of distinction. Saints and authors are of the same class."

43. Buchez et Roux, xxxv., 296. ("Institutions" by Saint-Just.) Meillan, "Mémoires," p. 17. Anne Plumptre, "A narrative of three years' residence in France, from 1802 to 1805," ii., 96. At Marseilles: "The two great crimes charged on those who were doomed to destruction, were here as elsewhere, wealth and aristocracy. . . . It had been decreed by the Terrorists that no person could have occasion for more than two hundred livres a year, and that no income should be permitted to exceed that sum."

come." "The richest Frenchman," says Robespierre, "ought not to have now more than three thousand *livres* rental." Beyond what is strictly necessary, no property is legitimate; we have the right to take the superfluous wherever we find it; not only today, because we now require it for the State and for the poor, but at all times, because the superfluous, in all times, confers on its possessor an advantage in contracts, a control of wages, an arbitrament over the means of living, in short, a supremacy of condition worse than preëminence in rank. Consequently, our hand is not against the nobles merely, but against the rich and well-to-do bourgeois,[44] also the large land-owners and capitalists; we are going to demolish their crafty feudalism from top to bottom.[45] In the first place, we prevent, and solely through the operation of new institutions, any recipient of a large income from levying on, as is customary with him, the best portion of the fruits of another's labor; the drones shall no longer annually consume the honey of other bees. To bring this about, we have only to let the assignats and the forced rate (at which they shall be received) work things out. Through the depreciation of paper-money, the indolent land-owner or capitalist sees his income melting away in his hands; his receipts consist only of nominal values. On the 1st of January, his tenant pays him really for a half

44. Archives Nationales, F[7], 4,437. (Address of the people's club of Clavisson (Gard), Messidor 7, year II.) "The Bourgeoisie, the merchants, the large land-owners have all the pretension of ex-nobles. The law provides no means for opening the eyes of the common people in relation to these new tyrants. The club desires that the revolutionary Tribunal should be empowered to condemn this proud class of individuals to a prompt partial confinement. The people would then see that they had committed a misdemeanor and would withdraw that sort of respect in which they hold them." A note in the hand-writing of Couthon: "Left to the decision of popular commissions."

45. Gouverneur Morris, in a letter of January 4, 1796, says that French capitalists have been financially ruined by assignats, and physically by the guillotine.—Buchez et Roux, xxx., 26. (Notes written by Robespierre in June, 1793.) "Internal dangers come from the bourgeois ... who are our enemies? The vicious and the rich."

term instead of a full term; on the 1st of March, his farmer settles his account with a bag of grain;[46] the effect is just the same as if we had made fresh contracts, and reduced by one-half, three-quarters, or, even more, the rate of interest on loans, the rent of houses and the leases of farm lands. Whilst the revenue of the landlord evaporates, his capital melts away, and we do the best we can to help this along. If he has claims on ancient corporations or civil and religious establishments of any description, whether provincial governments, congregations, associations, endowments or hospitals, we withdraw his special guarantee; we convert his title-deeds into a state annuity, we combine his private fortune with the public fortune whether he will or not, we drag him into the universal bankruptcy, toward which we are conducting all the creditors of the Republic.[47]

Besides, to effect his ruin, we have more direct and prompt means. If an *emigré*, and there are hundreds of thousands of *emigrés*, we confiscate his possessions; if he has been guillotined or transported, and there are tens of thousands of these, we confiscate his possessions; if he is "a marked enemy of the Revolution,"[48] and "all the rich pray for the counter-revolution,"[49] we sequestrate his property;

46. Narrative by M. Silvestre de Sacy (May 23, 1873): His father owned a farm bringing in four thousand francs per annum; the farmer offered him four thousand francs in assignats or a hog; M. de Sacy took the hog.

47. Buchez et Roux, xxxi., 441. (Report by Cambon on the institution of the *grand livre* of the public debt, August 15, 1793.)

48. *Ibid.*, xxxi., 311. Report by Saint-Just, February 26, 1794, and decree in accordance therewith, unanimously adopted. See, in particular, article 2.—*Moniteur*, 12 Ventose, year II. (meeting of the Jacobin club, speech by Collot d'Herbois). "The Convention has declared that prisoners must prove that they were patriots from the 1st of May, 1789. When the patriots and enemies of the Revolution shall be fully known, then the property of the former shall be inviolable and held sacred, while that of the latter will be confiscated for the benefit of the republic."

49. Buchez et Roux, xxvi., 1455. (Session of the Jacobin Club, May 10, 1793, speech by Robespierre.)—*Ibid.*, xxxi. (Report by Saint-Just, Feb. 26, 1794.) "He who has shown himself an enemy of his country cannot be one of its proprietors. Only he has patrimonial rights who has helped to free it."

we enjoy the usufruct of it until peace is declared, and we shall have the property after the war is over; usufruct or property, the State, in either case, inherits; at most, we may sometimes grant temporary aid to the family, which is not even entitled to food.

It is impossible to uproot fortunes more thoroughly. As to those which are not at once eradicated we get rid of them piece-meal, and against these we employ two axes. On the one hand, we decree the principle of progressive taxation, and on this basis we establish the forced loan:[50] in incomes, we distinguish between the essential and the surplus; we fix the essential at one thousand francs per head; according as the excess is greater or less we take a quarter, a third or the half of it, and, when above nine thousand francs, the whole; beyond its small alimentary reserve, the most opulent family will keep only four thousand five hundred francs income. On the other hand, we cut deep into capital through revolutionary taxes; our committees and provincial proconsuls levy arbitrarily what suits them, three hundred, five hundred, up to one million two hundred thousand francs,[51] on this or that banker, trader, bourgeois or widow, payable within a week; all the worse for the person taxed if he or she has no money on hand and is unable to borrow it; we declare them "suspects," we imprison them, we sequestrate their property and the State enjoys it in their place. In any event, even when the amount is paid, we force him or her to deposit their silver and gold coin in our hands, sometimes with assignats as security, and often nothing; henceforth, coin must circulate and the precious metals are in requisition;[52] everybody will deliver up what plate he possesses.

50. Buchez et Roux, xxxi., 93 and 130. (Speech by Robespierre on property, and the declaration of rights adopted by the Jacobin club.) Decree of Septem. 3, 1794 (articles 13 and 48).

51. *Moniteur,* xxii., 719. (Report by Cambon, Frimaire 6, year III.) At Bordeaux Raba was condemned to a fine of one million two hundred thousand francs, Péchotte to five hundred thousand, Martin-Martin to three hundred thousand.—Cf. Rodolphe Reuss, "Séligmann Alexandre, ou les Tribulations d'un Israélite de Strasbourg."

52. *Ibid.,* xviii., 486. (Report by Cambon, Frimaire 1, year II.) "The egotists who, some time ago, found it difficult to pay for the national domains they had

And let nobody presume to conceal his hoard; all treasure, whether silver-plate, diamonds, ingots, gold or silver, coined or uncoined, "discovered, or that may be discovered, buried in the ground or concealed in cellars, inside of walls or in garrets, under floors, pavements, or hearthstones, or in chimneys and other hiding places,"[53] becomes the property of the Republic, with a premium of twenty per cent. in assignats to the informer. As, furthermore, we make requisitions for bed-linen, beds, clothes, provisions, wines and the rest, along with specie and the precious metals, the condition of a mansion may be imagined, especially after we have lodged in it; it is the same as if the house had been on fire; all personal capital is gone, as well as other capital. Now that both are destroyed they must not be allowed to accumulate again. To ensure this, we abolish, according to rule, the freedom of bequest,[54] we prescribe equal and obligatory divisions of all inheritances;[55] we include bastards in this under the same title as legitimate children; we admit *représentation à l'infini*,[56] "in order to multiply heirs and parcel out inheritances;"[57]

---

acquired from the Republic, even in assignats, now bring us their gold. . . . Collectors of the revenue who had buried their gold have come and offered to pay what they owe the nation in ingots of gold and silver. These have been refused, the Assembly having decreed the confiscation of these objects."

53. Decree of Brumaire 23, year II. On taxes and confiscations in the provinces see M. de Martel, "Etude sur Fouché et Pieces authentiques servant à l'histoire de la revolution à Strasbourg." And further on the details of this operation at Troyes.—Meillan, 90: "At Bordeaux, merchants were heavily taxed, not on account of their *incivisme*, but on account of their wealth."

54. Decree of March 7–11, 1793.

55. *Moniteur*, xviii., 274, decrees of Brumaire 4, and *ibid.*, 305, decree of Brumaire 9, year II., establishing equal partition of inheritances with retroactive effect to July 14, 1789. Adulterous bastards are excepted. The reporter of the bill, Cambacèrés, laments this regretable exception.

56. Rights of inheritance allowed to the descendants of a deceased person who never enjoyed these rights, but who might have enjoyed them had he been living when they fell to him.—Tr.

57. Fenet, "Travaux du Code civil." (Report by Cambacèrés on the Code civil, August 9, 1793). The framer of the bill makes excuses for not having deprived the father of all the disposable portion. "The committee believed that such a clause would seriously violate our customs without being of any benefit

we reduce the disposable portion to one-tenth, in the direct line, and one-sixth in a collateral line; we forbid any gift to persons whose income exceeds one thousand quintals of grain; we inaugurate adoption, "an admirable institution," and essentially republican, "since it brings about a division of large properties without a crisis." Already, in the Legislative Assembly a deputy had stated that "equal rights could be maintained only by a persistent tendency to uniformity of fortunes."[58] We have provided for this for the present day and we likewise provide for it in the future. None of the vast excrescences which have sucked the sap of the human plant are to remain; we have cut them away with a few telling blows, while the steady-moving machine, permanently erected by us, will shear off their last tendrils should they chance to sprout again.

VI

Through this restoration of the natural man we have prepared for the advent of the social man. The object now is to form the citizen, and this is possible only through a levelling of conditions; "neither rich nor poor are necessary" in a well constituted society;[59] we have already destroyed the opulence which corrupts; it now remains for us to suppress the indigence which degrades. Under the tyranny of

---

to society or of any moral advantage. We assured ourselves, moreover, that there should always be a division of property." With respect to donations: "It is repugnant to all ideas of beneficence to allow donations to the rich. Nature is averse to the making of such gifts so long as our eyes dwell on misery and misfortune. *These affecting considerations* have determined us to fix a point, a sort of maximum, which prohibits gifts on the part of those who have reached that point."

58. *Moniteur*, xii., 730, (June 22, 1792) speech by Lamarque.—But this principle is encountered everywhere. "Equality, indeed, (is) the final aim of social art." (Condorcet, "Tableau des progrès de l'esprit humain," ii., 59.—"We desired," writes Baudot, "to apply to politics the equality which the Gospel awards to Christians." (Quinet, "Revolution Française," ii., 407.)

59. Buchez et Roux, xxxv., 296. (The words of Saint-Just.)—*Moniteur*, xviii., 505. (Ordinance of the Paris Commune, Frimaire 3. year II.), "Wealth and Poverty must alike disappear under the régime of equality."

material things, which is as oppressive as the tyranny of men, man falls below himself; never will a citizen be made out of a poor fellow condemned to remain valet, hireling, or beggar, to think only of himself and his daily bread, to ask in vain for work, to plod twelve hours a day at a monotonous pursuit, to live like a beast of burden and die in a hospital.[60] He must have his own bread, his own roof and all that is indispensable for life; he must not be overworked, nor suffer anxiety or constraint; "he must live independently, respect himself, have a tidy wife and healthy and robust children."[61] The community should guarantee him comfort, security, the certainty of not going hungry if he becomes infirm, and, if he dies, of not leaving his family in want. "It is not enough," says Barère,[62] "to bleed the rich, to pull down colossal fortunes; the slavery of poverty must be made to disappear from the soil of the Republic." "The unfortunate," says Saint-Just, "are the powerful of the earth; they have a right to speak as masters to the governments which neglect them;[63] they have a right to national beneficence. . . . In a democracy under organisation, everything should tend to raise each citizen above the prime necessities, by labor if he is fit for work, by education if he is a child, by succor if he is an invalid or in old age."[64] And never was there so propitious a moment. "Rich in domains, the Republic is calculating the millions intended by the rich for counter revolution, for the amelioration of the lot of its less fortunate citizens. . . . Those who would assassinate liberty have made it the richer. . . . The possessions of conspirators exist for the benefit of the unfor-

---

60. Buchez et Rouz, xxxv., 296. ("Institutions," by Saint-Just.) "A man is not made for trades, nor for a hospital, nor for an asylum; all this is frightful."— *Ibid.*, xxxi., 312. (Report of Saint-Just, Ventose 8, year II.) "Let Europe see that you will not allow a miserable man on French territory! . . . Happiness is a new idea in Europe."

61. Buchez et Roux, xxxv., 296. ("Institutions," by Saint-Just.)

62. *Moniteur*, xx., 444. (Report by Barère, Floréal 22, year II.) "Mendicity is incompatible with popular government."

63. *Ibid.*, xix., 568. (Report by Saint-Just, Ventose, year II.)

64. *Ibid.* Report by Barère, Floréal 22.

tunate."[65] Let the poor take with a quiet conscience: it is not a charity but "an indemnity" which we provide for them; we save their pride by providing for their comfort, and we solace them without humiliating them. "We leave charitable enterprises to monarchies; this vile and insolent way of furnishing assistance is fit only for slaves and masters; we substitute for it a system of national works, on a grand scale, over the whole territory of the Republic."[66] On the other hand, we cause a statement to be drawn up in each commune, of "the condition of citizens without property," and "of national possessions not disposed of"; we divide these possessions in small lots; we distribute them "in the shape of national sales" to poor folks able to work; we give, "through form of rental," an acre to each head of a family who has less than an acre of his own; "we thus bind all citizens to the country as well as to property; we restore to the soil idle and robust arms, and families lost or enervated in the workshops and in the towns." As to old and infirm farmers or me-

65. *Ibid.*, xix., 568. (Report by Saint-Just, Ventose 8, and decree of Ventose 13.) "The Committee of Public Safety will report on the means of *indemnifying* the unfortunate with property belonging to the enemies of the Revolution."

66. *Ibid.* xix., 484. (Report by Barère, Ventose 21, year II.)—*Ibid.*, xx., 445. (Report by Barère, Floréal 22, year II.)—Decrees on public assistance, June 28, 1793, July 25, 1793, Frimaire 2, and Floréal 22, year II.—This principle, moreover, was set forth in the Constitution of 1793. "Public help is a sacred obligation; society owes a subsistence to unfortunate citizens, whether by providing work for them, or by ensuring the means of existence to those who are not in a condition to work."—Archives Nationales, AF.II., 39. The character of this measure is very clearly expressed in the following circular of the Committee of Public Safety to its representatives on mission in the departments, Ventose, year II. "A summary act was necessary to put the aristocracy down. The national Convention has struck the blow. *Virtuous indigence was to recover property of which the usurpations of crime had deprived it.* The national Convention has proclaimed its rights. A general list of all prisoners should be sent to the Committee of General Security, charged with deciding on their fate. The Committee of Public Safety will receive the statement of the indigent in each commune so as to regulate what is due to them. Both these proceedings demand the utmost despatch and should go together. It is necessary that terror and justice be brought to bear on all points at once. The Revolution is the work of the people and it is time they should have the benefit of it."

chanics, also poor mothers, wives, and widows of mechanics and farmers, we keep in each department a "big ledger of national beneficence"; we inscribe thereon for every thousand inhabitants, four farmers, two mechanics, five women, either mothers or widows; each registered person shall be pensioned by the State, the same as a maimed soldier; labor-invalids are as respectable as war-invalids. Over and above those who are privileged on account of poverty, we relieve and elevate the entire poor class, not alone the thirteen hundred thousand indigent enumerated in France,[67] but, again, all who, having little or no means on hand, live from day to day on what they can earn. We have passed a law[68] by which the public treasury shall, through a tax on large fortunes, "furnish to each commune or district the necessary funds for adapting the price of bread to the rate of wages." Our representatives in the provinces impose on the wealthy the obligation of "lodging, feeding, and clothing all infirm, aged, and indigent citizens and orphans of their respective cantons."[69] Through the decree on monopolisation and the establishment of the *maximum* we bring within reach of the poor all objects of prime necessity. We pay them forty sous a day for attending district meetings; and three francs a day for serving on committees of surveillance. We recruit from amongst them our revolutionary army;[70] we select amongst them the innumerable custodians of *sequestrés:* in this way, hundreds of thousands of *sans-culottes* enter into the various public services. At last, the poor are taken out of a state of poverty: each will now have his plot of ground, his salary

67. *Moniteur,* xx., 449. (Report by Barère, Floréal 22, year II.)

68. Decree of April 2–5, 1793.

69. *Moniteur,* xviii., 505. (Orders of Fouché and Collot d'Herbois, dated at Lyons and communicated to the commune of Paris, Frimaire 3, year II.)—De Martel, "Etude sur Fouché," 132. Orders of Fouché on his mission in the Nievre, Sept. 19, 1793. "There shall be established in each district town a Committee of Philanthropy, authorised to levy on the rich a tax proportionate to the number of the indigent."

70. Decree of April 2–5, 1793. "There shall be organised in each large commune a guard of citizens selected from the *least fortunate*. These citizens shall be armed and paid at the expense of the Republic."

or pension; "in a well-ordered republic nobody is without some property."[71] Henceforth, among individuals, the difference in welfare will be small; from the maximum to the minimum, there will be only a degree, while there will be found in every dwelling about the same sort of household, a plain, simple household, that of the small rural proprietor, well-off farmer or factory foreman; that of Rousseau at Montmorency, or that of the Savoyard Vicar, or that of Duplay, the carpenter, with whom Robespierre lodges.[72] There will be no more domestic servitude: "only the bond of help and gratitude will exist between employer and employee."[73] "He who works for another citizen belongs to his family and sits at his table."[74] Through the transformation of low conditions into average conditions we restore men to their dignity, and out of the proletaire, the valet, and the workman, we begin to liberate the citizen.

VII

Two leading obstacles hinder the development of civism, and the first is egoism. Whilst the citizen prefers the community to himself, the egoist prefers himself to the community. He cares only for his own interest, he gives no heed to public necessities; he sees none of the superior rights which take precedence of his derived right; he supposes that his property is his own without restriction or condition; he forgets that, if he is allowed to use it, he must not use it to another's detriment.[75] Thus, even in the middle or low class, do those

71. *Moniteur*, xx., 449. (Report of Barère, Floréal 22, year II.)

72. *Ibid.*, xix., 689. (Report by Saint-Just, Ventose 23, year II.) "We spoke of happiness. It is not the happiness of Persepolis we have offered to you. It is that of Sparta or Athens in their best days, the happiness of virtue, that of comfort and moderation, the happiness which springs from the enjoyment of the necessary without the superfluous, the luxury of a cabin and of a field fertilised by your own hands. A cart, a thatched roof affording shelter from the frosts, a family safe from the lubricity of a robber—such is happiness!"

73. Buchez et Roux, xxxi., 402. (Constitution of 1793.)

74. *Ibid.*, xxxv., 310. ("Institutions," by Saint-Just.)

75. *Ibid.*, xxvi., 93 and 131. (Speech by Robespierre on property, April 24, 1793, and declaration of rights adopted by the Jacobin Club.)—Mallet-Dupan,

who possess the necessaries of life, act. The greater the demand for these the higher they raise their prices; soon, they sell only at an exorbitant rate, and worse still, stop selling and store their goods or products, in the expectation of selling them dearer. In this way, they speculate on another's wants; they augment the general distress and become public enemies. Nearly all the agriculturists, manufacturers, and tradesmen of the day, little and big, are public enemies—farmers, metayers, market-gardeners, cultivators of every degree, as well as foremen, shopkeepers, especially wine-dealers, bakers, and butchers. "All tradesmen are essentially antirevolutionists, and would sell their country to gain a few sous."[76] We will not tolerate this legal brigandage. Since "agriculture has done nothing for liberty and has sought only its own gain,"[77] we will put it under surveillance, and, if necessary, under control. Since "commerce has become a species of miserly tyrant," since "it has become self-paralysed," and, "through a sort of antirevolutionary contempt, neglected the manufacture, handling, and expedition of diverse materials," we will "defeat" the calculations of its barbarous arithmetic, and purge it of the aristocratic and corrupting fermentation which oppresses it." We make monopoly "a capital crime";[78] we call him a monopolist who

---

"Mémoires," i., 401. (Address of a deputation from Gard.) "Material wealth is no more the special property of any one member of the social body than base metal stamped as a circulating medium."

76. *Moniteur*, viii., 452. (Speech by Hébert in the Jacobin Club, Brumaire 26, year II.) "Un Séjour en France de 1792 à 1795," p. 218. (Amiens, Oct. 4, 1794.) "While waiting this morning at a shop door I overheard a beggar bargaining for a slice of pumpkin. Unable to agree on the price with the woman who kept the shop, he pronounced her 'gaugrened with aristocracy.' 'I defy you to prove it!' she replied. But, as she spoke, she turned pale and added, 'Your civism is beyond all question—but take your pumpkin.' 'Ah,' returned the beggar, 'what a good republican!'"

77. *Ibid.*, xviii., 320. (Meeting of Brumaire 11, year II. Report by Barère.)—Meillan, 17. Already, before the 31st May: "The tribune resounded with charges against monopoly, every man being a monopolist who was not reduced to living on daily wages or on alms."

78. Decrees of July 26, 1793, Sept. 11 and 29; Brumaire 11, and Ventose 6, year II.

"takes food and wares of prime necessity out of circulation," and "keeps them stored without daily and publicly offering them for sale." Penalty of death against whoever, within eight days, does not make a declaration, or if he makes a false one. Penalty of death against any person who keeps more bread on hand than he needs for his subsistence.[79] Penalty of death against the cultivator who does not bring his grain weekly to market. Penalty of death against the dealer who does not post up the contents of his warehouse, or who does not keep open shop. Penalty of death against the manufacturer who does not verify the daily use of his workable material. As to prices, we intervene authoritatively between buyer and seller; we fix the extreme price for all objects which, near or remotely, serve to feed, warm, and clothe man; we will imprison whoever offers or demands anything more. Whether the dealer or manufacturer pays expenses at this rate, matters not; if, after the maximum is fixed, he closes his factory, or gives up business, we declare him a "suspect"; we chain him down to his pursuit, we oblige him to lose by it. That is the way to clip the claws of beasts of prey, little and big! But the claws grow out again, and, instead of paring them down, it would, probably be better to pull them out. Some amongst us have already thought of that; the right of preemption might be applied to every article; "in each department, national storehouses might be established where cultivators, land-owners, and manufacturers would be obliged to deposit at a fixed price, paid down, the surplus of their consumption of every species of merchandise. The nation would distribute this merchandise to wholesale dealers, reserving a profit of six per centum. The profit of the wholesale dealer would be fixed at eight per centum and that of the retailer at twelve per centum."[80]

---

79. *Moniteur,* xviii., 359. "Brumaire 16, year II. Sentence of death of Pierre Gourdier, thirty-six years of age, stock-broker, resident in Paris, rue Bellefond, convicted of having monopolised and concealed in his house a large quantity of bread, in order to breed scarcity in the midst of abundance." He had gastritis and could eat nothing but panada made with toast, and the baker who furnished this gave him thirty pieces at a time (Wallon, ii., 155).

80. Journal of the debates of the Jacobin Club, No. 532, Brumaire 20, year

In this way, agriculturists, manufacturers, and merchants would all become clerks of the State, appointed on a premium or a discount; unable to gain a great deal, they would not be tempted to gain too much; they would cease to be greedy and soon cease to be egoists. Since, fundamentally, egoism is the capital vice and individual proprietorship the food that nourishes it, why not suppress individual proprietorship altogether? Our extreme logicians, with Baboeuf at the head of them, go as far as that, and Saint-Just seems to be of that opinion.[81] A decretal of the Agrarian law is not the point; the nation would reserve the soil to itself and divide among individuals, not lands but rents. The outcome of this principle affords us a glimpse of an order of things in which the State, sole proprietor of real-estate, sole capitalist, sole manufacturer, sole trader, having all Frenchmen in its pay and service, would assign to each one his task according to his aptitude, and distribute to each one his rations according to his wants. These various uncompleted plans still float in a hazy distance; but their common purpose is clearly distinguishable. "All which tends to concentrating human passions in the abjection of personality must be repudiated or repressed";[82] the point is, to annihilate special interests, to deprive the individual of the motives and means for self-isolation, to suppress preoccupations and ambitions by which he makes himself a centre at the expense of the veritable centre, in short, to detach him from himself in order to attach him wholly to the State.

This is why, outside the narrow egoism through which the individual prefers himself to the community, we follow out the broad egoism by which the individual prefers to the community the group of which he forms a part. Under no pretext must he separate himself

---

II. (Plan of citizen Dupré, presented in the Convention by a deputation of the Arcis Club.)—Dauban, "Paris en 1794," p. 483 (a project similar to the former, presented to the Committee of Public Safety by the Jacobin Club of Montereau, Thermidor, year II.)

81. Buchez et Roux, xxxv., 272. ("Institutions," by Saint-Just.)

82. Buchez et Roux, xxxi., 273. (Report by Robespierre, Pluviose 17, year II.)

934 / THE FRENCH REVOLUTION

from the whole; at no price, must he be allowed to form for himself a small patrimony within the large one, for, by the affection he entertains for the small one, he frustrates the objects of the large one. Nothing is worse than political, civil, religious and domestic federalism; we combat it under all its forms.[83] In this particular, the Constituent Assembly has paved the way for us, since it has broken up all the principal historic or material groups by which men have separated themselves from the masses and formed a band apart, provinces, clergy, nobles, parliaments, religious orders, and trades-unions. We complete its work: we destroy churches, we suppress literary or scientific associations, educational or benevolent societies, even down to financial companies.[84] We prohibit any departmental or commercial "local spirit": we find "odious and opposed to all principles, that, amongst municipalities, some should be rich and others poor, that one should have immense patrimonial possessions and another nothing but indebtedness."[85] We regard these possessions as the nation's, and we place indebtedness to the nation's account. We take grain from rich communes and departments, to feed poor communes and departments. We build the bridges, roads, and canals of each district, at the expense of the State; "we centralise the labor of the French people in a broad, opulent fashion."[86] We

83. *Moniteur,* xix., 653. (Report by Barère, Ventose 21, year II.) "You should detect and combat federalism in all your institutions, as your natural enemy. . . . A grand central establishment for all the work of the Republic is an efficacious means against federalism."—Buchez et Roux, xxxi., 351, and xxxii., 316. (Report by Saint-Just, Ventose 23, and Germinal 26, year II.) "Immorality is a federalism in the civil state. . . . Civil federalism, by isolating all parts of the state, has dried up abundance."

84. Decree of Germinal 26–29, year II. "Financial companies are and hereby remain suppressed. All bankers, commission merchants, and other persons, are forbidden to form any establishment of this order under any pretext or under any denomination."

85. "Mémoires de Carnot," i., 278. (Report by Carnot.) "That is not family life. If there are local privileges there will soon be individual privileges and local aristocracy will bring along in its train the aristocracy of inhabitants."

86. *Moniteur,* xix., 683. (Report by Barère, Ventose 21, year II.) This report

want no more local interests, souvenirs, idioms, and patriotisms. One tie only should subsist between individuals, that which attaches them to the social body; we sunder all others; we do not tolerate any special aggregation; we do the best we can to break up the most tenacious of all, the family. To this end, we assimilate marriage with ordinary contracts: we render this loose and precarious, as nearly resembling the free and transient union of the sexes as possible; it shall be dissolved at the option of both parties, and even of one of the parties, after one month of formalities and of probation; if the couple has lived separate six months, the divorce may be granted without any probation or delay; divorced parties may remarry. On the other hand, we suppress marital authority: since spouses are equal, each has equal rights over common property and the property of each other; we deprive the husband of its administration and render it "common" to both parties. We abolish "paternal authority"; "it is cheating nature to enforce her rights through constraint. ... The only rights that parents have are those of protection and watchfulness."[87] The father can no longer control the education of his children; the State takes charge of it. The father is no longer master of his possessions; the portion he can dispose of by donation or testament is of the smallest; we prescribe an equal and forced division of property. Finally, we preach adoption, we efface bastardy, we confer on children born of free love, or of a despotic will, the same rights as those of legitimate children. In short, we break up that sacred circle, that exclusive group, that aristocratic organisation which, under the name of the family, was created out of pride and egoism.[88] Henceforth, affection and obedience will no longer be frit-

---

should be read in full to comprehend the communistic and centralising spirit of the Jacobins.

87. Feret, "Travaux du Code civil," 105. (Reports by Cambacérès, August 9, 1793, and Septem. 9, 1794.)—Decrees of September 20, 1793, and Floréal 4, year II. (on Divorce.)—Cf. "Institutions," by Saint-Just. (Buchez et Roux, xxxv., 302.) "A man and woman who love each other are married; if they have no children they may keep their relationship secret."

88. This article of the Jacobin programme, like the others, has its practical

tered away; the miserable supports to which they have clung like ivy vines, castes, churches, corporations, provinces, communes, or families, are ruined and rooted out; on the ground which is thus levelled, the State alone remains standing, and it alone offers any point of adhesion; all these vines are about to twine themselves in one trunk about the great central column.

VIII

Let them not go astray, let us lead them on, let us direct minds and souls, and, to this end, let us enfold man in our doctrines. He needs general ideas and the daily experiences flowing out of them; he needs some theory explaining the origin and nature of things, one which

---

result.—"At Paris, in the twenty-seven months after the promulgation of the law of September, 1792, the courts granted five thousand nine hundred and ninety-four divorces, and in year VI. the number of divorces exceeded the marriages." (Glasson, "Le Mariage Civil et le Divorce," p. 51).—"The number of foundlings which, in 1790, in France, did not exceed twenty-three thousand, is now (year X.) more than sixty-three thousand. ("Statistique de la Sarthe," by Auvray, préfet, year X.).—In Lot-et-Garonne ("Statistique," by Pieyre, préfet, year X.), more than fifteen hundred foundlings are counted: "this extraordinary number increased during the Revolution through the too easy admission of foundlings into the asylums, through the temporary sojourning of soldiers in their homes, through the disturbance of every moral and religious principle."—"It is not rare to find children of thirteen and fourteen talking and acting in a way that would have formerly disgraced a young man of twenty." (Moselle, "Analyse," by Ferrière).—"The children of workmen are idle and insubordinate; some indulge in the most shameful conduct against their parents"; others try stealing and use the coarsest language." (Meurthe, "Statistique," by Marquis, préfet.)—Cf. Anne Plumptre (A narrative of three years residence in France, from 1802 to 1805, i., 46). "You would not believe it, madame, said a gardener to her at Nismes, that during the Revolution we dared not scold our children for their faults. Those who called themselves *patriots* regarded it as against the fundamental principles of liberty to correct children. This made them so unruly that, very often, when a parent presumed to scold its child the latter would tell him to mind his business, adding, 'we are free and equal, the Republic is our only father and mother; if you are not satisfied, I am. Go where you like it better.' Children are still saucy. It will take a good many years to bring them back to minding."

assigns him his place and the part he has to play in the world, which teaches him his duties, which regulates his life, which fixes the days he shall work and the days he shall rest, which stamps itself on his mind through commemorations, festivals and ceremonies, through a catechism and a calendar. Up to this time Religion has been the power charged with this service, interpreted and served by the Church; now it is to be Reason, interpreted and served by the State. In this connection, many among us, disciples of the encyclopedists, constitute Reason a divinity, and honor her with a system of worship; but it is plain that they personify an abstraction; their improvised goddess is simply an allegorical phantom; none of them see in her the intelligent cause of the world; in the depths of their hearts they deny this Supreme Cause, their pretended religion being merely a show or a sham. We discard atheism, not only because it is false, but again, and more especially, because it is disintegrating and unwholesome.[89] We want an effective, consolatory, and fortifying religion, and that religion is natural religion, which is social as well as true. "Without this," Rousseau says, "it is impossible to be a good citizen."[90] . . . The existence of divinity, the future life, the sacredness of the social contract and of the laws," all are its dogmas; "no one may be forced to believe in these, but whoever dares say that he does not believe in them, sets himself up against the French people, the human species and nature." Consequently, we decree that "the French people recognises the Supreme Being and the immortality of the soul." The important thing now is to plant this entirely philosophic faith in all hearts. We introduce it into the civil order of things, we take the calendar out of the hands of the Church, we purge it of its Christian imagery; we make the new era begin with the advent of the Republic; we divide the year according to the

89. Buchez et Roux, xxxii., 364. (Report by Robespierre, Floréal 8, year II.)—At Bayeux, the young girl who represented Liberty, had the following inscription on her breast or back: "Do not make me an instrument of licentiousness." (Gustave Flaubert, family souvenirs.)

90. *Ibid.*, 385. (Address of a Jacobin deputation to the Convention, Floréal 27, year II.)

metric system, we name the months according to the vicissitudes of the seasons, "we substitute, in all directions, the realities of reason for the visions of ignorance, the truths of nature for a sacerdotal prestige,"[91] the decade for the week, the *décadi* for Sundays, lay festivals for ecclesiastical festivals.[92] On each *décadi*, through solemn and appropriate pomp, we impress on the popular mind one of the highest truths of our creed; we glorify, in the order of their dates, Nature, Truth, Justice, Liberty, Equality, the People, Adversity, Humanity, the Republic, Posterity, Glory, Patriotism, Heroism, and other virtues. Besides this, we honor the important days of the Revolution, the taking of the Bastille, the fall of the Throne, the punishment of the tyrant, the expulsion of the Girondists. We, too, have our anniversaries, our relics, the relics of Chalier and Marat,[93] our processions, our services, our ritual,[94] and the vast system of visible pageantry by which dogmas are made manifest and propagated. But ours, instead of leading men off to an imaginary heaven, brings them back to a living patrimony, and, through our ceremonies as well as through our creed, we inculcate civism.

If it is important to preach this to adults, it is still more important to teach it to children, for children are more easily moulded than adults. Our hold on these still flexible minds is complete, and, through national education "we possess ourselves of coming gen-

91. Buchez et Roux, xxxi., 415. (Report by Fabre d'Eglantine. October 6, 1793.)—(Grégoire, "Mémoires," i., 341.) "The new calendar was invented by Romme in order to get rid of Sunday. That was his object; he admitted it to me."

92. *Ibid.*, xxxii., 274. (Report by Robespierre, Floréal 18, year II.) "National Festivals form an essential part of public education. . . . A system of national festivals is the most powerful means of regeneration."

93. *Ibid.*, xxviii., 335. Marat's heart, placed on a table in the Cordéliers Club, was an object of religious reverence.—(Grégoire, "Mémoires," i., 341.) "In some schools the pupils were obliged to make the sign of the cross at the names of Marat, Lazowski, etc."

94. De Martel, "Étude sur Fouché," 137. Fête at Nevers, on the inauguration of a bust of Brutus.—*Ibid.*, 222, civic festival at Nevers in honor of valor and morals.—Dauban, "Paris en 1704." Programme of the fête of the Supreme Being at Sceaux.

erations."[95] Naught is more essential and naught is more legitimate. "The country," says Robespierre, "has a right to bring up its own children; it cannot confide this trust to family pride nor to the prejudices of individuals, the eternal nourishment of aristocracies and of a domestic federalism which narrows the soul by keeping it isolated." We are determined to have *"education common and equal for all French people,"* and "we stamp on it a great character, analogous to the nature of our government and the sublime doctrines of our Republic. The aim is no longer to form *gentlemen* (messieurs) but citizens."[96] We oblige[97] teachers, male and female, to present certificates of civism, that is to say, of Jacobinism. We close their school if "precepts or maxims opposed to revolutionary morality" are taught in it, that is to say, in conformity with Christian morality. Children will learn to read in the Declaration of Rights and in the Constitution of 1793. Republican manuals and catechisms will be prepared for their use.[98] "They must be taught the virtuous traits which most honor free men, and especially the traits characteristic of the French Revolution, the best calculated to elevate the soul and render them worthy of equality and liberty." The 14th of July, 10th of August, 2d of September, 21st of January, and 31st of May must

95. An expression by Rabaut Saint-Etienne.

96. Buchez et Roux, xxxii., 373. (Report by Robespierre, Floréal 15, year II.)—Danton had expressed precisely the same opinion, supported by the same arguments, at the meeting of Frimaire 22, year II. (*Moniteur*, xviii., 654.) "Children first belong to the Republic before belonging to their parents. Who will assure me that these children, inspired by parental egoism, will not become dangerous to the Republic? What do we care for the ideas of an individual alongside of national ideas? ... Who among us does not know the danger of this constant isolation? It is in the national schools that the child must suck republican milk! ... The Republic is one and indivisible. Public instruction must likewise relate to this centre of unity."

97. Decree of Vendémiaire 30 and Brumaire 7, year II.—Cf. Sauzay, vi., 252, on the application of this decree in the provinces.

98. Albert Duruy, "L'Instruction publique et la Revolution," 164 to 172 (extracts from various republican spelling-books and catechisms).—Decree of Frimaire 29, year II., section i., art. 1, 83; section ii., art. 2; section iii., arts. 6 and 9.

be lauded or justified in their presence. They must be taken to meetings of the municipalities, to the law courts,[99] "and especially to the
popular clubs; from these pure sources they will derive a knowledge
of their rights, of their duties, of the laws, of republican morality,"
and, on entering society, they will find themselves imbued with all
good maxims. Over and above their political opinions we shape their
ordinary habits. We apply on a grand scale the plan of education
drawn out by Jean-Jacques (Rousseau).[100] We want no more literary
prigs; in the army, "the 'swell' breaks down the first campaign";[101]
we want young men able to endure privation and fatigue, toughened,
like Emile, "by hard work" and physical exercise. We have, thus far,
only sketched out this department of education, but the agreement
amongst the various plans shows the meaning and bearings of our
principle. "Children generally, without distinction and without exception," says Lepelletier de Saint-Fargeau,[102] "boys from five to
twelve, and girls from five to eleven years of age, must be brought
up in common at the expense of the Republic; all, under the sacred
law of equality, are to receive the same clothing, the same food, the
same education, the same attention" in boarding-schools distributed
according to cantons, and containing each from four to six hundred
pupils. "Pupils will be made to submit every day and every moment
to the same rigid rules. . . . Their beds must be hard, their food
healthy, but simple, their clothing comfortable, but coarse." Servants
will not be allowed; children must help themselves and, besides this,
they must wait on the old and infirm, lodged with or near them.
"Among daily duties, manual labor will be the principal thing; all
the rest will be accessory." Girls must learn to spin, sew and wash

99. *Moniteur,* xviii., 653. (Meeting of Frimaire 22, speech by Bouquier,
reporter.)

100. *Moniteur,* xviii., 351–359. (Meeting of Brumaire 15, year II., report by
Chénier.) "You have made laws—create habits. . . . You can apply to the public
instruction of the nation the same course that Rousseau follows in 'Emile.'"

101. The words of Bouquier, reporter. (Meeting of Frimaire 22, year II.)

102. Bouchez et Roux, xxiv., 57. (Plan by Lepelletier St. Fargeau, read by
Robespierre at the Convention, July 13, 1793.)—*Ibid.,* 35. (Draft of a decree
by the same hand.)

clothes; the boys will work the roads, be shepherds, ploughmen and work-hands; both will have tasks set them, either in the school-workshops, or in the fields and factories in the neighborhood; they will be hired out to surrounding manufacturers and to the tillers of the soil. Saint-Just is more specific and rigid.[103] "Male children from five to sixteen years of age, must be raised for their country. They must be clad in common cloth at all seasons, and have mats for beds, and sleep eight hours. They are to have common food only, fruits, vegetables, preparations of milk, bread and water. They must not eat meat before sixteen. . . . Their education, from ten to sixteen, is to be military and agricultural. They will be formed into companies of sixty; six companies make a battalion; the children of a district form a legion; they will assemble annually at the district town, en-camp there and drill in infantry tactics, in arenas specially provided for the purpose; they will also learn cavalry manoeuvres and every other species of military evolution. In harvest time they are to be distributed amongst the harvesters." After sixteen, "they enter the arts," along with some farmer, artisan, merchant, or manufacturer, who becomes their titulary "instructor," and with whom they are bound to remain up to the age of twenty-one, "under the penalty of being deprived for life of a citizen's rights.[104] . . . All children will dress alike up to sixteen years of age; from sixteen to twenty-one, they will dress as workmen; from twenty-one to twenty-five, they will dress as soldiers, if they are not in the magistracy." Already we show the effects of the theory by one striking example; we founded the "Ecole de Mars";[105] we select out of each district six boys from sixteen to seventeen and a half years old "among the children of

---

103. *Ibid.*, xxxv., 229. ("Institutions," by Saint-Just.)

104. Buchez et Roux, xxxi., 261. (Meeting of Nivose 17.) On the committee presenting the final draft of the decrees on public instruction the Convention adopts the following article: "All boys who, on leaving the primary schools of instruction, do not devote themselves to tillage, will be obliged to learn some science, art or occupation useful to society. Otherwise, on reaching twenty, they will be deprived of citizens' rights for ten years, and the same penalty will be laid on their father, mother, tutor or guardian."

105. Decree of Prairial 13, year II.

sans-culottes"; we summon them to Paris, "to receive there, through a revolutionary education, whatever belongs to the knowledge and habits of a republican soldier. They are schooled in fraternity, in discipline, in frugality, in good habits, in love of country and in detestation of kings." Three or four thousand young people are lodged at the Sablons, "in a palisaded enclosure, the intervals of which are guarded by *chevaux de frises* and sentinels."[106] We put them into tents; we feed them with bran bread, rancid pork, water, and vinegar; we drill them in the use of arms; we march them out on national holidays and stimulate them with patriotic harangues. Suppose all Frenchmen educated in such a school; the habits they acquire in youth will persist in the adult, and, in each adult we shall find the sobriety, energy and patriotism of a Spartan or Roman.

Already, under the pressure of our decrees, civism affects customs, and there are manifest signs, on all sides, of public regeneration. "The French people," says Robespierre, "seem to have outstripped the rest of humanity, by two thousand years; one might be tempted to regard them, living amongst them, as a different species. In the rest of Europe, a ploughman, an artisan, is an animal formed for the pleasures of a noble; in France, the nobles are trying to transform themselves into ploughmen and artisans, but do not succeed in obtaining that honor."[107] Life in all directions is gradually assuming democratic forms. Wealthy prisoners are prohibited from purchasing delicacies, or procuring special conveniences; they eat along with the poor prisoners the same ration, at the common mess.[108] Bakers

---

106. Langlois, "Souvenirs de l' Ecole de Mars."

107. Buchez et Roux, xxxii., 355. (Report by Robespierre, Floréal 18, year II.)

108. *Moniteur,* xviii., 326. (Meeting of the Commune, Brumaire 11, year II.) The commissary announces that, at Fontainebleau and other places, "he has established the system of equality in the prisons and places of confinement, where the rich and the poor partake of the same food."—*Ibid.,* 210. (Meeting of the Jacobins, Vendémiaire 29, year II. Speech by Laplanche on his mission to Gers.) "Priests had every comfort in their secluded retreats; the *sans-culottes* in the prisons slept on straw. The former provided me with mattresses for the latter."—*Ibid.,* xviii., 445. (Meeting of the Convention, Brumaire 26, year II.)

have orders to make but one quality of bread, the brown bread called equality bread, and, to obtain his ration, each person must place himself in line with the rest of the crowd. On holidays[109] everybody will bring his provisions down into the street and eat as one family with his neighbor; on the *décadi,* all are to sing and dance together, pell-mell, in the temple of the Supreme Being. The decrees of the Convention and the orders of the representatives impose the republican cockade on women; public opinion and example impose on men the costume and appearance of *sans-culottes;* we see even "swells" wearing mustaches, long hair, red cap, vest, and heavy wooden shoes.[110] Nobody calls a person *Monsieur* or *Madame;* the only titles allowed are *citoyen* and *citoyenne* while *thee* and *thou* is the general rule. Rude familiarity takes the place of monarchical politeness; all greet each other as equals and comrades. There is now only one tone, one style, one language; revolutionary forms constitute the tissue of speech, as well as of written discourse; thought now seems to consist entirely of our ideas and phrases. All names are transformed, those of months and of days, those of places and of monuments, baptismal names and names of families: St. Denis has become Franciade; Peter Gaspard is converted into Anaxagoras,

---

"The Convention decrees that the food of persons kept in places of confinement shall be simple and the same for all, the rich paying for the poor."

109. Archives Nationales. (AF.II., 37, order of Lequinio, Saintes, Nivose 1, year II.) "Citizens generally in all communes, are requested to celebrate the day of the decade by a fraternal banquet which, served without luxury or display ... will render the man bowed down with fatigue insensible to his forlorn condition; which will fill the soul of the poor and unfortunate with the sentiment of social equality and raise man up to the full sense of his dignity; which will suppress with the rich man the slightest feeling of pride and extinguish in the public functionary all germs of haughtiness and aristocracy."

110. Archives Nationales, AF.II., ii., 48 (Act of Floréal 25, year II.) "The Committee of Public Safety request David, representative of the people, to present his views and plans in relation to modifying the present national costume, so as to render it appropriate to republican habits and the character of the Revolution."—*Ibid.,* (Act of Prairial 5, year II.) for engraving and coloring twenty thousand impressions of the design for a civil uniform, and six thousand impressions of the three designs for a military, judicial, and legislative uniform.

and Antoine-Louis into Brutus; Leroi, the deputy, calls himself La-loi, and Leroy, the jurist, calls himself August-Tenth. By dint of thus shaping the exterior we reach the interior, and through outward civism we prepare internal civism. Both are obligatory, but the latter much more so than the former; for that is the fundamental princi-ple,[111] the mainspring which sustains and impels a democratic and popular government. "It is impossible to apply the social contract if everybody does not scrupulously observe the first clause of it, namely, the complete surrender of himself to the community; every-body, then, must give himself up entirely, not only actually but heartily, and devote himself to the public weal, which public weal is the regeneration of man as we have defined it. The veritable citizen is he who thus marches along with us. With him, as with us, abstract truths of philosophy control the conscience and govern the will. He starts with our articles of faith and follows them out to the end; he derives from them all the consequences which we derive from them; he endorses our acts, he recites our creed, he observes our discipline,

111. Buchez et Roux, xxxi., 271. (Report by Robespierre, Pluviose 1, year II.) "This sublime principle supposes a preference for public interests over all private interests; from which it follows that the love of country supposes again, or produces, all the virtues." "As the essence of a republic or of democracy is equality, it follows that love of country necessarily comprises a love of equality." "The soul of the Republic is virtue, equality."—Lavalette, "Mémoires," i., 254. (Narrated by Madame Lavalette.) She was compelled to attend public festivals, and, every month, the patriotic processions. "I was rudely treated by my as-sociates, the low women of the quarter; the daughter of an *emigré*, of a marquis, or of an imprisoned mother, ought not to be allowed the honor of their com-pany; . . . it was all wrong that she was not made an apprentice. . . . Hortense de Beauharnais was apprenticed to her mother's seamstress, while Eugene was put with a carpenter in the Faubourg St. Germain." The prevailing dogmatism has a singular effect with simple-minded people. (Archives Nationales, AF. II., 135, petition of Ursule Riesler, servant to citizen Estreich and arrested along with him, addressed to Garnerin, agent of the Committee of Public Safety. She begs citizen Garnerin to interest himself in obtaining her freedom. She will devote her life to praying to the Supreme Being for him, since he will redeem her life. He is to furnish her, moreover, with the means for espousing a future husband, a genuine republican, by whom she is pregnant, and who would not allow her to entertain any idea of fanatical capers.

he is a believing and practicing Jacobin, an orthodox Jacobin, un-sullied, and without taint of heresy or schism. Never does he swerve to the left toward exaggeration, nor to the right toward toleration; without haste or delay he travels along on the narrow, steep and straight path which we have marked out for him; this is the pathway of reason, for, as there is but one reason, there is but one pathway. Let no one swerve from the line; there are abysses on each side of it. Let us follow our guides, men of principles, the pure, especially Couthon, Saint-Just, and Robespierre; they are choice specimens, all cast in the true mould, and it is this unique and rigid mould in which all French men are to be recast.

❧ CHAPTER II ❧

I. *Retrograde conception of the State—Analogy between this idea of the State and that of antiquity—Difference between antique and modern society—Difference in circumstances— II. Difference between men's souls—Conscience and its Christian origin—Honour and its feudal origin—The individual of today refuses to surrender himself entirely—His motives—Additional motives in modern democracy—Character of the elective process and nature of the mandatory— III. Origin and nature of the modern State—Its functions, rights, and limits— IV. Temptation to encroachments—Precedents and reasons for its pretensions— V. Direct common interest—This consists in the absence of constraint—Two reasons in favor of freedom of action—Character, in general, of the individual man—Modern complications— VI. Indirect common interest—This consists in the most economical and most productive employment of spontaneous forces— Difference between voluntary labor and forced labor—Sources of man's spontaneous action—Conditions of their energy, work, and products—Motives for leaving them under personal control—Extent of the private domain—Individuals voluntarily extend it—What they leave to the State—Obligatory functions of the State—Optional functions of the State— VII. Fabrication of social instrumentalities—Application of this principle—How all kinds of useful laborers are formed—Respect for spontaneous sources, the essential and adequate condition— Obligation of the State to respect these—They dry up when it monopolizes them—The aim of Patriotism—The aim of other liberal dispositions—Impoverishment of all the productive faculties—Destructive effect of the Jacobin system— VIII. Comparison between despotisms—Philip II. and Louis XIV.— Cromwell and Frederic the Great—Peter the Great and the Sultans—Proportions of the weight they sustain and the forces they control—Disproportion between the Jacobins' attempt to raise this weight and their forces—Folly of their undertaking—Physical force the only governmental force they possess—They are com-*

pelled to exercise it—They are compelled to abuse it—Character of their gov-
ernment—Character requisite in their leaders.

THE LOGICAL creation of a curtailed type of humanity, the effort
to adapt the living man to this type, the interference of public authority in every branch of public endeavor, restrictions put upon
labor, exchanges, and property, upon the family and education, upon
worship, habits, customs, and sentiments, the sacrifice of the individual to the community, the omnipotence of the State—such is the
Jacobin theory. None could be more retrograde; for the modern
man is made to revert back to social forms which, for eighteen
centuries, he had already passed through and left behind him. During the historical era preceding our own, and especially in the old
Greek or Latin cities, in Rome and Sparta, which the Jacobins take
for their models,[1] human society was shaped after the pattern of an
army or convent. In a convent as in an army, one idea, absorbing
and unique, predominates: the aim of the monk is to please God at
any sacrifice; the soldier makes every sacrifice to obtain a victory;
accordingly, each renounces every other desire and entirely abandons himself, the monk to his rules and the soldier to his drill. In
like manner, in the antique world, two preoccupations were of supreme importance. In the first place, the city had its gods who were
both its founders and protectors: it was therefore obliged to worship
these in the most reverent and particular manner; otherwise, they
abandoned it; the neglect of any insignificant rite might offend them
and ruin it. In the second place, there was incessant warfare, and
the rights of war were atrocious; on a city being taken every citizen
might expect to be killed or maimed, or sold at auction, and see his
children and wife knocked down to the highest bidder.[2] In short,

1. Buchez et Roux, xxxii., 354. (Speech by Robespierre in the Convention,
Floréal 18, year II.) "Sparta gleams like a flash of lightning amidst profoundest
darkness."
2. Milos taken by the Athenians; Thebes, after Alexander's victory; Corinth,
after its capture by the Romans.—In the Peloponnesian war, the Plateans, who
surrender at discretion, are put to death. Nicias is murdered in cold blood after
his defeat in Sicily. The prisoners at Aegos-Potamos have their thumbs cut off.

the antique city, with its acropolis of temples and its fortified citadel surrounded by implacable and threatening enemies, resembles for us the institution of the Knights of St. John on their rocks at Rhodes or Malta, a religious and military confraternity encamped around a church. Liberty, under such conditions, is out of the question: public convictions are too imperious; public danger is too great. With this pressure upon him, and thus hampered, the individual gives himself up to the community, which takes full possession of him, because, to maintain its own existence, it needs the whole man. Henceforth, no one may develop apart and for himself; no one may act or think except within fixed lines. The type of man is distinctly and clearly marked out, if not logically at least traditionally; each life, as well as each portion of each life must conform to this type; otherwise public security is compromised: any falling off in gymnastic education weakens the army; passing the images of the gods and neglecting the usual libation draws down celestial vengeance on the city. Consequently, to prevent all deviations, the State, absolute master, exercises unlimited jurisdiction; no freedom whatever is left to the individual, no portion of himself is reserved to himself, no sheltered corner against the strong hand of public force, neither his possessions, his children, his personality, his opinions, or his conscience.[3] If, on voting days, he shares in the sovereignty, he is a subject all the rest of the year, even to his private sentiments. Rome, to serve these ends, had two censors; one of the archons of Athens was inquisitor of the faith; Socrates was put to death "for not believing in the gods in which the city believed."[4] In reality, not only in Greece and in Rome, but in Egypt, in China, in India, in Persia, in Judea, in Mexico, in Peru, during the first stages of civilisation,[5]

---

3. Fustel de Coulanges: "La Cité Antique," ch. xvii.

4. Plato, "The Apology of Socrates." See also in the "Crito" Socrates' reasons for not eluding the penalty imposed on him. The antique conception of the State is here clearly set forth.

5. Cf. the code of Manu, the Zendavesta, the Pentateuch, and the Tcheou-Li. In this last code (Biot's translation), will be found the perfection of the system, particularly in vol. i., 241, 247, ii., 393, iii., 9, 11, 21, 52. "Every district

the principle of human communities is still that of animal associations: the individual belongs to his community the same as the bee to its hive and the ant to its ant-hill; he is simply an organ within an organism. Under diverse forms and in diverse applications authoritative socialism alone prevails.

It is just the opposite in modern society; what was once the rule has now become the exception; the antique system survives only in temporary associations, like that of an army, or in special associations, as in a convent. The individual has liberated himself by degrees, and, from century to century, he has extended his domain; the two chains which once bound him fast to the community, are broken or become loosened. In the first place, public power has ceased to consist of a militia protecting a cult. Through the institution of Christianity, civil society and religious society have become two distinct empires, Christ himself having separated the two jurisdictions; "Render unto Caesar the things which are Caesar's, and unto God the things that are God's." On the other hand, through the rise of Protestantism, the great Christian Church is split into numerous sects which, unable to destroy each other, have been so compelled to live together that the State, even when preferring one of them, has found it necessary to tolerate the others. Finally, through the development of Protestantism, philosophy and the sciences, speculative beliefs have multiplied; there are almost as many faiths now-a-days as there are thinking men, and, as thinking men are becoming daily more numerous, opinions are daily becoming more numerous, so that, if the State should try to impose any one

---

chief, on the twelfth day of the first moon, assembles together the men of his district and reads to them the table of rules; he examines their virtue, their conduct, their progress in the right path, and in their knowledge, and encourages them; he investigates their errors, their failings and prevents them from doing evil. . . . Superintendents of marriages see that young people marry at the prescribed age." The reduction of man to a State automaton is plain enough in the institution of "Overseer of Gags . . ." "At all grand hunts, at all gatherings of troops, he orders the application of gags. In these cases gags are put in the soldiers' mouths; they then fulfill their duties without tumult or shoutings."

of these on society, this would excite opposition from an infinity of others; hence the wisdom of the State is found, first, in remaining neutral, and, next, in acknowledging that it is not qualified to interfere. In the second place, war has become less frequent and less destructive because men have not so many motives for waging it, nor the same motives to push it to the same extremes. Formerly, war was the main source of wealth; through victories man acquired slaves, subjects, and tributaries; he turned these to the best account; he leisurely enjoyed their forced labor. Nothing of this kind is seen now-a-days; people no longer think of providing themselves with human cattle; they have discovered that, of all animals, these are the most troublesome, the least productive, and the most dangerous. Comforts and security are obtained much more readily through free labor and machinery; the great object now is not to conquer, but to produce and interchange. Every day, man, pressing forward more eagerly in civil careers, is less disposed to put up with any obstacle that interferes with his aims; if he still consents to be a soldier it is not to become an invader, but to provide against invasion. Meanwhile, war has become more scientific and, through the complications of its machinery, more costly; the State can no longer call out and enlist for life every able-bodied man without ruining itself, nor put too many obstacles in the way of that free industry which, through taxation, provides for its expenses; however short-sighted the State may be, it consults civil interests, even in its military interest. Thus, of the two nets, in the toils of which it has enveloped all human activity, one is rent asunder and the other has relaxed its meshes. There is no longer any reason for making the community omnipotent; the individual need not alienate himself entirely; he may, without inconvenience, reserve to himself a part of himself, and, if now called upon to sign a social contract, you may be sure that he would make this reservation.

II

Outward circumstances, indeed, are not only changed, but the very depths of the soul are changed; the breast of man is animated by a sentiment which is repugnant to antique stipulations. Undoubtedly, in extreme cases and under the pressure of brutal necessity I may, without special instructions and for a time, give the State my signature in blank. But, never, with a full comprehension of the meaning of the terms, will I sign away in good faith the complete and permanent abandonment of myself: it would be against *conscience and honor,* which two possessions are not to be alienated. My honor and my conscience are not to go out of my keeping; I am their sole guardian and depositary; I would not even entrust them to my father. Both these terms are new and express two conceptions unknown to the ancients,[6] both being of profound import and of infinite reach. Through them, like a bud separated from its stem and taking root apart, the individual has separated himself from the primitive body, clan, family, caste, or city in which he has lived indistinguishable and lost in the crowd; he has ceased to be an organ and appendage; he has become a personality. The first of these conceptions is of Christian origin and the second of feudal origin; both, following each other and conjoined, measure the enormous distance which separates an antique soul from a modern soul.

Alone, in the presence of God, the Christian feels every tie dissolving like wax that binds him to the group around him; he stands face to face with the Great Judge, and this infallible judge sees all souls as they are, not confusedly and in masses, but distinctly and each by itself. At the bar of this tribunal no one is answerable for another; each answers for himself alone; one is responsible only for one's acts. But those acts are of infinite consequence, for the soul, redeemed by the blood of a God, is of infinite price; hence, according as it has or has not profited by the divine sacrifice, so will the reward or punishment be infinite; at the final judgment, an eternity of torment or bliss opens before it. All other interests vanish alongside of

6. These two words have no exact equivalents in Greek or Latin. *Conscientia, dignitas, honos* denote different shades of meaning. This difference is most appreciable in the combination of the two modern terms *delicate conscience, scrupulous conscience,* and the phrase of *stake one's honor on this or that, make it a point of honor,* the *laws of honor,* etc. The technical terms in antique morality, *beautiful, virtuous, sovereign good,* indicate ideas of another stamp and origin.

an interest of such vast disproportion; thenceforth, righteousness is the most serious of all aims, not in the eyes of man, but of God, and again, day after day, the soul renews within itself that tragic questioning in which the Judge interrogates and the sinner responds. Through this dialogue, which has been going on for eighteen centuries, and which is yet to continue, conscience has grown more and more sensitive, and man has conceived the idea of absolute justice. Whether this is vested in an all-powerful master, or whether it is a self-existent truth, like mathematical truths, in no wise takes away from its sacredness nor, consequently, from its authority. It commands with a superior voice and its commands must be obeyed, cost what it will: there are strict duties to which every man is rigorously bound. No pledge may relieve him of these duties; if not fulfilled because he has given contrary pledges he is no less culpable on this account, and besides, he is culpable for having pledged himself; the pledging of himself to crimes was in itself a crime. His fault thus appears to him twofold, and the inward prick galls him twice instead of once. Hence, the more sensitive the conscience, the greater its repugnance to self-abdication; it repels in advance any pact tending to wrong-doing, and refuses to give to men the right of imposing remorse.

At the same time another sentiment has arisen, not less precious and still more energetic, more human and more efficacious. Solitary in his stronghold, the feudal chieftain, at the head of his band, could depend on nobody but himself, for a public force did not then exist. It was necessary that he should protect himself, and, indeed, over-protect himself; whoever, in the anarchical and military society in which he lived, allowed the slightest encroachment, or left unpunished the slightest approach to insult, was regarded as weak or craven and at once became a prey; one had to be proud-spirited under penalty of death. And do not fancy this a difficult task for him. Sole proprietor and absolute sovereign, with no equals or peers on his domain, he lived there a unique being of a superior kind, and disproportionate with every one else.[7] Hence his soliloquising during

7. Montaigne, "Essais," book i., ch. 42. "Observe in the provinces far from

the long hours of a dreary solitude, which soliloquy has lasted for nine centuries.[8] Thus, in his own eyes, his person and all that depends on him are inviolable; rather than tolerate the slightest infringement on his prerogatives he will dare all and sacrifice all.[9] A proud sensibility (*orgueil exalté*) is the best of sentinels to protect a right; for, not only does it mount guard over the right to preserve it, but, again, and especially, for its own satisfaction; the imagination has conceived a character which befits the rank, and this character the man imposes on himself as a password. Henceforth, he not only forces the respect of others, but he respects himself; he possesses the sentiment of honor, a generous self-esteem which makes him regard himself as noble and incapable of doing anything mean. In discriminating between his actions, he may err; fashion or vanity may sometimes lead him too far, or lead him astray, either on the path of recklessness or on that of puerility; his point of honor may be fixed in the wrong direction. But, in sum, and thanks to this being a fixed point, he will maintain himself erect even under an absolute monarchy, under a Philip II. in Spain, under a Louis XIV. in France, under a Frederic II. in Prussia. From the feudal baron or gentleman of the court to the modern gentleman, this tradition persists and descends from story to story down to the lowest social substratum: today, every man of spirit, the bourgeois, the peasant, the workman, has his point of honor like the noble. He likewise, in spite of the social encroachments that gain on him, reserves to himself his private

---

the court, in Brittany for example, the retinue, the subjects, the duties, the ceremony, of a seignior living alone by himself, brought up among his dependents, and likewise observe the flights of his imagination than which nothing is more royal; he may allude to his superior once a year, as if he were the King of Persia. . . . The burden of sovereignty scarcely affects the French *gentilhomme* twice in his life, who cares only to nestle at his own hearthstone and who knows how to rule his household without dispute or trial; he is as free as the Duke of Venice."

8. "Mémoires de Chateaubriand," vol. i. ("Les Soirées au Chateau de Cambourg.")

9. In China, the moral principle is just the opposite. The Chinese, amidst obstacles and embarrassments, always enjoin *siao-sin,* which means, "abate thy affections." (Huc, "L'Empire Chinoise," i., 204.)

nook, a sort of moral stronghold wherein he preserves his faiths, his opinions, his affections, his obligations as son, husband, and father; it is the sacred treasury of his innermost being. This stronghold belongs to him alone; no one, even in the name of the public, has a right to enter it; to surrender it would be cowardice; rather than give up its keys he would die in the breach;[10] when this militant sentiment of honor is enlisted on the side of conscience it becomes virtue itself.[11] Such are, in these days, the two master ideas of our European morality.[12] Through the former the individual recognises duties from which nothing can exempt him; through the latter, he claims rights of which nothing can deprive him: our civilization has vegetated from these two roots, and still vegetates. Consider the

10. In the United States the moral order of things reposes chiefly on puritan ideas; nevertheless deep traces of feudal conceptions are found there; for instance, the general deference for women which is quite chivalric there, and even excessive.

11. Observe, from this point of view, in the woman of modern times the preservatives of female virtue. The sentiment of duty is the first safeguard of modesty, but this has a much more powerful auxiliary in the sentiment of honor, or deep innate pride.

12. The moral standard varies, but according to a fixed law, the same as a mathematical function. Each community has its own moral elements, organisation, history, and surroundings, and necessarily its peculiar conditions of vitality. When the queen bee in a hive is chosen and impregnated this condition involves the massacre of useless male and female rivals (Darwin). In China, it consists of paternal authority, literary education, and ritual observances. In the antique city, it consisted of the omnipotence of the State, gymnastic education, and slavery. In each century, and in each country, these vital conditions are expressed by more or less hereditary passwords which set forth or interdict this or that class of actions. When the individual feels the inward challenge he is conscious of *obligation;* when he does not respond he experiences *remorse:* the moral conflict consists in the struggle within himself between the universal password and personal desire. In our European society the vital condition, and thus the general countersign, is self-respect, coupled with respect for others (including women and children). This countersign, new in history, has a singular advantage over all preceding ones: each individual being respected, each can develop himself according to his nature; he can accordingly invent in every sense, bring forth every sort of production, and be useful to himself and others in every way, thus enabling society to develop indefinitely.

depth and extent of the historical soil in which they penetrate, and you may judge of their vigor. Consider the height and unlimited growth of the trees which they nourish, and you may judge of their healthiness. Everywhere else, one or the other having failed, in China, in the Roman Empire, in Islamism, the sap has dried downward and the tree has become stunted, or has fallen. Through them our civilisation lives and keeps on growing; they give substance to its noblest branches, to its best fruits; their human offshoots are more or less beautiful, according as the sap which reaches them is more or less pure, and these the Jacobin axe seeks to cut away. It is the modern man, who is neither Chinese, nor antique, nor Mussulman, nor negro, nor savage, the man formed by Christian education and taking refuge in his conscience as in a sanctuary, the man formed by feudal education and entrenched behind his honor as in a fortress, whose sanctuary and stronghold the new social contract bids him surrender.

Now, in this democracy founded on the preponderance of numbers, into whose hands am I required to make this surrender? Theoretically, to the community, that is to say, to a crowd in which an anonymous impulse is the substitute for individual judgment; in which action becomes impersonal because it is collective; in which nobody acknowledges responsibility; in which I am borne along like a grain of sand in a whirlwind; in which all sorts of outrages are condoned beforehand for reasons of state: practically, to the plurality of voices counted by heads, to a majority which, overexcited by the struggle for mastery, will abuse its victory and wrong the minority to which I may belong; to a provisional majority which, sooner or later, will be replaced by another, so that if I am today oppressor I am sure of being oppressed tomorrow; still more particularly, to six or seven hundred representatives, among whom I am called upon to choose but one. To elect this unique mandatory I have but one vote among ten thousand; and in helping to elect him I am only the ten-thousandth; I do not even count for a ten-thousandth in electing the others. And it is these six or seven hundred strangers to me to whom I give full power to decide for me—note the expression full

power—which means *unlimited power*, not alone over my possessions and life, but, again, over my conscience, with all its powers
combined; that is to say, with powers much more extensive than
those I confer separately on ten persons in whom I place the most
confidence—to my legal adviser who looks after my fortune, to the
teacher of my children, to the physician who cares for my health,
to the confessor who directs my conscience, to friends who are to
serve as executors of my last will and testament, to seconds in a duel
who decide on my life, on the waste of my blood, and who guard
my honor. Without reference to the deplorable farce, so often played
around the ballot-box, or to the forced and spurious elections which
put a contrary interpretation on public sentiment, or to the official
fictions by which, actually at this moment, a few fanatics and madmen, who represent nobody but themselves, assume to represent the
nation, measure what degree of confidence I may have, even after
honest elections, in mandatories who are thus chosen! Frequently, I
have voted for the defeated candidate; in which case I am represented by the other whom I did not want for a representative. In
voting for the elected candidate, I did it because I knew of no better
one, and because his opponent seemed to me worse. And even him
I have seen only half the time, at odd moments; I scarcely knew
more of him than the color of his coat, the tone of his voice, and
the way he has of thumping his breast. All I know of him is through
his "platform," vague and declamatory, through editorials, and
through drawing-room, coffee-house, or street gossip. His title to
my confidence is of the flimsiest and shallowest kind; there is nothing
to substantiate to me his integrity or competency; he has no diploma,
and no one to indorse him like the preceptor; he has no guarantee
from the incorporation to which he belongs, like the physician, the
priest or the lawyer; with certificates of character such as he has I
should hesitate in engaging a domestic. And all the more because
the class from which I am obliged to take him is almost always that
of politicians, a suspicious class, especially in countries in which
universal suffrage prevails; for, this class is not recruited among the
most independent, the ablest, and the most honest, but among vol-

uble, scheming men and zealous charlatans, who, having failed in private careers for lack of character, in situations where one is watched too closely and too nicely weighed in the balance, have fallen back on vicious courses in which the want of scrupulousness and discretion is a force instead of a weakness; to their indelicacy and impudence the doors of a public career stand wide open. Such is the august personage into whose hands, according to the theory, I am called upon to surrender my will, my will in full; certainly, if self-renunciation were necessary, I should risk less in giving myself up to a king or to an aristocracy, even hereditary; for then would my representatives be at least recommended by their evident rank and their probable competency. Democracy, in its nature and composition, is a system in which the individual awards to his representatives the least trust and deference; hence, it is the system in which he should entrust them with the least power. Conscience and honor everywhere enjoin a man to retain for himself some portion of his independence; but nowhere else will he cede so little of it. If, in every modern constitution the domain of the State ought to be limited, it is in modern democracy that it should be the most restricted.

III

Let us try to define these limits. After the turmoil of invasions and conquest, at the height of social disintegration, amidst the combats daily occurring between private parties, there arose in every European community a *public force*, which force, lasting for centuries, still persists in our day. How it was organised, through what early stages of violence it passed, through what accidents and struggles, and into whose hands it is now entrusted, whether temporarily or forever, whatever the laws of its transmission, whether by inheritance or election, is of secondary importance; the main thing is its functions and their mode of operation. Substantially, it is a mighty sword, drawn from its scabbard and uplifted over the smaller blades around it, with which private individuals once cut each others' throats. Menaced by it, the smaller blades repose in their scabbards; they have become inert, useless, and, finally, rusty; with few exceptions, everybody save malefactors, has now lost both the habit and the desire to use them, so that, henceforth, in this pacified society, the public sword is so formidable that all private resistance vanishes the moment it flashes. This sword is forged out of two interests; it was necessary to have one of its magnitude, first, against similar blades brandished by other communities on the frontier; and next, against the smaller blades which bad passions are always sharpening in the interior. People demanded protection against outside enemies and inside ruffians and murderers, and, slowly and painfully, after much groping and many retemperings, the hereditary banding-together of persistent energies has fashioned the sole arm which is capable of protecting lives and property with any degree of success.

So long as it does no more I am indebted to the State which holds the hilt: it gives me a security which, without it, I could not enjoy; in exchange for this security I owe it, for my quota, the means for keeping this weapon in good condition: any service rendered is worth its cost. Accordingly, there is between the State and myself, if not an express contract, at least a tacit understanding analogous to that which binds a child to its parent, a believer to his church, and, on both sides, this mutual understanding is clear and precise. The State engages to look after my security within and without; I engage to furnish the means for so doing, which means consist of my respect and gratitude, my zeal as a citizen, my services as a conscript, my contributions as a tax-payer, in short, whatever is necessary for the maintenance of an army, a navy, a diplomatic organisation, civil and criminal courts, a militia and police, central and local administrations, in short, a harmonious set of organs of which my obedience and loyalty constitute the food, the substance, and the blood. This loyalty and obedience, whatever I am, whether rich or poor, Catholic, Protestant, Jew or free-thinker, royalist or republican, individualist or socialist, I owe in honor and in conscience, for I have received their equivalent; I am very glad that I am not vanquished, assassinated, or robbed. I pay back to the State exactly what it expends in machinery and oversight for keeping down brutal cupidity, greedy appetites, deadly fanaticisms, the entire howling pack of passions and desires of which, sooner or later, I might become the prey, were it not constantly to extend over me its vigilant protection. When it demands its outlay of me it is not my property which it takes away, but its own property, which it resumes and, in this light, it may legitimately force me to pay. On condition, however, that it does not exact more than my liabilities, and this it does when it oversteps its original engagements; when it undertakes some extra material or moral work that I do not ask for; when it constitutes itself sectarian, moralist, philanthropist, or pedagogue; when it strives to propagate within its borders, or outside of them, any religious or philosophic dogma, or any special political or social system. For then, it adds a new article to the primitive pact, for which article there is not the same unanimous and assured assent that existed for the pact. We are all willing to be secured against violence and fraud; outside of this, and on almost any other point, there are divergent wills. I have my own religion, my own opinions, my habits, my customs, my peculiar views of life, and way of regarding the universe; now, this is just what constitutes my personality, what honor and conscience forbid me to alienate, that which the State has promised me to hold harmless. Consequently, when, through its additional article, it attempts to regulate these in a certain way, if that way is not my way, it fails to fulfill its primordial engagement and, instead of protecting me, it oppresses me. Even if it should have the support of a majority, even if all voters, less one, should agree to entrusting it with this supererogatory function, were there only one dissentient, he would be wronged, and in two ways. In the first place, and in all cases, the State, to fulfill its new task, exacts from him an extra amount of subsidy and service; for, every supplementary work brings along with it supplementary expenses; the *budget* is overburdened when the State takes upon itself the procuring of work for laborers or employment for artists, the maintenance of any particular industrial or commercial enterprise, the giving of alms, and the furnishing of education. To an expenditure of money add an expenditure of lives, should it enter upon a war of generosity or of propagandism. Now, to all these expenditures that it does not approve of, the minority contributes as well as the majority which does approve of them; so much the worse for the conscript and the tax-payer if they belong to the dissatisfied group; like it or not, the collector puts his hand in the tax-payer's pocket, and the sergeant lays his hand on the conscript's collar. In the second place, and in numerous cases, not only does the State take unjustly over and beyond my liability, but, again, it uses unjustly the money it extorts from me in the application of this to new constraints; such is the case when it imposes on me its theology or philosophy; when it prescribes for me, or interdicts, a cult; when it assumes to regulate my ways and habits, to limit my labor or expenditure, to direct the education of my children, to fix the prices of my wares or the rate of my wages. For then, in support of its commands or prohibitions, it enacts against the refractory light or serious penalties, all the way from political or civil incapacity to fine, imprisonment, exile, and the guillotine. In other words, the crown I do not owe it, and of which it robs me, pays for the persecution which it inflicts upon me; I am reduced to paying out of my own purse the wages of my inquisitors, my jailor, and my executioner. A more glaring oppression could not be imagined! Let us take heed of the encroachments of the State and not allow it to become anything more than a watchdog. Whilst the teeth and nails of other guests in the household have been losing their sharpness, its fangs have become formidable; it is now colossal and it alone still keeps up the practice of fighting. Let us supply it with nourishment against wolves; but never let it touch peaceable folks around the table. Appetite grows by eating; it would soon become a wolf itself, and the most ravenous wolf inside the fold. The important thing is to keep a chain around its neck and confine it within its own pale.

IV

Let us inspect this fold, which is an extensive one, and, through its angles, reaching into almost every nook of private life. Each private domain, indeed, physical or moral, offers temptations for its neighbors to trespass on it, and, to keep this intact, demands the superior intervention of a third party. To acquire, to possess, to sell, to give, to bequeath, to contract between husband and wife, father, mother, or child, between master or domestic, employer or employee, each act and each situation, involves rights limited by contiguous and adverse rights, and it is the State which sets up the boundary between them. Not that it creates this boundary; but, that this may be recognised, it draws the line and therefore enacts civil laws, which it applies through its courts and gendarmes in such a way as to secure to each individual what belongs to him. The State stands, accordingly, as regulator and controller, not alone of private possessions, but also of the family and of domestic life; its authority is thus legitimately introduced into that reserved circle in which the individual will has intrenched itself, and, as is the habit of all great powers, once the circle is invaded, its tendency is to occupy it fully and entirely. To this end, it alleges a new principle. Constituted as a moral personality, the same as a church, university, or charitable or scientific body, is not the State bound, like every corporate body that is to last for ages, to extend its vision far and near and prefer to private interests, which are only life-interests, the common interest which is eternal? Is not this the superior end to which all others should be subordinated, and must this interest, which is supreme over all, be sacrificed to two troublesome instincts which are often unreasonable and sometimes dangerous: to conscience, which overflows in mystic absurdities, and to honor, the excitements of which end in murder? Certainly not, and first, in its grandest works, when the State, as legislator, regulates marriages, inheritances, and testaments, it is not respect for the will of individuals which solely guides it; it does not content itself with obliging everybody to pay his debts, including even those which are tacit, involuntary, and innate; it takes into account the public interest; it calculates remote probabilities, future contingencies, all results singly and collectively. Manifestly, in allowing or forbidding divorce, in extending or restricting what a man may dispose of by testament, in favoring or interdicting substitutions, it is chiefly in view of some political, economical, or social advantage, either to refine or consolidate the union of the sexes, to implant in the family habits of discipline or sentiments of affection, to excite in children an initiatory spirit, or one of concord, to prepare for the nation a staff of natural chieftains, or an army of small proprietors, and always authorised by the universal assent. Moreover, and always with this universal assent, it does other things outside the task originally assigned to it, and nobody finds that it usurps, when it coins money, when it regulates weights and measures, when it establishes quarantines, when, on condition of an indemnity, it expropriates private property for public utility, when it builds lighthouses, harbors, dykes, canals, roads, when it defrays the cost of scientific expeditions, when it founds museums and public libraries; at times, toleration is shown for its support of universities, schools, churches, and theatres, and, to justify fresh drafts on private purses for such objects, no reason is assigned for it but the common interest. Why should it not, in like manner, take upon itself every enterprise for the benefit of all? Why should it hesitate in commanding the execution of every work advantageous to the community, and why abstain from interdicting every disadvantageous work? Now, observe this, that in human society every act of omission or of commission, even when the most carefully concealed or avowed, is a loss or gain to society: if I neglect to take care of my property or of my health, of my intellect, or of my soul, I undermine or weaken in my person a member of the community who is rich, healthy, and strong only through the richness, health, and strength of his fellow members, so that, from this point of view, my private actions are all public benefits or public injuries. Why then, from this point of view, should the State scruple about prescribing some of these to me and interdicting others? Why, in order to better exercise this right, and better fulfill this obligation, should it not constitute itself the universal contractor for labor, and the universal distributor of productions? Why should it not become the sole agriculturist, manufacturer, and merchant, the unique proprietor and administrator of all France? Precisely because this would be opposed to the common weal. Here the second principle, that advanced against individual independence, operates inversely, and, instead of being an adversary, it becomes a champion. Far from setting the State free, it puts another chain around its neck, and thus strengthens the pale within which modern conscience and modern honor have confined the public guardian.

V

In what, indeed, does the common weal consist? In the interest of each person, while that which interests each person is the things of which the possession is agreeable and the deprivation painful. The whole world would in vain gainsay this point; every sensation is personal. My suffering and my enjoyments are not to be contested any more than my inclination for objects which procure me the one, and my dislike of objects which procure me the other. There is, therefore, no arbitrary definition of each one's particular interest; this exists as a fact independently of the legislator; all that remains is to show what this interest is, and what each individual prefers. Preferences vary according to race, time, place, and circumstance; but, among the possessions which are ever desirable and the privation of which is ever dreaded, there is one which, directly desired, and for itself, becomes, through the progress of civilisation, more and more cherished, and of which the privation becomes, through the progress of civilisation, more and more grievous, and that is the entire disposition of one's self, the full ownership of one's body and property, the faculty of thinking, believing, and worshipping as one pleases, of associating with others, of acting separately or along with others, in all senses and without hindrance; in short, one's liberty. That this liberty may be as extensive as possible is, in all times, one of man's great needs, and, in our days, it is his greatest need. There are two reasons for this, one natural and the other historical. Man, in nature, is individual, that is to say a small distinct world in himself, a centre apart in an enclosed circle, a detached organism complete in itself and which suffers when his spontaneous inclinations are thwarted by the intervention of a foreign power. History has made him a complex organism, wherein three or four religions, five or six civilisations, thirty centuries of assiduous culture have left their imprint; in which its acquisitions are combined together, wherein heredities are intercrossed, wherein special traits have accumulated in such a way as to produce the most original and the most sensitive of beings; as civilisation increases, so does his complexity go on increasing: accordingly, his originality strengthens and his sensibilities become keener; from which it follows that, the more civilised he becomes, the greater his repugnance to constraint and uniformity. At the present day, each of us is the terminal and peculiar product of a vast elaboration of which the diverse stages occur in this order but once, a plant unique of its species, a solitary individual of superior and finer essence which, with its own inward structure and its own inalienable type, can bear no other than its own characteristic fruit. Nothing could be more adverse to the interest of the oak than to be tortured into bearing the apples of the apple-tree; nothing could be more adverse to the interest of the apple-tree than to be tortured into bearing acorns; nothing could be more opposed to the interests of both oak and apple-tree, also of other trees, than to be pruned, shaped, and twisted so as all to grow after a forced model, delineated on paper according to the rigid and limited imagination of a geometrician. The least possible constraint is, therefore, everybody's chief interest; if one particular restrictive agency is established, it is that every one may be preserved by it from other more powerful constraints, especially those which the foreigner and evildoers would impose. Up to that point, and no further, its intervention is beneficial; beyond that point, it becomes one of the evils it is intended to forestall. Such then, if the common weal is to be looked after, is the sole office of the State—to prevent constraint and, therefore, never to use it except to prevent worse constraints; to secure respect for each individual in his own physical and moral domain; never to encroach on this except for that purpose; to withdraw immediately; to abstain from all indiscreet meddling, and yet more, as far as is practicable, without any sacrifice of public security, to reduce old assessments, to exact only a minimum of subsidies and services, to gradually limit even useful action, to set itself as few tasks as possible, to let each one have all the room possible and the maximum of initiative, to slowly abandon monopolies, to refrain from competition with private parties, to rid itself of functions which they can fulfill equally well—all clearly showing that the limits prescribed to the State by the common good are just those which duty and right render obligatory.

VI

If we now take into consideration, no longer the direct, but the indirect interest of all; if, instead of caring for men we concern ourselves with their works; if we regard human society as a material and spiritual workshop, the perfection of which consists in its being the most productive and economical, and as well furnished and as well managed as possible—from this point of view again, with this secondary and subordinate aim, the domain of the State is scarcely less limited: very few new functions are to be attributed to it; nearly all the rest will be better fulfilled by independent persons, or by natural or voluntary associations. Contemplate the man who works for his own benefit, the agriculturist, the manufacturer, the merchant, and observe how attentive he is to his business. And because his interest and pride are involved; his welfare and that of those around him is at stake, his capital, his reputation, his social position and advancement; on the other side, are want, ruin, social degradation, dependence, bankruptcy, and the hospital. In the presence of this alternative he keeps close watch and becomes industrious; he thinks of his business even when abed or at his meals; he studies it, not afar off speculatively, in a general way, but on the spot, practically, in detail, in all its bearings and relationships, constantly calculating difficulties and resources, with such sharp insight and special information that for any other person to try to solve the daily problem which he solves, would be impossible, because nobody could possess or estimate as he can the precise elements which constitute it. Compare with this unique devotion and these peculiar qualifications the ordinary capacity and languid uniformity of an administrative head-clerk, even when an expert and honest. He is sure of his salary, provided he does his duty tolerably well, and this he does when he is occupied during official hours. Let his papers be correct, as the rules and traditions of his bureau demand, and nothing more is asked of him; he need not tax his brain beyond that. If he conceives any economical measure, or any improvement of his branch of the ser-vice, not he, but the public, an anonymous and vague impersonality, reaps all the benefit of it. Moreover, why should he care about it, since his project or reform ends in a report which finds its resting-place in a pigeon-hole? The machine is too vast and complicated, too unwieldy, too clumsy, with its rusty wheels, its "ancient rights and safe situations," to be made over anew, just as one likes, the same as a farm, a warehouse or a foundry. Accordingly, he has no idea of troubling himself further in the matter; on leaving his bureau he dismisses it from his mind; he lets things go on automatically, just as it happens, in a costly way and with indifferent results. Even in a country of as much probity as France, it is calculated that every enterprise managed by the State costs one-quarter more, and brings in one-quarter less, than when entrusted to private hands. Conse-quently, if work were withheld from individuals in order that the State might undertake it, the community, when the accounts came to be balanced, would suffer a loss of one-half.

Now, this is true of all work, whether spiritual or material not only of agricultural, industrial, and commercial products, but, again, of works of science and of art, of literature and philosophy, of char-ity, of education and of propagandism; not only when the motor is egoistic, like personal interest and vulgar vanity, but likewise when a disinterested sentiment is involved, like that which prompts the discovery of truth or the creation of beauty, the spread of a faith, the diffusion of convictions, religious enthusiasm, or natural gen-erosity, affection on a broad or on a narrow basis, from one who embraces all humanity to one who devotes himself wholly to his friends and kindred. The effect is the same in both cases, because the cause is the same. Always, in the shop directed by the free workman, the motive force is enormous, almost infinite, because it is a living spring which flows at all hours and is inexhaustible. The mother thinks constantly of her child, the savant of his science, the artist of his art, the inventor of his inventions, the philanthropist of his endowments, Faraday of electricity, Stephenson of his locomotive, Pasteur of his *microbes*, De Lesseps of his isthmus, sisters of charity of their poor. Through this peculiar concentration of thought, man derives every possible advantage from human faculties and surroundings; he himself gets to be a more and more perfect instrument, and, moreover, he fashions others: with this he daily reduces the friction of the powerful machine which he controls and of which he is the main wheel; he increases its yield; he economises, maintains, repairs, and improves it with a capability and success that nobody questions; in short, he fabricates in a superior way. But this living spring, to which the superiority of the product is due, cannot be separated from the producer, for it issues from his own affections and profoundest sentiments. It is useless without him; out of his hands, in the hands of strangers, the fountain ceases to flow and production stops. If, consequently, a good and large yield is required, he alone must have charge of the mill; he is the resident owner of it, the one who sets it in motion, the born engineer, installed and specially designed for that position. In vain may attempts be made to turn the stream elsewhere; there simply ensues a stoppage of the natural issue, a dam barring useful canals, a haphazard change of current not only without gain, but with loss, the stream subsiding in swamps or undermining the steep banks of a ravine. At the utmost, the millions of buckets of water, forcibly taken from private reservoirs, half fill with a good deal of trouble the great central artificial basin in which the water, low and stagnant, is never sufficient in quantity or force to move the huge public wheel that replaces the small private wheels, doing the nation's work.

Thus, even regarding men merely as manufacturers, in treating them simply as producers of what is valuable and serviceable, with no other object in view than to furnish society with supplies and to benefit consumers, the private domain comprehends all enterprises

undertaken by private individuals, either singly or associated together, through personal interest or personal taste: this suffices to
ensure their being better managed than by the State; it is by virtue
of this that they have devolved into their hands. Consequently, in
the vast field of labor, they themselves decide on what they will
undertake; they themselves, of their own authority, set their own
fences. They may therefore enlarge their own domain to any extent
they please, and reduce indefinitely the domain of the State. On the
contrary, the State cannot pretend to more than what they leave;
just in proportion to their advance on a partitioned soil with a doubtful frontier, it is bound to recede and leave the ground to them;
whatever pursuit they may follow the State must let that alone,
except in case of their default, or their prolonged absence, or on
proof of their having abandoned it. All the rest, therefore, falls to
the State; first, offices which they would never claim, and which they
are always glad to leave in its hands, because they have not, and it
withholds, the only instrumentality of any account, that special, indispensable instrumentality known as armed force—the protection
of the community against foreign communities, the protection of
individuals against one another, the levying of soldiers, the imposition of taxes, the execution of the laws, the administration of justice
and of the police. Next to this, come matters of which the accom-
plishment concerns everybody without directly interesting any one
in particular—the government of unoccupied territory, the administration of rivers, coasts, forests, and public highways, the task of
governing subject countries, the framing of laws, the coinage of
money, the conferring of a civil status, the negotiating in the name
of the community with local and special corporations, departments,
communes, banks, institutions, churches, and universities. Add to
these, according to circumstances, sundry optional cooperative services,[13] such as subsidies granted to institutions of great public utility,

13. When the function to be performed is of an uncertain or mixed character
the following rule may be applied in deciding whether the State or individuals
shall be entrusted with it; also, in determining, in the case of coöperation, what

for which private contributions could not suffice, now in the shape
of concessions to corporations for which equivalent obligations are
exacted, and, again, in those hygienic precautions which individuals
fail to take through indifference; occasionally, such provisional aid
as supports a man, or so stimulates him as to enable him some day
or other to support himself; and, in general, those discreet and
scarcely perceptible interpositions for the time being which prove
so advantageous in the future, like a far-reaching code and other
consistent regulations which, mindful of the liberty of the existing
individual, provide for the welfare of coming generations. Nothing
beyond that.

VII

Again, in this preparation for future welfare the same principle still
holds. Among precious productions, the most precious and important are, evidently, the animated instruments called men, since they
produce the rest. The object then, is to fashion men capable of
physical, mental, or moral labor, the most energetic, the most persistent, the most skillful, and the most productive; now, we already
know the conditions of their formation. It is essential, and this suffices, that each living spring as above described, should flow in its
own channel, each through its natural outlet, and under the control
of its owner. On this condition the jet becomes more vigorous, for
the acquired impetus increases the original outflow; the projector of
labor becomes more and more skillful, for he gains knowledge

---

portion of it shall be assigned to individuals and what portion to the State. As
a general rule, when individuals, either singly or associated together, have a
direct interest in, or are drawn toward, a special function, and the community
has no direct interest therein, the matter belongs to individuals and not to the
State. On the other hand, if the interest of the community in any function is
direct, and indirect for individuals singly or associated together, it is proper for
the State and not for individuals to take hold of it. According to this rule the
limits of the public and private domain can be defined, which limits, as they
change backward and forward, may be verified according to the changes which
take place in interests and preferences, direct or indirect.

through practise; those around him likewise become better work-men, inasmuch as they find encouragement in his success and avail themselves of his discoveries. Thus, simply because the State re-spects, and enforces respect, for these individual springs in private hands, it develops in individuals, as well as in those around them, the will and the talent for producing much and well, the faculty for, and desire to, keep on producing more and better; in other words, all sorts of energies and capacities, each of its own kind and in its own place, with all compatible fulness and efficiency. Such is the office, and the sole office, of the State, first in relation to the turbid and frigid springs issuing from selfishness and self-conceit, whose operations demand its oversight, and next, for still stronger reasons, in relation to the warm and pure springs whose beneficence is un-alloyed, as in the family affections and private friendships; again, in relation to those rarer and higher springs, such as the love of beauty, the yearning for truth, the spirit of association, patriotism, and love of mankind; and, finally, for still stronger reasons, in relation to the two most sacred and salutary of all springs, conscience which renders will subject to duty, and honor which makes will the support of right. Let the State prevent, as well as abstain from, any interference with either; let this be its object and nothing more; its abstention is as necessary as its vigilance. Let it guard both, and it will see ev-erywhere growing spontaneously, hourly, each in degree according to conditions of time and place, the most diligent and most com-petent workmen, the agriculturist, the manufacturer, the merchant, the savant, the artist, the inventor, the propagandist, the husband and wife, the father and mother, the patriot, the philanthropist and the sister of charity.

On the contrary, if, like our Jacobins, the State seeks to confiscate every natural force to its own profit, if it seeks to make affection for itself paramount, if it strives to suppress all other passions and interests, if it tolerates no other preoccupation than that which con-cerns the common weal, if it tries to forcibly convert every member of society into a Spartan or Jesuit, then, at enormous cost, will it not only destroy private springs, and spread devastation over the entire territory, but it will destroy its own fountain-head. We honor the State only for the services it renders to us, and proportionately to these services and the security it affords us, and to the liberty which it ensures us under the title of universal benefactor; when it deliberately wounds us through our dearest interests and tenderest affections, when it goes so far as to attack our honor and conscience, when it becomes the universal wrong-doer, our affection for it, in the course of time, turns into hatred. Let this system be maintained, and patriotism, exhausted, dries up, and, one by one, all other beneficent springs, until, finally, nothing is visible over the whole country, but stagnant pools or overwhelming torrents, inhabited by passive subjects or depredators. As in the Roman empire in the fourth century, in Italy in the seventeenth century, in the Turkish provinces in our own day, naught remains but an ill-conducted herd of stunted, torpid creatures, limited to their daily wants and animal instincts, indifferent to the public welfare and to their own prospective interests, so degenerate as to have lost sight of their own discoveries, unlearned their own sciences, arts and industries, and, in short, and worse than all, base, false, corrupted souls entirely wanting in honor or conscience. Nothing is more destructive than the unrestricted intermeddling of the State, even when wise and paternal; in Paraguay, under the discipline of Jesuits, so minute in its details, "Indian physiognomy appeared like that of animals taken in a trap." They worked, ate, drank, and gave birth by sound of bell, under watch and ward, correctly and mechanically, but showing no liking for anything, not even for their own existence, being transformed into so many automatons; the least that can be said is that the means employed to produce this result were gentle, while before this they were mere brutes. The revolutionist-Jesuit now undertakes to transform men into automatons, and by harsh means.

VIII

Frequently, in European history, despotisms almost equally harsh have borne down heavily on human effort; but never have any of them been so thoroughly inept; for none have ever attempted to raise so heavy a mass with so short a lever.

In the first place, however authoritative the despot might be there was a limit to his interference. Philip II. burned heretics, persecuted Moors, and drove out Jews; Louis XIV. forcibly converted Protestants; but both used violence only against dissenters, about a fifteenth or a twentieth of their subjects. If Cromwell, on becoming Protector, remained sectarian, and the compulsory servant of an army of sectarians, he took good care not to impose on other churches the theology, rites, and discipline of his own church;[14] on the contrary, he repressed fanatical outrages; protected the Anabaptists equally with his Independents, granted paid curates to the Presbyterians as well as the public exercise of their worship, also private worship with liberal toleration, to the Episcopalians; he maintained the two great Anglican universities and allowed the Jews to erect a synagogue. Frederick II. drafted into his army every able-bodied peasant that he could feed; he kept every man twenty years in the service, under a discipline worse than slavery, with the almost certain prospect of death; and in his last war, he sacrificed about one-sixth of his male subjects;[15] but they were serfs, and his conscription did not touch the bourgeois class. He put his hands in the pockets of the bourgeois and of every other man, and took every crown they had; when driven to it, he adulterated coin and stopped paying his functionaries; but, under the scrutiny of his eyes, always open, the administration was honest, the police effective, justice exact, toleration unlimited, and the freedom of the press complete; the King allowed the publication of the most cutting pamphlets against himself, and their public sale, even at Berlin. A little earlier, in the great empire of the East,[16] Peter the Great, with whip in hand, lashed his Muscovite bears and made them drill and dance in European fashion;

14. Carlyle: "Cromwell's Speeches and Letters," iii., 418. (Cromwell's address to the Parliament, September 17, 1656.)

15. Seeley, "Life and Times of Stein," ii., 143.—Macaulay, "Biographical Essays," Frederick the Great, 33, 35, 87, 92.

16. Eugene Schuyler, "Peter the Great," vol. 2.

but they were bears accustomed from father to son to the whip and chain; moreover, he stood as the orthodox head of their faith, and left their *mir* (the village commune) untouched. Finally, at the other extremity of Europe, and even outside of Europe, the caliph or sultan, in the seventh century, in the fifteenth century, an Omar or a Mahomet, a fanatical Arab or brutal Turk, who had just overcome Christians with the sword, himself assigned the limits of his own absolutism: if the vanquished were reduced to the condition of heavily ransomed tributaries and of inferiors daily humiliated, he allowed them their worship, civil laws, and domestic usages; he left them their institutions, their convents, and their schools; he allowed them to administer the affairs of their own community as they pleased under the jurisdiction of their patriarch, or other natural chieftains. Thus, whatever the tyrant may have been, he did not attempt to make man over again, nor recast all his subjects according to one pattern. Far as his tyranny went, it stopped in the soul at a certain point; that point reached, the sentiments were left free. However overwhelming this tyranny may have been, it affected only one class of men; the others, outside of its network, remained untrammelled. In touching all sensitive chords, it affected only those of a small minority incapable of self-defence; with the majority, able to protect itself, the main sensibilities were respected, especially the most sensitive, this one or that one, as the case might be, now the conscience which binds man to his religion, now that *amour-propre* on which honor depends, and now the habits which make man cling to customs, hereditary usages and outward observances. As far as the others were concerned, those which relate to property, personal welfare, and social position, it proceeded cautiously and with moderation. In this way the discretion of the ruler lessened the resistance of the subject, and a daring enterprise, even when mischievous, was not outrageous; it might be carried out; nothing was required but a force in hand equal to the resistance it provoked.

Again, on the other hand, the tyrant possessed this force. Very many and very strong arms stood behind the prince ready to coöperate with him and countervail any resistance. Behind Philip II. or

Louis XIV. stood the Catholic majority, either exciting or consenting to the oppression of dissenters, as fanatical or as illiberal as their king. To aid and coöperate with Philip II., Louis XIV., Frederick II. and Peter the Great, stood the entire nation, equally violent, rallied around the sovereign through his consecrated title and uncontested right, through tradition and custom, through a rigid sentiment of duty and the vague idea of public security. Peter the Great counted among his auxiliaries every eminent and cultivated man in the country; Cromwell had his disciplined and twenty-times victorious army; the caliph or sultan brought along with him his military and privileged population. Aided by cohorts of this stamp, it was easy to raise a heavy mass, and even maintain it in a fixed position. Once the operation was concluded, there followed a sort of equilibrium; the mass, kept in the air by a permanent counterbalance, only required a little daily effort to prevent it from falling.

Just the reverse with the measures of the Jacobins. According as these are carried out, their theory, more exacting, adds extra weight to the uplifted mass, and, finally, a burden of almost infinite weight. At first, the Jacobin confined his attacks to royalty, to nobility, to the Church, to parliaments, to privileges, to ecclesiastical and feudal possessions, in short, to mediaeval foundations; now, he attacks yet more ancient and more solid foundations—positive religion, property and the family. For four years he has contented himself with demolition; he now aims at reconstruction; his object is not merely to do away with a positive faith and suppress social inequality, to proscribe revealed dogmas, hereditary beliefs, an established cult, the supremacy of rank and superiority of fortunes, wealth, leisure, refinement and elegance, but, in addition to all this, he must refashion the citizen, create new sentiments, impose natural religion on the individual, civic education, uniform ways and habits, Jacobin conduct, Spartan virtue; in short, nothing is to be left in a human being that is not prescribed, enforced, and constrained. Henceforth, there is opposed to the Revolution, not alone the partisans of the ancient régime—priests, nobles, parliamentarians, royalists, and Catholics—but, again, every man imbued with European civilisation, every member of a regular family, any possessor of capital much or little; every kind or degree of proprietor, agriculturist, manufacturer, merchant, artisan, or farmer, even most of the revolutionists who, nearly all, count on themselves escaping the constraints they impose, and who like the straight-jacket only when it is on another's back. The pressure of resistant wills at this moment becomes incalculable. It would be easier to raise a mountain, while, just at this moment, the Jacobins have deprived themselves of every moral force through which a political engineer acts on human wills.

Unlike Philip II. and Louis XIV. they are not supported by the intolerance of a vast majority, for, instead of fifteen or twenty orthodox against one heretic, they count in their church scarcely more than one orthodox against fifteen or twenty heretics.[17] They have not at their back, like legitimate sovereigns, the stubborn loyalty of an entire population, following in the steps of its chieftain through the prestige of hereditary right and through habits of ancient fealty. On the contrary, their reign is only a day old and they themselves are interlopers, at first installed by a *coup d'état* and afterwards by

17. Cf. "The Revolution" vol. ii., pp. 46 and 323, and vol. iii., ch. 1. Archives des Affaires Etrangèrès, vol. 332. (Letter by Thiberge, Marseilles, Brumaire 14, year II.) "I have been to Marteygne, a small town ten leagues from Marseilles, along with my colleague Fournet; I found (*je trouvée*) seventeen patriots in a town of five thousand population."—*Ibid.* (Letter by Regulus Leclerc, Bergues, Brumaire 15, year II.) At Bergues, he says, "the municipality is composed of traders with empty stores, and brewers without beer since the law of the maximum." Consequently there is universal lukewarmness, "only forty persons being found to form a popular club, holding sessions as a favor every five days. . . . Public spirit at Bergues is dead; fanaticism rules."—Archives Nationales, F⁷, 7,164 (Department of Var, reports of year V. "general idea.")—"At Draguignan, out of seven thousand souls, forty patriots, *exclusifs*, despised or dishonest; at Vidauban, nine or ten *exclusifs*, favored by the municipality and who live freely without their means being known; at Brignolles, frequent robberies on the road by robbers said to have been very patriotic in the beginning of the Revolution: people are afraid of them and dare not name them; at Fréjus, nine leading *exclusifs* who pass all their time in the *café*."— Berryat-Saint-Prix, "La Justice Révolutionnaire," p. 146.—Brutus Thierry, grocer, member of the Rev. Com. of Angers, said that "in Angers, there were not sixty revolutionists."

the semblance of an election, having extorted or obtained by trick the suffrages through which they act, so familiar with fraud and violence that, in their own Assembly, the minority which succeeds has seized and held on to power by violence and fraud, putting down the majority by riots, and the departments by force of arms; while, to give to their brutalities the semblance of right, they improvise two pompous demonstrations, first, the sudden manufacture of a paper constitution, which moulders away in their archives, and next, the scandalous farce of a hollow and compulsory *plebiscite*. A dozen leaders of the faction centre unlimited authority in themselves; but, as admitted by them, their authority is derivative; it is the Convention which makes them its delegates; their precarious title has to be renewed monthly; a turn of the majority may sweep them and their work away tomorrow; an insurrection of the people, whom they have familiarised with insurrection, may tomorrow sweep them away, their work and their majority. They maintain only a disputed, limited and transient ascendency over their adherents. They are not military chieftains like Cromwell and Napoleon, generals of an army obeyed without a murmur, but common stump-speakers at the mercy of an audience that sits in judgment on them. There is no discipline in this audience: every Jacobin remains independent by virtue of his principles; if he accepts leaders, it is with a reservation of their worth to him; selecting them as he pleases, he is free to change them when he pleases; his trust in them is intermittent, his loyalty provisional, and, as his adhesion depends on a mere preference, he always reserves the right to discard the favorite of today as he has discarded the favorite of yesterday. In this audience, there is no such thing as subordination; the lowest demagogue, any subaltern brawler, a Hébert or Jacques Roux, who is ambitious to step out of the ranks, outvies the charlatans in office in order to obtain their places. Even with a complete and lasting ascendency over an organised band of docile supporters, the Jacobin leaders would be feeble for lack of reliable and competent instruments; for they have but very few partisans other than those of doubtful probity and of notorious incapacity. Cromwell had around him, to carry out the puritan programme, the moral élite of the nation, an army of rigorists, with narrow consciences, but much more strict towards themselves than towards others, men who never drank and who never swore, who never indulged for a moment in sensuality or idleness, who forbade themselves every act of omission or commission about which they held any scruples, the most honest, the most temperate, the most laborious, and the most persevering of mankind,[18] the only ones capable of laying the foundations of that practical morality on which England and the United States still subsist at the present day. Around Peter the Great, in carrying out his European programme, stood the intellectual élite of the country, an imported staff of men of ability associated with natives of moderate ability, every well-taught resident foreigner and indigenous Russian, the only ones able to organise schools and public institutions, to set up a vast central and regular system of administration, to assign rank according to service and merit, in short, to erect on the snow and mud of a shapeless barbarism a conservatory of civilisation which, transplanted like an exotic tree, grows and gradually becomes acclimated. Around Couthon, Saint-Just, Billaud, Collot, and Robespierre, with the exception of certain men devoted, not to Utopianism but to the country, and who, like Carnot, conform to the system in order to save France, there are but a few sectarians to carry out the Jacobin programme, men so short-sighted as not to clearly comprehend its fallacies, or sufficiently fanatical to accept its horrors, a lot of social outcasts and self-constituted statesmen, infatuated through incommensurate faculties with the parts they play, unsound in mind and superficially educated, wholly incompetent, boundless in ambition, with perverted, callous or deadened consciences, deluded by sophistry, cold-blooded through vain glory and vicious through crime, impunity and success.

Thus, whilst other despots raise a moderate weight, calling

---

18. Macaulay. "History of England," i., 152. "The Royalists themselves confessed that, in every department of honest industry, the discarded warriors prospered beyond other men, that none was charged with any theft or robbery, that none was heard to ask an alms, and that, if a baker, a mason, or a waggoner attracted notice by his diligence and sobriety, he was in all probability one of Oliver's old soldiers."

around them either the majority or the flower of the nation, employing the best strength of the country and lengthening their lever as much as possible, the Jacobins attempt to raise an incalculable weight, repel the majority as well as the flower of the nation, discard the best strength of the country, and shorten their lever to the utmost. They hold on only to the shorter end, the rough, clumsy, iron-bound, creaking, and grinding extremity, that is to say, to physical force, the means for physical constraint, the heavy hand of the gendarme on the shoulder of the suspect, the jailor's bolts and keys turned on the prisoner, the club used by the *sans-culottes* on the back of the bourgeois to quicken his pace, and, better still, the *Septembriseur's* pike thrust into the aristocrat's belly, and the blade falling on the neck held fast in the clutches of the guillotine. Such, henceforth, is the only machinery they possess for governing the country, for they have deprived themselves of all other. Their engine has to be exhibited, for it works only on condition that its bloody image be stamped indelibly on every body's imagination; if the negro monarch or the pacha desires to see heads bowing as he passes along, he must be escorted by executioners. They must abuse their engine because fear, losing its effect through habit, needs example to keep it alive; the negro monarch or the pacha who would keep the fear alive by which he rules, must be stimulated every day; he must slaughter too many to be sure of slaughtering enough; he must slaughter constantly, in heaps, indiscriminately, haphazard, no matter for what offence, on the slightest suspicion, the innocent along with the guilty. He and his are lost the moment they cease to obey this rule. Every Jacobin, like every African monarch or pacha, must observe it that he may be and remain at the head of his band. For this reason, the chiefs of the sect, its natural leaders designated beforehand, consist of theorists able to grasp its principles, and logicians able to arrive at its conclusions, narrow-minded enough not to see that their undertaking exceeds their powers and all human powers, shrewd enough to see that brutal force is their only instrumentality, inhuman enough to apply it unscrupulously and without reserve, and perverted enough to murder on all sides that they may stamp an impression of lasting terror.

BOOK SEVENTH

❧

The Governors

Psychology of the Jacobin leaders— I. *Marat*—*Disparity between his faculties and pretensions*—*The Maniac*—*The Ambitious delirium*—*Rage for persecution*—*A confirmed nightmare insanity*—*Homicidal frenzy*— II. *Danton*—*Richness of his faculties*—*Disparity between his condition and instincts*—*The Barbarian*—*His work*—*His weakness*— III. *Robespierre*—*Mediocrity of his faculties*—*The* Cuistre—*Absence of ideas*—*Study of phrases*—*Wounded self-esteem*—*Intensity of this trait*—*Satisfied self-esteem*—*His infatuation*—*He plays the victim*—*His gloomy fancies*—*His resemblance to Marat*—*Difference between him and Marat*—*The sincere hypocrite*—*The Festival in honor of the Supreme Being, and the law of Prairial 22*—*The external and internal characters of Robespierre and the Revolution.*

I

THREE men among the Jacobins, Marat, Danton, and Robespierre, merited distinction and possessed authority: owing to a malformation, or distortion, of head and heart, they fulfilled the requisite conditions. Of the three, Marat is the most monstrous; he borders on the lunatic, of which he displays the chief characteristics—furious exaltation, constant overexcitement, feverish restlessness, an inexhaustible propensity for scribbling, that mental automatism and tetanus of the will under the constraint and rule of a fixed idea, and, in addition to this, the usual physical symptoms, such as sleeplessness, a livid tint, bad blood, foulness of dress and person,[1] with,

1. Harmand (de la Meuse): "Anecdotes relatives à la Révolution." "He

during the last five months of his life, irritations and eruptions over his whole body.[2] Issuing from incongruous races, born of a mixed blood and tainted with serious moral commotions,[3] he harbors within him a singular germ: physically, he is an abortion, morally a pretender, and one who covets all places of distinction. His father, who was a physician, intended, from his early childhood, that he should be a savant; his mother, an idealist, meant that he should be a philanthropist, while he himself always steered his course towards both summits. "At five years of age," he says, "it would have pleased me to be a schoolmaster, at fifteen a professor, at eighteen an author, and a creative genius at twenty,"[4] and, afterwards, up to the last, an apostle and martyr to humanity. "From my earliest infancy I had an intense love of fame which changed its object at various stages of my life, but which never left me for a moment." He rambled over Europe or vegetated in Paris for thirty years, living a nomadic life in subordinate positions, hissed as an author, distrusted as a man of science and ignored as a philosopher, a third rate political writer, aspiring to every sort of celebrity and to every honor, constantly presenting himself as a candidate and as constantly rejected, too great a disproportion between his faculties and ambition! Talentless,[5]

---

dressed about like a cab-driver ill at his ease. He had a disturbed look and an eye always in motion; he acted in an abrupt, quick, and jerky way. A constant restlessness gave a convulsive contraction to his muscles and features which likewise affected his manner of walking so that he never stepped but jumped."

2. Chevremont, "Jean Paul Marat"; also Alfred Bougeard, "Marat" *passim*. These two works, with numerous documents, are panegyrics of Marat.—Bougeat, i., 11 (description of Marat by Fabre d'Eglantine); ii., 259 and i., 83.— "Journal de la République Française," by Marat, No. 93, January 9, 1793. "I devote only two out of the twenty-four hours to sleep, and only one hour to my meals, toilette, and domestic necessities. I have not had fifteen minutes playspell for more than three years."

3. Chevremont, i., pp. 1 and 2. His family, on the father's side, was Spanish, long settled in Sardinia. The father, Dr. Jean Mara, had abandoned Catholicism and removed to Geneva where he married a woman of that city; he afterwards established himself in the canton of Neufchatel.

4. "Journal de la République Française." No. 98, description of "l'Ami du peuple" by himself.

5. Read his novel "Les Aventures du jeune Comte Potowski," letter 5, by

possessing no critical acumen and of mediocre intelligence, he was fitted only to teach some branch of the sciences, or to practise some one of the arts, either as professor or doctor more or less bold and lucky, or to follow, with occasional slips on one side or the other, some path clearly marked out for him. "But," he says, "I never had any thing to do with a subject which did not hold out ... great results for myself, and show my originality, for I cannot make up my mind to treat a subject over again that has been well done, or to plod over the work of others." Consequently, when he tries to originate he merely imitates, or commits mistakes. His treatise on "Man" is a jumble of physiological and moral common-places, made up of ill-digested reading and words strung together haphazard,[6] of gratuitous and incoherent suppositions in which the doctrines of the seventeenth and eighteenth centuries, coupled together, end in empty phraseology. "Soul and Body are distinct substances with no essential relationship, being connected together solely through the nervous fluid"; this fluid is not gelatinous for the spirituous by which it is renewed contains no gelatine; the soul, excited by this, excites that; hence the place assigned to it "in the *meninges*." His "Optics"[7] is the reverse of the great truth already discovered by Newton more than a century before, and since confirmed by more than another century of experiment and calculation. On "Heat" and "Electricity" he merely puts forth feeble hypotheses and literary generalisations; one day, driven to the wall, he inserts a needle in a piece of rosin to make this a conductor, in which piece of scientific trickery he is

---

Lucile: "I think of Potowski only. My imagination, inflamed at the torch of love, ever presents to me his sweet image." Letter of Potowski after his marriage. "Lucile now grants to love all that modesty permits ... enjoying such transports of bliss, I believe that the gods are jealous of my lot."

6. Preface, xx. "Descartes, Helvetius, Haller, Lelat all ignored great principles; man, with them, is an enigma, an impenetrable secret." He says in a foot-note, "We find evidence of this in the works of Hume, Voltaire, Bonnet, *Racine*, and Pascal."

7. "Mémoires Académiques sur la Lumière," pref., vii. He especially opposes "the differential refrangibility of heterogeneous rays" which is "the basis of Newton's theory."

caught by the physicist Charles.[8] He is not even qualified to comprehend the great discoverers of his age, Laplace, Monge, Lavoisier, or Fourcroy; on the contrary, he libels them in the style of a low rebellious subordinate, who, without the shadow of a claim, aims to take the place of legitimate authorities. In Politics, he adopts every absurd idea in vogue growing out of the *Contrat-Social* based on natural right, and which he renders still more absurd by repeating as his own the arguments advanced by those bungling socialists, who, physiologists astray in the moral world, derive all rights from physical necessities. "All human rights issue from physical wants.[9] If a man has nothing, he has a right to any surplus with which another gorges himself. What do I say? He has a right to seize the indispensable, and, rather than die of hunger, he may cut another's throat and eat his throbbing flesh. . . . Man has a right to self-preservation, to the property, the liberty and even the lives of his fellow creatures. To escape oppression he has a right to repress, to bind and to massacre. He is free to do what he pleases to ensure his own happiness." It is plain enough what this leads to. But, let the consequences be what they may, whatever he writes or does, it is always in self-admiration and always in a counter sense, being as vain-glorious of his encyclopaedic impotence as he is of his social mischievousness. Taking his word for it, his discoveries in Physics will render him immortal.[10] "They will at least effect a complete transformation in Optics. . . . The true primitive colors were unknown before me." He is a Newton, and still better. Previous to his appearance "the place occupied by the electric fluid in nature, considered as an universal agent, was completely ignored. . . . I have made it known in such a way as to leave no further doubt about it."[11] As to the igneous fluid, "that existence

8. Chevremont, i., 74. (See the testimony of Arago, Feb. 24, 1844).

9. Ibid., i., 104. (Sketch of a declaration of the rights of man and of the citizen.)

10. See the epigraph of his "Mémoires sur la Lumière." "They will force their way against wind and tide."—Ibid., preface, vii. "Déconvertes de Monsieur Marat," 1780, 2nd ed., p. 140.

11. "Recherches physiques sur l'electricité," 1782, pp. 13, 17.

unknown before me, I have freed the theory from every hypothesis and conjecture, from every alembical argument; I have purged it of error, I have rendered it intuitive; I have written this out in a small volume which consigns to oblivion all that scientific bodies have hitherto published on that subject."[12] Anterior to his treatise on "Man," moral and physical relationships were incomprehensible. "Descartes, Helvetius, Haller, Lecat, Hume, Voltaire, Bonnet, held this to be an impenetrable secret, 'an enigma.'" He has solved the problem, he has fixed the seat of the soul, he has determined the medium through which the soul communicates with the body.[13] In the higher sciences, those treating of nature generally, or of human society, he reaches the climax. "I believe that I have exhausted every combination of the human intellect in relation to morals, philosophy, and political science."[14] Not only has he discovered the true theory of government, but he is a statesman, a practical expert, able to forecast the future and shape events. He makes predictions, on the average, twice a week, which always turn out right; he already claims, during the early sessions of the Convention, to have made "three hundred predictions on the leading points of the Revolution, all justified by the event."[15] In the face of the *Constituants* who demolish and reconstruct so slowly, he is sufficiently strong to take down, put up, and complete at a moment's notice. "If I were one of the people's tribunes[16] and were supported by a few thousand

---

12. Chevremont, i., 59.

13. "De l'Homme," preface vii. and book iv.

14. "Journal de la République Française," No. 98.

15. "Journal de la République Française," by Marat, No. 1.

16. "L'Ami du Peuple" No. 173 (July 26, 1790). The memories of conceited persons, given to immoderate self-expansion, are largely at fault. I have seen patients in asylums who, believing in their exalted position, have recounted their successes in about the same vein as Marat. (Chevremont, i., 40, 47, 54). "The reports of extraordinary cures effected by me brought me a great crowd of the sick. The street in front of my door was blocked with carriages. People came to consult me from all quarters. . . . The abstract of my experiments on Light finally appeared and it created a prodigious sensation throughout Europe; the newspapers were all filled with it. I had the court and the town in my house

determined men, I answer for it that, in six weeks, the Constitution would be perfected, the political machine well agoing, and the nation free and happy. In less than a year there would be a flourishing, formidable government which would remain so as long as I lived." If necessary, he could act as commander-in-chief of the army and always be victorious: having twice seen the Vendéans carry on a fight he would end the war "at the first encounter."[17] "If I could stand the march, I would go in person and carry out my views. At the head of a small party of trusty troops the rebels could be easily put down to the last man, and in one day. I know something of military art, and, without boasting, I can answer for success." On any difficulty occurring, it is owing to his advice not having been taken; he is the great political physician: his diagnosis from the beginning of the Revolution is always correct, his prognosis infallible, his therapeutics efficacious, humane, and salutary. He furnishes the panacea and he should be allowed to prescribe it; only, to ensure a satisfactory operation, he should himself administer the dose. Let the public lancet, therefore, be put in his hands that he may perform the humanitarian operation of blood-letting. "Such are my opinions. I have published them in my works. I have signed them with my name and I am not ashamed of it. . . . If you are not equal to me and able to comprehend me so much the worse for you."[18] In other words, in his own eyes, Marat is in advance of everybody else and, through his superior genius and character, he is the veritable saviour.

Such are the symptoms by which medical men recognise imme-

---

for six months. . . . The Academy, finding that it could not stifle my discoveries tried to make it appear that they had emanated from its body." Three academic bodies came in turn the same day to see if he would not present himself as a candidate. "Up to the present time several crowned heads have sought me and always on account of the fame of my works."

17. "Journal de la République Française," July 6, 1793.

18. *Moniteur* (Session of the Convention, Sep. 25, 1792). Marat, indeed, is constantly claiming the post of temporary dictator. ("L'Ami du peuple," Nos. 258, 268, 466, 668 and "Appel à la nation," p. 53).

diately one of those partial lunatics who may not be put in confinement, but who are all the more dangerous;[19] the malady, as they would express it in technical terms, may be called the *ambitious delirium,* well known in lunatic asylums. Two propensities, one a habitually perverted judgment, and the other a colossal excess of self-esteem,[20] constitute its sources, and nowhere are both more prolific than in Marat. Never did man with such diversified culture, possess such an incurably perverted intellect. Never did man, after so many abortive speculations and such repeated malpractices, conceive and maintain so high an opinion of himself. Each of these two sources in him augments the other: through his faculty of not seeing things as they are, he attributes to himself virtue and genius; satisfied that he possesses genius and virtue, he regards his misdeeds as merits and his crotchets as truths. Thenceforth, and spontaneously, his malady runs its own course and becomes complex; next to the ambitious delirium comes the *mania for persecution.* In effect, the evident or demonstrated truths which he supplies should strike the public at once; if they burn slowly or miss fire, it is owing to their being stamped out by enemies or the envious: manifestly, they have conspired against him, and against him plots have never ceased. First came the philosophers' plot: when his treatise on "Man" reached Paris from Amsterdam, "they felt the blow I struck at their principles and had the book stopped at the custom-house."[21] Next came the plot of the doctors, who "ruefully estimated my enormous gains. Were it necessary, I could prove that they often met together to consider the best way to destroy my reputation." Finally, came the plot of the Academicians; "the disgraceful persecution I had to undergo from the Academy of Sciences for two years, after being satisfied that my discoveries on Light upset all that it had done for

19. Cf. Moreau de Tours. "La Folie lucide."

20. Chevremont, ii., 81. "Shortly after the taking of the Bastille and obliged to oppose the Paris municipality, I stated that I was the eye of the people and that I was of more consequence in the triumph of liberty than an army of one hundred thousand men."

21. Chevremont, i., 40. (Marat's letters, 1793.)

a century, and that I was quite indifferent about becoming a member of its body. . . . Would it be believed that these scientific charlatans succeeded in underrating my discoveries throughout Europe, in exciting every society of savants against me, and in closing against me all the newspapers!"[22] Naturally, the would-be-persecuted man defends himself, that is to say, he attacks. Naturally, as he is the aggressor, he is repulsed and put down, and, after creating imaginary enemies, he creates real ones, especially in politics where, on principle, he daily preaches insurrection and murder. Naturally, in fine, he is prosecuted, convicted at the Chatelet court, tracked by the police, obliged to fly and wander from one hiding-place to another; to live like a bat "in a cellar, underground, in a dark dungeon";[23] once, says his friend Panis, he passed "six weeks on one of his buttocks" like a madman in his cell, face to face with his reveries. It is not surprising that, with such a system, the reverie should become more intense, more and more gloomy, and, at last settle down into a *confirmed nightmare;* that, in his distorted brain, objects should appear distorted; that, even in full daylight men and things should seem awry, as in a magnifying, dislocating mirror; that, frequently, on the numbers (of his journal) appearing too blood-thirsty, and his chronic disease too acute, his physician should bleed him to arrest these attacks and prevent their return.[24]

But he has taken his bent: henceforth, falsities spring up in his brain as on their native soil; planting himself on the irrational he cultivates the absurd, even physical and mathematical. "Taking an extreme view of it," he says, "the patriotic contribution of one-

---

22. Journal de la République Française, No. 98.

23. The words of Marat and Panes. (Chevremont, i., 197, 203; also "The Revolution" ii., 290, 2d note).

24. Michelet, "Histoire de la Révolution," ii., 89. (Narrated by M. Bourdier, Marat's physician, to M. Serre, the physiologist.) Barbaroux, "Mémoires," 355, (after a visit to Marat): "You should see how superficially Marat composed his articles. Without any knowledge of a public man he would ask the first person he met what he thought of him and this he wrote down, exclaiming 'I'll crush the rascal!'"

quarter of one's income will produce, at the very least, four billion eight hundred and sixty million francs, and perhaps twice that sum"; with this sum M. Necker may raise five hundred thousand men, which he calculates on for the subjugation of France.[25] Since the taking of the Bastille, "the municipality's defalcations alone amount to two hundred millions. The sums pocketed by Bailly are estimated at more than two millions; what 'Mottié' (Lafayette) has taken for the past two years is incalculable."[26] On the 15th of November, 1791, the gathering of *emigrés* comprises "at least one hundred and twenty thousand gentlemen and drilled partisans and soldiers, not counting the forces of the gentlemen-princes about to join them."[27] Consequently, as with his brethren in Bicêtre (a lunatic asylum), he raves incessantly on the horrible and the foul: the procession of terrible or disgusting phantoms has begun.[28] According to him, the savants who do not choose to admire him are fools, charlatans, and plagiarists. Laplace and Monge are even "automatons," so many calculating machines; Lavoisier, "reputed father of every discovery that makes any noise in the world, has not an idea of his own"; he steals from others without comprehending them, and "changes his system as he changes his shoes." Fourcroy, his disciple and horn-blower, is of still thinner stuff. All are scamps: "I could cite a hundred instances of dishonesty by the Academicians of Paris, a hundred breaches of trust"; twelve thousand francs were entrusted to them for the purpose of ascertaining how to direct balloons, and "they divided it among themselves, squandering it at the Rapée, the opera

25. Chevremont, i., 361. (From a pamphlet against Necker, by Marat, July, 1790).

26. "L'Ami du Peuple," No. 552. (August 30, 1791.)

27. *Ibid.*, No. 626. (Dec. 15, 1791). Cf. "The Revolution," ii., 129, on the number of armed emigrés. At this date the authorised number as published is four thousand.

28. His filthy imputations cannot be quoted. See in Buchez et Roux, ix., 419 (April 26, 1791), and x., 220 (Nos. for June 17, 19, and 21), his statement against Lafayette; again, his list with its vile qualifications of "rascals and rogues," who are canvassing for election, and his letters on the Academicians.

and in brothels."[29] In the political world, where debates are battles, it is still worse. The "Friend of the people" has merely rascals for adversaries. Praise of Lafayette's courage and disinterestedness, how absurd! If he went to America it was because he was jilted, "cast off by a Messalina"; he maintained a park of artillery there as "powder-monkeys look after ammunition-wagons"; these are his only exploits; besides, he is a thief. Bailly is also a thief, and Malouet a "clown." Necker has conceived the "horrible project of starving and poisoning the people; he has drawn on himself for all eternity the execration of Frenchmen and the detestation of mankind." What is the Constituent Assembly but a set of "low, rampant, mean, stupid fellows?" "Infamous legislators, vile scoundrels, monsters athirst for gold and blood, you traffic with the monarch, with our fortunes, with our rights, with our liberties, with our lives!" "The second legislative corps is no less rotten than the first one." In the Convention, Roland, "the officious Gilles and the forger Pasquin, is the infamous head of the monopolisers." "Isnard is a juggler, Buzot a Tartuffe, Vergniaud a police spy."[30] When a madman sees everywhere around him, on the floor, on the walls, on the ceiling, toads, scorpions, spiders, swarms of crawling, loathsome vermin, he thinks only of crushing them, and the disease enters on its last stage: after the ambitious delirium, the mania for persecution and the settled nightmare, comes the *homicidal mania*.

With Marat, this broke out at the very beginning of the Revo-

---

29. Buchez et Roux, x., 407 (Sept., 1791).—Cf. Ibid., 473. According to Marat, "It is useless to measure a degree of the meridian; the Egyptians having already given this measure. The Academicians obtained an appropriation of one thousand crowns for the expenses of this undertaking, a small cake which they have fraternally divided amongst themselves."

30. Chevremont, i., 238–249. "L'Ami du peuple," Nos. 419, 519, 543, 608, 641. Other falsities just as extravagant are nearly all grotesque. No. 630 (April 15, 1792). "Simonneau, mayor of d'Etampes, is an infamous ministerial monopoliser."—No. 627 (April 12, 1792). Delessart, the minister, "accepts gold to let a got-up decree be passed against him." No. 650 (May 10, 1792). "Louis XVI. desired war only to establish his despotism on an indestructible foundation."

lution. The disease was innate; he was inoculated with it beforehand. He had contracted it in good earnest, on principle; never was there a plainer case of deliberate insanity. On the one hand, having derived the rights of man from physical necessities, he concluded "that society owes to those among its members who have no property, and whose labor scarcely suffices for their support, an assured subsistence, the wherewithal to feed, lodge, and clothe oneself suitably, provision for attendance in sickness and when old age comes on, and for bringing up children. Those who wallow in wealth must (then) supply the wants of those who lack the necessaries of life." Otherwise, "the honest citizen whom society abandons to poverty and despair, reverts back to the state of nature and the right of forcibly claiming advantages which were only alienated by him to procure greater ones. All authority which is opposed to this is tyrannical, and the judge who condemns a man to death (through it) is simply a cowardly assassin."[31] Thus do the innumerable riots which the dearth excites, find justification, and, as the dearth is permanent, the daily riot is legitimate. On the other hand, having laid down the principle of popular sovereignty he deduces from this, "the sacred right of constituents to dismiss their delegates"; to seize them by the throat if they prevaricate, to keep them in the right path by fear, and wring their necks should they attempt to vote wrong or govern badly. Now, they are always subject to this temptation. "If there is one eternal truth of which it is important to convince man, it is that the mortal enemy of the people, the most to be dreaded by them, is the Government." "Any minister who remains twice twenty-four hours in office, when it is not impossible for the cabinet to operate against the Government is 'suspect.'"[32] Bestir yourselves, then, ye unfortunates in town and country, workmen without work, street stragglers sleeping under bridges, prowlers along the high-

31. Chevremont, i., 106. (Draft of a declaration of the rights of man and of the citizen, 1789).—*Ibid.*, i., 196.

32. "L'Ami du peuple," Nos. 24 and 274.—Cf. "Placard de Marat," Sept. 18, 1792. "The National Convention should always be under the eye of the people, so that the people may stone it if it neglects its duty."

ways, beggars without fuel or shelter, tattered vagabonds, cripples and tramps, and seize your faithless mandatories! On July 14th and October 5th and 6th, "the people had the right not only to execute some of the conspirators in military fashion, but to immolate them all, to put to the sword the entire body of royal satellites leagued together for our destruction, the whole herd of traitors to the country, of every condition and degree."[33] Never go to the Assembly "without filling your pockets with stones and throwing them at the impudent scoundrels who preach monarchical maxims; I recommend to you no other precaution but that of telling their neighbors to look out."[34] "We do not demand the resignation of the ministers—we demand their heads. We demand the heads of all the ministerialists in the Assembly, your mayor's, your general's, the heads of most of the staff-officers, of most of the municipal council, of the principal agents of the executive power in the kingdom." Of what use are half-way measures, like the sack of the hotel de Castries?[35] "Avenge yourselves wisely! Death! Death! is the sole penalty for traitors raging to destroy you! It is the only one that strikes terror into them. . . . Follow the example of your implacable enemies! Keep always armed, so that they may not escape through the delays of the law! Stab them on the spot or blow their brains out!" "Twenty-four millions of men shout in unison: If the black, gangrened, archigangrened ministerialists dare pass a bill reducing and reorganising the army, citizens, do you build eight hundred scaffolds in the Tuileries garden and hang on them every traitor to his country—that infamous Riquetti, Comte de Mirabeau, at the head of them—and, at the same time, erect in the middle of the fountain basin a big pile of logs to roast the ministers and their tools!"[36] Could "the Friend of the people" rally around him two thousand men determined "to save the country, he would go and tear the heart out of that infernal

33. "L'Ami du peuple," Nos. 108–111 (May 20–23, 1790).
34. Ibid., No. 258 (Oct. 22, 1790).
35. Ibid., No. 286 (Novem. 20, 1790).
36. Ibid., No. 198 (August 22, 1790).

Mottié in the very midst of his battalions of slaves; he would go and
burn the monarch and his imps in his palace, impale the deputies on
their benches, and bury them beneath the flaming ruins of their
den."[37] On the first cannon shot being fired on the frontier, "it is
indispensable that the people should close the gates of the towns and
unhesitatingly make way with every priest, public functionary and
antirevolutionist, known machinators and their accomplices." "It
would be wise for the people's magistrates to keep constantly manufacturing large quantities of strong, sharp, short-bladed, double-
edged knives, so as to arm each citizen known as a friend of his
country. Now, the art of fighting with these terrible weapons consists
in this: Use the left arm as buckler, and cover it up to the arm-pit
with a sleeve quilted with some woollen stuff, filled with rags and
hair, and then rush on the enemy, the right hand wielding the
knife."[38] Let us use these knives as soon as possible, for "what now
remains to us to end the evils which overwhelm us? I repeat it,
nothing but executions by the people."[39] The Throne is at last down;
but "be careful not to give way to false pity! . . . No quarter! I advise
you to decimate the antirevolutionist members of the municipality,
of the justices of the peace, of the members of the departments and
of the National Assembly."[40] At the outset, a few lives would have
sufficed: "five hundred heads ought to have fallen when the Bastille
was taken, and all would then have gone on well." But, through
lack of foresight and timidity, the evil was allowed to spread, and
the more it spread the larger the amputation should have been. With
the sure, keen eye of the surgeon, Marat gives its dimensions; he

37. *Ibid.*, Nos. 523 and 524 (July 19 and 20, 1791).
38. *Ibid.*, No. 626 (Decem. 15, 1791).
39. *Ibid.*, No. 668 (July 8, 1792).—Cf. No. 649 (May 6, 1792). He approves
of the murder of General Dillon by his men, and recommends the troops everywhere to do the same thing.
40. *Ibid.*, No. 677 (August 10, 1792). See also subsequent numbers, especially No. 680, Aug. 19th, for hastening on the massacre of the Abbaye prisoners. And Aug. 21st: "As to the officers, they deserve to be quartered like
Louis Capet and his *manège* toadies."

has made his calculation beforehand. In September, 1792, in the Council at the Commune, he estimates approximatively forty thousand as the number of heads that should be laid low.[41] Six weeks later, the social abscess having enormously increased, the figures swell in proportion; he now demands two hundred and seventy thousand heads,[42] always on the score of humanity, "to ensure public tranquillity," on condition that the operation be entrusted to him, as the summary, temporary justiciary. Save this last point, the rest is granted to him; it is unfortunate that he could not see with his own eyes the complete fulfilment of his programme, the batches condemned by the revolutionary Tribunal, the massacres of Lyons and Toulon, the drownings of Nantes. From first to last, he was in the right line of the Revolution, lucid on account of his blindness, thanks to his crazy logic, thanks to the concordance of his personal malady with the public malady, to the precocity of his complete madness alongside of the incomplete or tardy madness of the rest, he alone steadfast, remorseless, triumphant, perched aloft at the first bound on the sharp pinnacle which his rivals dared not climb or only stumbled up.

---

41. Buchez et Roux, xxviii., 105. (Letter of Chevalier St. Dizier, member of the first Committee of Surveillance, Sep. 10, 1792.)—Michelet, ii., 94. (In December, 1790, he already demands twenty thousand heads).

42. *Moniteur*, Oct. 26, 1792. (Session of the Convention, Oct. 24th.) "N——: I know a member of the Convention, who heard Marat say that, to ensure public tranquillity, two hundred and seventy thousand heads more should fall."

VERMONT: "I declare that Marat made that statement in my presence."
MARAT: "Well, I did say so; that's my opinion and I say it again."

Up to the last he advocates surgical operations. (No. for July 12, 1793, the eve of his death.) Observe what he says on the antirevolutionists. "To prevent them from entering into any new military body I had proposed at that time, as an indispensable prudent measure, cutting off their ears, or rather their thumbs." He likewise had his imitators. (Buchez et Roux, xxxii., 186, Session of the Convention, April 4, 1796.) Deputies from the popular club of Cette "regret that they had not followed his advice and cut off three hundred thousand heads."

II

There is nothing of the madman about Danton; on the contrary, not only is his intellect sound, but he possesses political aptitudes to an eminent degree, and to such an extent that, in this particular, none of his associates or adversaries compare with him, while, among the men of the Revolution, only Mirabeau equals or surpasses him. He is an original, spontaneous genius and not, like most of his contemporaries, a disputatious, quill-driving theorist,[43] that is to say, a fanatical pedant, an artificial being composed of his books, a mill-horse with blinkers, and turning around in a circle without an issue. His free judgment is not hampered by abstract prejudices: he does not carry about with him a social contract, like Rousseau, nor, like Sièyes, a social art and cabinet principles or combinations;[44] he has kept aloof from these instinctively and, perhaps, through contempt for them; he had no need of them; he would not have known what to do with them. Systems are crutches for the impotent, while he is able-bodied; formulas serve as spectacles for the short-sighted, while his eyes are good. "He had read and meditated very little," says a learned and philosophical witness;[45] "his knowledge was scanty and he took no pride in investigation; but he *observed* and *saw*. . . . His native capacity, which was very great and not absorbed by other things, was naturally closed to vague, complex, and false notions, and naturally open to every notion of experience the truth of which was made manifest." Consequently, "his perceptions of men and things, sudden, clear, impartial, and true, were instinct with solid,

43. Danton never wrote or printed a speech. "I am no writer," he says. (Garat, "Mémoires," 31.)

44. Garat, Mémoires," iii.: "Danton had given no serious study to those philosophers who, for a century past, had detected the principles of social art in human nature. He had not sought in his own organisation for the vast and simple combinations which a great empire demands. He had that instinct for the grand which constitutes genius and that silent circumspection which constitutes judgment."

45. Garat, *ibid.*, 311, 312.

practical discretion." To form a clear idea of the divergent or concordant dispositions, fickle or earnest, actual or possible, of different parties and of twenty-six millions of souls, to justly estimate probable resistances, and calculate available forces, to recognise and take advantage of the one decisive moment, to combine executive means, to find men of action, to measure the effect produced, to foresee near and remote contingencies, to regret nothing and take things coolly, to accept crimes in proportion to their political efficacy, to manoeuvre in the face of great obstacles, even in contempt of current maxims, to consider objects and men the same as an engineer contracting for machinery and calculating horse-power[46]—such are the faculties of which he gave proof on the 10th of August and the 2nd of September, during his effective dictatorship between the 10th of August and the 21st of September, afterwards in the Convention, on the first Committee of Public Safety, on the 31st of May and on the 2nd of June:[47] we have seen him busy at work. Up to the last, in spite of his partisans, he has tried to diminish or, at least, not add to, the resistance the government had to overcome. Nearly up to the last, in spite of his adversaries, he tried to increase or, at least, not destroy the available forces of the government. In defiance of the shoutings of the clubs, which clamor for the extermination of the Prussians, the capture of the King of Prussia, the overthrow of all thrones, and the murder of Louis XVI., he negotiated the

46. The head of a State may be considered in the same light as the superintendent of an asylum for the sick, the demented and the infirm. In the government of his asylum he undoubtedly does well to consult the moralist and the physiologist; but, before following out their instructions he must remember that in his asylum its inmates, including the keepers and himself, are more or less ill, demented, or infirm.

47. De Sybel: "Histoire de l'Europe pendant la Révolution Française," (Dosquet's translation from the German) ii., 303. "It can now be stated that it was the active operations of Danton and the first Committee of Public Safety which divided the coalition and gave the Republic the power of opposing Europe. . . . We shall soon see, on the contrary, that the measures of the "Mountain" party, far from hastening the armaments, hindered them."

almost pacific withdrawal of Brunswick;[48] he strove to detach Prussia from the coalition;[49] he wanted to turn a war of propagandism into one of interests;[50] he caused the Convention to pass the decree that France would not in any way interfere with foreign governments; he secured an alliance with Sweden; he prescribed beforehand the basis of the treaty of Basle, and had an idea of saving the King.[51] In spite of the distrust and attacks of the Girondists, who strove to discredit him and put him out of the way, he persists in offering them his hand; he declared war on them only because they refused to make peace,[52] and he made efforts to save them when they were

48. *Ibid.*, i., 558, 562, 585. (The intermediaries were Westermann and Du-mouriez.)

49. *Ibid.*, ii., 28, 290, 291, 293.

50. Buchez et Roux, xxv., 445. (Session of April 13, 1793.)

51. According to a statement made by Count Theodore de Lameth, the eldest of the four brothers Lameth and a colonel and also deputy in the Legislative Assembly. During the Assembly he was well acquainted with Danton. After the September massacre he took refuge in Switzerland and was put on the list of *emigrés*. About a month before the King's death he was desirous of making a last effort and came to Paris. "I went straight to Danton's house, and, without giving my name, insisted on seeing him immediately. Finally, I was admitted and I found Danton in a bath-tub. "You here!" he exclaimed. "Do you know that I have only to say the word and send you to the guillotine?" "Danton," I replied, "you are a great criminal, but there are some vile things you cannot do, and one of them is to denounce me." "You come to save the King?" "Yes." We then began to talk in a friendly and confidential way. "I am willing," said Danton, "to try and save the King, but I must have a million to buy up the necessary votes and the money must be on hand in eight days. I warn you that although I may save his life I shall vote for his death: I am quite willing to save his head but not to lose mine." M. de Lameth set about raising the money; he saw the Spanish Embassador and had the matter broached to Pitt who refused. Danton, as he said he would, voted for the King's death, and then aided or allowed the return of M. de Lameth to Switzerland. (I have this account through M . . . who had it from Count Theodore de Lameth's own lips.)

52. Garat. "Mémoires," 317. "Twenty times, he said to me one day, I offered them peace. They did not want it. They refused to believe me in order to reserve the right of ruining me."

down. Amidst so many ranters and scribblers whose logic is mere words and whose rage is blind, who grind out phrases like a hand-organ, or are wound up for murder, his intellect, always capacious and supple, went right to facts, not to disfigure and pervert them, but to accept them, to adapt himself to them, and to comprehend them. With a mind of this quality one goes far no matter in what direction; nothing remains but to choose one's path. Mandrin, under the ancient régime, was also, in a similar way, a superior man;[53] only he chose the highway.

Between the demagogue and the highwayman the resemblance is close: both are leaders of bands and each requires an opportunity to organise his band. Danton, to organise his band, required the Revolution. "Of low birth, without a patron," penniless, every office being filled, and "the Paris bar unattainable," admitted a lawyer after "a struggle," he for a long time strolled about the streets without a brief, or frequented the coffee-houses, the same as similar men now-adays frequent the beer-shops. At the Café de l'Ecole, the proprietor, a good natured old fellow "in a small round perruque, grey coat, and a napkin on his arm," circulated among his tables smiling blandly, while his daughter sat in the rear as cashier.[54] Danton chat-ted with her and demanded her hand in marriage. To obtain her, he had to mend his ways, purchase an attorneyship in the Court of the Royal Council and find bondsmen and endorsers in his small native town.[55] Wedded and lodged in the gloomy Passage du Commerce, "more burdened with debts than with causes," tied down to a sed-entary profession which demands vigorous application, accuracy, a moderate tone, a respectable style, and blameless deportment; obliged to keep house on so small a scale that, without the help of

53. Cf. the "Ancient Régime," p. 501.

54. "Danton," by Dr. Robinet, *passim*. (Notices by Béon, one of Danton's fellow-disciples.—Fragment by Saint Albin.)—"The Revolution," ii., p. 35, foot-note.

55. Emile Bos, "Les Avocats du Conseil du Roi," 515, 520. (See Danton's marriage-contract and the discussions about his fortune. From 1787 to 1791, he is found engaged as counsel only in three cases.)

a *louis* regularly advanced to him each week by his coffee-house father-in-law, he could not make both ends meet;[56] his free-and-easy tastes, his alternately impetuous and indolent disposition, his love of enjoyment and of having his own way, his rude, violent instincts, his expansiveness, creativeness and activity, all rebel: he is ill-calculated for the quiet routine of our civil careers; it is not the steady discipline of an old society that suits him, but the tumultuous brutality of a society going to pieces, or one in a state of formation. In temperament and character he is a *barbarian,* and a barbarian born to command his fellow-creatures, like this or that vassal of the sixth century or baron of the tenth century. A colossus with the head of a "Tartar," pitted with the small-pox, tragically and terribly ugly, with a mask convulsed like that of a growling "bull-dog,"[57] with small, cavernous, restless eyes buried under the huge wrinkles of a threatening brow, with a thundering voice and moving and acting like a combatant, full-blooded, boiling over with passion and energy, his strength in its outbursts seeming illimitable like the forces of nature, roaring like a bull when speaking, and heard through closed windows fifty yards off in the street, employing immoderate imagery, intensely in earnest, trembling with indignation, revenge, and pa-triotic sentiments, able to arouse savage instincts in the most tranquil breast and generous instincts in the most brutal,[58] profane, using emphatic terms,[59] cynical, not monotonously so and affectedly like Hébert, but spontaneously and to the point, full of crude jests worthy of Rabelais, possessing a stock of jovial sensuality and good-humor, cordial and familiar in his ways, frank, friendly in tone; in short, outwardly and inwardly the best fitted for winning the confidence and sympathy of a Gallic, Parisian populace, and all contributing to

56. Madame Roland, "Mémoires." (Statement of Madame Danton to Ma-dame Roland.)

57. Expressions used by Garat and Roederer. Larevilliere-Lepaux calls him "the Cyclop."

58. Fauchet describes him as "the Pluto of Eloquence."

59. Riouffe, "Mémoires sur les prisons." In prison "every utterance was mingled with oaths and gross expressions."

the formation of "his inborn, practical popularity," and to make of him "a grand-seigñior of *sans-culotterie*."[60] Thus endowed for playing a part, there is a strong temptation to act it the moment the theatre is ready, whether this be a mean one, got up for the occasion, and the actors rogues, scamps and prostitutes, or the part an ignoble one, murderous, and finally fatal to him who undertakes it. To withstand temptation of this sort would require a sentiment of repugnance which a refined or thorough culture develops in both sense and soul, but which was completely wanting in Danton. Nothing disgusts him physically or morally: he embraces Marat,[61] fraternises with drunkards, congratulates the *Septembriseurs*, retorts in blackguard terms to the insults of prostitutes, treats reprobates, thieves, and jail-birds as equals, Carra, Westermann, Huguenin, Rossignol, and the confirmed scoundrels whom he sends into the departments after the 2d of September. "Eh! f——, you think we ought to send young misses."[62] One must employ foul people to do foul work; one

60. Terms used by Fabre d'Eglantine and Garat. Beugnot, a very good observer, had a good idea of Danton.—M. Dufort de Cheverney (manuscript memoirs published by M. Robert de Crèvecoeur), after the execution of Baboeuf, in 1797, had an opportunity to hear Samson, the executioner, talk with a war commissary, in an inn between Vendôme and Blois. Samson recounted the last moments of Danton and Fabre d'Eglantine. Danton, on the way to the scaffold, asked if he might sing. "There is nothing to hinder," said Samson. "All right. Try to remember the verses I have just composed," and he sang the following to a tune in vogue:

> "Nous sommes menés au trépas
> Par quantité de scélérats,
>   C'est ce qui nous désole
> Mais bientot le moment viendra
> Où chacun d'eux y passera,
>   C'est ce qui nous console."

61. Buchez et Roux, xxi., 108. Speech (printed) by Pétion: "Marat embraced Danton and Danton embraced him. I certify that this took place in my presence."

62. Buchez et Roux, xxi., 126. ("To Maximilian Robespierre and his royalists," a pamphlet by Louvet.)—Beugnot, "Mémoires," i., 250, "On arriving in Paris as deputy from my department (to the Legislative Assembly) Danton

cannot stop one's nose when they come for their wages; one must pay them well, talk to them encouragingly, and leave them plenty of sea-room. Danton is willing to add fuel to the fire, and he humors vices; he has no scruples, and lets people scratch and take. He has taken himself as much to give as to keep, to maintain his role as much as to benefit by it, squaring accounts by spending the money of the Court against the Court, probably inwardly chuckling, the same as the peasant in a blouse on getting ahead of his well-duped landlord, or as the Frank, whom the ancient historian describes as leering on pocketing Roman gold the better to make war against Rome. The graft on this plebeian seedling has not taken; in our modern garden this remains as in the ancient forest; its vigorous sap preserves its primitive raciness and produces none of the fine fruits of our civilisation, a moral sense, honor, and conscience. Danton has no respect for himself nor for others; the nice, delicate limitations that circumscribe human personality, seem to him as legal conventionality and mere drawing-room courtesy. Like a Clovis, he tramples on this, and like a Clovis, equal in faculties, in similar expedients, and with a worse horde at his back, he throws himself athwart society, to stagger along, destroy and reconstruct it to his own advantage.

At the start, he comprehended the peculiar character and normal procedure of the Revolution, that is to say, the useful agency of popular brutality: in 1788 he had already figured in insurrections. He comprehended from the first the ultimate object and definite result of the Revolution, that is to say, the dictatorship of the violent minority. Immediately after the "14th of July," 1789, he organised in his quarter of the city[63] a small independent republic, aggressive

---

sought me and wanted me to join his party. I dined with him three times, in the Cour du Commerce, and always went away frightened at his plans and energy. . . . He contented himself by remarking to his friend Courtois and my colleague: 'Thy big Beugnot is nothing but a devotee—you can do nothing with him.'"

63. The Cordeliers district. (Buchez et Roux, iv., 27.) Assembly meeting of the Cordeliers district, November 11th, 1789, to sanction Danton's permanent

and predominant, the centre of the faction, a refuge for the riff-raff and a rendezvous for fanatics, a pandemonium composed of every available madcap, every rogue, visionary, shoulder-hitter, newspaper scribbler and stump-speaker, either a secret or avowed plotter of murder, Camille Desmoulins, Fréron, Hébert, Chaumette, Clootz, Théroigne, Marat, while, in this more than Jacobin State, the model in anticipation of that he is to establish later, he reigns, as he will afterwards reign, the permanent president of the district, commander of the battalion, orator of the club, and the concocter of bold undertakings. Here, usurpation is the rule: there is no recognition of legal authority; they brave the King, the ministers, the judges, the Assembly, the municipality, the mayor, the commandant of the National Guard. Nature and principle raise them above the law; the district takes charge of Marat, posts two sentinels at his door to protect him from prosecutions, and uses arms against the armed force sent with a warrant to arrest him.[64] And yet more, in the name of the city of Paris, "chief sentinel of the nation," they assume to govern France: Danton betakes himself to the National Assembly and declares that the citizens of Paris are the natural representatives of the eighty-three departments, and summons it, on their injunction, to cancel an act it has passed.[65] The entire Jacobin conception is therein expressed: Danton, with his keen insight, took it all in and proclaimed it in appropriate terms; to apply it at the present time on a grand scale,[66] he has merely to pass from the small theatre to the large one, from the Cordeliers club to the Commune, to the Ministry, and the Committee of Public Safety, and, in all these theatres, he plays the same part with the same end in view and the

---

presidency. He is always reelected, and unanimously. This is the first sign of his ascendency, although sometimes, to save the appearance of his dictatorship, he has his chief clerk Paré elected, whom he subsequently made minister.

64. Buchez et Roux, iv., 295, 298, 401; v., 140.

65. *Ibid.*, viii., 28 (October, 1790).

66. *Ibid.*, ix., 408; x., 144, 234, 297, 417.—Lafayette "Mémoires," i., 359, 366. Immediately after Mirabeau's death (April, 1791) Danton's plans are apparent, and his initiative is of the highest importance.

same results. A despotism formed by conquest and maintained by terror, the despotism of the Jacobin Parisian rabble, is the end to which he directly marches. He employs no other means and, adapting the means to the end and the end to the means, manages the important days and instigates the decisive measures of the Revolution—the 10th of August,[67] the 2d of September, the 31st of May, the 2d of June;[68] the decree providing for an army of paid *sans-culottes* "to keep down aristocrats with their pikes"; the decree in each commune where grain is dear, taxing the rich to put bread within reach of the poor;[69] the decree giving laborers forty sous for attending the meetings of the Section Assemblies;[70] the institution of the revolutionary Tribunal;[71] the proposal to erect the Committee of Public Safety into a provisional government; the proclamation of Terror; the concentration of Jacobin zeal on useful works; the employment of the eight thousand delegates of the primary assemblies, who had been sent home as recruiting agents for the universal armament;[72] the inflammatory expressions of young men on the frontier; the wise resolutions for limiting the levy *en masse* to men be-

---

67. "The Revolution," ii., 238 (Note) and 283.—Garat, 309: "After the 20th of June everybody made mischief at the chateau, the power of which was daily increasing. Danton arranged the 10th of August and the chateau was thunderstruck."—Robinet: "Le Procès des Dantonistes," 224, 229. ("Journal de la Société des amis de la Constitution," No. 214, June 5, 1792.) Danton proposes "the law of Valerius Publicola, passed in Rome after the expulsion of the Tarquins, permitting every citizen to kill any man convicted of having expressed opinions opposed to the law of the State, except in case of proof of the crime." (*Ibid.*, Nos. 230 and 231, July 13, 1792.) Danton induces the federals present "to swear that they will not leave the capital until liberty is established, and before the will of the department is made known on the fate of the executive power." Such are the principles and the instruments, of "August 10" and "September 2."

68. Garat, 314. "He was present for a moment on the Committee of Public Safety. The outbreaks of May 31 and June 2 occurred; he was the author of both these days."

69. Decrees of April 6 and 7, 1793.

70. Decree of September 5, 1793.

71. Decree of March 10, 1793.

72. August 1 and 12, 1793.

tween eighteen and twenty-five, which put an end to the scandalous
songs and dances by the populace in the very hall of the Convention.[73] In order to set the machine up, he cleared the ground, fused
the metal, hammered out the principal pieces, filed off the blisterings,
designed the action, adjusted the minor wheels, set it agoing, and
indicated what it had to do, and, at the same time, he forged the
plating which guarded it from the foreigner and against all outward
violence. The machine being his, why, after constructing it, did he
not serve as its engineer?

Because, if competent to construct it, he was not qualified to
manage it. In a crisis, he may take hold of the wheel himself, excite
an assembly or a mob in his favor, carry things with a high hand
and direct an executive committee for a few weeks. But he dislikes
regular, persistent labor; he is not made for studying documents, for
poring over papers and confining himself to administrative routine.[74]
Never, like Robespierre and Billaud can he attend to both official
and police duties at the same time, carefully reading minute daily
reports, annotating mortuary lists, extemporising ornate abstractions, coolly enunciating falsehoods and acting out the patient, satisfied inquisitor; and especially, he can never become the systematic
executioner. On the one hand, his eyes are not obscured by the grey
veil of theory: he does not regard men through the *Contrat-Social*
as a sum of arithmetical units,[75] but as they really are, living, suf-

73. See "The Revolution," vol. iii., ch. i.—Buchez et Roux, xxv., 285.
(Meeting of Nov. 26, 1793.)—*Moniteur,* xix., 726. Danton (March 16, 1794)
secures the passing of a decree that "hereafter prose only shall be heard at the
bar of the house."

74. Archives Nationales, Papers of the Committee of General Security, No.
134.—Letter of Delacroix to Danton, Lille, March 25, 1793, on the situation in
Belgium, and the retreat of Dumouriez. . . . "My letter is so long I fear that
you will not read it to the end. . . . Oblige me by forgetting your usual indolence."—Letter of Chabot to Danton, Frimaire 12, year II. "I know your genius,
my dear colleague, and consequently your natural indolent disposition. I was
afraid that you would not read me through if I wrote a long letter. Nevertheless
I rely on your friendship to make an exception in my favor."

75. Lagrange, the mathematician, and senator under the empire, was asked

fering, shedding their blood, especially those he knows, each with his peculiar physiognomy and demeanor. Compassion is excited by all this when one has any feeling, and he had. Danton had a heart; he had the quick sensibilities of a man of flesh and blood stirred by the primitive instincts, the good ones along with the bad ones, instincts which culture had neither impaired nor deadened, which allowed him to plan and permit the September massacre, but which did not allow him to practise daily and blindly, systematic and wholesale murder. Already in September, "cloaking his pity under his bellowing,"[76] he had shielded or saved many eminent men from the butchers. When the axe is about to fall on the Girondists, he is "ill with grief" and despair. "I am unable to save them," he exclaimed, "and big tears streamed down his cheeks." On the other hand, his eyes are not covered by the bandage of incapacity or lack of forethought. He detected the innate vice of the system, the inevitable and approaching suicide of the Revolution. "The Girondists forced us to throw ourselves upon the *sans-culotterie* which has devoured them, which will devour us, and which will eat itself up."[77] "Let Robespierre and Saint-Just alone, and there will soon be nothing left in France but a Thebiad of political Trappists."[78] At the end, he sees more clearly still. "On a day like this I organised the revolutionary Tribunal. . . . I ask pardon for it of God and man. . . . In Revolutions, authority remains with the greatest scoundrels. . . . It is better to be a poor fisherman than govern men."[79] Nevertheless, he professed to govern them; he constructed a new machine for the purpose, and, deaf to its creaking, it worked in conformity with its structure and the impulse he gave to it. It towers before him, this

---

how it was that he voted for the terrible annual conscriptions. "It had no sensible effect on the tables of mortality," he replied.

76. Garat, 305, 310, 313. "His friends almost worshipped him."

77. *Ibid.*, 317.—Thibeaudeau, "Mémoires," i., 59.

78. Quinet, "La Révolution," ii., 304. (According to the unpublished memoirs of Baudot.) These expressions by Danton's friends all bear the mark of Danton himself. At all events they express exactly his ideas.

79. Riouffe, 67.

sinister machine, with its vast wheel and iron cogs grinding all France, their multiplied teeth pressing out each individual life, its steel blade constantly rising and falling, and, as it plays faster and faster, daily exacting a larger and larger supply of human material, while those who furnish this supply are held to be as insensible and as senseless as itself. Danton cannot, or will not, be so. He gets out of the way, diverts himself, gambles,[80] forgets; he supposes that the titular decapitators will probably consent to take no notice of him; in any event they do not pursue him; "they would not dare do it." "No one must lay hands on me, I am the ark." At the worst, he prefers "to be guillotined rather than guillotine." Having said or thought this, he is ripe for the scaffold.

III

Even with the firm determination to remain decapitator-in-chief, Danton would not be the true representative of the Revolution. It is brigandage, but carried on philosophically; its creed includes robbery and assassination, but only as a knife in its sheath; the showy, polished sheath is for public display, and not the sharp and bloody blade. Danton, like Marat, lets the blade be too plainly visible. At the mere sight of Marat, filthy and slovenly, with his livid, frog-like face, round, gleaming and fixed eyeballs, bold, maniacal stare and steady monotonous rage, common-sense rebels; people do not accept for their guide a homicidal bedlamite. At sight of Danton, with his billingsgate expressions, his voice like a tocsin of insurrection, his cyclopean features and air of an exterminator, humanity takes alarm; one does not surrender oneself to a political butcher without repugnance. The Revolution demands another interpreter, wearing like itself a specious exterior, and such is Robespierre,[81] with his irre-

---

80. Miot de Melito, "Mémoires," i., 40, 42.—Michelet, "Histoire de la Révolution Française," vi., 34; v. 178, 184. (On the second marriage of Danton in June, 1793, to a young girl of sixteen. On his journey to Arcis, March, 1794.)— Riouffe, 68, In prison "He talked constantly about trees, the country, and nature."

81. We can trace the effect of his attitude on the public in the police reports,

proachable attire, well-powdered hair, carefully brushed coat,[82] strict habits, dogmatic tone, and formal, studied manner of speaking. No mind, in its mediocrity and incompetence, so well harmonises with the spirit of the epoch. The reverse of the statesman, he soars in empty space, amongst abstractions, always mounted on a principle and incapable of dismounting so as to see things practically. "That b—— there," exclaims Danton, "doesn't even know how to boil an egg!" "The vague generalities of his preaching," writes another contemporary,[83] "rarely culminated in any specific measure or legal provision. He combated everything and proposed nothing; the secret of his policy happily accorded with his intellectual impotence and with the nullity of his legislative conceptions." Once the thread of

---

especially at the end of 1793, and beginning of the year 1794. (Archives Nationales, F⁷, 3, 61, report of Charmont, Nivose 6, year II.) "Robespierre gains singularly in public estimation, especially since his speech in the Convention, calling on his colleagues to rally and crush out the monsters in the interior, also in which *he calls on all to support* the new revolutionary government with their intelligence and talents. . . . I have to state that I have everywhere heard his name mentioned with admiration. They wound up by saying that it would be well for all members of the Convention to adopt the measures presented by Robespierre."—(Report of Robin, Nivose 8.) "Citizen Robespierre is honored everywhere, in all groupes and in the *cafés*. At the Café Manouri it was given out that his views of the government were the only ones which, *like the magnet*, would attract all citizens to the Revolution. It is not the same with citizen Billaud-Varennes." (Report of the Purveyor, Nivose 9.) "In certain clubs and groups there is a rumor that Robespierre is to be appointed dictator. . . . The people do justice to his austere virtues; it is noticed that he has never changed his opinions since the Revolution began."

82. "Souvenirs d'un déporté" by P. Villiers (Robespierre's secretary for seven months in 1790), p. 2. "Of painstaking cleanliness."—Buchez et Roux, xxxiv., 94. Description of Robespierre, published in the newspapers after his death; "His clothes were exquisitely clean and his hair always carefully brushed."

83. D'Hericault, "La Révolution du 9 Thermidor," (as stated by Daunou).—Meillan, "Mémoires," p. 4. "His eloquence was nothing but diffusive declamation without order or method, and especially with no conclusions. Every time he spoke we were obliged to ask him what he was driving at. . . . Never did he propose any remedy. He left the task of finding expedients to others, and especially to Danton."

his revolutionary scholasticism has spun itself out, he is completely used up. As to financial matters and military art, he knows nothing and risks nothing, except to underrate or calumniate Carnot and Cambon who did know and who took risks.[84] In relation to a foreign policy his speech on the state of Europe is the amplification of a schoolboy; on exposing the plans of the English minister he reaches the pinnacle of chimerical nonsense;[85] eliminate the rhetorical passages, and it is not the head of a government who speaks, but the porter of the Jacobin club. On contemporary France, as it actually exists, he has not one just or precise idea: instead of men, he sees only twenty-six millions of automatons, who, duly penned in, work together in peace and harmony; they are, indeed, naturally good,[86] and, after a little necessary purification, they will become good again; accordingly, their collective will is "the voice of reason and public interest"; hence, on meeting together, they are wise. "The people's assembly of delegates should deliberate, if possible, in the presence of the whole body of the people"; the Legislative body, at least, should hold its sittings "in a vast, majestic edifice open to twenty thousand spectators." Note that for the past four years, in

84. Buchez et Roux, xxxiii., 437, 438, 440, 442. (Speech by Robespierre, Thermidor 8, year II.)

85. *Ibid.*, xxx., 225, 226, 227, 228 (Speech, Nov. 17, 1793), and xxxi., 255 (Speech, Jan. 26, 1794). "The policy of the London Cabinet largely contributed to the first movement of our Revolution. . . . Taking advantage of political tempests (the cabinet) aimed to effect in exhausted and dismembered France a change of dynasty and to *place the Duke of York on the throne of Louis XVI.* . . . Pitt . . . is an imbecile, whatever may be said of a reputation that has been much too greatly puffed up. A man who, abusing the influence acquired by him on an island *placed haphazard in the ocean,* is desirous of contending with the French people, could not have conceived of such an absurd plan elsewhere than in a madhouse."—Cf. *Ibid.*, xxx., 465.

86. *Ibid.*, xxvi., 433, 441 (Speech on the Constitution, May 10, 1793); xxxi., 275. "Goodness consists in the people preferring itself to what is not itself; the magistrate, to be good, must himself immolate himself to the people." . . . "Let this maxim be first adopted that the people are good and that its delegates are corruptible." . . . xxx., 464. (Speech, Dec. 25, 1793): "The virtues are the appanage of the unfortunate and the patrimony of the people."

the Constituent Assembly, in the Legislative Assembly, in the Convention, at the Hôtel-de-Ville, in the Jacobin Club, wherever Robespierre speaks, the galleries have kept up constant vociferations: such a positive, palpable experience would open anybody's eyes; his are closed through prejudice or interest; even physical truth finds no access to his mind, because he is unable to comprehend it, or because he has to keep it out. He is, accordingly, either obtuse or a charlatan, and both in fact, for both combine to form the *cuistre,* that is to say, the hollow, inflated mind which, filled with words and imagining that these are ideas, revels in its own declamation and dupes itself that it may dictate to others.

Such is his title, character, and the part he plays. In this artificial and declamatory tragedy of the Revolution he takes the leading part; the maniac and the barbarian slowly retire in the background on the appearance of the *cuistre;* Marat and Danton finally become effaced, or efface themselves, and the stage is left to Robespierre who absorbs attention.[87] If we would comprehend him we must look at him as he stands in the midst of his surroundings. At the last stage of an intellectual vegetation passing away, he remains on the last branch of the eighteenth century, the most abortive and driest offshoot of the classical spirit.[88] He has retained nothing of a worn-out system of philosophy but its lifeless dregs and well-conned formulae, the formulae of Rousseau, Mably, and Raynal, concerning "the people, nature, reason, liberty, tyrants, factions, virtue, morality," a ready-made vocabulary,[89] expressions too ample, the meaning of which, ill-defined by the masters, evaporates in the hands of the disciple.

87. Cf. *passim,* Hamel, "Histoire de Robespierre," 3 vols. An elaborate panegyric full of details. Although eighty years have elapsed, Robespierre still makes dupes of people through his attitudinising and rhetorical flourishes. M. Hamel twice intimates his resemblance to Jesus Christ. The resemblance, indeed, is that of Pascal's Jesuits to the Jesus of the Gospel.

88. "The Ancient Régime," p. 262.

89. Garat, "Mémoires," 84. Garat who is himself an ideologist, notes "his eternal twaddle about the rights of man, the sovereignty of the people, and other principles which he was always talking about, and on which he never gave utterance to one precise or fresh idea."

He never tries to get at this; his writings and speeches are merely long strings of vague abstract periods; there is no telling fact in them, no distinct, characteristic detail, no appeal to the eye evoking a living image, no personal, special observation, no clear, frank original impression. It might be said of him that he never saw anything with his own eyes, that he neither could nor would see, that false conceptions have intervened and fixed themselves between him and the object;[90] he combines these in logical sequence, and simulates the absent thought by an affected jargon, and this is all. The other Jacobins alongside of him likewise use the same scholastic jargon; but none of them expatiate on it so lengthily. For hours, we grope after him in the vague shadows of political speculation, in the cold and perplexing mist of didactic generalities, trying in vain to make something out of his colorless tirades, and we grasp nothing. We then, astonished, ask what all this talk amounts to, and why he talks at all; the answer is, that he has said nothing and that he talks only for the sake of talking, the same as a sectary preaching to his congregation, neither the preacher nor his audience ever wearying, the one of turning the dogmatic crank, and the other of listening. So much the better if the hopper is empty; the emptier it is the easier and faster the crank turns. And better still, if the empty term he selects is used in a contrary sense; the sonorous words justice, humanity, mean to him piles of human heads, the same as a text from the gospels means to a grand inquisitor the burning of heretics. Through this extreme perversity, the *cuistre* spoils his own mental instrument; thenceforth he employs it as he likes, as his passions dictate, believing that he serves truth in serving these.

Now, his first passion, his principal passion, is literary vanity. Never was the chief of a party, sect, or government, even at critical moments, such an incurable, insignificant rhetorician, so formal, so

90. Read especially his speech on the Constitution (May 10, 1793), his report on the principles of Republican Government (Dec. 15, 1793), his speech on the relationship between religious and national ideas and republican principles (May 7, 1794), and speech of Thermidor 8.—Carnot: "Mémoires," ii., 512. "He brought to bear nothing but vague generalities in all business deliberations."

pompous, and so vapid. On the eve of the 9th of Thermidor, when it was necessary to conquer or die, he enters the tribune with a set speech, written and rewritten, polished and repolished,[91] overloaded with studied ornaments and bits for effect,[92] coated by dint of time and labor, with the academic varnish, the glitter of symmetrical antitheses, rounded periods, exclamations, preteritions, apostrophes and other tricks of the pen.[93] In the most famous and important of his reports,[94] I have counted eighty-four instances of prosopopoeia imitated from Rousseau and the antique, many of them largely expanded, some addressed to the dead, to Brutus, to young Barra, and others to absentees, priests, and aristocrats, to the unfortunate, to French women, and finally to abstract substantives like Liberty and Friendship. With unshaken conviction and intense satisfaction, he deems himself an orator because he harps on the same old tune. There is no sign of true inspiration in his elaborate eloquence, nothing but recipes and those of a worn-out art, Greek and Roman common-places, Socrates and the hemlock, Brutus and his dagger, classic metaphors like "the flambeaux of discord," and "the vessel of State,"[95] words coupled together and beauties of style which a

91. Buchez at Roux, xxxiii., 406. (Speech delivered Thermidor 8th.) The printed copy of the manuscript with corrections and erasures.

92. *Ibid.*, 420, 422, 427.

93. *Ibid.*, 428, 435, 436. "O day forever blessed! What a sight to behold, the entire French people assembled together and rendering to the author of nature the only homage worthy of him! How affecting each object that enchants the eye and touches the heart of man! O honored old age! O generous ardor of the young of our country! O the innocent, pure joy of youthful citizens! O the exquisite tears of tender mothers! O the divine charms of innocence and beauty! What majesty in a great people happy in its strength, power and virtue!" "No, Charmette, No, death is not the sleep of eternity!" "Remember, O, People, that in a republic, etc." "If such truths must be dissembled then bring me the hemlock!"

94. Speech, May 7, 1794. (On moral and religious ideas in relation to republican principles.)

95. Buchez et Roux, xxxiii., 436. "The Verres and Catilines of our country." (Speech of Thermidor 8th.)—Note especially the speech delivered March 7, 1794, crammed full of classical reminiscences.

pupil in rhetoric aims at on the college bench;[96] sometimes a grand bravura air, so essential for parade in public;[97] oftentimes a delicate strain of the flute, for, in those days, one must have a tender heart;[98] in short, Marmontel's method in "Belisarius," or that of Thomas in his "Eloges," all borrowed from Rousseau, but of inferior quality, like a sharp, thin voice strained to imitate a rich, powerful voice; a sort of involuntary parody, and the more repulsive because a word ends in a blow, because a sentimental, declamatory Trissotin poses as statesman, because the studied elegances of the closet become pistol shots aimed at living breasts, because an epithet skilfully directed sends a man to the guillotine. The contrast is too great between his talent and the part he plays. With a talent as petty and false as his intellect, there is no employment for which he is less calculated than that of governing men; he was cut out for another, which, in a peaceable community, would have stood him in stead. Suppress the Revolution, and Marat would have probably ended his days in an asylum. Danton might possibly have become a legal fillibuster, a Mandrin or bravo under certain circumstances, and finally throttled or hung. Robespierre, on the contrary, might have continued as he began,[99] a busy, hard-working lawyer of good stand-

---

96. *Ibid.*, xxxiii., 421. "Truth has touching and terrible accents which reverberate powerfully in pure hearts as in guilty consciences, and which falsehood can no more counterfeit than Salome can counterfeit the thunders of heaven."—437: "Why do those who yesterday predicted such frightful tempests now gaze only on the fleeciest clouds? Why do those who but lately exclaimed 'I affirm that we are treading on a volcano,' now behold themselves sleeping on a bed of roses?"

97. *Ibid.*, xxxii., 360, 361. (Portraits of the encyclopaedists and Hébertists.)

98. *Ibid.*, xxxiii., 408. "Here I must give vent to my feelings."—xxxii., 475–478, the concluding part.

99. Hamel: "Histoire de Robespierre," i., 34–76. An attorney at 23, a member of the *Rosati* club at Arras at 24, a member of the Arras Academy at 25. The Royal Society of Metz awarded him a second prize for his discourse against the prejudice which regards the relatives of condemned criminals as infamous. His eulogy of Gresset is not crowned by the Amiens Academy. He reads before the Academy of Arras a discourse against the civil disabilities of bastards, and then another on reforms in criminal jurisprudence. In 1789, he is president of

ing, member of the Arras Academy, winner of competitive prizes, author of literary eulogiums, moral essays, and philanthropic pamphlets; his little lamp, lighted like hundreds of others of equal capacity at the focus of the new philosophy, would have burned moderately without doing harm to any one, and diffused over a provincial circle a dim, commonplace illumination proportionate to the little oil his lamp would hold.

But the Revolution bore him into the Constituent Assembly, where, for a long time on this great stage, the self-love that constitutes the sensitive chord of the *cuistre,* suffered terribly. He had already suffered on this score from his earliest youth, and his wounds being still fresh made him only the more sensitive. Left an orphan, poor, befriended by his bishop, becoming a bursar through favor at the college Louis-le-Grand, after this a clerk with Brissot under the revolutionary system of law-practice, and at length settled down in his gloomy rue des Rapporteurs as a pettifogger, living with a peevish sister, he adopts Rousseau, whom he had once seen and whom he ardently studies, for his master in philosophy, politics, and style. Fancying, probably, like other young men of his age and condition, that he could play a similar part and thus emerge from his blind alley, he published law pleadings for effect, contended for Academy prizes, and read papers before his Arras colleagues. His success was moderate: one of his harangues obtained a notice in the Artois Almanack; the Academy of Metz awarded him only a second prize; that of Amiens gave him no prize, while the critic of the "Mercure" spoke of his style as smacking of the provinces. In the National Assembly, eclipsed by men of great and spontaneous ability, he remains a long time in the shade, and, more than once, through over self-assertion or lack of tact, makes himself ridiculous. With his sharp, thin, attorney's visage, "dull, monotonous, coarse voice and wearisome delivery," "an artesian accent," and constrained air,[100] his

---

the Arras Academy, and publishes an eulogy of Dupaty and an address to the Artesian nation on the qualities necessary for future deputies.

100. See his eulogy of Rousseau in the speech of May 7, 1794. (Buchez et

constantly putting himself forward, his elaboration of common-
places, his evident determination to impose on cultivated people,
still a body of intelligent listeners, and the intolerable ennui he
caused them—all this is not calculated to render the Assembly indulgent to errors of sense and taste.[101] One day, referring to certain
acts of the "Conseil": "It is necessary that a noble and simple formula should announce national rights and carry respect for law into
the hearts of the people." Consequently, in the decrees as promulgated, after the words "Louis, by the grace of God," etc., these
words should follow: "People, behold the law imposed on you! Let
this law be considered sacred and inviolable for all!" Upon this, a
Gascon deputy arises and remarks in his southern accent, "Gentlemen, this formula is useless—we do not sing psalms (*cantique*)."
There is a general roar;[102] Robespierre keeps silent and bleeds internally: two or three discomfitures of this stamp render a man sore
from head to foot.

It is not that his folly is foolishness to him; no pedant taken in
the act and hissed would avow that he deserved such treatment; on
the contrary, he is content to have spoken as becomes a philosophic

---

Roux, xxxii., 369.)—Garat, 85. "I hoped that his selection of Rousseau for a
model of style and the constant reading of his works would exert some good
influence on his character."

101. Fievée, "Correspondence" (introduction). Fievée, who heard him at
the Jacobin Club, said that he resembled a "tailor of the ancient régime."
Laréveillère-Lepeaux, "Mémoires."—Buchez et Roux, xxxiv., 94.—Malouet,
"Mémoires," ii., 135. (Session of May 31, 1791, after the delivery of Abbé
Raynal's address.) "This is the first and only time I found Robespierre clear
and even eloquent. . . . He spun out his opening phrases as usual, which contained the spirit of his discourse, and which, in spite of his accustomed rigmarole, produced the effect he intended."

102. Courrier de Provence, iii., No. 52 (Octo. 7 and 8, 1789).—Buchez et
Roux, vi., 372. (Session of July 10, 1790.) Another similar blunder was committed by him on the occasion of an American deputation. The president had
made his response, which was "unanimously applauded." Robespierre wanted
to have his say notwithstanding the objections of the Assembly, impatient at his
verbiage, and which finally put him down. Amidst the laughter, "M. l'Abbé
Maury demands ironically the printing of M. Robespierre's discourse."

and moral legislator, and so much the worse for the narrow minds and corrupt hearts unable to comprehend him. Thrown back upon himself, his wounded vanity seeks inward nourishment and takes what it can find in the sterile uniformity of his bourgeois moderation. Robespierre, unlike Danton, has no cravings. He is sober; he is not tormented by his senses; if he gives way to them, it is only no further than he can help, and with a bad grace; in the rue Saintonge in Paris, "for seven months," says his secretary, "I knew of but one woman that he kept company with, and he did not treat her very well . . . very often he would not let her enter his room": when busy, he must not be disturbed; he is naturally steady, hard-working, studious and fond of seclusion, at college a model pupil, at home in his province an attentive advocate, a punctual deputy in the Assembly, everywhere free of temptation and incapable of going astray. "Irreproachable" is the word which from early youth an inward voice constantly repeats to him in low tones to console him for obscurity and patience. Thus has he ever been, is now, and ever will be; he says this to himself, tells others so, and on this foundation, all of a piece, he builds up his character. He is not, like Desmoulins, to be seduced by dinners, like Barnave, by flattery, like Mirabeau and Danton, by money, like the Girondists, by the insinuating charm of ancient politeness and select society, like the Dantonists, by the bait of joviality and unbounded license—he is the incorruptible. He is not to be deterred or diverted, like the Feuillants, Girondists, and Dantonists, like statesmen or specialists, by considerations of a lower order, by regard for interests or respect for acquired positions, by the danger of undertaking too much at once, by the necessity of not disorganising the service and of giving play to human passions, motives of utility and opportunity: he is the uncompromising champion of right.[103] "Alone, or nearly alone, I do not allow myself to be corrupted; alone or nearly alone, I do not compromise the right;[104]

103. P. Villiers, p. 2.

104. Cf. his principal speeches in the Constituent Assembly—against martial law; against the veto, even suspensive; against the qualification of the silver

which two merits I possess in the highest degree. A few others may live correctly, but they oppose or betray principles; a few others profess to have principles, but they do not live correctly. No one else leads so pure a life or is so loyal to principles; no one else joins to so fervent a worship of truth so strict a practice of virtue: I am the unique." What can be more agreeable than this mute soliloquy? It is gently heard the first day in Robespierre's address to the Third-Estate of Arras;[105] it is uttered aloud the last day in his great speech in the Convention;[106] during the interval, it crops out and shines through all his compositions, harangues, or reports, in exordiums, parentheses, and perorations, permeating every sentence like the drone of a bag-pipe.[107] Through the delight he takes in this he can listen to nothing else, and it is just here that the outward echoes supervene and sustain with their accompaniment the inward cantata which he sings to his own glory. Towards the end of the Constituent Assembly, through the withdrawal or the elimination of every man

---

marc and in favor of universal suffrage; in favor of admitting into the National Guard nonacting citizens; of the marriage of priests; of the abolition of the death penalty; of granting political rights to colored men; of interdicting the father from favoring any one of his children; of declaring the "Constituants" ineligible to the Legislative Assembly, etc. On royalty: "The King is not the representative but the clerk of the nation." On the danger of allowing political rights to colored men: "Let the colonies perish if they cost you your honor, your glory, your liberty!"

105. Hamel, i., 76, 77 (March, 1789). "My heart is an honest one and I stand firm; I have never bowed beneath the yoke of baseness and corruption." He enumerates the virtues that a representative of the Third Estate should possess (26, 83). He already shows his blubbering capacity and his disposition to regard himself as a victim: "They undertake making martyrs of the people's defenders. Had they the power to deprive me of the advantages they envy, could they snatch from me my soul and the consciousness of the benefits I desire to confer on them."

106. Buchez et Roux, xxxiii. "Who am I that am thus accused? The slave of freedom, a living martyr to the Republic, at once the victim and the enemy of crime!" See this speech in full.

107. Especially in his address to the French people (Aug., 1791), which, in a justificatory form, is his apotheosis.—Cf. Hamel, ii., 212; Speech in the Jacobin Club (April 27, 1792).

at all able or competent, he becomes one of the conspicuous tenors on the political stage, while in the Jacobin Club he is decidedly the tenor most in vogue. "Unique competitor of the Roman Fabricius," writes the branch club at Marseilles to him; "immortal defender of popular rights," says the Jacobin crew of Bourges.[108] One of two portraits of him in the exhibition of 1791 bears the inscription: "The Incorruptible." At the Molière Theatre a drama of the day represents him as launching the thunderbolts of his logic and virtue at Rohan and Condé. On his way, at Bapaume, the patriots of the place, the National Guard on the road, and the authorities, come in a body to honor the great man. The town of Arras is illuminated on his arrival. On the adjournment of the Constituent Assembly the people in the street greet him with shouts, crown him with oak wreaths, take the horses from his cab, and drag him in triumph to the rue St. Honoré, where he lodges with the carpenter Duplay. Here, in one of those families in which the semibourgeois class borders on the people, whose minds are unsophisticated, and on whom glittering generalities and oratorical tirades take full hold, he finds his worshippers; they drink in his words; they have the same opinion of him that he has of himself; to every soul in the house, husband, wife, and daughter, he is the great patriot, the infallible sage; he bestows benedictions night and morning; he inhales clouds of incense; he is a god installed in furnished apartments. The faithful, to obtain access to him form a line in the court;[109] they are admitted into the reception room, where they gather around portraits of him drawn with pencil and stump, in sepia and in water color, and before miniature busts in red or grey plaster; then, on the signal being given by him, they penetrate through a glass door into the sanctuary where he presides, in the private closet in which the best bust of him, with verses and mottoes, supplies his place during his absence. His worshippers adore him on their knees, and the women more than the men. On

108. Hamel, i., 517, 532, 559; ii., 5.

109. Laréveillère-Lepeaux, "Mémoires."—Barbaroux, "Mémoires," 358. (Both, after a visit to him.)

the day he delivers his apology before the Convention "the passages are lined with women[110] . . . seven or eight hundred of them in the galleries, and but two hundred men at most"; and how frantically they cheer him! He is a priest surrounded by devotees."[111] On spouting his "rigmarole" at the Jacobin Club "the most affecting sobbings, shoutings and stampings almost make the house tumble."[112] A looker-on who shows no emotion is greeted with murmurs and obliged to slip out, like a heretic that has strayed into a church on the elevation of the Host. The faster the revolutionary thunderbolts fall on other heads, so does Robespierre mount higher and higher in glory and deification. Letters are addressed to him as "the founder of the Republic, the incorruptible genius who foresees all and saves all, who can neither be deceived nor seduced";[113] who has "the energy of a Spartan and the eloquence of an Athenian";[114] "who shields

110. Robespierre's devotees constantly attend at the Jacobin Club and in the Convention to hear him speak and applaud him, and are called, from their condition and dress, "the fat petticoats."

111. Buchez et Roux, xx., 197. (Meeting of Nov. 1, 1792.)—"Chronique de Paris," Nov. 9, 1792, article by Condorcet. With the keen insight of the man of the world, he saw clearly into Robespierre's character. "Robespierre preaches, Robespierre censures; he is animated, grave, melancholy, deliberately enthusiastic and systematic in his ideas, and conduct. He thunders against the rich and the great; he lives on nothing and has no physical necessities. His sole mission is to talk, and this he does almost constantly. . . . His characteristics are not those of a religious reformer, but of the chief of a sect. He has won a reputation for austerity approaching sanctity. He jumps up on a bench and talks about God and Providence. He styles himself the friend of the poor; he attracts around him a crowd of women and 'the poor in spirit,' and gravely accepts their homage and worship. . . . Robespierre is a priest and never will be anything else." Among Robespierre's devotees Madame de Chalabre must be mentioned (Hamel, i., 525), a young widow (Hamel, iii., 524), who offers him her hand with an income of forty thousand francs. "Thou art my supreme deity," she writes to him, "and I know no other on this earth! I regard thee as my guardian angel, and would live only under thy laws."

112. Fievée, "Correspondance," (introduction).

113. Report of Courtois on the papers found in Robespierre's domicile. Justificatory documents No. 20, letter of the Secretary of the Committee of Surveillance of Saint Calais, Nivose 15, year II.

114. *Ibid.*, No. 18. Letter of V——, former inspector of "droits reservés," Feb. 5, 1792.

the Republic with the aegis of his eloquence";[115] who "illuminates the universe with his writings, fills the world with his renown and regenerates the human species here below";[116] whose "name is now, and will be, held in veneration for all ages, present and to come";[117] who is "the Messiah promised by the Eternal for universal reform."[118] "An extraordinary popularity," says Billaud-Varennes,[119] a popularity which, founded under the Constituent Assembly, "only increased during the Legislative Assembly," and, later on, so much more, that, "in the National Convention he soon found himself the only one able to fix attention on his person . . . and control public opinion. . . . With this ascendency over public opinion, with this irresistible preponderance, when he reached the Committee of Public Safety, he was already the most important being in France." In three years, a chorus of a thousand voices,[120] which he formed and led indefatigably, rehearses to him in unison his own litany, his most sacred creed, the hymn of three stanzas composed by him in his own honor, and which he daily recites to himself in a low tone of voice, and often in a loud one: "Robespierre alone has discovered the ideal citizen! Robespierre alone attains to it without exaggeration or shortcomings! Robespierre alone is worthy of and able to lead the Revolution!"[121] Cool infatuation carried thus far is equivalent to a raging fever, and Robespierre almost attains to the ideas and the ravings of Marat.

115. *Ibid.*, No. 8. Letter of P. Brincourt, Sedan, Aug. 29, 1793.

116. *Ibid.*, No. 1. Letter of Besson, with an address of the popular club of Menosque, Prairial 23, year II.

117. *Ibid.*, No. 14. Letter of D——, member of the Cordeliers Club, and former mercer, Jan. 31, 1792.

118. *Ibid.*, No. 12. Letter by C——, Chateau Thierry, Prairial 30, year II.

119. Hamel, iii., 682. (Copied from Billaud-Varennes' manuscripts, in the Archives Nationales).

120. *Moniteur*, xxii., 175. (Session of Vendémiaire 18, year III. Speech by Laignelot.) "Robespierre had all the popular clubs under his thumb."

121. Garat, 85. "The most conspicuous sentiment with Robespierre, and one, indeed, of which he made no mystery, was that the defender of the people could never see amiss."—(Bailleul, quoted in Carnot's Memoirs, i., 516.) "He regarded himself as a privileged being, destined to become the people's regenerator and instructor."

First, in his own eyes, he, like Marat, is a persecuted man, and, like Marat, he poses himself as a "martyr," but more skilfully and keeping within bounds, affecting the resigned and tender air of an innocent victim, who, offering himself as a sacrifice, ascends to Heaven, bequeathing to mankind the imperishable souvenir of his virtues.[122] "I excite against me the self-love of everybody;[123] I sharpen against me a thousand daggers. I am a sacrifice to every species of hatred. . . . It is certain that my head will atone for the truths I have uttered. I have given my life, and shall welcome death almost as a boon. It is, perhaps, Heaven's will that my blood should indicate the pathway of my country to happiness and freedom. With what transports I accept this glorious destiny!"[124] "One does not wage war against tyrants for existence, and, what is still more dangerous, against miscreants; . . . the greater their eagerness to put an end to my career here below, the more eager I shall be to fill it with actions serving the welfare of my fellow-creatures."[125] "These miscreants all revile me;[126] the most insignificant, the most legitimate actions of others are, in my case, crimes. Whoever becomes acquainted with me is at once calumniated. The luck of others is pardoned, my zeal is guilt. Deprive me of my conscience and I am the most wretched of men. I do not even enjoy the rights of a citizen.

122. Speech of May 16, 1794, and of Thermidor 8, year II.

123. Buchez et Roux, x., 295, 296. (Session June 22, 1791, of the Jacobin Club.)—*Ibid.*, 294.—Marat spoke in the same vein: "I have made myself a curse for all good people in France." He writes, the same date: "Writers in behalf of the people will be dragged to dungeons. 'The friend of the people,' whose last sigh is given for his country, and whose faithful voice still summons you to freedom, is to find his grave in a fiery furnace." The last expression shows the difference in their imaginations.

124. Hamel, ii., 122. (Meeting of the Jacobin Club, Feb. 10, 1792.) "To obtain death at the hands of tyrants is not enough—one must deserve death. If it be true that the earliest defenders of liberty became its martyrs they should not suffer death without bearing tyranny along with them into the grave."—Cf., *ibid.*, ii., 215. (Meeting of April 27, 1792.)

125. Hamel, ii., 513. (Speech in the Convention, Prairial 7, year II.)

126. Buchez et Roux, xxxiii., 422, 445, 447, 457. (Speech in the Convention, Thermidor 8, year II.)

I am not even allowed to perform my duty as a representative of the people. . . . To the enemies of my country, to whom my existence seems an obstacle to their heinous plots, I am ready to sacrifice it, if their odious empire is to endure; . . . let their road to the scaffold be the pathway of crime, ours shall be that of virtue; . . . let the hemlock be got ready for me, I await it on this hallowed spot. I shall at least bequeath to my country an example of constant affection for it, and to the enemies of humanity the disgrace of my death."

Naturally, as always with Marat, he sees around him only "evil-doers," "intriguers," and "traitors."[127] Naturally, as with Marat, common sense with him is perverted, and, like Marat again, he thinks at random. "I am not obliged to reflect," said he to Garat, "I always rely on first impressions." "For him," says the same authority, "the best reasons are suspicions,"[128] and nought makes headway against suspicions, not even the most positive evidence. On September 4, 1792, talking confidentially with Pétion, and hard pressed with the questions that he put to him, he ends by saying, "Very well, I think that Brissot is on Brunswick's side."[129] Naturally, finally, he, like Marat, imagines the darkest fictions, but they are less improvised, less grossly absurd, more slowly worked out, and more industriously interwoven in his calculating inquisitorial brain. "Evidently," he says to Garat, "the Girondists are conspiring."[130] "And where?" demands Garat. "Every where," he replies, "in Paris, throughout France, over all Europe. Gensonné, at Paris, is plotting in the Faubourg St. Antoine, going about among the shopkeepers and persuading them that we patriots mean to pillage their shops. The Gironde (department)

127. Buchez et Roux, xx., 11, 18. (Meeting of the Jacobin Club, Oct. 29, 1792.) Speech on Lafayette, the Feuillants, and Girondists, xxxi., 360, 363. (Meeting of the Convention, May 7, 1794.) On Lafayette, the Girondists, Dantonists, and Hébertists.—xxxiii., 427. (Speech of Thermidor 8, year II.)

128. Garat, "Mémoires," 87, 88.

129. Buchez et Roux, xxi., 107. (Speech of Pétion on the charges made against him by Robespierre.) Pétion justly objects that "Brunswick would be the first to cut off Brissot's head, and Brissot is not fool enough to doubt it."

130. Garat, 94. (After the King's death and a little before the 10th of March, 1793.)

has for a long time been plotting its separation from France so as to join England; the chiefs of its deputation are at the head of the plot, and mean to carry it out at any cost. Gensonné makes no secret of it; he tells all among them who will listen to him that they are not representatives of the nation, but plenipotentiaries of the Gironde. Brissot is plotting in his journal, which is simply a tocsin of civil war; we know of his going to England, and why he went; we know all about his intimacy with that Lebrun, minister of foreign affairs, a *Liegois* and creature of the Austrian house. Brissot's best friend is Clavière, and Clavière has plotted wherever he could breathe. Rabaut, treacherous like the Protestant and philosopher that he is, was not clever enough to conceal his correspondence with that courtier and traitor Montesquiou; six months ago they were working together to open Savoy and France to the Piedmontese. Servan was made general of the Pyrenean army only to give the keys of France to the Spaniards." "Is there no doubt of this in your mind?" asks Garat. "None, whatever."[131]

Such assurance, equal to that of Marat, is terrible and worse in its effect, for Robespierre's list of conspirators is longer than that of Marat. Political and social, in Marat's mind, the list comprehends only aristocrats and the rich; theological and moral in Robespierre's mind, it comprehends all atheists and dishonest persons, that is to say, nearly the whole of his party. In this narrow mind, given up to abstractions and habitually classifying men under two opposite headings, whoever is not with him on the good side is against him on the bad side, and, on the bad side, the common understanding between the factious of every flag and the rogues of every degree, is natural. "All aristocrats are corrupt, and every corrupt man is an aristocrat"; for, "republican government and public morality are one

---

131. *Ibid.*, 97. In 1789 Robespierre assured Garat that Necker was plundering the Treasury, and that people had seen mules loaded with the gold and silver he was sending off by millions to Geneva.—Carnot, "Mémoires," i., 512. "Robespierre," say Carnot and Prieur, "paid very little attention to public business, but a good deal to public officers: he made himself intolerable with his perpetual mistrust of these, never seeing any but traitors and conspirators."

and the same thing."[132] Not only do evil-doers of both species tend
through instinct and interest to league together, but their league is
already perfected. One has only to open one's eyes to detect "in all
its extent" the plot they have hatched, "the frightful system of destruction of public morality."[133] Guadet, Vergniaud, Gensonné, Danton, Hébert, "all of them artificial characters," had no other end in
view: "they felt[134] that, to destroy liberty, it was necessary to favor
by every means whatever tended to justify egoism, wither the heart
and efface that idea of moral beauty, which affords the only rule for
public reason in its judgment of the defenders and enemies of humanity." Their heirs remain; but let those be careful. Immorality is
a political offence; one conspires against the State merely by making
a parade of materialism or by preaching indulgence, by acting scan-
dalously, or by following evil courses, by stock-jobbing, by dining
too sumptuously; by being vicious, scheming, given to exaggeration,
or "on the fence"; by exciting or perverting the people, by deceiving
the people, by finding fault with the people, by distrusting the people,[135] in short, when one does not march straight along on the
prescribed path marked out by Robespierre according to principles:
whoever stumbles or turns aside is a scoundrel, a traitor. Now, not

132. Buchez et Roux, xxxiii., 417. (Speech of Thermidor 8, year II.)

133. *Ibid.*, xxxii., 361 (Speech May 7, 1794), and 359. "Immorality is the
basis of despotism, as virtue is the essence of the Republic."

134. *Ibid.*, 371.

135. Buchez et Roux, xxxiii., 195. (Report of Couthon and decree in conformity therewith, Prairial 22, year II.) "The revolutionary Tribunal is organised for the punishment of the people's enemies. . . . The penalty for all offences within its jurisdiction is death. Those are held to be enemies of the people
who shall have misled the people, or the representatives of the people, into
measures opposed to the interests of liberty; those who shall have sought to
create discouragement by favoring the undertakings of tyrants leagued against
the Republic; those who shall have spread false reports to divide or disturb the
people; those who shall have sought to misdirect opinion and impede popular
instruction, produce depravity and corrupt the public conscience, diminish the
energy and purity of revolutionary and republican principles, or stay their progress. . . . Those who, charged with public functions, abuse them to serve the
enemies of the Revolution, vex patriots, oppress the people, etc."

counting the Royalists, Feuillantists, Girondists, Hébertists, Dantonists, and others already decapitated or imprisoned according to their
deserts, how many traitors still remain in the Convention, on the
Committees, amongst the representatives on mission, in the administrative bodies not properly weeded out, amongst petty tyrannic
underlings and the entire ruling, influential class at Paris and in the
provinces? Outside of "about twenty political Trappists in the Convention," outside of a small devoted group of pure Jacobins in Paris,
outside of a faithful few scattered among the popular clubs of the
departments, how many Fouchés, Vadiers, Talliens, Bourdons, Col-
lots, remain amongst the so-called revolutionists? How many dis-
sentients are there, disguised as orthodox, charlatans disguised as
patriots, and pachas disguised as *sans-culottes?*[136] Add all this vermin
to that which Marat seeks to crush out; it is no longer by hundreds
of thousands, but by millions, exclaim Baudot, Jean Bon St. André
and Guffroy, that the guilty must be counted and heads laid low!
And all these heads, Robespierre, according to his maxims, must
strike off. He is well aware of this; hostile as his intellect may be to
precise ideas, he, when alone in his closet, face to face with himself,
sees clearly, as clearly as Marat. Marat's chimera, on first spreading
out its wings, bore its frenzied rider swiftly onward to the charnel
house; that of Robespierre, fluttering and hobbling along, reaches
the goal in its turn; in its turn, it demands something to feed on,
and the rhetorician, the professor of principles, begins to calculate
the voracity of the monstrous brute on which he is mounted. Slower
than the other, this one is still more ravenous, for, with similar claws
and teeth, it has a vaster appetite. At the end of three years Robes-

---

136. Buchez et Roux, xxxv., 290. ("Institutions," by Saint-Just.) "The Revolution is chilled. Principles have lost their vigor. Nothing remains but red-
caps worn by intrigue."—Report by Courtois, "Pièces justificatives" No. 20.
(Letter of Pays and Rompillon, president and secretary of the Committee of
Surveillance of Saint-Calais, to Robespierre, Nivose 15, year II.) "The Mountain
here is composed of only a dozen or fifteen men on whom you can rely as
on yourself; the rest are either deceived, seduced, corrupted, or enticed away.
Public opinion is debauched by the gold and intrigues of honest folks."

pierre has overtaken Marat, at the extreme point reached by Marat at the outset, and the theorist adopts the policy, the aim, the means, the work, and almost the vocabulary of the maniac:[137] armed dictatorship of the urban mob, systematic maddening of the subsidised populace, war against the bourgeoisie, extermination of the rich, proscription of opposition writers, administrators, and deputies. Both monsters demand the same food; only, Robespierre adds "vicious men" to the ration of his monster, by way of extra and preferable game. Henceforth, he may in vain abstain from action, take refuge in his rhetoric, stop his chaste ears, and raise his hypocritical eyes to heaven, he cannot avoid seeing or hearing under his immaculate feet the streaming gore, and the bones crashing in the open jaws of the insatiable monster which he has fashioned and on which he prances.[138] These ever open and hungry jaws must be daily fed with an ampler supply of human flesh; not only is he bound to let it eat, but to furnish the food, often with his own hands, except that

137. Report by Courtois, N. 43.—Cf. Hamel, iii., 43, 71.—(The following important document is on file in the Archives Nationales, F⁷, 4,446, and consists of two notes written by Robespierre in June and July, 1793): "Who are our enemies? *The vicious and the rich.* How may the civil war be stopped? Punish traitors and conspirators, especially guilty deputies and administrators; . . . make terrible examples; . . . proscribe perfidious writers and antirevolutionists; . . . internal danger comes from the bourgeois; to overcome the bourgeois, rally the people; . . . the present insurrection must be kept up; . . . It is necessary that the same plan of insurrection should go on step by step. . . . *The sans-culottes should be paid and remain in the towns.* They ought to be armed, *worked up,* taught."

138. The Committee of Public Safety, and Robespierre especially, knew of and commanded the drownings of Nantes, as well as the principal massacres by Carrier, Turreau, etc. (De Martel, "Etude sur Fouché," 257–265.)—*Ibid.*, ("Types révolutionnaires," 41–49.)—Buchez et Roux, xxxiii., 101 (May 26, 1794.) Report by Barère and decree of the Convention ordering that "No English prisoners should be taken." Robespierre afterwards speaks in the same sense. *Ibid.*, 458. After the capture of Newport, where they took five thousand English prisoners, the French soldiers were unwilling to execute the Convention's decree, on which Robespierre (speech of Thermidor 8) said: "I warn you that your decree against the English has been cruelly violated; England, illtreated in our discourses, is favored by our arms."

he must afterwards wash them, declaring, and even believing, that no spot of blood has ever soiled them. He is generally content to caress and flatter the brute, to excuse it, to let it go on. Nevertheless, more than once, tempted by the opportunity, he points out the prey and gives it the rein.[139] He is now himself starting off in quest of living prey; he casts the net of his rhetoric[140] around it; he fetches it bound to the open jaws; he thrusts aside with an absolute air the arms of friends, wives, and mothers, the outstretched hands of suppliants begging for lives;[141] he suddenly throttles the struggling victims[142] and, for fear that they might escape, he strangles them in time. Towards the last, this no longer suffices; the brute must have grander quarries, and, accordingly, a pack of hounds, beaters-up, and, willingly or not, Robespierre must equip, direct, and urge them on, at Orange, at Paris,[143] ordering them to empty the prisons, and be expeditious in doing their work. Destructive instincts, long repressed by civilisation, thus devoted to butchery, become aroused. His feline physiognomy, at first "that of a domestic cat, restless but mild, changes into the savage mien of the wildcat, and next to the ferocious mien of the tiger. In the Constituent Assembly he speaks with a whine, in the Convention he froths at the mouth."[144] The monotonous drone of a stiff subprofessor changes into the personal

139. On the Girondists, Cf. "The Revolution," ii., 216.

140. Buchez et Roux, xxx., 157. Sketch of a speech on the Fabre d'Eglantine factim.—*Ibid.*, 336. Speech at the Jacobin Club against Clootz.—xxxii., abstract of a report on the Chabot affair, 18.—*Ibid.*, 69. Speech on maintaining Danton's arrest.

141. *Ibid.*, xxx., 378. (Dec. 10, 1793.) With respect to the women who crowd the Convention in order to secure the liberty of their husbands: "Are republican women insensible to the proprieties of citizenship by remembering that they are wives?"

142. Hamel, iii., 196.—Michelet, v., 394, abstract of the judicial debates on the disposition of the Girondists: "The minutes of this decree are found in Robespierre's handwriting."

143. De Martel, "Types révolutionnaires," 44. The instructions sent to the revolutionary Tribunal at Orange are in Robespierre's handwriting.—(Archives Nationales, F⁷, 4,439.)

144. Merlin de Thionville.

accent of furious passion; he hisses and grinds his teeth;[145] sometimes, on a change of scene, he affects to shed tears.[146] But his wildest outbursts are less alarming than his affected sensibility. The festering grudges, corrosive envies and bitter schemings which have accumulated in his breast are astonishing. The gall vessels are full, and the extravasated gall overflows on the dead. He never tires of re-executing his guillotined adversaries, the Girondists, Chaumette, Hébert and especially Danton,[147] probably because Danton was the active agent in the Revolution of which he was simply the incapable pedagogue; he vents his posthumous hatred on this still warm corpse in artful insinuations and obvious misrepresentations. Thus, inwardly corroded by the venom it distils, his physical machine gets out of order, like that of Marat, but with other symptoms. When speaking in the tribune "his hands crisp with a sort of nervous contraction"; sudden tremors agitate "his shoulders and neck, shaking him convulsively to and fro."[148] "His bilious complexion becomes livid," his eyelids quiver under his spectacles, and how he looks! "Ah," said a *Montagnard*, "you would have voted as we did on the

145. Buchez et Roux, xxxii., 71. (On Danton.) "Before the day is over we shall see whether the Convention will shatter an idol a long time rotten. . . . In what respect is Danton superior to his fellow-citizens? . . . I say that the man who now hesitates is guilty. . . . The debate, just begun, is a danger to the country."—Also the speech in full, against Clootz.

146. *Ibid.*, xxx., 338. "Alas, suffering patriots, what can we do, surrounded by enemies fighting in our own ranks! . . . Let us watch, for the fall of our country is not far off," etc.—These cantatas, with the accompaniments of the celestial harp, are terrible to one who considers the circumstances. For instance, on the 3d of September, 1792, while the massacres are going on, Robespierre enters the tribune of the electoral assembly and "declares that he will calmly face the steel of the enemies of public good, and carry with him to his grave the satisfaction of having served his country, the certainty of France having preserved its liberty.—(Archives Nationales, C. ii., 58–76.)

147. Buchez et Roux, xxxii., 360, 371. (Speech of May 7, 1794.) "Danton, the most dangerous, if he had not been the most cowardly, of the enemies of his country. . . . Danton, the coldest, the most indifferent, during his country's greatest peril."

148. *Ibid.*, xxxiv., 94.—Cf. the description of him by Fievée, who saw him in the tribune at the Jacobin Club.

9th of Thermidor, had you seen his green eyeballs!" "Physically as well as morally," he becomes a second Marat, suffering all the more because his delirium is not steady, and because his policy, being a moral one, forces him to exterminate on a grander scale.

But he is a discreet Marat, of a timid temperament, anxious,[149] keeping his thoughts to himself, made for a school-master or a pleader, but not for taking the lead or for governing, always acting hesitatingly, and ambitious to be rather the pope, than the dictator of the Revolution.[150] He would prefer to remain a political Grandison; he keeps the mask on to the very last, not only to the public and to others, but to himself and in his inmost conscience. The mask, indeed, has adhered to his skin; he can no longer distinguish one from the other; never did impostor more carefully conceal intentions and acts under sophisms, and persuade himself that the mask was his face, and that in telling a lie, he told the truth.

Taking his word for it, he had nothing to do with the September events.[151] "Previous to these occurrences, he had ceased to attend the General Council of the Commune. . . . He no longer went there." He was not charged with any duty, he had no influence there; he had not provoked the arrest and murder of the Girondists.[152] All

149. Merlin de Thionville "A vague, painful anxiety, due to his temperament, was the sole source of his activity."

150. Barère, "Mémoires." "He wanted to rule France influentially rather than directly."—Buchez et Roux, xiv., 188. (Article by Marat.) During the early sessions of the Legislative Assembly, Marat saw Robespierre on one occasion, and explained to him his plans for exciting popular outbreaks, and for his purifying massacres. "Robespierre listened to me with dismay, turned pale, and kept silent for some moments. This interview confirmed me in the idea I always had of him, that he combined the enlightenment of a wise senator with the uprightness of a genuine good man and the zeal of a true patriot, but that he equally lacked the views and boldness of a statesman."—Thibaudeau, "Mémoires," 58.—He was the only member of the Committee of Public Safety who did not join the department missions.

151. Buchez et Roux, xx., 198. (Speech of Robespierre in the Convention, November 5, 1792.)

152. All these statements by Robespierre are opposed to the truth.—("Procès-verbaux des Séances de la Commune de Paris.") Sep. 1, 1792, Robes-

he did was to "speak frankly concerning certain members of the Committee of Twenty-one"; as "a magistrate" and "one of a municipal assembly." Should he not "explain himself freely on the authors of a dangerous plot?" Besides, the Commune "far from provoking the 2d of September did all in its power to prevent it." In fine, but one innocent person perished, "which is undoubtedly one too many. Citizens, mourn over this cruel mistake; we too have long

---

pierre *speaks twice at the evening session.*—The testimony of two persons, both agreeing, indicate, moreover, that he *spoke at the morning session,* the names of the speakers not being given. "The question," says Pétion (Buchez et Roux, xxi., 103), "was the decree opening the barriers." This decree is under discussion at the Commune at the morning session of September 1: "Robespierre, on this question, spoke in the most animated manner, wandering off in sombre flights of imagination: he saw precipices at his feet and plots of *liberticides;* he designated *the pretended conspirators.*"—Louvet (*ibid.,* 130), assigns the same date (except that he takes the evening for the morning session), for Robespierre's first denunciation of the Girondists: "Nobody, then," says Robespierre, "dare name the traitors? Very well, I denounce them. I denounce them for the security of the people. I denounce the *liberticide* Brissot, the Girondist faction, the villainous committee of twenty-one in the National Assembly. I denounce them for having sold France to Brunswick and for having received pay in advance for their baseness."—Sep. 2 ("Procès-verbaux de la Commune," evening session), "MM. Billaud-Varennes and Robespierre, in developing their civic sentiments, . . . denounce to the Conseil-Général the conspirators in favor of the Duke of Brunswick, whom a powerful party want to put on the throne of France."—September 3, at 6 o'clock in the morning (Buchez et Roux, 16, 132, letter of Louvet), commissioners of the Commune present themselves at Brissot's house with an order to inspect his papers; one of them says to Brissot that he has eight similar orders against the Gironde deputies and that he is to begin with Guadet. (Letter of Brissot complaining of this visit, *Moniteur,* Sep. 7, 1792.) This same day, Sep. 3, Robespierre presides at the Commune. (Granier de Cassagnac, "Les Girondins" ii., 63.) It is here that a deputation of the Mauconseil section comes to find him, and he is charged by the "Conseil" with a commission at the Temple.—Septem. 4 (Buchez et Roux, xxi., 106, Speech of Pétion), the Commune issues a warrant of arrest against Roland; Danton comes to the Mayoralty with Robespierre and has the warrant revoked; Robespierre ends by telling Pétion: "I believe that Brissot belongs to Brunswick."—*Ibid.,* 506. "Robespierre (before Septem. 2), took the lead in the Conseil."—*Ibid.,* 107. "Robespierre," I said, "you are making a good deal of mischief. Your denunciations, your fears, hatreds, and suspicions, excite the people."

mourned over it! But, as all things human come to an end, let your tears cease to flow." When the sovereign people resumes its delegated power and exercises its inalienable rights, we have only to bow our heads. Moreover, it is just, wise, and good: "in all that it undertakes, all is virtue and truth; nothing can be excess, error, or crime."[153] It must intervene when its true representatives are hampered by the law: "let it assemble in its sections and compel the arrest of faithless deputies."[154] What is more legal than such a motion, which is the only part Robespierre took on the 31st of May. He is too scrupulous to commit or prescribe an illegal act. That will do for the Dantons, the Marats, men of relaxed morals or excited brains, who if need be, tramp in the gutters and roll up their shirtsleeves; as to himself, he can do nothing that would ostensibly derange or soil the dress proper to an honest man and irreproachable citizen. In the Committee of Public Safety, he merely executes the decrees of the Convention, and the Convention is always free. He a dictator! He is merely one of seven hundred deputies, and his authority, if he has any, is simply the legitimate ascendency of reason and virtue.[155] He a murderer! If he has denounced conspirators, it is the Convention which summons these before the revolutionary Tribunal,[156] and the revolutionary Tribunal pronounces judgment on them. He a terrorist! He merely seeks to simplify the established proceedings, so as to secure a speedier release of the innocent, the punishment of the guilty, and the final purgation that is to render liberty and morals the order of the day.[157] Before uttering all this he almost believes it, and, when he has uttered it he believes it fully.[158]

153. Garat, 86.—Cf. Hamel, i., 264. (Speech, June 9, 1791.)

154. "The Revolution," ii., 338, 339. (Speech, Aug. 3, 1792.)

155. Buchez et Roux, xxxiii., 420. (Speech, Thermidor 8.)

156. *Ibid.*, xxxii., 71. (Speech against Danton.) "What have you done that you have not done freely?"

157. *Ibid.*, xxxiii., 199 and 221. (Speech on the law of Prairial 22.)

158. Mirabeau said of Robespierre: "Whatever that man has said, he believes in it."—Robespierre, Duplay's guest, dined every day with Duplay, a juryman in the revolutionary Tribunal and cooperator for the guillotine, at eighteen francs a day. The talk at the table probably turned on the current abstractions;

When nature and history combine, to produce a character, they succeed better than man's imagination. Neither Molière in his "Tartuffe," nor Shakespeare in his "Richard III.," dared bring on the stage a hypocrite believing himself sincere, and a Cain that regarded himself as an Abel. There he stands on a colossal stage, in the presence of a hundred thousand spectators, on the 8th of June, 1794, the most glorious day of his life, at the fête in honor of the Supreme Being, which is the glorious triumph of his doctrine and the official consecration of his popedom. Two characters are found in Robespierre, as in the Revolution which he represents: one, apparent, paraded, external, and the other hidden, dissembled, inward, the latter being overlaid by the former. The first one all for show, fashioned out of purely cerebral cogitations, is as artificial as the solemn farce going on around him. According to David's programme, the cavalcade of supernumeraries who file in front of an allegorical mountain, gesticulate and shout at the command, and under the eyes, of Henriot and his gendarmes,[159] manifesting at the appointed time the emotions which are prescribed for them. At five o'clock in the morning "friends, husbands, wives, relations, and children will embrace. . . . The old man, his eyes streaming with tears of joy, feels himself rejuvenated." At two o'clock, on the turf-laid terraces of the sacred mountain "all will show a state of commotion and excitement: mothers here press to their bosoms the infants they suckle, and there offer them up in homage to the author of Nature, while youths,

---

but there must have been frequent allusions to the condemnations *of the day*, and, even when not mentioned, they were in their minds. Only Robert Browning, at the present day, could imagine and revive what was spoken and thought in those evening conversations before the mother and daughters.

159. Buchez et Roux, xxxiii., 151.—Cf. Dauban, "Paris en 1794," p. 386 (illustration), and 392, "Fête de l'Etre Suprême à Sceaux," according to the programme drawn up by the patriot Palloy. "All citizens are requested to be at their windows or doors, even those occupying lodgings in by-streets."—*Ibid.*, 399. "Youthful citizens will strew flowers at each station, fathers will embrace their children and mothers turn their eyes upward to heaven."—*Moniteur*, xxx., 653. "Plan of the fête in honor of the Supreme Being, drawn up by David, and decreed by the National Convention."

aglow with the ardor of battle, simultaneously draw their swords and hand them to their venerable fathers. Sharing in the enthusiasm of their sons, the transported old men embrace them and bestow on them the paternal benediction. . . . All the men distributed around the 'Field of Reunion' sing in chorus the (first) refrain. . . . All the women distributed around the 'Field of Reunion' sing in unison the (second) refrain. . . . All Frenchmen partake of each other's sentiments in one grand fraternal embrace." Such an idyl, performed to the beating of drums, in the presence of moral symbols and colored pasteboard divinities, what could better please the counterfeit moralist, unable to distinguish the false from the true, and whose skin-deep sensibility is borrowed from sentimental authors! "For the first time" his glowing countenance beams with joy, while "the enthusiasm"[160] of the scribe overflows, as usual, in book phraseology: "Behold!" he exclaims, "that which is most interesting in humanity! The Universe is here assembled! O, Nature, how sublime, how exquisite is thy power! How tyrants must quail at the contemplation of this festival!" Is not he himself its most dazzling ornament? Was not he unanimously chosen to preside over the Convention and conduct the ceremonies? Is he not the founder of the new cult, the only pure worship on the face of the earth, approved of by morality and reason? Wearing the uniform of a representative, nankeen breeches, blue coat, tricolored sash, and plumed hat,[161] holding in his hand a bouquet of flowers and grain, he marches at the head of the Convention and officiates on the platform; he sets fire to the veil which hides from view the idol representing "Atheism," and suddenly, through an ingenious contrivance, the majestic statue of "Wisdom" appears in its place. He then addresses the crowd, over and over again, exhorting, apostrophising, preaching, elevating his soul to the Supreme Being, and with what oratorical combinations! What an academic swell of bombastic cadences, strung together to enforce his tirades! How cunning the even balance of adjective and

160. Buchez et Roux, xxxiii., 176. (Narrative by Valate.)
161. Hamel, iii., 541.

substantive![162] From these faded rhetorical flowers, arranged as if for a prize distribution or a funeral oration, exhales a sanctimonious, collegiate odor which he complacently breathes, and which intoxicates him. At this moment, he must certainly be in earnest; there is no hesitation or reserve in his self-admiration; he is not only in his own eyes a great writer and great orator, but a great statesman and great citizen: his artificial, philosophic conscience awards him only praise. But look underneath, or rather wait a moment. Signs of impatience and antipathy appear behind his back: Lecointre has braved him openly; numerous insults, and, worse than these, sarcasms, reach his ears. On such an occasion, and in such a place! Against the pontiff of Truth, the apostle of Virtue! The miscreants, how dare they! Silent and pale, he suppresses his rage, and,[163] losing his balance, closing his eyes, he plunges headlong on the path of murder: cost what it will, the miscreants must perish and without loss of time. To expedite matters, he must get their heads off quietly, and as "up to this time things have been managed confidentially in the Committee of Public Safety," he, alone with Couthon, two days after, without informing his colleagues,[164] draws up, brings to the Convention, and has passed the terrible act of Prairial which places everybody's life at his disposal. In his crafty, blundering haste, he has demanded too much; each one, on reflection, becomes alarmed

162. Buchez et Roux, xxviii., 178, 180.

163. *Ibid.*, 177 (Narrative by Vilate). *Ibid.*, 170, Notes by Robespierre on Bourdon (de l'Oise) 417. Passages erased by Robespierre in the manuscript of his speech of Thermidor 8.—249. Analogous passages in his speech as delivered, all these indications enable us to trace the depths of his resentment.

164. *Ibid.*, 183. Memoirs of Billaud-Varennes, Collot d'Herbois, Vadier, and Barère. "The next day after Prairial 22, at the morning session (of the Committee of Public Safety) ... I now see, says Robespierre, that I stand alone, with nobody to support me, and, getting violently excited, he launched out against the members of the Committee who had conspired against him. He shouted so loud as to collect together a number of citizens on the Tuileries terrace." Finally, "he pushed hypocrisy so far as to shed tears." The nervous machine, I imagine, broke down.—Another member of the Committee, Prieur (Carnot, "Mémoires," ii., 525), relates that, in the month of Floréal, after another equally long and violent session, "Robespierre, exhausted, became ill."

for himself; he is compelled to back out, to protest that he is mis-understood, admit that representatives are excepted, and, accord-ingly, to sheathe the knife he has already applied to his adversaries' throats. But he still holds it in his grasp. He watches them, and, pretending to retreat, affects a renunciation, crouched in his cor-ner,[165] waiting until they discredit themselves, so as to spring upon them a second time. He has not to wait long, for the exterminating machine he set up on the 22d of Prairial, is in their hands, and it has to work as he planned it, namely, by making rapid turns and almost haphazard: the odium of a blind sweeping massacre rests with them; he not only makes no opposition to this, but, while pretending to abstain from it, he urges it on. Secluded in the private office of his secret police, he orders arrests;[166] he sends out his principal blood-hound, Herman; he first signs and then despatches the resolution by which it is supposed that there are conspirators among those in confinement and which, authorising spies or paid informers, is to provide the guillotine with those vast batches which "purge and clean prisons out in a trice."[167] "I am not responsible," he states later

165. Carnot, "Mémoires," ii., 526. "As his bureau was in a separate place, where none of us set foot, he could retire to it without coming in contact with any of us, as in effect, he did. He even made a pretence of passing through the committee rooms, after the session was over, and he signed some papers; but he really neglected nothing, except our common discussions. He held frequent conferences in his house with the presidents of the revolutionary Tribunals, over which his influence was greater than ever."

166. Dauban, "Paris en 1794," 563.—Archives Nationales, AF.II., 58. The signature of Robespierre, in his own handwriting, is found affixed to many of the resolutions of the Committee of Public Safety, passed Thermidor 5 and 7, and those of Saint-Just and Couthon after this, up to Thermidor 3, 6, and 7. On the register of the minutes of the Committee of Public Safety, Robespierre is always recorded as present at all meetings between Messidor 1 and Thermidor 8, inclusive.

167. Archives Nationales, F[7], 4,438. Report to the Committee of Public Safety by Herman, Commissioner of the Civil and Police administrations and of the Courts, Messidor 3, year II. "The Committee charged with a general supervision of the prisons, and obliged to recognise that all the rascals mostly concerned with *liberticide* plots are . . . still in the prisons, forming a band apart, and rendering surveillance very troublesome; they are a constant source of

on. . . . "My lack of power to do any good, to arrest the evil, forced me for more than six weeks to abandon my post on the Committee of Public Safety."[168] To ruin his adversaries by murders committed by him, by those which he makes them commit and which he imputes to them, to whitewash himself and blacken them with the same stroke of the brush, what intense delight! If the natural conscience murmurs in whispers at moments, the acquired superposed conscience immediately imposes silence, concealing personal hatreds under public pretexts: the guillotined, after all, were aristocrats, and whoever comes under the guillotine is immoral. Thus, the means are good and the end better; in employing the means, as well as in pursuing the end, the function is sacerdotal.

Such is the scenic exterior of the Revolution, a specious mask with a hideous visage beneath it, under the reign of a nominal humanitarian theory, covering over the effective dictatorship of evil and low passions. In its true representative, as in itself, we see ferocity issuing from philanthropy, and, from the *cuistre,* the executioner.

---

disorder, always getting up attempts to escape, being a daily assemblage of persons devoting themselves wholly to imprecations against liberty and its defenders. . . . *It would be easy to point out in each prison, those who have served, and are to serve, the diverse factions, the diverse conspiracies. . . . It may be necessary, perhaps, to purge the prisons at once and free the soil of liberty of their filth, the refuse of humanity.*" The Committee of Public Safety consequently "charges the Commission to ascertain in the prisons of Paris . . . who have been more specially concerned in the diverse factions and conspiracies that the National Convention has destroyed." The word "approved" appears at the foot of the resolution in Robespierre's handwriting, then the signature of Robespierre, and lower down, those of Billaud and Barère. A similar resolution providing for the 7th of Messidor, signed by the same parties and five others, is despatched the same day. (M. de Martel came across and made use of this conclusive document before I did, most of it being quoted in "Les Types Révolutionnaires.")

168. Buchez et Roux, xxxiii., 434.

CHAPTER II

LET US follow the operations of the new government from the first to the last of its derivations, those of its ruling bodies and leaders, its assemblies, committees, delegates, administrators, and underlings of every kind and degree. Like living flesh stamped with a red-hot iron, so do their brows bear the imprint of two stigmata, each with its own cicatrice and discoloration. In vain do they, too, strive to conceal their scars: we detect under the crowns and titles they assume the brand of the slave or the mark of the tyrant.

I

At the Tuileries, the omnipotent Convention sits enthroned in the theatre, converted into an Assembly room. It carries on its deliberations daily, in grand style. Its decrees, received with blind obedience, startle France and upset all Europe. At a distance, its majesty is imposing, more august than that of the republican senate in Rome. Near by, the effect is quite otherwise; these undisputed sovereigns are serfs who live in trances, and justly so, for, nowhere, even in prison, is there more constraint and less security than on their benches. After the 2d of June, 1793, their inviolable precincts, the grand official reservoir from which legal authority flows, becomes a sort of tank, into which the revolutionary net plunges and successfully brings out its choicest fish, singly or by the dozen, and sometimes in vast numbers; at first, the sixty-seven Girondist deputies, who are executed or proscribed; then, the seventy-three members of the "Right," swept off in one day and lodged in the prison of La Force; next, the prominent Jacobins: Osselin, arrested on the 19th of Brumaire, Bazire, Chabot, and Delaunay, accused by decree on the 24th Brumaire, Fabre d'Eglantine, arrested on the 24th of Nivose, Bernard, guillotined on the 3d of Pluviose, Anacharsis Clootz guillotined on the 4th of Germinal, Hérault-Séchelles, Lacroix, Philippeaux, Camille Desmoulins and Danton, guillotined with four others on the 10th of Germinal, Simon, guillotined on the 24th of Germinal, and Osselin, guillotined on the 8th of Messidor. Naturally, the others take warning and are careful. At the opening of the session they are seen entering the hall, looking uneasy, "full of distrust,"[1]

1. Thibaudeau: "Mémoires," i., 47, 70.—Durand-Maillane, "Mémoires," 183.—Vatel, "Charlotte Corday et les Girondins," ii., 269. Out of the seventy-

like animals driven into a pen and suspicious of a trap. "Each," writes an eye-witness, "acted and spoke with circumspection, for fear of being charged with some crime: in effect, nothing was unimportant, the seat one took, a glance of the eye, a gesture, a murmur, a smile." Hence, they flock instinctively to the side which is best sheltered, the left side. "The tide flowed towards the summit of the Mountain; the right side was deserted. . . . Many took no side at all, and, during the session, often changed their seats, thinking that they might thus elude the spy by donning a mixed hue and keeping on good terms with everybody. The most prudent never sat down; they kept off the benches, at the foot of the tribune, and, on matters getting to be serious, slipped quietly out of the hall." Most of them took refuge in their committee-rooms; each tries to be overlooked, to be obscure, to appear insignificant or absent.[2] During the four months following the 2d of June, the hall of the Convention is half or three-quarters empty; the election of a president does not bring out two hundred and fifty voters;[3] only two hundred, one hundred, fifty votes, elect the Committees of Public Safety and General Security; about fifty votes elect the judges of the revolutionary Tribunal; less than ten votes elect their substitutes;[4] not one vote is cast for the adoption of the decree indicting the deputy, Dulaure;[5] "no member

---

six presidents of the Convention eighteen were guillotined, eight transported, twenty-two declared outlaws, six incarcerated, three who committed suicide, and four who became insane, in all sixty-one. All who served twice perished by a violent death.

2. *Moniteur*, xviii., 38. (Speech by Amar, reporter, Oct. 3, 1793.) "The apparently negative behavior of the minority in the Convention, since the 2d of June, is a new plot hatched by Barbaroux."

3. Mortimer-Ternaux, viii., 44. Election of Collot d'Herbois as president by one hundred and fifty-one out of two hundred and forty-one votes, June 13, 1793.—*Moniteur*, xvii., 366. Election of Hérault-Séchelles as president by one hundred and sixty-five out of two hundred and thirty-six votes, Aug. 3, 1793.

4. "The Revolution," vol. iii., ch. i.—Mortimer-Ternaux, vii., 435. (The three substitutes obtain, the first, nine votes, the second, six votes, and the third, five votes.)

5. Marcelin Boudet, "Les Conventionnels d' Auvergne," 206.

rises for or against it; there is no vote"; the president, nevertheless, pronounces the act passed and "the Marais lets things take their course." "Marais frogs" is the appellation bestowed on them before the 2d of June, when, amongst the dregs of the "Centre," they "broke" with the "Mountain"; now, they still number four hundred and fifty, three times as many as the *Montagnards;* but they purposely keep quiet; their old name "renders them, so to say, soft; their ears ring with eternal menaces; their hearts shrivel up with terror;[6] while their tongues, paralysed by habitual silence, cleave to the roofs of their mouths. In vain do they keep in the back-ground, consent to everything, ask nothing for themselves but personal safety, and surrender all else, their votes, their wills and their consciences; they feel that their life hangs by a thread. The greatest mute among them all, Siéyès, denounced in the Jacobin Club, barely escapes, and through the protection of his shoemaker, who rises and exclaims: "That Siéyès! I know him. He don't meddle with politics. He does nothing but read his book. I make his shoes and will answer for him."[7]

Of course, previous to the 9th of Thermidor, none of them open their mouths; it is only the *Montagnards* who make speeches, and on the countersign being given. If Legendre, the admirer, disciple, and confidential friend of Danton, dares at one time interfere in relation to the decree which sends his friend to the scaffold, asking that he may first be heard, it is only to retract immediately; that very evening, at the Jacobin club, for greater security, "he rolls in the mud";[8] he declares "that he submits to the judgment of the revolutionary Tribunal," and swears to denounce "whoever shall oppose any obstacle to the execution of the decree."[9] Has not Robespierre taught him a lesson, and in his most pedantic manner? What is more beau-

6. Dussault: "Fragment pour servir à l'histoire de la Convention."

7. Sainte-Beuve: "Causeries du Lundi," v., 216. (According to the unpublished papers of Siéyès.)

8. Words of Michelet.

9. *Moniteur,* xx., 95, 135. (Sessions of Germinal II. in the Convention and at the Jacobin club.)

tiful, says the great moralist, more sublime, than an Assembly which purges itself?[10] Thus, not only is the net which has already dragged out so many palpitating victims still intact, but it is enlarged and set again, only, the fish are now caught on the "Left" as well as on the "Right," and preferably on the topmost benches of the "Mountain."[11] And better still, through the law of Prairial 22, its meshes are reduced in size and its width increased; with such admirable tackle, the tank could not fail to be exhausted. A little before the 9th of Thermidor, David, who was one of Robespierre's devoted adherents, himself exclaimed: "Will twenty of us be left on the Mountain?" About the same time, Legendre, Thuriot, Léonard Bourdon, Tallien, Bourdon de l'Oise, and others, each has a spy all day long at his heels; there are thirty deputies to be proscribed and their names are whispered about; whereupon, sixty spring out of bed, feeling sure that they will be seized the next morning before they can get up.[12]

Subject to such a system, prolonged for so many months, people sink down and become discouraged. "Everybody stooped so as to pass beneath the popular yoke.[13] Everybody became one of the low

10. Buchez et Roux, xxxii., 17. (Sessions of Ventose 26, year II. Speech of Robespierre.) "In what country has a powerful senate ever sought in its own bosom for the betrayers of the common cause and handed them over to the sword of the law? Who has ever furnished the world with this spectacle? You, my fellow citizens."

11. Miót de Melito, "Mèmoires," i. 44. Danton, at table in the ministry of Foreign Affairs, remarked: "The Revolution, like Saturn, eats its own children." As to Camille Desmoulins, "His melancholy already indicated a presentiment of his fate; the few words he allowed to escape him always turned on questions and observations concerning the nature of punishment, inflicted on those condemned by the revolutionary Tribunal and the best way of preparing oneself for that event and enduring it."

12. Buchez et Roux, xxxiii., 363, 357. (Police reports on the deputies, Messidor 4, and following days.)—Vilate: "Coups secrètes de la Révolution du 9 et 10 Thermidor," a list designated by Barère.—Denunciation by Lecointre. (2d ed. p. 13.)

13. Thibaudeau, i., 47. "Just as in ordinary times one tries to elevate oneself, so does one strive in these times of calamity to lower oneself and be forgotten, or atone for one's inferiority by seeking to degrade oneself."

class. . . . Clothes, manners, refinement, cleanliness, the conveniences of life, civility and politeness were all renounced." People wear their clothes indecently and curse and swear; they try to resemble the *sans-culottes Montagnards* "who are profane and dress themselves like so many dock-loafers";[14] at Armonville, the carder, who presides (at a meeting) wears a woolen cap, and similarly at Cusset, a gauze-workman, who is always drunk. Only Robespierre can appear in neat attire; others, without his ascendency, "big-bellied" demi-suspects, the remains of the ancient régime, might become dangerous; they do well not to attract the attention of the foul-mouthed spy who cannot spell;[15] especially is it important at a meeting to be one of the crowd and remain unnoticed by the paid *claqueurs*, drunken swaggerers, and "fat petticoats" of the tribunes. It is even essential to shout in harmony with them and join in their bar-room dances. The deputations of the popular clubs come for fourteen months to the bar of the house and recite their commonplace or bombastic tirades, and the Convention is forced to applaud them. For nine months,[16] street ballad-singers and coffee-house ranters attend in full session and sing the rhymes of the day, while the

14. Madame Roland: "Mémoires," i., 23.

15. Archives Nationales, F⁷, 3,116⁷. This set of papers contains five hundred and thirty-seven police reports, especially those of Nivose, year II. The following is a sample Report of Nivose 25, year II. "Being on a deputation to the Convention, some *coleagues* took me to dine in the old Breteuil gardens, in a large room with a nice floor. . . . The bill-of-fare was called for, and I found that after having eaten a *ritz* soup, some meat, a bottle of wine, and two potatoes, I had spent, as they told me, eight francs twelve sous, because I am not rich. *'Foutre!'* I say to them, how much do the rich pay here? . . . It is well to state that I saw some deputies come into this large hall, also former marquises, counts, and knights of the poniard of the ancient régime . . . but I confess that I cannot remember the true names of these former nobles . . . for the devil himself could not recognise those b—— disguised like *sans-culottes*."

16. Buchez et Roux, xxviii., 237, 308. (July 5 and 14, 1793.)—*Moniteur*, xix., 716. (Ventose 26, year II.) Danton secures the passage of a decree "that nothing but prose shall be heard at the bar." Nevertheless, after his execution, this sort of parade begins again. On the 12th of Messidor, "a citizen admitted to the bar reads a poem composed by him in honor of the success of our arms on the Sambre." (*Moniteur*, xvi., 101.)

Convention is obliged to join in the chorus. For six weeks,[17] the profaners of churches come to the hall and display their dance-house buffooneries, and the Convention has not only to put up with these, but also to take part in them. Never, even in imperial Rome, under Nero and Heliogabalus, did a senate descend so low.

II

Observe one of their parades, that of Brumaire 20th, 22d, or 30th, which masquerade often occurs several times a week and is always the same, with scarcely any variation. Male and female wretches march in procession to the doors of the deputies' hall, still "drunk with the wine imbibed from chalices, after eating mackerel broiled in patens," besides refreshing themselves on the way. "Mounted astride of asses, covered with a chasuble and guided by a stole," they halt at each low smoking-den, holding a pyx in their hand; the bar-tender, with a mug in his hand, fills it, and, at each station, they toss off their bumpers, one after the other, in imitation of the Mass, and which they repeat in the street in their own fashion. On finishing this, they don copes, chasubles, and dalmatica, and, in two long lines, file before the benches of the Convention. Some of them bear on hand-barrows or in baskets, candelabra, chalices, gold and silver salvers, monstrances, and reliquaries; others hold aloft banners, crosses, and other ecclesiastical spoils. In the mean time "bands play the air of the *carmagnole* and 'Malbrook.' . . . On the entry of the dais, they strike up 'Ah! le bel oiseau' ";[18] all at once the masqueraders throw off their disguise, and, mitres, stoles, chasubles flung in the air, "disclose to view the defenders of the country in the national uniform." Peals of laughter, shouts and enthusiasm, while the instrumental din becomes louder! The procession, now in full blast,

17. *Moniteur,* xviii., 369, 397, 399, 420, 455, 469, 471, 479, 488, 492, 500, etc.—Mercier, "Le Nouveau Paris," ii., 96.—Dauban, "La Demagogie en 1793," 500, 505. (Articles by Prud'homme and Diurnal by Beaulieu.)

18. *Moniteur,* xviii., 420, 399.—"Ah, le bel oiseau," was a song chosen for its symbolic and double meaning, one pastoral and the other licentious.

demands the *carmagnole,* and the Convention consents; even some of the deputies descend from their benches and cut the pigeon-wing with the merry prostitutes. To wind up, the Convention decrees that it will attend that evening the fête of Reason and, in fact, they go in a body. Behind an actress in short petticoats wearing a red cap, representing Liberty or Reason, march the deputies, likewise in red caps, shouting and singing until they reach the new temple, which is built of planks and pasteboard in the choir of Notre Dame. They take their seats in the front rows, while the Goddess, and old frequenter of the suppers of the Duc de Soubise, along with "all the pretty dames of the Opera," display before them their operatic graces.[19] They sing the "Hymn to Liberty," and, since the Convention has that morning decreed that it must sing, I suppose that it also joined in.[20] After this there follows dancing; but, unfortunately, the authorities are wanting for stating whether the Convention danced or not. In any event, it is present at the dance, and thus consecrates an unique orgy, not Rubens's "Kermesse" in the open air, racy and healthy, but a nocturnal boulevard-jollification, a "Mardi-gras" composed of lean and haggard scape-graces. In the great nave of the Cathedral, "the dancers, almost naked, with bare necks and breasts, and stockings down at the heel," writhe and stamp, "howling the *carmagnole.*" In the side chapels, which are "shut off by high tapestries, prostitutes with shrill voices" pursue their avocation.[21] To descend to this low level so barefacedly, to fraternise with barrier sots, and wenches, to endure their embraces and hiccoughs, is bad enough, even for docile deputies. More than

19. De Goncourt, "La Société française pendant la Revolution," 418. (Article from "Père Duchesne.")—Dauban, *ibid.,* 506. (Article by Prud'homme.) "Liberty on a seat of verdure, receives the homage of republicans, male and female, . . . and then . . . *she turns and bestows a benevolent regard on her friends.*"

20. *Moniteur,* xviii., 399. Session of Brumaire 20, on motion of Thuriot: "I move that the Convention attends the temple of Reason to sing the hymn to Liberty."—"The motion of Thuriot is decreed."

21. Mercier, *ibid.,* 99. (Similar scenes in the churches of St. Eustache and St. Gervais.)

one half of them loathed it beforehand and remained at home; after this they do not feel disposed to attend the Convention.[22] But the "Mountain sends for them, and an officer brings them back"; it is necessary that they should coöperate through their presence and felicitations in the profanations and apostasies which ensue;[23] it is necessary that they should approve of and decree that which they hold in horror, not alone folly and nonsense, but crime, the murder of innocent people, and that of their friends. All this is done. "Unanimously, and with the loudest applause," the Left, united with the Right, sends Danton to the scaffold, its natural chieftain, the great promoter and leader of the Revolution.[24] "Unanimously, and with the loudest applause," the Right, united to the Left, votes the worse decrees of the revolutionary government.[25] "Unanimously," with approbatory and enthusiastic cheers, manifesting the warmest sympathy for Collot d'Herbois, Couthon, and Robespierre,[26] the Con-

22. Durand-Maillane, "Mémoires," 182.—Grégoire, "Mémoires," ii., 34. On the 7th of November, 1793, in the great scene of the abjurations, Grégoire alone resisted, declaring: "I remain a bishop; I invoke freedom of worship." "Outcries burst forth to stifle my voice the pitch of which I raised proportionately. . . . A demoniac scene occurred, worthy of Milton. . . . I declare that in making this speech I thought I was pronouncing sentence of death on myself." For several days, emissaries were sent to him, either deputies or bandits, to try and make him retract. On the 11th of November a placard posted throughout Paris declared him responsible for the continuance of fanaticism. "For about two years, I was almost the only one in Paris who wore the ecclesiastical costume."

23. Moniteur, xviii., 480. (Session of Brumaire 30.) N. . . . "I must make known the ceremony which took place here today. I move that the speeches and details of this day be inserted in full in the bulletin, and sent to all the departments." (Another deputy): "And do not neglect to state that the Right was never so well furnished." (Laughter and applause.)

24. Buchez et Roux, xxxii., 103. (Germinal 11.)—Moniteur, xx., 124. (Germinal 15.) Decree for cutting short the defence of Danton and his accused associates.

25. Moniteur, xx., 226. (Germinal 26. Report by Saint-Just and decree on the police.)—Ibid., xix., 54. (Report by Robespierre, and decree on the principles of revolutionary government, Nivose 5.)—Ibid., xx., 567, 589. Prairial 6 (Decree forbidding the imprisonment of any Englishman or Hanoverian), and xxi., 13. (Messidor 16.)

26. Moniteur, xx., 544. After the effort of Ladmiral against Collot d'Herbois, the latter appears in the tribune. "The loudest applause greets him from all

vention, through multiplied and spontaneous reelections, maintains
the homicidal government which the Plain detests, because it is homicidal, and which the Mountain detests, because it is decimated by
it. Plain and Mountain, by virtue of terror, majority after majority,
end in consenting to and bringing about their own suicide: on the
22nd of Prairial, the entire Convention has stretched out its neck;[27]
on the 8th of Thermidor, for a quarter of an hour after Robespierre's
speech,[28] it has again stretched this out, and would probably have
succumbed, had not five or six of them, whom Robespierre designated or named, Bourdon de l'Oise, Vadier, Cambon, Billaud, and
Panis, stimulated by the animal instinct of self-preservation, raised
their arms to ward off the knife. Nothing but imminent, personal,
mortal danger could, in these prostrated beings, supplant long-
continued fear with still greater fear. Later on, Siéyès, on being asked
how he acted in these times, replied, "I lived." In effect, he and
others are reduced to that; they succeeded in doing this, at all costs,
and at what a price![29] His private notes, still redolent of his daily
disgust, his most secret memoranda, confirm the statement;[30] on the

---

sides of the house."—*Ibid.*, xxi., 173. (Messidor 21.) On the report of Barère
who praises the conduct of Joseph Lebon, criticising nothing but "somewhat
harsh formalities," a decree is passed to the order of the day, which is "adopted
unanimously with great applause."

27. *Moniteur*, xx., 698, 715, 716, 719. (Prairial 22 and 24.) After the speeches
of Robespierre and Couthon, "Loud and renewed applause; the plaudits begin
over again and are prolonged." Couthon, having declared that the Committee
of Public Safety was ready to resign, "on all sides there were cries of No,
No."—*Ibid.*, xxi., 268. (Thermidor 2.) Eulogy of the revolutionary government
by Barère and decree of the police "unanimously adopted amidst the loudest
applause."

28. *Moniteur*, xxi., 329.

29. Lafayette, "Mémoires," iv., 330. "At last came the 9th of Thermidor. It
was not due to people of common sense. Their terror was so great that an
estimable deputy, to whom one of his colleagues put the question, no witness
being present, 'how long must we endure this tyranny?' was upset by it to such
a degree as to denounce him."

30. Sainte-Beuve, "Causeries du Lundi," v., 209. (Siéyès' unpublished papers.)—*Moniteur*, xviii., 631, containing an example of both the terror and style
of the most eminent men, among others of Fourcroy the celebrated chemist,
then deputy, and later, Counsellor of State and Minister of Public Instruction.

Committee of March 20, "Paillasse, half drunk, gives a dissertation on the way to carry on the war, and interrogates and censures the Minister; the poor Minister turns his questions with *café* gossip and a narrative of campaigns. These are the men placed at the head of the government to save the Republic!" "H——, in his distraction, had the air of a lucky dog inwardly smiling at his own knavish thoughts." "*Ruit irrevocabile vulgus. . . . Jusque datum sceleri.*" "You keep your mouth shut?" he is told: "Of what use is my glass of wine in this torrent of ardent spirits?" All this is very well, but he did not merely keep silent and abstain. He voted, legislated, and decreed, along with the unanimous Convention; he was a collaborator, not only passively, through his presence, but also through his active participation in the acts of the government which he elected and enthroned, reelected twelve times, cheered every week, and flattered daily, authorising and keeping on to the end its work of spoliation and massacre. "Everybody is guilty here," said Carrier in the Convention, "even to the president's bell." In vain do they constantly repeat to themselves that they were forced to obey under penalty of death: the conscience of the purest among them, if he has any, replies: "You too, in spite of yourself, I admit; less than others, if you please, but you were a terrorist, that is to say, a brigand and an assassin."[31]

He is accused in the Jacobin Club, Brumaire 18, year II., of not addressing the Convention often enough, to which he replies: "After twenty years' devotion to the practice of medicine I have succeeded in supporting my *sans-culotte* father and my *sans-culottes* sisters. . . . As to the charge made by a member that I have given most of my time to science. . . . I have attended the Lycée des Arts but three times, and then only for the purpose of *sans-culotteising* it."

31. Michelet, "Histoire de la Révolution," v., preface xxx (3rd ed.). "A young man and trying to find something to do, I was directed to an ultra Review, to a well-known philanthropist, devoted to education, to the people, and to the welfare of humanity. I found a very small man of a melancholy, mild and tame aspect. We were in front of the fire, on which he fixed his eyes without looking at me. He talked a long time, in a didactic, monotonous tone of voice. I felt ill at ease and sick at heart, and got away as soon as I could. It was this little man, I afterwards learned, who hunted down the Girondists, and had them guillo-

III

On a man becoming a slave, said old Homer, the Gods take away the half of his soul; the same is true of a man who becomes a tyrant. In the Pavillon de Flore, alongside of and above the enslaved Convention, sit the twelve kings it has enthroned, twice a day,[32] ruling over it as well as over France.[33] Of course, some guarantee is re-

---

tined, and which he accomplished at the age of twenty."—His name is Julien de la Drôme. I saw him once when quite young. He is well known: first, through his correspondence, and next, by his mother's diary. ("Journal d'une bourgeoise pendant la Revolution," ed. Locroy.)—We have a sketch of David ("La Demagogie à Paris en 1793," by Dauban, a fac-simile at the beginning of the volume), representing Queen Marie Antoinette led to execution. Madame Julien was at a window along with David looking at the funeral convoy, whilst he made the drawing.—Madame Julien writes in her "Journal," September 3, 1792: "To attain this end we must will the means. No barbarous humanity! The people are aroused, the people are avenging the crimes of the past three years."—Her son, a sort of raw, sentimental Puritan, fond of bloodshed, was one of Robespierre's most active agents. He remembered what he had done, as is evident by Michelet's narrative, and cast his eyes down, well knowing that his present philanthropy could not annihilate past acts.

32. Archives Nationales, AF. II., 46. Register of the Acts of the Committee of Public Safety, vol. ii., orders of August 3, 1793.

33. On the concentration and accumulation of business, cf. Archives Nationales, *ibid.*, acts of Aug. 4, 5, 6, 1793; and AF. II., 23, acts of Brumaire 1 and 15, year II.—On the distribution and despatch of business in the Committee and the hours devoted to it, see Acts of April 6, June 13, 17, 18, Aug. 3, 1793, and Germinal 27, year II.—After August 3, two sessions were held daily, from 8 o'clock in the morning to 1 o'clock in the afternoon, and from 7 to 10 o'clock in the evening; at 10 o'clock, the Executive Council met with the Committee of Public Safety, and papers were signed about 2 or 3 o'clock in the morning.— The files of AF. II., 23 to 42, contain an account of the doings of the Committee, the minutes of its meetings and of its correspondence. A perusal of these furnishes full details concerning the initiative and responsibility of the Committee. For example (Nivose 4, year II., letters to Fréron and Barras, at Marseilles), "The Committee commend the vigorous measures you have sanctioned in your orders at Marseilles. Marseilles, through you, affords a great example. Accustomed, as you are, to wielding thunderbolts, you are best calculated for still governing it. . . . How glorious, citizen colleagues, to be able like you, after long continued labors and immortal fame, how gratifying, under such auspices,

quired from those who fill this place; there is not one of them who is not a revolutionist of long standing, an impenitent regicide, a fanatic in essence and a despot through principle; but the fumes of omnipotence have not intoxicated them all to the same degree. Three or four of them, Robert Lindet, Jean Bon St. André, Prieur de la Côte d'Or and Carnot, confine themselves to useful and secondary duties; this suffices to keep them partially safe. As specialists, charged with an important service, their first object is to do this well, and hence they subordinate the rest to this, even theoretical exigencies and the outcries of the clubs. Lindet's prime object is to feed the departments that are without corn, and the towns that are soon to be short of bread; Prieur's business is to see that biscuits, brandy, clothes, shoes, gunpowder, and arms are manufactured;[34] Jean Bon, that vessels are equipped and crews drilled; Carnot, to draw up campaign plans and direct the march of armies: the despatch of so many bags of grain during the coming fortnight to this or that town, or warehouse in this or that district; the making up of so many weekly rations, to be transported during the month to certain places on the frontier; the transformation of so many fishermen into artillerymen or marines, and to set afloat so many vessels in three months; to expedite certain corps of cavalry, infantry, and artillery, so as to arrive by such and such roads at this or that pass—these

---

to return to the bosom of the National Convention!"—(AF. II., 36, Pluviose 7, year II., letter to the representatives on mission at Bordeaux, approving of the orders issued by them against merchants.) "Concealed behind the obscurity of its complots, mercantilism cannot support the ardent, invigorating atmosphere of Liberty; Sybaritic indolence quails before Spartan virtue."—(AF. II., 37, Pluviose 20, letter to Prieur de la Marne, sent to Nantes to replace Carrier.) "Carrier, perhaps, has been badly surrounded; . . . his ways are harsh, the means he employs are not well calculated to win respect for the national authority: . . . he is used up in that city. He is to leave and go elsewhere."—(AF. II., 36, Nivose 21, letter to Fouché, Laporte, and Albitte, at Commune-affranchie, signed by Billaud-Varennes and composed by him.) "The Convention, Nivose 1, has approved of the orders and other measures taken by you. We can add nothing to its approval. The Committee of Public Safety subjects all operations to the same principles, that is to say, it conforms to yours and acts with you."

34. Sainte-Beuve, "Nouveaux Lundis," viii., 105. (Unpublished report by Vice-admiral Villaret-Joyeuse, May 28, 1794.)

are precise combinations which purge the brain of dogmatic phrases, which force revolutionary jargon into the background and keep a man sensible and practical; and all the more because three of them, Jean Bon, former captain of a merchantman, Prieur and Carnot, engineer officers, are professional men and go to the front to put their shoulders to the wheel on the spot. Jean Bon, always visiting the coasts, goes on board a vessel of the fleet leaving Brest to save the great American convoy; Carnot, at Watignies, orders Jourdan to make a decisive move, and, shouldering his musket, marches along with the attacking column.[35] Naturally, they have no leisure for speechmaking in the Jacobin club, or for intrigues in the Convention: Carnot lives in his own office and in the committee-room; he does not allow himself time enough to eat with his wife, dines on a crust of bread and a glass of lemonade, and works sixteen and eighteen hours a day;[36] Lindet, more overtasked than any body else, because hunger will not wait, reads every report himself, and "passes days and nights at it";[37] Jean Bon, in wooden shoes and woolen vest, with a bit of coarse bread and a glass of bad beer,[38] writes and dictates until his strength fails him, and he has to lie down and sleep on a mattress on the floor. Naturally, again, when interfered with, and the tools in their hands are broken, they are dissatisfied; they know well the worth of a good instrument, and for the service, as they comprehend it, good tools are essential, competent, faithful employees, regular in attendance at their offices, and not at the club. When they have a subordinate of this kind they defend him, often at the risk of their lives, even to incurring the enmity of Robespierre. Cambon,[39] who, on his financial committee, is also a sort of sover-

35. Carnot, "Mémoires," i., 107.

36. *Ibid.*, i., 450, 523, 527, "we often ate only a morsel of dry bread on the Committee's table."

37. *Moniteur*, xxi., 362. (Speech by Cambon, Session of Thermidor 11, year II.)

38. Beugnot, "Mémoires," ii., 15. (Stated by Jean Bon himself in a conversation at Mayence in 1813.)

39. Gaudia, duc de Gaéte, "Mémoires," i., 16, 28. "I owed my life to Cambon personally, while, through his firmness, he preserved the whole Treasury department, continually attacked by the all-powerful Jacobin club."—On the

eign, retains at the Treasury five or six hundred employees unable to procure their certificate of civism, and whom the Jacobins incessantly denounce so as to get their places. Carnot saves and employs eminent engineers, D'Arcon, de Montalembert, d'Obenheim, all of them nobles, and one of them an anti-Jacobin, without counting a number of accused officers whom he justifies, replaces, or maintains.[40] Through these courageous and humane acts, they solace themselves for their scruples, at least partially and for the time being; moreover, they are statesmen only because the occasion and superior force makes it imperative, more led by others than leading, terrorists through accident and necessity, rather than through system and instinct. If, in concert with ten others, Prieur and Carnot order wholesale robbery and murder, if they sign orders by twenties and hundreds, amounting to assassinations, it is owing to their forming part of a body. When the whole committee deliberates, they are bound, in important decrees, to submit to the preponderating opinion of the majority, after voting in the negative. In relation to secondary decrees, in which there has been no preliminary discussion in common, the only responsible member is the one whose signature stands first; the following signatures affixed, without reading the document, are simply a "formality which the law requires," merely a *visa*, necessarily mechanical; with "four or five hundred business matters to attend to daily," it is impossible to do otherwise; to read over and

---

8th of Thermidor, Robespierre was "very severe on the administration of the Treasury, which he accused of an aristocratic and antirevolutionary spirit. . . . Under this pretext, it was known that the orator meant to propose an act of accusation against the representative charged with its surveillance, as well as against the six commissioners, and bring them before the revolutionary Tribunal, whose verdict could not be doubtful."—Buchez et Roux, xxxiii., 431, 436, 441. Speech by Robespierre, Thermidor 8, year II. . . . "Machiavellian designs against the small fund-holders of the State. . . . A contemptible financial system, wasteful, irritating, devouring, absolutely independent of your supreme oversight. . . . Antirevolution exists in the financial department. . . . Who are its head administrators? Brissotins, Feuillants, aristocrats, and well-known knaves—the Cambons, the Mallarmés, the Ramels!"

40. Carnot, "Mémoires," i., 425.

vote in every case, would be "a physical impossibility."[41] Finally, as things are, "is not the general will, at least the apparent general will, that alone on which the government can decide, itself ultrarevolutionary?"[42] In other words, should not the five or six rascals in a State who vociferate, be listened to, rather than a hundred honest folks who keep their mouths shut? With this sophism, gross as it is, but of pure Jacobin manufacture, Carnot ends by hoodwinking his honor and his conscience; otherwise intact, and far more so than his colleagues, he likewise undergoes moral and mental mutilation; constrained by the duties of his post and the illusions of his creed, he succeeded in an inward decapitation of the two noblest of human faculties, common-sense, the most useful, and the moral sense, the most exalted of all.

IV

If such are the ravages which are made in an upright, firm and healthy soul, what must be the havoc in corrupt or weak natures, in which bad instincts already predominate! And observe this, that they are without the protection afforded to Carnot and other occupied men, who are pursuing some specific and evidently useful object. They bear the title of "government men," "revolutionists" properly

41. *Moniteur,* xxiv., 47, 50. (Session of Germinal 2, year II.) Speeches by Lindet and Carnot with confirmatory details.—Lindet says that he had signed twenty thousand papers.—*Ibid.,* xxxiii., 591. (Session of Ventose 12, year III. Speech by Barère.) "The labor of the Committee was divided amongst the different members composing it, but all, without distinction, signed each other's work. I, myself, knowing nothing of military affairs, have perhaps, in this matter, given four thousand signatures."—*Ibid.,* xxiv., 74. (Session of Germinal 6, year III.) Speech of Lavesseur, witness of an animated scene between Carnot and Robespierre concerning two of Carnot's clerks, arrested by order of Robespierre.—Carnot adds "I had myself signed this order of arrest without knowing it."—*Ibid.,* xxii., 116. (Session of Vendémiaire 8, year II., speech by Carnot in narrating the arrest of General Huchet for his cruelties in Vendée.) On appearing before the Committee of Public Safety, Robespierre defended him and he was sent back to the army and promoted to a higher rank: I was obliged to sign in spite of my opposition."

42. Carnot, "Mémoires," i., 572. (Speech by Carnot, Germinal 2, year III.)

so-called, "folks who carry things with a high hand";[43] in effect, they direct all things according to their conception of unity. The creation, organisation, and application of Terror belongs wholly to them; they are the constructors, regulators, and engineers of the machine,[44] the recognised heads of the party, of the sect, and of the government, especially Billaud and Robespierre, who never serve on missions,[45] nor relax their hold for a moment on the central motor; the former, an active politician, with Collot for his second, is charged with urging on the constituted authorities, the districts, the municipalities, the national agents, the revolutionary committees, and the representatives on mission in the interior;[46] the latter, a theologian, moralist, titular doctor, and preacher, is charged with ruling the Convention and indoctrinating the Jacobins with sound principles; behind him stands Couthon, his lieutenant, with Saint-Just, his disciple and executor of works of great importance; in their midst, Barère, the Committee's mouthpiece, is merely a tool, but indispensable, conveniently at hand and always ready to start whatever drum-beating is required on any given theme in honor of the party which stuffs

43. Sénart, "Mémoires," 145, 153. (Details on the members of the two committees.)

44. Reports by Billaud on the organisation of the revolutionary government, November 18, 1793: and on the theory of democratic government, April 20, 1794.—Reports by Robespierre on the political situation of the Republic, November 17, 1793; and on the principles of revolutionary government, December 5, 1793.—Information on the genius of revolutionary laws, signed principally by Robespierre and Billaud, November 29, 1793.—Reports by Robespierre on the principles of political morality which ought to govern the Convention, February 5, 1794; and on the relationship between religious and moral ideas and republican principles, May 7, 1794.

45. Billaud no longer goes on mission after he becomes one of the Committee of Public Safety. Robespierre never went. Barère, who is of daily service, is likewise retained at Paris.—All the others serve on the missions and several repeatedly, and for a long time.

46. *Moniteur*, xxiv., 60. The words of Carnot, session of Germinal 2, year III.—*Ibid.*, xxii., 138, words of Collot, session of Vendémiaire 12, year III. "Billaud and myself have sent into the departments three hundred thousand written documents, and have made at least ten thousand minutes (of meetings) with our own hand."

his brain; below these comes the Committee of General Security, Vadier, Amar, Vouland, Guffroy, Panis, David, Jagot, and the rest, those who undertook, reported on, and acted in behalf of universal proscription. All these bear the imprint of their service; they could be recognised by "their pallid hue, hollow and bloodshot eyes,"[47] habits of omnipotence stamped "on their brows, and on their deportment, something indescribably haughty and disdainful. The Committee of General Security reminded one of the former lieutenants of police, and the Committee of Public Safety, of the former ministers of state." In the Convention, "it is considered an honor to talk with them, and a privilege to shake hands with them; one seems to read one's duty on their brows." On the days on which their orders are to be converted into laws "the members of the Committee and the reporter of the bill, keep people waiting, the same as the heads and representatives of the former sovereign power; on their way to the Assembly hall, they are preceded by a group of courtiers who seem to announce the masters of the world."[48] In fact, they reign—but observe on what conditions.

"Make no complaints," said Barère,[49] to the composer of an opera, the performance of which had just been suspended: "as times go, you must not attract public attention. Do we not all stand at the foot of the guillotine, *all, beginning with myself?*" Again, twenty years later, in a private conversation, on being interrogated as to the veritable object, the secret motive of the Committee of Public Safety, he replied: "As we were animated by but one sentiment,[50] my dear sir, that of self-preservation, we had but one desire, that of maintaining an existence which each of us believed to be menaced. You had your neighbor guillotined to prevent your neighbor from guillotining you."[51] The same apprehension exists in stouter souls,

---

47. Dussault, "Fragment pour servir à l'histoire de la Convention."
48. Thibaudeau, i., 49.
49. Arnault, "Souvenirs d'un Sexagénaire," ii., 78.
50. "Mémoires d'un Bourgeois de Paris," by Véron, ii., 14. (July 7, 1815.)
51. Cf. Thibaudeau, "Mémoires," i., 46. "It seemed, then, that to escape

although there may have been, along with fear, motives of a less debased order. "How many times," says Carnot,[52] "we undertook some work that required time, with the conviction that we should not be allowed to complete it!" "It was uncertain[53] whether, the next time the clock struck the hour, we should not be standing before the revolutionary Tribunal on our way to the scaffold without, perhaps, having had time to bid adieu to our families. . . . We pursued our daily task so as not to let the machine stand still, as if a long life were before us, when it was probable that we should not see the next day's sun." It is impossible to count on one's life, or that of another, for twenty-four hours; should the iron hand which holds one by the throat tighten its grasp, all will be over that evening. "There were certain days so difficult that one could see no way to control circumstances; those who were directly menaced resigned themselves wholly to chance."[54] "The decisions for which we are so much blamed," says another,[55] "were not generally thought of two days, or one day, beforehand; they sprung out of the crisis of the moment. We did not desire to kill for the sake of killing . . . but to *conquer at all hazards, remain masters, and ensure the sway of our principles.*" That is true, they are subjects as well as despots. At the Committee table, during their nocturnal sessions, their sovereign presides, a formidable figure, the revolutionary Idea which confers on them the right to slay, on condition of exercising it against everybody, and therefore on themselves. Towards two o'clock, or three o'clock in the morning, exhausted, out of words and ideas, not knowing where to slay, on the right or on the left, they anxiously turn to this figure and try to read its will in its fixed eyes. "Who

---

imprisonment, or the scaffold, there was no other way than to put others in your place."

52. Carnot, "Mémoires," i., 508.

53. Carnot, i., 527. (Words of Prieur de la Cote d'Or.)

54. Carnot, *ibid.*, 527. (The words of Prieur.)

55. "La Nouvelle Minerve," i., 355, (Notes by Billaud-Varennes, indited at St. Domingo and copied by Dr. Chervin.) "We came to a decision only after being wearied out by the nightly meetings of our Committee."

shall fall tomorrow?" Ever the same reply steadily expressed on the features of the impassable phantom: "the antirevolutionists," under which name is comprised all who by act, speech, thought, or inmost sentiment, either through irritation or carelessness, through humanity or moderation, through egoism or nonchalance, through passive, neutral, or indifferent feeling, serve well or ill the Revolution.[56] All that remains is to add names to this horribly comprehensive decree. Shall Billaud do it? Shall Robespierre do it? Will Billaud put down Robespierre's name, or Robespierre put down Billaud's, or each the name of the other, with those he chooses to select from among the two Committees? Osselin, Chabot, Bazire, Julien de Toulouse, Lacroix, Danton, were on them, and when they left, their heads fell.[57] Hérault-Séchelles, again, was on them, maintained in office with honor through the recent approbation of the Convention,[58] one of the titular twelve, and on duty when an order issued by the other eleven suddenly handed him over to the revolutionary Tribunal for execution. Whose turn is it now among the eleven? Seized unawares, the docile Convention unanimously applauding, after three days of a judicial farce, the cart will bear him to the Place de la Révolution; Samson will tie him fast, shouters at thirty sous a day will clap their

56. Decree of September 17, 1793, on "Suspects." Ordinance of the Paris Commune, October 10, 1793, extending it so as to include "those who, having done nothing against the Revolution, do nothing for it."—Cf. "Papers seized in Robespierre's apartments," ii., 370, letter of Payan. "Every man who has not been for the Revolution has been against it, for he has done nothing for the country. . . . In popular commissions, individual humanity, the moderation which assumes the veil of justice, is criminal."

57. Mortimer-Ternaux, viii., 394, and following pages; 414 and following pages (on the successive members of the two committees).

58. Wallon, "Histoire du Tribunal Révolutionaire," iii., 129–131. Hérault de Séchelles, allied with Danton, and accused of being indulgent, had just given guarantees, however, and applied the revolutionary régime in Alsace with a severity worthy of Billaud. (Archives des Affaires Étrangérès, vol. v., 141.) "Instructions for civil commissioners by Hérault, representative of the people" (Colmar, Frimaire 2, year II.), with suggestions as to the categories of persons that are to be "sought for, arrested, and immediately put in jail," probably embracing nineteen-twentieths of the inhabitants.

hands, and, on the following morning, the popular politicians will congratulate each other on seeing the name of a great traitor on the bulletin of the guillotined.[59] To this end, to enable this or that king of the day to pass from the national Almanac to the mortuary list, merely required an understanding among his colleagues, and, perhaps, this is already arrived at. Among whom and against whom? It is certain that, as this idea occurs to the eleven, seated around the table, they eye each other with a shudder; they calculate the chances and turn things over in their minds; words have been uttered that are not forgotten. Carnot often made this charge against Saint-Just: "You and Robespierre are after a dictatorship."[60] Robespierre replied to Carnot: "I am ready for you on the first defeat."[61] On another occasion, Robespierre, in a rage, exclaimed: "The Committee is conspiring against me!" and, turning to Billaud, "I know you, now!" Billaud retorted, "I know you too, you are an antirevolutionist!"[62]

---

59. Dauban, "Paris en 1794," 285, and following pages. (Police Reports, Germinal, year II.) Arrest of Hébert and associates "Nothing was talked about the whole morning but the atrocious crimes of the conspirators. They were regarded as a thousand times more criminal than Capet and his wife. They ought to be punished a thousand times over. . . . The popular hatred of Hébert is at its height. . . . The people cannot forgive Hébert for having deceived them. . . . Popular rejoicings were universal on seeing the conspirators led to the scaffold."

60. *Moniteur*, xxiv., 53. (Session of Germinal 2, year III.) Words of Prieur de la Côte d'Or: "The first quarrel that occurred in the Committee was between Saint-Just and Carnot; the latter says to the former, 'I see that you and Robespierre are after a dictatorship.' "—*Ibid.*, 74. Levasseur makes a similar statement.—*Ibid.*, 570. (Session of Germinal 2, year III., words of Carnot): "I had a right to call Robespierre a tyrant every time I spoke to him. I did the same with Saint-Just and Couthon."

61. Carnot, i., 525. (Testimony of Prieur.) *Ibid.*, 522. Saint-Just says to Carnot: "You are in league with the enemies of the patriots. It is well for you to know that a few lines from me could send you to the guillotine in two days."

62. Buchez et Roux, xxx., 185. (Reply of Billaud, Collot, Vadier, and Barère to the renewed charges against them by Lecointre.)—*Moniteur*, xxiv., 84. (Session of Germinal 7, year III.) Words of Barère: "On the 4th of Thermidor, in the Committee, Robespierre speaks like a man who had orders to give and victims to point out."—"And you, Barère," he replies, "remember the report you made on the 2nd of Thermidor."

There are conspirators and antirevolutionists, then, on the committee itself; what can be done to avoid this appellation, which is a sentence of death? Silently, the fatal phantom enthroned in their midst, the Erynnes through which they rule, renders his oracle and all take it to heart: "All who are unwilling to become executioners are conspirators and antirevolutionists."

V

Thus do they march along during twelve months, goaded on by the two sharp thongs of theory and fear, traversing the red pool which they have created, and which is daily becoming deeper and deeper, all together and united, neither of them daring to separate from the group, and each spattered with the blood thrown in his face by the others' feet. It is not long before their eyesight fails them; they no longer see their way, while the degradation of their language betrays the stupor of their intellect. When a government brings to the tribune and moves the enactment of important laws, it confronts the nation, faces Europe, and takes a historical position. If it cares for its own honor it will select reporters of bills that are not unworthy, and instruct them to support these with available arguments, as closely reasoned out as possible; the bill, discussed and adopted in full council, will show the measure of its capacity, the information it possesses and its common-sense. To estimate all this, read the bills put forth in the name of the Committee; weigh the preambles, remark the tone, listen to the two reporters usually chosen, Saint-Just, who draws up the acts of proscription, special or general, and Barère, who draws up all acts indifferently, but particularly military announcements and decrees against the foreigner; never did public personages, addressing France and posterity, use such irrational arguments and state falsehoods with greater impudence.[63]

63. Saint-Just, report on the Girondists, July 8, 1793; on the necessity of imprisoning persons inimical to the Revolution, Feb. 26, 1794; on the Hébertists, March 13; on the arrest of Hérault-Séchelles and Simond, March 17; on the arrest of Danton and associates, March 31; on a general policy, April 15.—Cf., likewise, his report on declaring the government revolutionary until peace is declared, Oct. 10, 1793, and his report of the 9th of Thermidor, year II.

The former, stiff in his starched cravat, posing "like the Holy Ghost," more didactic and more absolute than Robespierre himself, comes and proclaims to Frenchmen from the tribune, equality, probity, frugality, Spartan habits, and a rural cot with all the voluptuousness of virtue;[64] this suits admirably the chevalier Saint-Just, a former applicant for a place in the Count d'Artois' body-guard, a domestic thief, a purloiner of silver plate which he takes to Paris, sells and spends on prostitutes, imprisoned for six months on complaint of his own mother,[65] and author of a lewd poem which he succeeds in rendering filthy by trying to render it fanciful. Now, indeed, he is grave; he no longer leers; he kills—but with what arguments, and what a style![66] The young Laubardemont, the paid informers and prosecutors of imperial Rome, have less disgraced the human intellect, for these creatures of a Tiberius or a Richelieu still used plausible arguments in their reasoning, and with more or less adroitness. With Saint-Just, there is no connection of ideas; there is no sequence or march in his rhapsody; like an instrument strained to the utmost, his mind plays only false notes in violent fits and starts; logical continuity, the art then so common of regularly developing a theme, has disappeared; he stumbles over the ground, piling up telling aphorisms and dogmatic axioms. In dealing with facts there is nothing in his speech but a perversion of the truth; impostures abound in it of pure invention, palpable, as brazen as those of a charlatan in his booth;[67] he does not even deign to disguise

64. Buchez et Roux, xxxi., 346. (Report of March 13, 1794.)—xxxii., 314. (Report of April 15.)

65. See "The Revolution," ii., 313.

66. A single phrase often suffices to give the measure of a man's intellect and character. The following by Saint-Just has this merit. (Apropos of Louis XVI. who, refraining from defending himself, left the Tuileries and took refuge in the Assembly on the 10th of August.) "He came amongst you; he forced his way here. . . . He resorted to the bosom of the legislature; his soldiers burst into the asylum. . . . He made his way, so to say, by *sword thrusts into the bowels of his country* that he might find a place of concealment."

67. Particularly in the long report on Danton containing a historic survey of the factions (Buchez et Roux, xxxii., 76), and the report on the general police

them with a shadow of probability; as to the Girondists, and as to
Danton, Fabre d'Eglantine, and his other adversaries, whoever they
may be, old or new, any rope to hang them with suffices for him;
any rough, knotted, badly-twisted cord he can lay his hands on, no
matter what, provided it strangles, is good enough; there is no need
of a finer one for confirmed conspirators; with the gossip of the club
and an Inquisition catechism, he can frame his bill of indictment.
Accordingly, his intellect grasps nothing and yields him nothing; he
is a sententious and over-excited declaimer, an artificial spirit always
on the stretch, full of affectations,[68] his talent reducing itself down
to the rare flashes of a sombre imagination, a pupil of Robespierre,
as Robespierre himself is a pupil of Rousseau, the exaggerated
scholar of a plodding scholar, always rabidly ultra, furious through
calculation, deliberately violating both language and ideas,[69] confining himself to theatrical and funereal paradoxes, a sort of "grand
vizier"[70] with the airs of an exalted moralist and the bearing of the
sentimental shepherd.[71] Were one of a mocking humor one might

---

(*Ibid.*, 304), with another historic document of the same order. "Brissot and
Ronsin (were) recognised royalists. . . . Since Necker a system of famine has
been devised. . . . Necker had a hand in the Orleans faction. . . . Double rep-
resentation (of the Third Estate) was proposed for it." Among other charges
made against Danton; after the fusillade on the Champ de Mars in July, 1791:
"You went to pass happy days at Arcis-sur-Aube, if it is possible for a conspirator against his country to be happy. . . . When you knew that the tyrant's
fall was prepared and inevitable you returned to Paris on the 9th of August.
You wanted to go to bed on that evil night. . . . Hatred, you said, is insupportable to me and (yet) you said to us 'I do not like Marat,' etc." There is an
apostrophe of nine consecutive pages against Danton, who is absent.

68. Buchez et Roux, *Ibid.*, 312. "Liberty emanated from the bosom of tempests; its origin dates with that of the world issuing out of chaos along with
man, who is born dissolved in tears." (Applause.)—*Ibid.*, 308. Cf. his portrait,
got up for effect, of the "revolutionary man" who is "a treasure of good sense
and probity."

69. *Ibid.*, 312. "Liberty is not the chicanery of a palace; it is rigidity towards
evil."

70. Barère, "Mémoires," i. 347. "Saint-Just . . . discussed like a vizier."

71. Buchez et Roux, xxxii., 314. "Are the lessons furnished by history, the
examples afforded by all great men, lost to the universe? These all counsel us

shrug one's shoulders; but, in the present state of the Convention, there is no room for anything but fear. Launched in imperious tones, his phrases fall upon their ears in monotonous strokes, on bowed heads, and, after five or six blows from this leaden hammer, the stoutest are stretched out stupified on the ground; discussion is out of the question; when Saint-Just, in the name of the Convention, affirms anything, it must be believed; his dissertation is a peremptory injunction and not an effort of reason; it commands obedience; it is not open to examination; it is not a report which he draws from his coat pocket, but a bludgeon.

The other reporter, Barère, is of quite another stamp, a "patent-right" haranguer, an amusing Gascon, alert, "free and easy," fond of a joke, even on the Committee of Public Safety,[72] unconcerned in the midst of assassinations, and, to the very last, speaking of the Reign of Terror as "the simplest and most innocent thing in the world."[73] No man was ever less trammeled by a conscience; in truth, he has several, that of two days ago, that of the previous day, that of the present day, that of the morrow, of the following day, and still others, as many as you like, all equally pliant and supple, at the service of the strongest against the weakest, ready to swing round at once on the wind changing, but all joined together and working to one common end through physical instinct, the only one that lasts in the immoral, adroit and volatile being who circulates nimbly about, with no other aim than self-preservation, and to amuse him-

---

to lead obscure lives; the *lowly cot and virtue form the grandeurs of this world. Let us seek our habitations on the banks of streams, rock the cradles of our children* and educate them in Disinterestedness and Intrepidity."—As to his political or economic capacity and general ideas, read his speeches and his "Institutions" (Buchez et Roux, xxviii., 133; xxx., 305, xxxv., 369), a mass of chemical and abstract rant.

72. Carnot, i., 527. (Narrated by Prieur.) "Often when hurriedly eating a bit of dry bread at the Committee table, Barère with a jest, brought a smile on our lips."

73. Véron, ii., 14.—Arnault, ii., 74.—Cf., *passim*, "Mémoires de Barère," and the essay on Barère by Macaulay.

self.[74] In his dressing-gown, early in the morning, he receives a crowd of solicitors, and, with the ways of a "dandified minister," graciously accepts the petitions handed to him; first, those of ladies, "distributing gallantries among the prettiest"; he makes promises, and smiles, and then, returning to his cabinet, throws the papers in the fire: "There," he says, "my correspondence is done." He sups twice every decade in his fine house at Clichy, along with three more than accommodating pretty women; he is gay, awarding flatteries and attentions quite becoming to an amiable protector: he enters into their professional rivalries, their spites against the reigning beauty, their jealousy of another who wears a blonde perruque and pretends "to set the fashion." He sends immediately for the National Agent and gravely informs him that this head-dress, borrowed from the guillotined, is a rallying point for antirevolutionists, whereupon, the next day, perruques are denounced at the Commune-council, and suppressed; "Barère roared with laughter on alluding to this piece of fun." The humor of an undertaker and the dexterity of a commercial drummer: he plays with Terror. In like manner he plays with his reports, and at this latter exercise, he improvises; he is never embarrassed; it is simply necessary to turn the faucet and the water runs. "Had he any subject to treat, he would fasten himself on Robespierre, Hérault, Saint-Just, or somebody else, and draw them out; he would then rush off to the tribune and spin out their ideas; "they were all astonished at hearing their thoughts expressed as fully as if reflected in a mirror." No individual on the Committee, or in the Convention, equalled him in promptness and fluency, for the reason that he was not obliged to think before he spoke: with him, the faculty of speaking, like an independent organ, acted by itself, the empty brain or indifferent heart contributing nothing to his loquacity. Naturally, whatever issues from his

---

74. Vilate, Barère Edition, 184, 186, 244. "Fickle, frank, affectionate, fond of society, especially that of women, in quest of luxuries and knowing how to spend money."—Carnot, ii., 511. In Prieur's eyes, Barère was simply "a good fellow."

mouth comes forth in ready-made bombast, the current jargon of the Jacobin club, sonorous, nauseous commonplace, schoolboy metaphors and similes derived from the shambles.[75] Not an idea is found in all this rhetoric, nothing acquired, no real mental application. When Bonaparte, who employed everybody, and even Fouché, were disposed to employ Barère, they could make nothing out of him for lack of substance, except as a low newsmonger, common spy, or agent engaged to stir up surviving Jacobins; later on, a listener at keyholes, and a paid weekly collector of public rumors, he was not even fit for this vile service, for his wages were soon stopped; Napoleon, who had no time to waste, cut short his drivelling verbiage. It is this verbiage which, authorised by the Committee of Public Safety, now forms the eloquence of France; it is this manufacturer of phrases by the dozen, this future sneak and prison-spy under the empire, this frolicking inventor of the blonde-perruque conspiracy, that the government sends into the tribune to announce victories, trumpet forth military heroism and proclaim war unto death. On the 7th of Prairial,[76] Barère, in the name of the committee, proposes a return to savage law: "No English or Hanoverian prisoner shall henceforth be made"; the decree is endorsed by Carnot and passes the Convention unanimously. Had it been executed, as reprisals, and according to the proportion of prisoners, there would have been for one Englishman shot, three Frenchmen hung: honor and humanity

75. *Moniteur,* xxi., 173. (Justification of Joseph Lebon and "his somewhat harsh ways.") "The Revolution is to be spoken of with respect, and revolutionary measures with due regard. Liberty is a virgin, to raise whose veil is a crime."—And again: "The tree of Liberty grows when watered with the blood of tyrants."

76. *Moniteur,* xx., 580, 582, 583, 587.—"Campagnes de la Revolution Française dans les Pyrénées Orientals," by Fervel, ii., 36 and following pages.—General Dugommier, after the capture of Toulouse, spared the English general O'Harra, taken prisoner in spite of the orders of the Convention, and received the following letter from the Committee of Public Safety. "The Committee accepts your victory and your wound as compensations." On the 24th of December, Dugommier, that he may not be present at the Toulon massacres, asks to return to the Convention and is ordered off to the army of the eastern Pyrenees.—In 1797, there were thirty thousand French prisoners in England.

disappeared from the camps; the hostilities maintained by Christians became as exterminating as among negroes. Happily, French soldiers felt the nobleness of their profession; on the order being given to shoot the prisoners, a brave sergeant replied: "We will not shoot— send them to the Convention. If the representatives delight in killing prisoners—let them do it themselves, and eat them, too, savages as they are!" The sergeant, a rough sort of fellow, is not on a level with the Committee, or with Barère; and yet Barère did his best in a bill of indictment of twenty-seven pages, full of grand flourishes, every possible ritornello, glaring falsehood and silly inflation, explaining how "the britannic leopard" paid assassins to murder the representatives; how the London cabinet had armed little Cécile Renault "the new Corday," against Robespierre; how the Englishman, naturally barbarous, "does not give the lie to his origin"; how he descends from the Carthaginians and Phenicians, and formerly dealt in the skins of wild beasts and slaves; how his trading occupation is not changed; how Caesar, formerly, on landing in the country, found nothing but a ferocious tribe battling with wolves in the forest and threatening to burn every building which tried to encroach; and how it still is the same." A consultation with a strolling operator who uses big words to recommend a deep amputation, a clumsy show-prospectus that does not deceive a poor sergeant, such is the exposition of motives by a government for the purpose of enforcing a decree that might have been drawn up by redskins; to horrible acts he adds debased language, and employs the inept to justify atrocities.

VI

About one hundred representatives sent by the Committee of Public Safety, sometimes singly and, again, in groups of two or three, go and succeed each other in the provinces, "with unlimited power," to establish, enforce, or aggravate the revolutionary government, their proclamations at once declaring the nature of this government.[77]

77. *Moniteur*, xviii., 291. (Speech by Barère, session of Brumaire 8, year II.) At this rate, there are one hundred and forty deputies on mission to the armies

"Brave and vigorous *sansculottes!*" writes a deputy on leaving a mission and announcing his successor,[78] "You seem to have desired a good b—— of a representative, who has never swerved from his principles, that is to say, a regular *Montagnard*. I have fulfilled your wishes, and you will have the same thing in citizen Ingrand. Remember, brave *sans-culottes*, that, with the patriot Ingrand, you can do everything, get anything, cancel whatever you please, imprison, bring to trial, transport and guillotine everybody and regenerate society. Don't f—— him a minute's patience! Let everybody tremble through him; let everything crumble, and order be at once restored!" The representative arrives at headquarters by post, and presents his credentials. All the authorities at once bow to the ground. In the evening, in his sabre and plume, he harangues the popular club, blowing into a flame the smouldering embers of Jacobinism. Then, according to his personal acquaintances, if he has any in the place, or according to the votes of the Committee of General Security, if he is a new-comer, he selects five or six of the "warmest *sans-culottes*" there, and, forming them into a revolutionary committee, installs them permanently at his side, sometimes in the same building, in a room next to his own, where, on lists or with verbal com-

---

and in the departments.—Before the institution of the Committee of Public Safety (April 7, 1793), there were one hundred and sixty representatives in the departments, sent there to hasten the levy of two hundred thousand men. (*Moniteur*, xvii., 99, speech by Cambon, July 11, 1793.)—The Committee gradually recalled most of these representatives and, on the 16th July, only sixty-three were on mission.—(*Ibid.*, xvii., 152, speech by Gossuin, July 16.)—On the 9th of Nivose, the Committee designated fifty-eight representatives for settling up the revolutionary government in certain places and fixing the limits of their jurisdictions. (Archives Nationales, AF., II., 22.) Subsequently, several were recalled, and replaced by others.—The letters and orders of the representatives on mission are classed in the National Archives according to departments, in two series, one of which comprises missions previous to Thermidor 9, and the other missions after that date.

78. Thibaudeau, "Histoire du Terrorisme dans le department de la Vienne," p. 4. "Paris, Brumaire 15, the *sans-culotte* Piorry, representative of the people to the *sans-culottes* composing the popular club of Poitiers."

munications furnished to him, he works with a will and without stopping.[79]

First comes a purification of all the local authorities. They must always remember that "there can be no exaggeration in behalf of the people; he who is not imbued with this principle, who has not put it in practice, cannot remain on an advanced post;"[80] consequently, at the popular club, in the department, in the district, in the municipality, all doubtful men are excluded, discharged, or incarcerated; if a few weak ones are retained provisionally, or by favor, they are berated and taught their duty very summarily: "They will strive, by a more energetic and assiduous patriotism, to atone for the evil committed by them in not doing all the good they could do." Sometimes, through a sudden change of scene, the entire administrative staff is kicked out so as to give place to a no less complete staff, which the same kick brings up out of the ground. Considering that "everything drags in Vaucluse, and that a frightful *moderantisme* paralyses the most revolutionary measures," Maignet, in one order[81] appoints the administrators and secretary of the de-

---

79. Archives Nationales, AF., II., 116. (Letter of Laplanche, Orleans, September 10, 1793.—"Also *procès-verbaux* of the Orleans sections, September 7.) "I organised them, after selecting them from the popular club, into a revolutionary Committee. They worked under my own eye, their bureau being in an adjoining chamber. . . . I required sure, local information, which I could not have had without collaborators of the country. . . . The result is that I have arrested this night more than sixty aristocrats, strangers or 'suspects.'"—De Martel, "Études sur Fouché," 84. Letter of Chaumette, who posted Fouché concerning the Nevers Jacobins. "Surrounded by royalists, federalists, and fanatics, representative Fouché had only 3 or 4 persecuted patriots to advise him."

80. Archives Nationales, AF., II., 88. Speech by Rousselin, Frimaire 9.—*Ibid.*, F⁷, 4,421. Speech and orders issued by Rousselin, Brumaire 25.—Cf. Albert Babeau, "Histoire de Troyes pendant la Revolution," vol. ii. Missions of Garnier de Rousselin and Bô.

81. Archives Nationales, AF., II., 145. (Order of Maignet, Avignon, Floréal 13, year II., and proclamation of Floréal 14.)—*Ibid.*, AF., II., 111, Grenoble. Prairial 8, year II. Similar orders issued by Albitte and Laporte, for renewing all the authorities of Grenoble.—*Ibid.*, AF., II., 135. Similar order of Ricord at Grasse, Pluviose 28, and throughout the Var.—*Ibid.*, AF., II., 36. Brumaire, year II., circular of the Committee of Public Safety to the representatives on

partment, the national agent, the administrators and council-general
of the district, the administrators, council-general and national agent
of Avignon, the president, public prosecutor and recorder of the
criminal court, members of the Tribunal de Commerce, the collector
of the district, the post-master, and the head of the squadron of
gendarmerie. And the new functionaries will certainly go to work
at once, each in his office. The summary process, which has
brusquely swept away the first set of puppets, is going to brusquely
install the second one. "Each citizen appointed to any of the above
mentioned offices, shall betake himself immediately to his post, *under
penalty of being declared suspect,*" on the simple notification of his
appointment. Universal and passive obedience of governors, as well
as of the governed! There are no more elected and independent
functionaries; all the authorities, confirmed or created by the representative, are in his hands; there is not one among them who does
not subsist or survive solely through his favor; there is not one of
them who acts otherwise than according to his approval or by his
order. Directly, or through them, he makes requisitions, sequestrates,
or confiscates as he sees fit, taxes, imprisons, transports, or decapitates as he sees fit, and, in his circumscription, he is the pacha.

But he is a pacha with a chain around his neck, and at short
tether. From and after December, 1793, he is directed "to conform
to the orders of the Committee of Public Safety and report to it
every ten days."[82] The circumscription in which he commands is
rigorously "limited"; "he is reputed to be without power in the other
departments,"[83] while he is not suffered to grow old on his post. "In
every magistrature the grandeur and extent of power is compensated
by the shortness of its duration. Overprolonged missions would soon
be considered as birthrights."[84] Therefore, at the end of two or three

mission in the departments: "Before quitting your post, you are to effect the most
complete purification of the constituted authorities and public functionaries."

82. Decrees of Frimaire 6 and 14, year II.

83. Archives Nationales, AF., II., 22. Acts of the Committee of Public
Safety, Nivose 9, year II.

84. *Ibid.,* AF., II., 37. Letter to the Committee on the War, signed by Barère
and Billaud-Varennes, Pluviose 23, year II.

months, often at the end of a month, the incumbent is recalled to Paris or despatched elsewhere, at short notice, on the day named, in a prompt, absolute, and sometimes threatening tone, not as a colleague one humors, but as a subordinate who is suddenly and arbitrarily revoked or displaced because he is deemed inadequate, or "used up." For greater security, oftentimes a member of the Committee, Couthon, Collot, Saint-Just, or some near relation of a member of the Committee, a Lebas or young Robespierre, goes personally to the spot to give the needed impulsion; sometimes, agents simply of the Committee, taken from outside the Convention, and without any personal standing, quite young men, Rousselin, Julien de la Drôme, replace or watch the representative with powers equal to his. At the same time, from the top and from the centre, he is pushed on and directed: his local counsellors are chosen for him, and the directors of his conscience;[85] they rate him soundly on the choice of his agents or of his lodgings;[86] they force dismissals on

85. *Ibid.*, AF., II., 36. Letter of the Committee of Public Safety to Lecarpentier, on mission in l'Orne, Brumaire 19, year II. "The administrative bodies of Alençon, the district excepted, are wholly gangrened; all are Feuillants, or infected with a no less pernicious spirit. . . . For the choice of subjects, and the incarceration of individuals, you can refer to the *sans-culottes:* the most nervous are Symaroli and Préval.—At Montagne, the administration must be wholly removed, as well as the collector of the district, and the post-master; . . . purify the popular club, expel nobles and limbs of the law, those that have been turned out of office, priests, *muscadins,* etc. . . . Dissolve two companies, one the grenadiers and the other the infantry who are very *muscadin* and too fond of processions. . . . Reform the staff and officers of the National Guard. To secure more prompt and surer execution of these measures of security you may refer to the present municipality, the Committee of Surveillance and the Cannoneers."

86. *Ibid.*, AF., II., 37. To Ricord, on mission at Marseilles, Pluviose 7, year II. He is rudely lectured: he softens, he went and lodged with N. Même, a suspect; he is too favorable to the Marseilles people who, during the siege "made sacrifices to procure subsistances"; he blamed their arrest, etc.—Floréal 13, year II., to Bouret on mission in the Manche and at Calvados. "The Committee are under the impression that you are constantly deceived by an insidious secretary who, by the bad information he has given you, has often led you to give favorable terms to the aristocracy, etc."—Ventose 6, year II., to Guimberteau, on mission near the army on the coasts of Cherbourg: "The Committee is astonished to find that the military commission established by you, undoubtedly

him, appointments, arrests, executions; they spur him on in the path of terror and suffering. Around him are paid emissaries,[87] while others watch him gratis and constantly write to the Committees of Public Safety and General Security, often to denounce him, always to report on his conduct, to judge his measures and to provoke the measures which he does not take.[88]

Whatever he may have done or may do, he cannot turn his eyes toward Paris without seeing danger ahead, a mortal danger which, on the Committee, in the Convention, at the Jacobin Club, increases or will increase against him, like a tempest. Briez, who, in Valenciennes under siege, showed courage, and whom the Convention had just applauded and added to the Committee of Public Safety, hears himself reproached for being still alive: "He who was at Valenciennes when the enemy took it will never reply to this question— are you dead?"[89] He has nothing to do now but to declare himself incompetent, decline the honor mistakenly conferred on him by the Convention, and disappear. Dubois-Crancé took Lyons, and, as pay for this immense service, he is stricken off the roll of the Jacobin Club; because he did not take it quick enough, he is accused of treachery; two days after the capitulation, the Committee of Public Safety withdraw his powers; three days after the capitulation, the

---

for striking off the heads of conspirators, was the first to let them off. Are you not acquainted with the men who compose it? For what have you chosen them? If you do not know them, how does it happen that you have summoned them for such duties?"—*Ibid.*, and Ventose 23, order to Guimberteau to investigate the conduct of his secretary.

87. See especially in the "Archives des Affaires Étrangéres," vols. 324 to 334, the correspondence of secret agents sent into the interior.

88. Archives Nationales, AF., II., 37, to Fromcastel on mission in Indre-et-Loire, Floréal 13, year II. "The Committee sends you a letter from the people's club of Chinon, demanding the purging and organisation of all the constituted authorities of this district. The Committee requests you to proceed at once to carry out this important measure."

89. Words of Robespierre, session of the Convention September 24, 1793.— On another representative, Merlin de Thionville, who likewise stood fire, Robespierre wrote as follows: "Merlin de Thionville, famous for surrendering Mayence, and more than suspected of having received his reward."

Committee of Public Safety has him arrested and sent to Paris under escort.[90] If such men after such services are thus treated, what is to become of the others? After the mission of young Julien, Carrier at Nantes, Ysabeau and Tallien at Bordeaux, feel their heads shake on their shoulders; after the mission of young Robespierre in the East and South, Barras, Fréron and Bernard de Saintes believe themselves lost.[91] Fouché, Rovère, Javogue, and how many others, compromised by the faction of which they are, or were, Hébertists or Dantonists, are sure of perishing if their patrons of the Committee succumb; not sure of living if their patrons keep their place; not knowing whether their heads will not be exchanged for others; restricted to the narrowest, the most rigorous and most constant orthodoxy; guilty and condemned should their orthodoxy of today become the heterodoxy of tomorrow; all of them menaced, at first the hundred and eighty autocrats who, before the concentration of the revolutionary government, ruled for eight months uncontrollable in the provinces; next, and above all, the fifty hard-fisted *Montagnards*, unscrupulous fanatics or dissipated despots, who, at this moment, tread human flesh under foot and allot themselves power, the same as wild boars in a forest, or wallow in scandal, like swine in a mud-pool.

There is no refuge for them, other than temporary, and not temporary refuge, otherwise than in zealous and tried obedience, such as the Committee demands proof of, that is to say, through rigor. "The Committees so wanted it," says Maignet, later on, the incendiary of Bédouin; "The Committees did every thing. . . . Circumstances controlled me. . . . The patriotic agents conjured me not to give way. . . . I did not fully carry out the most imperative orders."[92]

90. Guillon, ii., 207.—"Fouché," by M. de Martel, 292.

91. Hamel, iii., 395, and following pages.—Buchez et Roux, xxx., 435. (Session of the Jacobin Club, Nivose 12, year II. Speech of Collot d'Herbois.) "Today I no longer recognise public opinion; had I reached Paris three days later, I should probably have been indicted."

92. Marcelin Boudet, "Les Conventionnels d'Auvergne," 438. (Unpublished memoir of Maignet.)

Similarly, the great exterminator of Nantes, Carrier, when urged to spare the rebels who surrendered of their own accord: "Do you want me to be guillotined? It is not in my power to save those people."[93] And another time: "I have my orders; I must observe them; I do not want to have my head cut off!" Under penalty of death, the representative on mission is a Terrorist, like his colleagues in the Convention and on the Committee of Public Safety, but with a much more serious disturbance of his nervous and his moral system; for he does not operate like them on paper, at a distance, against categories of abstract, anonymous, and vague beings; his work is not merely an effort of the intellect, but also of the senses and the imagination. If he belongs to the region, like Lecarpentier, Barras, Lebon, Javogue, Couthon, André, Dumont, and many others, he is well acquainted with the families he proscribes; names to him are not merely so many letters strung together, but they recall personal souvenirs and evoke living forms. At all events, he is the spectator, artisan and beneficiary of his own dictatorship; the silver-plate and money he confiscates passes under his eye, through his hands; he sees the "suspects" he incarcerates march before him; he is in the court-room on the rendering of the sentence of death; frequently, the guillotine he has supplied with heads works under his windows; he sleeps in the mansion of an *emigré;* he makes requisitions for the furniture, linen, and wine belonging to the decapitated and the imprisoned,[94] lies in their beds, drinks their wine and revels with plenty

---

93. Buchez et Roux, xxxiv., 165, 191. (Evidence of witnesses on the trial of Carrier.)—Paris, ii., 113, "Histoire de Joseph Lebon." "The prisons," says Le Bon, "overflowed at St. Pol. I was there and released two hundred persons. Well, in spite of my orders, several were put back by the Committee of Surveillance, authorised by Lebas, a friend of Darthé. What could I do against Darthé supported by Saint-Just and Lebas? *He would have denounced me.*"— *Ibid.,* 128, apropos of a certain Lefèvre, "veteran of the Revolution," arrested and brought before the revolutionary Tribunal by order of Lebon. "It was necessary to take the choice of condemning him, or of being denounced and persecuted myself, without saving him."—Beaulieu, "Essai," v., 233. "*I am afraid and I cause fear* was the principle of all the revolutionary atrocities."

94. Ludovic Sciout, "Histoire de la Constitution civile du Clergé," iv., 136.

of company at their expense, and in their place. In like manner, a bandit chief who neither kills nor robs with his own hands, has murder and robbery committed in his presence, by which he substantially profits, not by proxy, but personally, through the well-directed blows ordered by him. To this degree, and in such proximity to physical action, omnipotence is a mephitic atmosphere which no state of health can resist. Restored to the conditions which poisoned man in barbarous times or countries, he is again attacked by moral maladies from which he was thenceforth believed to be exempt; he retrogrades even to the strange corruptions of the Orient and the Middle Ages; forgotten leprosies, apparently extinct, with exotic pestilences to which civilised lands seemed closed, reappear in his soul with their issues and tumors.

VII

"It seems," says a witness who was long acquainted with Maignet, "that all he did for these five or six years was simply the delirious phase of an illness, after which he recovered, and lived on as if nothing had happened."[95] And Maignet himself writes: "I was not made for these tempests." That is true of all, and first of the coarser

---

(Orders of Pinét and Cavaignac, Pluviose 22, and Ventose 2.)—*Moniteur,* xxiv., 469. (Session of Prairial 30, year III., denunciation of representative Laplanche at the bar of the house, by Boismartin.) On the 24th of Brumaire, year II., Laplanche and General Seepher installed themselves at St. Lô in the house of an old man of seventy, a M. Lemonnier then under arrest. "Scarcely had they entered the house when they demanded provisions of every kind, linen, clothes, furniture, jewelry, plate, vehicles and title-deeds—all disappeared." Whilst the inhabitants of St. Lô were living on a few ounces of brown bread, "the best bread, the choicest wines, pillaged in the house of Lemonnier, were lavishly given in pans and kettles to General Seepher's horses, also to those of representative Laplanche." Lemonnier, set at liberty, could not return to his emptied dwelling then transformed into a storehouse. He lived at the inn, stripped of all his possessions, valued at sixty thousand livres, having saved from his effects only one silver table-service, which he had taken with him into prison.

95. Marcelin Boudet, 446. (Notes of M. Ignace de Barante.) Also 440. (Unpublished memoir of Maignet).

natures; subordination would have restrained them; a dictatorship brings them out; the brutal instinct of the old soldier or of the faun breaks out in an eruption. Contemplate a Duquesnoy, a sort of bull-dog, always barking and biting when satiated more furiously than ever. Delegate to the army of the Moselle, and passing by Metz[96] he summoned before him Altmayer, the public prosecutor, although he had sat down to dinner. The latter waits three hours and a half in the ante-chamber, is not admitted, returns, and, at length received, is greeted with a thundering exclamation: "Who are you?" "The public prosecutor," he replies. "You look like a bishop—you were once a *curé* or monk—you can't be a revolutionist. . . . I have come to Metz with unlimited powers. Public opinion here is not satisfactory. I am going to drill it. I am going to set folks straight here. I mean to shoot, here in Metz, as well as in Nancy, five or six hundred every fortnight." The same at the house of General Bessières, commandant of the town; encountering there M. Cledat, an old officer, the second in command, he measures him from head to foot: "You look like a *muscadin*. Where did you come from? You must be a bad republican—you look as if you belonged to the ancient régime." "My hair is gray," he responds, "but I am not the less a good

96. Archives Nationales, AF., II., 59. Extract from the minutes of the meetings of the People's Club of Metz, and depositions made before the Committee of Surveillance of the Club, Floréal 12, year II., on the conduct of representative Duquesnoy, arrived at Metz the evening before at six o'clock.—There are thirty-two depositions, and among others those of M. Altmayer, Joly, and Clédat. One of the witnesses states: "As to these matters, I regarded this citizen (Duquesnoy) as tipsy or drunk, or as a man beside himself."—This is customary with Duquesnoy.—Cf. Paris, "His. de Joseph Lebon," i., 273, 370.—"Archives des Affaires Étrangérès," vol. 329. Letter of Gadolle, September II, 1793. "I saw Duquesnoy, the deputy, dead drunk at Bergues, on Whit-Monday, at 11 o'clock in the evening."—"Un Séjour en France, 1792 to 1796, p. 136. "His naturally savage temper is excited to madness by the abuse of strong drink. General de —— assures us that he saw him seize the mayor of Avesnes, a respectable old man, by the hair on his presenting him with a petition relating to the town, and throw him down with the air of a cannibal." "He and his brother were dealers in hops at retail, at Saint Pol. He made this brother a general."

republican: you may ask the General and the whole town." "Be off! Go to the devil, and be quick about it, or I will have you arrested!" The same, in the street, where he lays hold of a man passing, on account of his looks; the justice of the peace, Joly, certifies to the civism of this person, and he "eyes" Joly: "You too, you are an aristocrat! I see it in your eyes! I never make a mistake." Whereupon, tearing off the Judge's badge, he sends him to prison. Meanwhile, a fire, soon extinguished, breaks out in the army bakehouse; officers, townspeople, laborers, peasants, and even children form a line (for passing water) and Duquesnoy appears to urge them on in his way: using his fists and his foot, he falls on whoever he meets, on an employee in the commissariat, on a convalescent officer, on two men in the line, and many others. He shouts to one of them, "You are a *muscadin!*" To another: "I see by your eyes that you are an aristocrat!" To another: "You are f—— beggar, an aristocrat, a rascal," and he strikes him in the stomach; he seizes a fourth by his collar and throws him down on the pavement.[97] In addition to this, all are imprisoned. The fire being extinguished, an indiscreet fellow, who stood by looking on, "recommends" the dispenser of blows "to wipe his forehead." "You can't see straight—who are you? Answer me, I am the representative." The other replies mildly: "Representative, nothing could be more respectable." Duquesnoy gives the unlucky courtier a blow under the nose: "You are disputing—go to prison," "which I did at once," adds the docile subject. That same evening, "whereas, in the conflagration, none of the inhabitants in good circumstances offered their services in extinguishing the fire,[98] and none

---

97. Alexandrine des Echerolles, "Une famille noble sous la Terreur," 209. At Lyons, Marin, the commissioner, "a tall, powerful, robust man with stentorian lungs," opens his court with a volley of "republican oaths." . . . The crowd of solicitors melts away. One lady alone dared present her petition. "Who are you?" She gives her name. "What! You have the audacity to mention a traitor's name in this place?" Get away! and, giving her a push, he put her outside the door with a kick.

98. *Ibid.* A mass of evidence proves, on the contrary, that people of every class gave their assistance, owing to which the fire was almost immediately extinguished.

but *sans-culottes* came thereto, from the garrison as well as from the commune," Duquesnoy orders "that a tax of forty thousand livres be imposed on the commune of Metz, levied on the fortunes of the rich and distributed among the poor, payable within the decade."[99] "*Fais moi f . . . dedans tous ces b . . . là,*"[100] "*quatre j . . . f . . . à raccourcir;*"[101] at Arras, as at Metz, the lout is ever the ruffian and the butcher.

Others are either jolly fellows, or blackguards. A certain André Dumont, an old village attorney, now king of Picardie, or sultan, as occasion offers, "figures as a white negro," sometimes jovial, but generally as a rude hardened cynic, treating female prisoners and petitioners as in a *kermesse*.[102] One morning a lady enters his ante-room, and waits amidst about twenty *sans-culottes*, to solicit the release of her husband. Dumont appears in a morning-gown, seats himself and listens to the petitioner. "Sit down, *citoyenne*." He takes her on his lap, thrusts his hand in her bosom and exclaims: "Who would suppose that the bust of a marchioness would feel so soft to

99. *Ibid.* The popular club unanimously attests these facts, and despatches six delegates to enter a protest at the Convention. Up to the 9th of Thermidor, no relief is granted, while the tax imposed by Duquesnoy is collected. On the 5th Fructidor, year II., the order of Duquesnoy is cancelled by the Committee of Public Safety, but the money is not paid back.

100. Paris, i., 370. (Words of Duquesnoy to Lebon.)

101. Carnot, "Mémoires," i., 414. (Letter of Duquesnoy to the central bureau of representatives at Arras.)

The import of these untranslatable profanities being sufficiently clear I let them stand as in the original.—TR.

102. "Un Séjour en France," 158, 171.—Manuscript journal of Mallet-Dupan (January, 1795).—Cf. his letters to the Convention, the jokes of jailors and *sbirri*, for instance.—(*Moniteur*, xviii., 214, Brumaire 1, year II.)—Lacretelle, "Dix Années d' Epreuves," 178. "He ordered that everybody should dance in his fief of Picardy. They danced even in prison. Whoever did not dance was "suspect." He insisted on a rigid observance of the fêtes in honor of Reason, and that everybody should visit the temple of the Goddess each decadi, which was the cathedral (at Noyon). Ladies, *bourgeoises*, seamstresses, and cooks, were required to form what was called the chain of Equality. We dragoons were forced to be performers in this strange ballet."

one of the people's representatives." The *sans-culottes* shout with laughter. He sends the poor woman away and keeps her husband locked up. In the evening he may write to the Convention that he investigates things himself, and closely examines aristocrats. To maintain this revolutionary strain at this point requires a drop too much in one's head, and most of them take precautions in this direction. At Lyons,[103] "the representatives sent to ensure the people's welfare, Albitte and Collot," call upon the Committee of Sequestrations to deliver at their house two hundred bottles of the best wine to be found, and five hundred bottles more of Bordeaux red wine, first quality, for table use." In three months, at the table of the representatives who devastate la Vendée, nineteen hundred and seventy-four bottles of wine are emptied,[104] taken from the houses of the *emigrés* belonging to the town; for, "when one has helped to preserve a commune one has a right to drink to the Republic." Representative Bourbotte presides at this bar; Rossignol touches his glass, an ex-jeweler and then a September *massacreur*, all his life a debauchee and brigand, and now a major-general; alongside of Rossignol, stand his adjutants, Grammont, an old actor, and Hazard, a former priest; along with them is Vacheron, a good *républiquain*, who ravishes women and shoots them when they refuse to succumb;[105] in addition to these are some "brilliant" young ladies, undoubtedly brought from Paris, "the prettiest of whom share their nights between Rossignol and Bourbotte," whilst the others serve

103. De Martel, "Fouché," 418. (Orders of Albitte and Collot, Nivose 13, year II.)

104. Camille Boursier, "Essai sur la Terreur en Anjou," 225. Letter of Vacheron, Frimaire 15, year II. "*Républiquain*, it is absolutely necessary, immediately, that you have sent or brought into the house of the representatives, a lot of red wine, of which the consumption is greater than ever. People have a right to drink to the Republic when they have helped to preserve the Commune you and yours live in. I hold you responsible for my demand." Signed, le *républiquain*, Vacheron."

105. *Ibid.*, 210. Deposition of Madame Edin, apropos of Quesnoy, a prostitute, aged twenty-six, Brumaire 12, year III.; and of Rose, another prostitute. Similar depositions by Benaben and Scotty.

their subordinates: the entire band, male and female, is installed in a Hotel de Fontenay, where they begin by breaking the seals, so as to confiscate "for their own benefit, furniture, jewelry, dresses, feminine trinkets, and even procelains."[106] Meanwhile, at Chantonney, representative Bourdon de l'Oise drinks with General Tunck, becomes "frantic" when tipsy, and has patriotic administrators seized in their beds at midnight, whom he had embraced the evening before. Nearly all of them, like the latter, have too bad wine, Carrier at Nantes, Petit-Jean at Thiers, Duquesnoy at Arras, Cusset at Thionville, Monestier at Tarbes. At Thionville, Cusset drinks like a "Lapithe" and, when drunk, gives the orders of a "vizier," which orders are executed.[107] At Tarbes, Monestier "after a heavy meal and much excited," warmly harangues the court, examines the prisoner himself, M. de Lasalle, an old officer, whom he has condemned to death, and signs the order to have him guillotined at once; M. de Lasalle is guillotined that very evening, at midnight, by torchlight. The following morning Monestier says to the president of the court:

106. Dauban, "La Demagogie en 1793," p. 369. (Extracts from the unpublished memoirs of Mercier de Rocher.)—*Ibid.*, 370. "Bourdon de l'Oise had lived with Tuncq at Chantonney, where they kept busy emptying bottles of fine wine. Bourdon is an excellent patriot, a man of sensibility, but, in his fits of intoxication, he gives himself up to impracticable views." "Let those rascally administrators," he says, "be arrested!" Then, going to the window—he heard a runaway horse galloping in the street—"That's another antirevolutionist! Let 'em all be arrested!"—Cf. "Souvenirs," by General Pélleport, p. 21. At Perpignan, he attended the fête of Reason. "The General in command of the post made an impudent speech, even to the most repulsive cynicism. Some prostitutes, well known to this wretch, filled one of the tribunes; they waved their handkerchiefs and shouted "*Vive la Raison!*" After listening to similar harangues by representatives Soubrang and Michaud, Pélleport, although half cured (of his wound) returns to camp: "I could not breathe freely in town, and did not think that I was safe until facing the enemy along with my comrades."

107. Archives des Affaires Étrangéres, vol. 332; correspondence of secret agents, October, 1793. "Citizen Cusset, representative of the people, shows no dignity in his mission; he drinks like a Lapithe, and when intoxicated commits the arbitrary acts of a vizier." For the style and orthography of Cusset, see one of his letters. (Dauban, "Paris en 1794," p. 14.)—Berryat St. Prix, "La Justice Révolutionnaire" (2d ed.), 339.

"Well, we gave poor Lasalle a famous fright last night, didn't we?"
"How a famous fright? He is executed!" Monestier is astonished—
he did not remember having issued the order.[108] With others, wine,
besides sanguinary instincts, brings out the foulest instincts. At
Nismes, Borie, in the uniform of a representative, along with Cour-
bis, the mayor, Géret, the justice and a number of prostitutes, dance
the *farandole* around the guillotine. At Auch, one of the worst tyrants
in the South, Dartigoyte, always heated with liquor "vomited every
species of obscenity" in the faces of women that came to demand
justice; "he compels, under penalty of imprisonment, mothers to take
their daughters to the popular club," to listen to his filthy preaching;
one evening, at the theatre, probably after an orgy, he apostrophises
all the women between the acts, lets loose upon them his smutty
vocabulary, and, by way of demonstration, or as a practical conclusion, ends by stripping himself naked.[109] This time, the genuine brute

108. *Ibid.*, 371. (According to "Piecés et Documents" published by M.
Fajon.)—*Moniteur*, xxiv., 453. (Session of Floréal 24, year III.) Address of the
Commune of St. Jean du Gard.—xxi., 528. (Session of Fructidor 2, year III.)
Address of the Popular Club of Nismes.

109. *Moniteur*, xxiv., 602. (Session of Prairial 13, year III.) Report of
Durand-Meillan: "This denunciation is only too well supported by documents.
It is for the Convention to say whether it will hear them read. I have to state
beforehand that it can hear nothing more repulsive nor better authenticated."—
De Martel, "Fouché, 246. (Report of the constituted authorities of la Nièvre on
the missions of Collot d'Herbois, Laplanche, Fouché, and Pointe, Prairial 19,
year III.) Laplanche, a former Benedictine, is the most foul-mouthed." In his
speech to the people of Moulins-Engelbert, St. Pierre-le-Montier, and Nevers,
Laplanche asked girls to surrender themselves and let modesty go. "Beget children," he exclaims, "the Republic needs them. Continence is the virtue of fools."
Bibliotheque Nationale, Lb. 41, No. 1802. (Denunciation, by the six sections of
the Dijon commune to the Convention, of Leonard Bourdon and Piochefer
Bernard de Saintes, during their mission in Côte d' Or.) Details on the orgies
of Bernard with the municipality, and on the drunkenness and debaucheries of
Bourdon with the riff-raff of the country; authentic documents proving the
robberies and assassinations committed by Bernard. He pillaged the house of
M. Micault, and, in four hours, had this person arrested, tried and guillotined;
he attended the execution himself, and that evening, in the dead man's house,
danced and sung before his daughter with his acolytes.

appears. The clothing thrown around him by centuries and with which civilisation had protected him, the last drapery of humanity, falls to the ground. Nothing remains but the primitive animal, the ferocious, lewd gorilla supposed to be tamed, but which still subsists indefinitely and which a dictatorship, joined to drunkenness, revives in an uglier guise than in remotest times.

VIII

If intoxication is needed to awaken the brute, a dictatorship suffices to arouse the madman. The mental equilibrium of most of these new sovereigns is disturbed; the distance between what the man once was and what he now is, is too great; formerly, a petty lawyer, village doctor, or schoolmaster, an unknown mover of a resolution in a local club, and only yesterday one voter in the Convention out of seven hundred and fifty; behold him now, the arbiter, in one of the departments, of all fortunes and liberties, and master of five thousand lives. Like a pair of scales into which a disproportionate weight has been thrown, his reason totters on the side of pride. Some of them regard their competency unlimited, like their powers, and having just joined the army, claim the right of being appointed major-generals.[110] "Declare officially," writes Fabre to the Committee of Public Safety,[111] "that, in future, generals shall be simply the lieu-

---

110. "Souvenirs," by General Pélleport, p. 8. He, with his battalion, is inspected in the Place du Capitale, at Toulouse, by the representative on mission. "It seems as if I could see that actor. He tossed his hideous, plumed head and dragged along his sabre like a toy soldier, that he might appear brave. It made me feel sad."

111. Fervel, "Campagnes des Français dans les Pyrénées Orientals," i., 169. (October, 1793.)—*Ibid.*, 201, 206.—Cf. 188. Plan of Fabre for seizing Roses and Figuières, with eight thousand men, without provisions or transports. "Fortune is on the side of fools," he said. Naturally the scheme fails. Collioure is lost, and disasters accumulate. As an offset to this the worthy general Dagobert is removed. Commandant Delatre and chief-of-staff Ramel are guillotined. In the face of the impracticable orders of the representatives the commandant of artillery commits suicide. On the devotion of the officers and enthusiasm of the troops. *Ibid.*, 105, 106, 130, 131, 162.

tenants of the delegates to the Convention." Awaiting the required declaration, they claim command and, in reality, exercise it. "I know of neither generals nor privates," says Gaston, a former justice of the peace, to the officers; "as to the Minister, he is a dog on a skittle-ground; I am in command here and must be obeyed." "What are generals good for?" adds his colleague Guiter; "the old women in our faubourgs know as much as they do. Plans, formal manoeuvres, tents, camps, redoubts? All this is of no use! The only war suitable to Frenchmen after this will be a rush with side arms." To turn out of office, guillotine, disorganise, march blindly on, waste lives haphazard, force defeat, sometimes get killed themselves, is all they know, and they would lose all if the effects of their incapacity and arrogance were not redeemed by the devotion of the officers and the enthusiasm of the soldiers. The same spectacle is visible at Charleroy where, through his absurd orders, Saint-Just does his best to compromise the army, leaving that place with the belief that he is a great man.[112] There is the same spectacle in Alsace, where Lacoste, Baudot, Ruamps, Soubrany, Milhaud, Saint-Just, and Lebas, through their excessive rigor, do their best to break up the army and then boast of it. The revolutionary Tribunal is installed at headquarters, soldiers are urged to denounce their officers, the informer is promised money and secrecy, he and the accused are not allowed to confront each other, no investigation, no papers allowed, even to make exception to the verdict—a simple examination without any notes, the accused arrested at eight o'clock, condemned at nine o'clock, and shot at ten o'clock.[113] Naturally, under such a system,

112. Sybel (Dosquet's translation [French]), ii., 435; iii., 132, 140. (For details and authorities, cf. the Memoirs of Marshal Soult.)

113. Gouvion St. Cyr, "Mémoires sur les campagnes de 1792 à la paix de Campio-Formio," i., pp. 91 to 139.—*Ibid.*, 229. "The effect of this was to lead men who had any means to keep aloof from any sort of promotion."—Cf., *ibid.*, ii., 131 (November, 1794), the same order of things still kept up. By order of the representatives the army encamps during the winter in sheds on the left bank of the Rhine, near Mayence, a useless proceeding and mere literary parade. "They would listen to no reason; a fine army and well-mounted artillery were to perish with cold and hunger, for no object whatever, in quarters that might

no one wants to command; already, before Saint-Just's arrival, Meunier had consented to act as major-general only *ad interim;* "every hour of the day" he demanded his removal; unable to secure this, he refused to issue any order; the representatives, to procure his successor, are obliged to descend down to a depot captain, Carlin, bold enough or stupid enough to allow himself to take a commission under their lead, which was a commission for the guillotine. If such is their presumption in military matters, what must it be in civil affairs! On this side there is no external check, no Spanish or German army capable of at once taking them *in flagrante delicto,* and of profiting by their ambitious incapacity and mischievous interference. Whatever the social instrumentality may be—judiciary, administration, credit, commerce, manufactures, agriculture—they can dislocate and mar it with impunity. They never fail to do this, and, moreover, in their despatches, they take credit to themselves for the ruin they cause. That, indeed, is their mission; otherwise, they would be regarded as bad Jacobins; they would soon become "suspects"; they rule only on condition of being infatuated and destructive; the overthrow of common-sense is with them an act of State grace, a necessity of the office, and, on this common ground of compulsory unreason, every species of physical delirium may be implanted.

With those that we can follow closely, not only is their judgment perverted, but the entire nervous apparatus is affected; permanent overexcitement has begun, and a morbid restlessness. Consider Joseph Lebon, son of a sergeant-at-arms, subsequently, a teacher with the *Oratoriens* of Beaune, next, *curé* of Neuville-Vitasse, repudiated as an interloper by the élite of his parishioners, not respected, without house or furniture, and almost without a flock.[114] Two years after this, finding himself sovereign of his province, his head is turned; much less would make it turn; it is only a twenty-eight-

---

have been avoided." The details are heart-rending. Never was military heroism so sacrificed to the folly of civilian commanders.

114. See Paris, "Histoire de Joseph Lebon," i., ch. I, for biographical details and traits of character.

year-old head, not very solid, without any inside ballast,[115] already disturbed by vanity, ambition, rancor, and apostasy, by the sudden and complete wheeling-about which put him at variance with his past educational habits and most cherished affections: it breaks down under the vastness and novelty of this greatness. In the costume of a representative, a Henry IV. hat, tricolor plume, waving scarf, and sabre dragging the ground, Lebon orders the bell to be rung and summons the villagers into the church, where, aloft in the pulpit in which he had formerly preached in a threadbare cassock, he displays his metamorphosis. "Who would believe that I should have returned here with unlimited powers!"[116] And that, before his counterfeit majesty, each person would be humble, bowed down and silent! To a member of the municipality of Cambray who, questioned by him, looked straight at him and answered curtly, and who, to a query twice repeated in the same terms, dared to answer twice in the same terms, he says: "Shut up! You *disrespect* me, you do not behave properly to the national representative." He immediately commits him to prison.[117] One evening, at the theatre, he enters a box in which the ladies, seated in front, keep their places. In a rage, he goes out, rushes on the stage and, brandishing his great sabre, vociferates and threatens the audience, taking immense strides across the boards and acting and looking so much like a wild beast that several of the ladies faint away: "Look there!" he shouts, "at those *muscadines* who do not condescend to move for a representative of twenty-five millions of men! Everybody used to make way for a prince—they will not budge for me, a representative, *who am more than a king!*"[118]

115. *Ibid.*, i., 13. His mother became crazy and was put in an asylum. Her derangement, he says, was due to "her indignation at his vows and at his appointment to the curacy of Nouvelle-Vitasse."

116. *Ibid.*, i., 123. Speech by Lebon in the church of Beaurains.

117. *Ibid.*, ii., 71, 72.—Cf. 85. "Citizen Chamonart, wine-dealer, standing at the entrance of his cellar, sees the representative pass, looks at him and does not salute him. Lebon steps up to him, arrests him, treats him as an "agent of Pitt and Cobourg." . . . "They search him, take his pocket-book and lead him off to the Anglaises (a prison)."

118. *Ibid.*, ii., 84.

The word is spoken. But this king is frightened, and he is one who thinks of nothing but conspiracy;[119] in the street, in open daylight, the people who are passing him are plotting against him either by words or signs. Meeting in the main street of Arras a young girl and her mother talking Flemish, that seems to him "suspect." "Where are you going?" he demands. "What's that to you?" replies the child, who does not know him. The girl, the mother, and the father are sent to prison.[120] On the ramparts, another young girl, accompanied by her mother, is taking the air, and reading a book. "Give me that book," says the representative. The mother hands it to him; it is the "History of Clarissa Harlowe." The young girl, extending her hand to receive back the book, adds, undoubtedly with a smile: "That is not 'suspect.'" Lebon deals her a blow with his fist on her stomach which knocks her down; both women are searched and he personally leads them to the guard-room. The slightest expression, a gesture, puts him beside himself; any motion that he does not comprehend makes him start, as with an electric shock. Just arrived at Cambray, he is informed that a woman who had sold a bottle of wine below the *maximum*, had been released after a *procès-verbal*. On reaching the Hôtel-de-Ville, he shouts out: "Let everybody here pass into the Consistory!" The municipal officer on duty opens a door leading into it. Lebon, however, not knowing who he is, takes alarm. "He froths at the mouth," says the municipal officer, "and cries out as if possessed by a demon. 'Stop, stop, scoundrel, you are running off!' He draws his sabre and seizes me by the collar; I am dragged and borne along by him and his men. 'I have hold of him, I have hold of him!' he exclaims, and, indeed, he did hold me with his teeth, legs, and arms, like a madman. At last, 'Scoundrel, monster, b——,' says he, 'are you a marquis?' 'No,' I replied, 'I am a *sans-culotte*.' 'Ah, well! people, you hear what he says,' he exclaims, 'he says that he is a *sans-culotte*, and that is the way he greets a denunciation on

119. *Moniteur,* xxv., 201. (Session of Messidor 22, year III.) "When in the tribune (of the Convention) prison conspiracies were announced . . . my dreams were wholly of prison conspiracies."

120. *Ibid.,* 211. (Explanations given by Lebon to the Convention.)—Paris, ii., 350, 351. (Verdict of the jury.)

the *maximum!* I remove him. Let him be f—— in prison!' "[121] It is certain that the King of Arras and Cambray is not far from a raging fever; with such symptoms an ordinary individual would be sent to an asylum.

Not so vain, less fond of parading his royalty, but more savage and placed in Nantes amidst greater dangers, Carrier, under the pressure of more sombre ideas, is much more furious and constant in his madness. Sometimes his attacks reach hallucination. "I have seen him," says a witness, "so carried away in the tribune, in the heat of his harangue when trying to overrule public opinion, as to cut off the tops of the candles with his sabre," as if they were so many aristocrats' heads.[122] Another time, at table, after having declared that France could not feed its too numerous population, and that it was decided to cut down the excess, all nobles, magistrates, priests, merchants, etc., he becomes excited and exclaims, "Kill, kill!" as if he were already engaged in the work and ordering the operation.[123] Even when fasting, and in an ordinary condition, he is scarcely more cooled down. When the administrators of the department come to consult with him,[124] they gather around the door to see if he looks enraged, and is in a condition to hear them. He not only insults petitioners, but likewise the functionaries under him who make reports to him, or take his orders; his foul nature rises to his lips and overflows in the vilest terms: "Go to —— and be ——. I have no time."[125] They consider themselves lucky if they get off with a volley of obscene oaths, for he generally draws his sabre: "The first —— that mentions supplies, I will —— his head off."[126] And to the president of the military commission, who demands that verdicts be rendered before ordering executions: "You,

121. Paris, ii., 85.

122. Buchez et Roux, xxxiv., 181. (Depositions of Monneron, a merchant.).

123. *Ibid.*, 184. (Deposition of Chaux.)—Cf. 200. (Depositions of Monneron and Villemain, merchants.).

124. *Ibid.*, 204. (Deposition of Lamarie, administrator of the department.).

125. *Ibid.*, 173. (Deposition of Erard, a copyist.)—168. (Deposition of Thomas, health officer.) "To all his questions, Carrier replied in the grossest language."

126. *Ibid.*, 203. (Deposition of Bonami, merchant.)

you old rascal, you old ——, you want verdicts, do you! Go ahead! If the whole pen is not emptied in a couple of hours I will have you and your colleagues shot!" His gestures, his look have such a powerful effect upon the mind that the other, who is also a "bruiser," dies of the shock a few days after.[127] Not only does he draw his sabre, but he uses it; among the petitioners, a boatman, whom he is about to strike, runs off as fast as he can; he draws General Moulins into the recess of a window and gives him a cut.[128] People "tremble" on accosting him, and yet more in contradicting him. The envoy of the Committee of Public Safety, Julien de la Drôme, on being brought before him, takes care to "stand some distance off, in a corner of the room," wisely trying to avoid the first spring; wiser still, he replies to Carrier's exclamations with the only available argument: "If you put me out of the way today, you yourself will be guillotined within a week!"[129] On coming to a stand before a mad dog one must aim the knife straight at its throat; there is no other way to escape its tusks and slaver. Accordingly, with Carrier, as with a mad dog, the brain is mastered by the steady mechanical reverie, by persistent images of murder and death. He exclaims to President Tronjolly, apropos of the Vendéan children: "The guillotine, always the guillotine!"[130] In relation to the drownings: "You judges must

127. *Ibid.*, 156. (Deposition of Vaujois, public prosecutor to the military commission.)

128. *Ibid.*, 169. (Deposition of Thomas.)—Berryat Saint-Prix, pp. 34, 35.—Buchez et Roux, 118. "He received the members of the popular club with blows, also the municipal officers with sabre thrusts, who came to demand supplies." . . . "He draws his sabre (against the boatman) and strikes at him, which he avoids only by running away."

129. Buchez et Roux, xxxiv., 196. (Deposition of Julien.) "Carrier said to me in a passion: 'It is you, is it, you d—— beggar, who presumes to denounce me to the Committee of Public Safety. . . . As it is sometimes necessary for the public interests to get rid of certain folks quickly, I won't take the trouble to send you to the guillotine, I'll be your executioner myself!"

130. *Ibid.*, 175. (Deposition of Tronjolly.) 295. (Depositions of Jean Lavigne, a shopkeeper; of Arnandan, civil commissioner; also of Corneret, merchant.) 179. (Deposition of Villemain).—Berryat Saint-Prix, 34. "Carrier, says the gendarme Desquer, who carried his letters, was a roaring lion rather than an officer

have verdicts; pitch them into the water, which is much more simple." Addressing the popular club of Nantes, he says: "The rich, the merchants, are all monopolisers, all antirevolutionists; denounce them to me, and I will have all their heads under the national razor. Tell me who the fanatics are that shut their shops on Sunday and I will have them guillotined." "When will the heads of those rascally merchants fall?" "I see beggars here in rags; you are as big fools at Ancenis as at Nantes. Don't you know that the money, the wealth of these old merchants, belongs to you, and is not the river there?" "My brave b———, my good *sans-culottes* your time is come! Denounce them to me! The evidence of two good *sans-culottes* is all I want to make the heads of those old merchants tumble!" "We will make France a grave-yard rather than not regenerate it in our own way."[131] His steady howl ends in a cry of anguish: "We shall all be guillotined, one after the other!"[132] Such is the mental state to which the office of representative on mission leads. Below Carrier, who is on the extreme verge, the others, less advanced, likewise turn pale at the lugubrious vision, which is the inevitable effect of their work and their mandate. Beyond every grave they dig, they catch a glimpse of the grave already dug for them. There is nothing left for the grave-digger but to dig mechanically day after day, and, in the meantime, make what he can out of his place; he can at least render himself insensible by having "a good time."

IX

Most of them follow this course, some instinctively and through lassitude, and others because the display they make adds to their authority. "Dragged along in carriages with six horses, surrounded by guards, seated at sumptuous tables set for thirty persons, eating

---

of the people." "He looked at once like a charlatan and a tiger," says another witness.

131. *Ibid.*, xxxiv., 204. (Deposition of Lamarie.)
132. *Ibid.*, 183. (Deposition of Caux.)

to the sound of music along with a cortege of actors, courtezans, and pretorians,"[133] they impress the imagination with an idea of their omnipotence, and people bow all the lower because they make a grand show. At Troyes, on the arrival of young Rousselin, cannon are discharged as if for the entry of a prince. The entire population of Nevers is called upon to honor the birth of Fouché's child; the civil and military authorities pay their respects to him, and the National Guards are under arms.[134] At Lyons, "The imposing display of Collot d'Herbois resembles that of the Grand Turk. It requires three successive applications to obtain an audience; nobody approaches nearer than a distance of fifteen feet; two sentinels with muskets stand on each side of him, with their eyes fixed on the petitioners."[135] Less menacing, but not less imposing, is the pomp which surrounds the representatives at Bordeaux; to approach them, requires "a pass from the captain of the guards,"[136] through several squads of sentinels. One of them, Ysabeau, who, after having guillotined to a considerable extent, has become almost tractable, allows adulation, and, like a Duc de Richelieu coming down from Versailles, tries to play the popular potentate, with all the luxuries which the situation affords. At the theatres, in his presence, they give a ballet in which shepherds form with garlands of flowers the words "Ysabeau, Liberty, Equality." He allows his portrait to pass from hand to hand, and condescendingly smiles on the artist who inscribes these words at the bottom of an engraving of the day: "*An occurrence which took place under Ysabeau, representative of the people.*" "When he passes in the street people take off their hats to him, cheer him, and shout '*Hurrah for Ysabeau! Hurrah for the saviour of Bordeaux, our friend and father!*' The children of aristocrats come and apostrophise him in this way, even at the doors of his carriage; for he has

---

133. Mallet-Dupan, "Mémoires," ii., 6. (Memorial of Feb. 1, 1794.) On André Dumont, "Un Séjour en France," 158, 171.—On Merlin de Thionville, Michelet, vi., 97.

134. De Martel, "Fouché," 109.

135. Mallet-Dupan, ii., 46.

136. Buchez et Roux, xxxii., 413, 423. (Letter of Julien to Robespierre.)

a carriage, and several of them, with a coachman, horses, and the equipage of a former noble, gendarmes preceding him everywhere, even on excursions into the country," where his new courtiers call him "great man," and welcome him with "Asiatic magnificence." There is good cheer at his table, "superb white bread," called "representatives' bread," whilst the rustics of the neighborhood live on roots, and the inhabitants of Bordeaux can scarcely obtain over four ounces per diem of musty bread. There is the same feasting with the representatives at Lyons, in the midst of similar distress. In the reports made by Collot we find a list of bottles of brandy at four francs each, along with partridges, capons, turkeys, chickens, pike, and crawfish; also white bread, "equality bread," the other kind, assigned to simple mortals, offending this august palate. Add to this the requisitions made by Albitte and Fouché, seven hundred bottles of fine wine, in one lot, another of fifty pounds of coffee, one hundred and sixty ells of muslin, three dozen silk handkerchiefs for cravats, three dozen pairs of gloves, and four dozen pairs of stockings: they provide themselves with a good stock.[137] Among so many

---

137. Archives Nationales, AF., II., 111. An order issued by Bourbotte, Tours, Messidor 5, year II., "requiring the district administration to furnish him personally, as well as for the citizens attached to his commission, forty bottles of red wine and thirty of white wine, to be taken from the cellars of *emigrés,* or from those of persons condemned to death; and, besides this, fifty bottles of common wine other than white or red."—On the 2d of Messidor, ale is drank and there is a fresh order for fifty bottles of red wine, fifty of common wine, and two bottles of brandy.—De Martel, "Fouché," 419, 420.—*Moniteur,* xxiv., 604. (Session of Prairial 13, par iii.) "Dugué reads the list of charges brought against Mallarmé. He is accused ... of having put in requisition whatever pleased him for his table and for other wants, without paying for anything, not even for the post-horses and postillions that carried him."—*Ibid.* 602. Report of Perès du Gers. "He accuses Dartigoyte ... of having taken part with his secretaries in the auction of the furniture of Daspe, who had been condemned; of having kept the most valuable pieces for himself, and afterwards fixing their price; of having warned those who had charge of the sale that confinement awaited whoever should bid on the articles he destined for himself."—Laplanche, ex-Benedictine, said in his mission in Loiret, that "those who did not like the Revolution must pay those who make it."

perambulating satraps, the most audaciously sensual is, I believe, Tallien, the *Septembriseur* at Paris and *guillotineur* at Bordeaux, but still more rake and robber, caring mostly for his palate and stomach. Son of the cook of a grand seignor, he is doubtless swayed by family traditions: for his government is simply a larder where, like the head-butler in "Gil Blas," he can eat and turn the rest into money. At this moment, his principal favorite is Teresa Cabarrus, a woman of society, or one of the *demi-monde,* whom he took out of prison; he rides about the streets with her in an open carriage, "with a courier behind and a courier in front," sometimes wearing the red cap and holding a pike in her hand,[138] thus exhibiting his goddess to the people. And this is the sentiment which does him the most credit; for, when the crisis comes, the imminent peril of his mistress arouses his courage against Robespierre, and this pretty woman, who is good-natured, begs him, not for murders, but for pardons. Others, as gallant as he is, but with less taste, obtain recruits for their pleasures in a rude way, either as fast-livers on the wing, or because fear subjects the honor of women to their caprices, or because the public funds defray the expenses of their guard-room habits. At Blois, for this species of expenditure, Guimberteau discharges his obligations by drafts on the proceeds of the revolutionary tax.[139] Carrier, at Nantes, appropriates to himself the house and garden of a private person for "his seraglio"; the reader may judge whether, on desiring to be a third party in the household, the husband would make objections; at other times, in the hotel Henry IV., "with his friends and prostitutes brought under requisition, he has an orgy"; he allows himself the same indulgence on the galiot, at the drownings; there at the end of a drunken frolic, he is regaled with merry songs, for example, "la gamelle":[140] he must be amused. Some, who

138. Buchez et Roux, xxxii., 426. (Extract from the Memoirs of Sénart.)—Hamel, iii., 565. (Description of Teresa's domicile by the Marquis de Paroy, a petitioner and eye-witness.)

139. Buchez et Roux, xxxiii., 12. (Extract from the Memoirs of Sénart.) "The certified copies of these drafts are on file with the Committee of General Security."

140. Report of Courtois, 360. (Letters of Julien to Robespierre, Pluviose 15

are shrewd, think of the more substantial and look out for the future. Foremost among these is Tallien, the king of robbers, but prodigal, whose pockets, full of holes, are only filled to be at once emptied; Javogues, who makes the most of Montbrison; Rovère, who, for eighty thousand francs in assignats, has an estate adjudged to him worth five hundred thousand francs in coin; Fouché, who, in Nièvre, begins to amass the twelve or fourteen millions which he secures later on;[141] and so many others, who were either ruined or impoverished previous to the outbreak of the Revolution, and who are rich when it ends: Barras with his domain of Gros Bois; André Dumont, with the Hotel de Plouy, its magnificent furniture, and an estate worth four hundred thousand livres; Merlin de Thionville, with his country-houses, equipages, and domain of Mont-Valérien, and other domains; Salicetti, Rewbell, Rousselin, Chateauneuf-Randon, and the rest of the corrupt Directory cormorants. Without mentioning the taxes and confiscations of which they render no account, they have, for their hoard, the ransoms offered underhandedly by "suspects" and their families; what is more convenient?[142] And all the more, because the Committee of General Security, even when informed, let things take their course: to prosecute *Montagnards,* would be "making the Revolution take a step backward."

---

and 16, year II.)—Buchez et Roux, xxxiv., 199, 200, 202, 203, 211. (Depositions of Villemain, Monneron, Legros, Robin.)—Berryat Saint-Prix, 35. (Depositions of Fourrier and of Louise Courant, sempstress.)

141. See, on Tallien, "Mémoires de Sénart."—On Javogues, *Moniteur,* xxiv., 461, Floréal 24, III. Petition against Javogues, with several pages of signatures, especially those of the inhabitants of Montbrison: "In the report made by him to the Convention he puts down coin and assignats at seven hundred and seventy-four thousand six hundred and ninety-six francs, while the spoils of one person provided him with five hundred thousand francs in cash."—On Fouché, De Martel, 252.—On Dumont, Mallet-Dupan, "Manuscript notes." (January, 1795.)—On Rovère, Michelet, vi., 256.—Carnot, ii., 87. (According to the Memoirs of the German Olsner, who was in Paris under the Directory): "The tone of Barras' *Salon* was that of a respectable gambling house; the house of Rewbell resembled the waiting-room of an inn at which the mail-coach stops."

142. Buchez et Roux, xxxii., 391, and xxxiii., 9. (Extracts from the Memoirs of Sénart.)

One is bound to humor useful servants who have such hard work, like that of September; irregularities, as with these September people, must be overlooked; it is necessary to allow them a few perquisites and give them gratuities.[143]

All this would not suffice to keep them at work if there were not an attraction of superior force. To the common run of civilised men, the office of *Septembriseur* is at first disagreeable; but, after a little practice, especially with a tyrannical nature, which, under cover of the theory, or under the pretext of public safety, can satiate its despotic instincts, all repugnance subsides. There is keen delight in the exercise of absolute power; one is glad, every hour, to assert one's omnipotence and prove it by some act, the most conclusive of all acts being some act of destruction. The more complete, radical and prompt the destruction is, the more conscious one is of one's strength. However great the obstacle, one is not disposed to recede or stand still; one breaks away all the barriers which men call good sense, humanity, justice, and the satisfaction of breaking them down is great. To crush and to subdue becomes voluptuous pleasure, to which pride gives keener relish, affording a grateful incense of the holocaust which the despot consumes on his own altar; at this daily sacrifice, he is both idol and priest, offering up victims to himself that he may be conscious of his divinity. Such is Saint-Just, all the more a despot because his title of representative on mission is supported by his rank on the Committee of Public Safety: to find natures strained to the same pitch as his, we must leave the modern world and go back to a Caligula, or to a caliph Hakem in Egypt in the tenth century.[144] He also, like these two monsters, but with different formulae, regards himself as a God, or God's vicegerent on earth,

143. Carnot, "Mémoires," i. 416. Carnot, having shown to the Committee of Public Safety, proofs of the depredations committed on the army of the North, Saint-Just got angry and exclaimed: "It is only an enemy of the Republic that would accuse his colleagues of depredations, *as if patriots hadn't a right to everything!*"

144. As to Caligula see Suetonius and Philo.—With respect to Hakem, see "L'Exposé de la Religion des Druses," by M. de Sacy.

invested with absolute power through Truth incarnated in him, the representative of a mysterious, limitless and supreme power, known as the People; to worthily represent this power, it is essential to have a soul of steel.[145] Such is the soul of Saint-Just, and only that. All other sentiments merely serve to harden it; all the metallic agencies that compose it—sensuality, vanity, every vice, every species of ambition, all the frantic outbursts, and melancholy vaporings of his youth—are violently commingled and fused together in the revolutionary mould, so that his soul may take the form and rigidity of trenchant steel. Suppose this an animated blade, feeling and willing in conformity with its temper and structure; it would delight in being brandished, and would need to strike; such is the need of Saint-Just. Taciturn, impassible, keeping people at a distance, as imperious as if the entire will of the people and the majesty of transcendent reason resided in his person, he seems to have reduced his passions to the desire of dashing everything to atoms, and to creating dismay. It may be said of him that, like the conquering Tartars, he measures his self-attributed grandeur by what he fells; no other has so extensively swept away fortunes, liberties and lives; no other has so terrifically heightened the effect of his deeds by laconic speech and the suddenness of the stroke. He orders the arrest and close confinement of all former nobles, men and women, in the four departments, in twenty-four hours; he orders the bourgeoisie of Strasbourg to pay over nine millions in twenty-four hours; ten thousand persons in Strasbourg must give up their shoes in twenty-four hours; random and immediate discharges of musketry on the officers of the Rhine army—such are the measures.[146] So much the worse for the innocent; there is no time to discern who they are; "a blind man hunting for

---

145. Saint-Just, speaking in the Convention, says: "What constitutes a republic is the utter destruction of whatever is opposed to it."

146. Orders issued by Saint-Just and Lebas for the departments of Pas-de-Calais, Nord, la Somme et l'Aisne.—Cf. "Histoire de l'Alsace," by Stroebel, and "Recueil de pièces authentiques pour servir à l'histoire de la Révolution à Strasbourg," 3 vols.—Archives Nationales AF., II., 135, orders issued Brumaire 10, year II., and list of the one hundred and ninety-three persons taxed.

a pin in a dust-heap takes the whole heap."[147] And, whatever the order, even when it cannot be executed, so much the worse for him to whom it is given, for the captain who, directed by the representative to establish this or that battery in a certain time, works all night with all his forces, "with as many men as the place will hold."[148] The battery not being ready at the hour named, Saint-Just sends the captain to the guillotine. The sovereign having once given an order it cannot be counter-manded; to take back his words would be weakening himself;[149] in the service of omnipotence, pride is insatiable, and, to mollify it, no barbaric act is too great. The same appetite is visible in Collot d'Herbois, who, no longer on the stage, plays before the town the melo-dramatic tyrant with all becoming ostentation. One morning, at Lyons, he directs the revolutionary Tribunal to arrest, examine and sentence a youthful "suspect" before the day is over. "Towards six o'clock,[150] Collot being at table enjoying an orgy with prostitutes, buffoons, and executioners, eating and drinking to choice music, one of the judges of the Tribunal enters; after the usual formalities, he is led up to the Representative, and informs him that the young man had been arrested and examined, and the strictest enquiries made concerning him; he is found irreproachable and the Court decided to set him free. Collot, *without looking at the judge,* raises his voice and says to him: 'I ordered you to punish that young man and I want him out of the way before night. If the innocent are spared, too many of the guilty will escape. Go.' The music and gaiety begin again, and in an hour the young man is shot." And so with most of the other pachalics; if any head mentally

147. Buchez et Roux, xxxi., 32. (Saint-Just's reply to Mayor Monet.)—De Sybel, ii., 447, 448. At the first interview Saint-Just said to Schneider: "Why use so much ceremony? You know the crimes of the aristocrats? In the twenty-four hours taken for one investigation you might have twenty-four condemned."

148. "Journal de marche du sergent Fricasse," p. 34. (Narrative by Marshal Soult.)

149. Cf. in the Bible, the story of Ahasuerus who, out of respect for his own majesty, cannot retract the order he has issued against the Jews, but he turns the difficulty by allowing them to defend themselves.

150. Mallet-Dupan, ii., 47.

condemned by the pacha escapes or does not fall soon enough, the latter is indignant at the delays and forms of justice, also against the judges and juries, often selected by himself. Javogues writes an insulting letter to the commission of Feurs which has dared acquit two former nobles. Laignelot, Lecarpentier, Michaud, Monestier, Lebon, break up, recompose, or replace the commissions of Fontenoy, St. Malo, and Perpignan, and the tribunals of Pau, Nismes, and Arras, whose judgments did not please them.[151] Lebon, Bernard de Saintes, Dartigoyte, and Fouché rearrest prisoners on the same charge, solemnly acquitted by their own tribunals. Bô, Prieur de la Marne, and Lebon, send judges and juries to prison that do not always vote death.[152] Barras and Fréron despatch, from brigade to brigade, to the revolutionary Tribunal in Paris, the public prosecutor and president of the revolutionary Tribunal of Marseilles, for being indulgent to antirevolutionists, because, out of five hundred and twenty-eight prisoners, they guillotined only one hundred and sixty-two.[153] To contradict the infallible Representative! That of itself is an offence. He owes it to himself to punish those who are not docile, to rearrest absolved delinquents, and to maintain cruelty with cruelty.

When one has long imbibed a strong and disagreeable draught, not only does the palate get accustomed to the draught, but it often acquires a taste for it; it soon wants to have it stronger; finally, it swallows it pure, completely raw, with no admixture or condiment to disguise its repulsiveness. Such, to certain imaginations, is the spectacle of human gore; after getting accustomed to it they take delight in seeing it. Lequinio, Laignelot, and Lebon invite the exe-

---

151. Berryat Saint-Prix, "La Justice Révolutionnaire," xvii.—Marcelin Boudet, "Les Conventionnels d'Auvergne," 269.—*Moniteur*, Brumaire 27, year III., report by Calès.

152. Paris, "Histoire de Joseph Lebon," i., 371; ii., 341, 344.—De Martel, "Fouché," 153.—Berryat Saint-Prix, 347, 348.

153. Berryat Saint-Prix, 390. *Ibid.*, 404. (On Soubrié, executioner at Marseilles, letter of Lazare Giraud, public prosecutor): "I put him in the dungeon for having shed tears on the scaffold, in executing the antirevolutionists we sent to be executed."

cutioner to dine with them;[154] Monestier, with his cut-throats, is going himself in search of prisoners in the dungeons, so that he may accompany them to the Tribunal and overwhelm them with charges, if they are disposed to defend themselves; after their condemnation, he assists in uniform at their execution.[155] Fouché, lorgnette in hand, looks out of his window upon a butchery of two hundred and ten Lyonnese. Collot, Laporte, and Fouché feast together in a large company on shooting days, and, at each discharge, stand up and cheer lustily, waving their hats.[156] At Toulon, Fréron, in person, orders and sees executed, the first grand massacre on the Champ de Mars.[157] On the Place d'Arras, M. de Vielfort, already tied and stretched out on the plank, awaits the fall of the knife. Lebon appears on the balcony of the theatre, makes a sign to the executioner to stop, opens the newspaper, and, in a loud voice, reads off the recent successes of the French armies; then, turning to the condemned man, exclaims: "Go, wretch, and take the news of our victories to your brethren."[158] At Feurs, where the shootings take place at the house of M. du Rosier, in the great avenue of the park, his daughter, quite a young woman, advances in tears to Javogues, and asks for the release of her husband. "Oh, yes, my dear," replies Javogues, "you shall have him home tomorrow." In effect, the next day, her husband is shot, and buried in the avenue.[159] It is evident that they get to liking the business. Like their September predecessors, they find amusement in murdering: people around them allude gaily to "the

---

154. *Moniteur*, xviii., 413. (Session of the Convention, letter of Lequinio and Laignelot, Rochefort, Brumaire 17, year II.) "We have appointed the patriot Anse *guilloteneur* and we have invited him, in dining with us, to come and assume his prescribed powers, and water them with a libation in honor of the Republic."—Paris, ii., 72.

155. Marcelin Boudet, 270. (Testimony of Bardanèche de Bayonne.)

156. Guillon, "Histoire de la ville de Lyons pendant la Révolution," ii., 427, 431, 433.

157. "Mémoire du Citoyen Fréron," (in the Barrière collection), p. 357. (Testimony of a survivor.)

158. Paris, ii., 32.

159. Delandine, "Tableaux des prisons de Lyons," p. 14.

red theatre" and "the national razor." An aristocrat is said to be "putting his head at the national window," and "he has put his head through the cat-hole."[160] They themselves enjoy the style and humor of the occupation. "Tomorrow, at seven o'clock," writes Hugues, "let the sacred guillotine be erected!" "The *demoiselle* guillotine," writes Lecarlier, "keeps steadily agoing."[161] "The relatives and friends of *emigrés* and of refractory priests," writes Lebon, "monopolise the guillotine.[162] . . . Day before yesterday, the sister of the former Comte de Bethune sneezed in the sack." Carrier loudly proclaims "the pleasure he has derived" from seeing priests executed: "I never laughed in my life as I did at the faces they made in dying."[163] This is the extreme perversity of human nature, that of a Domitian who watches the features of the condemned, to see the effect of suffering, or, better still, that of the negro who holds his sides with laughter at the aspect of a man being impaled. And this delight of contemplating death throes, Carrier finds it in the sufferings of children. Notwithstanding the remonstrances of the revolutionary Tribunal and the entreaties of President Phelippes,[164] he

160. Camille Boursier, "Essai sur la Terreur en Anjou," 164. (Letter of Boniface, ex-Benedictine, president of the Revolutionary Committee, to Representative Richard, Brumaire 3, year II.) "We send you the said Henri Verdier, called de la Saurinière. . . . It will not be long before you will see that we make the guillotine a present. . . . The Committee begs you to send him *sacram sanctam guillotinam*, and the republican minister of his worship. . . . Not an hour of the day passes that new members do not come to us whom we desire to initiate in its mysteries, (sic)."

161. Thibaudière, "Histoire du Terrorisme dans le départment de la Vienne," 34, 48.—Berryat Saint-Prix, 239.

162. Archives Nationales F[7], 4,435. (Letter of Lebon, Floréal 23, year II.) —Paris, i., 241.

163. Buchez et Roux, xxxiv., 184, 200. (Depositions of Chaux, Monnéron and Villemain.)

164. Register of the revolutionary Tribunal of Nantes, copied by M. Chevrier. (M. Chevrier has kindly sent me his manuscript copy.)—Berryat Saint-Prix, 94.—Archives Nationales, F[7], 4,591. (Extract from the acts of the Legislative Committee, session of Floréal 3, year III. Restitution of the confiscated property of Alexander Long to his son.) Dartigoyte, at Auch, did what Carrier did at Nantes. "It follows from the above abstract duly signed that on the 27th

signs on the 29th of Frimaire, year II., a positive order to guillotine without trial twenty-seven persons, of whom seven are women, and, among these, four sisters, Mesdemoiselles de la Metayrie, one of these twenty-eight years old, another twenty-seven, the third twenty-six, and the fourth seventeen. Two days before, notwithstanding the remonstrances of the same tribunal and the entreaties of the same president, he signed a positive order to guillotine twenty-six artisans and farm-hands, among them two boys of fourteen, and two of thirteen years of age. He was driven "in a cab" to the place of execution and he followed it up in detail. He could hear one of the children of thirteen, already bound to the board, but too small and having only the top of the head under the knife, ask the executioner, "Will it hurt me much?" What the triangular blade fell upon may be imagined! Carrier saw this with his own eyes, and whilst the executioner, horrified at himself, died a few days after in consequence of what he had done, Carrier put another in his place, began again and continued operations.

Germinal, year II., between eight and nine o'clock in the evening, Alexandre Long, Sr., was put to death on the public square of the commune of Auch by the executioner of criminal sentences, without any judgment having been rendered against the said Long."—In many places an execution becomes a spectacle for the Jacobins of the town and a party of pleasure. For instance, at Arras, on the square devoted to executions, a gallery was erected for spectators with a room for the sale of refreshments, and, during the execution of M. de Montgon, the "Ca ira" is played on the bass drum. (Paris, ii., 158, and i., 159.) A certain facetious representative has rehearsals of the performance in his own house. "Lejeune, to feed his bloodthirsty imagination, had a small guillotine put up, on which he cut off the heads of all the poultry consumed at his table. . . . Often, in the middle of the repast, he had it brought in and set to work for the amusement of his guests." (*Moniteur*, xxiv., 607, session of June 1, 1795, letter from the district of Besançon, and with the letter, the confirmatory document.) "This guillotine, says the reporter, is deposited with the Committee of Legislation."

CHAPTER III

The Rulers (continued)— I. *The administrative body at Paris—Composition of the group out of which it was recruited—Deterioration of this group—Weeding-out of the Section Assemblies—Weeding-out of the popular clubs—Pressure of the government—* II. *Quality of the subaltern leaders—How they rule in the section assemblies—How they seize and hold office—* III. *A Minister of Foreign Affairs—A General in command—The Paris Commune—A Revolutionary Committee—* IV. *The administrative staff in the provinces—Jacobinism less in the departmental towns than in Paris—Less in the country than in the towns—The Revolutionary Committees in the small communes—Municipal bodies lukewarm in the villages—Jacobins too numerous in bourgs and small towns—Unreliable or hampered as agents when belonging to the administrative bodies of large or moderate-sized towns—Local rulers recruited on the spot inadequate—* V. *Importation of a foreign staff—Paris Jacobins sent into the provinces—Jacobins of enthusiastic towns transported to moderate ones—The Jacobins of a* chef-lieu *spread through the district—Resistance of public opinion—Distribution and small number of really Jacobin agents—* VI. *Quality of the staff thus formed—Social state of the agents—Their unfitness and bad conduct—The administrators in Seine-et-Marne—Drunkenness and feastings—Committees and Municipalities in the Côte d'Or—Waste and extortions—Traffickers in favors at Bordeaux—Seal-breakers at Lyons—Monopolisers of national possessions—Sales of personal property—Embezzlements and Frauds—A* procès-verbal *in the office of the mayor of Strasbourg—Sales of real-estate—Commissioners on declarations at Toulouse—The administrative staff and clubs of buyers in Provence—The Revolutionary Committee of Nantes—* VII. *The Armed Force—National Guard and Gendarmerie—Its composition and operations—The Revolutionary Armies in Paris and in the departments—Quality of the recruits—Their employment—Their expeditions into the country towns—Their exploits in the vicinity of Paris and Lyons—The company of Maratists, the American Hussars and the German Legion at Nantes—General character of the Revolutionary government and of the administrative staff of the Reign of Terror.*

I

TO PROVIDE these local sovereigns with the subordinate lieutenants and agents which they require, we have the local Jacobin population, and we know how this is recruited[1]—outcasts, the infatuated and perverted of every class and degree, especially the lowest, envious and rancorous dependents, small shopkeepers in debt, strolling and dissipated work-men, coffee-house and bar-room idlers, vagrants, tramps, abject prostitutes—in short, every species of "antisocial vermin," male and female,[2] including a few honest crack-brains into which the fashionable theory had freely found its way; the rest, and by far the largest number, are veritable beasts of prey, speculating on the established order of things and adopting the revolutionary faith only because it provides food for their appetites. In Paris, they number five or six thousand, and, after Thermidor, there is about

1. "The Revolution," ii., pp. 298–304, and p. 351.

2. Should the foregoing testimony be deemed insufficient, the following, by those foreigners who had good opportunities for judging, may be added: (Gouverneur Morris, letter of December 3, 1794.) "The French are plunged into an abyss of poverty and slavery, a slavery all the more degrading because the men who have plunged them into it *merit the utmost contempt.*"—Meissner, "Voyage à Paris" (at the end of 1795), p. 160. "The (revolutionary) army and the revolutionary committees were really associations organised *by crime for committing every species of injustice, murder, rapine, and brigandage with impunity.* The government had deprived all men of any talent or integrity of their places and given these to its creatures, that is to say, to *the dregs of humanity.*"—Baron Brinckmann, Chargé d'Affaires from Sweden. (Letter of July 11, 1799.) "I do not believe that the different classes of society in France are more corrupt than elsewhere; but I trust that no people may ever be ruled by as imbecile and cruel scoundrels as those that have ruled France since the advent of its new state of freedom. . . . *The dregs of the people,* stimulated from above by sudden and violent excitement, have everywhere brought to the surface *the scum of immorality.*"

the same number, the same appetites rallying them around the same dogma,[3] levellers and terrorists, "some because they are poor, others because they have ceased working at their trade," infuriate "against the *porte-cochère* scoundrels, the rich holders of objects of prime necessity," many "having taken a hand in the Revolution, and ready to do it again provided the rich rascals, monopolists, and merchants can all be killed," all "frequenters of popular clubs who think themselves philosophers, although most of them are unable to read," at the head of them the remnant of the most notorious political bandits, the famous post-master, Drouet, who, in the tribune at the Convention, declared himself a "brigand,"[4] Javogues, the robber of Montbrison and the "Nero of Ain,"[5] the sot Casset, formerly a silk-hand and afterwards the pacha of Thionville, Bertrand, the friend of Charlier, the ex-mayor and executioner of Lyons, Darthé, ex-secretary of Lebon and the executioner at Arras, Rossignol and nine other *Septembriseurs* of the Abbaye and the Carmelites, and, finally, the great apostle of despotic communism, Baboeuf, who, sentenced to twenty years in irons for the falsification of public contracts, and as needy as he is vicious, rambles about Paris airing his disappointed ambitions and empty pockets along with the swaggering crew who, if not striving to reach the throne by a new massacre,[6] tramp through the streets slipshod, for lack of money "to redeem a pair of boots at the shoemakers," or to sell some snuff-box, their last resource,

3. Fleury, "Baboeuf," 139, 150.—Granier de Cassagnac, "Histoire du Directoire," ii., 24–170.—(Trial of Baboeuf, *passim*.) The above quotations are from documents seized in Baboeuf's house, also from affidavits made by witnesses, and especially by Captain Grizel.

4. *Moniteur*, session of September 5, 1793. "Since our virtue, our moderation, our philosophic ideas, are of no use to us, let us be brigands for the good of the people; let us be brigands!"

5. An expression of Couthon's on Javogues.

6. Baboeuf, "Le Tribune du Peuple," No. 40. Apologising for the men of September, he says that "they are simply priests, the sacrificers of a just immolation for public security. If anything is to be regretted it is that a larger and more general Second of September did not sweep away all starvers and all despoilers."

for a morning dram.[7] In this class we see the governing rabble fully and distinctly. Separated from its forced adherents and the official automatons who serve it as they would any other power, it stands out pure and unalloyed by any neutral afflux; we recognise here the permanent residue, the deep, settled slime of the social sewer. It is to this sink of vice and ignorance that the revolutionary government betakes itself for its staff-officers and its administrative bodies.

Nowhere else could they be found. For the daily task imposed upon them, and which must be done by them, is robbery and murder; excepting the pure fanatics, who are few in number, only brutes and blackguards have the aptitudes and tastes for such business. In Paris, as in the provinces, it is from the clubs or popular associations in which they congregate, that they are sought for. Each section of Paris contains one of these clubs, in all forty-eight, rallied around the central club in the Rue St. Honoré, forty-eight district alliances of professional rioters and brawlers, the rebels and blackguards of the social army, all the men and women incapable of devoting themselves to a regular life and useful labor,[8] especially those who, on the 31st of May and 2d of June, had aided the Commune and the "Mountain" in violating the Convention. They recognise each other by this sign that, "each would be hung in case of a counter-revolution,"[9] laying it down "as an incontestable fact that, should a single aristocrat be spared, all of them would mount the scaffold."[10] They are naturally wary and they cling together: in their clique

7. Granier de Cassagnac, ii., 90. (Deposition of Grisel.) Rossignol says, "That snuff-box is all I have to live on." "Massard could not obtain a pair of boots belonging to him at the shoemaker's, because he had no money."

8. Archives Nationales, Cf. 3,116[7]. (Report of Robin, Nivose 9.) "The women always had a deliberative voice in the popular assemblies of the Pantheon section," and in all the other clubs they attended the meetings.

9. *Moniteur*, xix., 103. (Meeting of the Jacobin club, Dec. 28, 1793.) Dubois-Crancé puts the following question to each member who passes the weeding-out vote: "What have you done that would get you hung in case of a counter-revolution?"

10. *Ibid.*, xvii., 410. (Speech by Montaut, Jacobin club, Brumaire 21, year II.)

"every thing is done on the basis of good fellowship;"[11] no one is admitted except on the condition of having proved his qualifications "on the 10th of August and 31st of May."[12] And, as they have made their way into the Commune and into the revolutionary committees behind victorious leaders, they are able, through the certificates of civism which these arbitrarily grant or refuse, to exclude, not only from political life but, again, from civil life, whoever is not of their coterie. "See," writes one of Danton's correspondents,[13] "the sort of persons who easily obtain these certificates, the Ronsins, the Jourdans, the Maillards, the Vincents, all bankrupts, keepers of gambling-hells, and cut-throats. Ask these individuals whether they have paid the patriotic contribution, whether they regularly pay the usual taxes, whether they give to the poor of their sections, to the volunteer soldiers, etc.; whether they mount guard or see it regularly done, whether they have made a loyal declaration for the forced loan. You will find that they have not. . . . The Commune issues certificates of civism to its satellites and refuses them to the best citizens." The monopoly is obvious; they make no attempt to conceal it; six weeks later,[14] it becomes official: "several revolutionary committees decide not to grant certificates of civism to citizens who are not members of a popular club." And strict exclusion goes on increasing from month to month. Old certificates are cancelled and new ones imposed, which new certificates have new formalities added to them, a larger number of endorsers being required and certain kinds of guarantees being rejected; there is greater strictness in relation to

11. Dauban, "Paris in 1794," 142. (Police report of Ventose 13, year II.)

12. Morellet, "Mémoires," ii.

13. Dauban, 26, 35. (Note drawn up in January, 1794, probably by the physician Quevremont de Lamotte.)—*Ibid.*, 82.—Cf. Morellet, ii., 434–470. (Details on the issue of certificates of civism, in September, 1793.)

14. Archives Nationales, F⁷, 3,116⁷. (Report by Latour-Lamontagne, Ventose 1, year II.) "It is giving these associations too much influence; it is destroying the jurisdiction of the general assemblies (of the section.) We find accordingly, that these are being deserted and that the cabalists and intriguers succeed in making popular clubs the centres of public business in order to control affairs more easily."

the requisite securities and qualifications; the candidate is put off until fuller information can be obtained about him; he is rejected at the slightest suspicion:[15] he is only too fortunate if he is tolerated in the Republic as a passive subject, if he is content to be taxed and taxed when they please, and if he is not sent to join the "suspects" in prison; whoever does not belong to the band does not belong to the community.

Amongst themselves and in their popular club it is worse, for "the eagerness to get any office leads to every one denouncing each other";[16] consequently, at the Jacobin club in the rue St. Honoré, and in the branch clubs of the quarter, there is constant weeding-out, and always in the same sense, until the faction is purged of all honest or passable alloy and only a minority remains, which has its own way at every balloting. One of them announces that, in his club, eighty doubtful members have already been got rid of; another that, in his club, one hundred are going to be excluded.[17] On Ventose 23, in the "Bon-Conseil" club, most of the members examined are rejected: "they are so strict that a man who cannot show that he acted energetically in critical times, cannot form part of the assembly; he is set aside for a mere trifle." On Ventose 13, in the same club, "out of twenty-six examined, seven only are admitted; one citizen, a tobacco dealer, aged sixty-eight, who has always performed his duty, is rejected for having called the president *Monsieur*, and

---

15. Dauban, *ibid.*, 203. (Report by Bacon, Ventose 19.) "In the general assembly of the Maison Commune section all citizens of any rank in the companies have been weeded out. The slightest stain of *incivism*, the slightest negligence in the service, caused their rejection. Out of twenty-five who passed censorship—nineteen at least were rejected. . . . Most of them are either shoe-makers, cooks, carpenters, tailors, or eating-house keepers."

16. *Ibid.*, 141. (Report by Charmont, Ventose 12.)—*Ibid*, 140. "There is only one way, it is said at the Café des Grands Hommes, on the boulevard, to keep from being arrested, and that is to cabal for admission into the civil and revolutionary committees when there happens to be a vacancy. Before salaries were attached to these places nobody wanted them; since that, there are disputes as to who shall be appointed."

17. *Ibid.*, 307. (Report of Germinal 7.)

for having spoken in the tribune bareheaded; two members, after this, insisted on his being a Moderate, which is enough to keep him out." Those who remain, consist of the most restless and most loquacious, the most eager for office, the self-mutilated club being thus reduced to a knot of charlatans and rogues.

To these spontaneous eliminations through which the club deteriorates, add the constant pressure through which the Committee of Public Safety frightens and degrades it. The lower the revolutionary government sinks, and the more it concentrates its power, the more servile and sanguinary do its agents and employees become. It strikes right and left as a warning; it imprisons or decapitates the turbulent among its own clients, the secondary demagogues who are impatient at not being principal demagogues, the bold who think of striking a fresh blow in the streets, Jacques Roux, Vincent, Momoro, Hébert, leaders of the Cordeliers club and of the Commune; after these, the indulgent who are disposed to exercise some discernment or moderation in terrorism, Camille Desmoulins, Danton and their adherents; and lastly, many others who are more or less doubtful, compromised or compromising, wearied or eccentric, from Maillard to Chaumette, from Antonelle to Chabot, from Westermann to Clootz. Each of the proscribed has a gang of followers, and suddenly the whole gang are obliged to be turncoats; those who are able to lead, flag, while those who can feel pity, become hardened. Henceforth, amongst the subaltern Jacobins, the roots of independence, humanity, and loyalty, hard to extirpate even in an ignoble and cruel nature, are eradicated even to the last fibre, the revolutionary staff, already so debased, becoming more and more degraded, until it is worthy of the office assigned to it. The confidants of Hébert, those who listen to Chaumette, the comrades of Westermann, the officers of Ronsin, the faithful readers of Camille, the admirers and devotees of Danton, all are bound to publicly repudiate their incarcerated friend or leader and approve of the decree which sends him to the scaffold, to applaud his calumniators, to overwhelm him on trial: this or that judge or juryman, who is one of Danton's partisans, is obliged to stifle a defence of him, and, knowing him to be innocent, pronounce him guilty; one who had often dined with Desmoulins is not only to guillotine him, but, in addition to this, to guillotine his young widow. Moreover, in the revolutionary committees, at the Commune, in the offices of the Committee of General Safety, in the bureau of the Central Police, at the headquarters of the armed force, at the revolutionary Tribunal, the service to which they are restricted becomes daily more onerous and more repulsive. To denounce neighbors, to arrest colleagues, to go and seize innocent persons, known to be such, in their beds, to select in the prisons the thirty or forty unfortunates who form the daily food of the guillotine, to "amalgamate" them haphazard, to try them and condemn them in a lot, to escort octogenarian women and girls of sixteen to the scaffold, even under the knife-blade, to see heads dropping and bodies swinging, to contrive means for getting rid of a multitude of corpses, and for removing the too-visible stains of blood—of what species do the beings consist, who can accept such a task, and perform it day after day, with the prospect of doing it indefinitely? Fouquier-Tinville himself succumbs. One evening, on his way to the Committee of Public Safety, "he feels unwell" on the Pont-Neuf and exclaims: "I think I see the ghosts of the dead following us, especially those of the patriots I have had guillotined!"[18] And at another time: "I would rather plough the ground than be public prosecutor. If I could, I would resign." The government, as the system becomes aggravated, is forced to descend lower still that it may find suitable instruments; it finds them now only in the lowest depths; in Germinal, to renew the Commune, in Floréal, to renew the ministries, in Prairial, to recompose the revolutionary Tribunal, month after month, purging and reconstituting the committees of each quarter[19] of the city. In vain does Robespierre, writing and rewriting his secret

---

18. Wallon, "Histoire du Tribunal Revolutionaire," iv., 129.

19. Archives Nationales, AF., II., 46. (Act of the Committee of Public Safety, Prairial 15.) "Citizens Pillon, Gouste and Né, members of the Revolutionary Committee of the Marat section, are removed. Their duties will be performed by citizens Martin, Majon, and Merel. Manville, rue de la Liberté, No. 32, is appointed on the said Revolutionary Committee to complete it, composed only of eleven members." And other similar acts.

lists, try to find men able to maintain the system; he always falls back on the same names, those of unknown persons, illiterate, about a hundred knaves or fools with four or five second-class despots or fanatics among them, as malevolent and as narrow as himself. The purifying crucible has been long and too often used; it has been overheated; what was sound, or nearly so, in the elements of the primitive fluid has been forcibly evaporated; the rest has fermented and become acid; nothing remains in the bottom of the vessel but the lees of stupidity and wickedness, their concentrated and corrosive dregs.

II

Such are the subordinate sovereigns[20] who, for fourteen months in Paris, dispose of fortunes, liberties, and lives as they please. And first, in the section assemblies, which still maintain a semblance of popular sovereignty, they rule despotically and uncontested. "A dozen or fifteen men wearing a red cap,[21] well-informed or not, claim the exclusive right of speaking and acting, and if any other citizen with honest motives happens to propose measures which he thinks proper, and which really are so, no attention is paid to these measures, or, if it is, it is only to show the members composing the assemblage of how little account they are. These measures are accordingly rejected, solely because they are not presented by one of the men in a red cap, or by somebody like themselves, initiated in the mysteries of the section." "Sometimes," says one of the leaders,[22] "we find only ten of the club at the general assembly of the section;

---

20. Duverger, decree of Frimaire 14, year II. "The application of revolutionary laws and measures of general security and public safety is confided to the municipalities and revolutionary committees." See, in chapter ii., the extent of the domain thus defined. It embraces nearly everything. It suffices to run through the registers of a few of the revolutionary committees, to verify this enormous power and see how they interfere in every detail of individual life.

21. Archives Nationales, F[7], 3,116[7]. (Report, Nivose 1, year II., by Leharival.)

22. Dauban, *ibid.*, 307. (Report of March 29, 1794.) It here relates to the "Piques" Section, Place Vendome.

but there are enough of us to intimidate the rest. Should any citizen of the section make a proposition we do not like, we rise and shout that he is an intriguer, or a signer (of former constitutional petitions). In this way we impose silence on those who are not in unison with the club." The operation is all the easier inasmuch as since September, 1793, the majority, composed of beasts of burden, mind the lash. "When something has to be effected that depends on intrigue or on private interest,[23] the motion is always put by one of the members of the revolutionary committee of the section, or by one of those fanatical patriots who join in with the committee, and commonly act as its spies. Immediately the ignorant men, to whom Danton has allowed forty sous for each meeting, and who, *since that time, flock to the assembly in crowds, where they never came before*, welcome the proposition with loud applause, *calling for a vote*, and the act is passed unanimously, notwithstanding the contrary opinions of all well-informed and honest citizens. Should any one dare make an objection, he would run the risk of imprisonment as a 'suspect,'[24] after being treated as an aristocrat or federalist, or at least, refused a certificate of civism, if he had the misfortune to need one, did his subsistence depend on this, either as employee or pensioner." In the Maison-Commune section, most of the auditory are masons, "excellent patriots," says one of the clubbists of the quarter:[25] "they always vote on our side; we make them do what we want." Numbers of day-laborers, cab-drivers, cartmen and workmen of every class, thus earn their forty sous, and have no idea of other demands being made on them. On entering the hall, when the meeting opens, they

23. Dauban, 308. (Note found among Danton's papers and probably written by the physician, Quevremont de Lamotte.)

24. Dauban, *ibid.*, 125. (Report of Bérard, Ventose 10.) In the words of a woman belonging to the Bonne-Novelle section: "My husband has been in prison four months. And what for? He was one of the first at the Bastille: he has always refused places so that the good *sans-culottes* might have them, and, if he has made enemies, it was because he was unwilling to see these filled by ignoramuses or new-comers, who, vociferating and apparently thirsting for blood, have created a barrier of partisans around them."

25. Dauban, *ibid.*, 307. (Report of March 29, 1794.)

write down their names, after which they go out "to take a drink," without thinking themselves obliged to listen to the rigmarole of the orators; towards the end, they come back, make all the noise that is required of them with their lungs, feet and hands, and then go and "take back their card and get their money."[26] With paid applauders of this stamp, they soon get the better of any opponents, or, rather, all opposition is suppressed beforehand. "The best citizens keep silent" in the section assemblies, or "stay away"; these are simply "gambling-shops" where "the most absurd, the most unjust, the most impolitic of resolutions are passed at every moment.[27] Moreover, citizens are ruined there by the unlimited sectional expenditure, which exceeds the usual taxation and the communal expenses, already very heavy. At one time, some carpenter or locksmith, member of the Revolutionary Committee, wants to construct, enlarge or decorate a hall, and it is necessary to agree with him. Again, a poor speech is made, full of exaggeration and political extravagance, of which three, four, five, and six thousand impressions are ordered to be printed. Then, to cap the climax, following the example of the Commune, *no accounts are rendered*, or, if this is done for form's sake, no fault must be found with them, under penalty of suspicion, etc." Proprietors and distributors of civism, the twelve leaders have only to agree amongst themselves to share the profits, each according to his appetite; henceforth, cupidity and vanity are free to sacrifice the common weal, under cover of the common interest. The

26. *Ibid.*, 150. (Report of Ventose 14.)—Archives Nationales, F⁷, 3,116⁷. (Reports of Nivose 9 and 25.) "A great many citizens are found in the sections who are called out after the meeting, to get forty sous. I notice that most of them are masons, and even a few coach drivers belonging to the nation, who can do without the nation's indemnity, which merely serves them for drink to make them very noisy." "The people complain, because the persons to whom the forty sous are given, to attend the section assemblies, do nothing all day, being able to work at different trades . . . and depending on these forty sous."

27. Dauban, *ibid.*, 312. (Note by Quevremont.)—*Moniteur*, xviii., 568. (Meeting of the Commune, Frimaire 11, year II.) "The Beaurepaire section advertises that wishing to put a stop to the cupidity of the wine-dealers of the arrondissement, it has put seals on all their cellars."

provender is enormous and the summons to it comes from above. "I am very glad," says Henriot, in one of his orders of the day,[28] "to announce to my brethren in arms that all the offices are at the disposal of the government. The actual government, which is revolutionary, whose intentions are pure, and which merely desires the happiness of all, . . . goes to garrets for virtuous men, . . . poor and genuine *sans-culottes,*" and it has the wherewithal to satisfy them—thirty-five thousand places of public employment in the capital alone:[29] it is a rich mine; already, before the month of May, 1793, "the Jacobin club boasted of having placed nine thousand agents in the administration,"[30] and since the 2d of June, "virtuous men, poor, genuine *sans-culottes,*" arrive in crowds from "their garrets," dens and hired rooms, each to grab his share. Setting aside the old offices in the War, Navy, and Public-Works departments, in the Treasury and Ministry of Foreign Affairs, which they besiege, and where they install themselves by hundreds and rule, where they constantly denounce all the able employees who stay there, and make vacancies in order to fill them,[31] there are twenty new administrative departments which they keep for themselves: commissioners of the first

28. Dauban, *ibid.,* 345. (Order of the day by Henriot, Floréal 9.)

29. Mallet-Dupan, ii., 56. (March, 1794.)

30. Buchez et Roux, xxvii., 10. (Speech by Barbaroux, May 14, 1793.)—Report on the papers found in Robespierre's apartment, by Courtois, 285. (Letter by Collot d'Herbois Frimaire 3, year II., demanding that Paris Jacobins be sent to him at Lyons.) "If I could have asked for our old ones I should have done . . . but they are necessary at Paris, almost all of them having been made mayors."

31. Meissner, "Voyage à Paris" (at the end of 1795), 160. "Persons who can neither read nor write obtain the places of accountants of more or less importance."—Archives des Affaires Étrangérès, vol. 324. (Denunciations of Pio to the club, against his colleagues.) Dauban, *ibid.,* 35. (Note by Quevremont, Jan., 1794.) "The honest man who knows how to work cannot get into the ministerial bureaux, especially those of the War and Navy departments, as well as those of Commerce and of the Departments, without having his feelings tried.—Offices are mostly filled by creatures of the Commune who very often have neither talent nor integrity. Again, the denumciations, always welcomed, however frivolous and baseless they may be, turn everything upside down."

confiscation of national property, commissioners of national property arising from emigrants and the convicted, commissioners of
conscripted carriage-horses, commissioners on clothing, commissioners on the collecting and manufacturing of saltpetre, commissioners on monopolies, civil-commissioners in each of the forty-
eight sections, commissioners on propagandism in the departments,
commissioners on subsistences, and many others; fifteen hundred
places are counted in the single department of subsistence in Paris,[32]
and all are salaried. Here, already, are a number of desirable offices.
Some are for the lowest rabble, two hundred, at twenty sous a day,
paid to "stump-speakers," employed to direct opinion in the Palais-
Royal, also among the Tuileries groups, as well as in the tribunes
of the Convention and of the Hôtel-de-Ville;[33] two hundred more
at four hundred francs per annum, to waiters in coffee-houses,
gambling-saloons, and hotels, for watching foreigners and customers; hundreds of places at two, three, and five francs a day with
meals, for the guardians of seals, and for garrisoning the domiciles
of "suspects"; thousands, with premiums, pay, and full license, for
brigands who, under Ronsin, compose the revolutionary army, and
for the gunners, paid guard, and gendarmes of Henriot. The principal posts, however, are those which subject lives and liberties to
the discretion of those who occupy them: for, through this more
than regal power, they possess all other power, and such is that of
the men composing the forty-eight revolutionary committees, the

32. *Moniteur*, xxiv., 397. (Speech of Dubois-Crancé in the Convention Floréal 16, year III.)—Archives Nationales, F⁷, 3,116⁷. (Report by Rolin, Nivose
7, year II.) "The same complaints are heard against the civil Commissioners of
the section, most of whom are unintelligent, not even knowing how to read."

33. Archives des Affaires Étrangérès, vol. 1411. (August, 1793.) "Plan
adopted" for the organisation of the Police, "excepting executive modifications."
In fact, some months later, the number of *claqueurs*, male and female, is much
greater, and finally reaches a thousand. (Beaulieu, "Essais," v., 110.)—The same
plan comprehends fifteen agents at two thousand four hundred francs, "selected
from the frequenters of the clubs," to revise the daily morning lists; thirty at
one thousand francs, for watching popular clubs, and ninety to twelve hundred
francs for watching the section assemblies.

bureaux of the Committee of General Security and of the Commune, and the staff-officers of the armed force. They are the prime-movers and active mainsprings of the system of Terror, all picked Jacobins and tested by repeated selection, all designated or approved by the Central Club, which claims for itself the monopoly of patriotism, and which, erected into a supreme council of the sect, issues no patent of orthodoxy except to its own instruments.[34]

They immediately assume the tone and arrogance of dictatorship. "Pride has reached the highest point":[35] "One who, yesterday, had nothing to do, and was amiable and honest, has become haughty and insolent because, deceived by appearances, his fellow-citizens have elected him commissioner, or given him some employment or other." Henceforth, he demeans himself like an aga amongst infidels, and, in command, carries things with a high hand. On the 20th of Vendémiaire, year II., "in the middle of the night," the committee of the Piques section summons M. Bélanger, the architect. He is notified that his house is wanted immediately for a new bastille. "But, said he, 'I own no other, and it is occupied by several tenants; it is decorated with models of art, and is fit only for that purpose.'

34. Archives Nationales, F[7], 4,436. (Letter of Bouchotte, Minister of War, Prairial 5, year II.) "The appointment of Ronsin, as well as of all his staff, again excited public opinion. The Committee, to assure itself, sent the list to the Jacobin club, where they were accepted."—*Ibid.*, AF., II., 58. "Paris, Brumaire 11, year II., club of the Friends of Liberty and Equality, in session at the former Jacobin club, rue St. Honoré. List of the citizens who are to set out for Lyons and act as national commissioners. (Here follow their names.) All the citizens designated have undergone the inspection of the said club, at its meeting this day." (Here follow the signatures of the President and three secretaries.)— "Journal des Débats et Correspondence de la Société des Jacobins, No. 545, 5th day of the 3d month of the year II.—In relation to the formation of a new Central club: "Terrasson is of opinion that this club may become *liberticide,* and demands a committee to examine into it and secure its extinction. The committee demanded by Terrasson is appointed." It is evident that they hold on energetically to this monopoly.—Cf. *Moniteur,* xix., 637. (Ventose 13.) Motion adopted in the Jacobin club, obliging the ministers to turn out of office any individual excluded from the club.

35. Dauban, *ibid.*, 307. (Report of Germinal 9.)

'Your house or a prison.' 'But I shall be obliged to indemnify my tenants.' 'Either your house or a prison; as to indemnities, we have vacant lodgings for your tenants, as well as for yourself, in La Force, or St. Pelagie.' Twelve sentinels on the post start off at once and take possession of the premises; the owner is allowed six hours to move out and is forbidden, henceforth, to return; the bureaux, to which he appeals, interpret his obedience as 'tacit adhesion,' and, very soon, he himself is locked up."[36] Administrative tools that cut so sharply need the greatest care, and, from time to time, they are carefully oiled:[37] on the 20th of July, 1793, two thousand francs are given to each of the forty-eight committees, and eight thousand francs to General Henriot, "for expenses in watching antirevolutionary manoeuvres"; on the 7th of August, fifty thousand francs "to indemnify the less successful members of the forty-eight committees"; three hundred thousand francs to Gen. Henriot "for thwarting conspiracies and securing the triumph of liberty"; fifty thousand francs to the mayor, "for detecting the plots of the malevolent"; on the 10th of September, forty thousand francs to the mayor, president and *procureur-syndic* of the department, "for measures of security"; on the 13th of September, three hundred thousand francs to the mayor "for preventing the attempts of the malevolent"; on the 15th of November, one hundred thousand francs to the popular clubs, "because these are essential to the propagation of sound principles." Moreover, besides gratuities and a fixed salary, there are the gratifications and perquisites belonging to the office.[38] Henriot ap-

36. *Moniteur,* xxii., 353. (Session of Brumaire 20, year III. Reclamation made by M. Bélanger at the bar of the Convention.)

37. Archives Nationales, AF., II., 40. (Acts passed by the Committee of Public Safety at the dates indicated.) Beaulieu, "Essais," v., 200. (*Ibid.*) The registers of the Committee of Public Safety contain a number of similar gratuities paid to provincial clubs and patriots, for instance, AF., II. 58 (Brumaire 8), fifty thousand francs to Laplanche, and (Brumaire 9), fifty thousand francs to Couthon, "to maintain public spirit in Calvados, to revive public spirit in Lyons," "to aid, as required, the less successful patriots who zealously devote their time to the service of their country."

38. Dauban, *ibid.,* 171 (report of Ventose 17), and 243 (report of Ventose

points his comrades on the staff of paid spies and denunciators, and, naturally, they take advantage of their position to fill their pockets; under the pretext of *incivism,* they multiply domiciliary visits, make the master of the house ransom himself, or steal what suits them on the premises.[39] In the Commune, and on the revolutionary committees, every extortion can be, and is, practiced. "I am acquainted," says Quevremont, "with two citizens who have been put in prison, without being told why, and, at the end of three weeks or a month, let out—and do you know how? By paying, one of them, fifteen thousand livres, and the other, twenty-five thousand. . . . Gambron, at La Force, pays one thousand five hundred livres a month not to live amongst lice, and besides this, he had to pay a bribe of two thousand livres on entering. This happened to many others who, again, dared not speak of it, except in a whisper."[40] Woe to the imprudent who, never concerning themselves with public affairs, and relying on their innocence, discard the officious broker and fail to pay up at once! Brichard, the notary, having refused or tendered too late, the hundred thousand crowns demanded of him, is to put his head "at the red window." And I omit ordinary rapine, the vast field open to extortion through innumerable inventories, sequestrations and adjudications, through the enormities of contractors, through

---

25), on the civil-committees and revolutionary committees, who order meat served to them before serving it to the sick, and who likewise serve the good friends of their wives.—*Ibid.,* 146. (Report of Ventose 10.) . . . Archives Nationales, F⁷, 2,475. (Register of the deliberations of the Revolutionary Committee of the Piques sections, Brumaire 27, year II.) "The Committee orders that the two-horse cab belonging to Lemarche be henceforth at the service of the section and of the Committee when measures of security are concerned." In this register, and others of the same series, we clearly see the inside of a committee and its vast despotism. Style and orthography, with almost all, are of the same low order.

39. Archives des Affaires Étrangérès, vol. 1411. (Report of Aug. 21 and 22, 1793.) "General Henriot sent me several . . . who made use of the authority of the Committee of Public Safety and General Security, as well as of that which he delegated to me, to make domiciliary visits at the houses of individuals who were not assured patriots; but that did not warrant their *receiving money* and even *abstracting it.*"

40. Dauban, *ibid.,* 36 and 48. (Case of the Notary, Brichard.)

hastily executed purchases and deliveries, through the waste of two or three millions given weekly by the government to the Commune for supplies for the capital, through the requisitions of grain which give fifteen hundred men of the revolutionary army an opportunity to clean out all the neighboring farms, as far as Corbeil and Meaux, and benefit by this after the fashion of the *chauffeurs*.[41] Considering the parties, as above, who have the places, the anonymous robberies are not surprising. Beboeuf, the falsifier of public contracts, is secretary for subsistences to the Commune; Maillard, the Abbaye *Septembriseur*, receives eight thousand francs for his direction, in the forty-eight sections, of the ninety-six observers and leaders of public opinion; Chrétien, whose smoking-shop serves as the rendezvous of rowdies, becomes a juryman at eighteen francs a day in the revolutionary Tribunal, and leads his section with uplifted sabre;[42] De Sade, professor of crimes, is now the oracle of his quarter, and, in the name of the Piques section, he reads addresses to the Convention.

III

Let us examine some of these figures closely: the nearer they are to the eye and foremost in position, the more the importance of the duty brings into light the unworthiness of the potentate. There is already one of them, whom we have seen in passing, Buchot, twice noticed by Robespierre under his own hand as "a man of probity, energetic, and capable of fulfilling the most important functions,"[43] appointed by the Committee of Public Safety "Commissioner on

41. Cf. "The Revolution," ii., 302, 303.—Mercier, "Paris pendant la Révolution," i., 151.—*Moniteur*, xviii., 660. (Session of Frimaire 24, speech by Lecomtre in the Convention.)—On robberies and the bribes paid, see, among other documents, "Mémoires sur les Prisons," i., 290. (Eighty thousand francs of bribes given to the head of the police force by Perisial, keeper of an eating-house, for the privilege of feeding prisoners in St. Lazare.)

42. Buchez et Roux, xxxv., 77. (Trial of Fouquier-Tinville.) Testimony of Robillard: "Another day, in the general assembly, he struck a citizen with his sabre."

43. Buchez et Roux, xxxv., 407. (Lists in Robespierre's handwriting.)

External Relations," that is to say, Minister of Foreign Affairs, and kept in this important position for nearly six months. He is a schoolmaster from the Jura,[44] recently disembarked from his small town and whose "ignorance, low habits, and stupidity surpass any thing that can be imagined. . . . The chief clerks have nothing to do with him; he neither sees nor asks for them. He is never found in his office, and when it is indispensable to ask for his signature on any legislative matter, the sole act to which he has reduced his functions, they are compelled to go and force it from him in the Café Hardy, where he usually passes his days." It must be borne in mind that he is envious and spiteful, avenging himself for his incapacity on those whose competency makes him sensible of his incompetency; he denounces them as Moderates, and, at last, succeeds in having a warrant of arrest issued against his four chief clerks; on the morning of Thermidor 9, with a wicked leer, he himself carries the news to one of them, M. Miot. Unfortunately for him, after Thermidor, he is turned out and M. Miot is put in his place. With diplomatic politeness, the latter calls on his predecessor and "expresses to him the usual compliments." Buchot, insensible to compliments, immediately

---

44. Miot de Melito, "Mémoires," i., 46–51.—Buchot is not the only one of his species in the ministry of Foreign Affairs. In the archives of this ministry, vol. 324, may be found the sayings and doings of a certain Pio, an Italian refugee who slipped into the place, simulating poverty, and displaying patriotism, and who denounces his chief and colleagues.—The ex-notary Pigeot, condemned to twenty years in irons and put in the pillory, Frimaire 9, year III., will come to the surface; he is encountered under the Directory as introducer of ambassadors.—Concerning one of the envoys of the Directory to Switzerland, here is a note by Mallet-Dupan. ("Anecdotes manuscrites," October, 1797.) "The Directorial ambassador, who has come to exact from the Swiss the expulsion of the body-guard, is named Mingot, of Belfort, a relation of Rewbell's, former body-guard to M. le Comte d'Artois.—He came to Zurich with a prostitute, a seamstress of Zurich, established in Berne. He was living with her at the expense of the Zurich government. Having invited the family of this creature, that is to say a common horse-driver with his wife and some other persons, to dinner, they drank and committed such excesses that the driver's wife, who was big with child, gave birth to it in the midst of the banquet. This creature gave Mingot a disease which has laid him up at Basle."

thinks of the substantial, and the first thing he asks for is to keep provisionally his apartment in the ministry. On this being granted, he expresses his thanks and tells M. Miot that it was very well to appoint him, but "for myself, it is very disagreeable. I have been obliged to come to Paris and quit my post in the provinces, and now they leave me in the street." Thereupon, with astounding impudence, he asks the man whom he wished to guillotine to give him a place as ministerial clerk. M. Miot tries to make him understand that for a former minister to descend so low would be improper. Buchot regards such delicacy as strange, and, seeing M. Miot's embarrassment, he ends by saying: "If you don't find me fit for a clerk, I shall be content with the place of a servant." This estimate of himself shows his proper value.

The other, whom we have also met before, and who is already known by his acts,[45] general in Paris of the entire armed force, commander-in-chief of one hundred and ten thousand men, is that former servant or under-clerk of the *procureur* Formey, who, dismissed by his employer for robbery, shut up in Bicêtre, by turns a spy and bully for a travelling show, barrier-clerk, and September butcher, purged the Convention on the 2d of June—in short, the famous Henriot, and now a common soldier and sot. In this latter capacity, spared on the trial of the Hébertists, he is kept as a tool, for the reason, doubtless, that he is narrow, coarse, and manageable, more compromised than anybody else, good for any job, without the slightest chance of becoming independent, unemployed in the army,[46] having no prestige with true soldiers, a general for street

---

45. "The Revolution," ii., 338, 348, 354.

46. Martel, "Types Révolutionnaires," 136–144.—The Minister of War appoints Henriot brigadier-general, July 3, 1793, and major-general on the 19th of September, and says in a postscript, "Please communicate to me the order of your services," unknown in the ministry because they were of no account.—On the orgies at Choisy-sur-Seine, v. (Archives, W., 2, 500–501), see investigation of Thermidor 18 and 19, year II., made at Boisy-sur-Seine by Blache, agent of the Committee of General Security. Boulanger, brigadier-general, and Henriot's first lieutenant, was an ex-companion jeweller.

parade and an interloper and lower than the lowest of the mob; his mansion, his box at the Opera-Comique, his horses, his importance at festivals and reviews, and, above all, his orgies make him perfectly content. Every evening, in full uniform, escorted by his aides-de-camp, he gallops to Choisy-sur-Seine, where, in the domicile of a flatterer named Fauvel, along with some of Robespierre's confederates or the local demagogues, he revels. They toss off the wines of the Duc de Coigny, smash the glasses, plates and bottles, betake themselves to neighboring dance-rooms and kick up a row, bursting in doors, and breaking benches and chairs to pieces—in short, they have a good time. The next morning, having slept himself sober, he dictates his orders for the day, veritable masterpieces in which the silliness, imbecility, and credulity of a numskull, the sentimentality of the drunkard, the clap-trap of a mountebank, and the tirades of a cheap philosopher form an unique compound, at once sickening and irritating, like the fiery, pungent mixtures of low groggeries, which suit his audience better because they contain the biting, mawkish ingredients that compose the adulterated brandy of the Revolution. He is posted on foreign transactions, and knows what makes the famine: "A lot of bread has been lately found in the privies: the Pitts and Cobourgs and other rascals who want to enslave justice and reason, and assassinate philosophy, must be called to account for this. Headquarters, etc."[47] He has theories on religions and preaches civic modesty to all dissenters: "The ministers and sectaries of every form of worship are requested not to practice any

47. Archives des Affaires Étrangérès, vol. 1411. Orders of the day by Henriot, September 16, Vendémiaire 29, year II., and Brumaire 19, year II. Many of these orders of the day are published in Dauban ("Paris en 1794"), p. 33. "Let our enemies pile up their property, build houses and palaces, let them have them, what do we care, we republicans, we do not want them! All we need to shelter us is a cabin, and as for wealth, simply the habits, the virtues and the love of our country. Headquarters, etc."—P. 43: "Yesterday evening a fire broke out in the Grand Augustins. . . . Everybody worked at it and it was put out in a very short time. Under the ancient régime the fire would have lasted for days. Under the system of freemen the fire lasted only an hour. What a difference! . . . Headquarters, etc."

further religious ceremonies outside their temples. Every good sectarian will see the propriety of observing this order. The interior of
a temple is large enough for paying one's homage to the Eternal,
who requires no rites that are repulsive to every thinking man. The
wise agree that a pure heart is the sublimest homage that Divinity
can desire. Headquarters, etc." He sighs for the universal idyllic
state, and invokes the suppression of the armed force: "I beg my
fellow-citizens, who are led to the criminal courts out of curiosity,
to act as their own police; this is a task which every good citizen
should fulfill wherever he happens to be. In a free country, justice
should not be secured by pikes and bayonets, but through reason
and philosophy. These must maintain a watchful eye over society;
these must purify it and proscribe thieves and evil-doers. Each individual must bring his small philosophic portion with him and, with
these small portions, compose a rational totality that will enure to
the benefit and welfare of all. Oh, for the time when functionaries
shall be rare, when the wicked shall be overthrown, when the law
shall become the sole functionary in society! Headquarters, etc."
Every morning, he preaches in the same pontifical strain. Imagine
the scene—Henriot's levee at headquarters, and a writing table,
with, perhaps, a bottle of brandy on it; on one side of the table, the
rascal who, while buckling on his belt or drawing on his boots,
softens his husky voice, and, with his nervous twitchings, flounders
through his humanitarian homily; on the other side the mute, uneasy
secretary, who may probably spell, but who dares not materially
change the grotesque phraseology of his master.

The Commune which employs the commanding-general is of
about the same alloy, for, in the municipal sword, the blade and hilt,
forged together in the Jacobin shop, are composed of the same base
metal. Fifty-six, out of eighty-eight members, whose qualifications
and occupations are known, are decidedly illiterate, or nearly so,
their education being rudimentary, or none at all.[48] Some of them

48. Wallon, "Histoire du Tribunal Révolutionnaire de Paris," v. 252, 420.
(Names and qualifications of the members of the Commune of Paris, guillotined

are petty clerks, counter-jumpers and common scribblers, one
among them being a public writer; others are small shopkeepers,
pastry-cooks, mercers, hosiers, fruit-sellers and wine-dealers; others,
finally, are simple mechanics or even laborers, carpenters, joiners,
cabinet-makers, locksmiths, and especially three tailors, four hair-
dressers, two masons, two shoemakers, one cobbler, one gardener,
one stone-cutter, one paver, one office-runner, and one domestic.
Among the thirty-two who are instructed, one alone has any reputation, Paris, professor at the University and the assistant of Abbé
Delille. Only one, Dumetz, an old engineer, steady, moderate, and
attending to the supplies, seems a competent and useful workman.
The rest, collected from amongst the mass of unknown demagogues,
are six art-apprentices or bad painters, six business-agents or ex-
lawyers, seven second- or third-rate merchants, one teacher, one
surgeon, one unfrocked married priest, all of whom, under the political direction of Mayor Fleuriot-Lescot and Payen, the national
agent, bring to the general council no administrative ability, but the
faculty for verbal argumentation, along with the requisite amount
of talk and scribbling indispensable to a deliberative assembly. And
it is curious to see them in session. Toward the end of September,
1793,[49] one of the veterans of liberal philosophy and political econ-

---

Thermidor 10 and 11.) The professions and qualifications of some of its members are given in Eymery's Biographical Dictionary, in Morellet's Memoirs and
in Arnault's Souvenirs.—*Moniteur*, xvi., 710. (Verdicts of the revolutionary
Tribunal, Fructidor 15, year II.) Forty-three members of the civil or revolutionary committees, sectional commissioners, officers of the National Guard and
of the cannoneers, signed the list of the Council-general of the Commune as
present on the 9th of Thermidor and are put on trial as Robespierre's adherents.
But they promptly withdrew their signatures, all being acquitted except one.
They are leaders in the Jacobin quarter and are of the same sort and condition
as their brethren of the Hôtel-de-Ville. One only, an ex-collector of *rentes*, may
have had an education; the rest are carpenters, floor-tilers, shoemakers, tailors,
wine-dealers, eating-house keepers, cartmen, bakers, hair-dressers, and joiners.
Among them we find one ex-stone-cutter, one ex-office runner, one ex-domestic,
and two sons of Samson the executioner.

49. Morellet, "Mémoires," i., 436–472.

omy, belonging to the French Academy and ruined by the Revolution, the old Abbé Morellet, needs a certificate of civism, to enable him to obtain payment of the small pension of one thousand francs, which the Constituent Assembly had voted him in recompense for his writings; the Commune, desiring information about this, selects three of its body to enquire into it. Morellet naturally takes the preliminary steps. He first writes "a very humble, very civic note," to the president of the General Council, Lubin Jr., formerly an art-apprentice who had abandoned art for politics, and is now living with his father a butcher, in the rue St. Honoré; he calls on this authority, and passes through the stall, picking his way amongst the slaughter-house offal; admitted after some delay, he finds his judge in bed, before whom he pleads his cause. He then calls upon Bernard, an ex-priest, "built like an incendiary and ill-looking," and respectfully bows to the lady of the house, "a tolerably young woman, but very ugly and very dirty." Finally, he carries his ten or a dozen volumes to the most important of the three examiners, Vialard, "ex-ladies' hair-dresser"; the latter is almost a colleague, "for," says he, "I have always liked mechanicians, having presented to the Academy of Sciences a top which I invented myself." Nobody, however, had seen the petitioner in the streets on the 10th of August, nor on the 2d of September, nor on the 31st of May; how can a certificate of civism be granted after such evidences of lukewarmness? Morellet, not disheartened, awaits the all-powerful hair-dresser at the Hôtel-de-Ville, and accosts him frequently as he passes along. He, "with greater haughtiness and distraction than the most unapproachable Minister of War would show to an infantry lieutenant," scarcely listens to him and walks on; he goes in and takes his seat, and Morellet, much against his will, has to be present at ten or twelve of these meetings. What strange meetings, to which patriotic deputations, volunteers and amateurs come in turn to declaim and sing; where the president, Lubin, "decorated with his scarf," shouts the Marseilles Hymn five or six times, "*Ca Ira,*" and other songs of several stanzas, set to tunes of the Comic Opera, and always "out of time, displaying the voice, airs, and songs of an exquisite Leander.

... I really believe that, at the last meeting, he sung alone in this manner three quarters of an hour at different times, the assembly repeating the last line of the verse." "How odd!" exclaims a common woman alongside of Morellet, "how droll, passing all their time here, singing in that fashion! Is that what they come here for?" Not alone for that: after the circus-parade is over, the ordinary haranguers, and especially the hair-dresser, come and propose measures for murder "in infuriate language and with fiery gesticulation." Such are the good speakers[50] and men for show. The others, who remain silent, and hardly know to write, act and do the rough work. A certain Chalaudon, member of the Commune,[51] is one of this order, president of the revolutionary committee of the section of "L'Homme armé," and probably an excellent man-hunter; for "the government committees assigned to him the duty of watching the right bank of the Seine, and, with extraordinary powers conferred on him, he rules from his back shop one half of Paris. Woe to those he has reason to complain of, those who have withdrawn from, or not given him, their custom! Sovereign of his quarter up to Thermidor 10, his denunciations are death-warrants. Some of the streets, especially that of Grand Chantier, he "depopulates." And this Marais exterminator is a "cobbler," a colleague in leather, as well as in the Commune,

50. On the ascendency of the talkers of this class see Dauban ("Paris en 1794," pp. 118–143). Details on an all-powerful clothes-dealer in the Lombards Section. If we may believe the female citizens of the Assembly "he said everywhere that whoever was disagreeable to him should be turned out of the popular club." (Ventose 13, year II.)

51. Arnault, "Souvenirs d'un Sexagénaire," iii., 111. Details on another member of the Commune, Bergot, ex-employee at the Halle-aux-Cuirs and police administrator, may be found in "Mémoires des Prisons," i., 232, 239, 246, 289, 290. Nobody treated the prisoners more brutally, who protested against the foul food served out to them, than he. "It is too good for b—— who are going to be guillotined." . . . "He got drunk with the turnkeys and with the commissioners themselves. One day he staggered in walking, and spoke only in hiccoughs: he would go in in that condition. The house-guard refused to recognize him; he was arrested" and the *concierge* had to repeat her declarations to make the officer of the post "give up the hog."

of Simon the shoemaker, the preceptor and murderer of the young Dauphin.

Still lower down than this admirable municipal body, let us try to imagine, from at least one complete example, the forty-eight revolutionary committees who supply it with hands. There is one of them of which we know all the members, where the governing class, under full headway, can be studied to the life.[52] This consists of the nomadic and interloping class which is revolutionary only through its appetites; no theory and no convictions animate it; during the first three years of the Revolution it pays no attention to, or cares for, public matters; if, since the 10th of August, and especially since the 2d of June, it takes any account of these, it is to get a living and gorge itself with plunder. Out of eighteen members, simultaneously or in succession, of the "Bonnet Rouge," fourteen, before the 10th of August and especially since the 2d of June, are unknown in this quarter, and had taken no part in the Revolution. The most prominent among these are three painters, heraldic, carriage and miniature, evidently ruined and idle on account of the Revolution, a candle-dealer, a vinegar-dealer, a manufacturer of saltpetre, and a locksmith; while of these seven personages, four have additionally enhanced the dignity of their calling by vending tickets for small lotteries, acting as pawnbrokers or as keepers of a *biribi*[53] saloon. Seated along with these are two upper-class domestics, a hack-driver, an ex-gendarme dismissed from the corps, a cobbler on the street corner, a runner on errands who was once a carter's boy, and another who, two months before this, was a scavenger's apprentice, the latter penniless and in tatters before he became one of the Committee, and since that, well clad, lodged and furnished; finally, a former dealer in lottery-tickets, himself a counterfeiter by his own admission, and a jail-bird. Four others have been dismissed from their places for

52. "Mémoires sur les Prisons," i., 211. ("Tableau Historique de St. Lazare.") The narrator is put into prison in the rue de Sèvres in October, 1793.— II., 186. ("An historical account of the jail in the rue de Sèvres.") The narrator was confined there during the last months of the Reign of Terror.

53. A game of chance.

dishonesty or swindling, three are known drunkards, two are not even Frenchmen, while the ring-leader, the man of brains of this select company is, as usual, a seedy, used-up lawyer, the ex-notary Pigeot, and expelled from his professional body on account of bankruptcy. He is probably the author of the following speculation: After the month of September, 1793, the Committee, freely arresting whomsoever it pleased in the quarter, and even out of it, makes a haul of "three hundred heads of families" in four months, with whom it fills the old barracks it occupies in the rue de Sèvres. In this confined and unhealthy tenement, more than one hundred and twenty prisoners are huddled together, sometimes ten in one room, two in the same bed, and, for their keeping, they pay three hundred francs a day. As sixty-two francs of this charge are verified, there is of this sum (not counting other extortions or concessions which are not official), two hundred and thirty-eight francs profit daily for these honest contractors. Accordingly, they live freely and have "the most magnificent dinners" in their assembly chamber; the contribution of ten or twelve francs apiece is "nothing" for them. But, in this opulent St. Germain quarter, so many rich and noble men and women form a herd which must be conveniently stalled, so as to be the more easily milked. Consequently, toward the end of March, 1794, the Committee, to increase its business and fill up the pen, hires a large house on the corner of the boulevard possessing a court and a garden, where the high society of the quarter is assigned lodgings of two rooms each, at twelve francs a day, which gives one hundred and fifty thousand livres per annum, and, as the rent is twenty-four hundred francs, the Committee gain one hundred and forty-seven thousand six hundred livres by the operation; we must add to this twenty sorts of profit in money and other matters—taxes on the articles consumed and on supplies of every description, charges on the despatch and receipt of correspondence and other gratuities, such as ransoms and fees. A penned-up herd refuses nothing to its keepers,[54] and this one less than any other; for if this herd

54. "Un Séjour en France de 1792 à 1795," 281. "We had an appointment

is plundered it is preserved, its keepers finding it too lucrative to send it to the slaughter-house. During the last six months of Terror, but two out of the one hundred and sixty boarders of the "Bonnet Rouge" Committee are withdrawn from the establishment and handed over to the guillotine. It is only on the 7th and 8th of Thermidor that the Committee of Public Safety, having undertaken to empty the prisons, breaks in upon the precious herd and disturbs the well-laid scheme, so admirably managed. It was only too well-managed, for it excited jealousy; three months after Thermidor, the "Bonnet Rouge" committee is denounced and condemned; ten are sentenced to twenty years in irons, with the pillory in addition, and, among others, the clever notary,[55] amidst the jeerings and insults of

---

in the afternoon with a person employed by the Committee on National Domains; he was to help my friend with her claims. This man was originally a valet to the Marquise's brother; on the outbreak of the Revolution he set up a shop, failed, and became a rabid Jacobin, and, at last, member of a revolutionary committee. As such, he found a way . . . to intimidate his creditors and obtain two discharges of his indebtedness without taking the least trouble to pay his debts." . . . "I know an old lady who was kept in prison three months for having demanded from one of these patriots three hundred livres which he owed her." (June 3, 1795.) "I have generally noticed that the republicans are either of the kind I have just indicated, coffee-house waiters, jockeys, gamblers, bankrupts, and low scribblers, or manual laborers more earnest in their principles, more ignorant and more brutal, all spending what they have earned in vulgar indulgence."

55. Schmidt, "Tableaux Historiques de la Révolution Française," ii., 248, 249. (Agent's reports, Frimaire 8, year III.) "The prosecution of Carrier is approved by the public, likewise the condemnation of the former revolutionary committee called the "Bonnet-Rouge." Ten of its members are condemned to twenty years in irons. The public is overjoyed."—*Ibid.*, (Frimaire 9), "The people rushed in crowds to the square of the old commune building to see the members of the former revolutionary committee of the Bonnet-Rouge sections, who remained seated on the bench until six o'clock, in the light of flambeaux. They had to put up with many reproaches and much humiliation."—"Un Séjour en France," 286, (June 6, 1795). "I have just been interrupted by a loud noise and cries under my window; I heard the names Scipio and Solon distinctly pronounced in a jeering and insulting tone of voice. I sent Angelique to see what was the matter and she tells me that it is a crowd of children following a shoemaker of the neighborhood who was member of a revolutionary committee

the crowd. And yet these are not the worst; their cupidity had mollified their ferocity. Others, less adroit in robbing, show greater cruelty in murdering. In any event, in the provinces as well as in Paris, in the revolutionary committees paid three francs a day for each member, the quality of one or the other of the officials is about the same. According to the pay-lists which Barère keeps, there are twenty-one thousand five hundred of these committees in France.[56]

IV

Had the laws of March 21 and September 5, 1793, been strictly enforced, there would have been forty-five thousand of these revolutionary committees, instead of twenty-one thousand five hundred, composed of five hundred and forty thousand members and costing the public five hundred and ninety-one millions per annum.[57] This would have made the regular administrative body, already twice as numerous and twice as costly as under the ancient régime, an extra corps expending, "simply in surveillance," one hundred millions more than the entire taxation of the country, the greatness of which had excited the people against the ancient régime. Happily, the poisonous and monstrous mushroom obtains but one-half its growth; neither the Jacobin seed nor the bad atmosphere it required

---

... and had called himself Scipio Solon. As he had been caught in several efforts at stealing he could no longer leave his shop without being reviled for his robberies and hooted at under his Greek and Roman names."

56. Barère, "Mémoires," ii., 324.

57. *Moniteur,* xxii., 742. (Report by Cambon, Frimaire 6, year II.)—*Ibid.,* 22.—Report by Lindet, September 20, 1794): "The land and navy forces, war and other services, deprive agricultural pursuits and other professions of more than one million five hundred thousand citizens. It would cost the Republic less to support six million men in all the communes."—"Le Departement des Affaires Étrangérès," by Fr. Masson, 382. (According to "Paris à la fin du dix-huitieme siècle," by Pujoulx, year IX.): "At Paris alone there are more than thirty thousand (government) clerks; six thousand at the most do the necessary writing; the rest cut away quills, consume ink and blacken paper. In old times, there were too many clerks in the bureaux relatively to the work; now, there are three times as many, and there are some who think that there are not enough."

to make it spread could be found anywhere. "The people of the provinces," says a contemporary,[58] "are not up to the level of the Revolution; it opposes old habits and customs and the resistance of inertia to innovations which it does not understand." "The plough-man is an estimable man," writes a missionary representative, "but he is generally a poor patriot."[59] In effect, there is on the one hand, less of human sediment in the departmental towns than in the great Parisian sink, and, on the other hand, the rural population, preserved from intellectual miasmas, better resists social epidemics than the urban population. Less infested with vicious adventurers, less fruitful in disordered intellects, the provinces supply a corps of inquisitors and terrorists with greater difficulty.

And first, in the thousands of communes which have less than five hundred inhabitants,[60] in many other villages of greater popu-lation, but scattered[61] and purely agricultural, especially in those in

58. "Souvenirs de M. Hua," a parliamentary advocate, p. 96. (A very ac-curate picture of the bourg Coucy-le-Chateau, in Aisne, from 1792 to 1794.)— "Archives des Affaires Étrangéres," vol. 334. (Letter of the agents, Thionville, Ventose 24, year II.) The district of Thionville is very patriotic, submits to the maximum and requisitions, but not to the laws prohibiting outside worship and religious assemblies. "The apostles of Reason preached in vain to the people, telling them that, up to this time, they had been deceived and that now was the time to throw off the yoke of prejudice: 'we are willing to believe that, thus far, we have been deceived, but who will guarantee us that you will not deceive us in your turn?'"

59. Lagros: "La Revolution telle qu'elle est." (Unpublished correspondence of the Committee of Public Safety, i., 366. Letter of Prieur de la Marne.) "In general, the towns are patriotic; but the rural districts are a hundred leagues removed from the Revolution. . . . Great efforts will be necessary to bring them up to the level of the Revolution."

60. According to the statistics of 1866 (published in 1869) a district of one thousand square kilometres contains on an average, thirty-three communes above five hundred souls, twenty-three from five hundred to one thousand, seventeen bourgs and small towns from one thousand to five thousand, and one average town, or very large one, about five thousand. Taking into account the changes that have taken place in seventy years, one may judge from these figures of the distribution of the population in 1793. This distribution explains why, instead of forty-five thousand revolutionary committees, there were only twenty-one thousand five hundred.

61. "Souvenirs des M. Hua," 179. "This country (Coucy-le-Chateau) pro-

which patois is spoken, there is a scarcity of suitable subjects for a revolutionary committee. People make use of their hands too much; hands with a tough skin do not write easily; nobody wants to take up a pen, especially to keep a register that may be preserved and some day or other prove compromising. It is already a difficult matter to recruit a municipal council, to find a mayor, the two additional municipal officers, and the national agent which the law requires; in the small communes, these are the only agents of the revolutionary government, and I fancy that, in most cases, their Jacobin fervor is moderate. Municipal officer, national agent or mayor, the real peasant of that day belongs to no party, neither royalist nor republican;[62] he has too few ideas, too transient and too sluggish, to enable him to form a political opinion. All he comprehends of the Revolution is that which nettles him, or that which he sees every day around him, with his own eyes; to him '93 and '94 are and will remain "the time of bad paper (money) and great fright," and nothing more.[63] Patient in his habits, he submits to the new as he did to the ancient régime, bearing the load put on his shoulders, and stooping down for fear of a heavier one. He is often mayor or national agent in spite of himself; he has been obliged to take the place and would gladly throw the burden off. For, as times go, it is onerous; if he executes decrees and orders, he is certain to make enemies; if he does not execute them, he is sure to be imprisoned; he had better remain, or go back home "Gros-jean," as he was before. But he has no choice; the appointment being once made

---

tected by its bad roads and still more by its nullity, belonged to that small number in which the revolutionary turmoil was least felt."

62. Among other documents of use in composing this tableau I must cite, as first in importance, the five files containing all the documents referring to the mission of the representative Albert, in Aisne and Marne. (Ventose and Germinal, year III.) Nowhere do we find more precise details of the sentiments of the peasant, of the common laborer and of the lower bourgeois from 1792 to 1795. (Archives Nationales, D. §§ 2 to 5.)

63. Dauban, "La Demagogie en 1793," xii. (The expression of an old peasant, near St. Emilion, to M. Vatel engaged in collecting information on the last days of Pétion, Guadet and Buzot.)

and confirmed, he cannot decline, nor resign, under penalty of being a "suspect"; he must be the hammer in order not to become the anvil. Whether he is a wine-grower, miller, ploughman or stone-breaker, he must act accordingly in self-defence, unless to "petition for his removal," when Terror begins to decide, on the ground that "he writes badly," that "he knows nothing whatever about law and is unable to enforce it"; that "he has to support himself with his own hands"; that "he has a family to provide for, and is obliged to drive his own cart" or vehicle; in short, entreating that he "may be relieved of his charge."[64] These involuntary recruits are evidently nothing more than common laborers; if they drag along the revolutionary cart they do it like their horses, because they are pressed into the service.

Above the small communes, in the large villages possessing a revolutionary committee, and also in certain bourgs, the horses in harness often pretend to draw and do not, for fear of crushing some one. At this epoch, a straggling village, especially when isolated, in an out-of-the-way place and on no highway, is a small world in itself, much more secluded than now-a-days, much less accessible to Parisian verbiage and outside pressure; local opinion here pre-ponderates; neighbors support each other; they would shrink from denouncing a worthy man whom they had known for twenty years;

---

64. Archives Nationales, D. § I., 5. (Petition of Claude Defert, miller, and national agent of Turgy.) Numbers of mayors, municipal officers, national agents, administrators and notables of districts and departments solicit succes-sors, and Albert compels many of them to remain in office.—(Joint letter of the entire municipality of Landreville; letter of Charles, stone-cutter, mayor of Trannes; Claude Defert, miller, national agent of Turgy; of Elegny, meat-dealer; of a wine-grower; municipal official at Merrex, etc.) The latter writes: "The Republic is great and generous; it does not desire that its children should ruin themselves in attending to its affairs; on the contrary, its object is to give salaried (*emolumentaires*) places to those who have nothing to live on."—Another, Ma-geure, appointed mayor of Bar-sur-Seine writes, Pluviose 29, year III.: "I learned yesterday that some persons of this community would like to procure for me the insidious gift of the mayoralty," and he begs Albert to turn aside this cup.

the moral sway of honest folks suffices for keeping down "black-guards."[65] If the mayor is republican, it is only in words, perhaps for self-protection, to protect his commune, and because one must howl along with the other wolves. Moreover, in other bourgs, and in the small towns, the fanatics and rascals are not sufficiently numerous to fill all the offices, and, in order to fill the vacancies, those who are not good Jacobins have been pushed forward or admitted into the new administrative corps, lukewarm, indifferent, timid, or needy men, who take the place as an asylum or ask for it as a means of subsistence. "Citizens," one of the recruits, more or less under restraint, writes later on,[66] "I was put on the Committee of Surveillance of Aignay by force, and installed by force." Three or four madmen on it ruled, and if one held any discussion with them, "it was always threats. . . . Always trembling, always afraid, that is the way I passed eight months doing duty in that miserable place." Finally, in medium-sized or large towns, the dead-lock produced by collective dismissals, the pell-mell of improvised appointments, and

65. "Souvenirs de M. Hua," 178–205. "M. P——, mayor of Crépy-au-Mont, knew how to restrain some low fellows who would have been only too glad to revolutionise his village. . . . And yet he was a republican. . . . One day, speaking of the revolutionary system, he said: 'They always say that it will not hold on; meanwhile, it sticks like lime.' " "A general assembly of the inhabitants of Coucy and its outskirts was held, in which everybody was obliged to undergo an examination, stating his name, residence, birth-place, present occupation, and what he had done during the Revolution." Hua avoids telling that he had been a representative in the Legislative Assembly, a notorious fact in the neighborhood. "Not a voice was raised to compromise me." *Ibid.,* 183. (Reply of the Coucy Revolutionary Committee to that of Meaux.)

66. "Frochot," by Louis Passy, 175. (Letter of Pajot, member of the Revolutionary Committee of Troyes, Vendémiaire, year III.)—Archives Nationales, F⁷, 4,421. (Register of the Revolutionary Committee of Troyes.) Brumaire 27, year II. Incarceration of various suspects, among others of "Lerouge, former lawyer, under suspicion of having constantly and obstinately refused revolutionary offices." Also, a person named Corps, for "having refused the presidency of the district tribunal at the time of its organisation, under the pretext of consulting the Chambre des Comptes; also for being the friend of suspects, and for having accepted office only after the Revolution had assumed an imposing character."

the sudden renewal of an entire set of officials, threw into the administration, willingly or not, a lot of pretended Jacobins who, at heart, are Girondists or Feuillantists, but who, having been over-oratorical, are assigned offices on account of their stump-speeches, and who thenceforth sit alongside of the worst Jacobins, in the worst employment. "Member of the Feurs Revolutionary Committee— those who make that objection to me," says a Clermont advocate,[67] "are persuaded that those only who secluded themselves, felt the Terror. They are not aware, perhaps, that nobody felt it more than those who were compelled to execute its decrees. Remember that the handwriting of Couthon which designated some citizen for an office also conveyed a threat, and in case of refusal, of being declared 'suspect,' a threat which promised in perspective the loss of liberty and the sequestration of property! Was I free, then, to refuse?" Once installed, the man must act, and many of those who do act let their repugnance be seen in spite of themselves: at best, they cannot be got to do more than mechanical service. "Before going to court," says a judge at Cambray, "I swallowed a big glass of spirits to give me strength enough to preside." He leaves his house with no other intention than to finish the job, and, the sentence once pronounced, to return home, shut himself up, and close his eyes and ears. "I had to pronounce judgment according to the jury's declaration—what could I do?"[68] Nothing, but remain blind and deaf: "*I drank. I tried to ignore everything, even the names of the accused.*" It is plain enough that, in the local official body, there are too many agents who are weak, not zealous, without any push, unreliable, or even

---

67. Marcelin Boudet, "Les Conventionnels d'Auvergne," 161. (Justification of Etienne Bonarmé, the last months of 1794.)

68. Paris, "Histoire de Joseph Lebon," ii., 92. (Declaration by Guérard, lawyer, appointed judge at Cambrai, by the Cambrai Revolutionary Committee.)—*Ibid.*, 54. (Declaration by Lemerre, appointed juryman without his knowledge, in the Cambrai court.) "What was my surprise, I, who never was on a jury in my life! The summons was brought to me at a quarter to eleven (*à onze heur moin un car*—specimen of the orthography) and I had to go at eleven without having time to say good-by to my family."

secretly hostile; these must be replaced by others who are energetic and reliable, and the latter must be taken wherever they can be found.[69] This reservoir in each department or district is the Jacobin nursery of the principal town; from this, they are sent into the bourgs and communes of the conscription. The central Jacobin nursery for France is in Paris, from whence they are despatched to the towns and departments.

V

Consequently, swarms of Jacobin locusts from Paris constantly overspread the provinces, also from the local country-towns, the surrounding country. In this cloud of destructive insects, there are diverse figures and of diverse shapes: in the front rank, are the representatives on mission, who are to take command in the departments; in the second rank, "the political agents," who, assigned the duty of watching the neighboring frontier, take upon themselves the additional duty of leading the popular club of the town they reside in, or of urging on its administrative body.[70] Besides that, there issue from the Paris headquarters in the rue St. Honoré, select

69. Report by Courtois on the papers found in Robespierre's domicile, 370. (Letter of Maignet to Payan, administrator of the department of Drôme, Germinal 20, year II.) "You know the dearth of subjects here. . . . Give me the names of a dozen outspoken republicans. . . . If you cannot find them in this department (Vaucluse) hunt for them either in the Drôme or the Isère, or in any other. I should like those adapted to a revolutionary Tribunal. I should even like, in case of necessity, to have some that are qualified to act as national agents."

70. Archives des Affaires Étrangérès, vols. 322 to 334, and 1409 to 1411.— These agents reside in Nismes, Marseilles, Toulouse, Tarbes, Bordeaux, Auch, Rochefort, Brest, Bergues, Givèt, Metz, Thionville, Strasbourg, Colmar, Belfort, and Grenoble, and often betake themselves to towns in the vicinity. The fullest reports are those of Chépy, at Grenoble, whose correspondence is worthy of publication; although an ultra Jacobin, he was brought before the revolutionary Tribunal as a moderate, in Ventose, year II. Having survived (the Revolution) he became under the Empire a general Commissary of Police at Brest. Almost all of them are veritable Jacobins, absolutist at bottom, and they became excellent despotic tools.

sans-culottes, who, empowered by, or delegates from, the Committee of Public Safety, proceed to Lyons, Marseilles, Bordeaux, Tonnerre, Rochefort, and elsewhere, to act as missionaries among the too inert population, or form the committees of action and the tribunals of extermination that are recruited with difficulty on the spot.[71] Sometimes also, when a town is in bad repute, the popular club of a sounder-minded city sends its delegates there, to bring it into line; thus, four deputies of the Metz club arrive without notice in Belfort, catechise their brethren, associate with them the local Revolutionary Committee, and, suddenly, without consulting the municipality, or any other legal authority, draw up a list of "moderates, fanatics, and egoists," on whom they impose an extraordinary tax of one hundred and thirty-six thousand six hundred and seventeen livres;[72] in like manner, sixty delegates from the club of Côte d'Or, Haute-Marne, Vosges, Moselle, Saone-et-Loire and Mont-Terrible, all "tempered by the white heat of *Père Duchesne,*" proceed to Strasbourg at the summons of the representatives, where, under the title of "propagandists," they are to regenerate the town.[73] At the same time, in

71. Buchez et Roux, xxx., 425.—Twenty-four commissioners, drawn by lot from the Jacobins of Paris, are associated with Collot d'Herbois. One of them, Marino, becomes president of the temporary Committee of Surveillance, at Lyons. Another, Parrien, is made president of the Revolutionary Committee.— Archives Nationales, AF., II., 59. (Deliberations in the Paris Jacobin Club, appointing three of their number to go to Tonnerre and request the Committee of Public Safety "to give them the necessary power, to use it as circumstances may require, for the best good of the Republic." Frimaire 6, year II.)—Order of the Committee of Public Safety, allowing two thousand francs to the said parties for their travelling expenses."—Archives des Affaires Étrangérès, vol. 333. The agents sent to Marseilles affix their signatures, "*sans-culottes,* of Paris," and one of them, Brutus, becomes president of the Marseilles revolutionary Tribunal.

72. Archives Nationales, AF., II., 49. Papers relating to the revolutionary tax of Belfort, giving all the amounts and names. (Brumaire 30, year II.) Here is the formula: "Citizen X . . . (male or female) will pay in one hour the sum of ————, under penalty of being considered suspect and treated as such."

73. "Recueil des Pièces Authentiques Concernant la Révolution à Strasbourg," i., 128, 187. (Expressions of the representative Baudot in a letter dated Brumaire 29, year II.)

each department, the Jacobins of the principal town are found scattered along the highways, that they may inspect their domain and govern their subjects. Sometimes, it is the representative on mission, who, personally, along with twenty "hairy devils," makes his round and shows off his peregrinating dictatorship; again, it is his secretary or delegate who, in his place and in his name, comes to a second-class town and draws up his documents.[74] At another time, it is "a committee of investigation and propagandism" which, "chosen by the club and provided with full powers," comes, in the name of the representatives, to work up for a month all the communes of the district.[75] Again, finally, it is the revolutionary committee of the principal town, which, "declared central for the whole department,"[76] delegates one or the other of its members to go outside the walls, and purge and recompose suspected municipalities. Thus does

74. Archives Nationales: the acts and letters of the representatives on mission are classed by departments.—On the delegates of the representatives on mission, I will cite but one text. (Archives des Affaires Étrangérès, vol. 333, letter of Garrigues, Auch, Pluviose 24, year II.) "A delegate of Dartigoyte goes to l'Isle and, in the popular club, wants the *curé* of the place to get rid of his priestly attributes. The man answers, so they tell me, that he would cheerfully abstain from his duties, but that, if, in addition to this, they used force he would appeal to the Convention, which had no idea of interfering with freedom of opinion. 'Very well,' replied Dartigoyte's emissary, 'I appeal to a gendarme,' and he at once ordered his arrest."

75. Lallier, "Une Commission D'énquête et de Propagande," p. 7. (It is composed of twelve members, selected by the club of Nantes, who overrun the district of Ancenis, six thousand francs of fees being allowed it.)—Babeau, ii., 280. (Despatch of sixty commissioners, each at six francs a day by the Troyes administration, to ascertain the state of the supplies on hand, Prairial, year II.)

76. For example, at Bordeaux and at Troyes.—Archives Nationales F[7], 4,421. Register of the Revolutionary Committee of Troyes, fol. 164. Two members of the Committee betake themselves to the commune of Lusigny, dismiss the mayor and justice, and appoint in the place of the latter "the former *curé* of the country, who, some time ago, abjured sacerdotal fanaticism."—Archives des Affaires Étrangérès, vol. 332. (Letter of Desgranges, Bordeaux, Brumaire 15, year II.) The representatives have just instituted "a revolutionary committee of surveillance composed of twelve members, selected with the greatest circumspection. All the committees established in the department are obliged to correspond with it, and fulfill its requisitions."

Jacobinism descend and spread itself, step by step, from the Parisian centre to the smallest and remotest commune: throughout the province, whatever its hue may be, positive or indistinct, the administration, imported into or imposed upon this, stamps it with its red stigma.

But the stamp is only superficial; for the *sans-culottes*, naturally, are not disposed to confer offices on any but men of their own kidney, while in the provinces, especially in the rural districts, these men are rare. As one of the representatives says: there is a "dearth of subjects." At Macon, Javogues tries in vain;[77] he finds in the club only "disguised federalists"; the people, he says, "will not open their eyes: it seems to me that this blindness is due to the physique of the country, which is very rich." Naturally, he storms and dismisses; but, even in the revolutionary committee, none but dubious candidates are presented to him for selection; he does not know how to manage in order to renew the local authorities. "They play into each others' hands," and he ends by threatening to transfer the public institutions of the town elsewhere, if they persist in proposing to him none but bad patriots. At Strasbourg,[78] Couturier, and Dentzel, on mission, report that: "owing to an unexampled coalition among all the capable citizens, obstinately refusing to take the office of mayor, in order, by this course, to clog the wheels, and subject the representatives to repeated and indecent refusals," he is compelled to appoint a young man, not of legal age, and a stranger in the department. At Marseilles, write the agents,[79] "in spite of every effort

77. Archives Nationales, AF., II., 58. (Letter of Javogues to Collot d'Herbois, Brumaire 28, year II.)

78. "Recueil des Pièces Authentiques," etc., i., 195. (Acts passed Jan. 21, 1793.)

79. Archives des Affaires Étrangérès, vol. 326. (Letters from Brutus, September 24; from Topino-Lebrun, jr., September 25 and October 6, 1793.)— Vol. 330. (Letters from Brutus, Nivose 6, year II.) The character of the agent is often indicated orthographically. For example, vol. 334, letter from Galon-Boyer, Brumaire 18, year II. "The public spirit is (*et* for *est*) generally bad. Those who claim to be patriots know no restraint (*frin* for *frein*). The rest are lethargic (*en létargie*) and federalism appears innate."

and our ardent desire to republicanise the Marseilles people, our pains and fatigues are nearly all fruitless. . . . Public spirit among owners of property, mechanics and journeymen is everywhere detestable. . . . The number of discontented seems to increase from day to day. All the communes in Var, and most of those in this department are against us. . . . It is a race to be destroyed, a country to be colonised anew." . . . "I repeat it, the only way to work out the Revolution in the federalised departments, and especially in this one, is to transport all the indigenous population who are able to bear arms, scatter them through the armies and put garrisons in their places, which, again, will have to be changed from time to time." At the other extremity of the territory, in Alsace, "republican sentiments are still in the cradle; fanaticism is extreme and incredible; the spirit of the inhabitants in general is in no respect revolutionary. . . . Nothing but the revolutionary army and the venerated guillotine will cure them of their conceited aristocracy. The execution of the laws depends on striking off the heads of the guilty, for nearly all the rural municipalities are composed only of the rich, of clerks of former bailiffs, almost always devoted to the ancient régime."[80] And in the rest of France, the population, less refractory, is not more Jacobin; here where the people appear "humble and submissive" as in Lyons and Bordeaux, the inspectors report that it is wholly owing to terror;[81] there, where opinion seems enthusiastic, as at Rochefort and Grenoble, they report that it is "artificial heat."[82] At Rochefort,

80. Archives des Affaires Étrangérès, vol. 1411. (Letter of Haupt, Brumaire 26, year II.)—Vol. 333. (Letter of Blessman and Haüser, Pluviose 4, year II.)

81. Archives des Affaires Étrangérès, vol. 333. (Letter of Chartres and of Caillard, Commune Affranchie, Nivose 21.)—Vol. 331. (Letters of Desgranges, at Bordeaux, Brumaire 8 and Frimaire 3.) "The offerings in plate and coin multiply indefinitely; all goes right. The court-martial has condemned Dudon to death, son of the *ex-procureur-général* in the former parliament at Bordeaux, Roullat, *procureur-syndic* of the department, Sallenave, merchant. These executions excite sympathy, but nobody murmurs."

82. *Ibid.,* vol. 333. (Letter of Cuny, sr., Nivose 20.) Vols. 331, 332. (Letters of Chépy, *passim,* and especially those dated Frimaire 11.)—Vol. 329. (Letter of Chépy, August 24, 1793.) "At Annecy, the women have cut down the liberty-

zeal is maintained only "by the presence of five or six Parisian Jacobins." At Grenoble, Chépy, the political agent and president of the club, writes that "he is knocked up, worn out, and exhausted, in trying to keep up public spirit and maintain it on a level with events," but he is "conscious that, if he should leave, all would crumble." There are none other than Moderates at Brest, at Lille, at Dunkirk; if this or that department, the Nord, for instance, hastened to accept the *Montagnard* constitution, it is only a pretence: "an infinitely small portion of the population answered for the rest."[83] At Belfort, where "from one thousand to twelve hundred fathers of families alone are counted," writes the agent,[84] "one popular club of thirty or forty members, at the most, maintains and enforces the love of liberty." In Arras, "out of three or four hundred members composing the popular club" the weeding-out of 1793 has spared but "sixty-three, one-tenth of whom are absent."[85] At Toulouse, "out of about fourteen hundred members" who form the club, only three or four hundred remain after the weeding-out of 1793,[86]

---

pole and burnt the archives of the club and of the commune. At Chambéry, the people wanted to do the same thing."—*Ibid.* (September 18, 1793.) "The inhabitants around Mont Blanc show neither spirit nor courage; the truth is, an antirevolutionary spirit animates all minds."—*Ibid.* (Letter of August 8, 1793.) "Not only have the citizens of Grenoble, who were drawn by lot, not set out on the expedition to Lyons, but, even of those who have obeyed the laws, several have returned with their arms and baggage. No commune between St. Laurent and Lyons would march. The rural municipalities, badly tainted with the federal malady, ventured to give the troops very bad quarters, especially those who had been drafted."

83. *Ibid.* (Letter of Cuny, jr., Brest, Brumaire 6.) "There are, in general, very few patriots at Brest; the inhabitants are nearly all moderates."—(Letter of Gadolle, Dunkirk, July 26, 1793.)—(Letter of Simon, Metz, Nivose, year II.) "Yesterday, on the news of the capture of Toulon being announced in the theatre, . . . I noticed that only about one-third of the spectators gave way to patriotic enthusiasm; the other two-thirds remained cold, or put on a long face."

84. *Ibid.* (Letter of Haupt, Belfort, September 1, 1793.)

85. Report by Courtois on the papers found in Robespierre's domicile, p. 274. (Letter of Darthé, Ventose 29, year II.)

86. "Tableau des Prisons de Toulouse," by citizen Pescayre (published in year III.), p. 101.

"mere machines, for the most part," and "whom ten or a dozen intriguers lead as they please." The same state of things exists elsewhere, a dozen or two determined Jacobins—twenty-two at Troyes, twenty-one at Grenoble, ten at Bordeaux, seven at Poitiers, as many at Dijon—constitute the *active* staff of a large town:[87] the whole number might sit around one table. The Jacobins, straining as they do to swell their numbers, only scatter their band; careful as they are in making their selections, they only limit their number. They remain what they always have been, a small feudality of brigands superposed on conquered France.[88] If the terror they spread around multiplies their serfs, the horror they inspire diminishes their proselytes, while their minority remains insignificant because, for their collaborators, they can have only those just like themselves.

87. Archives Nationales, F[7], 4,421. (Register of the Revolutionary Committee, established at Troyes, Brumaire 11, year II.)—Albert Babeau, vol. ii., *passim.*—Archives des Affaires Étrangérès, vol. 332, Chépy (letter, Brumaire 6, Grenoble). "The sections had appointed seven committees of surveillance. Although weeded out by the club, they nevertheless alarmed the *sans-culottes.* . . . Representative Petit-Jean has issued an order, directing that there shall be but one committee at Grenoble composed of twenty-one members. This measure is excellent and ensures the triumph of *sans-culotteism.*"—Archives Nationales, F[7], 4,434. (Letter of Pérrieu to Brissot, Bordeaux, March 9, 1793.) Before June 2, the national club "of Bordeaux, composed of Maratists, did not comprise more than eight or ten individuals at most."—*Moniteur,* xxii., 133. (Speech by Thibeaudeau on the popular club of Poitiers, Vendémiaire 11, year III.)—*Ibid.* (Session of Brumaire 5, year III., letter of Calès, and session of Brumaire 17, year III., report by Calès.) "The popular club of Dijon made all neighboring administrative bodies, citizens and districts tremble. All were subject to its laws, and three or four men in it made them. This club and the municipality were one body." "The Terror party does not exist here, or, if it does exist, it does not amount to much: out of twenty thousand inhabitants there are not six who can legitimately be suspected of belonging to it."

88. Baroly, "Les Jacobins Demasqués," (iv. 8vo., of 8pp., year III). "The Jacobin club, with its four hundred active members at Paris, and the four thousand others in the provinces, not less devoted, represent the living force of the Revolution."

VI

Thus, on closely observing the final set of officials of the revolutionary government, in the provinces as well as at Paris, we find few besides the eminent in vice, dishonesty, and misconduct, or, at the very least, in stupidity and grossness. First, as is indicated by their name, they all must be, and nearly all are, *sans-culottes*, that is to say, men who live from day to day on their daily earnings, possessing no income from capital, confined to subordinate places, to petty trading, to manual services, lodged or encamped on the lowest steps of the social ladder, and therefore requiring pay to enable them to attend to public business;[89] it is on this account that decrees and orders allow them wages of three, five, six, ten, and even eighteen francs a day. At Grenoble, the representatives form the municipal body and the revolutionary committee, along with two health-officers, three glovers, two farmers, one tobacco-merchant, one perfumer, one grocer, one belt-maker, one innkeeper, one joiner, one shoemaker, one mason, while the official order by which they are installed, appoints "Teyssière, *licoriste*," national agent.[90] At Troyes,[91] among the men in authority we find a confectioner, a weaver, a journeyman-weaver, a hatter, a hosier, a grocer, a carpenter, a dancing-master, and a policeman, while the mayor, Gachez,

89. Archives Nationales, D. § I., 10. (Orders of representatives Delacroix, Louchet, and Legendre, Nivose 12, year II.) "On the petition of the Committee of Surveillance of Evreux, which sets forth that all its members are without means, and that it will be impossible for them to continue their duties since they are without resources for supporting their families," the representatives allow three of them two hundred and seventy francs each, and a fourth one hundred and eighty francs, as a gratuity (outside of the three francs a day).

90. *Ibid*. AF., II., iii. (Order of Albitte and Laporte, Prairial 18, year II.)

91. Albert Babeau, ii., 154–157.—*Moniteur*, xxii., 425. (Session of Brumaire 13, year III. Speech by Cambon.) "A government was organised in which surveillance alone cost five hundred and ninety-one millions per annum. Every man who tilled the ground or worked in a shop, at once abandoned his pursuit for a place on the Revolutionary Committees ... where he got five francs a day."

formerly a common soldier in the regiment of Vexin, was, when appointed, a school-teacher in the vicinity. At Toulouse,[92] a man named Terrain, a pie-dealer, is installed as president of the administration; the revolutionary committee is presided over by Pio, a journeyman-barber; the inspiration, "the soul of the club," is a *concierge*, that of the prison. The last and most significant trait is found at Rochefort,[93] where the president of the popular club is the executioner. If such persons form the select body of officials in the large towns, what must they be in the small ones, in the bourgs and in the villages? "Everywhere they are of the *meanest*,"[94] cartmen, *sabot*- (wooden shoe) makers, thatchers, stone-cutters, dealers in rabbit-skins, day laborers, idle mechanics, many without any pursuit, or mere vagabonds who had already participated in riots or jacqueries, loungers in the groggeries, having given up work and designated for a public career only by their irregular habits and incompetency to follow a private career. Even in the large towns, it is evident that discretionary power has fallen into the hands of nearly raw barbar-

92. "Tableau des Prisons de Toulouse," by citizen Pescare, 162, 166, 435.

93. Berryat Saint-Prix, "La Justice Révolutionaire," (second edition) p. xix.—*Ibid.*, xiv. At Rochefort there is on the revolutionary Tribunal a mason, a shoemaker, a calker, and a cook; at Bordeaux, on the military commission, an actor, a wine-clerk, a druggist, a baker, a journeyman-gilder, and later, a cooper and a leather-dresser.

94. I give this as I got it in my conversations with old peasants.—Archives Nationales, AF., II., 111. (Order of the Representative Ichon, Messidor 18, year II.) "The popular club of Chinon will be immediately regenerated. Citizens (I omit their names), the following showing their occupations: shoemaker, police-man, *sabot*-maker, cooper, carter, shoemaker, joiner, butcher, carpenter, and mason, will form the committee which is to do the weeding-out and choose successors among those that offer to become members of the club."—*Ibid.*, D., §1, 10. (Orders of the Representatives Delacroix, Louchet, and Legendre, on mission in the department of Seine-Inférieure for the purpose of removing, at Conchez, the entire administration, and for forming there a new revolutionary committee, with full powers, Frimaire 9, year II.) The members of the committee, the nature of which is indicated, are two coopers, one gardener, two carpenters, one merchant, a coach-driver, and a tailor. (One finds in the archives, in the correspondence of the representatives, plenty of orders appointing authorities of the same sort.)

ians; one has only to note in the old documents, at the Archives, the orthography and style of the committees empowered to grant or refuse civic cards, and draw up reports on the opinions and pursuits of prisoners. "His opinions appear insipid (*Ces opignons paroisse insipide*).[95] ... He is married (but) without children." (*Il est marie cent (sans) enfants*). .... Her profession is wife of Paillot-Montabert, her income is living on her income; these relations are with a woman we pay no attention to; we presume her opinions are like her husband's."[96] The handwriting, unfortunately, cannot be represented here, being that of a child five years old.[97]

"As stupid as they are immoral,"[98] says Representative Albert, of the Jacobins he finds in office at Troyes. Low, indeed, as their condition may be, their feeling and intelligence are yet lower because, in their professions or occupations, they are the refuse instead of the élite, and, especially on this account, they are turned out after Thermidor, some, it is true, as Terrorists, but the larger number as either dolts, scandalous or crazy, mere interlopers, or mere valets. At Rheims, the president of the district is[99] "a former bailiff, on

95. Albert Babeau, ii., 296.

96. *Sa profession est fame de Paillot-Montabert; son revenu est vivre de ses revenus; ces relation son d'une fame nous ny portons pas d'atantion; ces opignons nous les presumons semblable, à ceux de son mary.*

97. Archives Nationales, F⁷, 4,421. Order of the Committee of Surveillance of the third section of Troyes, refusing civic certificates to seventy-two persons, or sending them before the Central Committee as "marchands d'argant, aristocrate, douteux, modére, intrigant, egoiste fanatique. Fait et areté par nous, membre du commité le ans et jour susdit."—"Mémoire des Commissaires de la 5e seiscion dite de la liberté nommé par le citoyen de Baris (Paris) pour faire les visite de l'argenteri ché les citoyens de la liste fait par les citoyens Diot et Bailly et Jaquin savoir depence du 13 et 14 et 15 Frimaire pour leur nouriture du troyes jour monte à 24 fr.

98. Albert Babeau, ii., 154.

99. Archives Nationales, D., § 1, 5. (Mission of Representative Albert, in Aube and in Marne.)—These notes are made on the spot, with a thorough knowledge of the situation, by zealous republicans who are not without common-sense and of average honesty (chiefly in Pluviose and Ventose, year III).—Letter of Albert to the directories of the two departments.—Prairial 3,

familiar terms with the spies of the Robespierre régime, acting in concert with them, but without being their accomplice, possessing none of the requisite qualities for administration"; another administrator is likewise "a former bailiff, without means, negligent in the highest degree and a confirmed drunkard": alongside of these sit "a horse-dealer, without any means, better suited for jockeying than governing, moreover a drunkard; a dyer, lacking judgment, open to all sorts of influences, pushed ahead by the Jacobin faction, and having used power in the most arbitrary manner, rather, perhaps, through ignorance than through cruelty; a shoemaker, entirely uninstructed, knowing only how to sign his name," and others of the same character. In the Tribunal, a judge is noted as "true in principle, but whom poverty and want of resources have driven to every excess, a turncoat according to circumstances in order to get a place, associated with the leaders in order to keep the place, and yet not without sensibility, having, perhaps, acted criminally merely to keep himself and his family alive." In the municipal body, the majority is composed of an incompetent lot, some of them being journeymen-spinners or thread-twisters, and others second-hand dealers or shop-keepers, "incapable," "without means," with a few crack-brains among them: one, "his brain being crazed, absolutely of no account, anarchist and Jacobin"; another, "very dangerous through lack of judgment, a Jacobin, overexcited"; a third, "an instrument of tyranny, a man of blood capable of every vice, having assumed the name of Mutius Scaevola, of recognised depravity and unable to write." Similarly, in the Aube districts, we find some of the heads feverish with the prevailing epidemic, for instance, at Nogent, the national agent, Delaporte, "who has the words 'guillotine' and 'revolutionary tribunal' always on his lips, and who declares that if he were the government he would imprison doctor, surgeon, and lawyer, who delights in finding people guilty and says that he is never content except when he gets three pounds' weight of denunciations

---

year II. "I am satisfied, during the course of my mission, of the necessity of reorganising the municipalities throughout both departments."

a day." But, apart from these madcaps, most of the administrators or judges are either people wholly unworthy of their offices, because they are "inept," "too uneducated," "good for nothing," "too little familiar with administrative forms," "too little accustomed to judicial action," "without information," "too busy with their own affairs," "unable to read or write," or, because "they have no delicacy," are "violent," "agitators," "knaves," "without public esteem," and more or less dishonest and despised.[100] A certain fellow from Paris, was, at first, at Troyes, a baker's apprentice,[101] and afterwards a dancing-master; he next figured at the Club, making headway, doubtless, through his Parisian chatter, until he stood first and soon became a member of the district. Appointed an officer in the sixth battalion of Aube, he behaved in such a manner in Vendée that, on his return, "his brethren in arms" broke up the banner presented to him, "declaring him unworthy of such an honor, because he cowardly fled before the enemy." Nevertheless, after a short plunge, he came again to the surface and, thanks to his civil compeers, was reinstated in his administrative functions; during the Terror, he was intimate with all the Terrorists, being one of the important men of Troyes. The mayor of the town, Gachez, an old soldier and exschoolmaster, is of the same stuff as this baker's apprentice. He, likewise, was a Vendéan hero; only, he was unable to distinguish himself as much as he liked, for, after enlisting, he failed to march; having pocketed the bounty of three hundred livres, he discovered that he had infirmities and, getting himself invalided, he served the nation in a civil capacity. "His own partisans admit that he is a

100. *Ibid.* Orders of Albert, Ventose 5, and Pluviose 29, year III., reorganising the courts and administrations in the districts of Ervy, Arcis and Nogent-sur-Seine, with a tabular statement of the names of those removed and the reasons for so doing.

101. Petition of Jean Nicolas Antoine, former member of the Directory of the district of Troyes for twenty-eight months. (Ventose 9, year III.) Shut up in Troyes, he asks permission to go to Paris, "I have a small lot of goods which it is necessary for me to sell in Paris. It is my native town and I know more people there than anywhere else."—*Ibid.* Information furnished on Antoine by the Conseil-général of the Commune of Troyes.

drunkard and that he has committed forgery." Some months after Thermidor he is sentenced to eight years imprisonment and put in the pillory for this crime. Hence, "almost the entire commune is against him; the women in the streets jeer him, and the eight sections meet together to request his withdrawal." But Representative Bô reports that he is every way entitled to remain, being a true Jacobin, an admirable terrorist and "the only *sans-culotte* mayor which the commune of Troyes has to be proud of."[102]

It would be awarding too much honor to men of this stamp, to suppose that they had convictions or principles; they were governed by animosities and especially by their appetites,[103] to satiate which they[104] made the most of their offices. At Troyes, "all provisions and

102. Archives Nationales, AF., II., 59. (Memorials dated Messidor 28, year II., by an emissary of the Committee of Public Safety, sent to Troyes, Prairial 29, to report on the situation of things and on the troubles in Troyes.)—Albert Babeau, ii., 203, 205 and 112, 122.—Cf. 179. "Gachez, intoxicated, about eleven o'clock at night, with several women as drunk as himself, compelled the keeper of the Temple of Reason to open the doors, threatening him with the guillotine."—*Ibid.*, 166. He addressed the *sans-culottes* in the popular club: "Now is the time to put yourselves in the place of the rich. Strike, and don't put it off!"—*Ibid.*, 165. "Forty-two thousand six hundred and thirty-three livres were placed in the hands of Gachez and the committee, as secret revolutionary service money. . . . Between December 4 and 10 Gachez received twenty thousand livres, in three orders, for revolutionary expenses and provisional aid." "The leaders of the party disposed of these sums without control and, it may be added, without scruple." Gachez hands over only four thousand livres to the sectional poor-committee. On Nivose 12, there remains in the treasury of the poor fund only three thousand seven hundred and thirty-eight livres, twelve thousand having been diverted or squandered.

103. "Frochot," by Louis Passy, 172. (Letter of Pajot, member of the revolutionary committee of Aignay-le-Duc.) "Denunciations occupied most of the time at our meetings, and it is there that one could see the hatreds and vengeance of the colleagues who ruled us."

104. Archives Nationales, D., § 1, No. 4. The following is a sample among others of the impositions of the revolutionary committees. (Complaint of Mariotte, proprietor, former mayor of Chatillon-sur-Seine, Floréal 27, year II.) "On Brumaire 23, year II., I was stopped just as I was taking post at Mussy, travelling on business for the Republic, and provided with a commission and passport from the Minister of War. . . . I was searched in the most shameful manner;

eatables are drawn upon to supply the table of the twenty-four" *sans-culottes*[105] to whom Bô entrusted the duty of weeding-out the popular club; before the organisation of "this regenerating nucleus" the revolutionary committee, presided over by Rousselin, the civil commissioner, carried on its "feastings" in the Petit-Louvre tavern, "passing nights in tippling" and in the preparation of lists of suspects.[106] In the neighboring provinces of Dijon, Beaune, Semur and Aignay-le-Duc, the heads of the municipality and of the club always meet in taverns and groggeries. At Dijon, we see "the ten or twelve Hercules of patriotism traversing the town, each with a chalice under his arm":[107] this is their drink-cup; each has to bring his own to the *Montagnard* inn; there, they imbibe copiously, frequently, and between two glasses of wine "declare who are outlaws." At Aignay-le-Duc, a small town with only half a dozen patriots "the majority of whom can scarcely write, most of them poor, burdened with families, and living without doing anything, never quit the groggeries, where, night and day, they revel"; their chief, a financial *ex-*

---

citizen Ménétrier, member of the committee, used towards me the foulest language. . . . I was confined in a tavern; instead of two gendarmes which would have been quite sufficient to guard me, I had the whole brigade, who passed that night and the next day drinking, until, in wine and brandy the charge against me in the tavern amounted to sixty francs. And worse still, two members of the same committee passed a night guarding me and made me pay for it. Add to this, *they said openly before me that I was a good pigeon to pluck.* . . . They gave me the escort of a state criminal of the highest importance, three national gendarmes, mounted, six National Guards, and even to the Commandant of the National Guard; citizen Mièdan, member of the Revolutionary Committee, put himself at the head of the cortege, ten men to conduct one! . . . I was obliged to pay my executioners, fifty francs to the commandant, and sixty to his men."

105. *Moniteur,* xxi., 261. (Speech by an inhabitant of Troyes in the Jacobin Club, Paris, Messidor 26, year II.)

106. Albert Babeau, ii., 164. (Depositions of the tavern-keeper and of the commissioner, Garnier.)

107. "Frochot," by Louis Passy, 170, 172. (Letter by Pajot and petition of the Aignay municipality, March 10, 1795.)—Bibliotheque Nationale, L., 41. No. 1802. (Denunciation by six sections of the commune of Dijon to the National Convention.)

procureur, now "*concierge*, archivist, secretary, and president of the popular club," holds municipal council in the bar-room. "On leaving, they put for female aristocrats," while one of them declares "that if the half of Aignay were slaughtered the other half would be all the better for it." There is nothing like drinking to excite ferocity to the highest pitch. At Strasbourg the sixty propagandist mustachioed patriots lodged in the college in which they are settled fixtures, have a cook provided for them by the town, and they revel day and night "on the choice provisions put in requisition," "on wines destined to the defenders of the country."[108] It is, undoubtedly, on issuing from these orgies that they proceed, sword in hand, to the popular club,[109] vote and force others to vote "death to all prisoners confined in the Seminary to the number of seven hundred, of every age and of both sexes, without any preliminary trial." For a man to become a good cut-throat, he must first get intoxicated;[110] such was the course pursued in Paris by those who did the work in September: the revolutionary government being an organised, prolonged, and permanent *Septembrisade*, most of its agents are obliged to drink hard.[111]

108. "Recueil de Pièces Authentiques sur la Révolution de Strasbourg," i., 187, and letter of Burger, Thermidor 25, year II.

109. Archives Nationales, D., § 1, 6 (file 37).—Letter of the members of the Strasbourg Revolutionary Committee, Ventose 13, year III., indicating to the mayor and municipal officers of Chalons-sur-Marne certain Jacobins of the town as suitable members of the Propaganda at Strasbourg.

110. "Recueil de Pièces Authentiques Concernant la Révolution à Strasbourg," i., 71. Deposition of the recorder Weis on the circuit of the revolutionary Tribunal, composed of Schneider, Clavel, and Taffin. "The judges never left the table without having become intoxicated with everything of the finest, and, in this state, they resorted to the tribunal and condemned the accused to death."—Free living and "extravagant expenditure" were common even "among the employees of the government." "I encountered," says Meissner, "government carters served with chickens, pastry and game, whilst at the traveller's table there was simply an old leg of mutton and a few poor side-dishes." ("Voyage en France," toward the end of 1795, p. 371.)

111. Some of them, nevertheless, are not ugly, but merely sots. The following is a specimen. A certain Velu, a born vagabond, formerly in the hospital

For the same reasons when the opportunity, as well as the temptation, to steal, presents itself, they steal. At first, during six months, and up to the decree assigning them pay, the revolutionary com-

---

and brought up there, then a shoemaker or a cobbler, afterwards teaching school in the Faubourg de Vienne, and at last a haranguer and proposer of tyrannicide motions, short, stout and as rubicund as his cap, is made President of the Popular club at Blois, then delegate for domiciliary visits, and, throughout the Reign of Terror, he is a principal personage in the town, district, and department. (Dufort de Cheverney, "Mémoires," (MS.) March 21, 1793 and June, 1793.) In June, 1793, this Velu is ordered to visit the chateau de Cheverney, to verify the surrender of all feudal documents. He arrives unexpectedly, meets the steward, Bambinet, enters the mayor's house, who keeps an inn, and drinks copiously, which gives Bambinet time to warn M. Dufort de Cheverney and have the suspicious registers concealed.—This done, "Velu is obliged to leave his bottle and march to the chateau.—He assumed haughtiness and aimed at familiarity; he would put his hand on his breast and, taking yours, address you: "Good-day, brother."—He came there at nine o'clock in the morning, advanced, took my hand and said: "Good-day, brother, how are you?" "Very well, citizen, and how are you?" "You do not *tutoyer*—you are not up to the Revolution?" "We'll see—will you step in the parlor?" "Yes, brother, I'll follow you."—We enter; he sees my wife who, I may say, has an imposing air. He boldly embraces her and, repeating his gesture on the breast, takes her hand and says: "Good-day, sister." "Come," I interpose, "let us take breakfast, and, if you please, you shall dine with me." "Yes, but on one condition, that *tu me tutoie.*" "I will try, but I am not in the habit of it." After warming up his intellect and heart with a bottle of wine, we get rid of him by sending him to inspect the archives-room, along with my son and Bambinet. It is amusing, for he can only read print. . . . Bambinet, and the *procureur,* read the titles aloud, and pass over the feudalisms. Velu does not notice this and always tells them to go on.—After an hour, tired out, he comes back: "All right," he says, "now let me see your chateau, which is a fine one." He had heard about a room where there were *fantocini,* in the attic. He goes up, opens some play-books, and, seeing on the lists of characters the name of King and Prince, he says to me: "You must scratch those out, and play only republican pieces." The descent is by a back-stairs. On the way down he encounters a maid of my wife's, who is very pretty; he stops and, regarding my son, says: "You must as a good Republican, sleep with that girl and marry her." I look at him and reply: "Monsieur Velu, listen; we are well behaved here, and such language cannot be allowed. You must respect the young people in my house." A little disconcerted, he tames down and is quite deferential to Madame de Cheverney.—"You have pen and ink on your table," he says, "bring

mittees "take their pay themselves";[112] they then add to their legal
salary of three and five francs a day about what they please: for it
is they who assess the extraordinary taxes, and often, as at Montbrison, "without making any list or record of collections." On Frimaire 16, year II., the financial committee reports that "the collection
and application of extraordinary taxes is unknown to the government; that it was impossible to supervise them, the National treasury
having received no sums whatever arising from these taxes."[113] Two
years after, four years after, the accounts of revolutionary taxation,
of forced loans, and of pretended voluntary gifts, still form a bottomless pit; out of forty billions of accounts rendered to the National
Treasury only twenty are found to be verified; the rest are irregular

them here." "What for," I ask, "to take my inventory?" "No, but I must make
a *procès-verbal*. You help me; it will be better for you, as you can fix it to suit
you." This was not badly done, to conceal his want of knowledge.—We go in
to dinner. My servants waited on the table; I had not yielded to the system of
a general table for all of us, which would not have pleased my servants any
more than myself. Curiosity led them all to come in and see us dining together.—"Brother," says Velu to me, "don't these people eat with you?" (He
saw the table set for only four persons.) I reply: "Brother, that would not be
any more agreeable to them than to myself. Ask them."—He ate little, drank
like an ogre, and was talkative about his amours; getting excited, he was sufficiently venturesome in his stories and excited my wife, but he did not go far.
Apropos of the Revolution, and the danger we incurred, he said innocently:
"Don't I run as much risk as anybody? It is my opinion that, in three months,
I shall have my head off! But we must all take our chance!"—Now and then,
he indulged in *sans-culottisms*. He seized the servant's hand, who changed his
plate: "Brother, I beg you to take my place, and let me wait on you in my
turn!" He drank the cordials, and finally left, pleased with his reception.—
Returning to the inn, he stays until nine o'clock at night and stuffs himself, but
is not intoxicated. One bottle had no effect on him; he could empty a cask and
show no signs of it.

112. *Moniteur*, xxii., 425. (Session of Brumaire 13, year III.) Cambon, in
relation to the revolutionary committees, says: "I would observe to the Assembly that they were never paid." A member replies: "They took their pay themselves." ("Yes, yes."—Applause.)

113. *Moniteur*, xxii., 711. (Report by Cambon, Frimaire 6, year III.)—Cambon stated, indeed, Frimaire 26, year II. (*Moniteur*, xviii., 680), concerning these
taxes: "Not one word, not one sou has yet reached the Treasury; they want to
override the Convention which made the Revolution."

and worthless. Besides, in many cases, not only is the voucher worth-less or not forthcoming, but, again, it is proved that the sums col-lected disappeared wholly or in part. At Villefranche, out of one hundred and thirty-eight thousand francs collected, the collector of the district deposited but forty-two thousand; at Baugency, out of more than five hundred thousand francs collected, there were only fifty thousand deposited; at la Réole, out of at least five hundred thousand francs collected, there were but twenty-two thousand six hundred and fifty deposited. "The rest," says the collector at Ville-franche, "were wasted by the Committee of Surveillance." "The tax-collectors," writes the national-agent at Orleans, "after having employed terror gave themselves up to orgies and are now building palaces."[114] As to the expenses which they prove, they almost always consist of "indemnities to members of revolutionary committees, to patriots, and to defray the cost of patriotic missions," to maintaining and repairing the meeting-rooms of the popular clubs, to military expeditions, and to succoring the poor, so that three or four hundred millions in gold or silver, extorted before the end of 1793, hundreds of millions of assignats extorted in 1793 and 1794, in short, almost the entire product of the total extraordinary taxation[115] was con-

114. *Ibid.*, 720. "The balances reported, of which the largest portion is al-ready paid into the vaults of the National Treasury, amount to twenty millions one hundred and sixty-six thousand three hundred and thirty livres."—At Paris, Marseilles, and Bordeaux, in the large towns where tens of millions were raised in three-quarters of the districts, Cambon, three months after Thermidor, could not yet obtain, I will not say the returns, but a statement of the sums raised. The national agents either did not reply to him, or did it vaguely, or stated that in their districts there was neither civic donation nor revolutionary tax, and particularly at Marseilles, where a forced loan had been made of four millions.— Cf. De Martel, "Fouché," p. 245. (Memorial of the Central administration of Nièvre, Prairial 10, year III.) "The account returned by the city of Nevers amounts to eighty thousand francs, the use of which has never been verified. . . . This tax, in part payment of the war subsidy, was simply a trap laid by the political actors in order to levy a contribution on honest, credulous citizens."— *Ibid.*, 217. On voluntary gifts and forced taxation cf. at Nantes, the use made of revolutionary taxes, brought out on the trial of the revolutionary committee.

115. Ludovic Sciout, iv., 19. Report of Representative Becker. (Journal des Débats et Décrets, p. 743, Prairial, year III.) He returns from a mission to

sumed on the spot and by the *sans-culottes*. Seated at the public
banqueting table they help themselves first, and help themselves
copiously.

A second windfall, equally gross. Enjoying the right to dispose
arbitrarily of fortunes, liberties and lives, they can traffic in these,
while no traffic can be more advantageous, both for buyers and
sellers. Any man who is rich or well-off, in other words, every man
who is likely to be taxed, imprisoned, or guillotined, gladly consents
"to compound," to redeem himself and those who belong to him.
If he is prudent, he pays, before the tax, so as not to be overtaxed;
he pays, after the tax, to obtain a diminution or delays; he pays to
be admitted into the popular club. When danger draws near he pays
to obtain or renew his certificate of civism, not to be declared "suspect," not to be denounced as a conspirator. After being denounced,
he pays to be allowed imprisonment at home rather than in the jail,
to be allowed imprisonment in the jail rather than in the general
prison, to be well treated if he gets into this, to have time to get
together his proofs in evidence, to have his record (*dossier*) placed
and kept at the bottom of the file among the clerk's registers, to
avoid being inscribed on the next batch of cases in the revolutionary
Tribunal. There is not one of these favors that is not precious;
consequently, ransoms without number are tendered, while the rascals[116] who swarm on the revolutionary committees, need but open
their hands to fill their pockets. They run very little risk, for they
are held in check only by their own kind, or are not checked at all.

Landau and renders an account of the executions committed by the Jacobin
agents in the Rhenish provinces. They levied taxes, sword in hand, and threatened the refractory with the guillotine at Strasbourg. The receipts which passed
under the reporter's eyes "presented the sum of three millions three hundred
and forty-five thousand seven hundred and eighty-five livres, two deniers, whilst
our colleague, Cambon, reports only one hundred and thirty-eight thousand
paid in."

116. *Moniteur*, xxii., 754. (Report of Grégoire, Frimaire 24, year III.) "*Ras-
callery*—this word recalls the old revolutionary committees, most of which
formed the scum of society and which showed so many aptitudes for the double
function of robber and persecutor."

In any large town, two of them suffice for the issue of a warrant of arrest "save a reference to the Committee within twenty-four hours," with the certainty that their colleagues will kindly return the favor.[117] Moreover, the clever ones know how to protect themselves beforehand. For example, at Bordeaux, where one of these clandestine markets had been set up, M. Jean Davilliers, one of the partners in a large commercial house, is under arrest in his own house, guarded by four *sans-culottes;* on the 8th of Brumaire, he is taken aside and told "that he is in danger if he does not come forward and meet the indispensable requirements of the Revolution in its secret expenditures." A prominent man, Lemoal, member of the

---

117. Archives Nationales, AF., II., 107. (Orders of Representatives Ysabeau and Tallien, Bordeaux, Brumaire 11 and 17, year II.)—Third order, promulgated by the same parties, Frimaire 2, year II., replacing this committee by another of twelve members and six deputies, each at two hundred francs a month. Fourth order, Pluviose 16, year II., dismissing the members of the foregoing committee, as *exagérés* and disobedient. It is because they regard their local royalty in quite a serious light.—*Ibid.,* AF., II., 46. ("Extracts from the minutes of the meetings of the Revolutionary Committee of Bordeaux," Prairial, year II.) This extract, consisting of eighteen pages, shows in detail the inside workings of a Revolutionary committee; the number of arrested goes on increasing; on the 27th of Prairial there are one thousand five hundred and twenty-four. The committee is essentially a police office; it delivers certificates of civism, issues warrants of arrest, corresponds with other committees, even very remote, at Limoges, and Clermont-Ferrand, delegates any of its members to investigate concerning this or that "suspect," to affix seals, to make domiciliary visits. It receives and transmits denunciations, summons the denounced to appear before it, reads interrogations, writes to the Committee of Public Safety, etc. The following are samples of its warrants of arrest: "Citoyen Héry, formerly a (man) milliner, makes a denunciation in this office against Citizen Tauray and wife, in accordance with which the Committee orders their arrest, and seals put on their papers." "Muller, a riding-master, will be confined in the former Petit Seminaire, under suspicion of aristocracy, according to public opinion." Another example, Archives Nationales, F[7], 2,475. Register of the *procès-verbaux* of the Revolutionary Committee of the Piquos section, Paris, June 3, 1793. Warrant of arrest against Boucher, grocer, rue Neuve du Luxembourg, "suspect" of *incivisme* and "having cherished wicked and perfidious intentions against his wife." Boucher, arrested, declares that, "what he said and did in his house, concerned nobody but himself." On which he was led to prison.

revolutionary committee and administrator of the district, had spoken of these requirements and thought that M. Davilliers should contribute the sum of one hundred and fifty thousand livres. Upon this, a knock at the door is heard; Lemoal enters and all present leave the room, while Lemoal merely asks: "Do you consent?" "But I cannot thus dispose of my partners' property." "Then you will go to prison." At this threat the poor man yields and gives his note to Lemoal at twenty days, payable to bearer, for one hundred and fifty thousand livres, and, at the end of a fortnight, by dint of pushing his claims, obtains his freedom. Thereupon, Lemoal thinks the matter over, and deems it prudent to cover up his private extortion by a public one. Accordingly, he sends for M. Davilliers: "It is now essential for you to openly contribute one hundred and fifty thousand livres more for the necessities of the Republic. I will introduce you to the representatives to whom you should make the offer." The chicken being officially plucked in this way, nobody would suppose that it had been first privately plucked, and, moreover, the inquisitive, if there were any, would be thrown off the scent by the confusion arising from two sums of equal amount. M. Davilliers begs to be allowed to consult his partners, and, as they are not in prison, they refuse. Lemoal, on his side, is anxious to receive the money for his note, while poor Davilliers, "struck with terror by nocturnal arrests," and seeing that Lemoal is always on the top of the ladder, concludes to pay; at first, he gives him thirty thousand livres, and next, the charges, amounting in all to forty-one thousand livres, when, being at the end of his resources, he begs and entreats to have his note returned to him. Lemoal, on this, considering the chicken as entirely stripped, becomes mollified, and tears off in presence of his debtor "the signature in full of the note," and, along with this, his own receipts for partial payments underneath. But he carefully preserves the note itself, for, thus mutilated, it will show, if necessary, that he had not received anything, and that, through patriotism, he had undoubtedly wished to force a contribution from a merchant, but, finding him insolvent, had humanely cancelled the written obligation.[118] Such are the precautions taken in this business. Others, less shrewd, rob more openly, among others the mayor, the seven members of the military commission surnamed "the seven mortal sins," and especially their president, Lacombe, who, by promising releases, extracts from eight or nine captives three hundred and fifty-nine thousand six hundred livres.[119] Through these manoeuvres, writes a strict Jacobin,[120] "Many of those who had been declared outlaws returned to Bordeaux by paying; of the number who thus redeemed their lives, some did not deserve to lose it, but, nevertheless, they were threatened with execution if they did not consent to everything. But material proofs of this are hard to obtain. These men now keep silent, for fear, through open denunciation, of sharing in the penalty of the traffickers in justice, and being unwilling to expose (anew) the life they have preserved." In short, the plucked pigeon is mute, so as not to attract attention, as well as to avoid the knife; and all the more, because those who pluck him hold on to the knife and might, should he cry out, despatch him with the more celerity. Even if he makes no outcry, they sometimes despatch him so as to stifle in advance any possible outcry, which happened to the Duc du Châtelet and others. There is but one mode of self-preservation[121] and that is, "to pay one's patrons by instalments, like

118. Archives Nationales, AF., II., 30 (No. 105). Examination of Jean Davilliers, and other ransomed parties.

119. Berryat Saint-Prix, 313. (Trial of Lacombe and his accomplices after Thermidor.)

120. Archives Nationales, AF., II., 46. (Letter of Julien to the Committee of Public Safety, Bordeaux, Messidor 12, year II.)—*Moniteur*, xxii., 713. (Report by Cambon, Frimaire 6, year III.) At Verins, citizens were imprisoned and then set at liberty "on consideration of a fee."—Albert Babeau, ii., 164, 165, 206. (Report by Cambon, Frimaire 6, year II.) "Citoyenne (madame) Deguerrois, having come to procure the release of her husband, a public functionary demanded of her ten thousand livres, which he reduced to six thousand for doing what she desired. . . . One document attests that Massey paid two thousand livres, and widow Delaporte six hundred livres, to get out of prison."

121. Mallet-Dupan, "First letter to a Geneva merchant," (March 1, 1796), pp. 33–35. "One of the wonders of the Reign of Terror is the slight attention

nurses by the mouth, on a scale proportionate to the activity of the guillotine." In any event, the pirates are not disturbed, for the trade in lives and liberties leaves no trace behind it, and is carried on with impunity for two years, from one end of France to the other, according to a tacit understanding between sellers and buyers.

There is a third windfall, not less large, but carried on in more open sunshine and therefore still more enticing. Once the "suspect" is incarcerated, whatever he brings to prison along with him, whatever he leaves behind him at home, becomes plunder; for, with the

---

given to the trafficking in life and death, characteristic of terrorism. We scarcely find a word on the countless bargains through which 'suspect' citizens bought themselves out of captivity, and imprisoned citizens bought off the guillotine. . . . Dungeons and executions were as much matters of trade as the purchase of cattle at a fair." This traffic "was carried on in all the towns, bourgs and departments surrendered to the Convention and Revolutionary Committees." "It has been established since the 10th of August."—"I will only cite among a multitude of instances the unfortunate Duc du Châtelet; never did anybody pay more for his execution!"—Wallon, "Histoire du Tribunal Révolutionnaire de Paris," vi., 88. Denunciation of Fouquier-Tinville, signed Saulnie. According to Saulnie he dined regularly twice a week at No. 6 rue Serpente, with one Demay, calling himself a lawyer and living with a woman named Martin. In this den of orgies, the freedom or death of those in prison was bargained for in money with impunity. One head alone, belonging to the house of Boufflers, escaping the scaffold through the intrigues of these vampires, was worth to them thirty thousand livres, of which one thousand were paid down and a bond given for the rest, payable on being set at liberty.—Mallet-Dupan, "Mémoires," ii., 495. "Fouquier-Tinville received a pension of one thousand crowns a month from Mesdames de Boufflers; the ransom increased one quarter each month on account of the atrocity of the circumstances. This method saved these ladies, whilst those who paid a sum in gross lost their lives. . . . It was Du Vaucel, *fermier-general,* who saved the Princess of Tarente . . . for five hundred louis . . . after having saved two other ladies for three hundred louis, given to one of the Jacobin leaders."—Morellet, "Mémoires," ii., 32. The agent of Mesdames de Boufflers was Abbé Chevalier, who had formerly known Fouquier-Tinville in the office of a *procureur an Parliament* and who, renewing the acquaintance, came and drank with Fouquier. "He succeeded in having the papers of the ladies Boufflers, which were ready to be sent to the Tribunal, placed at the bottom of the file."

incompleteness, haste and irregularity of papers,[122] with the lack of surveillance and known connivance, the vultures, great and small, could freely use their beaks and talons. At Toulouse, as in Paris and elsewhere, commissioners take from prisoners every object of value and, accordingly, in many cases, all gold, silver, assignats, and jewelry, which, confiscated for the Treasury, stop half-way in the hands of those who make the seizure.[123] At Poitiers, the seven scoundrels

122. "Tableau des Prisons de Toulouse," 324. Coudert, of the Municipal Council, shoemaker, charged with the duty of taking silver-plate from the accused, did not know how, or was unwilling, to draw up any other than an irregular and valueless *procès-verbal*. On this, an accused party objected and refused to sign. "Take care, you," exclaims Coudert in a rage, "with your —————— cleverness, you are playing the stubborn. You are nothing but a —————— fool! You are getting into a bad box! If you don't sign, I'll have you guillotined." Frequently, there are no papers at all. (De Martel, "Fouché," p. 236. Memorial by the authorities of Allier, addressed to the Convention, document 9.) October 30, 1793. Order of the revolutionary committee enjoining nocturnal visits in all "suspect" houses in Moulins, to remove all gold, silver and copper. "Eleven parties are made up . . . each to visit eight or ten houses. Each band is headed by one of the committee, with one municipal officer, accompanied by locksmiths and a revolutionary guard. The dwellings of the accused and other private individuals are searched. They force secretaries and wardrobes of which they do not find the keys. They pillage the gold and silver coin. They carry off plate, jewels, copper utensils, and other effects, bed-clothes, clocks, vehicles, etc. *No receipt is given.* No statement is made of what is carried off. They rest content by *at the end of the month,* reporting, in a sort of *procès-verbal,* drawn up at a meeting of the committee, that, according to returns of the visits made, *very little plate was found,* and only a *little money in gold and silver,* all without any calculation or enumeration."—"Souvenirs et Journal d'un Bourgeois d'Evreux," p. 93. (February 25, 1795.) The meetings of the popular club "were largely devoted to reading the infamous doings and robberies of the revolutionary committee. . . . The members who designated 'suspects' often arrested them themselves, and drew up a *procès-verbal* in which they *omitted to state the jewels and gold they found.*"

123. *Ibid.,* 461. (Vendémiaire 24, year III. Visit of Representative Malarmé.) The former Duc de Narbonne-Lorra, aged eighty-four, says to Malarmé: "Citizen representative, excuse me if I keep my cap on; I lost my hair in that prison, without having been able to get permission to have a wig made; it is worse than being robbed on the road." "Did they steal anything from you?" "They

who form the ruling oligarchy, admit, after Thermidor, that they stole the effects of arrested parties.[124] At Orange, "*Citoyenne* Riot," wife of the public prosecutor, and "*citoyennes* Fernex and Ragot," wives of two judges, come in person to the record-office to make selections from the spoils of the accused, taking for their wardrobe silver shoe-buckles, laces, and fine linen.[125] But all that the accused, the imprisoned and fugitives can take with them, amounts to but little in comparison with what they leave at home, that is to say, under sequestration. All the religious or seignorial chateaux and mansions in France are in this plight, along with their furniture, and likewise most of the fine bourgeois mansions, together with a large

---

stole one hundred and forty-five louis d'or and paid me with an acquittance for a tax for the *sans-culottes,* which is another robbery done to the citizens of this commune where I have neither home nor possessions." "Who committed this robbery?" "It was Citizen Berger, of the municipal council." "Was nothing else taken from you?" "They took a silver coffee-pot, two soap-cases and a silver shaving-dish." "Who took those articles?" "It was Citizen Miot (a notable of the council)." Miot confesses to having kept these objects and not taken them to the Mint.—*Ibid.,* 178. (Ventose 20, year II.) Prisoners all have their shoes taken, even those who had but one pair, a promise being made that they should have *sabots* in exchange, which they never got. Their cloaks also were taken with a promise to pay for them, which was never done.—"Souvenirs et Journal d'un Bourgeois d'Evreux," p. 92. (February 25, 1795.) The sessions of the popular club were largely devoted to reading the infamies and robberies of the revolutionary committee. Its members, who designated the suspects, often arrested them themselves; they made levies and reports of these in which they omitted the gold and jewels found."

124. *Moniteur,* xxii., 133. (Session of Vendémiaire 11, year III.) Report by Thibaudeau. "These seven individuals are reprobates who were dismissed by the people's representatives for having stolen the effects of persons arrested. A document is on record in which they make a declaration that, not remembering the value of the effects embezzled, they agree to pay damages to the nation of twenty-two francs each."

125. Berryat Saint-Prix, 447. Judge Ragot was formerly a joiner at Lyons, and Viot, the public prosecutor, a former deserter from the Penthièvre regiment. "Other accused persons were despoiled. Little was left them other than their clothes, which were in a bad state. Nappier, the bailiff, was, later (Messidor, year III.), condemned to irons for having appropriated a part of the effects, jewels, and assignats belonging to persons under accusation."

number of minor residences, well-furnished, and supplied through provincial economy; besides these, nearly every warehouse and store belonging to large manufacturers and leading commercial houses; all this forms colossal spoil, such as was never seen before, consisting of objects one likes to possess, gathered in vast lots, which lots are distributed by hundreds of thousands over the twenty-six thousand square miles of territory. There are no owners for this property but the nation, an indeterminate, imperceptible personage; no barrier other than so many seals exists between the spoils and the despoilers, that is to say, so many strips of paper held fast by two ill-applied and indistinct stamps. Bear in mind, too, that the guardians of the spoil are the *sans-culottes* who have made a conquest of it; that they are poor; that such a profusion of useful or precious objects makes them feel the bareness of their homes all the more; that their wives would dearly like to lay in a stock of furniture; moreover, has it not been held out to them from the beginning of the Revolution, that "forty-thousand mansions, palaces, and chateaux, two-thirds of the property of France, would be the reward of their valor"?[126] At this very moment, does not the representative on mission authorise their greed? Are not Albitte and Collot d'Herbois at Lyons, Fouché at Nevers, Javogues at Montbrison, proclaiming that the possessions of antirevolutionists and a surplus of riches form "the patrimony of the *sans-culottes*"?[127] Do they not read in the proclamations of Monestier,[128] that the peasants "before leaving home may survey and measure off the immense estates of their seigneurs, choose, for example, on their return, whatever they want to add to their farm . . . tacking on a bit of field or rabbit-warren belonging to the former count or marquis"? Why not take a portion of his furniture, any of

126. The words of Camille Desmoulins in "La France Libre" (August, 1782).

127. De Martel, "Fouché," 362.—*Ibid.*, 132, 162, 179, 427, 443.—Lecarpentier, in La Manche, constantly stated: "Those who do not like the Revolution, must pay those who make it."

128. Marcelin Boudet, 175. (Address of Monestier to the popular clubs of Puy-de-Dome, February 23, 1793.)

his beds or clothes-presses? It is not surprising that, after this, the slip of paper which protects sequestrated furniture and confiscated merchandise should be ripped off by gross and greedy hands! When, after Thermidor, the master returns to his own roof it is generally to an empty house; in this or that habitation in the Morvan,[129] the removal of the furniture is so complete that a bin turned upside down serves for a table and chairs, when the family sit down to their first meal.

In the towns the embezzlements are often more brazenly carried out than in the country. At Valenciennes, the Jacobin chiefs of the municipality are known under the title of "seal-breakers and patriotic robbers."[130] At Lyons, the Maratists, who dub themselves "the friends of Chalier," are, according to the Jacobins' own admission, "brigands, thieves, and rascals."[131] They compose, to the number of three or four hundred, the thirty-two revolutionary committees; one hundred and fifty of the leading ones, "all administrators," form the popular club; in this town of one hundred and twenty thousand souls they number, as they themselves state, three thousand, and they firmly rely on "sharing with each other the wealth of Lyons." This huge cake belongs to them; they do not allow that strangers, Parisians, should have a slice,[132] and they intend to eat the whole of it, at discretion, without control, even to the last crumb. As to their

129. Alexandrine des Echerolles, "Une famille noble sous la Terreur."

130. Archives Nationales, AF., II., 65. (Letter of General Kermorvan to the president of the Committee of Public Safety, Valenciennes, Fructidor 12, year III.)

131. Report by Courtois, "Sur les papiers de Robespierre," (Pieces justificatives, pp. 312–324), Letters of Reverchon, Germinal 29, Floréal 7 and 23, and by Laporte, Germinal 24, year II.

132. *Ibid.* Letter by Laporte: "I do not know what fatality induces patriots here not to tolerate their brethren whom they call strangers. . . . They have declared to us that they would not suffer any of them to hold office." The representatives dared arrest but two robbers and despoilers, who are now free and declaiming against them at Paris. "Countless grave and even atrocious circumstances are daily presented to us on which we hesitate to act, lest we should strike patriots, or those who call themselves such. . . . Horrible depredations are committed."

mode of operations, it consists in "selling justice, in trading on denunciations, in holding under sequestration at least four thousand households," in putting seals everywhere on dwellings and warehouses, in not summoning interested parties who might watch their proceedings, in expelling women, children, and servants who might testify to their robberies, in not drawing up inventories, in installing themselves as "guardians at five francs a day," themselves or their boon companions, and in "general squandering, in league with the administrators." It is impossible to stay their hands or repress them, even for the representatives. "Take them in the act,[133] and you must shut your eyes or they will all shout at the oppression of patriots; they do this systematically so that nobody may be followed up. . . . We passed an order forbidding any authority to remove seals without our consent, and, in spite of the prohibition, they broke into a storehouse under sequestration, . . . forced the locks and pillaged, under our own eyes, the very house we occupy. And who are these devastators? Two commissioners of the Committee who emptied the storehouse without our warrant, and even without having any power from the Committee." It is a sack in due form, and day after day; it began on the 10th of October, 1793; it continued after, without interruption, and we have just seen that, on Floréal 28, year II., that is to say, April 26, 1794, after one hundred and twenty-three days, it is still maintained.

The last haul and the richest of all. In spite of the subterfuges of its agents, the Republic, having stolen immensely, and although robbed in its turn, could still hold on to a great deal; and first, to

133. *Ibid.* Letter by Reverchon: "These fanatics all want the Republic simply for themselves." . . . "They call themselves patriots only to cut the throats of their brethren and get rich."—Guillon de Montléon, "Histoire de la Ville de Lyons Pendant la Révolution," iii., 166. (Report by Fouché, April, 1794.) "Innocent persons, acquitted by the terrible tribunal of the Revolutionary Committee, were again consigned to the dungeons of criminals through the despotic orders of the thirty-two committees, because they were so unfortunate as to complain that, on returning home, they could not find the strictly necessary objects they had left there."

articles of furniture which could not be easily abstracted, to large lots of merchandise, also to the vast spoil of the palaces, chateaux, and churches; next, and above all, to real estate, fixtures, and buildings. Its necessities require it to put all this on the market, and whoever wants anything has only to come forward as a buyer, the last bidder becoming the legal owner and at a cheap rate. The wood cut down in one year very often pays for a whole forest.[134] Sometimes a chateau can be paid for by a sale of the iron-railings of the park, or the lead on the roof. Here are found chances for a good many bargains, and especially with objects of art. "The titles alone of the articles carried off, destroyed, or injured, would fill volumes."[135] On the one hand, the commissioners on inventories and adjudications, "having to turn a penny on the proceeds of sales," throw on the market all they can, "avoiding reserving" objects of public utility and sending collections and libraries to auction with a view to get their percentages. On the other hand, nearly all these commissioners are brokers or second-hand dealers who alone know the value of rarities, and openly depreciate them in order to buy them in themselves, "and thus ensure for themselves exorbitant profits." In certain cases the official guardians and purchasers who are on the look-out take the precaution to "disfigure" precious articles "so as to have them bought by their substitutes and accomplices": for instance, they convert sets of books into odd volumes, and take machines to pieces; the tube and object-glass of a telescope are separated, which pieces the rogues who have bought them cheap know how to put together again." Often, in spite of the seals, they take in advance "antiques, pieces of jewelry, medals, enamels, and engraved stones"; nothing is easier, for "even in Paris in Thermidor,

---

134. Meissner, "Voyage en France dans les Derniers Mois de 1705," p. 343. "A certain domain was handed over to one of their creatures by the revolutionary departments for almost nothing, less than the proceeds of the first cut of wood."—*Moniteur*, xxiii., 397. (Speech by Bourdon de l'Oise, May 6, 1795.) "A certain farmer paid for his farm worth five thousand francs by the sale of one horse."

135. *Moniteur*, xxii., 82. (Report by Grégoire, Fructidor 14, year II.) *Ibid.*, 775. (Report by Grégoire, Frimaire 24, year III.)

year II., agents of the municipality use anything with which to make a stamp, buttons, and even large pennies, so that whoever has a sou can remove and restamp the seals as he pleases"; having been successful, "they screen their thefts by substituting cut pebbles and counterfeit stones for real ones." Finally, at the auction sales, "fearing the honesty or competition of intelligent judges, they offer money (to these) to stay away from the sales; one case is cited of a bidder being knocked down." In the meantime, at the club, they shout with all their might; this, with the protection of a member of the municipality or of the Revolutionary Committee, shelters them from all suspicion. As for the protector, he gets his share without coming out into the light. Accuse, if you dare, a republican functionary who secretly, or even openly, profits by these larcenies; he will show clean hands. Such is the incorruptible patriot, the only one of his species, whom the representatives discover at Strasbourg, and whom they appoint mayor at once. On the 10th of Vendémiaire, year III.,[136] there is found "in his apartments" a superb and complete assortment of ecclesiastical objects, "forty-nine copes and chasubles, silk or satin, covered with gold or silver; fifty-four *palles* of the same description;" a quantity of "reliquaries, vases and spoons, censers, laces, silver and gold fringe, thirty-two pieces of silk," etc. None of these fine things belong to him; they are the property of citizen Mouet, his father. This prudent parent, taking his word for it, "deposited them for safe keeping in his son's house during the month of June, 1792 (old style)"; could a good son refuse his father such a slight favor? It is very certain that, in '93 and '94, during the young man's municipal dictatorship, the elder did not pay the Strasbourg Jew brokers too much, and that they did business in an offhand way. By what right could a son and magistrate prevent his father, a free individual, from looking after "his own affairs" and buying according to trade principles, as cheap as he could?

If such are the profits on the sale of personal property, what must

---

136. "Recueil de Pièces Authentiques sur la Révolution à Strasbourg," ii. p. 1. (*Procès-verbal*, drawn up in the presence of the elder Mouet and signed by him.)

they be on the sale of real estate? It is on this traffic that the fortunes of the clever terrorists are founded. It accounts for the "colossal wealth peaceably enjoyed," after Thermidor, of the well-known "thieves" who, before Thermidor, were so many "little Robespierres," each in his own canton, "the patriots" who, around Orleans, "built palaces," who, "exclusives" at Valenciennes, "having wasted both public and private funds, possess the houses and property of emigrants, knocked down to them at a hundred times less than their value."[137] On this side, their outstretched fingers shamelessly clutch all they can get hold of; for the obligation of each arrested party to declare his name, quality and fortune, as it now is and was before the Revolution, gives local cupidity a known, sure, direct and palpable object. At Toulouse, says a prisoner,[138] "the details and value of an object were taken down as if for *a succession*," while the commissioners who drew up the statement, "our assassins, proceeded, beforehand and almost under our eyes, to take their share, disputing with each other on the choice and suitableness of each object, comparing the cost of adjudication with the means of lessening it, discussing the certain profits of selling again and of the transfer, and consuming in advance the pickings arising from sales and leases." In Provence, where things are more advanced and corruption is greater than elsewhere, where the purport and aims of the Revolution were comprehended at the start, it is still worse. Nowhere did Jacobin rulers display their real character more openly, and nowhere, from 1789 to 1799, was this character so well maintained. At Toulon, the demagogues in the year V., as in the year II., are[139] "former workmen and clerks in the Arsenal who had become 'bosses' by acting as informers and through terrorism, getting property for nothing, or at an insignificant price, and plotting sales of national

---

137. *Moniteur,* xxii., 775. (Report of Grégoire, Frimaire 24, year III.)—*Ibid.,* 711. (Report by Cambon, Frimaire 6, year III.)—Archives Nationales, AF., II., 65. (Letter of General Kermorvan, Valenciennes, Fructidor 12, year III.)

138. "Tableau des Prisons de Toulouse," 184. (Visit of Ventose 27, year II.)

139. Archives Nationales, F⁷, 7,164. (Department of Var "Ideé générale et appréciation auc détails sur chaque canton," year V.)

possessions, petty traders from all quarters with stocks of goods acquired in all sorts of ways, through robberies, through purchases of stolen goods from servants and employees in the civil, war, and navy departments, and through abandoned or bought-up claims; in fine, from refugees from other communes who pass their days in coffee-houses and their nights in houses of ill-fame." The leading officials at Draguignan, Brignolles, Vidauban, and Fréjus, are of this sort. At Marseilles, after Thermidor, the intermittent returns to Terrorism always restore to office,[140] the same justiciary and police gangs, "once useful mechanics, but tired of working, and whom the profession of paid clubbists, idle guardians," and paid laborers "has totally demoralized," scoundrels in league with each other and making money out of whatever they lay their hands on, like thieves at a fair, habitually living at the expense of the public, "bestowing the favors of the nation on those who share their principles, harboring and aiding many who are under the ban of the law and calling themselves model patriots, in fine, in the pay of gambling-hells and houses of prostitution."[141] In the rural districts, the old bands "con-

140. *Ibid.*, F^7, 7,171 (No. 7,915).—(Department of Bouches-du-Rhone, "Ideé générale," year V.)—(Letters of Miollis, Commissioner of the Directory in the department, Ventose 14 and 16, year V. Letter of Gen. Willot to the Minister, Ventose 10, and of Gen. Merle to Gen. Willot, Ventose 17, year V.) "Several sections of anarchists travel from one commune to another exciting weak citizens to riots and getting them to take part in the horrors they are meditating."—*Ibid.*, F^7, 7,164. Letter of Gen. Willot to the Minister, Arles, Pluviose 12, year V:, with supporting documents, and especially a letter of the director of the jury, on the violence committed by, and the reign of, the Jacobins in Arles.) Their party "is composed of the vilest mechanics and nearly all the sailors." The municipality recruited amongst former terrorists, "has enforced for a year back the agrarian law, devastation of the forests, pillage of the wheat-crops, by bands of armed men under pretext of the right of gleaning, the robbery of animals at the plough as well as of the flocks," etc.

141. *Ibid.*, F^7, 7,171. "These commissioners (of the quarter) notify the exclusives, and even swindlers, when warrants are out against them. . . . The same measures carried out in the primary assemblies on the 1st of Thermidor last, in the selection of municipal officers, have been successfully revived in the organisation of the National Guard—threats, insults, vociferations, assaults, compulsory ejection from meetings then governed by the amnestied, finally, the

sisting of hordes of homeless brigands" who worked so well during the anarchy of the Constituent and Legislative assemblies, form anew during the anarchy of the Directory; they make their appearance in the vicinity of Apt "commencing with petty robberies and then, strong in the impunity and title of *sans-culottes,* break into farm-houses, rob and massacre the inmates, strip travelers, put to ransom all who happen to cross their path, force open and pillage houses in the commune of Gorges, stop women in the streets, tear off their rings and crosses," and attack the hospital, sacking it from top to bottom, while the town and military officers, just like them, allow them to go on.[142] Judge by this of their performances in the

---

appointment of the latter to the principal offices. In effect, all, beginning with the places of battalion leaders and reaching to those of corporals, are exclusively filled by their partisans. The result is that the honest, to whom serving with men regarded by them with aversion is repugnant, employ substitutes instead of mounting guard themselves, the security of the town being in the hands of those who themselves ought to be watched."

142. Archives Nationales, F^7, 3,273. (Letter of Mérard, former administrator and judge in 1790 and 1791, in years III., IV., and V., to the Minister, Apt, Pluviose 15, year III., with personal references and documentary evidence.) "I can no longer refrain at the sight of so many horrors. . . . The justices of the peace and the director of the jury excuse themselves on the ground that no denunciations or witnesses are brought forward. Who would dare appear against men arrogating to themselves the title of superior patriots, foremost in every revolutionary crisis, and with friends in every commune and protectors in all high places? The favor they enjoyed was such that the commune of Gordes was free of any levy of conscripts and from all requisitions. People thus disposed, they said, to second civic and administrative views, could not be humored too much. . . . This discouraging state of things simply results from the weakness, inexperience, ignorance, apathy, and immorality of the public functionaries who, *since the 18th of Fructidor, year V.,* swarm, with a few exceptions only, among the constituted authorities. *Whatever is most foul and incompetent* is in office, *every good citizen being frightened to death."—Ibid.* (Letter of Montauban, director of the registry since 1793 to the Minister of the Interior, a compatriot, Avignon, Pluviose 7, year VII.) "Honest folks are constantly annoyed and put down by the authors and managers of the 'Glacière' . . . by the tools of the bloody tribunal of Orange and the incendiaries of Bedouin." He enjoins secrecy on this letter, which, "if known to the Glacièrists, or Orangeists, would cost him his life."

time of Robespierre, when the vendors and administrators of the national possessions exercised undisputed control. Everywhere, at that time, in the departments of Var, Bouches-du-Rhone, and Vaucluse, "a club of would-be patriots" had long prepared the way for their exactions. It had "paid appraisers" for depreciating whatever was put up for sale, and false names for concealing real purchasers; "a person not of their clique, was excluded from the auction-room; if he persisted in coming in they would, at one time, put him under contribution for the privilege of bidding," and, at another time, make him promise not to bid above the price fixed by the league, while, to acquire the domain, they paid him a bonus. Consequently, "national property" was made way with "for almost nothing," the sharpers who acquired it never being without a satisfactory warrant for this in their own eyes. Into whose hands could the property of antirevolutionists better fall than into those of patriots? According to Marat, the martyr apostle and canonised saint of the Revolution, what is the object of the Revolution but to give to the lowly the fortunes of the great?[143] In all national sales everywhere, in guarding sequestrations, in all revolutionary ransoms, taxes, loans and seizures, the same excellent argument prevails; nowhere, in printed documents or in manuscripts, do I find any revolutionary committee which is at once terrorist and honest. Only, it is rare to find specific and individual details regarding all the members of the same committee. Here, however, is one case, where, owing to the lucky accident of an examination given in detail, one can observe in one nest, every variety of the species and of its appetites, the dozen or fifteen types of the Jacobin hornet, each abstracting what suits him from whatever he lights on, each indulging in his favorite sort of rapine. At Nantes, "Pinard, the great purveyor of the Committee,[144] orders everything that each member needs for his daily use to be

143. *Ibid.*, F⁷, 7,164. (Department of Var, year V., "Ideé Générale.") "National character is gone; it is even demoralised: an office-holder who has not made his fortune quickly is regarded as a fool."

144. *Moniteur,* xxii., 240. (Indictment of the fourteen members of the Revolutionary Committee of Nantes, and the summing-up of the examination, Ven-

carried to his house." "Gallou takes oil and brandy," and especially "several barrels from citizen Bissonneau's house." "Durassier makes domiciliary visits and exacts contributions"; among others "he compels citizen Lemoine to pay twenty-five hundred livres, to save him from imprisonment." "Naud affixes and removes seals in the houses of the incarcerated, makes nocturnal visits to the dwellings of the accused and takes what suits him." "Grandmaison appropriates plate under sequestration, and Bachelier plate given as a present." "Joly superintends executions and takes all he can find, plate, jewelry, precious objects." "Bolognié forces the return of a bond of twenty thousand livres already paid to him." "Perrochaux demands of *citoyenne* Ollemard-Dudan fifty thousand livres, to prevent her imprisonment," and confiscates for his own benefit sixty thousand livres' worth of tobacco, in the house of the widow Daigneau-Mallet, who, claiming it back, is led off by him to prison under the pretext of interceding for her. "Chaux frightens off by terrorism his competitors at auction sales, has all the small farms on the Baroissière

---

démiaire 23, year II.) When there is no special information concerning the other committees the verdict, on the whole, is nearly always as overwhelming.—*Ibid*. (Session of Vendémiaire 12, year III. Complaint of a deputation from Ferney.—Voltaire.) "The Gex district was, for over a year, a prey to five or six scoundrels who took refuge there. Under the mask of patriotism they succeeded in getting possession of all the offices. Vexations of every kind, robberies of private houses, squandering of public money, were committed by these monsters." (The Ferney deputies brought with them the testimony of witnesses.)—*Ibid.*, 290. (Letters of Representative Goupilleau, Beziers, Vendémiaire 28, year III. on the terrorists of Vaucluse.) "These carnivorous fellows, regretting the times when they could rob and massacre with impunity. . . . Who, six months ago, were starving, and who now live in the most scandalous opulence. . . . Squanderers of the public funds, robbers of private fortunes. . . . Guilty of rapine, of forced contributions, of extortions," etc.—Prudhomme, "Les Crimes de la Révolution," vi., 79. (On the Revolutionary Committee installed by Fouché at Nevers.) The local investigation shows that the eleven leaders were men of vile character, unfrocked and disreputable priests, lawyers and notaries driven out of their professional bodies, and even from the popular clubs, on account of their dishonesty, penniless actors, surgeons without patients, depraved, ruined, incapable men, and two jail-birds.

domain knocked down to him, and exclaims concerning a place which suits him, 'I know how to get it! I'll have the owner arrested. He'll be very glad to let me have his ground to get out of prison.'" The collection is complete, and ranged around a table, it offers samples which, elsewhere in France, are found scattered about.

VII

The last manipulators of the system remain, the hands which seize, the armed force which takes bodily hold of men and things. The first who are employed for this purpose are the National Guard and the ordinary gendarmerie. Since 1790, these bodies are of course constantly weeded out until only fanatics and instruments are left;[145] nevertheless, the weeding-out continues as the system develops itself. At Strasbourg,[146] on Brumaire 14, the representatives have dismissed, arrested, and sent to Dijon the entire staff of the National Guard to serve as hostages until peace is secured; three days afterwards, considering that the cavalry of the town had been mounted and equipped at its own expense, they deem it aristocratic, bourgeois, and "suspect," and seize the horses and put the officers in arrest. At Troyes, Rousselin, "National civil commissioner," dismisses, for the same reason, and with not less despatch, the whole of the gendarmes at one stroke, except four, and "puts under requisition their horses, fully equipped, also their arms, so as to at once mount well-known and tried *sans-culottes*." On principle, the poor *sans-culottes*, who are true at heart and in dress, alone have the right to bear arms, and should a bourgeois be on duty he must have only a pike, care being taken to take it away from him the moment he finishes his rounds.[147]

But, alongside of the usual armed force, there is still another,

145. Beaulieu, iii., 754.—Cf. "The Revolution," vol. ii., ch. i., § 9.

146. "Recueil de Pièces Authentiques sur la Révolution à Strasbourg," i., 21.—Archives Nationales D., I., § 6. (Orders by Rousselin, Frimaire 11, year II.)

147. "Un Séjour en France de 1792 à 1795," p. 409.

much better selected and more effective, the reserve gendarmerie, a special, and, at the same time, movable and resident body, that is to say, the "revolutionary army," which, after September 5, 1793, the government had raised in Paris and in most of the large towns. That of Paris, comprising six thousand men, with twelve hundred cannoneers, sends detachments into the provinces—two thousand men to Lyons, and two hundred to Troyes;[148] Ysabeau and Tallien have at Bordeaux a corps of three thousand men; Salicetti, Albitte, and Gasparin, one of two thousand men at Marseilles; Ysoré and Duquesnoy, one of one thousand men at Lille; Javogues, one of twelve hundred at Montbrison; others, less numerous, ranging from six hundred down to two hundred men, hold Moulins, Grenoble, Besançon, Belfort, Bourg, Dijon, Strasbourg, Toulouse, Auch, and Nantes.[149] When, on March 27, 1794, the Committee of Public Safety, threatened by Hébert, has them disbanded for being Hébertists, many of them are to remain at least as a nucleus, under various forms and names, either as kept by the local administration under the title of "paid guards,"[150] or as disbanded soldiers, loitering about

148. I have not found a complete list of the towns and departments which had a revolutionary army. The correspondence of representatives on mission and published documents verify the presence of revolutionary armies in the towns mentioned.

149. De Martel, "Fouché," 338. (Text of the orders of the Commissioners of Public Safety.) The detachment sent to Lyons comprises twelve hundred fusileers, six hundred cannoneers, one hundred and fifty horses. Three hundred thousand livres are remitted as travelling expenses to the commissary, fifty thousand to Collot d'Herbois, and nineteen thousand two hundred to the Jacobin civilians accompanying them.

150. *Moniteur.* (Session of Brumaire 17, year III.) Letter of Representative Calès to the Convention. "Under the pretext of guarding the prisons, the municipality (of Dijon) had a revolutionary army which I broke up two days ago, as it cost six thousand francs a month, and would not obey the commander of the armed force, and served as a support to intriguers. These soldiers, who were all workmen out of employment, do nothing but post themselves in the tribunes of the clubs, where they, with the women they bring along with them, applaud the leaders, and so threaten citizens who are disposed to combat them, and force these to keep their mouths shut."—De Martel, "Fouché," 425. "Javogues, to elude a decree of the Convention (Frimaire 14) suppressing the

and doing nothing, getting themselves assigned posts of rank in the National Guard of their town on account of their exploits; in this way they keep themselves in service, which is indispensable, for it is through these that the régime is established and lasts. "The revolutionary army,"[151] say the orders and decrees promulgated, "is intended to repress antirevolutionists, to execute, whenever it is found necessary, revolutionary laws and measures for public safety," that is to say, "to guard those who are shut up, arrest 'suspects,' demolish chateaux, pull down belfries, ransack vestries for gold and silver objects, seize fine horses and carriages," and especially "to seek for private stores and monopolies," in short, to exercise manual constraint and strike every one on the spot with physical terror. We readily see what sort of soldiers the revolutionary army is composed of.

Naturally, as it is recruited by voluntary enlistments, and all candidates have passed the purifying scrutiny of the clubs, it comprises none but ultra Jacobins. Naturally, the pay being forty sous a day, it comprises none but the very lowest class. Naturally, as the work is as loathsome as it is atrocious, it comprises but few others[152] than those out of employment and reduced to an enlistment to get a living, "hairdressers without customers, lackeys without places, vag-

---

revolutionary army in the departments, converted the twelve hundred men he had embodied in it in the Loire into paid soldiers."—*Ibid.*, 132. (Letter of Goulin, Bourg, Frimaire 23.) "Yesterday, at Bourg-Régeriéré, I found Javogues with about four hundred men of the revolutionary army whom he had brought with him on the 20th instant."

151. Buchez et Roux, xxix., 45.—*Moniteur*, xx., 67. (Report of Barère, Germinal 7.)—Sauzay, iv., 303. (Orders of Representative Bassal at Bésançon.)

152. We see by Barère's report (Germinal 7, year II.) that the revolutionary army of Paris, instead of being six thousand men, was only four thousand, which is creditable to Paris.—Mallet-Dupan, ii., 52. (Cf. "The Revolution," ii., 353.)—Gouvion St. Cyr, i., 137. "In these times, the representatives had organised in Haut-Rhin what they called a revolutionary army, composed of deserters and all the vagabonds and scamps they could pick up who had belonged to the popular club; they dragged along after it what they called judges and a guillotine."—"Hua, "Souvenirs d'un Avocat," 196.

abonds, wretches unable to earn a living by honest labor,"
"shoulder-hitters" who have acquired the habit of bullying, knock-
ing down, and keeping honest folks under their pikes, a gang of
confirmed scoundrels making public brigandage a cloak for private
brigandage, inhabitants of the slums glad to bring down their former
superiors into the mud, and themselves take precedence and strut
about in order to prove by their arrogance and self-display that they,
in their turn, are princes. "Take a horse, the nation pays for it!"[153]
exclaim water-carriers and *commissionaires* to their comrades in the
street, and who, "in a splendid procession," of three carriages, each
drawn by six horses, escorted by a body of *sans-culottes* on horseback, behind, in front, and each side the doors, are conducting
Riouffe and two other "suspects" to prison. The commander of the
squad who guards prisoners on the way to Paris, and who "starves
them along the road to speculate on them," is an ex-cook of Agen,
having become a gendarme; he makes them travel forty leagues
extra, "purposely to glorify himself," and "let all Agen see that he
has government money to spend, and that he can put citizens in
irons." Accordingly, in Agen, "he keeps constantly and needlessly
inspecting the vehicle," winking at the spectators, "more triumphant
than if he had made a dozen Austrians prisoners and brought them
along himself"; at last, to show the crowd in the street the importance of his capture, he summons two blacksmiths to come out and
rivet, on the legs of each prisoner, a cross-bar cannon-ball weighing
eighty pounds.[154] The more display these *sbirri* make of their brutality, the greater they think themselves. At Belfort, a patriot of the
club dies, and a civic interment takes place; a detachment of the

153. Riouffe, "Mémoires d'un détenu," p. 31.

154. *Ibid.*, 37. "These balls were brought out ostentatiously and shown to
the people beforehand. The tying of our hands and passing three ropes around
our waists did not seem to him sufficient. We kept these irons on the rest of
the route, and they were so heavy that, if the carriage had tilted to one side,
we should inevitably have had our legs broken. The gate-keepers of the Conciergerie of Paris, who had held their places nineteen years, were astonished
at it."

revolutionary army joins the procession; the men are armed with axes; on reaching the cemetery, the better to celebrate the funeral, "they cut down all the crosses (over the graves) and make a bonfire of them, while the *carmagnole* ends this ever memorable day."[155] Sometimes the scene, theatrical and played by the light of flambeaux, makes the actors think that they have performed an extraordinary and meritorious action, "that they have saved the country." "This very night," writes the agent at Bordeaux,[156] "nearly three thousand men have been engaged in an important undertaking, with the members of the Revolutionary Committee and of the municipality at the head of it. They visited every wholesale dealer's store in town and in the Faubourg des Chartrons, taking possession of their letter-books, sealing up their desks, arresting the merchants and putting them in the Seminiare. . . . Woe to the guilty!" If the prompt confinement of an entire class of individuals is a fine thing for a town, the seizure of a whole town itself is still more imposing. Leaving Marseilles with a small army,[157] commanded by two *sans-culottes*, they surround Martigne and enter it as if it were a mill. The catch is superb; in this town of five thousand souls there are only seventeen patriots; the rest are Federalists or Moderates. Hence a general disarmament and domiciliary visits. The conquerors depart, carrying off every able-bodied boy, "five hundred lads subject to the conscription, and leave in the town a company of *sans-culottes* to enforce obedience." It is certain that obedience will be maintained and that the garrison, joined to the seventeen patriots, will do as they like with their conquest.

In effect, all, both bodies and goods, are at their disposal, and they consequently begin with the country round about, entering private houses to get at their stores, also the farmhouses to have the grain threshed, in order to verify the declarations of their owners

---

155. Archives des Affaires Étrangérès, vol. 331. (Letter of Haupt, Belfort, Frimaire 13, year II.)

156. *Ibid.* (Letter by Desgranges, Bordeaux, Frimaire 10.)

157. *Ibid.*, vol. 332. (Letter of Thiberge, Marseilles, Frimaire 14.) "I surrounded the town with my small army."

and see if these are correct: if the grain is not threshed out at once it will be done summarily and confiscated, while the owner will be sentenced to twelve months in irons; if the declaration is not correct, he is condemned as a monopolist and punished with death. Armed with this order,[158] each band takes the field and gathers together not only grain, but supplies of every description. "That of Grenoble, the agent writes,[159] does wonderfully; in one little commune alone, four hundred measures of wheat, twelve hundred eggs, and six hundred pounds of butter had been found. All this was quickly on the way to Grenoble." In the vicinity of Paris, the forerunners of the throng, provided "with pitchforks and bayonets, rush to the farms, take oxen out of their stalls, grab sheep and chickens, burn the barns, and sell their booty to speculators."[160] "Bacon, eggs, butter, and chickens—the peasants surrender whatever is demanded of them,

158. *Ibid.,* 331. (Orders of Representative Bassal, Besançon, Frimaire 5.) "No citizen shall keep in his house more than four months' supplies. . . . Every citizen with more than this will deposit the surplus in the granary *'d'abondance'* provided for the purpose. . . . Immediately on receipt of the present order, the municipality will summon all citizens that can thresh and proceed immediately, without delay, to the threshing-ground, under penalty of being prosecuted as refractory to the law. . . . The revolutionary army is specially charged with the execution of the articles of this order, and the revolutionary tribunals, following this army with the enforcement of the penalties inflicted according to this order."—Other documents show us that the revolutionary army, organised in the department of Doubs and in the five neighboring departments, comprises, in all, two thousand four hundred men. (*Ibid.,* vol., 1411. Letter of Meyenfeld to Minister Desforges, Brumaire 27, year II.)—Archives Nationales, AF., II., 111. (Order of Couthon, Maignet, Chateauneuf, Randon, Laporte, and Albitte, Commune-Affranchie, Brumaire 9, year II., establishing in the ten surrounding departments a revolutionary army of one thousand men per department, for the conscription of grain. Each army is to be directed by commissioners, strangers to the department, and is to operate in other departments than in the one where it is raised.)

159. Archives des Affaires Étrangérès, 331. (Letter of Chépy, Frimaire 11.)—Writing one month before this (Brumaire 6), he says: "The farmers show themselves very hostile against the towns and the law of the *maximum*. Nothing can be done without a revolutionary army."

160. Mercier, "Paris Pendant la Revolution," i., 357.

and thenceforth have nothing that they can take to market. They curse the Republic which has brought war and famine on them, and nevertheless they do what they are told: on being addressed, 'Citizen peasant, I require of you on peril of your head,' . . . there is no longer any retreat."[161] Accordingly, they are only too glad to be let off so cheaply. On Brumaire 19, about seven o'clock in the evening, at Tigery, near Corbeil, twenty-five men "with sabres and pistols in their belts, most of them in the uniform of the National Guards and calling themselves the revolutionary army," enter the house of Gibbon, an old ploughman, seventy-one years of age, while fifty others guard all egress from it, so that the expedition may not be interfered with. Turlot, captain, and aid-de-camp to General Henriot, wants to know where the master of the house is. "In his bed," is the reply. "Wake him up." The old man rises. "Give up your arms." His wife hands over a fowling-piece, the only arm on the premises. The band immediately falls on the poor man, "strikes him down, ties his hands, and puts a sack over his head," and the same thing is done to his wife and to eight male and two female servants. "Now, give us the keys of your closets"; they want to be sure that there are no *fleur-de-lys* or other illegal articles. They search the old man's pockets, take his keys, and, to despatch business, break into the chests and seize or carry off all the plate, "twenty-six table-dishes, three soup-ladles, three goblets, two snuff-boxes, forty counters, two watches, another gold watch and a gold cross." "We will draw up a *procès-verbal* of all this at our leisure in Meaux. Now, where's your silver? If you don't say where it is, the guillotine is outside and I will be

161. Hua, 197. I do not find in any printed or manuscript document but one case of resistance, that of the brothers Chaperon, in the hamlet of Loges, near Sens, who declare that they have no wheat except for their own use, and who defend themselves by the use of a gun. The gendarmerie not being strong enough to overcome them, the tocsin is sounded and the National Guard of Sens and the neighborhood is summoned; bringing cannon, the affair ends with the burning of the house. The two brothers are killed. Previously, however, they had struck down the captain of the National Guard of Sens and killed or wounded nearly forty of their assailants. A surviving brother and a sister are guillotined. (June, 1794. Wallon, iv., 352.)

your executioner." The old man yields and merely requests to be untied. But it is better to keep him bound, "so as to make him 'shell out.'" They carry him into the kitchen and "put his feet into a heated brazier." He shouts with pain, and indicates another chest which they break open and then carry off what they find there, "seventy-two francs in coin and five or six thousand livres in assignats, which Gibbon had just received for the requisitions made on him for corn." Next, they break open the cellar doors, set a cask of vinegar running, carry wine upstairs, eat the family meal, get drunk and, at last, clear out, leaving Gibbon with his feet burnt, and garroted, as well as the other eleven members of his household, quite certain that there will be no pursuit.[162] In the towns, especially in federalist districts, however, these robberies are complicated with other assaults. At Lyons, whilst the regular troops are lodged in barracks, the revolutionary army is billeted on the householders, two thousand vile, sanguinary blackguards from Paris, and whom their general, Ronsin himself, calls "scoundrels and brigands," alleging, in excuse for this, that "honest folks cannot be found for such business." How they treat their host, his wife and his daughters may be imagined; contemporaries glide over these occurrences and, through decency or disgust, avoid giving details.[163] Some simply use

162. *Moniteur*, xviii., 663. (Session of Frimaire 24, report by Lecointre.) "The communes of Thieux, Jully, and many others were victims to their brigandage." "The stupor in the country is such that the poor sufferers dare not complain of these vexations because, they say, they are only too lucky to have escaped with their lives."—This time, however, these public brigands made a mistake. Gibbon's son happens to be Lecointre's farmer. Moreover, it is only accidentally that he mentions the circumstance to his landlord; "he came to see him for another purpose."—Cf. "The Revolution," vol. ii., 302. (There is a similar scene in the house of one Ruelle, a farmer, in the Commune of Lisse.)

163. Cf., *passim* Alfred Lallier, "Le sans-culotte Goullin."—Wallon. "Histoire du Tribunal Révolutionnaire de Paris," v., 368. (Deposition of Lacaille.)— In addition to this, the most extraordinary monsters are met with in other administrative bodies, for example, in Nantes, a Jean d'Héron, tailor, who becomes inspector of military stores. "After the rout at Clisson, says the woman Laillet, he appeared in the popular club with a brigand's ear attached to his hat by way of cockade. His pockets were full of ears, which he took delight in

brutal force; others get rid of a troublesome husband by the guillotine; in the most exceptional cases they bring their wenches along
with them, while the housekeeper has to arouse herself at one o'clock
at night and light a fire for the officer who comes in with the jolly
company. And yet, there are others still worse, for the worst attract
each other. We have seen the revolutionary committee at Nantes,
also the representative on mission in the same city; nowhere did the
revolutionary Sabbat rage so furiously, and nowhere was there such
a traffic in human lives. With such band-leaders as Carrier and his
tools on the Committee, one may be sure that the instrumentalists
will be worthy.

Accordingly, several members of the Committee themselves over-
see executions and lend a hand in the massacres. One of these,
Goullin, a creole from St. Domingo, sensual and nervous, accustomed to treating a negro as an animal and a Frenchman as a white
negro, a *Septembriseur* on principle, chief instigator and director of
the "drownings," goes in person to empty the prison of Bouffay,
and, ascertaining that deaths, the hospital and releases, had lessened
the number of the imprisoned, adds, of his own authority, fifteen
names, taken haphazard, to complete his list. Joly, a commissioner
on the Committee, very expert in the art of garroting, ties the hands
of prisoners together two and two and conducts them to the river.[164]
Grandmaison, another member of the Committee, a former dancing-
master, convicted of two murders and pardoned before the Revolution, strikes down with his sabre the uplifted hands stretched out
to him over the planks of the lighter.[165] Pinard, another Committee-
commissioner, ransoms, steals off into the country and himself kills,
through preference, women and children.[166] Naturally, the three

---

making the women kiss. He exposed other things which he made them kiss and
the woman Laillet adds certain details which I dare not transcribe." ("Le patriote
d'Héron," by L. de la Sicotière, pp. 9 and 10. Deposition of the woman Laillet,
fish-dealer, also the testimony of Mellinet, vol. viii., p. 256.)

164. Wallon, v., 368. (Deposition of de Laillet.)
165. *Ibid.,* v., 371. (Deposition of Tabouret.)
166. *Ibid.,* v., 373. (Deposition of Mariotte.)

bands which operate along with them, or under their orders, comprise only men of their species. In the first one, called the Marat company, each of the sixty members swears, on joining it, to adopt Marat's principles and carry out Marat's doctrine. Goullin,[167] one of the founders, demands in relation to each member, "Isn't there some one still more rascally? For we must have that sort to bring the aristocrats to reason!"[168] After Frimaire 5 "the Maratists" boast of their arms being "tired out" with striking prisoners with the flat of their sabres to make them march to the Loire,[169] and we see that, notwithstanding this fatigue, the business suited them, as their officers intrigued with Carrier to be detailed on the "drowning" service and because it was lucrative. The men and women sentenced to death, were first stripped of their clothes down to the shirt, and even the shift; it would be a pity to let valuable objects go to the bottom with their owners, and therefore the drowners divide these amongst themselves; a wardrobe in the house of the adjutant Richard is found full of jewelry and watches.[170] This company of sixty must

167. *Moniteur,* xxii., 321. (Deposition of Philippe Troncjolly.)—Berryat Saint-Prix, "La Justice Révolutionnaire," 39.

168. Campardon, "Histoire du Tribunal Révolutionnaire," ii., 30. They have ten francs a day, and full powers conferred on them. (Orders of Carrier and Francastel, October 28, 1793.) "The representatives . . . confer collectively and individually, on each member of the revolutionary company, the right of surveillance over all 'suspect' citizens in Nantes, over strangers who come to or reside there, over monopolists of every sort. . . . The right to make domiciliary visits wherever they may deem it advisable. . . . The armed force will everywhere respond to the demands made upon it in the name of the company, or of any individual member composing it."—Berryat Saint-Prix, p. 42.—Alfred Lallier, "Les Noyades de Nantes," p. 20. (Deposition of Gauthier.) *Ibid.,* p. 22. "D——," exclaims Carrier, "I kept that execution for Lamberty. I'm sorry that it was done by others."

169. Alfred Lallier, *ibid.,* pp. 21 and 90.—Cf. *Moniteur,* xxii., 331. (Deposition of Victoire Abraham.) "The drowners made quite free with the women, even using them for their own purposes when pleased with them, which women, in token of their kindness, enjoyed the precious advantage of not being drowned."

170. Campardon, ii., 8. (Deposition of Commeret.)—Berryat Saint-Prix, p. 42.—*Ibid.,* p. 28. Other agents of Carrier, Fouquet, and Lamberty, were

have made handsome profits out of the four or five thousand drowned. The second band, called "the American Hussars," and who operated in the outskirts, was composed of blacks and mulattoes, numerous enough in this town of privateers. It is their business to shoot women, whom they first violate; "they are our slaves," they say; "we have won them by the sweat of our brows." "Those who have the misfortune to be saved by them, become in their hands idiotic in a couple of days; in any event they are rearrested shortly afterwards and shot. The last band, which is styled "The German Legion," is formed out of German deserters and mercenaries who can scarcely speak French, or not at all, employed by the Military Commission to despatch the Vendéans picked up along the highways, and who are usually shot in groups of twenty five. "I came," says an eye-witness,[171] "to a sort of gorge where there was a semi-circular quarry; there, I noticed the corpses of seventy-five women . . . naked and lying on their backs." The victims of that day consisted of girls from sixteen to eighteen years of age. One of them says to her conductor, "I am sure you are taking us to die," and the German replies in his broken jargon, probably with a coarse laugh, "No, it is for a change of air." They are placed in a row in front of the bodies of the previous day and shot. Those who do not fall, see

---

condemned specially, "for having saved from national vengeance Madame de Martilly and her maid. . . . They shared the woman Martilly and the maid between them." In connection with the "dainty taste" of Jacobins for silk dresses M. Berryat Saint-Prix cites the following answer of a Jacobin of 1851 to the *judge d' instruction* of Rheims; on the objection being made to him that the Republic, as he understood it, could not last long, he replied: "Possibly, but say it lasts three months. That's long enough to fill one's pocket and belly and rumple silk dresses?" Another of the same species said in 1871: "We shall anyhow have a week's use of it." Observers of human nature will find analogous details in the history of the Sepoy rebellion in India against the English in 1803, also in the history of the Indians in the United States. The September massacres in Paris and the history of the combat of 1791 and 1792 have already provided us with the same characteristic documents.

171. Alfred Lallier, "Les Fusillades de Nantes," p. 23. (Depositions of Picard, commander of the National Guards of the escort.—Cf. the depositions of Jean Jounet, paver, and of Henri Ferdinand, joiner.)

the guns reloaded; these are again shot and the wounded despatched with the butt ends of the muskets. Some of the Germans then rifle the bodies, while others strip them and "place them on their backs." To find workmen for this task, it is necessary to descend, not only to the lowest wretches in France but, again, to the brutes of a foreign race and tongue, and yet lower still, to an inferior race degraded by slavery and perverted by license.

Such, from the top to the bottom of the ladder, at every stage of authority and obedience, is the ruling staff of the revolutionary government.[172] Through its recruits and its work, through its morals and modes of proceeding, it evokes the almost forgotten image of its predecessors, for there is an image of it in the period from the fourteenth to the seventeenth century. At that time also, society was frequently overcome and ravaged by barbarians; dangerous nomads, malevolent outcasts, bandits turned into soldiers suddenly pounced down on an industrious and peaceful population. Such was the case in France with the "Routiers" and the "Tard-venus," at Rome with the army of the Constable of Bourbon, in Flanders with the bands of the Duke of Alba and the Duke of Parma, in Westphalia and in Alsace, with Wallenstein's veterans, and those of Bernard of Saxe-Weimar. They lived upon a town or province for six months, fifteen months, two years, until the town or province was exhausted, alone

---

172. Sauzay, "Histoire de la Persécution Révolutionnaire dans le Département du Doubs," vii., 687. (Letter of Grégoire, December 24, 1796.) "An approximative calculation makes the number of the authors of so many crimes three hundred thousand, for in each commune there were about five or six of these ferocious brutes who, named Brutus, perfected the art of removing seals, drowning, and cutting throats. They consumed immense amounts in constructing 'Mountains,' in revellings, and in fêtes every three months which, after the first parade, became parodies, represented by three or four actors in them, and with no audience. These consisted, finally, of a drum-beater and the musical officer; and the latter, ashamed of himself, often concealed his scarf in his pocket, on his way to the Temple of Reason. . . . But these three hundred thousand brigands had two or three hundred directors, members of the National Convention, who cannot be called anything but scoundrels, since the language provides no other epithet so forcible."

armed, master of the inhabitant, using and abusing things and persons according to their caprices. But they were declared bandits, calling themselves scorchers (*ecorcheurs*), riders and adventurers, and not pretenders to being humanitarian philosophers. Moreover, beyond an immediate and personal enjoyment, they demanded nothing; they employed brutal force only to satiate their greed, their cruelty, their lust. The latter add to private appetites a far greater devastation, the systematic and gratuitous ravages enforced upon them by the superficial theory with which they are imbued.

BOOK VIII

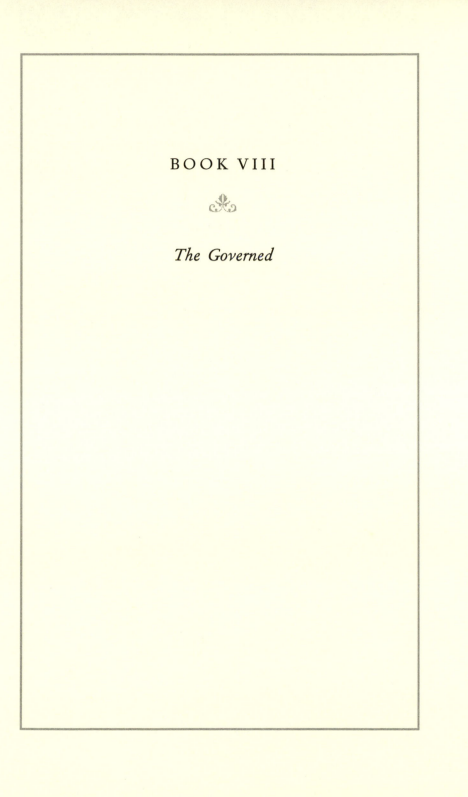

The Governed

CHAPTER I

The Oppressed— I. Magnitude of revolutionary destructiveness—The four ways of effecting it—Expulsion from the country through forced emigration and legal banishment—Number of those expelled—Privation of liberty—Different sorts of imprisonment—Number and situation of those imprisoned—Murders after being tried, or without trial—Number of those guillotined or shot after trial—Indication of the number of other lives destroyed—Necessity of and plan for wider destruction—Spoliation—Its extent—Squandering—Utter losses—Ruin of individuals and the State—The Notables the most oppressed— II. The value of Notables in society—Various kinds and degrees of Notables in 1789—The great social staff—Men of the world—Their breeding—Their intellectual culture—Their humanity and philanthropy—Their moral temper—Practical men—Where recruited—Their qualifications—Their active benevolence—Scarcity of them and their worth to a community— III. The three classes of Notables—The Nobility—Its physical and moral preparation through feats of arms—The military spirit—High character—Conduct of officers in 1789–1792—Service for which these nobles were adapted— IV. The Clergy—Where recruited—Professional inducements—Independence of ecclesiastics—Their substantial merits—Their theoretical and practical information—Their distribution over the territory—Utility of their office—Their conduct in 1790–1800—Their courage, their capacity for self-sacrifice— V. The Bourgeoisie—Where recruited—Difference between the functionary of the ancient régime and the modern functionary—Property in offices—Guilds—Independence and security of office-holders—Their limited ambition and contentedness—Fixed habits, seriousness and integrity—Ambition to secure esteem—Intellectual culture—Liberal ideas—Respectability and public zeal—Conduct of the bourgeoisie in 1789–1791— VI. The demi-notables—Where recruited—Village and trade syndics—Competency of their electors—Their interest in making good selections—Their capacity and integrity—The sorting

1181

of men under the ancient régime—Conditions of a family's maintenance and advancement—Hereditary and individual right of the Notable to his property and rank— VII. Principle of socialistic equality—All superiorities illegitimate—Bearing of this principle—Incivique benefits and enjoyments—How revolutionary laws reach the lower class—Whole populations affected in a mass—Proportion of the lowly in the proscription lists—How the revolutionary laws specially affect those who are prominent among the people— VIII. Their rigor increases according to the elevation of the class—The Notables properly so called attacked because of their being Notables—Orders of Taillefer, Milhaud, and Lefiot—The public atonement of Montargis— IX. Two characteristics of the upper class, wealth and education—Each of these is criminal—Measures against rich and well-to-do people—Affected in a mass and by categories—Measures against cultivated and polite people—Danger of culture and distinction—Proscription of "honest folks"— X. The Governors and the Governed—Prisoners in the rue de Sèvres and the "Croix-Rouge" revolutionary committee—The young Dauphin and Simon his preceptor—Judges, and those under their jurisdiction—Trenchard and Coffinhal, Lavoisier and André Chénier.

I

THE OBJECT of the Jacobin, first of all, is the destruction of his adversaries, avowed or presumed, probable or possible. Four violent measures concur, together or in turn, to bring about the physical or social extermination of all Frenchmen who no longer belong to the sect or the party.

The first operation consists in expelling them from the territory. Since 1789, they have been chased off through a forced emigration; handed over to jacqueries in the country, and to insurrections in the cities,[1] defenceless and not allowed to defend themselves, three-fourths of them have left France, simply to escape popular brutalities against which neither the law nor the government afforded them any protection. According as the law and the administration, in becoming more Jacobin, became more hostile to them, so did they leave in greater crowds. After the 10th of August and 2d of Septem-

---

1. Cf. "The Revolution," book i., ch. 3, and book iii., chs. 9 and 10.

ber, the flight necessarily was more general; for, henceforth, if any one persisted in remaining after that date it was with the almost positive certainty that he would be consigned to a prison, to await a massacre or the guillotine. About the same time, the law added to the fugitive the banished, all unsworn priests, almost an entire class consisting of nearly forty thousand persons.[2] It is calculated that, on issuing from the Reign of Terror, the total number of fugitives and banished amounted to one hundred and fifty thousand;[3] the list would have been still larger, had not the frontier been guarded by patrols and one had to cross it at the risk of one's life; and yet, many do risk their lives in attempting to cross it, in disguise, wandering about at night, in mid-winter, exposed to gunshots, determined to escape cost what it will, into Switzerland, Italy, or Germany, and even into Hungary, in quest of security and the right of praying to God as one pleases.[4] If any exiled or transported person ventures to

2. Grégoire, "Mémoires," ii., 172. "About eighteen thousand ecclesiastics are enumerated among the *emigrés* of the first epoch. About eighteen thousand more took themselves off, or were sent off, after the 2d of September."

3. *Ibid.*, 26. "The chief of the *emigré* bureau in the police department (May 9, 1805) enumerates about two hundred thousand persons reached, or affected, by the laws concerning emigration."—Lally-Tolendal, "Défense des Emigrés," (2d part, p. 62 and *passim*). Several thousand persons inscribed as *emigrés* did not leave France. The local administration recorded them on its lists either because they lived in another department, and could not obtain the numerous certificates exacted by the law in proof of residence, or because those who made up the lists treated these certificates with contempt. It was found convenient to manufacture an *emigré* in order to confiscate his possessions legally, and even to guillotine him, not less legally, as a returned *emigré*.—Message of the Directory to the "Five Hundred," Ventose 3, year V.: "According to a rough estimate, obtained at the Ministry of Finances, the number enrolled on the general list of emigrés amounts to over one hundred and twenty thousand; and, again, the lists from some of the departments have not come in."—Lafayette, "Mémoires," vol. ii., 181. (Letters to M. de Maubourg, Oct. 17, 1799 (*noté*) Oct. 19, 1800.) According to the report of the Minister of Police, the list of *emigrés*, in nine vols., still embraced one hundred and forty-five thousand persons, notwithstanding that thirteen thousand were struck off by the Directory, and twelve hundred by the consular government.

4. Cf. Mémoires of Louvet, Dulaure, and Vaublanc.—Mallet-Dupan, "Mé-

return, he is tracked like a wild beast, and, as soon as taken, he is guillotined.[5] For example, M. de Choiseul, and other unfortunates, wrecked and cast ashore on the coast of Normandy, are not sufficiently protected by the law of nations. They are brought before a military commission; saved temporarily through public commiseration, they remain in prison until the First Consul intervenes between them and the homicidal law and consents, through favor, to transport them to the Dutch frontier. If they have taken up arms against the Republic they are cut off from humanity; a Pandour prisoner is treated as a man; an *emigré* made prisoner is treated like a wolf—they shoot him on the spot. In some cases, even the pettiest legal formalities are dispensed with. "When I am lucky enough to catch 'em," writes Gen. Vandamme, "I do not trouble the military commission to try them. They are already tried—my sabre and pistols do their business."[6]

The second operation consists in depriving "suspects" of their liberty, of which deprivation there are several degrees; there are various ways of getting hold of people. Sometimes, the "suspect" is "adjourned," that is to say, the order of arrest is simply suspended; he lives under a perpetual menace that is generally fulfilled; he never knows in the morning that he will not sleep in a prison that night.

moires," ii., 7. "Several, to whom I have spoken, literally made the tour of France in various disguises, without having been able to find an outlet; it was only after a series of romantic adventures that they finally succeeded in gaining the Swiss frontier, the only one at all accessible."—Sauzay, v., 210, 220, 226, 276. (Emigration of fifty-four inhabitants of Charquemont, setting out for Hungary.)

5. *Ibid.*, vols. iv., v., vi., vii. (On the banished priests remaining and still continuing their ministrations, and on those who returned to resume them.)—To obtain an idea of the situation of the *emigrés* and their relations and friends, it is necessary to read the law of Sep. 15, 1794 (Brumaire 25, year III.), which renews and generalises previous laws; children of fourteen years and ten years are affected by it. It was with the greatest difficulty, even if one did not leave France, that a person could prove that he had not emigrated.

6. *Moniteur*, xviii., 215. (Letter of Brigadier-general Vandamme to the Convention, Ferney, Brumaire 1, year II.) The reading of this letter calls forth "reiterated applause."

Sometimes, he is put on the limits of his commune. Sometimes, he is confined to his house with or without guards, and, in the former case, he is obliged to pay them. Again, finally, and which occurs most frequently, he is shut up in this or that common jail. In the single department of Doubs, twelve hundred men and women are "adjourned," three hundred put on the limits of the commune, fifteen hundred confined to their houses, and twenty-two hundred imprisoned.[7] In Paris, thirty-six such prisons and more than ninety-six lock-ups, or temporary jails, constantly filled by the revolutionary committees, do not suffice for the service,[8] while it is estimated that, in France, not counting more than forty thousand provisional jails, twelve hundred prisons, full and running over, contain each more than two hundred inmates.[9] At Paris, notwithstanding the daily void created by the guillotine, the number of the imprisoned on Floréal 9, year II., amounts to seven thousand eight hundred and forty; and, on Messidor 25 following, notwithstanding the large batches of fifty and sixty persons led in one day, and every day, to the scaffold, the number is still seven thousand five hundred and two.[10] There are more than one thousand persons in the prisons of Arras, more than one thousand five hundred in those of Toulouse, more than three thousand in those of Strasbourg, and more than thirteen thousand in those of Nantes. In the two departments alone of Bouches-du-Rhone and Vaucluse, Representative Maignet, who is on the spot, reports from twelve thousand to fifteen thousand arrests.[11] "A little

7. Sauzay, v., 196. (The total is five thousand two hundred. Some hundreds of names might be added, inasmuch as many of the village lists are wanting.)

8. Buchez et Roux, xxxiv., 434. (Trial of Fouquier-Tinville, deposition of Therriet-Grandpré, one of the heads of the Commission on Civil Police and Judicial Administration, 51st witness.)

9. Report by Saladin, March 4, 1795.

10. Wallon, "La Terreur," ii., 202.

11. Duchatelier, "Brest Pendant la Terreur," p. 105.—Paris, "Histoire de Joseph Lebon," ii., 370.—"Tableau des Prisons de Toulouse," by Pescayre, p. 409.—"Recueil de Pièces Authentiques sur la Révolution à Strasbourg," i., 65. (List of arrests after Prairial 7, year II.) "When the following arrests were made there were already over three thousand persons confined in Strasbourg."—

before Thermidor," says Representative Beaulieu, "the number of incarcerated arose to nearly four hundred thousand, as is apparent on the lists and registers then before the Committee of General Security."[12] Among these poor creatures, there are children, and not alone in the prisons of Nantes where the revolutionary battures have collected the whole of the rural population; in the prisons of Arras, among twenty similar cases, I find a coal-dealer and his wife with their seven sons and daughters, from seventeen down to six years of age; a widow with her four children from nineteen down to twelve years of age; another noble widow with her nine children, from seventeen down to three years of age, and six children, without father or mother, from twenty-three down to nine years of age.[13]

Alfred Lallier, "Les Noyades de Nantes," p. 90.—Berryat Saint-Prix, p. 436. (Letter of Maignet to Couthon, Avignon, Floréal 4, year II.)

12. Beaulieu, "Essais," v., 283. At the end of December, 1793, Camille Desmoulins wrote: "Open the prison doors to those two hundred thousand citizens whom you call 'suspects'!"—The number of prisoners largely increased during the seven following months. ("Le Vieux Cordelier," No. iv., Frimaire 30, year II.)—Beaulieu does not state precisely what the Committee of General Security meant by the word *détenu*. Does it merely relate to those incarcerated? Or must all who were confined at their own houses be included?—We are able to verify his statement and determine the number, at least approximatively, by taking one department in which the rigor of the revolutionary system was average and where the lists handed in were complete. According to the census of 1791, Doubs contained two hundred and twenty-one thousand inhabitants; France had a population of twenty-six millions; and we have just seen the number of each category that were under confinement; the proportion for France gives two hundred and fifty-eight thousand persons incarcerated, and one hundred and seventy-five thousand confined to their houses, and one hundred and seventy-five thousand persons besides these on the limits in their communes, or *ajournées*, that is to say, six hundred and eight thousand persons deprived of their liberty. The first two categories from a total of four hundred and thirty-three thousand persons, sufficiently near Beaulieu's figures.

13. Paris, "Histoire de Joseph Lebon, ii., 371, 372, 375, 377, 379, 380.—"Les Angoisses de la Mort," by Poirier and Monjay of Dunkirk (second edition, year III.). "Their children and trusty agents still remained in prison; they were treated no better than ourselves. . . . We saw children coming in from all quarters, infants of five years, and, to withdraw them from paternal authority, they

These prisoners of State were treated, almost everywhere, worse than robbers and assassins under the ancient régime. They began by subjecting them to *rapiotage,* that is to say, stripping them naked or, at best, feeling their bodies under their shirts; women and young girls fainted away under this examination, formerly confined to convicts on entering the bagnio.[14] Frequently, before consigning them to their dungeons or shutting them up in their cells, they would be left two or three nights pell-mell in a lower hall on benches, or in the court on the pavement, "without beds or straw." "The feelings are wounded in all directions, every point of sensibility, so to say, being played upon. They are deprived one after the other of their property, assignats, furniture, and food, of daylight and lamp-light, of the assistance which their wants and infirmities demand, of a knowledge of public events, of all communication, either immediate or written, with fathers, sons, and husbands."[15] They are obliged to pay for their lodgings, their keepers, and for what they eat; they are robbed at their very doors of the supplies they send for outside; they are compelled to eat at a mess-table; they are furnished with scant and nauseous food, "spoilt codfish, putrid herrings, and meat, rotten vegetables, all this accompanied with a mug of Seine water colored red with some drug or other."[16] They starve them, bully

---

had sent to them from time to time, commissioners who used immoral language with them."

14. "Mémoires sur les Prisons," (Barrière et Berville collection), ii., 354, and appendix F. *Ibid.,* ii., 2,262. "The women were the first to pass under *rapiotage.*" (Prisons of Arras and that of Plessis, at Paris.)

15. "Documents on Daunou," by Taillandier. (Narrative by Daunou, who was imprisoned in turn in La Force, in the Madelonettes, in the English Benedictine establishment, in the Hotel des Fermes, and in Port-Libre.)—On prison management cf., for the provinces, "Tableaux des Prisons de Toulouse," by Pescayré; "Un Séjour en France," and "Les Horreurs des Prisons d' Arras," for Arras and Amiens; Alexandrines des Echerolles, "Une Famille noble sous la Terreur," for Lyons; the trial of Carrier for Nantes; for Paris, "Histoire des Prisons" by Nougaret, 4 vols., and the "Mémoires sur les Prisons," 2 vols.

16. Testimony of Representative Blanqui, imprisoned at La Force, and of Representative Beaulieu, imprisoned in the Luxembourg and at the Madelonettes.—Beaulieu, "Essais," v., 290: "The Conciergerie was still full of wretches

them, and vex them purposely as if they meant to exhaust their patience and drive them into a revolt, so as to get rid of them in a mass, or, at least, to justify the increasing rapid strokes of the guillotine. They are huddled together in tens, twenties, and thirties, in one room at La Force, "eight in a chamber, fourteen feet square," where all the beds touch, and many overlap each other, where two out of the eight inmates are obliged to sleep on the floor, where vermin swarm, where the closed sky-lights, the standing tub, and the crowding together of bodies poisons the atmosphere. In many places, the proportion of the sick and dying is greater than in the hold of a slave-ship. "Of ninety individuals with whom I was shut up two months ago," writes a prisoner at Strasbourg, "sixty-six were taken to the hospital in the space of eight days."[17] In the prisons of Nantes, three thousand out of thirteen thousand prisoners die of typhoid fever and of the rot in two months.[18] Four hundred

---

held for robbery and assassination, poverty-stricken and repulsive.—It was with these that counts, marquises, voluptuous financiers, elegant dandies, and more than one wretched philosopher, were shut up, pell-mell, in the foulest cells, waiting until the guillotine could make room in the chambers filled with camp-bedsteads. They were generally put with those on the straw, on entering, where they sometimes remained a fortnight. . . . It was necessary to drink brandy with these persons; in the evening, after having dropped their excrement near their straw, they went to sleep in their filth. . . . I passed those three nights half-sitting, half-stretched out on a bench, one leg on the ground and leaning against the wall."—Wallon, "La Terreur," ii., 87. (Report of Grandpré on the Conciergerie, March 17, 1793. "Twenty-six men collected into one room, sleeping on twenty-one mattresses, breathing the foulest air and covered with half-rotten rags." In another room forty-five men and ten straw-beds; in a third, thirty-nine poor creatures dying in nine bunks; in three other rooms, eighty miserable creatures on sixteen mattresses filled with vermin, and, as to the women, fifty-four having nine mattresses and standing up alternately.—The worst prisons in Paris were the Conciergerie, La Force, Le Plessis, and Bicêtre.—"Tableau des Prisons de Toulouse," p. 316. "Dying with hunger, we contended with the dogs for the bones intended for them, and we pounded them up to make soup with."

17. "Recueil de Pièces, etc.," i., p. 3. (Letter of Frederic Burger, Prairial 2, year II.)

18. Alfred Lallier, "Les Noyades de Nantes," p. 90.—Campardon, "Histoire de Tribunal Révolutionnaire de Paris" (trial of Carrier), ii., 55. (Deposition of

priests[19] confined on a vessel between decks, in the roadstead of Aix, stowed on top of each other, wasted with hunger, eaten up by vermin, suffocated for lack of air, half-frozen, beaten, mocked at, and constantly threatened with death, suffer still more than negroes in a slavehold; for, through interest in his freight, the captain of the slaver tries to keep his human consignment in good health, whilst, through revolutionary fanaticism, the crew of the Aix vessel detests its cargo of "black-frocks" and would gladly send them to the bottom. According to this system, which, up to Thermidor 9, grows worse and worse, imprisonment becomes a torture, oftentimes mortal, slower and more painful than the guillotine, and to such an extent that, to escape it, Champfort opens his veins and Condorcet swallows poison.[20]

The third expedient consists of murder, with or without trial. One hundred and seventy-eight tribunals, of which forty are ambulatory, pronounce in every part of the territory sentences of death which are immediately executed on the spot.[21] Between April 6, 1793, and Thermidor 9, year II., that of Paris has two thousand six hundred and twenty-five persons guillotined,[22] while the provincial judges do as much work as the Paris judges. In the small town of

---

the health-officer, Thomas.) "I saw perish in the revolutionary hospital (at Nantes) seventy-five prisoners in two days. None but rotten mattresses were found there, on each of which the epidemic had consumed more than fifty persons. At the Entrepot, I found a number of corpses scattered about here and there. I saw children, still breathing, drowned in tubs full of human excrement."

19. Narrative of the sufferings of unsworn priests, transported in 1794, in the roadstead of Aix, *passim*.

20. "Histoire des Prisons," i., 10. "Go and visit," says a contemporary (at the Conciergerie), the dungeons called 'the great Caesar,' 'Bombié,' 'St. Vincent,' 'Bel Air,' etc., and say whether death is not preferable to such an abode." Some persons, indeed, the sooner to end the matter, wrote to the public prosecutor, accusing themselves, demanding a king and priests, and are at once guillotined, as they hoped to be.—Cf. the narrative of "La Translation des 132 à Nantois Paris," and Riouffe, "Mémoires," on the sufferings of prisoners on their way to their last prison.

21. Berryat Saint-Prix, p. ix., *passim*.

22. Campardon, ii., 224.

Orange alone, they guillotine three hundred and thirty-one persons. In the single town of Arras they have two hundred and ninety-nine men and ninety-three women guillotined. At Nantes, the revolutionary tribunals and military committees have, on the average, one hundred persons a day guillotined, or shot, in all one thousand nine hundred and seventy-one. In the city of Lyons, the revolutionary committee admit one thousand six hundred and eighty-four executions, while Cadillot, one of Robespierre's correspondents, advises him of six thousand.[23] The statement of these murders is not complete, but seventeen thousand have been enumerated,[24] "most of them effected without any formality, evidence or direct charge," among others the murder of "more than one thousand two hundred women, several of whom were octogenarians and infirm";[25] particularly the murder of sixty women or young girls, condemned to death, say the warrants, for having attended the services of unsworn priests, or for having neglected the services of a sworn priest. "The accused, ranged in order, were condemned at sight. Hundreds of death-sentences took about a minute per head. Children of seven, five, and four years of age, were tried. A father was condemned for the son, and the son for the father. A dog was sentenced to death. A parrot was brought forward as a witness. Numbers of accused persons whose sentences could not be written out were executed." At Angers, the sentences of over four hundred men and three hundred and sixty women, executed for the purpose of relieving the prisons, were mentioned on the registers simply by the letters S or G (shot or

23. Berryat Saint-Prix, 445.—Paris, "Histoire de Joseph Lebon," ii., 352.—Alfred Lallier, p. 90.—Buchez et Roux, xxxii., 394.

24. Berryat Saint-Prix, pp. 23, 24.

25. Berryat Saint-Prix, p. 458. "At Orange, Madame de Latour-Vidan, aged eighty and idiotic for many years, was executed with her son. It is stated that, on being led to the scaffold, she thought she was entering a carriage to pay visits and so told her son."—*Ibid.*, 471. After Thermidor, the judges of the Orange commission having been put on trial, the jury declared that "they refused to hear testimony for the defence and to allow the accused lawyers to defend them."

guillotined).[26] At Paris, as in the provinces, the slightest pretext[27] served to constitute a crime. The daughter of the celebrated painter, Joseph Vernet,[28] was guillotined for being a "receiver," for having kept fifty pounds of candles in her house, distributed among the employees of La Muette by the liquidators of the civil list. Young de Maillé,[29] aged sixteen years, was guillotined as a conspirator, "for having thrown a rotten herring in the face of his jailor, who had served it to him to eat." Madame de Puy-Verin was guillotined as "guilty" because she had not taken away from her deaf, blind, and senile husband a bag of card-counters, marked with the royal effigy. In default of any pretext,[30] there was the supposition of a conspiracy; blank lists were given to paid emissaries, who undertook to search the various prisons and select the requisite number of heads; they wrote names down on them according to their fancy, and these provided the batches for the guillotine. "As for myself," said the juryman Vilate, "I am never embarrassed. I am always convinced. In a revolution, all who appear before this tribunal ought to be condemned." At Marseilles, the Brutus Commission,[31] "sentencing

26. Camille Boursier, "La Terreur en Anjou," p. 228. (Deposition of Widow Edin.) "La Persac, a nun ill and infirm, was ready to take the oath. Nicolas, Vacheron's agent, assisted by several other persons, dragged her out of bed and put her on a cart; from ninety to ninety-four others were shot along with her."

27. Berryat Saint-Prix, p. 161. The following are samples of these warrants: "S. (shot), Germinal 13, Widow Menard, seventy-two years old, an old aristocrat, liking nobody, habitually living by herself."—Warrant of the Marseilles committee, Germinal 28, year II., condemning one Cousinéri "for having continually strayed off as if to escape popular vengeance, to which he was liable on account of his conduct and for having detested the Revolution."—Camille Boursier, p. 72, Floréal 15, year II., execution of "Gérard, guilty of having scorned to assist at the planting of a Liberty-pole, in the commune of Vouille, Sep., 1792, and inducing several municipal officers to join him in his insolent and *liberticide* contempt."

28. Wallon, "Histoire du Tribunal Révolutionnaire de Paris," v., 145.

29. *Ibid.*, v., 109. (Deposition of Madame de Maillé.)—V., 189. (Deposition of Lhullier.)—Cf. Campardon, in the same affairs.

30. Campardon, ii., 189, 189, 193, 197. (Depositions of Beaulieu, Duclos, Tirard, Ducray, etc.)

31. Berryat Saint-Prix, 395. (Letter of Representative Moyse Bayle.)—*Ibid.*,

without public prosecutor or jurymen, sent to the prisons for those it wished to put to death. After having demanded their names, professions, and wealth they were sent down to a cart standing at the door of the Palais de Justice; the judges then stepped out on the balcony and pronounced the death-sentence." The same proceedings took place at Cambrai, Arras, Nantes, Le Mans, Bordeaux, Nismes, Lyons, Strasbourg, and elsewhere. Evidently, the judicial comedy is simply a parade; they make use of it as one of the respectable means, among others less respectable, to exterminate people whose opinions are not what they should be, or who belong to the proscribed classes;[32] Samson, at Paris, and his colleagues in the provinces, the execution-platoons of Lyons and Nantes, are simply the collaborators of murderers properly so called, while legal massacres complete other massacres pure and simple.

Of this latter description, the *fusillades* of Toulon come first, where the number of those who are shot largely surpasses one thousand;[33] next the great drownings of Nantes, in which four thousand eight hundred men, women, and children perished,[34] and other

---

216. (Words of Representative Lecarpentier at Saint-Malo.) "Why such delays? Of what use are these eternal examinations? What need is there of going so deep into this matter? The name, profession, and the upshot, and the trial is over."—He publicly stated to the informers: "You don't know what facts you require to denounce the Moderates? Well, a gesture, one single gesture, suffices."

32. Letter of Payan to Roman Formosa, judge at Orange: "In the commissions charged with punishing the conspirators, no formalities should exist; the conscience of the judge is there as a substitute for these. . . . The commissions must serve as political courts; they must remember that all the men who have not been on the side of the Revolution are against it, since they have done nothing for the country. . . . I say to all judges, in the name of the country, do not risk saving a guilty man."—Robespierre made the same declaration in the Jacobin Club. Frimaire 19, year II.: "We judge, in politics, with the suspicions of an enlightened patriotism."

33. "Mémoires de Fréron" and on Fréron (collection Barrière et Berville), p. 364. Letter of Fréron, Toulon, Nivose 16. "More than eight hundred Toulonese have already been shot."

34. Lallier, p. 90. (The eleven distinct drownings ascertained by M. Lallier extend up to Pluviose 12, year II.)

drownings, in which the number of dead is not fixed;[35] next, the innumerable slaughterings committed by the people between July 14, 1789, and August 10, 1792; the massacre of one thousand three hundred prisoners in Paris, in September, 1792; the long train of assassinations which, in July, August, and September, 1789, extends over the entire territory; finally, the despatch of the prisoners, either shot or sabred, without trial at Lyons and in the West. Even excepting those who had died fighting or who, taken with arms in their hands, were shot down or sabred on the spot, there were ten thousand persons slaughtered without trial in the province of Anjou alone:[36] accordingly, the instructions of the Committee of Public Safety, also the written orders of Carrier and Francastel, direct generals to "bleed freely" the insurgent districts,[37] and spare not a life: it is estimated that, in the eleven western departments, the dead of both sexes and of all ages exceeded four hundred thousand.[38] Considering the programme and principles of the Jacobin sect this is no great number; they might have killed a good many more. But time was wanting; during their short reign they did what they could with the instrument in their hands. Look at their machine, the gradual

35. *Monitenur*, xxii., 227. (Official documents read in the Convention, Ventose 21, year III.) These documents authenticate an ulterior drowning. Ventose 9, year II., by order of Lefévre, adjutant general, forty-one persons were drowned, among whom were two men seventy-eight years of age and blind, twelve women, twelve young girls, fifteen children, of which ten were between six and ten years old, and five at the breast. The drowning took place in the Bourgneuf bay.—Carrier says in the Convention (*Moniteur*, xxii., p. 578), in relation to the drowning of pregnant women: "At Laval, Angers, Saumur, Chaban-Gontier, everywhere the same things took place as at Nantes."

36. Camille Boursier, p. 159.

37. *Ibid.*, 203. Representative Francastel announces "the firm determination to purge, to bleed freely this Vendean question." This same Francastel wrote to General Grignon: "Make those brigands tremble! Give them no quarter! The prisons in Vendée are overflowing with prisoners! . . . The conversion of this country into a desert must be completed. Show no weakness and no mercy. . . . These are the views of the Convention. . . . I swear that Vendée shall be depopulated."

38. Granier de Cassagnac, "His. du Directoire," ii., 241.—(Letter of General Hoche to the Minister of the Interior, Feb. 2, 1796.) "Only one out of five remains of the population of one thousand seven hundred and eighty-nine."

construction of its parts, the successive stages of its operation from its starting up to Thermidor 9, and see how limited the period of its operation was. Organised March 30 and April 6, 1793, the revolutionary committees and the revolutionary Tribunal had but seventeen months in which to do their work. They did not drive ahead with all their might until after the fall of the Girondists, and especially after September, 1763, that is to say for a period of eleven months. Its loose wheels were not screwed up and the whole was not in running order under the impulse of the central motor until after December, 1793, that is to say during eight months. Perfected by the law of Prairial 22, it works for the past two months, faster and better than before, with an energy and rapidity that increase from week to week. At that date, and even before it, the theorists have taken the bearings of their destinies and accepted the conditions of their undertaking. Being sectarians, they have a faith, and as orthodoxy tolerates no heresy, and as the conversion of heretics is never sincere or durable, heresy can be suppressed only by suppressing heretics. "It is only the dead," said Barère, Messidor 16, "who never return." On the 2d and 3d of Thermidor,[39] the Committee of Public Safety sends to Fouquier-Tinville a list of four hundred and seventy-eight accused persons with orders "to bring the parties named to trial at once." Baudot and Jean Bon St. André, Carrier, Antonelle and Guffroy, had already estimated the lives to be taken at several millions and, according to Collot d' Herbois, who had a lively imagination, "the political perspiration should go on freely, and not stop until from twelve to fifteen million Frenchmen had been destroyed."[40]

39. Campardon ii., 247, 249, 251, 261, 321. (Examination of Fouquier-Tinville, Cambon's words.)

40. Article by Guffroy, in his journal *Le Rougiff:* "Down with the nobles, and so much the worse for the good ones, if there are any! Let the guillotine stand permanently throughout the Republic. Five millions of inhabitants are enough for France!"—Berryat Saint-Prix, 445. (Letter of Fauvety, Orange, Prairial 14, year II.) "We have but two confined in our arrondissement. What a trifle!"—*Ibid.,* 447. (Letter of the Orange Committee to the Committee of

To make amends, in the fourth and last division of their work, that is to say, in spoliation, they went to the last extreme: they did all that could be done to ruin individuals, families, and the State; whatever could be taken, they took. The Constituent and Legislative Assemblies had, on their side, begun the business by abolishing tithes and all feudal rights without indemnity, and by confiscating all ecclesiastical property; the Jacobin operators continue and complete the job; we have seen by what decrees and with what hostility against collective and individual property, whether they attribute to the State the possession of all corporations whatever, even laic, such as colleges, schools, and scientific or literary societies, hospitals and communes, or whether they despoil individuals, indirectly through assignats and the *maximum,* or directly through the forced loan, revolutionary taxes,[41] seizures of gold and silver coin, requisitions

---

Public Safety, Messidor 3.) As soon as the Committee gets fully agoing it is to try all the priests, rich merchants, and ex-nobles."—(Letter of Juge, Messidor 2.) "Judging by appearances more than three thousand heads will fall in the department."—*Ibid.,* 311. At Bordeaux, a huge scaffold is put up, authorised by the Military Committee, with seven doors, two of which are large and like barn-doors, called a four-bladed guillotine, so as to work faster and do more. The warrant and orders for its construction bear date Thermidor 3 and 8, year II.—Berryat Saint-Prix, 285. Letter of Representative Blutel, on mission at Rochefort, after Thermidor: "A few men, sunk in debauchery and crime, dared proscribe (here) virtues, patriotism, because it was not associated with their sanguinary excitement; the tree of Liberty, they said, required for its roots ten feet of human gore."

41. "Recueil de Pièces Authentiques, Concernant le Revolution à Strasbourg," i., 174, 178. Examples of revolutionary taxes.—Orders of Representatives Milhaud, Ruamps, Guyadin, approving of the following contributions, Brumaire 20, year II.

On	3	individuals of	Stutzheim	150,000	livres.
"	3	"	Offenheim	30,000	"
"	21	"	Molsheim	367,000	"
"	17	"	Oberenheim	402,000	"
"	84	"	Rosheim	503,000	"
"	10	"	Mutzig	114,000	"

Another order by Daum and Tisseraud, members of the Committee who

of common useful utensils,[42] sequestrations of prisoners' property, confiscations of the possessions of emigrants and exiles and of those transported or condemned to death. No capital invested in real or personal property, no income in money or produce, whatever its source, whether leases, mortgages, private credits, pensions, agricultural, industrial, or commercial gains, the fruits of economy or labor, from the farmers', the manufacturers', and the merchant's stores to the robes, coats, shirts and shoes, even to the beds and bed-rooms of private individuals—nothing escapes their rapacious grasp: in the country, they carry off even seed reserved for planting; at Strasbourg and in the Upper Rhine, all kitchen utensils; in Auvergne and elsewhere, even the pots used by the cattle-tenders. Every object of value, even those not in public use, comes under

---

temporarily replace the district administrators: "Whereas, it is owing to the county aristocrats that the Republic supports the war," they approve of the following taxes:

On the aristocrats of	Geispolzheim	400,000 livres.
"	"	Oberschoeffolsheim	200,000 "
"	"	Düttlenheim	150,000 "
"	"	Duppigheim	100,000 "
"	"	Achenheim	100,000 "

List of contributions raised in the rural communes of the district of Strasbourg, according to an assessment made by Stamm, *procureur* pro tem. of the district, amounting to three millions one hundred and ninety-six thousand one hundred livres.

42. "Recueil des Pièces Authentiques, etc., i., 23. By order of the representatives under date of Brumaire 25, year II. "The municipality of Strasbourg stripped the whole commune of shoes in twenty-four hours, sending for them from house to house."—*Ibid.*, p. 32. Orders of Representatives Lemaire and Baudot, Frimaire 1, year II., declaring that kitchen-utensils, boilers, sauce-pans, stew-pans, kettles, and other copper and lead vessels, as well as copper and lead not worked-up, found at Strasbourg and in the departments, be levied on."— Archives Nationales, AF., I., 92. (Orders of Taillefer, Brumaire 3, year II., Villefranche l' Avergnon.) Formation of a committee of ten persons directed to make domiciliary visits, and authorised to take possession of all the iron, lead, steel, and copper found in the houses of "suspects," all of which kitchen utensils, are to be turned into cannon.—Mallet-Dupan, "Mémoires," i., 15.

requisition: for instance,[43] the Revolutionary Committee of Bayonne seizes a lot of "dimities and muslins," under the pretext of making "breeches for the country's defenders." On useful objects being taken it is not always certain that they will be utilised; between their seizure and putting them to service, robbery and waste intervene; at Strasbourg,[44] on a requisition being threatened by the representatives, the inhabitants strip themselves and, in a few days, bring to the municipality "six thousand eight hundred and seventy-nine coats, breeches and vests, four thousand seven hundred sixty-seven pairs of stockings, sixteen thousand nine hundred and twenty-one pairs of shoes, eight hundred and sixty-three pairs of boots, one thousand three hundred and fifty-one cloaks, twenty thousand five hundred and eighteen shirts, four thousand five hundred and twenty-four hats, five hundred and twenty-three pairs of gaiters, one hundred and forty-three skin vests, two thousand six hundred and seventy-three sheets, nine hundred blankets, besides twenty-nine quintals of lint, twenty-one quintals of old linen, and a large number of other articles."

But "most of these articles remain piled up in the storehouses, part of them rotten, or eaten by rats, the rest being abandoned to the first-comer. . . . *The end of spoliation was attained.*" Utter loss to individuals and no gain, or the minimum of a gain, to the State.

---

43. *Moniteur,* xxv., 188. (Speech by Blutels, July 9, 1795.)

44. "Recueil du Pièces Authentiques," etc., i., 24.—Grégoire, reports on Vandalism, Fructidor 14, year II., and Brumaire 14, year III. (*Moniteur,* xxii., 86 and 751.)—*Ibid.,* Letter of December 24, 1796: "Not millions, but billions have been destroyed."—*Ibid.,* "Mémoires," i., 334: "It is incalculable, the loss of religious, scientific and literary objects. The district administrations of Blanc (Indre) notified me that to ensure the preservation of a library, they had the books put in casks."—Four hundred thousand francs were expended in smashing statues of the Fathers of the Church, forming a circle around the dome of the Invalides.—A great many objects became worthless through a cessation of their use: for example, the cathedral of Meaux was put up at auction and found no purchaser at six hundred francs. The materials were valued at forty-five thousand francs, but labor (for taking it down) was too high. (Narrative by an inhabitant of Meaux.)

Such is the net result of the revolutionary government. After having laid its hand on three-fifths of the landed property of France; after having wrested from communities and individuals from ten to twelve billions of real and personal estate; after having increased, through assignats and territorial warrants, the public debt, which was not five billions in 1789, to more than fifty billions;[45] no longer able to pay its employees; reduced to supporting its armies as well as itself by forced contributions on conquered territories, it ends in bankruptcy; it repudiates two-thirds of its debt, and its credit is so low that the remaining third which it has consolidated and guaranteed afresh, loses eighty-three per cent. the very next day. In its hands, the State has itself suffered as much as individuals. Of the latter, more than twelve hundred thousand have suffered in their persons: several millions, all who possessed anything, great or small, have suffered through their property.[46] But, in this multitude of the oppressed, it is the notables who are chiefly aimed at and who, in their possessions as well as in their persons, have suffered the most.

II

On estimating the value of a forest you begin by dividing its vegetation into two classes; on the one hand the full-grown trees, the large or medium-sized oaks, beeches and aspens, and, on the other, the saplings and the undergrowth. In like manner, in estimating society, you divide the individuals composing it into two groups, one consisting of its notables of every kind and degree, and the

---

45 "Les Origines du Système Financier Actuel," by Eugene Sturm, p. 53, 79.

46. Meissner, "Voyage à Paris," (end of 1795), p. 65. "The class of those who may have really gained by the Revolution ... is composed of brokers, army contractors, and their subordinates, a few government agents and *fermiers*, enriching themselves by their new acquisitions, and who are cool and shrewd enough to hide their grain, bury their gold and steadily refuse assignats."—*Ibid.*, 68, 70. "On the road, he asks to whom a fine chateau belongs, and they tell him with a significant look, 'to a former low fellow.'—'Oh, monsieur,' said the landlady at Vesoul, 'for one that the Revolution has made rich, you may be sure that it has made a thousand poor.'"

other, of the common run of men. If the forest is an old one and has not been too badly managed, nearly the whole of its secular growth is found in its clusters of full-grown trees; a few thousands of large trunks, with three or four hundred old or new staddles belonging to the reserve, contain more useful or precious timber than all the twenty or thirty millions of shrubs, bushes, and brambles put together. It is the same in a community which has existed for a long time under a tolerably strict system of justice and police; almost the entire gain of a secular civilisation is found concentrated in its notables, which, taking it all in all, was the state of French society in 1789.[47]

Let us first consider the most prominent personages. It is certain, that, among the aristocracy, the wealthiest and most conspicuous families had ceased to render services proportionate to the cost of their maintenance. Most of the seigniors and ladies of the Court, the worldly bishops, abbés, and parliamentarians of the drawing-room, knew but little more than how to solicit with address, make a graceful parade of themselves and spend lavishly. An ill-understood system of culture had diverted them from their natural avocations, and converted them into showy and agreeable specimens of vegetation, often hollow, blighted, sapless and overpruned, besides being very costly, overmanured and too freely watered; and the skilful gardening which shaped, grouped, and arranged them in artificial forms and bouquets, rendered their fruit abortive that flowers might be multiplied. But the flowers were exquisite, and even in a moralist's eyes, such an efflorescence is of some account. On the side of civility, good-breeding and deportment, the manners and customs of high life had reached a degree of perfection, which never, in France or elsewhere, had been attained before, and which has never since been

---

47. The following descriptions and appreciations are the fruit of extensive investigation, scarcely one tenth of the facts and texts that have been of service being cited. I must refer the reader, accordingly, to the series of printed and written documents of which I have made mention in this and the three preceding volumes.

revived;[48] and of all the arts through which men have emancipated themselves from primitive coarseness, that which teaches them mutual consideration is, perhaps, the most precious. The observance of this, not alone in the drawing-room, but in the family, in business, in the street, with regard to relatives, inferiors, servants, and strangers, gives dignity, as well as a charm, to human intercourse. Delicate regard for what is proper becomes a habit, an instinct, a second nature, which nature, superimposed on the original nature, is the best, inasmuch as the internal code which governs each detail of action and speech, prescribes the standard of behavior and respect for oneself, as well as respect and refined behavior towards others. To this merit, add mental culture. Never was there an aristocracy so interested in general ideas and refinement of expression; it was even too much so; literary and philosophical preoccupations excluded all others of the positive and practical order; they talked, instead of acting. But, in this limited circle of speculative reason and of pure literary forms, it excelled; writings and how to write furnished the ordinary entertainment of polite society; every idea uttered by a thinker caused excitement in the drawing-room: the talent and style of authors were shaped by its taste;[49] it was in the drawing-rooms that Montesquieu, Voltaire, Rousseau, d'Alembert, the Encyclopedists, great and little, Beaumarchais, Bernardin de Saint-Pierre, Champfort, and Rivarol, involuntarily sought listeners and found them, not merely admirers and entertainers, but friends, protectors, patrons, benefactors, and followers. Under the teachings of the masters, the disciples had become philanthropists; moreover, the amenities of manners developed in all souls compassion and benevolence: "Nothing was more dreaded by opulent men than to be regarded as insensible."[50] They concerned themselves with children, with the poor, with the peasantry, setting their wits to work to afford

48. "The Ancient Régime," book ii., ch. 2, § iv.
49. *Ibid.*, book iv., chs. i., ii., iii.
50. Lacretelle, "Histoire de France au 18ᵉᵐᵉ Siecle," v., 2.—"The Ancient Régime," pp. 163, 300.

them relief; their zeal was aroused against oppression, their pity was excited for every misfortune. Even those whose duties compelled them to be rigid tempered their rigidity with explanations or concessions. "Ten years before the Revolution," says Roederer,[51] "the criminal courts of France no longer bore their own likeness. . . . Their former spirit had become changed. . . . All the young magistrates, and this I can bear witness to, for I was one myself, pronounced judgments more in accordance with the principles of Beccaria, than according to law." As to the men in authority, military administrators and commandants, it was impossible to be more patient, more careful of spilling blood; likewise, on the other hand, their qualities turned into defects, for, through excess of humanity, they were unable to maintain order, as is evident when facing the insurrections that took place between 1789 and 1792. Even with the force in their own hands, amidst gross insults and extreme dangers, they dreaded to make use of it; they could not bring themselves to repressing brutes, rascals, and maniacs: following the example of Louis XVI., they considered themselves as shepherds of the people, and let themselves be trampled upon rather than fire upon their flock. In reality, they had noble, and even generous and big hearts: in the bailiwick assemblies, in March, 1789, long before the night of August 4, they voluntarily surrendered every pecuniary privilege; under severe trials, their courage, heightened by polished manners, adds even to their heroism, elegance, tact, and gaiety. The most corrupt, a Duke of Orleans, the most frivolous and the most blasé, a Duc de Biron, meet death with stoical coolness and disdain.[52] Delicate

51. Morellet, "Mémoires," i., 166. (Letter by Roederer to Beccaria's daughter, May 20, 1797.)

52. Mallet-Dupan, "Mémoires," ii., 493. "While the Duke of Orleans was undergoing his examination he read a newspaper."—*Ibid.*, 497. "Nobody died with more firmness, spirit and dignity than the Duke of Orleans. He again became a royal prince. On being asked in the revolutionary Tribunal whether he had any defence to make, he replied, 'Decide if I may die today rather than tomorrow.'" His request was granted.—The Duc de Biron refused to escape, considering that, in such a dilemma, it was not worth while. "He passed his time in bed, drinking Bordeaux wine. . . . Before the Tribunal, they asked his

women who complain of a draught in their drawing-rooms, make
no complaint of a straw mattress in a damp, gloomy dungeon, where
they sleep in their clothes so that they may not wake up stiffened,
and they come down into the court of the Conciergerie with their
accustomed cheerfulness. Men and women, in prison, dress themselves as formerly, with the same care, that they may meet and talk
together with the same grace and spirit, in a corridor with an iron
grating within a step of the revolutionary Tribunal, and on the eve
of the scaffold.[53] This moral temper is evidently of the rarest; if it
errs on either side it is on that of being over refined, bad for use,
good for ornament.

And yet, in the upper class there were associated with two or
three thousand idlers amongst a frivolous aristocracy, as many serious men, who, to their drawing-room experience, added experience
in business. Almost all who held office or had been in the service,

---

name and he replied, 'Cabbage, turnip, Biron, as you like, one is as good as
the other.' 'How!' exclaimed the judges, 'you are insolent!' 'And you—you are
prosy! Come to the point; you have only to say Guillotine, while I have nothing
to say.'" Meanwhile they proceeded to interrogate him on his pretended treachery in Vendée, etc. "'You do not know what you are talking about! You ignoramuses know nothing about war! Stop your questions. I reported at the time
to the Committee of Public Safety, which approved of my conduct. Now, it has
changed and ordered you to take my life. Obey, and lose no more time.' Biron
asked pardon of God and the King. Never did he appear better than on the
(executioner's) cart."

53. Morellet, ii., 31.—"Mémoires de la Duchesse de Tourzel," "—— de
Mdlle. des Echerolles," etc.—Beugnot, "Mémoires, i.," 200–203. "The wittiest
remarks, the most delicate allusions, the most brilliant repartees were exchanged
on each side of the grating. The conversation was general, without any subject
being dwelt on. There, misfortune was treated as if it were a bad child to be
laughed at, and, in fact, they did openly make sport of Marat's divinity, Robespierre's sacerdoce, and the magistracy of Fouquier. They seemed to say to all
these bloody menials: 'You may slaughter us when you please, but you cannot
hinder us from being agreeable.'" —Archives Nationales, F[7], 3,116[7]. (Report
by the watchman, Charmont, Nivose 29, year II.) "The people attending the
executions are very much surprised at the firmness and courage they show (sic)
on mounting the scaffold. They say that it looks (sic) like going to a wedding.
People cannot get used to it, some declaring that it is supernatural."

were of this number, either ambassadors, general officers, or former ministers, from Marshal de Broglie down to Machaut and Malesherbes; resident bishops, like Monseigneur de Durfort, at Besançon;[54] vicars-general and canons who really governed their dioceses on the spot; prelates, like those in Provence, Languedoc, and Brittany, who, by right, had seats in the provincial "Etats"; agents and representatives of the clergy at Paris; heads of Orders and Congregations; the chief and lieutenant commandants of the seventeen military departments, intendants of each *generalité*, head-clerks of each ministry, magistrates of each parliament, farmers-general, collectors-general, and, more particularly in each province, the dignitaries and local proprietors of the two first orders, and all leading manufacturers, merchants, ship-owners, bankers, and prominent bourgeois; in short, that élite of the nobles, clergy, and Third Estate, which, from 1778 to 1789, constituted the twenty-one provincial assemblies, and which certainly formed in France the great social staff. Not that they were superior politicians: for in those days there were none, scarcely a few hundred competent men, almost all of them being specialists. But, in these few men were summed up pretty much the entire political capacity, information, and good sense of France; outside of their heads the other twenty-six millions of brains contained but little else than dangerous and barren formulas; as they alone had commanded, negotiated, deliberated, and governed, they were the only ones who understood men and things tolerably well, and, con-

---

54. Sauzay, i., introduction.—De Tocqueville, "L'Ancien Régime et la Revolution," 166. "I have patiently read most of the reports and debates of the provincial 'Etats,' and especially those of Languedoc, where the clergy took much greater part than elsewhere in administrative details, as well as the *procès-verbaux* of the provincial assemblies between 1779 and 1787, and, entering on the study with the ideas of my time, I was surprised to find bishops and abbés, among whom were several as eminent for their piety as their learning, drawing up reports on roads and canals, treating such matters with perfect knowledge of the facts, discussing with the greatest ability and intelligence the best means for increasing agricultural products, for ensuring the well-being of the people and the property of industrial enterprises, oftentimes much better than the laymen who were interested with them in the same affairs."

sequently, the only ones who were not completely disqualified for their management. In the provincial Assemblies they were seen originating and conducting the most important reforms; they had devoted themselves to these effectively and conscientiously, with as much equity and patriotism as intelligence and thoroughness; most of the heads and subheads of the leading public and private branches of the service, guided by philosophy and supported by current opinion for twenty years, had likewise given evidence of active benevolence.[55] Nothing is more precious than men of this stamp, for they are the life and soul of their respective branches of service, and are not to be replaced in one lot, at a given moment, by persons of equal merit. In diplomacy, in the finances, in judicature, in administration, in extensive commerce and large manufacturing, a practical, governing capacity is not created in a day; affairs in all these are too vast and too complicated; there are too many diverse interests to take into account, too many near and remote contingencies to foresee; lacking a knowledge of technical details, it is difficult to grasp the whole; one tries to make short work of it, one shatters right and left and ends with the sword, obliged to fall back on systematic brutality to complete the work of audacious bungling. Except in war, where an apprenticeship is more quickly got through with than elsewhere, the good government of men and the management of capital requires ten years' practice, besides ten years of preparatory education; add to this, against the temptations of power which are strong, a stability of character established through pro-

---

55. "The Ancient Régime," p. 300.—"The Revolution," vol. i., p. 116.—Buchez et Roux, i., 481. The list of notables convoked by the King in 1787 gives an approximate idea of this social staff. Besides the leading princes and seigniors we find, among one hundred and thirty-four members, twelve marshals of France, eight Councillors of State, five *maitres de requetes*, fourteen bishops and archbishops, twenty presidents and seventeen *procureurs-généraux* of parliaments, or of royal councils, twenty-five mayors, *prévots-de-marchands, capitouls* and equerries of large towns, the deputies of the "Etats" of Burgundy, Artois, Brittany, and Languedoc, three ministers and two chief clerks.—The capacities were all there, on hand, for bringing about a great reform; but there was no firm, strong, controlling hand, that of a Richelieu or Frederic II.

fessional honor, and, if it so happens, by family traditions. After having directed financial matters for two years, Cambon is not yet aware that the functions of the *fermiers-généraux* of indirect taxes differ from those of the *receveurs-généraux* of direct taxes;[56] accordingly, he includes, or allows to be included, the forty-eight *receveurs* in the decree which sends the sixty *fermiers* before the revolutionary Tribunal, that is to say, to the guillotine; and, in fact, all of them would have been sent there had not a man familiar with the business, Gaudin, Commissioner of the Treasury, heard the decree proclaimed in the street and run to explain to the Committee on Finances that "there was nothing in common" between the two groups of outlaws; that the *fermiers* were holders of leases on probable profits while the *receveurs* were paid functionaries at a fixed salary, and the crimes of the former, proved or not proved, were not imputable to the latter. Great astonishment on the part of these improvised financiers! "They make an outcry," says Gaudin, "and assert that I am mistaken. I insist, and repeat what I have told the President, Cambon; I affirm on my honor and offer to furnish them the proof of it; finally, they are satisfied and the President says to one of the members, 'Since that is so, go to the bureau of *procès-verbaux* and *scratch out the term receveurs-généraux from the decree passed this morning.*'" Such are the gross blunders committed by interlopers, and even carried out, when not warned and restrained by veterans in the service. Cambon, accordingly, in spite of the Jacobins, retains in his bureaux all whom he can among veteran officials. If Carnot manages the war well, it is owing to his being himself an educated officer and to maintaining in their positions d'Arcon, d'Obenheim, de Grimoard, de Montalembert, and Marescot, all eminent men bequeathed to him by the ancient régime.[57] Reduced, before the 9th of Thermidor, to perfect

---

56. "Mémoires de Gaudin," duc de Gaëte.

57. Mallet-Dupan, "Mémoires," ii., 25, 24. "The War Committee is composed of engineer and staff-officers, of which the principal are Meussuer, Favart, St. Fief, d'Arcon, Lafitte-Clavé and a few others. D'Arcon directed the raising of the siege of Dunkirk and that of Maubenge. . . . These officers were selected with discernment; they planned and carried out the operations; aided by im-

nullity, the Ministry of Foreign Affairs is not again to become useful and active until the professional diplomats, Miot, Colchen, Otto, and Reinhart,[58] resume their ascendency and influence. It is a professional diplomat, Barthélemy, who, after the 9th of Thermidor, really directs the foreign policy of the Convention, and brings about the peace of Basle.

III

Three classes, the nobles, the clergy and the *bourgeoisie*, provided these élite superiorities, and, compared with the rest of the nation, they themselves formed an élite. Thirty thousand gentlemen, scattered through the provinces, had been brought up from infancy to the profession of arms; generally poor, they lived on their rural estates without luxuries, comforts or curiosity, in the society of wood-rangers and game-keepers, frugally and with rustic habits, in the open air, in such a way as to ensure robust constitutions. A child, at six years of age, mounted a horse; he followed the hounds, and hardened himself against inclemencies;[59] afterwards, in the academies, he rendered his limbs supple by exercise and obtained that

---

mense resources, in the shape of maps, plans, and reconnaissances preserved in the war department, they really operated according to the experience and intelligence of the great generals under the monarchy."

58. Miot de Melito, "Mémoires," i., 47.—Andre Michel, "Correspondance de Mallet-Dupan avec la Cour de Vienne," i., 26. (January 3, 1795.) "The Convention feels so strongly the need of suitable aids to support the burden of its embarrassments as to now seek for them among pronounced royalists. For instance, it has just offered the direction of the royal treasury to M. Dufresne, former chief of the department under the reign of the late King, and retired since 1790. It is the same spirit and making a still more extraordinary selection, which leads them to appoint M. Gerard de Rayneval to the Commissariat of Foreign Affairs, chief-clerk of correspondence since the ministry of the Duc de Choiseul until that of the Comte de Montmorin inclusive. He is a man of decided opinions and an equally decided character; in 1790 I saw him abandon the department through aversion to the maxims which the Revolution had forcibly introduced into it."

59. Marshal Marmont, "Mémoires." At nine years of age he rode on horseback and hunted daily with his father.

rugged health which is necessary for living under a tent and follow-ing a campaign. From early childhood, he was imbued with a mili-tary spirit; his father and uncles at table talked of nothing but their perils in war and feats of arms; his imagination took fire; he got accustomed to looking upon their pursuits as the only ones worthy of a man of rank and feeling, and he plunged ahead with a preco-ciousness which we no longer comprehend. I have read many re-cords of the service of gentlemen who were assassinated, guillotined, or *emigrés;* they nearly always began their careers before the age of sixteen, often at fourteen, thirteen, and eleven.[60] M. des Echerolles,[61] captain in the Poitou regiment, had brought along with him into the

60. Among other manuscript documents, a letter of M. Symn de Carneville, March 11, 1781. (On the families of Carneville and Montmorin St. Hérem, in 1789.) The latter family remains in France; two of its members are massacred, two executed, a fifth "escaped the scaffold by forestalling the justice of the people"; the sixth, enlisted in the revolution armies, received a shot at nineteen years of age which made him blind. The other family emigrated, and its chiefs, the Count and Viscount Carneville commanded, one, a free company in the Austrian service, and the other, a regiment of hussars in Condé's army. Twelve officers of these two corps were brothers-in-law, nephews, first-cousins, and cousins of the two commanders, the first of whom entered the service at fifteen, and the second at eleven.—Cf. "Mémoires du Prince de Ligne." At seven or eight years of age I had already witnessed the din of battle, I had been in a besieged town, and saw three sieges from a window. A little older, I was sur-rounded by soldiers; old retired officers belonging to various services, and living in the neighborhood, fed my passion.—Turenne said "I slept on a gun-carriage at the age of ten. My taste for war was so great as to lead me to enlist with a Captain of the 'Royal Vaissiaux,' in garrison two leagues off. If war had been declared I would have gone off and let nobody know it. I joined his company, determined not to owe my fortune to any but valorous actions."—Cf. also "Mémoires du Maréchal de Saxe." A soldier at twelve, in the Saxon legion, shouldering his musket, and marching with the rest, he completed each stage on foot from Saxony to Flanders, and before he was thirteen took part in the battle of Malplaquet.

61. Alexandrine des Echerolles, "Un Famille Noble sous la Terreur," p. 25.—Cf. "Correspondance de Madelle de Féring," by Honore Bonhomme. The two sisters, one sixteen and the other thirteen, disguised as men, fought with their father in Dumouriez' army.—See the sentiment of young nobles in the works of Berquin and Marmontel. (Les Rivaux d'Eux-meme.)

army his only son, aged nine, and a dozen little cousins of the same age. Those children fought like old soldiers; one of them had his leg fractured by a ball; young des Echerolles received a sabre stroke which cut away his cheek from the ear to the upper lip, and he was wounded seven times; still young, he received the cross of St. Louis. To serve the State, seek conflict, and expose one's life, seemed an obligation of their rank, a hereditary debt; out of nine or ten thousand officers who discharged this debt most of them cared only for this and looked for nothing beyond. With no fortune and without patrons, they had renounced promotion, fully aware that the higher ranks were reserved for the heirs of great families and the courtiers at Versailles. After serving fifteen or twenty years, they returned home with a captain's commission and the cross of St. Louis, sometimes with a small pension, contented with having done their duty and conscious of their own honor. On the approach of the Revolution, this old spirit, illumined by the new ideas, became an almost civic virtue:[62] we have seen how they behaved between 1789 and 1792, their moderation, their forbearance, their sacrifice of self-love, their abnegation and their stoical impassibility, their dislike to strike, the coolness with which they persisted in receiving without returning blows, and in maintaining, if not public order, at least the last semblance of it. Patriots as much as soldiers, through birth, education and conviction, they formed a natural, special nursery, eminently worthy of preserving, inasmuch as it furnished society with ready-made instruments for defence, internally against rascals and brutes, and externally against the enemy. Less calm in disposition and more given to pleasure than the rural nobles of Prussia, under slacker discipline and in the midst of greater worldliness, but more genial, more courteous, and more liberal-minded, the twenty-six thousand noble families of France upheld in their sons the traditions and prejudices, the habits and aptitudes, those energies of body,

62. "The Revolution," i., 158, 325. *Ibid.*, the affair of M. de Bussy, 306; the affair of the eighty-two gentlemen of Caen, 316.—See in Rivarol ("Journal Politique Nationale") details of the admirable conduct of the Body-guards at Versailles, Oct. 5 and 6, 1789.

heart, and mind[63] through which the Prussian "junkers" were able to constitute the Prussian army, organise the German army, and make Germany the first power of Europe.

IV

In like manner, in the Church, nearly all its officials, the whole of the lower and middle-class clergy, *curés,* vicars, canons, and collegiate chaplains, professors and directors of schools, colleges, and seminaries, more than sixty-five thousand ecclesiastics, formed a healthy, well-organised body, worthily fulfilling its duties. "I do not know," says de Tocqueville,[64] "if taking all in all and notwithstanding the vices of some of its members, there ever was in the world a more remarkable clergy than the Catholic clergy of France when the Revolution took them by surprise, more enlightened, more national, less intrenched behind their private virtues, better endowed with public virtues, and, at the same time, more strong in the faith. . . . I began the study of the old social system full of prejudices against them; I finish it full of respect for them." And first, which is a great point, most of the incumbents in the town parishes, in the three hundred collegial churches, in the small canonicates of the cathedral chapters, belonged to better families than at the present day.[65] Children were then more numerous, not merely among the peasants, but among the inferior nobles and the upper bourgeoisie;

63. The noble families under the ancient régime may be characterised as so many families of soldiers' children.

64. "L'Ancien Régime et la Revolution," by M. de Tocqueville, p. 169. My judgment, likewise based on the study of texts, and especially manuscript texts, coincides here as elsewhere with that of M. de Tocqueville. Biographies and local histories contain documents too numerous to be cited.

65. Sauzay, i., introduction, and Ludovic Sciout, "Histoire de la Constitution Civile du Clergé," i., introduction. (See in Sauzay, biographical details and the grades of the principal ecclesiastical dignitaries of the diocese Besançon.) The cathedral chapter, and that of the Madeleine, could be entered only through nobility or promotion; it was requisite for a graduate to have a noble for a father, or a doctor of divinity, and himself be a doctor of divinity or in canon law. Analogous titles, although lower down, were requisite for collegiate canons, and for chaplains or *familiers.*

each family, accordingly, was glad to have one of its sons take orders, and no constraint was necessary to bring this about. The ecclesiastical profession then had attractions which it no longer possesses; it had none of the inconveniences incident to it at the present time. A priest was not exposed to democratic distrust and hostility; he was sure of a bow from the laborer in the street as well as from the peasant in the country; he was on an equal footing with the local bourgeoisie, almost one of the family, and among the first; he could count on passing his life in a permanent situation, honorably and serenely, in the midst of popular deference and enjoying the good will of the public. On the other hand, he was not bridled as in our day. A priest was not a functionary salaried by the State; like his private income, his pay, put aside in advance, furnished through special appropriations, through local taxes, out of a distinct treasury, could never be withheld on account of a préfet's report, or through ministerial caprice, or be constantly menaced by budget difficulties and the ill-will of the civil powers. In relation to his ecclesiastical superiors he was respectful but independent. The bishop in his diocese was not what he has become since the Concordat, an absolute sovereign free to appoint and remove at will nine *curés* out of ten. In three vacancies out of four, and often in fourteen out of fifteen,[66] it was not the bishop who made the appointment; the new incumbent was designated sometimes by the cathedral chapter or corporation; again, by a collegial church or corporation; again, by the metropolitan canon or by the abbé or prior, the patron of the place; again, by the seignior whose ancestors had founded or endowed the Church; in certain cases by the Pope, and, occasionally, by the King or commune. Powers were limited through this multiplicity and intercrossing of authorities. Moreover, the canon or *curé* being once appointed he possessed guarantees; he could not be arbitrarily dismissed; in most cases, his removal or suspension required a previous trial according to prescribed formalities, accompanied with an ex-

---

66. "The Revolution," i., 233.—Cf. Emile Ollivier, "L'Eglise et l'Etat au Concile du Vatican," i., 134, ii., 511.

amination, pleadings, and arguments before the *officialité* or ecclesiastical court. He was, in fact, permanently placed, and very generally his personal merit sufficed to keep him in his place. For, if the highest positions were bestowed according to birth and favor, the intermediate positions were reserved to correct habits and attainments. Many canons and vicars-general, and almost all the *curés* in the towns were doctors of divinity or of canon law, while ecclesiastical studies, very thorough, had occupied eight or nine years of their youth.[67] Although the method was out of date, much was learned at the Sorbonne and St. Sulpice; at the very least, one became a good logician through prolonged and scientific intellectual gymnastics. "My dear Abbé," said Turgot, smiling, to Morellet, "it is only you and I who have taken our degree who can reason closely." Their theological drill, indeed, was about as valuable as our philosophical drill; if it expanded the mind less, it supplied this better with applicable conceptions; less exciting, it was more fruitful. In the Sorbonne of the nineteenth century, the studies consist of the speculative systems of a few isolated, divergent intellects who have exercised no authority over the multitude, while in the Sorbonne of the eighteenth century, the studies consisted of the creed, morality, discipline, history, and canons of a Church which had already existed seventeen centuries and which, comprising one hundred and fifty millions of souls, still sways one-half of the civilised world. To a theoretical education add practical education. A *curé*, and with still more reason, a canon, an archdeacon, a bishop, was not a passing

67. Morellet, "Mémoires," i., 8, 31. The Sorbonne, founded by Robert Sorbon, Confessor to St. Louis, was an association resembling one of the Oxford or Cambridge colleges, that is to say, a corporation possessing a building, revenues, rules, regulations, and boarders; its object was to afford instruction in the theological sciences; its titular members, numbering about a hundred, were mostly bishops, vicars-general, canons, *curés* in Paris and in the principal towns. Men of distinction were prepared in it at the expense of the Church.—The examinations for the doctorate were the *tentative*, the *mineure*, the *Sorbonique* and the *majeure*. A talent for discussion and argument was particularly developed.—Cf. Ernest Renan, "Souvenirs d'Enfance et de Jeunesse," p. 279 (on St. Sulpice and the study of Theology).

stranger, endowed by the State, wearing a surplice, as little belonging to his age through his ministry as through his dress, and wholly
confined to his spiritual functions: he managed the revenues of his
dotation, he granted leases, made repairs, built, and interested himself in the probabilities of the crops, in the construction of a highway
or canal, while his experiences in these matters were equal to those
of any lay proprietor. Moreover, being one of a small proprietary
corporation, that is to say, a chapter or local vestry, and one of a
great proprietary corporation of the diocese and Church of France,
he took part directly or indirectly in important temporal affairs, in
assemblies, in deliberations, in collective expenditures, in the establishment of a local budget and of a general budget, and hence, in
public and administrative matters, his competence was analogous
and almost equal to that of a mayor, subdelegate, farmer-general or
intendant. In addition to this he was liberal: never has the French
clergy been more earnestly so, from the latest *curés* back to the first
archbishops.[68] Remark, in fine, the distribution of the clergy over
the territory. There was a *curé* or vicar in the smallest of the forty
thousand villages. In thousands of small, poor, remote communes,
he was the only man who could readily read and write; none other
than he in many of the larger rural communes,[69] except the resident
seignior and some man of the law or half-way schoolmaster, was at
all learned.[70] In effect, for a man who had finished his studies and

68. Cf. the files of the clergy in the States-General, and the reports of
ecclesiastics in the provincial assemblies.

69. "The Revolution," p. 72.

70. In some dioceses, notably that of Besançon, the rural parishes were
served by distinguished men. (Sauzay, i., 16.) "It was not surprising to encounter
a man of European reputation, like Bergier, so long *curé* of Flangebouche; an
astronomer of great merit, like M. Mongin, *curé* of Grand 'combe des Bois,
whose works occupy an honorable place in Lalande's bibliography, all passing
their lives in the midst of peasants. At Rochejean, a priest of great intelligence
and fine feeling, M. Boillon, a distinguished naturalist, had converted his house
into a museum of natural history as well as into an excellent school. . . . It was
not rare to find priests belonging to the highest social circles, like MM. de
Trevillers, of Trevillers, Balard de Bonnevaux of Bonétage, de Mesmay of

knowing Latin, to consent, for six hundred francs or three hundred francs a year, to live isolated, and a celibate, almost in indigence, amongst rustics and the poor, he must be a priest; the quality of his office makes him resigned to the discomforts of his situation. A preacher of the Word, a professor of morality, a minister of Charity, a guide and dispenser of spiritual life, he taught a theory of the world, at once consoling and self-denying, which he enforced with a cult, and this cult was the only one adapted to his flock; manifestly, the French, especially those devoted to manual and hard labor, could not regard this world as ideal, except through his formulas; history, the supreme judge, had on this point rendered its verdict without appeal; no heresy, no schism, not the Reformation nor Jansenism, had prevailed against hereditary faith; through infinitely multiplied and deeply penetrating roots this faith suited national customs, temperament, and peculiar social imagination and sensibility. Possessing the heart, the intellect, and even the senses, through fixed, immemorial traditions and habits, it had become an unconscious, almost corporeal necessity, and the Catholic orthodox *curé,* in communion with the Pope, was about as indispensable to the village as the public fountain; he also quenched thirst, the thirst of the soul; without him, the inhabitants could find no drinkable water. And, if we keep human weaknesses in mind, it may be said that nobleness of character in the clergy corresponded with nobleness of profession; in all points no one could dispute their capacity for self-sacrifice, for they willingly suffered for what they believed to be the truth. If, in 1790, a number of priests took the oath to the civil constitution of the clergy, it was with reservations, or because they deemed the oath licit; but, after the dismissal of the bishops and the Pope's disapprobation, many of them withdrew it at the risk of their lives, so as not to fall into schism; they fell back into the ranks and gave themselves up

---

Mesmay, du Bouvot, at Osselle, cheerfully burying themselves in the depths of the country, some on their family estates, and, not content to share their income with their poor parishioners, but on dying, leaving them a large part of their fortunes."

voluntarily to the brutality of the crowd and the rigors of the law. Moreover, and from the start, notwithstanding threats and temptations, two-thirds of the clergy would not take the oath; in the highest ranks, among the mundane ecclesiastics whose scepticism and laxity were notorious, honor, in default of faith, maintained the same spirit; nearly the whole of them, great and small, had subordinated their interests, welfare and security to the maintenance of their dignity or to scruples of conscience. They had allowed themselves to be stripped of everything; they let themselves be exiled, imprisoned, tortured, and made martyrs of, like the Christians of the primitive church; through their invincible meekness, they were going, like the primitive Christians, to exhaust the rage of their executioners, wear out persecutions, transform opinion and compel the admission, even with those who survived in the eighteenth century, that they were true, deserving, and courageous men.

V

Below the nobles and the clergy, a third class of notables, the bourgeoisie, almost entirely confined to the towns,[71] bordered on the former classes through its upper circles, while its diverse groups, ranging from the parliamentarian to the rich merchant or manufacturer, comprised the remainder of those who were tolerably well-educated, say one hundred thousand families, recruited on the same conditions as the bourgeoisie of the present day: they were "bourgeois living nobly," meaning by this, living on their incomes, large manufacturers and traders, engaged in liberal pursuits—lawyers, notaries, *procureurs,* physicians, architects, engineers, artists, professors, and especially the government officials; the latter, however, very numerous, differed from ours in two essential points. On the one hand, their office, as nowadays with the notaries' *étude,* or a membership of the stock-board, was personal property. Their places, and many others, such as posts in the judiciary, in the finances, in

---

71. De Tocqueville, "L'Ancien Régime," 134, 137.

bailiwicks, in the *Présidial*, in the *Election*,[72] in the salt-department, in the customs, in the Mint, in the department of forests and streams, in presidencies, in councils, as *procureurs du roi* in various civil, administrative, and criminal courts, holding places in the treasury, auditors and collectors of the various branches of the revenue—all of which offices, and many others, had been alienated for more than a century by the State in return for specified sums of ready money; thenceforth, they fell into the hands of special purchasers; the title of each possessor was as good as that of a piece of real property, and he could legally sell his title, the same as he had bought it, at a given price, on due advertisement![73] On the other hand, the different groups of local functionaries in each town formed their own associations, similar to our notarial chambers, or those of our stock-brokers; these small associations had their own by-laws, meetings, and treasury, frequently a civil status and the right of pleading, often a political status and the right of electing to the municipal council;[74] consequently, besides his personal interests, each member cherished

72. Terms signifying certain minor courts of law.

73. Albert Babeau, "La Ville sous l'Ancien Régime," p. 26.—(Advertisements in the "Journal de Troyes," 1784, 1789.) "For sale, the place of Councillor in the Salt-department at Sézannes. Income from eight to nine hundred livres. Price ten thousand livres."—"A person desires to purchase in this town (Troyes) an office in the Magistracy or Finances, at from twenty-five thousand to sixty thousand livres; cash paid down if required."

74. De Tocqueville, "L'Ancien Régime," p. 356. The municipal body of Angers comprised, among other members, two deputies of the *présidial*, two of the Forest and Streams department, two of the *Election*, two of the Salt-department, two of the Customs, two of the Mint, two Council judges. The system of the ancient régime, universally, is the grouping together of all individuals in one body with a representative of all these bodies, especially those of the notables. The municipal body of Angers, consequently, comprises two deputies of the society of lawyers and *procureurs*, two of the notarial body, one of the University, one of the Chapter, a Syndic of the clerks, etc.—At Troyes (Albert Babeau, "Histoire de Troyes Pendant la Révolution," p. 23.) Among the notables of the municipality may be found one member of the clergy, two nobles, one officer of the bailiwick, one officer of the other jurisdictions, one physician, one or two bourgeois, one lawyer, one notary or *procureur*, four merchants and two members of the trade guild.

the professional interests of his guild. Thus was his situation different from what it now is, and, through a natural reaction, his character, manners, and tastes were different. First, he was much more
independent; he was not afraid of being discharged or transferred
elsewhere, suddenly, unawares, on the strength of an intendant's
report, for political reasons, to make room for a deputy's candidate
or a minister's tool. This would have cost too much: it would have
required first of all a reimbursement of the sum paid for his office,
and at a rate of purchase ten times, at least, the revenue of the office.[75]
Besides, in defending himself, in protesting against and forestalling
his disgrace, he would have been supported by his entire professional
guild, oftentimes by other similar bodies, and frequently by the
whole town, filled with his relations, clients, and comrades. The
entire hive protected the bee against the caprices of favoritism and
the brutalities of despotism. At Paris, a certain *procureur,* supported
by his colleagues, is known to have imposed on a noble who had
insulted him, the most humiliating atonement.[76] In fact, under the

75. Albert Babeau, "La Ville," p. 26. (Cf. note on preceding page.) The
"Returns" at Reteil, in 1746, is sold at one hundred and fifty thousand livres;
it brings in from eleven thousand to fourteen thousand livres.—The purchaser,
besides, has to pay to the State the "right of the gold maré" (a tax on the
transfer of property); in 1762, this right amounted to nine hundred and forty
livres for the post of Councillor to the bailiwick of Troyes. D'Espremenil,
councillor in the Paris Parliament, had paid fifty thousand livres for his place,
besides ten thousand livres for the tax of the "gold marc."

76. Emile Bos, "Les Avocats au Conseil du Roi," p. 340. Master Peruot,
procureur, was seated on the balcony of the Théâtre Français when Count More-
ton Chabrillant arrives and wants his place. The *procureur* resists and the Count
calls the guard, who leads him off to prison. Master Peruot enters a complaint;
there is a trial, intervention of the friends of M. de Chabrillant before the *garde
des sceaux,* petitions of the nobles and resistance of the entire guild of advocates
and *procureurs.* M. de Chabrillant, senior, offers Peruot forty thousand livres to
withdraw his suit, which Peruot refuses to do. Finally, the Count de Chabrillant
is condemned, with six thousand livres damages (which are given to the poor
and to prisoners), as well as to the expense of printing two hundred impressions
of the verdict.—Duport de Cheverney, "Mémoires" (unpublished), communicated by M. Robert de Crêvecoeur: "Formerly a man paid fifty thousand livres
for an office with only three hundred livres income; the consideration, however,

ancient régime, it was almost impossible for a functionary to be removed; hence, he could fulfill his duties securely and with dignity, without being obliged to keep daily watch of the capital, to go to Paris to see how the official wind blew, to look after all the influences in his favor, to nurse his relations with the government and live like a bird on a branch. In the second place, there was a limit to his ambition; he did not keep constantly thinking of mounting a step higher in the hierarchy; or how to pass from a small town to a large one and hold on to his title; this would have been a too troublesome and complicated matter; he would first have had to find a purchaser and then sell his place, and next find a seller and buy another at a higher price; a stock broker at Bordeaux, a notary at Lyons, is not an aspirant for the post of stock broker or notary at Paris. Nothing then bore any resemblance to the ambulant colony of the present day which, in obedience to orders from above, travels about governing each of our towns, strangers on the wing, with no personal standing, without local landed property, interests or means, encamped in some hired apartment, often in a furnished room, sometimes stopping at a hotel, eternal nomads awaiting a telegram, always prepared to pack up and leave for another place a hundred leagues off in consideration of a hundred crowns extra pay, and doing the same detached work over again. Their predecessor, belonging to the country, was a stable fixture and contented; he was not tormented by a craving for promotion; he had a career within the bounds of his corporation and town; cherishing no wish or idea of leaving it, he accommodated himself to it; he became proud of his office and professional brethren, and rose above the egoism of the individual; his self-love was bent on maintaining every prerogative and interest belonging to his guild. Established for life in his native town, in the midst of old colleagues, numerous relatives, and youthful companions, he esteemed their good opinion. Exempt from vexatious or

---

he enjoyed through it, and the certainty of remaining in it for life, compensated him for the sacrifice, while the longer he kept it, the greater was the influence of himself and children."

burdensome taxes, tolerably well off, owning at least his own office, he was above sordid preoccupations and common necessities. Used to old fashioned habits of simplicity, soberness, and economy, he was not tormented by a disproportion between his income and expenses, by the requirements of show and luxury, by the necessity of annually adding to his revenue. Thus guided and unembarrassed, the instincts of vanity and generosity, the essence of French character, took the ascendant; the councillor or comptroller, the King's agent, regarded himself as a man above the common run, as a noble of the Third-Estate; he thought less of making money than of gaining esteem; his chief desire was to be honored and honorable; "he passed life comfortably and was looked up to, . . . in the discharge of his duty, . . . with no other ambition than to transmit to his children . . . along with their inheritance an unsullied reputation."[77]

77. Albert Babeau, "La Ville," p. 27;—"Histoire de Troyes," p. 21.—This portrait is drawn according to recollections of childhood and family narrations. I happen to have known the details of two or three small provincial towns, one of about six thousand inhabitants where, before 1800, nearly all the notables, forty families, were relations; today all are scattered. The more one studies documents, the more does Montesquieu's definition of the mainspring of society under the ancient régime seem profound and just, this mainspring consisting of *honor*. In the *bourgeoisie* who were confounded with the nobility, namely the Parliamentarians, their functions were nearly gratuitous; the magistrate received his pay in deference. (*Moniteur*, v., 520. Session of August 30, 1790, speech by d'Espremenil.) "Here is what it cost a Councillor; I take myself as an example. He paid fifty thousand livres for his place, and ten thousand more for the tax of the 'marc d'or.' He received three hundred and eighty-nine livres ten sous salary, from which three hundred and sixty-seven livres 'capitation' had to be deducted. The King allowed us forty-five livres for extra service of 'La Tournelle.' How about the fees? is asked. The (grande chambre) superior court, asserted to have received the largest amount, was composed of one hundred and eighty members; the fees amounted to two hundred and fifty thousand livres, which were not a burden on the nation, but on the litigants. M. Thouret, who practised in the Rouen parliament, will bear witness to this. I appeal to him to say conscientiously what sum a Councillor derived from his office—not five hundred livres. . . . When a judgment cost the litigant nine hundred livres the King's portion was six hundred livres. . . . To sum up, the profits of an office were seven livres ten sous."

Among the other groups of the bourgeoisie the same corporate system, the same settled habits, the same security, the same frugality,
the same institutions, the same customs,[78] promoted the growth of
nearly the same sentiments, while the intellectual culture of these
men was not insignificant. Having leisure, they were given to reading; as they were not overwhelmed with newspapers they read books
worth reading; I have found in old libraries in the provinces, in the
houses of the descendants of a manufacturer or lawyer in a small
town, complete editions of Voltaire, Rousseau, Montesquieu, Buffon,
and Condillac, with marks in each volume showing that the volume
had been read by some one in the house before the close of the
eighteenth century. Nowhere else, likewise, had all that was sound
and liberal in the philosophy of the eighteenth century found such
a welcome; it is from this class that the patriots of 1789 were recruited; it had furnished not only the majority of the Constituent
Assembly, but again all the honest men who, from July, 1789 to the
end of 1791 performed their administrative duties so disinterestedly,
and with such devotion and zeal, amidst so many difficulties, dangers, and disappointments. Composed of Feuillants or Monarchists,
possessing such types of men as Huez of Troyes or Dietrich of
Strasbourg, and for representatives such leaders as Lafayette and
Bailly, it comprised the superior intelligence and most substantial
integrity of the Third-Estate. It is evident that, along with the nobles
and clergy, the best fruits of history were gathered in it, and most

78. Albert Babeau, "La Ville," ch. ii., and "Histoire de Troyes," i., ch. i.
At Troyes, fifty merchants, notables, elected the judge-consul and two consuls;
the merchants' guild possessed its own hall and had its own meetings. At Paris,
the drapers, mercers, grocers, furriers, hatters, and jewellers formed the six
bodies of merchants. The merchants' guild everywhere took precedence of other
industrial communities and enjoyed special privileges. "The merchants," says
Loyseau, "hold rank (*qualité d'honneur*), being styled honorable men, honest
persons and bourgeois of the towns, qualifications not attributed to husbandmen,
nor to *sergents*, nor to artisans, nor to manual laborers."—On paternal authority
and domestic discipline in these old bourgeois families see the History of Beaumarchais and his father. ("Beaumarchais," by M. de Loménie, vol i.)

of the mental and moral capital accumulated, not only by the century, but, again, by preceding centuries.

VI

Like a fire kindled on an eminence in a cold and obscure district, maintained amidst human barbarism on the summits at great cost, civilisation radiates only as its rays grow dim; its light and heat diminish just as its gleams reach remoter and deeper strata; nevertheless, both penetrate to a great distance and to a certain depth before wholly dying out. If, then, we would estimate their power in France at the close of the eighteenth century we must add to the notables the half-notables of society, namely, the men who, like the people, were devoted to manual labor, but who, among the people, kept at the head, say one hundred and fifty thousand families, consisting of well-to-do farmers, small rural proprietors, shopkeepers, retailers, foremen and master-workmen, village syndics and guild syndics,[79] those who were established and had some capital, owning

79. Albert Babeau, "Le Village sous l' Ancien Régime," p. 56, ch. iii and iv. (on the village syndics), and pp. 357 and 359. "The peasants had the right to deliberate on their own affairs directly and to elect their principal agents. They understood their own wants, what sacrifices to impose for school and church . . . for repairs of the town clock and the belfry. They appointed their own agents and generally elected the most capable."—*Ibid.*, "La Ville sous l' Ancien Régime," p. 29. The artisans' guilds numbered at Paris one hundred and twenty-four, at Amiens sixty-four, and at Troyes fifty, also Chalons-sur-Marne, at Angers twenty-seven. The edicts of 1776 reduced them to forty-four at Paris, and to twenty as the maximum for the principal towns within the jurisdiction of the Paris parliament.—"Each guild formed a city within a city. . . . Like the communes, it had its special laws, its selected chiefs, its assemblies, its own building or, at least, a chamber in common, its banner, coat-of-arms and colors."—*Ibid.*, "Histoire de Troyes Pendant la Révolution," i., 13, 329. Trade guilds and corporations bear the following titles, drawn up in 1789, from the files of complaints: apothecaries, jewellers and watch-makers, booksellers and printers, master-barbers, grocers, wax and candle-makers, bakers and tailors, master shoemakers, eating-house-keepers, inn-keepers and hatters, master-masons and plasterers in lime and cement, master-joiners, coopers and cabinet-makers, master-cutlers, armorers, and polishers; founders, braziers, and pin-makers; master-locksmiths, ironmongers, tinsmiths and other metal workers, vinegar-makers, master-shearers, master rope-makers, master-tanners, deal-

a lot of ground and a house, with a business or stock of tools, and a set of customers, that is to say, with something ahead and credit, not being obliged to live from hand to mouth, and therefore, beginning to be independent and more influential, in short, the overseers of the great social work-house, the sergeants and corporals of the social army. They, too, were not unworthy of their rank. In the village or trade community, the syndic, elected by his equals and neighbors, was not blindly nominated; all his electors in relation to him were competent; if peasants, they had seen him turning up the soil; if blacksmiths or joiners, they had seen him at work in his forge, or at the bench. And, as their direct, present, and obvious interests were concerned, they chose him for the best, not on the strength of a newspaper recommendation, in deference to a vague declamatory platform or sounding, empty phrases, but according to their personal experiences, and the thorough knowledge they had of him. The delegate sent by the village to the intendant and by the guild to the Hôtel-de-Ville, was its most capable, and most creditable man, one of those, probably, who, through his application, intelligence, honesty, and economy, had proved the most prosperous, some master-workman or farmer that had gained experience through long years of assiduity, familiar with details and precedents, of good judgment and repute, more interested than anybody else in supporting the interests of the community and with more leisure than others to attend to public affairs.[80] This man, through the nature of things, imposed himself on the attention, confidence, and deference of his peers, and, because he was their natural representative, he was their legal representative.

Upon the whole, if, in this old society, the pressure was unequally distributed, if the general equilibrium was unstable, if the upper parts

---

ers and master-dyers and dressers; master saddle and harness-makers, charcoal-burners, carters, paper-makers and band-box-makers, cap-makers and associates in arts and trades.—In some towns one or two of these natural guilds kept up during the Revolution and still exist, as, for example, that of the butchers at Limoges.

80. F. Leplay, "Les Ouvriers Européens," v., 456, 2d ed., (on workmen's guilds), Charpentier, Paris.

bore down too heavily on the lower ones, the sorting, at least, which goes on in every civilised State, constantly separating the wheat from the chaff, went on tolerably well; except at the centre and at the Court, where the winnowing machine had worked haphazard and, frequently, in an opposite sense for a century, the separation proceeded regularly, undoubtedly slower, but, perhaps, more equitably than in our contemporary democracy. The chance that a notable by right could become a notable *de facto* was then much greater: it was less difficult, and the inclination to found, maintain, and perpetuate a family or a work was much stronger; people oftener looked beyond mere self; the eyes naturally turned outside the narrow circle of one's personality, looking backward as well as beyond this present life. The institution of an equal partition of property, the system of obligatory partition, the rule of partition in kind, with other prescriptions of the civil code, does not split up a heritage and ruin the home.[81] Parental remissness and the cool self-possession of children had not yet weakened the principle of authority and abolished respect in the family. Useful and natural associations were not yet

81. F. Leplay, "Les Ouvriers Européens," (2d ed.), iv., 377, and the monographs of four families (Bordier of Lower Brittany, Brassier of Armagnac, Savonnier of Lower Provence, Paysan of Lavedan, ch. 7, 8 and 9).—*Ibid.*, "L'Organization de la Famille," p. 62, and the whole volume.—M. Leplay, in his exact, methodical and profound researches, has rendered a service of the highest order to political science and, consequently, to history. He has minutely observed and described the scattered fragments of the old organisation of society; his analysis and comparison of these fragments shows the thickness and extent of the stratum almost gone, to which they belonged. My own observations on the spot, in many provinces in France, as well as the recollections of my youth, agree with M. Leplay's discoveries.—On the stable, honest, and prosperous families of small rural proprietors, Cf. *ibid.*, p. 68 (Arthur Young's observation in Béarn), and p. 75. Many of these families existed in 1789, more of them than at the present time, especially in Gascony, Languedoc, Auvergne, Dauphiny, Franche-Comté, Alsace, and Normandy.—*Ibid.*, "L'Organization du Travail," pp. 499, 503, 508. (Effects of the "Code Civile" on the transmission of a manufactory and a business establishment in France, and on cultivation in Savoy; the number of suits in France produced by the system of forced partition of property.)

stifled in the germ nor arrested in their development by the systematic hostility of the law. The facility and cheapness of transportation, the promiscuousness of schools, the excitement of competition, the common rush for every office, the increasing irritation of every ambition and lust, had not immeasurably multiplied the class of irresponsible malcontents and mischievous nomads. In the political order of things, inaptitude, envy, brutality were not sovereign; universal suffrage did not exclude from power the men, born, bred, and qualified to exercise it; the innumerable public offices were not offered as a prey to charlatanism and to the intrigues of politicians. France was not then, as now-a-days, in a way to become a vast lodging-house managed by a chance overseer, condemned to periodical failures, peopled with anonymous inmates, indifferent to each other, without local attachments, with no corporate interests or affections, merely tenants and passing consumers, placed in the order of their numbers around a common mess-table where each thinks only of himself, gets served quickly, consumes what he can lay his hands on, and ends by finding out that, in a place of this sort, the best condition, the wisest course, is to put all one's property into an annuity and live a bachelor. Formerly, among all classes and in all the provinces, there were a large number of families that had taken root on the spot, living there a hundred years and more. Not only among the nobles, but among the bourgeoisie and the Third-Estate, the heir of any enterprise was expected to continue his calling; as with the seignorial chateau and extensive domain, as with the bourgeois dwelling and patrimonial office, the humble rural domain, farm, shop, and factory, were transmitted intact from one generation to another.[82] Great or small, the individual was not wholly interested in himself; his thoughts travelled forward to the future and back to the past, on the side of ancestors and on that of descendants, along the endless chain of which his own life was but a link; he possessed

82. F. Leplay, "L'Organization de la Famille," p. 212. (History of the Mélonga family from 1856 to 1869 by M. Cheysson.) Also p. 269. (On the difficulty of partitions among *ascendants*, by M. Claudio Jannet.)

traditions, he felt bound to set examples. Under this twofold title, his domestic authority was uncontested;[83] all who belonged to him followed his instructions without swerving and without resistance. When, by virtue of this home discipline, a family had maintained itself upright and respected on the same spot for a century, it could easily mount a degree; it could introduce one of its members into the upper class, pass from the plough or trade to petty offices, and from these to the higher ones and to parliamentary dignities, from the four thousand posts that ennoble to the legalised nobility, from the lately made nobles to the old nobility. Apart from the two or three thousand gilded drones living on the public honey at Versailles, apart from the court parasites and their valets, three or four hundred thousand notables and half-notables of France thus acquired and kept their offices, consideration and fortune; they were therefore their legitimate possessors. The peasant-proprietor and master-artisan had risen from father to son, at four o'clock in the morning, toiled all day and never drank. From father to son, the trader, notary, lawyer, and office-holder, had been careful, economical, skillful, and attentive to business, correct in their papers, precise in their accounts. From father to son, the gentleman had served bravely, the parliamentarian had judged equitably, on honor, with a salary less than the interest of the sum paid by him to acquire his rank or post. Each of these men received no more than his due; his possessions and his rank were the savings of his race, the price of social services rendered by the long file of deserving dead, all that his ancestors, his father and himself had created or preserved of any stable value; each piece of gold that remained in the hereditary purse represented the balance of a lifetime, the enduring labor of someone belonging to his line, while among these gold pieces, he himself had provided his share. For, personal services counted, even among the upper nobil-

83. Rétif de la Bretonne, "Vie de mon Pêre," (paternal authority in a peasant family in Burgundy). The reader, on this point, may test the souvenirs of his grand-parents. With reference to the *bourgeoisie* I have cited the family of Beaumarchais. Concerning the nobles, see the admirable letter by Buffon June 22, 1787 (correspondence of Buffon, two vols., published by M. Nadaud de Buffon), prescribing to his son how he ought to act on account of his wife's behavior.

ity; and all the more among the lower class, in the Third-Estate, and among the people. Among the notables of every degree just described, most of them, in 1789, were certainly full-grown, many of them mature, a goodly number advanced in years, and some quite aged; consequently, in justification of his rank and emoluments, or of his gains and his fortune, each could allege fifteen, twenty, thirty, and forty years of labor and honorability in private or public situations, the grand-vicar of the diocese as well as the chief-clerk of the ministry, the intendant of the *généralité* as well as the president of the royal tribunal, the village curé, the noble officer, the office-holder, the lawyer, the *procureur*, the large manufacturer, the wholesale dealer, as well as the well-to-do farmer, and the well-known handicraftsman. Thus, not only were they an élite corps, the most valuable portion of the nation, the best timber of the forest, but again, the wood of each branch belonged to that trunk; it grew there, and was the product of its own vegetation; it sprung out of the trunk wholly through the unceasing and spontaneous effort of the native sap, through time-honored and recent labor, and, on this account, it merited respect. Through a double onslaught, at once against each human branch and against the entire French forest, the Jacobin wood-choppers seek to clear the ground. Their theory results in this precept, that not one of the noble trees of this forest, not one valuable trunk from the finest oak to the tenderest sapling, should be left standing.

VII

Not that the ravages which they make stop there! The principle extended far beyond that. The fundamental rule, according to Jacobin maxims, is that every public or private advantage which any citizen enjoys not enjoyed by another citizen, is illegitimate. On Ventose 19, year II., Henriot, general in command, having surrounded the Palais Royal and made a sweep of "suspects," renders an account of his expedition as follows:[84] "One hundred and thirty *muscadins* have been arrested. . . . These gentlemen are transferred

84. *Moniteur*, xix., 669.

to the Petits-Pêres. They are not *sans-culottes*, being *well-fed and plump*." Henriot was right, for, to live well is *incivique*. Whoever lays in stores of provisions is criminal, even if he has gone a good ways for them, even if he has not overpaid the butcher of his quarter, even if he has not diminished by an ounce of meat the ration of his neighbor; on this being discovered, he is obliged to disgorge and be punished. "A citizen[85] had a little pig brought to him from a place six leagues from Paris, and killed it at once. Three hours afterwards, the pig was seized by commissioners and distributed among the people, without the owner getting a bit of it"; moreover, the said owner "was imprisoned." He is a monopolist! To Jacobin people, to empty stomachs, there is no greater crime; this misdeed, to their imaginations, explains the arrest of Hébert, their favorite: "It is said at the Halle[86] that he has monopolised one of St. Anthony's friends[87] together with a pot of twenty-five pounds of Brittany butter," which is enough; they immediately and "unanimously consign Père Duchesne to the guillotine." Of all privileges, accordingly, that of having a supply of food is the most offensive; "it is now necessary for one who has two dishes to give one of them to him who has none";[88] every man who manages to eat more than another is a robber; for, in the first place, he robs the community, the sole legitimate owner of aliments, and next, he robs, and personally, all who have less to eat than he has.

The same rule applies to other things of which the possession is either agreeable or useful: in an equalising social system, that now established, every article of food possessed by one individual to the exclusion of others, is a dish abstracted from the common table and held by him to another's detriment. On the strength of this, the theorists who govern agree with the reigning tatterdemalions. Who-

---

85. Dauban, "Paris en 1794," p. 245. (Report by Bacon, Ventose 25, year II.)

86. *Ibid.* (Report by Perrière, Ventose 26.)

87. Ironical, slang for a hog. TR.

88. *Ibid.*, 245. (Report by Bacon, speech of an orator to the general assembly of the section "Contrat-Social," Ventose 25.)

ever has two good coats is an aristocrat, for there are many who have only one poor one.[89] Whoever has good shoes is an aristocrat, for many wear wooden ones, and others go barefoot. Whoever owns and rents lodgings is an aristocrat, for others, his tenants, instead of receiving money, pay it out. The tenant who furnishes his own rooms is an aristocrat, for many lodge in boarding-houses and others sleep in the open air. Whoever possesses capital is an aristocrat, even the smallest amount in money or in kind, a field, a roof over his head, half-a-dozen silver spoons given to him by his parents on his wedding-day, an old woollen stocking into which twenty or thirty crowns have been dropped one by one, all one's savings, whatever has been laid by or economised, a petty assortment of eatables or merchandise, one's crop for the year and stock of groceries, especially if, disliking to give them up and letting his dissatisfaction be seen, he, through revolutionary taxation and requisitions, through the *maximum* and the confiscation of the precious metals, is constrained to surrender his small savings gratis, or at half their value. Fundamentally, it is only those who have nothing of their own that are held to be patriots, those who live from day to

---

89. "Un Séjour en France." (Sep., 1792.) Letter of a Parisian: "It is not yet safe to walk the streets in decent clothes. I have been obliged to procure and put on pantaloons, jacket, colored cravate, and coarse linen, before attempting to go outdoors."—Beaulieu, "Essais," v., 281. "Our dandies let their moustaches grow long; while they rumpled their hair, dirtied their hands and donned nasty garments. Our philosophers and literary men wore big fur caps with long fox-tails dangling over their shoulders; some dragged great trailing sabres along the pavement—they were taken for Tartars. . . . In public assemblies, in the theatre boxes, nothing was seen in the front rows but monstrous red bonnets. All the *galériens* of all the convict prisons in Europe seem to have come and set the fashion in this superb city which had given it to all Europe."—"Un Séjour en France," p. 43. (Amiens, September, 1792.) "Ladies in the street who are well-dressed or wear colors that the people regard as aristocratic are commonly insulted. I, myself, have been almost knocked down for wearing a straw hat trimmed with green ribbons."—Nolhac, "Souvenirs de Trois Années de la Révolution at Lyons," p. 132. "It was announced that whoever had two coats was to fetch one of them to the Section, so as to clothe some good republican and ensure the reign of equality."

day,[90] "the wretched," the poor, vagabonds, and the famished; the humblest laborer, the least instructed, the most ill at his ease, is treated as criminal, as an enemy, solely because he is suspected of having some resources; in vain does he show his scarified or callous hands; he escapes neither spoliation, the prison, nor the guillotine. At Troyes, a poor shop-girl who had set up a small business on borrowed money, but who is ruined by a bankruptcy and completely so by the *maximum*, infirm, and consuming piecemeal the rest of her stock, is taxed five hundred livres.[91] In the villages of Alsace, an order is issued to arrest the five, six, or seven richest persons in the Commune, even if there are no rich; consequently, they seize the least poor, simply because they are so; for instance, at Heiligenberg, six "farmers" one of whom is a day-laborer, "or journeyman," "suspect," says the register of the jail, "because he is comfortably off."[92] On this account nowhere are there so many "suspects" as

90. Buchez et Roux, xxvi., 455. (Speech by Robespierre, in the Jacobin Club, May 10, 1793.) "The rich cherish hopes for an antirevolution; it is only the wretched, only the people who can save the country."—*Ibid.*, xxx. (Report by Robespierre to the Convention, December 25, 1793.) "Virtue is the appanage of the unfortunate and the people's patrimony."—Archives Nationales, AF., II., 72. (Letter of the municipality of Montauban, Vendémiaire 23, year IV.) Many workmen in the manufactories have been perverted "by excited demagogues and club orators who have always held out to them equality of fortunes and presented the Revolution as the prey of the class they called *sans-culottes*. . . . The law of the 'maximum,' at first tolerably well carried out, the humiliation of the rich, the confiscation of the immense possessions of the rich, seemed to be the realisation of these fine promises."

91. Archives Nationales, F[7], 4,421. Petition of Madeleine Patris.—Petition of Quetreut Cogniér, weaver, "*sans-culotte*, and one of the first members of the Troyes national guard." (Style and orthography of the most barbarous kind.)

92. *Ibid.*, AF., II. 135. (Extract from the deliberations of the Revolutionary Committee of the commune of Strasbourg, list of prisoners and reasons for arresting them.) At Oberschaeffelsheim, two farmers "because they are two of the richest private persons in the commune."—"Recueil de Pièces, etc.," i. 225. (Declaration by Welcher, revolutionary commissioner). "I, the undersigned, declare that, on the orders of citizen Clauer, commissioner of the canton, I have surrendered at Strasbourg seven of the richest in Obershaeffelsheim without knowing why." Four of the seven were guillotined.

among the people; the shop, the farm, and the work-room harbor more aristocrats than the rectory and the chateau. In effect, according to the Jacobins,[93] "nearly all farmers are aristocrats"; "the merchants are all essentially antirevolutionary,"[94] and especially all dealers in articles of prime necessity, wine-merchants, bakers and butchers; the latter especially are open "conspirators," enemies "of the interior," and "whose aristocracy is insupportable." Such, already, among the lower class of people, are the many delinquents who are punished.

But there are still more of them to punish, for, besides the crime of not being indigent, of possessing some property, of withholding articles necessary for existence, there is the crime of aristocracy, necessarily so called, namely, repugnance to, lack of zeal, or even indifference for the established régime, regret for the old one, relationship or intercourse with a condemned or imprisoned *emigré* of the upper class, services rendered to some outlaw, the resort to some priest; now, numbers of poor farmers, mechanics, domestics, and women servants, have committed this crime;[95] and in many provinces

93. Buchez et Roux, xxvi., 341. (Speech by Chasles in the Convention, May 2, 1793.)

94. *Moniteur,* xviii., 452. (Speech by Hébert in the Jacobin Club, Brumaire 26.)—Schmidt, "Tableaux de la Révolution Française," 19. (Reports of Dutard, June 11.—Archives Nationales. F7, 3,116⁷. (Report of the *Pourvoyeur,* Nivose 6, year II.) "The people complain (*se plain*) that there are still some conspirators in the interior, such as butchers and bakers, but particularly the former, who are (*son*) an intolerable aristocracy. They (*il*) will sell no more meat, etc. It is frightful to see what they (*il*) give the people."

95. "Recueil de Police," etc., i., 69 and 91. At Strasbourg a number of women of the lower class are imprisoned as "aristocrats and fanatics," with no other alleged motive. The following are their occupations: dressmaker, upholsteress, housewife, midwife, baker, wives of coffee-house keepers, tailors, potters, and chimney-sweeps.—*Ibid.,* ii., 216. "Ursule Rath, servant to an *emigré,* arrested for the purpose of knowing what her master had concealed. . . . Marie Faber, on suspicion of having served in a priest's house."—Archives Nationales, AF., II., 135. (List of the occupations of the suspected women detained in the cabinets of the National college.) Most of them are imprisoned for being either mothers, sisters, wives, or daughters of *emigrés* or exiled priests, and many are the wives of shopkeepers or mechanics. One, a professional nurse, is an "aris-

and in many of the large cities nearly the whole of the laboring population commits it and persists in it; such is the case, according to Jacobin reports, in Alsace, Franche-Comté, Provence, Vaucluse, Anjou, Poitou, Vendée, Brittany, Picardie and Flanders, and in Marseilles, Bordeaux, and Lyons. In Lyons alone, writes Collot d'Herbois, "there are sixty thousand persons who never will become republicans. They should be disbanded and prudently distributed over the surface of the Republic."[96] Finally, add to the persons of the lower class, prosecuted on public grounds, those who are prosecuted on private grounds. Among peasants in the same village, workmen of the same trade and shopkeepers in the same quarter, there is always envy, enmities, and spites; those who are Jacobins become local pachas and are able to gratify local jealousies with impunity, which they never fail to do.[97]

Hence, on the lists of the guillotined, the incarcerated and of *emigrés*, the men and women of inferior condition are in much

---

tocrat and fanatic." (Another list describes the men); a cooper as "aristocrat"; a tripe-seller as "very *incivique,* never having shown any attachment to the Revolution"; a mason has never shown "patriotism," a shoemaker is "aristocrat at all times, having accepted a porter's place under the tyrant"; four foresters "do not entertain patriotic sentiments," etc.—"Recueil de Pièces, etc.," ii., 220. *Citoyenne* Genet, aged 75, and her daughter, aged 44, are accused of having sent, May 22, 1792, thirty-six francs in silver to the former's son, an *emigré,* and were guillotined.—Cf. Sauzay, vols. iii., iv. and v. (appendices), lists of *emigrés* and prisoners in Doubs, where titles and professions, with motives for confining them, will be found.—At Paris, even (Archives Nationales, F[7], 3,116[7], report of Latour-Lamontagne, September 20, 1793), aversion to the government descends very low. "Three women (market-women) all agree on one point— the necessity of a new order of things. They complain of the authorities without exception. . . . If the King is not on their lips, it is much to be feared that he is already in their hearts. A woman in the Faubourg St. Antoine, said: If our husbands made the Revolution we shall know how to put it down if necessary."

96. See above ch. v., § 4.—Archives Nationales, F[7], 4,435, No. 10. (Letter of Collot d'Herbois to Couthon, Frimaire 11, year II.)

97. Archives des Affaires Étrangérès, vol. 331. (Letter of Bertrand, Nismes, Frimaire 3.) "We are sorry to see patriots here not very delicate in the way they cause arrests, in ascertaining who are criminal, and the precious class of mechanics is no exception."

greater number, far greater than their companions of the superior and middle classes all put together. Out of twelve thousand condemned to death whose rank and professions have been ascertained, seven thousand five hundred and forty-five[98] are peasants, cultivators, ploughmen, workmen of various sorts, innkeepers, wine-dealers, soldiers, and sailors, domestics, women, young girls, servants, and seamstresses. Out of one thousand nine hundred *emigrés* from Doubs, nearly one thousand one hundred belong to the lower class. Towards the month of April, 1794, all the prisons in France overflow with farmers;[99] in the Paris prisons alone, two months before Thermidor 9, there are two thousand of them.[100] Without mentioning the eleven western departments in which four or five hundred square leagues of territory are devastated and twenty towns and one thousand eight hundred villages destroyed,[101] where the avowed purpose of the Jacobin policy is a systematic and total destruction of the country, man and beast, buildings, crops, and even trees, there are cantons and even provinces where the entire rural and working population is arrested or put to flight. In the Pyrenees, the old Basque populations "torn from their natal soil, crowded into the churches with no means of subsistence but that of charity," in the middle of winter, so that sixteen hundred of those incarcerated die "mostly of cold and hunger";[102] at Bédouin, a town of two thousand souls, in which a tree of liberty is cut down by some unknown persons, four hundred and thirty-three houses are demolished or burned, sixteen persons guillotined and forty-seven shot, while the rest of the inhabitants are driven out, reduced to living like vaga-

98. Berryat Saint-Prix, "La Justice Révolutionnaire," 1st ed., p. 229.

99. "Un Séjour en France," p. 186. "I notice that most of the arrests now made are farmers." (In consequence of the requisitions for grain, and on account of the applications of the law of the maximum.)

100. "Bulletin du Tribunal Révolutionnaire," No. 431. (Testimony of Tontin, secretary of the court.) Twelve hundred of these poor creatures were set free after Thermidor 9.

101. *Moniteur,* session of June 29, 1797. (Report of Luminais.)—Danican, "Les Brigands Démasqués," p. 194.

102. Meillan, "Mémoires," p. 166.

bonds on the mountain, or in holes which they dig in the ground;[103] in Alsace, fifty thousand farmers who, in the winter of 1793, take refuge with their wives and children on the other side of the Rhine.[104] In short, the revolutionary operation is a complete prostration of people of all classes, the trunks as well as the saplings being felled, and often in such a way as to clear the ground entirely.

In this general prostration, however, the notables of the people, making all due allowances, suffer more than the common run; the Jacobin wood-chopper manifestly selects out and fells with the greatest fury and persistency, the veterans of labor and economy, the large cultivators who from father to son and for many generations have possessed the same farm, the master-mechanics whose shops are well stocked and who have good customers, all respectable, well-patronised retailers, who owe nothing; the village-syndics and trades-syndics, all those showing more deeply and visibly than the rest of their class, the five or six blazes which warrant the stroke of the axe. They are better off, better provided with desirable comforts and conveniences, which is of itself an offence against equality. Hav-

---

103. Berryat Saint-Prix, "La Justice Révolutionnaire," p. 419.—Archives Nationales, AF., II., 145. (Orders issued by Representative Maignet, Floréal 14, 15 and 17, year II.) "The criminal court will try and execute the principal criminals; the rest of the inhabitants will abandon their houses in twenty-four hours, and take their furniture along with them. The town will then be burnt. All rebuilding or tillage of the soil is forbidden. The inhabitants will be apportioned among neighboring communes; nobody is allowed to leave the commune assigned to him under penalty of being treated as an *emigré*. All must appear once in a decade at the municipality under penalty of being declared 'suspect' and imprisoned."

104. "Recueil de Pieces, etc.," i., 52. (Carret de Beudot and La Coste, Pluviose 6, year II.) "Whereas, it being impossible to find jurors within an extent of one hundred leagues, two-thirds of the inhabitants having emigrated."— *Moniteur*, Aug. 28 and 29, 1797. (Report by Harmand de la Meuse.)—*Ibid.*, xix., 714. (Session of Ventose 26, year II., speech by Baudot.) "Forty thousand persons of all ages and both sexes in the districts alone of Hagnenau and Wissembourg, fled from the French territory on the lines being retaken. The names are in our hands, their furniture in the depot at Saverne and their property is made over to the Republic."

ing accumulated a small hoard, a few pieces of plate, sometimes a few crowns,[105] a store of linen and clothes, a stock of provisions or goods, they do not willingly submit to being plundered, which is the offence of egoism. Being egoists, it is presumed that they are hostile to the system of fraternity, at least indifferent to it, as well as lukewarm toward the Republic, that is to say, Moderates, which is the worst offence of all.[106] Being the foremost of their class, they are haughty like the nobles or the bourgeois and regard themselves as superior to a poor man, to a vagabond, to a genuine *sans-culotte*, the fourth and most inexcusable of all offences. Moreover, from the fact of their superior condition, they have contracted familiarities and formed connections with the proscribed class; the farmer, the intendant, the overseer is often attached to his noble proprietor or patron;[107] many of the farmers, shopkeepers, and mechanics belonging to old families are considered as affiliated with the bourgeoisie or the clergy,[108] through a son or brother who has risen a degree in

105. Albert Babeau, "Histoire de Troyes," ii., 160. "A gardener had carefully accumulated eight thousand two hundred and twenty-three livres in gold, the fruit of his savings; threatened with imprisonment, he was obliged to give them up."

106. Archives Nationales, AF., II., 116. (Orders of Representative Paganel, Toulouse, Brumaire 12, year II.) "The day has arrived when apathy is an insult to patriotism, and indifference a crime. We no longer reply to the objections of avarice; we will force the rich to fulfil the duties of fraternity which they have abjured."—*Ibid*. (Extract from the minutes of the meetings of the Central Committee of Montauban, April 11, 1793, with the approval of the representative, Jean Bon St. André.) "The moment has at length come when moderatism, royalism and pusillanimity, and all other traitorous or useless sects to the country, should disappear from the soil of Liberty." All opinions opposed to those of *sans-culotterie* are blamable and merit punishment.

107. Archives Nationales, F⁷, 2,471. (Minutes of the Revolutionary Committee of the Tuileries section, meeting of September 17, 1793.) List of seventy-four persons put under arrest and among them, M. de Noailles, with the following note opposite his name: "The entire family to be arrested, including their heir Guy, and Hervet, their old intendant, rue St. Honoré."

108. Archives des Affaires Étrangéres, vol. 322. (Letters of Ladonay, Chalons, September 17 and 20, 1792.) "At Meaux, the brigands have cut the throats of fifteen prisoners, seven of whom are priests *whose relations belong to the town*

trade, or by some industrial pursuit, or who, having completed his studies, has become a *curé* or lawyer, or else through some daughter, or well-married sister, or through one who has become a nun: now, this relation, ally, friend, or comrade of a "suspect" is himself a "suspect," the last antirevolutionary and decisive barrier. Sober and well-behaved persons, having prospered or maintained themselves under the ancient régime, must naturally cherish respect for former institutions; they must involuntarily retain a deep feeling of veneration for the King, and especially for religion; they are devout Catholics, and therefore are chagrined to see the churches shut up, worship prohibited, and ecclesiastics persecuted, and would again be glad to go to Mass, honor Easter, and have an orthodox *curé* who could administer to them available sacraments, a baptism, an absolution, a marriage-rite, and veritable extreme unction.[109] Under all these headings, they have made personal enemies of the rascals who hold office; on all these grounds, they are struck down; what was once meritorious with them is now disgraceful. Thus, the principal swath consists of the élite of the people, selected from amongst the people itself; it is against the "subordinate aristocracy," those most capable of doing and conducting manual labor, the most creditable workmen, through their activity, frugality, and good habits, that the Revolution, in its rigor against the inferior class, rages with the greatest fury.

VIII

For the same reason, as far as the notables, properly so-called, are concerned, it bears down still more heavily, not merely on the nobles because of ancient privileges, not merely on ecclesiastics on the score of being insubordinate Catholics, but on nobles, ecclesiastics, and bourgeois in their capacity of notables, that is to say, born and bred

---

or *its environs*. Hence an immense number of malcontents."—Sauzay, i., 97. "The country *curés* are generally recruited from among the rural bourgeoisie and the most respected farmers' families."

109. Sauzay, *passim*, especially vols. 3, 4, 5, and 6.

above others, and respected by the masses on account of their superior condition. In the eyes of the genuine Jacobin, the notables of the third class are no less criminal than the members of the two superior classes. "The bourgeois,[110] the merchants, the large proprietors," writes a popular club in the South, "all have the pretension of the old set (*des ci-dévants*)." And the club complains of "the law not providing means for opening the eyes of the people with respect to these new tyrants." It is horrible! The stand they take is an offence against equality and they are proud of it! And what is worse, this stand attracts public consideration! Consequently, "the club requests that the revolutionary Tribunal be empowered to consign this *proud* class to temporary confinement," and then "the people would see the crime it had committed and recover from the sort of esteem in which they had held it." Incorrigible and contemptuous heretics against the new creed, they are only too lucky to be treated somewhat like infidel Jews in the middle-ages. Accordingly, if they are tolerated, it is on the condition that they let themselves be pillaged at discretion, covered with opprobrium, and subdued through fear. At one time, with insulting irony, they are called upon to prove their dubious civism by forced donations. "Whereas,"[111] says Represen-

---

110. Archives Nationales, F[7], 4,437. Address of the popular club of Clavisson (Gard.), Messidor 7, year II.—Rodolphe Reuss, "Séligman Alexandre, sur les Tribulations d'un Israelite Strasbourgeois Pendant la Terreur," p. 37. Order issued by General Dieche to Coppin, in command of the "Séminaire" prison. "Strive with the utmost zeal to suppress the cackle of aristocrats." Such is the sum of the instructions to jail keepers.

111. Archives Nationales, AF., II., 88. (Edict issued by Representative Milhaud, Narbonne, Ventose 9, year II.) Article ii. "The patriotic donation will be doubled if, in three days, all boats are not unloaded and all carts loaded as fast as they arrive." Article iv. "The municipality is charged, on personal responsibility, to proportion the allotment on the richest citizens of Narbonne." Article vii. "If this order is not executed within twenty-four hours, the municipality will designate to the commandant of the post the rich egoists who may have refused to furnish their contingent, etc." Article viii. "The commandant is specially charged to report (the arrests of the refractory rich) to the representative of the people within twenty-four hours, he being *responsible on his head* for the punctual execution of the present order."—*Ibid.*, AF., II., 135. (Orders

tative Milhaud, "all the citizens and *citoyennes* of Narbonne being in requisition for the discharge and transport of forage; whereas, this morning, the Representative, in person, having inspected the performance of this duty," and having observed on the canal "none but *sans-culottes* and a few young citizens; whereas, not finding at their posts any *muscadin* and no *muscadine;* whereas, the persons, whose hands are no doubt too delicate, even temporarily, for the glorious work of robust *sans-culottes,* have, on the other hand, greater resources in their fortune, and, *desiring to afford to the rich of Narbonne the precious advantage of being equally useful to the Republic,*" hereby orders that "the richest citizens of Narbonne pay within twenty-four hours" a patriotic donation of one hundred thousand livres, one-half to be assigned to the military hospitals, and the other half, on the designation thereof by a "Committee of Charity, composed of three reliable revolutionary *sans-culottes,*" to be distributed among the poor of the Commune. Should any "rich egoist refuse to contribute his contingent he is to be immediately transferred to the jail at Perpignan." Not to labor with one's own hands, to be disqualified for work demanding physical strength, is of itself a democratic stain, and the man who is sullied by this draws down on himself, not alone an augmentation of pecuniary taxation, but frequently an augmentation of personal compulsory labor. At Villeneuve, Aveyron, and throughout the department of Cantal,[112] Representative Taillefer and his delegate Deltheil, instruct the revolutionary committees to "place under military requisition and conscription all *muscadins* above the first class," that is to say, all between twenty-five and forty years of age who are not reached by the law. "By *muscadins* is meant all citizens of that age not married, and exercising no useful profession," in other words, those who live on their income. And, that none of

---

of Saint-Just and Lebas, Strasbourg, Brumaire 10, year II.) The following is equally ironical; the rich of Strasbourg are represented as "soliciting a loan on opulent persons and severe measures" against refractory egoists.

112. Archives Nationales, AF., II., 92. Orders of Representative Taillefer, Villefranche, Aveyron, Brumaire 3, year II., and of his delegate, Deltheil, Brumaire 11, year II.

the middle or upper class may escape, the edict subjects to special rigor, supplementary taxes, and arbitrary arrest, not alone property-holders and fund-holders, but again all persons designated under the following heads—aristocrats, Feuillants, moderates, Girondists, federalists, *muscadins,* the superstitious, fanatics, the abettors of royalism, of superstition and of federation, monopolists, jobbers, egoists, "suspects" of incivism, and, generally, all who are indifferent to the Revolution, of which local committees are to draw up the lists.

Occasionally, in a town, some steps taken collectively, either a vote or petition, furnish a ready-made list;[113] it suffices to read this to know who are notables, the most upright people of the place; henceforth, under the pretext of political repression, the levellers may give free play to their social rancor. At Montargis, nine days after the attempt of June 20, 1792,[114] two hundred and twenty-eight notables sign an address in testimony of their respectful sympathy for the King; a year and nine months later, in consequence of a retroactive stroke, all are hit, and, with the more satisfaction, inasmuch as in their persons the most respected in the town fall beneath the blow, all whom flight and banishment had left there belonging to the noble, ecclesiastic, bourgeois, or popular aristocracy. Already, "on the purification of the constituted authorities of Montargis, the representative had withdrawn every signer from places of public

113. This is the case in Lyons, Bordeaux, Marseilles, and at Paris, as we see in the signatures of the petition of the eight thousand, or that of the twenty thousand, and for members of the Feuillants clubs, etc.

114. Archives Nationales, AF., II., 116. (Minutes of the public session of Ventose 20, year II., held at Montargis, in the Temple of Reason, by Benon, "national agent of the commune and special agent of the people's representative." Previous and subsequent orders, by Representative Lefert.) Eighty-six persons signed, subject to public penance, among them twenty-four wives or widows, which, with the four names sent to the Paris tribunal and the thirty-two imprisoned, makes one hundred and twenty-two. It is probable that the one hundred and six who are wanting to complete the list of two hundred and twenty-eight had emigrated, or been banished in the interval as unsworn priests.—*Ibid.,* D.S., I., 10. (Orders by Delacroix, Bouchet, and Legendre, Conches, Frimaire 8 and 9, year II.) The incarceration of the municipal officers of Conches for an analogous petition and other marks of Feuillantism.

trust and kept them out of all offices." But this is not sufficient; the punishment must be more exemplary. Four of them, the ex-mayor, an ex-collector, a district administrator and a notable are sent to the revolutionary Tribunal in Paris, to be guillotined in deference to principles. Thirty-two former officers—*chevaliers* of St. Louis, *mousquetaires,* nobles, priests, an ex-*procureur-royal,* an ex-treasurer of France, a former administrator of the department, and two ladies, one of them designated as "calling herself a former marchioness"— are confined, until peace is secured, in the jail at Montargis. Other former municipal officers and officers in the National Guard—men of the law, notaries and advocates, physicians, surgeons, former collectors, police commissioners, postmasters, merchants and manufacturers, men and women, married or widows, and widowers—are to make public apology and be summoned to the Temple of Reason to undergo there the humiliation of a public penance on the 20th of Ventose, at three o'clock in the afternoon. They all go, for the summons says, "whoever does not present himself on the day and hour named will be arrested and confined until peace is declared." On reaching the church, purified by Jacobin adoration, "in the presence of the constituted authorities of the popular club and of the citizens convoked in general assembly," they mount one by one into "a tribune raised three steps above the floor," in such a way as to be in full sight. One by one the national agent, or the mayor, reprimands them in the following language: "You have been base enough to sign a fawning address to Louis XVI., the most odious and the vilest of tyrants, an ogre of the human species guilty of every sort of crime and debauchery. You are hereby censured by the people. You are moreover warned that on committing the first act of *incivisme,* or manifesting any antirevolutionary conduct, the surveillance of the constituted authorities will be extended to you in the most energetic manner; the tribunals will show you less leniency and the guillotine will insure prompt and imposing justice." Each, called by name, receives in turn the threatened admonition, and, descending from the tribune amidst hues and cries, all sign the *procès-verbal.* But compunction is often wanting, and some of them seem to be not sufficiently penitent. Consequently, at the close of the ceremony, the National Agent calls the attention of the assembly to "the impudence manifested by certain aristocrats, so degraded that even national justice fails to make them blush"; and the Revolutionary Committee, "considering the indifference and derisive conduct of four women and three men, just manifested in this assembly; considering the necessity of punishing an inveterate aristocracy which seems to make sport of corrective acts that bear only (*sic*) on morals, in a most exemplary manner," decides that the seven delinquents "shall be put under arrest, and confined in the jail of Ste. Marie." The three who have shown indifference, are to be confined three months; the four who have shown derision, are to be confined until peace is restored. Besides this, the decree of the National Agent and the minutes of the meeting are to be printed and six thousand impressions struck off at the expense of the signers, "the richest and most 'suspect' "—a former treasurer of France, a notary, a grocer, the wife of the former commandant of the gendarmerie, a widow and another woman—all, says the agent, "of very solid wealth and aristocracy." "Bravo!" shouts the assembly, at this witticism; applause is given and it sings "the national hymn." It is nine o'clock in the evening. This public penitence lasts six hours and the Jacobins of Montargis retire, proud of their work; having punished as a public affront, an old and legal manifestation of respect for the public magistrate; having sent either to the scaffold or to prison, and fined or disgraced the small local élite; having degraded to the level of prostitutes and felons under surveillance, reputable women and honorable men who are, by law, most esteemed under a normal system of government and who, under the revolutionary system are, by law, the least so.[115]

---

115. The real sentiments and purposes of the Jacobins are well shown at Strasbourg. ("Recueil de Pièces, etc.," i., 77. Public meeting of the municipal body, and speech by Bierlyn, Prairial 25, year II.) "How can the insipid arrogance of these (Strasbourg) people be represented to you, their senseless attachment to the patrician families in their midst, the absurd *feuillantism* of some and the vile sycophancy of others? How is it, they say, that moneyless inter-

IX

Two advantages, fortune and education, each involving the other, cause a man to be ranked in the upper class; hence, one or the other, whether each by itself or both together, mark a man out for spoliation, imprisonment, and death. In vain may he have demonstrated his Jacobinism, and Jacobinism of the ultra sort. Hérault-Séchelles, who voted for murdering the King, who belongs to the Committee of Public Safety, who, in the Upper-Rhine, has just carried out the worst revolutionary ordinances,[116] but who has the misfortune to be rich and a man of the world, is led to the scaffold, and those devoted to the guillotine readily explain his condemnation: he is no patriot, how could he be, enjoying an income of two hundred thousand livres, and, moreover, is he not a general-advocate?[117] One of these offences is sufficient. Alone and by itself, "opulence," writes Saint-Just, "is a disgrace," and, according to him, a man is opulent "who supports fewer children than he has thousands of livres income"; in

lopers, scarcely ever heard of before, dare assume to have credit in a town of sensible inhabitants and honest families, from father to son, accustomed to governing and renowned for centuries?"—*Ibid.*, 113. (Speech of the mayor Mouet, Floréal 21, year II.) "Moral purification (in Strasbourg) has become less difficult through the reduction of fortunes and the salutary terror excited among those covetous men. . . . Civilization has encountered mighty obstacles in this great number of well-to-do families who have nourished souvenirs of, and who regret the privileges enjoyed by, these families under the Emperors; they have formed a caste apart from the State; carefully preserving the gothic pictures of their ancestors they were united only amongst themselves. They are excluded from all public functions. Honest artisans, now taken from all pursuits, impel the revolutionary cart with a vigorous hand."

116. Archives des Affairs Étrangérès, vol. 1411. (Instructions for the civil commissioners by Hérault, representative of the people, Colmar, Frimaire 2, year II.) He enumerates the diverse categories of persons who were to be arrested, which categories are so large and numerous as to include nine out of ten of the inhabitants.

117. Dauban, "Paris en 1794," p. 264. (Report of Pourveyeur, Ventose 29.) "They remark (*sic*) that one is not (*sic*) a patriot with twenty-thousand livres (*sic*) income, and especially a former advocate-general."

effect, among the persons confined as "rich and egoists" we find, according to the very declaration of the Revolutionary Committee, persons with incomes of only four thousand, three thousand seven hundred, one thousand five hundred, and even five hundred livres.[118] Moreover, a fortune or a competence, inspires its possessor with antirevolutionary sentiments; consequently, he is for the moment an obstruction; "You are rich," says Cambon, making use of a personification, "you cherish an opinion, which compels us to be on the defensive; pay then, so as to indemnify us and be thankful for our indulgence which, precautionary and until peace is declared, keeps you under bolt and bar."[119] "Rich, antirevolutionary, and vicious," according to Robespierre,[120] "these three traits depend on each other, and, therefore, the possession of the superfluous is an infallible sign of aristocracy, a visible mark of *incivisme*" and, as Fouché says, "a stamp of reprobation." "The superfluous is an evident and unwarrantable violation of the people's rights; every man who has more than his wants call for, cannot use, and therefore he must only abuse."[121] Whoever does not make over to the masses the excess of what is strictly necessary . . . places himself in the rank of 'suspects.' Rich egoists, you are the cause of our misfortunes!"[122] "You dared to smile contemptuously on the appellation of *sans-culottes;*[123] you have enjoyed much more than your brethren along-

118. De Martel, "Fouché," p. 226, 228. For instance, at Nevers, a man of sixty-two years of age, is confined "as rich, egoist, fanatic, doing nothing for the Revolution, a proprietor, and having five hundred livres revenue."

119. Buchez et Roux, xxvi., 177. (Speech by Cambon, April 27, 1793.)

120. "Who are our enemies? The vicious and the rich."—"All the rich are vicious, in opposition to the Revolution." (Notes made by Robespierre in June and July, 1793, and speech by him in the Jacobin Club, May 10, 1793.)

121. Guillon, ii., 355. (Instructions furnished by Collot d'Herbois and Fouché, Brumaire 26, year II.)

122. De Martel, 117, 181. (Orders of Fouché, Nevers, August 25 and October 8, 1793.)

123. Guillon.—Archives des Affaires Étrangérès, F. 1411. Reports by observers at Paris, Aug. 12 and 13, 1793. "The rich man is the sworn enemy of the Revolution."

side of you dying with hunger; you are not fit to associate with them, and since you have disdained to have them eat at your table, they cast you out eternally from their bosom and condemn you, in turn, to wear the shackles prepared for them by your indifference or your manoeuvres." In other words, whoever has a good roof over his head, or wears good clothes, man or woman, idler or industrious, noble or commoner, is available for the prison or the guillotine, or, at the very least, he is a taxable and workable serf at pleasure; his capital and accumulations, if not spontaneously and immediately handed over, form a criminal basis and proof of conviction. The orders of arrest are generally issued against him on account of his wealth; in order to drain a town of these offenders one by one, all are penned together according to their resources; at Strasbourg,[124] one hundred and ninety-three persons are taxed, each from six thousand to three hundred thousand livres, in all nine million livres, payable within twenty-four hours, by the leading men of each profession or trade, bankers, brokers, merchants, manufacturers, professors, pastors, lawyers, physicians, surgeons, publishers, printers, upholsterers, glass-dealers, rope-makers, master-masons, coffeehouse and tavern keepers. And let there be no delay in responding to these orders within the prescribed time! Otherwise the delinquents will be placed in the stocks, on the scaffold, face to face with the guillotine. "One of the best citizens in the Commune, who had steadily manifested his attachment to the Revolution, being unable to realise a sum of two hundred and fifty thousand livres in one day,

124. Archives Nationales, AF., II., 135. (Orders of Saint-Just and Lebas, Strasbourg, Brumaire 10, year II., with the list of names of one hundred and ninety-three persons taxed, together with their respective amounts of taxation.)—Among others, "a widow Franck, banker, two hundred thousand livres."—*Ibid.*, AF., II., 49. (Documents relating to the revolutionary tax at Belfort.) "Vieillard, Moderate and egoist, ten thousand francs; Keller, rich egoist, seven thousand; as aristocrats, of whom the elder and younger brother are imprisoned, Barthélémy the younger ten thousand, Barthélémy senior, three thousand five hundred, Barthélémy junior seven thousand, *citoyenne* Barthélémy, mother, seven thousand, etc."

was fastened in the pillory."[125] Sometimes the orders affected an entire class, not alone nobles or priests, but all the members of any bourgeois profession or even of any handicraft. At Strasbourg, a little later, "considering that the thirst for gold has always controlled the brewers of the Commune," they are condemned to two hundred and fifty thousand livres fine, to be paid in three days under penalty of being declared rebels, with the confiscation of their possessions"; then, upon another similar consideration, the bakers and flour dealers are taxed three hundred thousand livres.[126] In addition to this, writes Representative Milhaud, at Guyardin,[127] "We have ordered the arrest of all bankers, stock-brokers and notaries. . . . All their wealth is confiscated; we estimate the sums under seal at two or three millions in coin, and fifteen or sixteen millions in assignats." There is the same haul of the net at Paris. By order of Rhuillier, *procureur* of the department, "seals are placed in the offices of all the bankers, stock-brokers, silversmiths, etc.," and they themselves are shut up in the Madelonettes; a few days after, that they may pay their drafts, they are let out as a favor, but on condition that they remain under arrest in their homes, at their own expense, under guard of two good *sans-culottes*.[128] In like manner, at Nantes,[129] Lyons, Marseilles, and Bordeaux, the prisons are filled and the guil-

125. "Recueil de Pièces, etc.," i., 22. (Letter of the Strasbourg authorities.) De Martel, p. 288. (Letter of the authorities of Allier.) "Citizens Sainay, Balome, Heulard, and Lavaleisse were exposed on the scaffold in the most rigorous season for six hours (at Moulins) with this inscription—"bad citizen who has given nothing to the charity-box."

126. "Recueil de Pièces, etc.," i., 16.

127. *Ibid.*, i., 159. (Orders of Brumaire 15, year II.)

128. Archives Nationales, F⁷, 2,475. (Minutes of the Revolutionary Committee of the Piques section.) September 9, 1793, at 3 o'clock in the morning, the committee declares that, for its part, "it has arrested twenty-one persons of the category below stated." October 8, it places two *sans-culottes* as guards in the houses of all those named below, in the quarter, even those who could not be arrested on account of absence. "It is time to take steps to make sure of all whose indifference (*sic*) and moderatism is ruining the country."

129. Berryat Saint-Prix, pp. 36, 38. Carrier declares *suspect* "merchants and the rich."

lotine works according to the categories. At one time they are "all of the Grand Théatre," or the principal merchants, "to the number of more than two hundred," are incarcerated at Bordeaux in one night.[130] At another time, Paris provides a haul of farmer-generals or parliamentarians. Carts leave Toulouse conveying its parliamentarians to Paris to undergo capital punishment. At Aix, writes an agent,[131] "the guillotine is going to work on former lawyers; a few hundred heads legally taken off will do the greatest good." And, as new crimes require new terms to designate them, they add to "*incivisme*" and "*moderantisme*," the term "*negociantisme*," all of which are easily stated and widespread crimes. "The rich and the merchants," writes an observer,[132] "are here, as elsewhere, born enemies of equality and amateurs of hideous federalism, the only aristocracy that remains to be crushed out." Barras, with still greater precision, declares in the tribune that, "commerce is usurious, monarchical, and antirevolutionary."[133] Considered in itself, it may be defined as an appeal to bad instincts; it seems a corrupting, *incivique*, antifraternal institution, many Jacobins having proposed either to interdict it to private persons and attribute it wholly to the State, or suppress it along with the arts and manufactures which nourish it, in order that only a population of agriculturists and soldiers may be left in France.[134]

130. *Moniteur*, xviii., 641. (Letter of the representatives imprisoned at Bordeaux, Frimaire 10, year II.)

131. Archives des Affaires Étrangéres, vol. 329. (Letter of Brutus, October 3, 1793.)

132. *Ibid.*, vol. 329. (Letter of Charles Duvivier, Lille, Vendémiaire 15, year II.)

133. Speech by Barère, Ventose 17, year II.

134. Archives des Affaires Étrangéres, vol. 331. Letter by Darbault, political agent, Tarbes, Frimaire 11, year II. (Project for doing away with middle men in trade, brokers, and bankers.) "The profession of a banker is abolished. All holders of public funds are forbidden to sell them under a year and one day after the date of their purchase. No one must be at the same time wholesale and retail dealer, etc." Projects of this sort are numerous. As to the establishment of a purely agricultural and military Republic, see the papers of Saint-Just, and the correspondence of the Lyons Terrorists. According to them the new France

The second advantage and the second crime of the notables is superiority of education. "In all respectable assemblages," writes a Dutch traveler in 1795,[135] "you may be sure that one-half of those present have been in prison." Add the absent, the guillotined, the exiled, *emigrés*, the transported, and note this, that, in the other favored half, those who did not quaff the prison cup had had a foretaste of it for, each expected daily to receive his warrant of arrest; "the worst thing under Robespierre, as several old gentlemen have told me, was that one never knew in the morning whether one would sleep in one's own bed at night." There was not a well-bred man who did not live in dread of this; examine the lists of "suspects," of the arrested, of exiles, of those executed, in any town, district or department,[136] and you will see immediately, through their quality and occupations, first, that three-quarters of the cultivated are inscribed on it, and next, that intellectual culture in itself is "suspect." "They were equally criminal,"[137] write the Strasbourg administrators, "whether rich or cultivated. . . . The (Jacobin) municipality declared the University federalist; it proscribed public instruction and, consequently, the professors, regents, and heads of schools, with all instructors, public as well as private, even those provided with

----

needs no silk-weavers. The definite formulas of the system are always found among the Babeuvists. "Let the arts perish, if it must be so, provided real Equality remains." (Sylvain Maréchal, "Maniféste des Egaux.")

135. "Revue Historique," November, 1878. (Letter of M. Falk, Paris, Oct. 19, 1795.)

136. "Etude sur l'histoire de Grenoble Pendant la Terreur," by Paul Thibault. (List of notorious "suspects" and of ordinary "suspects" for each district in the Isère, April and May, 1793.)—Cf. the various lists of Doubs in Sauzay, and of Troyes, in Albert Babeau.

137. "Recueil de Pièces, etc.," i., 19, and the second letter of Frederic Burger, Thermidor 25.—Archives Nationales, AF., II., III. (Order of Representatives Merlincourt and Amar, Grenoble, April 27, 1793.) "The persons charged with the actual government of and instruction in the public establishments known in this town under the titles of, 1st, Orphelines; 2d, Présentins; 3d, Capuchins; 4th, Le Propagation; 5th, Hospice for female servants . . . are put under arrest and are forbidden to take any part whatever in the functions relating to teaching, education, or instruction."

certificates of *civisme*, were arrested; . . . every Protestant minister and teacher in the Lower-Rhine department was incarcerated, with a threat of being transferred to the citadel at Besançon." Fourcroy, in the Jacobin Club at Paris, excusing himself for being a savant, for giving lectures on chemistry, for not devoting his time to the rantings of the Convention and of the clubs, is obliged to declare that he is poor, that he lives by his work, that he supports "his father, a *sans-culotte*, and his *sans-culotte* sisters"; although a good republican, he barely escapes, and the same with others like him. "All educated men were persecuted," he states a month after Thermidor 9;[138] "to have acquaintances, to be literary, sufficed for arrest, as an aristocrat. . . . Robespierre . . . with devilish ingenuity, abused, calumniated and overwhelmed with gall and bitterness all who were devoted to serious studies, all who professed extensive knowledge; . . . he felt that cultivated men would never bend the knee to him. . . . Instruction was paralysed; they wanted to burn the libraries. . . . Must I tell you that at the very door of your assembly errors in orthography are seen? Nobody learns how to read or write." At Nantes, Carrier boasts of having "dispersed the literary chambers," while in his enumeration of the evil-minded he adds "to the rich and merchants," "all *gens d'esprit*."[139] Sometimes on the turnkey's register we read that such a one was confined "for being clever and able to do mischief," another for saying "good-day, gentlemen, to the municipal councillors."[140] Politeness, like other evidences of a good education, becomes a stigma; good-breeding seems not only a remnant of the ancient régime, but a revolt against new institutions; now, as the governing principle of these is, theoretically, abstract equality and, practically, the ascendency of the low class, there is an uprising against the established order of things when this consists in repudiating coarse companions, familiar oaths, and the indecent ex-

138. *Moniteur*, xxi., 645. (Session of the Convention, Fructidor 14, year II.)
139. *Moniteur*, xviii., 51. (Letter by Carrier, Brumaire 17, year II.)—Berryat Saint-Prix, pp. 36 and 38.
140. *Ibid.*, 140. (The imprisoned at Brest.)

pressions of the common workman and the soldier. In sum, Jacobinism, through its doctrines and deeds, its dungeons and executioners, proclaims to the nation over which it holds the rod:[141] "Be rude, that you may become republican, return to barbarism that you may show the superiority of your genius; abandon the customs of civilised people that you may adopt those of galley slaves; mar your language with a view to improve it; use that of the populace under penalty of death. Spanish mendicants treat each other in a dignified way; they show respect for humanity although in tatters. We, on the contrary, order you to assume our rags, our patois, our terms of intimacy. Don the *carmagnole* and tremble; become rustics and dolts, and prove your civism by the absence of all education." Education,[142] amiable qualities, gentle ways, a mild physiognomy, bodily graces, culture (literary), all natural endowments are henceforth "the inevitable causes of proscription." One is self-condemned if one has not converted oneself into a *sans-culotte* and proletaire, in accordance with affected modes, air, language, and dress. Hence, "through a hypocritical contest hitherto unknown men who were not vicious deemed it necessary to appear so." And worse still, "one was even afraid to be oneself; one changed one's name, one went in disguise, wearing a vulgar and tasteless attire; everybody shrunk from being what he was." For, according to the Jacobin programme, all Frenchmen must be recast in one uniform mould; they must be taken when small; all must be subject to the same enforced education, that of a mechanic, rustic, and soldier's boy. Be warned, ye adults, by the guillotine, reform yourselves beforehand according to the prescribed pattern! No more costly, elegant or delicate crystal or gold vases! All are shattered or are still being shattered. Henceforth, only common ware is to be tolerated or ordered to be made, all alike in substance, shape, and color, manufactured by thousands at wholesale

141. Mallet-Dupan, "Correspondance Politique," introduction, p. viii. (Hamburg, 1796.)

142. Portalis, "De la Révision des Jugements," 1795. (Saint-Beuve, "Causeries du Lundi," v., 452.)

and in public factories, for the common and plain uses of rural and military life; all original and superior forms are to be rejected. "The masters of the day," writes Daunou,[143] "deliberately aimed their sword thrusts at superior talent, at energetic characters; they mowed down as well as they could in so short a time," the flower and hope of the nation. In this respect they were consistent; equality-socialism allows none but automatic citizens, mere tools in the hands of the State, all alike, of a rudimentary fashion and easily managed, without personal conscience, spontaneity, curiosity, or integrity; whoever has cultivated himself, whoever has thought for himself and exercised his own will and judgment rises above the level and shakes off the yoke; to obtain consideration, to be intelligent and honorable, to belong to the élite, is to be antirevolutionary. In the popular club of Bourg-en-Bresse, Representative Javogues declared that "the Republic could be established only on the corpse of the last of the honest men."[144]

X

On one side, the élite of France, deprived of common rights, in exile, in prison, under pikes, and on the scaffold, almost every person of rank, fortune, family, and merit, those eminent for intelligence, culture, talent, and virtue; on the other side, those above all rights, possessing every office and omnipotent in the irresponsible dictatorship, in the despotic proconsulships, in the sovereignty of justice, a horde of the outcasts of all classes, the parvenus of fanaticism,

143. Granier du Cassagnac, "Histoire du Directoire," i., 107. (Trial of Baboeuf, extracts from Buonarotti, programme des "Egaux.") All literature in favor of Revelation must be prohibited: children are to be brought up in common; the child will no longer bear his father's name; no Frenchman shall leave France; towns shall be demolished, chateaux torn down and books proscribed; all Frenchmen shall wear one special costume; armies shall be commanded by civil magistrates; the dead shall be prosecuted and obtain burial only according to the favorable decision of the court; no written document shall be published without the consent of the government, etc."—Cf. "Les Méditations de Saint-Just."

144. Guillon, ii., 174.

charlatanism, imbecility, and crime; often, through the coupling together of these personages, one sees the contrast between the governed and the governors in such strong relief that one almost regards
it as calculated and arranged beforehand; the colors and brush of
the painter, rather than words, are necessary to represent it. In the
western section of Paris, in the prisons of the rue de Sèvres[145] the
prisoners consist of the most distinguished personages of the Quar-
tier St. Germain, prelates, officers, grand-seigniors, and noble ladies—Monseigneur de Clermont-Tonnerre, Monseigneur de Crussol
d'Amboise, Monseigneur de Hersaint, Monseigneur de St. Simon,
bishop of Agde, the Comtesse de Narbonne-Pelet, the Duchesse de
Choiseul, the Princesse de Chimay, the Comtesse de Raymond-
Narbonne and her daughter, two years of age, in short, the flower
of that refined society which Europe admired and imitated and
which, in its exquisite perfection, equalled or surpassed all that
Greece, Rome, and Italy had produced in brilliancy, polish, and
amiability. Contrast with these the arbiters of their lives and deaths,
the potentates of the same quarter who issue the warrants of arrest
against them, who pen them in to speculate on them, and who revel
at their expense and before their eyes: these consist of the members
of the revolutionary committee of the Croix-Rouge, the eighteen
convicted rogues and debauchees previously described,[146] ex-cab-
drivers, porters, cobblers, street-messengers, stevedores, bankrupts,
counterfeiters, former or future jail-birds, all the police or hospital
riff-raff. At the other end of Paris, in the east, in the tower of the
Temple, separated from his sister and torn from his mother, still
lives the Dauphin: no one in France merits any pity or respect. For,
if there is a France, it is owing to the thirty-five military chiefs and
crowned kings of which he is the last direct scion; without their
thousand years of hereditary rule and preserving policy the intruders
into the Tuileries who have just profaned their tombs at St. Denis

145. "Mémoires sur les Prisons," i., 211, ii., 187.—Beaulieu, "Essais," v.,
320. "The prisons became the rendezvous of polite society."
146. "The Revolution," vol. 3, ch. 6, *ante.*

and thrown their bones into a common ditch,[147] would not be Frenchmen. At this moment, were suffrages free, the immense majority of the people, nineteen Frenchmen out of twenty, would recognise this innocent and precious child for their King, the heir of the race to which they owed their nationality and patrimony, a child of eight years, of rare precociousness, as intelligent as he is good, and of a gentle and winning expression. Look at the other figure alongside of him, his fist raised and with insults on his lips, with a hang-dog face, bloated with brandy, titular governor, official preceptor, and absolute master of this child, the cobbler Simon, malignant, foul-mouthed, mean in every way, forcing him to become intoxicated, starving him, preventing him from sleeping, thrashing him, and who, obeying orders, instinctively visits on him all his brutality and corruption that he may pervert, degrade, and deprave him.[148] In the Palais de Justice, midway between the tower of the Temple and the prison in the rue de Sèvres, an almost similar contrast, transposing the merits and demerits, daily brings together in opposition the innocent with the vile; and there are days when the contrast, still more striking, seats criminals on the judges' bench and judges on the bench of criminals. On the first and second of Floréal, the old representatives and trustees of liberty under the monarchy, twenty-five magistrates of the Paris and Toulouse parliaments, many of them being eminent intellects of the highest culture and noblest character, embracing the greatest historical names of the French magistracy—Etienne Pasquier, Lefèvre d'Ormesson, Molé de Champlatreux, De Lamoignon, de Malesherbes—are sent to the

147. Chateaubriand: "Génie du Christianisme," part 4, book ii., notes on the exhumations at St. Denis taken by a monk, an eye-witness. Destruction, August 6 and 8, 1793, of fifty-one monuments. Exhumation of bodies, October 12 and 25, 1793.—Camille Boursier, "Essai sur la Terreur en Anjou," p. 223. (Testimony of Bordier-Langlois.) "I saw the head of our good Duke Réné, deposited in the chapel of St. Bernardin, in the Cordéliers at Angers, tossed like a ball by some laborers from one to the other."

148. R. Chantelauze, "Louis XVII." (according to unpublished documents). This book, free of declamation and composed according to the critical method, sets this question at rest.

guillotine[149] by the judges and juries familiar to us, assassins or brutes who do not take the trouble, or who have not the capacity, to give proper color to their sentences. M. de Malesherbes exclaims, after reading his indictment, "If that were only common-sense!" In effect those who pronounce judgment are, by their own admission, "substantial jurymen, good *sans-culottes*, men of nature." And such a nature! One of these, Trenchard, an Auvergnat carpenter, portrays himself to the life in the following note addressed to his wife before the trial comes on: "If you are not alone, and your companion can work, you may come, my dear, and see the twenty-four gentlemen condemned, all of them former presidents or councillors in the parliaments of Toulouse and Paris. I recommend you to bring something along with you (to eat), it will be three hours before we finish. I embrace you, my dear friend and wife."[150] In the same court, Lavoisier, the founder and organiser of chemistry, the great discoverer, and condemned to death, asks for a reprieve of his sentence for a fortnight to complete an experiment, and the president, Coffinhal, another Auvergnat, replies, "The Republic has no need of savants."[151] And it has no need of poets. The first poet of the epoch, André Chénier, the delicate and superior artist who reopens antique sources of inspiration and starts the modern current, is guillotined; we possess the original manuscript indictment of his examination, a veritable master-piece of gibberish and barbarism, of which a full copy is necessary to convey an idea of its "turpitudes of sense and orthography."[152] The reader may there see, if he pleases, a man of

---

149. Wallon, "Histoire du Tribunal Révolutionnaire," iii., 285.—Campardon, "His. du Tribunal Révolutionnaire de Paris," i., 306. Brochet, one of the jury, was formerly a lackey.

150. The above simply conveys the sense of the document, which is here given in the original: "Si tu n'èst pas toute seulle et que le compagnion soit a travailier tu peus ma chaire amie venir voir juger 24 mesieurs tous si-deven president on conselier au parlement de Paris et de Toulouse. Je t' ainvite a prendre quelque choge aven de venir parcheque nous naurons pas fini de 3 hurres. Je tembrase ma chaire amie et epouge."

151. Wallon, iii., 402.

152. Campardon, ii., 350.—Cf. "Causeries du Lundi," ii., 164. Saint-Beuve's

genius delivered up to brutes, coarse, angry, despotic animals, who
listen to nothing, who comprehend nothing, who do not even understand terms in common use, who stumble through their queries,
and who, to ape intelligence, draggle their pens along in supreme
stupidity.

The overthrow is complete. France, subject to the revolutionary
government, resembles a human being forced to walk with his head
down and to think with his feet.

---

comment on the examination. "André Chénier, natife de Constentinoble . . .
son frère vice-consulte en Espagne. "Remark the questions on his health and
correspondence and the cock-and-bull story about the 'maison à cotté.' "—They
ask him where his servant was on the 10th of August, 1792, and he replies that
he could not tell. "A lui representé qua lepoque de cette journée que touts les
bons citoyent ny gnoroit point leurs existence et quayant enttendue batte la
générale cettait un motife de plus pour reconnoitre tous les bons citoyent et le
motife au quelle il setait employée pour sauvée la Republique. A repondue quil
avoit dite l'exacte véritée. A lui demandée quel etoit dite l'exacte veritée—a
repondue que cetoit toutes ce qui etoit cy dessue."

CHAPTER II

*State the only depositary and distributor of food—Efforts made to establish a
conscription of labor—Discouragement of the Peasant—He refuses to cultivate—
Decrees and orders compelling him to harvest—His stubbornness—Cultivators
imprisoned by thousands—The Convention is obliged to set them at liberty—
Fortunate circumstances which save France from extreme famine— VI. Relaxation of the Revolutionary system after Thermidor—Repeal of the Maximum—
New situation of the peasant—He begins cultivation again—Requisition of grain
by the State—The cultivator indemnifies himself at the expense of private persons—Multiplication and increasing decline of assignats—The classes who have
to bear the burden—Famine and misery during year III. and the first half
of year IV.—In the country—In the small towns—In large towns and cities—
VII. Famine and misery at Paris—Steps taken by the government to feed the
capital—Monthly cost to the Treasury—Cold and hunger in the winter of 1794–
1795—Quality of the bread—Daily rations diminished—Suffering, especially
of the populace—Excessive physical suffering, despair, suicides, and deaths from
exhaustion in 1795—Government dinners and suppers—Number of lives lost
through want and war—Socialism as applied, and its effects on comfort, well-
being and mortality.*

I

SUPPOSE a man forced to walk with his feet in the air and his head
downward. By using extremely energetic measures he might, for a
while, be made to maintain this unwholesome attitude, and certainly
at the expense of a bruised or broken skull; it is very probable,
moreover, that he would use his feet convulsively and kick terribly.
But it is certain that if this course were persisted in, the man would
experience intolerable pain and finally sink down; the blood would
stop circulating and suffocation would ensue; the trunk and limbs
would suffer as much as the head, and the feet would become numb
and inert. Such is about the history of France under its Jacobin
pedagogues; their rigid theory and persistent brutality impose on
the nation an attitude against nature; consequently she suffers, and
each day suffers more and more; the paralysis increases; the functions get out of order and cease to act, while the last and principal
one,[1] the most urgent, namely, physical support and the daily nour-

---

1. On the other more complicated functions, such as the maintenance of

ishment of the living individual, is so badly accomplished, against so many obstacles, interruptions, uncertainties, and deficiencies, that the patient, reduced to extreme want, asks if tomorrow will not be worse than today, and whether his semistarvation will not end in complete starvation.

Nothing, apparently, is simpler, and yet really more complex, than the physiological process by which, in the organised body, the proper restorative food flows regularly to the spot where it is needed, among the innumerably diverse and distant cells. In like manner, nothing is simpler at the first glance, and yet more complex, than the economical process by which, in the social organism, subsistences and other articles of prime necessity, flow of themselves to all points of the territory where they are needed and within reach of each consumer. It is owing to this that, in the social body as in the organised body, the terminal act presupposes many others anterior to and coördinate with it, a series of elaborations, a succession of metamorphoses, one elimination and transportation after another, mostly invisible and obscure, but all indispensable, and all of them carried out by infinitely delicate organs, so delicate that, under the slightest pressure, they get out of order, so dependent on each other that an injury to one affects the operations of the rest, and thus suppresses or perverts the final result to which, nearly or remotely, they all contribute.

Consider, for a moment, these precious economical organs and their mode of operation. In any tolerably civilised community that has lasted for any length of time, they consist, first in rank, of those who possess wealth arising from the accumulation of old and recent savings, that is to say, those who possess any sort of security, large or small, in money, in notes, or in kind, whatever its form, whether

---

roads, canals, harbors, public buildings, lighting, cleanliness, hygiene, superior secondary and primary education, hospitals, and other asylums, highway security, the suppression of robbery and kindred crimes, the destruction of wolves, etc., see Rocquain, "Etat de la France au 18 Brumaire," and the "Statistiques des Départements," published by the préfets, from years IX. to XIII.—These branches of the service were almost entirely overthrown; the reader will see the practical results of their suppression in the documents referred to.

in lands, buildings or factories, in canals, shipping or machinery, in cattle or tools, as well as in every species of merchandise or produce. And see what use they make of these: each person, reserving what he needs for daily consumption, devotes his available surplus to some enterprise, the capitalist his ready money, the real-estate owner his land and tenements, the farmer his cattle, seed, and farming implements, the manufacturer his mills and raw material, the common-carrier his vessels, vehicles, and horses, the trader his ware-houses and stock of goods for the year, and the retailer his shop and supplies for a fortnight, to which everybody, the agriculturist, mer-chant, and manufacturer, necessarily adds his cash on hand, the deposits in his bank for paying the monthly salaries of his clerks, and at the end of the week, the wages of his workmen. Otherwise, it would be impossible to till the soil, to build, to fabricate, to trans-port, to sell; however useful the work might be, it could not be perfected, or even begun, without a preliminary outlay in money or in kind; in every enterprise, the crop presupposes labor and seed-planting; if I want to dig a well I am obliged to hire a pick and the arms to wield it, or, in other terms, to make certain *advances*. But these advances are made only on two conditions: first, that he who makes them is *able to make them*, that is to say, that he is the pos-sessor of an available surplus; and next, being the owner of this surplus, that he *desires* to make them, with this proviso that he may gain instead of losing by the operation. If I am wholly or partially ruined, if my tenants and farmers do not pay their rent,[2] if my lands or goods do not bring half their value in the market, if the net proceeds of my possessions are threatened with confiscation or pil-lage, not only have I fewer securities to dispose of, but, again, I become more and more uneasy about the future; over and above my immediate consumption I have to provide for a prospective con-

2. "St. John de Crèvecoeur," by Robert de Crèvecoeur, p. 216. (Letter of Mdlle. de Gouves, July, 1800.) "We are negotiating for the payment of, at least, the arrearages since 1789 on the Arras property." (M. de Gouves and his sisters had not emigrated, and yet they had had no income from their property for ten years.)

sumption; I add to my reserve stores especially of coin and provisions; I hold on to the remnant of my securities for myself and those who belong to me; they are no longer available and I can no longer make loans or enter upon my enterprise. And, on the other hand, if the loan or enterprise, instead of bringing me a profit, brings me loss; if the law is powerless or fails to do me justice and adds extra to ordinary risks; if my work once perfected is to become the prey of the government, of brigands, or of whoever pleases to seize it; if I am compelled to surrender my wares and merchandise at one-half their cost; if I cannot produce, put in store, transport, or sell except by renouncing all profit and with the certainty of not getting back my advances, I will no longer make loans or enter upon any undertaking whatever.

Such is the disposition and situation of people able to make advances in anarchical times, when the State falters and no longer performs its customary service, when property is no longer adequately protected by the public force, when jacqueries overspread the country and insurrections break out in the towns, when chateaux are sacked, archives burnt, shops broken into, provisions carried off and transportation is arrested, when rents and leases are no longer paid, when the courts dare no longer convict, when the constable no longer dares serve a warrant, when the gendarmerie holds back, when the police fails to act, when repeated amnesties shield robbers and incendiaries, when a revolution brings into local and central power dishonest and impoverished adventurers hostile to every one that possesses property of any kind. Such is the disposition and situation of all possessors of advances in socialistic times; when the usurping State, instead of protecting private property, destroys or seizes it; when it takes for itself the property of many of the great corporations; when it suppresses legally established credits without indemnity; when, by dint of expenditure and the burdens this creates, it becomes insolvent; when, through its paper-money and forced circulation, it annuls indebtedness in the hands of the creditor, and allows the debtor to go scot free; when it arbitrarily seizes current capital; when it makes forced loans and requisitions; when its tax on productions surpasses the cost of production and on merchandise the profit on its sale; when it constrains the manufacturer to manufacture at a loss and the merchant to sell at a loss; when its principles, judged by its acts, indicate a progression from partial to a universal confiscation. Through a certain affiliation, every phase of evil engenders the evil which follows, as may be said of a poison the effects of which spread or strike in, each function, affected by the derangement of one contiguous to it, becoming disturbed in its turn. The perils, mutilation, and suppression of property diminish available securities more and more, also the courage that risks them, that is to say, the mode of, and disposition to, make advances; through a lack of advances, useful enterprises languish, die out or are not undertaken; consequently, the production, supply, and sale of indispensable articles slacken, become interrupted, and cease altogether. There is less soap and sugar and fewer candles at the grocery, less wood and coal in the wood-yard, fewer oxen and sheep in the markets, less meat at the butcher's, less grain and flour at the corn-exchange, and less bread at the bakeries. As articles of prime necessity are scarce they become dear; as people contend for them their dearness increases; the rich man ruins himself in the struggle to get hold of them, while the poor man never gets any, the first of all necessities becoming unattainable.

II

Such is the misery existing in France at the moment of the completion of the Jacobin conquest, and of which the Jacobins are the authors; for, for the past four years, they have waged systematic war against property. From below, they have provoked, excused and amnestied, or tolerated and authorised, all the popular attacks on property,[3] countless insurrections, seven successive jacqueries, some of them so extensive as to cover eight or ten departments at the same time, the last one let loose on all France, that is to say, universal and lasting brigandage, the arbitrary rule of paupers, vagabonds,

3. Cf. "The Revolution," vol. i., 254–261, 311–352; vol. ii., 234–272.

and ruffians; every species of robbery, from a refusal to pay rents
and leases to the sacking of chateaux and ordinary domiciles, even
to the pillage of markets and granaries, free scope to mobs which,
under a political pretext, tax and ransom the "suspects" of all classes
at pleasure, not alone the noble and the rich but the peaceable farmer
and well-to-do artisan, in short, reverting back to the state of nature,
to the dominion of appetites and lusts, and to a savage, primitive
life in the forests. Only a short time before, in the month of February, 1793, through Marat's recommendation, and with the connivance of the Jacobin municipality, the Paris riff-raff had broken into
twelve hundred groceries and divided on the spot, either gratis or
at the price it fixed, sugar, soap, brandy, and coffee. From above,
they had undertaken, carried out, and multiplied the worst assaults
on property, vast spoliations of every sort—the suppression of hundreds of millions of incomes and the confiscation of billions of capital; the abolition without indemnity of tithes and quitrents; the
expropriation of the property of the clergy, of *emigrés*, that of the
order of Malta, that of the pious, charitable, and educational associations and endowments, even laic; seizures of plate, of the sacred
vessels and precious ornaments of the churches. And, since they are
in power, others still more vast; after August 10, their newspapers
in Paris and their commissioners in the departments,[4] preached "the
agrarian law, the holding of all property in common, the levelling
of fortunes, the right of each fraction of the sovereignty" to help
itself by force to all food and investments at the expense of the
owner, to hunt down the rich, proscribe "land-owners, leading merchants, financiers, and all men in possession of whatever is superfluous." Rousseau's dogma that "the fruit belongs to everybody and
the soil to no one" is established at an early date as a maxim of State
in the Convention, while in the deliberations of the sovereign assembly socialism, openly avowed, becomes ascendant, and, afterwards, supreme. According to Robespierre,[5] "whatever is essential

---

4. Cf. "The Revolution," ii., 273–276.
5. Buchez et Roux, xxii., 178. (Speech by Robespierre in the Convention,

to preserve life is *common property to society at large;* only the excess may be given up to individuals and surrendered to commercial enterprise." With still greater solemnity, the pontiff of the sect, in the Declaration of Rights which, unanimously adopted by the all-powerful Jacobin club, is to serve as the corner-stone of the new institutions, pens the following formulae big with their consequences:[6] "Society must provide for the support of all its members. The aid required by indigence is a debt of the rich to the poor. The right of property is limited," and applies "only to that portion which the law guarantees. Every ownership, any trade, which bears prejudicially on the existence of our fellow-creatures is necessarily illicit and immoral." The sense of this is clear, and yet more: the Jacobin populace, having decided that the possession of, and trade in, groceries was prejudicial to its existence, the grocers' monopoly is, therefore, immoral and illicit, and consequently, it pillages their shops. Under the rule of the populace and of the "Mountain," the Convention applies the theory, seizes capital wherever it can be found, and notifies the poor, in its name, "that they will find in the pocket-books of the rich whatever they need to supply their wants."[7]

Over and above these striking and direct attacks, an indirect and

---

December 2, 1792.)—Mallet-Dupan, "Mémoires," i., 400. About the same date, "a deputation from the department of Gard expressly demands a sum of two hundred and fifty millions, as indemnity to the cultivator, for grain which it calls *national property*." This fearful sum of two hundred and fifty millions, they add, is only a *fictive* advance, placing at its disposal *real* and purely national wealth, *not belonging in full ownership to any distinct member of the social body any more than the pernicious metals minted as current coin.*"

6. Buchez et Roux, xxvi., 95. (Declaration of Rights presented in the Jacobin Club, April 21, 1793.)

7. Decrees in every commune establishing a tax on the rich in order to render the price of bread proportionate to wages, also in each large city to raise an army of paid *sans-culottes*, that will keep aristocrats under their pikes, April 5–7.—Decree ordering the forced loan of a billion on the rich, May 20–25.—Buchez et Roux, xxv., 156. (Speech by Charles, March 27.—Gorsas, "Courrier des Départments," No. for May 15, 1793. (Speech by Simon in the club at Annecy.)—Speech by Guffroy at Chartres, and of Chalier and associates at Lyons, etc.

secret attack, but still more significant, slowly undermines the basis of all present and future property. State affairs are everybody's affairs, and, when the State ruins itself, everybody is ruined along with it. For, it is the country's greatest debtor and its greatest creditor, while there is no debtor so free of seizure and no creditor so absorbing, since, making the laws and possessing the force, it can, firstly, repudiate indebtedness and send away the fund-holder with empty hands, and next, increase taxation and empty the taxpayer's pocket of his last penny. There is no greater menace to private fortunes than the bad administration of the public fortune. Now, under the pressure of Jacobin principles and of the Jacobin faction, the trustees of France have administered as if they purposely meant to ruin their ward; every known means for wasting a fortune have been brought into play by them. In the first place, they have deprived him of three-fourths of his income. To please the people and enforce the theory, the taxes on articles consumed, on salt, with the excise subsidies and the *octroi* duties on liquors, meat, tobacco, leather, and gunpowder, have been abolished, while the new imposts substituted for the old ones, slowly fixed, badly apportioned and raised with difficulty have brought in no returns; on the 1st of February, 1793,[8] the Treasury had received on the real and personal taxation of 1791, but one hundred and fifty millions instead of three hundred millions; on the same taxes for 1792, instead of three hundred millions it had obtained nothing at all. At this date, and during the four years of the Revolution, the total arrears of taxation amounted to six hundred and thirty-two millions—a bad debt that can hardly be recovered, and, in fact, it is already reduced one-half, since, even if the debtor could and was disposed to pay, he would pay in assignats, which, at this time, were at a discount of fifty per cent. In the second place,

8. Report by Minister Claviéres, February 1, 1793, p. 27.—Cf. Report of M. de Montesquiou, September, 9, 1791, p. 47. "During the first twenty-six months of the Revolution the taxes brought in three hundred and fifty-six millions less than they should naturally have done."—There is the same deficit in the receipts of the towns, especially on account of the abolition of the *octroi*. Paris, under this head, loses ten millions per annum.

the new managers had quadrupled the public expenditure.[9] What with the equipment and excursions of the National Guards, federations, patriotic festivals, and parades, the writing, printing, and publication of innumerable documents, reimbursements for suppressed offices, the installation of new administrations, aid to the indigent and to its charity workshops, purchases of grain, indemnities to millers and bakers, it was under the necessity of providing for the cost of the universal demolition and reconstruction. Now, the State had, for the most part, defrayed all these expenses. At the end of April, 1793, it had already advanced to the city of Paris alone, one hundred and ten million francs, while the Commune, insolvent, kept constantly extorting fresh millions.[10] By the side of this gulf, the Jacobins had dug another, larger still, that of the war. For the first half of the year 1793 they threw into this pit first, one hundred and forty millions, then one hundred and sixty millions, and then one hundred and ninety million francs; in the second six months of 1793 the war and subsistences swallowed up three hundred million francs per month, and the more they threw into the two gulfs the deeper they became.[11]

9. Report by Cambon, Pluviose 3, year III. "The Revolution and the war have cost in four years five thousand three hundred and fifty millions above the ordinary expenses." (Cambon, in his estimates, purposely exaggerates ordinary expenses of the monarchy. According to Necker's budget, the expenditure in 1759 was fixed at five hundred and thirty-one millions and not, as Cambon states, seven hundred millions. This raises the expenses of the Revolution and of the war to seven thousand one hundred and twenty-one millions for the four and a half years, and hence to one thousand five hundred and eighty-one millions per annum, that is to say, to triple the ordinary expenses.) The expenses of the cities are therefore exaggerated like those of the State and for the same reasons.

10. Schmidt, "Pariser Zustände," i. 93, 96. "During the first half of the year 1789 there were seventeen thousand men at twenty sous a day in the national workshops at Montmartre. In 1790, there were nineteen thousand. In 1791, thirty-one thousand costing sixty thousand francs a day. In 1790, the State expends seventy-five millions for maintaining the price of bread in Paris at eleven sous for four pounds.—*Ibid.*, 113. During the first six months of 1793 the State pays the Paris bakers about seventy-five thousand francs a day to keep bread at three sous the pound.

11. *Ibid.*, i., 139–144.

Naturally, when there is no collecting a revenue and expenses go on increasing, one is obliged to borrow on one's resources, and piecemeal, as long as these last. Naturally, when ready money is not to be had on the market, one draws notes and tries to put them in circulation; one pays tradesmen with written promises in the future, and thus exhausts one's credit. Such is paper-money and the assignats, the third and most efficient way for wasting a fortune and which the Jacobins did not fail to make the most of. Under the Constituent Assembly, through a remnant of good sense and good faith, efforts were at first made to guarantee the fulfillment of written promises; the holders of assignats were almost secured by *a first mortgage* on the national possessions, which had been given to them coupled with an engagement not to raise more money on this guarantee, as well as not to issue any more assignats.[12] But they did not keep faith. They rendered the security afforded by this mortgage inoperative and, as all chances of repayment disappeared, its value declined. Then, on the 27th of April, 1792, according to the report of Cambon, there begins an unlimited issue; according to the Jacobin financiers, nothing more is necessary to provide for the war than to turn the wheel and grind out promises to pay: in June, 1793, assignats to the amount of four billion three hundred and twenty millions have already been manufactured, and everybody sees that the mill must grind faster. This is why the guarantee, vainly increased, no longer suffices for the monstrous, disproportionate mortgage; it exceeds all limits, covers nothing, and sinks through its own weight. At Paris, the assignat of one hundred francs is worth in specie, in the month of June, 1791, eighty-five francs, in January, 1792, only sixty-six francs, in March, 1792, only fifty-three francs; rising in value at the end of the Legislative Assembly, owing to fresh confiscations, it falls back to fifty-five francs in January, 1793, to forty-seven francs in

---

12. Decree of September 27, 1790. "The circulation of assignats shall not extend beyond one billion two hundred millions. . . . Those which are paid in shall be destroyed and there shall be no other creation or emission of them, without a decree of the Corps Legislatif, always subject to this condition that they shall not exceed the value of the national possessions nor obtain a circulation above one billion two hundred millions.

April, to forty francs in June, to thirty-three francs in July.[13] Thus are the creditors of the State defrauded of a third, one-half, and two-thirds of their investment, and not alone the creditors of the State but every other creditor, since every debtor has the right to discharge his obligations by paying his debts in assignats. Enumerate, if possible, all who are defrauded of private claims, all money-lenders, and stock-holders who have invested in any private enterprise, either manufacturing or mercantile, those who have loaned money on contracts of longer or shorter date, all sellers of real-estate, with stipulations in their deeds for more or less remote payment, all land-owners who have leased their grounds or buildings for a term of years, all holders of annuities on private bond or on an estate, all manufacturers, merchants and farmers who have sold their wares, goods, and produce on time, all clerks on yearly salaries, and even all other employees, underlings, servants, and workmen receiving fixed salaries for a specified term. There is not one of these persons whose capital, or income payable in assignats, is not at once crippled in proportion to the decline in value of assignats, so that not only the State falls into bankruptcy but likewise every creditor in France, legally bankrupt along with it through its fault.

In such a situation how can any enterprise be commenced or maintained? Who dares take a risk, especially when disbursements are large and returns remote? Who dares lend on long credits? If loans are still made they are not for a year but for a month, while the interest which, before the Revolution was six, five, or even four per cent. *per annum,* is now "two per cent. *a month* on securities." It soon runs up higher and, at Paris and Strasbourg we see it rising, as in India and the Barbary States, to four, five, six, and even seven per cent. a month.[14] What holder of raw material, or of manufactured

13. Schmidt, *ibid.,* i., 104, 138, 144.

14. Felix Rocquain, "L'Etat de la France au 18 Brumaire," p. 240. (Report by Lacuée, year IX.)—Reports by préfets under the Consulate. (Reports of Laumont, préfet of the Lower-Rhine, year X.; of Colchen, préfet of the Moselle, year XI., etc.)—Schmidt, "Pariser Zustände," iii., 205. ("The rate of interest during the Revolution was from four to five per cent. per month; in 1796 from

goods, would dare make entries on his books as usual and allow his customer the indispensable credit of three months? What large manufacturer would presume to make goods up, what wholesale merchant would care to make shipments, what man of wealth or with a competence would build, drain, and construct dams and dykes, repair, or even maintain them with the positive certainty of delays in getting back only one-half his advances and with the increasing certainty of getting nothing? Large establishments fail from year to year in all directions; after the ruin of the nobles and the departure of wealthy foreigners, every craft dependent on luxurious tastes, those of Paris and Lyons, which are the standard for Europe, all the manufactories of rich stuffs, and furniture, and other artistic, elegant, and fashionable articles; after the insurrection of the blacks in St. Domingo, and other troubles in the West Indies, the great colonial trade and remarkable prosperity of Nantes and Bordeaux, including all the industrial enterprises by which the production, transportation, and circulation of cotton, sugar, and coffee were affected;[15] after the declaration of war with England, the shipping interest; after the declaration of war with all Europe, the commerce of the continent.[16]

---

six to eight per cent. per month, the lowest rate being two per cent. per month with security.")

15. Arthur Young, "Voyage en France," ii., 360. (Fr. translation.) "I regard Bordeaux as richer and more commercial than any city in England except London."

16. *Ibid.*, ii., 357. The statistics of exports in France in 1787 give three hundred and forty-nine millions, and imports three hundred and forty millions (leaving out Lorraine, Alsace, the three Evéchés, and the West Indies).—*Ibid.*, 360. In 1786 the importations from the West Indies amounted to one hundred and seventy-four millions, of which St. Domingo furnished one hundred and thirty-one millions; the exports to the West Indies amounted to sixty-four millions, of which St. Domingo had forty-four millions. These exchanges were effected by five hundred and sixty-nine vessels carrying one hundered and sixty-two thousand tons, of which Bordeaux provided two hundred and forty-six vessels, carrying seventy-five thousand tons.—On the ruin of manufactures cf. the reports of préfets in the year X., with details from each department.—Arthur Young (ii., 444) states that the Revolution affected manufactures more seriously than any other branch of industry.

Failure after failure, an universal crash, utter cessation of extensively organised and productive labor: instead of productive industries, I see none now but destructive industries, those of the agricultural and commercial vermin, those of brokers and speculators who dismantle mansions and abbeys, and who demolish chateaux and churches so as to sell the materials as cheap as dirt, who bargain away national possessions, so as to make a profit on the transaction. Imagine the mischief a temporary owner, steeped in debt, needy and urged on by the maturity of his engagements, can and must do to an estate held under a precarious title and of suspicious acquirement, which he has no idea of keeping, and from which, meanwhile, he derives every possible benefit:[17] not only does he put no spokes in the mill-wheel, no stones in the dyke, no tiles on the roof, but he buys no manure, exhausts the soil, devastates the forest, alienates the fields, and dismembers the entire farm, damaging the ground and the stock of tools and injuring the dwelling by selling its mirrors, lead and iron, and oftentimes the window-shutters and doors; he turns all into cash, no matter how, at the expense of the domain, which he leaves in a run-down condition, unfurnished, and for a long time unproductive. In like manner, the communal possessions, ravaged, pillaged, and then pieced out and divided off, are so many organisms which are sacrificed for the immediate relief of the village poor, but of course to the detriment of their future productiveness and an abundant yield.[18] Alone, amongst these millions of men who

17. Reports of préfets. (Orme, year IX.) "The purchasers have speculated on the profits for the time being, and have exhausted their resources. Many of them have destroyed all the plantations, all the enclosures and even the fruit trees."—Felix Rocquain, *ibid.*, 116. (Report by Fourcroy on Brittany.) "The condition of rural structures everywhere demands considerable capital. But no advances, based on any lasting state of things, can be made."—*Ibid.*, 236. (Report of Lacuée on the departments around Paris.) "The doubtful owners of national possessions cultivate badly and let things largely go to ruin."

18. Reports by préfets, years X. and XI. In general, the effect of the partition of communal possessions was disastrous, especially pasture and mountain grounds.—(Doubs.) "The partition of the communal property has contributed, in all the communes, rather to the complete ruin of the poor than to any

have stopped working, or work the wrong way, the petty cultivator labors to advantage; free of taxes, of tithes, and of feudal imposts, possessing a scrap of ground which he has obtained for almost nothing or without stretching his purse-strings, he works in good spirits;[19] he is sure that henceforth his crop will no longer be eaten up by the levies of the seignior, of the *décimateur,* and of the King, that it will belong to him, that it will be wholly his, and that the worse the famine in the towns, the dearer he will sell his produce. Hence, he has ploughed more vigorously than ever; he has even cleared waste ground; getting the soil gratis, or nearly so, and having to make but few advances, having no other use for his advances, consisting of seed, manure, the work of his cattle and of his own hands, he has planted, reaped, and raised grain with the greatest energy. Perhaps other articles of consumption will be scarce; it may be that, owing to the ruin of other branches of industry, it will be hard to get dry-goods, shoes, sugar, soap, oil, candles, wine, and brandy; it may happen that, owing to the bungling way in which agricultural transformations have been effected, all produce of the secondary order, meat, vegetables, butter, and eggs, may become scarce. In any event, French aliment *par excellence* is on hand, standing in the field or stored in sheafs in the barns; in 1792 and 1793, and even in 1794, there is enough grain in France to provide every French inhabitant with his daily bread.[20]

---

amelioration of their fate."—(Lozére.) "The partition of the communal property by the law of June 10, 1792, has proved very injurious to cultivation." These partitions were numerous. (Moselle.) "Out of six hundred and eighty-six communes, one hundred and seven have divided per capitum, five hundred and seventy-nine by families, and one hundred and nineteen have remained intact."

19. *Ibid.* (Moselle.) Births largely increase in 1792. "But this is an exceptional year. All kinds of abuses, paper-money, the nonpayment of taxes and claims, the partition in the communes, the sale for nothing of national possessions, has spread so much comfort among the people that the poorer classes, who are the most numerous, have had no dread of increasing their families, to which they hope some day to leave their fields and render them happy."

20. Mallet-Dupan, "Mémoires," ii., 29. (February 1, 1794.) "The late crop

But that is not enough. In order that each Frenchman may obtain his bit of bread every day, it is still essential that grain should reach the markets in sufficient quantities, and that the bakers should every day have enough flour to make all the bread that is required; moreover, the bread offered for sale in the bakeries should not exceed the price which the majority of consumers can afford to pay. Now, in fact, through a forced result of the new system, neither of these conditions is fulfilled. In the first place, wheat, and hence bread, is too dear. Even at the old rate, these would still be too dear for the innumerable empty or half-empty purses, after so many attacks on property, industry, and trade, now that so many hundreds of workmen and employees are out of work, now that so many landowners and bourgeois receive no rents, now that incomes, profits, wages, and salaries have diminished by hundreds of thousands. But wheat, and, consequently, bread, has not remained at old rates. Instead of a sack of wheat being worth in Paris fifty francs in February, 1793, it is worth sixty-five francs; in May, 1793, one hundred francs and then one hundred and fifty; and hence bread, in Paris, early in 1793, instead of being three sous the pound, costs six sous, in many of the southern departments seven and eight sous, and in other places ten and twelve sous.[21] The reason is, that, since August 10, 1792, after the King's fall and the wrenching away of the ancient keystone of the arch which still kept the loosened stones of the social edifice in place, the frightened peasant would no longer part with his produce; he determined not to take assignats, not to let his grain go for

---

in France was generally good, and, in some provinces, it was above the average. . . . I have seen the statements of two returns made from twenty-seven departments; they declare an excess of fifteen, twenty, thirty, and thirty-five thousand bushels of grain. There is no real dearth."

21. Schmidt, *ibid.*, i., 110, and following pages.—Buchez et Roux, xx., 416. (Speeches of Lequinio, November 27, 1792.)—*Moniteur*, xvii., 2. (Letter by Clement, Puy-de-Dome, June 15, 1793.) "For the past fifteen days bread has been worth sixteen and eighteen sous the pound. There is the most frightful distress in our mountains. The government distributes one-eighth of a bushel to each person, everybody being obliged to wait two days to take his turn. One woman was smothered and several were wounded."

anything but ringing coin. To exchange good wheat for bad, dirty paper rags seemed to him a trick, and justly so, for, on going to town every month he found that the dealers gave him less merchandise for these rags. A hoarder, and so distrustful, he must have good, old fashioned crowns, of the old stamp, so as to lay them away in a jar or old woollen stocking; give him specie or he will keep his grain. For he is not, as formerly, obliged to part with it as soon as it is cut, to pay taxes and rent; the bailiff and sheriff are no longer there to distrain him; in these times of disorder and demagogism, under impotent or partial authorities, neither the public nor the private creditor has the power to compel payment, while the spurs which formerly impelled the farmer to seek the nearest market are blunted or broken. He therefore stays away, and he has excellent reasons for so doing. Vagabonds and the needy stand by the roadside and at the entrances of the towns to stop and pillage the loaded carts; in the markets and on the open square, women cut open bags of grain with their scissors and empty them, or the municipality, forced to do it by the crowd, fixes the price at a reduced rate.[22] The larger a town is the greater the difficulty in supplying its market; for its subsistences are drawn from a distance; each department, each canton, each village keeps its own grain for itself by means of legal requisitions or by brutal force; it is impossible for wholesale dealers in grain to make bargains; they are styled monopolists, and the mob, breaking into their storehouses, hangs them out of preference.[23] As

22. Cf. "La Revolution," i., 208; ii., 294, 205, 230.—Buchez et Roux, xx., 431. (Report of Lecointe-Puyraveau, Nov. 30, 1792.) (Mobs of four, five, and six thousand men in the departments of Eure-et-Loire, Eure, Orme, Calvados, Indre-et-Loire, Loiret, and Sarthe cut down the prices of produce. The three delegates of the Convention disposed to interfere have their lives saved only on condition of announcing the rate dictated to them.—*Ibid.*, 409. (Letter of Roland, Nov. 27, 1792.)—xxi., 198. (Another letter by Roland, Dec. 6, 1792.) "All convoys are stopped at Lissy, la Ferté, Milan, la Ferté-sous-Jouarre. . . . Carts loaded with wheat going to Paris have been forced to go back near Lonjumeau and near Meaux."

23. Archives Nationales, F⁷, 3,265. (Letter of David, cultivator, and administrator of the department of Seine-Inférieure, Oct. 11, 1792; letter of the

the government, accordingly, has proclaimed their speculations "crimes," it is going to interdict their trade and substitute itself for them.[24] But this substitution only increases the penury still more; in vain do the towns force collections, tax their rich men, raise money on loan, and burden themselves beyond their resources;[25] they only make the matter worse. When the municipality of Paris expends twelve thousand francs a day for the sale of flour at a low price in the markets, it keeps away the flour-dealers, who cannot deliver flour at such low figures; the result is that there is not flour enough in the market for the six hundred thousand mouths in Paris; when it expends seventy-five thousand francs daily to indemnify the bakers, it attracts the outside population, which rushes into Paris to get bread cheap, and for the seven hundred thousand mouths of Paris and the suburbs combined, the bakers have not an adequate supply. Whoever comes late finds the shop empty; consequently, everybody tries to get there earlier and earlier, at dawn, before daybreak, and then five or six hours before daybreak. In February, 1793, long lines of people

---

special committee of Rouen, Oct. 22; letter of the delegates of the executive power, Oct. 20, etc.) "Reports from all quarters state that the farmers who drive to market are considered and treated in their parishes as aristocrats. . . . Each department keeps to itself: they mutually repel each other."

24. Buchez et Roux, xx., 409. (Letter of Roland, Nov. 27, 1792.) "The circulation of grain has for a long time encountered the greatest obstacles; scarcely a citizen now dares to do that business."—*Ibid.*, 417. (Speech by Lequinio.) "The monopoly of wheat by land-owners and farmers is almost universal. Fright is the cause of it. . . . And where does this fear come from? From the general agitation, and threats, with the bad treatment in many places of the farmers, land-owners, and traffickers in wheat known as *bladiers*."—Decrees of Sep. 16, 1792, and May 4, 1793.

25. Buchez et Roux, xix. (Report by Cambon, Sep. 22, 1792.) "The taxes no longer reach the public treasury, because they are used for purchasing grain in the departments." *Ibid.*, xix., 29. (Speech by Cambon, Oct. 12, 1792.) "You can bear witness in your departments to the sacrifices which well-to-do people have been obliged to make in helping the poor class. In many of the towns extra taxes have been laid for the purchase of grain and for a thousand other helpful measures."

are already waiting at the bakers' door, these lines growing longer and longer in April, while in June they are enormously long.[26] Naturally, for lack of bread, people fall back on other aliments, which also grow dearer; add to this the various contrivances and effects of Jacobin politics which still further increase the dearness of food of all sorts, and also of every other necessary article: for instance, the extremely bad condition of the roads, which renders transportation slower and more costly; the prohibition of the export of coin and hence the obtaining of food from abroad; the decree which obliges each industrial or commercial association, at present or to come, to "pay annually into the national treasury one-quarter of the amount of its dividends"; the revolt in Vendée, which deprives Paris of six hundred oxen a week; the feeding of the armies, which takes one-half of the cattle brought to the Poissy market; shutting off the sea and the continent, which ruins manufacturers and extensive commercial operations; the insurrections in Bordeaux, Marseilles, and the South, which still further raise the price of groceries, sugar, soap, oil, candles, wine, and brandy.[27] Early in 1793, a pound of beef in France is worth on the average, instead of six sous twenty sous; in May, at Paris, brandy which, six months before, cost thirty-five sous, costs ninety-four sous; in July, a pound of veal, instead of five sous, costs twenty-two sous. Sugar, from twenty sous, advances to four francs ten sous; a candle costs seven sous. France, pushed on by the Jacobins, approaches the depths of misery, entering the first circle of its Inferno; other circles follow down deeper and deeper, narrower still and yet more sombre; under Jacobin impulsion is she to descend to the lowest?

26. Buchez et Roux, xx., 409. (Letter of Roland, Nov. 29, 1792.)—xxi., 199. (Deliberations of the provisional executive council, Sep. 3, 1792.)—Dauban, "La Demagogie en 1793," p. 64. (Diary kept by Beaulieu.)—*Ibid.*, 150.)

27. Schmidt, i., 110–130.—Decrees against the export of coin or ingots, Sep. 5 and 15, 1792.—Decree on stocks or bonds payable to bearer, Aug. 14, 1792.

III

It is evident that when nutrition in the social organism goes on slowly and is interrupted in some places, it is owing to the derangement of one of the inmost fibres of the economical machine. It is evident that this fibre consists of the sentiment by which man holds on to his property, fears to risk it, refuses to depreciate it, and tries to increase it. It is evident that, in man as he actually is, as now fashioned, this intense, tenacious sentiment, always on the alert and active, is the magazine of inward energy which provides for three-fourths, almost the whole, of that sustained effort, that extreme cautiousness, that determined perseverance which leads the individual to undergo privation, to contrive and to exert himself, to turn to profitable account the labor of his hands, brain, and capital, and to produce, save, and create for himself and for others various resources and comforts.[28] Thus far, this sentiment has been only partially affected, and the injury has been confined to the well-to-do and wealthy class; hence, only one-half of his useful energy has been destroyed, and the services of the well-to-do and wealthy class have been only specially dispensed with; but little else than the labor of the capitalist, proprietor, and man of enterprise has been suppressed, that far-reaching, combined, comprehensive labor, the products of which consist of objects of luxury and comfort, abundant supplies always on hand, and the ready and spontaneous distribution of indispensable commodities. There remains to crush out what is left of this laborious and nutritive fibre; the remnant of useful energy has to be destroyed down to its extirpation among the people; there

28. It is probable that disinterested motives, pure love for one's neighbor, for humanity, for country, do not form a hundredth part of the total energy that produces human activity. It must not be forgotten that the actions of men are alloyed with motives of a lower order, such as love of fame, the desire of self-admiration and of self-approval, fear of punishment and hope of reward beyond the grave, all of these being interested motives, and without which disinterested motives would be inoperative excepting in two or three souls among ten thousand.

must be a suppression, as far as possible, of all manual, rude labor on a small scale, and of its rudimentary fruits; the discouragement of the insignificant shopkeeper, mechanic and ploughman must be effected; the corner-grocer must be prevented from selling his sugar and candles, and the cobbler from mending shoes: the miller must think of giving up his mill and the wagoner of abandoning his cart; the farmer must be convinced that the best thing he can do is to get rid of his horses, eat his pork himself,[29] let his oxen famish and leave his crops to rot on the ground. The Jacobins are to do all this, for it is the inevitable result of the theory that they have proclaimed and which they apply. According to this theory the stern, strong, deep-seated instinct through which the individual stubbornly holds on to what he has, to what he makes for himself and for those that belong to him, is just the unwholesome fibre that must be rooted out or paralysed at any cost; its true name is "egoism, *incivism,*" and its operations consist of outrages on the community, which is the sole legitimate proprietor of property and products, and, yet more, of all persons and services. Body and soul, all belongs to the State, nothing to individuals, and, if need be, the State has the right to take not only lands and capital, but, again, to claim and tax at whatever rate it pleases all corn and cattle, all vehicles and the animals that draw them, all candles and sugar; it has the right to

---

29. Archives Nationales, D., 55, I., file 2. (Letter by Joffroy, national agent in the district of Bar-sur-Aube, Germinal 5, year III.) "Most of the farmers, to escape the requisition, have sold their horses and replaced them with oxen."— Memoirs (in ms.) of M. Dufort de Cheverney (communicated by M. Robert de Crêvecoeur). In June, 1793, "the requisitions fall like hail, every week, on wheat, hay, straw, oats, etc.," all at prices fixed by the contractors, who make deductions, postpone and pay with difficulty. Then come requisitions for hogs. "This was depriving all the country folks of what they lived on." As the requisitions called for live hogs, there was a hog St. Bartholomew. Everybody killed his pig and salted it down." (Environs of Blois.) In relation to refusing to gather in crops, see further on.—Dauban, "Paris in 1794," p. 229. (Ventose 24, general orders by Henriot.) "Citizen Guillon being on duty outside the walls, saw with sorrow that citizens were cutting their wheat to feed rabbits with."

appropriate to itself and tax at whatever rate it pleases, the labor of shoemaker, tailor, miller, wagoner, ploughman, reaper, and thrasher. The seizure of men and things is universal, and the new sovereigns do their best at it; for, in practice, necessity urges them on; insurrection thunders at their door; their supporters, all crackbrains with empty stomachs, the poor and the idle, and the Parisian populace, listen to no reason and blindly insist on things haphazard; they are bound to satisfy their patrons at once, to issue one on top of the other all the decrees they call for, even when impracticable and mischievous; to starve the provinces so as to feed the city, to starve the former tomorrow so as to feed the latter today. Subject to the clamors and menaces of the street they despatch things rapidly; they cease to care for the future, the present being all that concerns them; they take and take forcibly; they uphold violence by brutality, they support robbery with murder; they expropriate persons by categories and appropriate objects by categories, and after the rich they despoil the poor. During fourteen months the revolutionary government thus keeps both hands at work, one hand completing the confiscation of property, large and medium, and the other proceeding to the entire abolition of property on a small scale.

Against large or medium properties it suffices to extend and aggravate the decrees already passed. The spoliation of the last of existing corporations must be effected: the government confiscates the possessions of hospitals, communes, and all scientific or literary associations.[30] There is the spoliation of State credits and all other credits: it issues in fourteen months five billions one million of assignats, often one billion four hundred millions and two billions at a time, under one decree, and thus condemns itself to complete

---

30. Decree of Messidor 23, year II., on the consolidation with the national domain of the assets and liabilities of hospitals and other charitable institutions. (See reports of préfets on the effect of this law, on the ruin of the hospitals, on the misery of the sick, of foundlings, and the infirm, from years IX. to XIII.)— Decrees of August 8 and 12, 1793, and July 24, 1794, on academies and literary societies.—Decree of August 24, 1793, § 29, on the assets and liabilities of communes.

future bankruptcy; it calls in the one billion five hundred million of assignats bearing the royal stamp (*à face royale*) and thus arbitrarily converts and reduces the public debt on the Grand Ledger, which is already, in fact, a partial and declared bankruptcy. Six months imprisonment for whoever refuses to accept assignats at par, twenty years in irons if the offence is repeated and the guillotine if there is an *incivique* intention or act, which suffices for all other creditors.[31] The spoliation of individuals, a forced loan of a billion on the rich, requisitions for coin against assignats at par, seizures of plate and jewels in private houses, revolutionary taxes so numerous as not only to exhaust the capital, but likewise the credit, of the person taxed,[32] and the resumption by the State of the public domain pledged to private individuals for the past three centuries: how many years of labor are requisite to bring together again so much available capital, to reconstruct in France and to refill the private reservoirs in which all the accumulated savings will flow out, like a power-giving mill-stream, on the great wheel of general enterprise? Take into account, moreover, the enterprises which are directly destroyed, root and branch, by revolutionary executions, enforced against the manufacturers and traders of Lyons, Marseilles, and Bordeaux, proscribed in a mass,[33] guillotined, imprisoned, or put to flight, their

31. Schmidt, i., 144. (Two billions September 27, 1793; one billion four hundred millions June 19, 1794.)—Decree of August 24, September 13, 1793, on the conversion of title-deeds and the formation of the Grand Ledger.— Decrees of July 31, August 30 and September 5, on calling in the assignats *à face royale*.—Decrees of August 1 and September 5, 1793, on the refusal to accept assignats at par.

32. Archives Nationales, F[7], 4,421. (Documents on the revolutionary taxes organised at Troyes, Brumaire 11, year II.) Three hundred and seventy-three persons are taxed, especially manufacturers, merchants, and land-owners; the minimum of the tax is one hundred francs, the maximum fifty thousand francs, the total being one million seven hundred and sixty-two thousand seven hundred francs. Seventy-six petitions attached to the papers show exactly the situation of things in relation to trade, manufactures, and property, the state of fortunes and credit of the upper and lower bourgeois class.

33. Mallet-Dupan, "Mémoires," ii., 17. "I have seen the thirty-second list of *emigrés* at Marseilles, merely of those whose possessions have been confis-

factories stopped, their storehouses put under sequestration, with their stocks of brandy, soap, silk, muslins, leather, paper, serges, cloth, canvas, cordage, and the rest; the same at Nantes under Carrier, at Strasbourg under Saint-Just, and everywhere else.[34] "Commerce is annihilated," writes a Swiss merchant,[35] from Paris, and the government, one would say, tries systematically to render it impossible. On the 27th of June, 1793, the Convention closes the Bourse; on the 15th of April, 1794, it suppresses "financial associations" and "prohibits all bankers, merchants and other persons from organising any establishment of the said character under any pretext or title whatsoever." On the 8th of September, 1793, the Commune places seals "in all the counting-houses of bankers, stock-brokers, agents and silver-dealers,"[36] and locks up their owners; as a favor, considering that they are obliged to pay the drafts drawn on them, they are let out, but provisionally, and on condition that they remain under arrest at home, "under the guard of two good citizens," at their own expense. Such is the case in Paris and in other cities, not

---

cated and sold; there are twelve thousand of them, and the lists were not finished."—Reports of préfets. (Var by Fanchet, year IX.) "The emigration of 1793 throws upon Leghorn and the whole Italian coast a very large number of Marseilles and Toulon traders. These men, generally industrious, have established (there) more than one hundred and sixty soap factories and opened a market for the oil of this region. This event may be likened to the Revocation of the Edict of Nantes."—Cf. the reports on the departments of the Rhone, Aude, Lot, and Garonne, Lower Pyrenees, Orme, etc.

34. Archives des Affaires Étrangéres, vol. 332. (Letter of Désgranges, Bordeaux, Brumaire 12, year II.) "Nobody here talks about trade any more than if it had never existed."

35. Dr. Jaïn, "Choix de documents et lettres privées trouvées dans des papiers de famille," p. 144. (Letter of Gédéon Jaïn, banker at Paris, November 18, 1793.) "Business carried on with difficulty and at a great risk occasion frequent and serious losses, credit and resources being almost nothing."

36. Archives Nationales, F⁷, 2,475. (Letters of Thullier, *procureur-syndic* of the Paris department, September 7 and 10, 1793.—Report by a member of the Piques section, September 8 and 10, 1793.—Cf. the petitions of traders and lawyers imprisoned at Troyes, Strasbourg, Bordeaux, etc.—Archives Nationales, AF., II., 271. Letter of Francastel: "At least three thousand monopolist aristocrats have been arrested at Nantes . . . and this is not the last purification."

alone with prominent merchants, but likewise with notaries and lawyers, with whom funds are on deposit and who manage estates; a *sans-culotte* with his pike stands in their cabinet whilst they write, and he accompanies them in the street when they call on their clients. Imagine the state of a notary's office or a counting-room under a system of this sort! The master of it winds up his business as soon as he can, no matter how, makes no new engagements, and does as little as possible. Still more inactive than he, his colleagues, condemned to an indefinite listlessness, under lock and key in the common prison, no longer attend to their business. There is a general, total paralysis of those natural organs which, in economic life, produce, elaborate, receive, store, preserve, exchange, and transmit in gross masses; and which, on the reverse side, hamper, throttle, or consume all the lesser subordinate organs to which the superior ones no longer provide outlets, intermediary agencies or aliment.

It is now the turn of the lowly. Whatever their sufferings may be they are to do their work as in healthy epochs, and they must do it perforce. The Convention, pursuing its accustomed rigid logical course with its usual shortsightedness, lays on them its violent and inept hands; they are trodden down, trampled upon and mauled for the purpose of curing them. Farmers are forbidden to sell their produce except in the markets, and obliged to bring to these a quota of so many sacks per week, and accompanied with military raids which compel them to furnish their quotas.[37] Shopkeepers are ordered "to expose for sale, daily and publicly, all goods and provisions of prime necessity" that they have on hand, while a maximum price

37. Decrees of May 4, 15, 19, 20 and 23, and of August 30, 1793.—Decrees of July 26, August 15, September 11, 1793, and February 24, 1794.—Camille Boursier, "Essai sur la Terreur en Anjou," p. 254. (Letter of Buissart to his friend Maximilian Robespierre, Arras, Pluviose 14, year II.) "We are dying with starvation in the midst of abundance; I think that the mercantile aristocracy ought to be killed out like the nobles and priests. The communes, under the favor of a storehouse of food and goods must alone be allowed to trade. This idea, well carried out, can be realised; then, the benefits of trade will turn to the advantage of the Republic, that is to say, to the advantage of buyer and seller."

is established, above which no one shall sell "bread, flour and grain, vegetables and fruits, wine, vinegar, cider, beer and brandy, fresh meat, salt meat, pork, cattle, dried, salted, smoked or pickled fish, butter, honey, sugar, sweet-oil, lamp-oil, candles, firewood, charcoal and other coal, salt, soap, soda, potash, leather, iron, steel, castings, lead, brass, hemp, linen, woollens, canvas and woven stuffs, *sabots,* shoes and tobacco." Whoever keeps on hand more than he consumes is a monopolist and commits a capital crime; the penalty, very severe, is imprisonment or the pillory, for whoever sells above the established price:[38] such are the simple and direct expedients of the rev-

---

38. Archives Nationales, AF., II., 49. (Documents on the levy of revolutionary taxes, Belfort, Brumaire 30, year II.) "Verneur, sr., taxed at ten thousand livres, for having withheld goods deposited with him by his sister, in order to save them from the coming taxation." Campardon, i., 292. (Judgments of the revolutionary commission at Strasbourg.)—"The head-clerk in Hecht's apothecary shop is accused of selling two ounces of rhubarb and manna at fifty-four sous; Hecht, the proprietor, is condemned to a fine of fifteen thousand livres. Madeleine Meyer, at Rosheim, a retailer, is accused of selling a candle for ten sous and is condemned to a fine of one thousand livres, payable in three days. Braun, butcher and bar-keeper, accused of having sold a glass of wine for twenty sous, is condemned to a fine of forty thousand francs, to be imprisoned until this is paid, and to exposure in the pillory before his own house for four hours, with this inscription: *debaser of the national currency.*"—"Recueil de Pieces, etc., at Strasbourg," (supplement, pp. 21, 30, 64). "Marie Ursule Schnellen and Marie Schultzmann, servant, accused of monopolising milk. The former is sentenced to the pillory for one day under a placard, *monopoliser of milk,* and to hold in one hand the money and, in the other, the milk-pot; the other, a servant with citizen Benner . . . he, the said Benner, is sentenced to a fine of three hundred livres, payable in three days." "Dorothy Franz, convicted of having sold two heads of salad at twenty sous, and of thus having depreciated the value of assignats, is sentenced to a fine of three thousand livres, imprisonment for six weeks and exposure in the pillory for two hours."—*Ibid.,* i., 18. "A grocer, accused of having sold sugar-candy at lower than the rate, although not comprised in the list, is sentenced to one hundred thousand livres fine and imprisonment until peace is declared."—Orders by Saint-Just and Lebas, Nivose 3, year II. "The criminal court of the department of the Lower-Rhine is ordered to destroy the house of any one convicted of having made sales below the rates fixed by the *maximum,*" consequently, the house of one Schauer, a furrier, is torn down, Nivose 7.

olutionary government, and such is the character of its inventive faculty, like that of the savage who hews down a tree to get at its fruit. For, after the first application of the *maximum* the shopkeeper is no longer able to carry on business; his customers, attracted by the sudden depreciation in price of his wares, flock to his shop and empty it in a few days;[39] having sold his goods for half what they cost him,[40] he has got back only one-half of his advances; therefore, he can only one-half renew his assortment, less than a half, since he has not paid his bills, and his credit is declining, the representatives on mission having taken all his coin, plate, and assignats. Hence, during the following month, buyers find on his unfurnished counters nothing but scraps and refuse.

In like manner, after the proclamation of the *maximum*,[41] the peasant refuses to bring his produce to market, while the revolutionary army is not everywhere on hand to take it from him by

39. Archives des Affaires Étrangérès, vol. 322. (Letter by Haupt, Belfort, Brumaire 3, year II.) "On my arrival here, I found the law of the *maximum* promulgated and in operation . . . (but) the necessary steps have not been taken to prevent a new monopoly by the rustics, who have flocked in to the shops of the dealers, carried off all their goods and created a factitious dearth."

40. Archives Nationales, F⁷, 4,421. (Petitions of merchants and shopkeepers at Troyes in relation to the revolutionary tax, especially of hatters, linen, cotton and woollen manufacturers, weavers, and grocers. There is generally a loss of one-half, and sometimes of three-fourths of the purchase money.)

41. Archives des Affaires Étrangérès, vol. 330. (Letter of Brutus, Marseilles, Nivose 6, year II.) "Since the *maximum* everything is wanting at Marseilles."— *Ibid.* (Letter by Soligny and Gosse, Thionville, Nivose 5, year II.) "No peasant is willing to bring anything to market. . . . They go off six leagues to get a better price and thus the communes which they once supplied are famishing. . . . According as they are paid in specie or assignats the difference often amounts to two hundred per cent., and nearly always to one hundred per cent."—"Un Séjour en France," pp. 188–189.—Archives Nationales, D., § I., file 2. (Letter of Representative Albert, Germinal 19, year II., and of Joffroy, national agent, district of Bar-sur-l Aube, Germinal 5, year III. "The municipalities have always got themselves exempted from the requisitions, which all fall on the farmers and proprietors unable to satisfy them. . . . The allotment among the tax-payers is made with the most revolting inequality. . . . Partiality through connections of relatives and of friendship."

force: he leaves his crop unthrashed as long as he can, and complains of not finding the men to thrash it. If necessary, he hides it or feeds it out to his animals. He often barters it away for wood, for a side of bacon or in payment for a day's work. At night, he carts it off six leagues to a neighboring district, where the local *maximum* is fixed at a higher rate. He knows who, in his own vicinity, still has specie in his pocket and he underhandedly supplies him with his stores. He especially conceals his superabundance and, as formerly, plays the sufferer. He is on good terms with the village authorities, with the mayor and national agent who are as interested as he is in evading the law, and, on a bribe being necessary, he gives it. At last, he allows himself to be sued, and his property attached; he goes to prison and tires the authorities out with his obstinacy. Hence, from week to week, less flour and grain and fewer cattle come to market, while meat becomes scarcer at the butcher's, and bread at the baker's. Having thus paralysed the lesser organs of supply and demand the Jacobins now have only to paralyse labor itself, the skilled hands, the active and vigorous arms. To do this, it suffices to substitute for the independent private workshop, the compulsory national work-shop, piece-work for work by the day, the attentive, energetic work-man who minds his business and expects to earn money, for the littleness and laxity of the workman picked up here and there, poorly paid and paid even when he botches and strolls about. This is what the Jacobins do by forcibly commanding the services of all sorts of laborers,[42] "all who help handle, transport and retail produce and articles of prime necessity," "country people who usually get in the

---

42. Decrees of September 29, 1793 (articles 8 and 9); of May 4 and 20, and June 26, 1794.—Archives Nationales, AF., II., 68–72. (Orders of the Committee of Public Safety, Prairial 26, year II.) "The horses and wagons of coal peddlers, the drivers accustomed to taking to Paris by law a portion of the supply of coal used in baking in the department of Seine-et-Marne, are drafted until the 1st of Brumaire next, for the transportation of coal to Paris. During this time they cannot be drafted for any other service." (A good many orders in relation to subsistences and articles of prime necessity may be found in these files, mostly in the handwriting of Robert Lindet.)

crops," and, more particularly, thrashers, reapers, carters, raftsmen, and also shoemakers, tailors, blacksmiths, and the rest. At every point of the social organism, the same principle is applied with the same result. Substitute everywhere an external, artificial, and mechanical constraint for the inward, natural, and animating stimulant, and you get nothing but an universal atrophy; deprive people of the fruits of their labor, and yet more, force them to produce by fear, confiscate their time, their painstaking efforts and their persons, reduce them to the condition of fellahs, create in them the sentiments of fellahs, and you will have nothing but the labor and productions of fellahs, that is to say, a minimum of labor and production, and hence, insufficient supplies for sustaining a very dense population, which, multiplied through a superior and more productive civilisation, will not long subsist under a barbarous, inferior, and unproductive régime. When this systematic and complete expropriation terminates we see the final result of the system, no longer a dearth, but famine, famine on a large scale, and the destruction of lives by millions. Among the Jacobins,[43] some of the maddest who are clearsighted, on account of their fury, Guffroy, Antonelle, Jean Bon St.-André, Collot d'Herbois, foresee the consequences and accept them along with the principle; others, who avoid seeing it, are only the more determined in the application of it, while all together work with all their might to aggravate the misery of which the lamentable spectacle is so vainly exposed under their eyes.

IV

Collot d'Herbois wrote from Lyons on November 6, 1793: "There is not two days' supply of provisions here." On the following day: "The present population of Lyons is one hundred and thirty thousand souls at least, and there is not sufficient subsistence for three

---

43. Cf. "The Revolution," ii., 69.—Dauban, "Paris en 1794." (Report by Pouvoyeur, March 15, 1794.) "A report has been long circulated that all the aged were to be slaughtered; there is not a place where this falsehood is not uttered."

days." Again the day after: "Our situation in relation to food is deplorable." Then, the next day: "Famine is beginning."[44] Near by, in the Montbrison district, in February, 1794, "there is no food or provisions left for the people"; all has been taken by requisition and carried off, even seed for planting, so that the fields lie fallow.[45] At Marseilles, "since the *maximum*, everything is lacking; even the fishermen no longer go out (on the sea) so that there is no supply of fish to live on."[46] At Cahors, in spite of multiplied requisitions, the Directory of Lot and Representative Taillefer[47] state that "the inhabitants, for more than eight days, are reduced wholly to maslin bread composed of one-fifth of wheat and the rest of barley, barley-malt, and millet." At Nismes,[48] to make the grain supply last, which is giving out, the bakers and all private persons are ordered not to bolt meal, but to leave the bran in it and knead and bake the "dough such as it is." At Grenoble,[49] "the bakers have stopped baking; the country people no longer bring wheat in; the dealers hide away their goods, or put them in the hands of neighborly officials, or send them off." "It goes from bad to worse," write the agents of Huningue;[50] "one might say even, that they would give this or that article to their cattle rather than sell it in conformity with the tax." The inhabitants of towns are everywhere put on rations, and so small a

44. Archives Nationales, F[7], 4,435, file 10, letters of Collot d'Herbois, Brumaire 17 and 19, year II.—De Martel, "Fouché," 340, 341. Letters of Collot d'Herbois, November 7 and 9, 1793.

45. De Martel, *ibid.*, 462. (Proclamation by Javogues, Pluviose 13, year II.)

46. Archives des Affaires Étrangérès, vol. 330. (Letter of Brutus, political agent, Nivose 6.)

47. Archives Nationales, AF., II., 116. (Orders of Taillefer and Marat-Valette, and Deliberations of the Directory of Lot, Brumaire 20, year II.)

48. Archives des Affaires Étrangérès, vol. 331. (Letter of the agent Bertrand, Frimaire 3.)

49. *Ibid.*, vol. 1332. (Letter of the agent Chépy, Brumaire 2.)

50. *Ibid.*, vol. 1411. (Letter of Blessmann and Hauser, Brumaire 30.)—*Ibid.* (Letter of Haupt, Belfort, Brumaire 29.) "I believe that Marat's advice should be followed here and a hundred scaffolds be erected; there are not guillotines enough to cut off the heads of the monopolists. I shall do what I can to have the pleasure of seeing one of these d—— b—— play hot cockles."

ration as to scarcely keep them from dying with hunger. "Since my
arrival in Tarbes," writes another agent,[51] "every person is limited
to half a pound of bread a day, composed one-third of wheat and
two-thirds of corn meal." The next day after the *fête* in honor of
the tyrant's death there was absolutely none at all. "A half-pound
of bread is also allowed at Evreux,[52] "and even this is obtained with
a good deal of trouble, many being obliged to go into the country
and get it from the farmers with coin." And even "they have got
very little bread, flour or wheat, for they have been obliged to bring
what they had to Evreux for the armies and for Paris."

It is worse at Rouen and at Bordeaux: at Rouen, in Brumaire, the
inhabitants have only one-quarter of a pound per head per diem of
bread; at Bordeaux, "for the past three months," says the agent,[53]
"the people sleep at the doors of the bakeries, to pay high for bread
which they often do not get. . . . There has been no baking done
today, and tomorrow only half a loaf will be given to each person.
This bread is made of oats and beans. . . . On days that there is
none, beans, chestnuts, and rice are distributed in very small quantities," four ounces of bread, five of rice or chestnuts. "I, who tell
you this, have already eaten eight or ten meals without bread; I
would gladly do without it if I could get potatoes in place of it, but
these, too, cannot be had." Five months later, fasting still continues,
and it lasts until after the reign of Terror, not alone in the town,
but throughout the department. "In the district of Cadillac," says
Tallien,[54] "absolute dearth prevails; the citizens of the rural districts
contend with each other for the grass in the fields; I have eaten

---

51. *Ibid.*, vol. 333. (Letter of Garrigues, Pluviose 16.)

52. "Souvenirs et Journal d'un Bourgeois d'Evreux," pp. 83–85. (June and
July 1794.)—*Ibid.*, at Nantes.—Dauban, "Paris en 1794," p. 194, March 4.

53. Archives des Affaires Étrangérès, vols. 331 and 332. (Letters of Désgranges, Frimaire 3 and 8 and 10.) "Many of the peasants have eaten no bread
for a fortnight. Most of them no longer work." Buchez et Roux, xviii., 346.
(Session of the Convention, Brumaire 14, speech by Legendre.)

54. *Moniteur,* xix., 671. (Speech by Tallien, March 12, 1794.) Buchez et Roux,
xxxii., 423. (Letter of Jullien, June 15, 1794.)

bread made of dog-grass." Haggard and worn out, the peasant, with his pallid wife and children, resorts to the marsh to dig roots, while there is scarcely enough strength in his arms to hold the plough. The same spectacle is visible in places which produce but little grain, or where the granaries have been emptied by the revolutionary drafts. "In many of the Indre districts," writes the representative on missions,[55] "food is wanting absolutely. Even in some of the communes, many of the inhabitants are reduced to a frightful state of want, feeding on acorns, bran and other unhealthy food. . . . The districts of Châtre and Argenton, especially, will be reduced to starvation unless they are promptly relieved. . . . The cultivation of the ground is abandoned; most of the persons in the jurisdiction wander about the neighboring departments in search of food." And it is doubtful whether they find it. In the department of Cher, "the butchers can no longer slaughter; the dealers' stores are all empty." In Allier, "the slaughter-houses and markets are deserted, every species of vegetable and aliment having disappeared; the inns are closed." In one of the Lozère districts, composed of five cantons, of which one produces an extra quantity of rye, the people live on requisitions imposed on Gard and the Upper Loire; the extortions of the representatives in these two departments "were distributed among the municipalities, and by these to the most indigent: many entire families, many of the poor and even of the rich, suffered for want of bread during six or eight days, and this frequently.[56] Nevertheless they do not riot; they merely supplicate and stretch forth their hands "with tears in their eyes." Such is the diet and submission of the

---

55. Archives Nationales, AF., II., 111. (Letters of Michaud, Chateauroux, Pluviose 18 and 19, year II.)

56. Dauban, "Paris en 1794," 410, 492, 498. (Letters from the national agent of the district of Sancoins, Thermidor 9, year II.; from the Directory of Allier, Thermidor 9; from the national agent of the district of Villefort, Thermidor 9.)—Gouverneur Morris, April 10, 1794, says in a letter to Washington that the famine in many places is extremely severe. Men really die of starvation who have the means to buy bread if they could only get it.

stomach in the provinces. Paris is less patient. For this reason, all the rest is sacrificed to it,[57] not merely the public funds, the Treasury from which it gets one or two millions per week,[58] but whole districts are starved for its benefit, six departments providing grain, twenty-six departments providing pork,[59] at the rate of the *maximum*, through requisitions, through the prospect of imprisonment and of the scaffold in case of refusal or concealment, under the predatory bayonets of the revolutionary army. The capital, above all, has to be fed. Let us see, under this system of partiality, how people live in Paris and what they feed on.

"Frightful crowds" at the doors of the bakeries, then at the doors of the butchers and grocers, then at the markets for butter, eggs, fish, and vegetables, and then on the quay for wine, firewood, and charcoal—such is the steady refrain of the police reports.[60] And this lasts uninterruptedly during the fourteen months of revolutionary government: long lines of people waiting in turn for bread, meat,

57. Volney, "Voyage en Orient," ii., 344. "When Constantinople lacks food twenty provinces are starved for its supply."

58. Archives Nationales, AF., II., 46, 68. (Decree of Committee of Public Safety.) The Treasury pays over to the city of Paris for subsistence, on Aug. 1, 1793, two millions, August 14, three, and 27, one million; September 8, 16, and 13, one million each, and so on. One million each on Frimaire 10 and 17, two each on the 22d and 26th: Nivose 17, two and 26, two; Pluviose 5, two and 20, one; Ventose 7, one and 24, two; Germinal 7, two and 15, two. Between August 7, 1793 and Germinal 19, year II., the Treasury paid over to Paris, thirty-one millions.

59. *Ibid.*, AF., II., 68. Decrees of Brumaire 14, Nivose 7 and Germinal 22 on the departments assigned to the supply of Paris.—Buchez et Roux, xxviii., 489. (Speech by Danton in Jacobin club, Aug. 28, 1793.) "I constantly asserted that it was necessary to give all to the mayor of Paris if he exacted it to feed its inhabitants. . . . Let us sacrifice one hundred and ten millions and save Paris and through it, the Republic."

60. Archives des Affaires Étrangères, vols. 1410 and 1411. Reports of June 20 and 21, 1793, July 21, 22, 28, 29 and 31, and every day of the months of August and September, 1793. Schmidt, "Tableaux de la Révolution Française," vol. II., *passim.*—Dauban, "Paris in 1794" (especially throughout Ventose, year II.)—Archives Nationales, F[7], 3,116[7]. (Reports for Nivose, year II.)

oil, soap, and candles, "*queues* for milk, for butter, for wood, for charcoal, *queues* everywhere!"[61] "There was one *queue* beginning at the door of a grocery in the Petit-Carreau stretching half-way up the rue Montorgueil."[62] These *queues* form at three o'clock in the morning, one o'clock, and at midnight, increasing from hour to hour. Picture to yourself, reader, the file of wretched men and women sleeping on the pavement when the weather is fine[63] and when not fine, standing up on stiff tottering legs; above all in winter, "the rain pouring on their backs," and their feet in the snow, for so many weary hours in dark, foul, dimly lighted streets strewed with garbage; for, for want of oil, one-half of the the street lamps are extinguished, and for lack of money, there is no repavement, no more sweeping, the offal being piled up against the walls.[64] The crowd draggles along through it, likewise, nasty, tattered and torn, people with shoes full of holes, because the shoemakers do no more work for their customers, and in dirty shirts, because no more soap can be had to wash with, while, morally as well as physically, all these forlorn beings elbowing each other render themselves still fouler. Promiscuousness, contact, weariness, waiting, and darkness afford free play to the grosser instincts; especially in summer, natural bestiality and Parisian mischievousness have full play.[65] "Lewd

61. Dauban, "Paris en 1794," 138. (Report of Ventose 2.)

62. Mercier, "Paris Pendant la Révolution," i., 355.

63. Archives des Affaires Étrangérès, 1411. (Reports of August 1 and 2, 1763.) "At one o'clock in the morning, we were surprised to find men and women lying along the sides of the houses patiently waiting for the shops to open."—Dauban, 231. (Report of Ventose 24.) To obtain the lights of a hog, at the slaughter-house near the Jardin des Plantes, at the rate of three francs ten sous, instead of thirty sous as formerly, women "were lying on the ground with little baskets by their side and waiting four and five hours."

64. Archives Nationales, F^7, 3,116^7. (Reports of Nivose 9 and 28.) "The streets of Paris are always abominable; they are certainly afraid to use those brooms." Dauban, 120. (Ventose 9.) "The rue St. Anne is blocked up with manure. In that part of it near the Rue Louvois, heaps of this stretch along the walls for the past fortnight."

65. Archives des Affaires Étrangérès, vol. 1411. (Reports of August 9,

women" pursue their calling standing in the row; it is an interlude for them; "their provoking expressions, their immoderate laughter," is heard some distance off and they find it a convenient place: two steps aside, on the flank of the row, are "half-open doors and dark alleys" which invite a confab; many of these women who have brought their mattresses "sleep there and commit untold abominations." What an example for the wives and daughters of steady workmen, for honest servants who hear and see! "Men stop at each row and choose their dulcinea, while others, less shameless, pounce on the women like bulls and kiss them one after the other." Are not these the fraternal kisses of patriotic Jacobins? Do not Mayor Pache's wife and daughter go to the clubs and kiss drunken *sansculottes?* And what says the guard? It has enough to do to restrain another blind and deaf animal instinct, aroused as it is by suffering, anticipation, and deception.

On approaching each butcher's stall before it opens "the porters, bending under the weight of a side of beef, quicken their steps so as not to be assailed by the crowd which presses against them, seeming to devour the raw meat with their eyes." They force a passage, enter the shop in the rear, and it seems as if the time for distributing the meat had come; the gendarmes, spurring their horses to a gallop, scatter the groups that are too dense; "rascals, in pay of the Commune," range the women in files, two and two, "shivering" in the cold morning air of December and January, awaiting their turn. Beforehand, however, the butcher, according to law, sets aside the portion for the hospitals, for pregnant women and others who are confined, for nurses, and besides, notwithstanding the law, he sets aside another portion for the revolutionary committee of the section, for the assistant commissioner and superintendent, for the pachas

---

1793.)—Mercier, i., 353.—Dauban, 530. (Reports of Fructidor 27, year II.) "There are always great gatherings at the coal depots. They begin at midnight, one, two o'clock in the morning. Many of the *habitués* take advantage of the obscurity and commit all sorts of indecencies."

and semipachas of the quarter, and finally for his rich customers who pay him extra.[66] To this end, "porters with broad shoulders form an impenetrable rampart in front of the shop and carry away whole oxen"; after this is over, the women find the shop stripped, while many, "after wasting their time for four mortal hours," go away empty handed. With this prospect before them the daily assemblages get to be uneasy and the waves rise; nobody, except those at the head of the row, is sure of his pittance; those that are behind regard enviously and with suppressed anger the person ahead of them. First come outcries, then jeerings, and then scuffling; the women rival the men in struggling and in profanity,[67] and they hustle each other. The line suddenly breaks; each rushes to get ahead of the other; the foremost place belongs to the most robust and the most brutal, and to secure it they have to trample down their neighbors.

There are fisticuffs every day.[68] When an assemblage remains quiet the spectators take notice of it. In general "they fight,[69] snatch bread out of each other's hands; those who cannot get any forcing whoever gets a loaf weighing four pounds to share it in small pieces.

66. Schmidt, "Tableaux de la Révolution Française," ii., 155. (Reports of Ventose 25.)—Dauban, 188. (Reports of Ventose 19.)—*Ibid.*, 69. (Reports of Ventose 2.) *Ibid.*, 126. (Reports of Ventose 10.)—Archives Nationales, F[7], 3,116[7]. (Reports of Nivose 28, year II.) The women "denounce the butchers and pork-sellers who pay no attention to the *maximum* law, giving only the poorest meat to the poor."—*Ibid.* (Reports of Nivose 6.) "It is frightful to see what the butchers give the people."

67. Mercier, *ibid.*, 363. "The women struggled with all their might against the men and contracted the habit of swearing. The last on the row knew how to worm themselves up to the head of it."—Buchez et Roux, xxviii., 364. ("Journal de la Montague," July 28, 1793.) "One citizen was killed on Sunday, July 21, one of the Gravilliers (club) in trying to hold on to a six-pound loaf of bread which he had just secured for himself and family. Another had a cut on his arm the same day in the Rue Froid-Manteau. A pregnant woman was wounded and her child died in her womb."

68. Dauban, 256. (Reports of Ventose 27.) Market of Faubourg St. Antoine. "On ne se f—— pas de coups de poing depuis deux on trois jours."

69. Archives des Affaires Étrangérès, vol. 1410. (Reports of August 6 and 7, 1793.)

The women yell frightfully. . . . Children sent by their parents are beaten," while the weak are pitched into the gutter. "In distributing the meanest portions of food[70] it is force which decides," the strength of loins and arms; "a number of women this morning came near losing their lives in trying to get four ounces of butter." More sensitive and more violent than men, "they do not, or will not, listen to reason,[71] they pounce down like harpies" on the market-wagons; they thrash the drivers, strew the vegetables and butter on the ground, tumble over each other and are suffocated through the impetuosity of the assault; some, "trampled upon, almost crushed, are carried off half-dead." Everybody for himself. Empty stomachs feel that, to get anything, it is important to get ahead, not to await for the distribution, the unloading, or even the arrival of the supplies. "A boat laden with wine having been signalled, the crowd rushed on board to pillage it and the boat sunk," probably along with a good many of its invaders.[72] Other gatherings at the barriers stop the peasants' wagons and take their produce before they reach the markets. Outside the barriers, children and women throw stones at the milkmen, forcing them to get down from their carts and distribute milk on the spot. Still further out, one or two leagues off on the highways, gangs from Paris go at night to intercept and seize the supplies intended for Paris. "This morning," says a watchman, "all the Faubourg St. Antoine scattered itself along the Vincennes road and pillaged whatever was on the way to the city; some paid, while others carried off without paying. . . . The unfortunate peasants

70. Dauban, 144. (Reports of Ventose 19.)

71. Dauban, 199. (Reports of Ventose 19.)—Dauban, "La Demagogie en 1793," p. 470. "Scarcely had the peasants arrived when harpies in women's clothes attacked them and carried off their goods. . . . Yesterday, a peasant was beaten for wanting to sell his food at the *maximum* rate." (October 19, 1793.)—Dauban, "Paris en 1794," 144, 173, 199. (Reports of Ventose 13, 17 and 19.)—Archives des Affaires Étrangérès, vol. 1410. (Reports of June 26 and 27, 1793.) Wagons and boats are pillaged for candles and soap.

72. Dauban, 45. (Reports of Pluviose 17.)—222. (Reports of Ventose 23.)—160. (Reports of Ventose 15.)—340. (Reports of Germinal 28.)—87. (Reports of Ventose 5.)

swore that they would not fetch anything more," the dearth thus increasing through the efforts to escape it.

In vain the government makes its requisitions for Paris as if in a state of siege, and fixes the quantity of grain on paper which each department, district, canton, and commune, must send to the capital. Naturally, each department, district, canton, and commune strives to retain its own supplies, for charity begins at home.[73] Especially in a village, the mayor and members of a municipality, themselves cultivators, are lukewarm when the commune is to be starved for the benefit of the capital; they declare a less return of grain than there really is; they allege reasons and pretexts; they mystify or suborn the commissioner on subsistences, who is a stranger, incompetent and needy; they make him drink and eat, and, now and then, fill his pocket-book; he slips over the accounts, he gives the village receipts on furnishing three-quarters or a half of the demand, often in spoilt or mixed grain or poor flour, while those who have no rusty wheat get it of their neighbors; instead of parting with a hundred quintals they part with fifty, while the quantity of grain in the Paris markets is not only insufficient, but the grain blackens or sprouts and the flour grows musty. In vain the government makes clerks and depositaries of butchers and grocers, allowing them five or ten per cent. profit on retail sales of the food it supplies them with at wholesale, and thus creates in Paris, at the expense of all France, an artificial decline. Naturally, the bread[74] which, thanks to the State,

73. Archives Nationales, AF., II., 116. (Order of Paganel, Castres, Pluviose 6 and 7, year II. "The steps taken to obtain returns of food have not fulfilled the object. . . . The statements made are either false or inexact.") Cf., for details, the correspondence of the other representatives on mission.—Dauban, "Paris en 1794," 190. (Speech by Fouquier-Tinville in the Convention, Ventose 19.) "The mayor of Pont St. Maxence has dared to say that 'when Paris sends us sugar we will then see about letting her have our eggs and butter.'"

74. Archives des Affaires Étrangérès, vol. 1411. (Reports of August 7 and 8, 1793.) "Seven thousand five hundred pounds of bread, about to be taken out, have been stopped at the barriers."—Dauban, 45. (Orders of the day, Pluviose 17.) Lamps are set up at all the posts, "especially at la Grève and Passy, so as to light up the river and see that no eatables pass outside."—Mercier, i., 355.—

costs three sous in Paris, is furtively carried out of Paris into the suburbs, where six sous are obtained for it; there is the same furtive leakage for other food furnished by the State on the same conditions to other dealers; the tax is a burden which forces them to go outside their shops; food finds its level like water, not alone outside of Paris, but in Paris itself. Naturally, "the grocers peddle their goods" secretly, "sugar, candles, soap, butter, dried vegetables, meat-pies, and the rest," amongst private houses, in which these articles are bought at any price. Naturally, the butcher keeps his large pieces of beef and choice morsels for the large eating-houses, and for rich customers who pay him whatever profit he asks. Naturally, whoever is in authority, or has the power, uses it to supply himself first, largely, and in preference; we have seen the levies of the revolutionary committees, superintendents and agents; as soon as rations are allotted to all mouths, each potentate will have several rations delivered for his mouth alone; in the meantime[75] the patriots who guard the barriers appropriate all provisions that arrive, and the next morning, should any scolding appear in the orders of the day, it is but slight.

Such are the two results of the system: not only is the food which is supplied to Paris scant and poor, but the regular consumers of it, those who take their turn to get it, obtain but a small portion, and

---

Dauban, 181. (Reports of Ventose 18.)—210. (Reports of Ventose 21.)—190. Speech by Fouquier, Ventose 19.) "The butchers in Paris who cannot sell above the *maximum* carry the meat they buy to the Sèvres butchers and sell it at any price they please."—257. (Reports of Ventose 27.) "You see, about ten o'clock in the evening, aristocrats and other egoists coming to the dealers who supply Egalité's mansion (the Duke of Orleans) and buy chickens and turkeys which they carefully conceal under their overcoats."

75. Dauban, 255. (Orders of the day by Henriot, Ventose 27.) "I have to request my brethren in arms not to take any rations whatever. This little deprivation will silence the malevolent who seek every opportunity to humble us."—*Ibid.*, 359. "On Floréal 29, between five and six o'clock in the morning, a patrol of about fifteen men of the Bonnet-Rouge section, commanded by a sort of commissary, stop subsistences on the Orleans road and take them to their section."

that the worst.[76] A certain inspector, on going to the corn-market for a sample of flour, writes "that it cannot be called flour;[77] it is ground bran," and not a nutritive substance; the bakers are forced to take it, the markets containing for the most part no other supply than this flour." Again, three weeks later, "Food is still very scarce and poor in quality. The bread is disagreeable to the taste and produces maladies with which many citizens are suffering, like dysentery and other inflammatory ailments." The same report, three months later in Nivose: "Complaints are constantly made of the poor quality of flour, which, it is said, makes a good many people ill; it causes severe pain in the intestines, accompanied with a slow fever." In Ventose, "the scarcity of every article is extremely great,"[78] especially of meat. Some women in the Place Maubert, pass six hours in a line waiting for it, and do not get the quarter of a pound; in many stalls there is none at all, not "an ounce" being obtainable to make broth for the sick. Workmen do not get it in their shops and do without their soup; they live on "bread and salted herrings." A great many people groan over "not having eaten bread for a fortnight"; women say that "they have not had a dish of meat and vegetables (*pot-au-feu*) for a month." Meanwhile "vegetables are astonishingly scarce and excessively dear . . . two sous for a miserable carrot, and as much for two small leeks"; out of two thousand women who wait at the central market for a distribution of beans, only six hundred receive any; potatoes increase in price in one week from two to three francs a bushel, and oatmeal and ground

76. Dauban, 341. (Letter of the Commissioner on Subsistences, Germinal 23.) "The supplies are stolen under the people's eyes, or what they get is of inferior quality." The commissioner is surprised to find that, having provided so much, so little reaches the consumers.

77. Archives des Affaires Étrangérès, vol. 1411. (Reports of August 11–12 and 31, and Sept. 1, 1793.)—Archives Nationales, F[7], 3,116[7]. (Reports of Nivose 7 and 12, year II.)

78. Dauban, "Paris en 1794," 60, 68, 69, 71, 82, 93, 216, 231.—Schmidt, "Tableaux de Paris," 187, 190.—Archives Nationales, F[7], 3,116[7]. (Report of Leharivel, Nivose 7.)—The gunsmiths employed by the government likewise state that they have for a long time had nothing to eat but bread and cheese.

peas triple in price. "The grocers have no more brown sugar, even for the sick," and sell candles and soap only by the half-pound. A fortnight later candles are wholly wanting in certain quarters, except in the section storehouse, which is almost empty, each person being allowed only one; a good many households go to rest at sundown for lack of lights and do not cook any dinner for lack of coal. Eggs, especially, are "honored as invisible divinities," while the absent butter "is a god."[79] "If this lasts," say the workmen, "we shall have to cut each other's throats, since there is nothing left to live on."[80] "Sick women,[81] children in their cradles, lie outstretched in the sun, in the very heart of Paris, in rue Vivienne, on the Pont-Royal, and remain there "late in the night, demanding alms of the passers-by." "One is constantly stopped by beggars of both sexes, most of them healthy and strong," begging, they say, for lack of work. Without counting the feeble and the infirm who are unable to stand in a line, whose sufferings are visible, who gradually waste away and die without a murmur at home, "one encounters in the streets and markets" only famished and eager visages, "an immense crowd of citizens running and dashing against each other," crying out and weeping, "everywhere presenting an image of despair."[82]

V

If this penury exists, say the Jacobins, it is owing to the decrees against monopoly, and sales above the *maximum* not being executed according to the letter of the law; the egoism of the cultivator and the cupidity of dealers are not restrained by fear; delinquents escape too frequently from the legal penalty. Let us enforce this penalty rigorously; let us augment the punishment against them and their instruments; let us screw up the machine and give them a new

79. Dauban, 231. (Report of Perriére, Ventose 24.) "Butter of which they make a god."

80. *Ibid.*, 68. (Report of Ventose 2.)

81. Archives Nationales, F^7, 3,116^7, (Report of Nivose 28.)—Dauban, 144. (Report of Nivose 14.)

82. Dauban, 81. (Report of Latour-Lamontagne, Ventose 4.)

wrench. A new estimate and verification of the food-supply takes place, domiciliary perquisitions, seizures of special stores regarded as too ample,[83] limited rations for each consumer, a common and obligatory mess-table for all prisoners, brown, *égalité* bread, mostly of bran, for every mouth that can chew, prohibition of the making of any other kind, confiscation of bolters and sieves,[84] the "individual," personal responsibility of every administrator who allows the people he rules to resist or escape furnishing the supplies demanded, the sequestration of his property, imprisonment, fines, the pillory, and the guillotine to hurry up requisitions, or stop free trading—every terrifying engine is driven to the utmost against the farmers and cultivators of the soil.

After April, 1794,[85] crowds of this class are seen filling the prisons to overflowing; the Revolution has struck them also. They stroll about in the court-yard, and wander through the corridors with a sad, stupified expression, no longer comprehending the way things are going on in the world. In vain are efforts made to explain to them that "their crops are national property and that they are simply

83. "Souvenirs et Journal d'un Bourgeois d'Evreux," 83. "Friday, June 15, 1794, a proclamation is made that all who have any provisions in their houses, wheat, barley, rye, flour and even bread, must declare them within twenty-four hours under penalty of being regarded as an enemy of the country and declared 'suspect,' put under arrest and tried by the courts."—Schmidt, "Tableaux de la Révolution Française," ii., 214. A seizure is made at Passy of two pigs and forty pounds of butter, six bushels of beans, etc., in the domicile of citizen Lucet who had laid in supplies for sixteen persons of his own household.

84. Archives Nationales, AF., II., 68. Orders of the Committee of Public Safety, Pluviose 23, referring to the law of Brumaire 25, forbidding the extraction of more than fifteen pounds of bran from a quintal of flour. Order directing the removal of bolters from bakeries and mills; he who keeps or conceals these on his property "shall be treated as 'suspect' and put under arrest until peace is declared."—Berryat Saint-Prix, 357, 362. At Toulouse, three persons are condemned to death for monopoly. At Montpelier, a baker, two dealers and a merchant are guillotined for having invoiced, concealed and kept "a certain quantity of gingerbread cakes intended solely for consumption by antirevolutionists."

85. "Un Séjour en France" (April 22, 1794).

its depositaries";[86] never had this new principle entered into, nor will it enter, their rude brains; always, through habit and instinct, will they work against it. Let them be spared the temptation. Let us relieve them from, and, in fact, take their crops; let the State in France become the sole depositary and distributor of grain; let it solely buy and sell grain at a fixed rate. Consequently, at Paris,[87] the Committee of Public Safety first puts "in requisition all the oats that can be found in the Republic; every holder of oats is required to deposit his stock on hand within eight days, in the storehouse indicated by the district administration" at the *maximum* price; otherwise he is " 'suspect' and must be punished as such." In the meantime, through still more comprehensive orders issued in the provinces, Paganel in the department of Tarn, and Dartigoyte in those of Gers and the Upper-Garonne,[88] enjoin each commune to establish public granaries. "All citizens are ordered to bring in whatever produce they possess in grain, flour, wheat, maslin, rye, barley, oats, millet, buckwheat" at the *maximum* rate; nobody shall keep on hand more than one month's supply, fifty pounds of flour or wheat for each person; in this way, the State, which holds in its hands the keys of the storehouses, may "carry out the salutary equalisation of subsistences" between department and department, district and district, commune and commune, individual and individual. A storekeeper will look after each of these well-filled granaries; the mu-

86. Ludovic Sciout, iv., 236. (Proclamation of the representatives on mission in Finisterre.) "Magistrates of the people tell all farmers and owners of land that their crops belong to the nation and that they are simply its depositaries."—Archives Nationales, AF., II., 92. (Orders by Bô, representative in Cautal, Pluviose 8.) "Whereas, as all citizens in a Republic form one family . . . all those who refuse to assist their brethren and neighbors under the specious pretext that they have not sufficient supplies must be regarded as 'suspect' citizens."

87. Archives Nationales, AF., II., 68. (Orders of the Committee of Public Safety, Prairial 28.) The *maximum* price is fourteen francs the quintal; after Messidor 30, it is not to be more than eleven francs.

88. *Ibid.*, AF., II., 116 and 106, orders of Paganel, Castres, Pluviose 6 and 7. Orders of Dartigoyte, Floréal 23, 25, and 29.

nicipality will itself deliver rations and, moreover, "take suitable steps to see that beans and vegetables, as they mature, be economically distributed under its supervision," at so much per head, and always at the rate of the *maximum*. Otherwise, dismissal, imprisonment and prosecution "in the extraordinary criminal tribunal." This being accomplished, and the fruits of labor duly allotted, there remains only the allotment of labor itself. To effect this, Maignet,[89] in Vaucluse, and in the Bouches-du-Rhone, prescribes for each municipality the immediate formation of two lists, one of day-laborers and the other of proprietors; "all proprietors in need of a cultivator by the day," are to appear and ask for one at the municipality, which will assign the applicant as many as he wants, "in order on the list," with a card for himself and numbers for the designated parties. The laborer who does not enter his name on the list, or who exacts more than the *maximum* wages, is to be sentenced to the pillory with two years in irons. The same sentence with the addition of a fine of three hundred livres, is for every proprietor who employs any laborer not on the list or who pays more than the *maximum* rate of wages. After this, nothing more is necessary, in practice, than to draw up and keep in sight the new registries of names and figures made by the members of thirty thousand municipal boards, who cannot keep accounts and who scarcely know how to read and write; build a vast public granary, or put in requisition three or four barns in each commune, in which half dried and mixed grain may rot; pay two hundred thousand incorruptible storekeepers and measurers who will not divert anything from the depots for their friends or themselves; add to the thirty-five thousand employees of the Committee on Subsistences,[90] five hundred thousand municipal scribes disposed to quit their trades or ploughs for the purpose of making daily distributions gratuitously; but more precisely, to maintain four or

89. *Ibid.*, AF., II., 147. (Orders of Maignet, Avignon, Prairial 2.)

90. *Moniteur*, xxiii., 397. (Speech by Dubois-Crancé, May 5, 1795.) "The Committee on Commerce (and Supplies) had thirty-five thousand employees in its service."

five millions of perfect gendarmes, one in each family, living with it, to help along the purchases, sales, and transactions of each day and to verify at night the contents of the locker—in short, to set one-half of the French people as spies on the other half. These are the conditions which secure the production and distribution of food, and which suffice for the institution throughout France of a conscription of labor and the captivity of grain.

Unfortunately, the peasant does not understand this theory, but he understands business; he makes close calculations, and the positive, patent, vulgar facts on which he reasons lead to other conclusions.[91] "In Messidor last they took all my last years' oats, at fourteen francs in assignats, and, in Thermidor, they are going to take all this year's oats, at eleven francs in assignats. At this rate I shall not sow at all. Besides, I do not need any for myself, as they have taken my horses for the army-wagons. To raise rye and wheat, as much of it as formerly, is also working at a loss; I will raise no more than the little I want for myself, and again, I suppose that this will be put in requisition, even my supplies for the year! I had rather let my fields lie fallow. Just see now, they are taking all the live three-months' pigs! Luckily, I killed mine beforehand and it is now in the pork-barrel. But they are going to claim all salt provisions like the rest. The new grabbers are worse than the old ones. Six months

91. Archives Nationales, AF., II., 68. (Orders of the Committee of Public Safety, Prairial 28.)—Decree of Messidor 8, year II. "All kinds of grain and the hay of the present crop are required by the government."—A new estimate is made, each farmer being obliged to state the amount of his crop; verification, confiscation in case of inaccurate declarations, and orders to thrash out the sheaves.—Dauban, 490. (Letter of the national agent of Villefort, Thermidor 19.) Calculations and the reasoning of farmers with a view to avoid sowing and planting: "Not so much on account of the lack of hands as not to ruin oneself by sowing and raising an expensive crop which, they say, affords them small returns when they sell their grain at so low a price."—Archives Nationales, AF., II., 106. (Letter of the national agent in Gers and Haute-Garonne, Floréal 25.) "They say here, that as soon as the crop is gathered, all the grain will be taken away, without leaving anything to live on. It is stated that all salt provisions are going to be taken and the agriculturists reduced to the horrors of a famine."

more, and we shall all die of hunger. It is better to cross one's arms at once and go to prison; there, at least, we shall be fed and not have to work." In effect, they allow themselves to be imprisoned, the best of the small cultivators and proprietors by thousands, and Lindet,[92] at the head of the Commission on Subsistences, speaks with dismay of the ground being no longer tilled, of cattle in France being no more abundant than the year before, and of nothing to be had to cut this year.

For a strange thing has happened, unheard of in Europe, almost incredible to any one familiar with the French peasant and his love of work. This field which he has ploughed, manured, harrowed, and reaped with his own hands, its precious crop, the crop that belongs to him and on which he has feasted his eyes for seven months, now that it is ripe, he will not take the trouble to gather it; it would be bothering himself for some one else; as the crop that he sees there is for the government, let the government defray the final cost of getting it in; let it do the harvesting, the reaping, the putting it in sheaves, the carting, and the thrashing in the barn. Thereupon, the representatives on mission exclaim, each shouting in a louder or lower key, according to his character. "Many of the cultivators," writes Dartigoyte,[93] "affect a supreme indifference for this splendid

92. *Moniteur*, xxii., 21. (Speech by Lindet, September 7, 1794.) "We have long feared that the ground would not be tilled, that the meadows would be covered with cattle while the proprietors and farmers were kept in prison." Archives Nationales, D., § 1, No. I. (Letter from the district of Bar-sur-Seine, Ventose 14, year III.) "The *maximum* causes the concealment of grain. The quit-claims ruined the consumers and rendered them desperate. How many wretches, indeed, have been arrested, attacked, confiscated, fined, and ruined for having gone off fifteen or twenty leagues to get grain with which to feed their wives and children?"

93. AF., II., 106. (Circular by Dartigoyte, Floréal 25.) "You must apply this rule, that is, make the municipal officers responsible for the noncultivation of the soil." "If any citizen allows himself a different kind of bread, other than that which all the cultivators and laborers in the commune use, I shall have him brought before the courts conjointly with the municipality as being the first culprit guilty of having tolerated it. . . . Reduce, if necessary, three-fourths of

crop. One must have seen it, as I have, to believe how great the neglect of the wheat is in certain parts, how it is smothered by the grass. . . . Draft, if the case requires it, a certain number of inhabitants in this or that commune to work in another one. . . . Every man who refuses to work, except on the 'decade' day, must be punished as an ill-disposed citizen, as a *royalist.*" "Generous friends of nature," writes Ferry,[94] "introduce amongst you, perpetuate around you, the habit of working in common, and begin with the present crop. Do not spare either indolent women or indolent men, those social parasites, many of whom you doubtless have in your midst. What! allow lazy men and lazy women where we are! Where should we find a Republican police? . . . Immediately on the reception of this present order the municipal officers of each commune will convoke all *citoyennes* in the Temple of the Eternal and urge them, in the name of the law, to devote themselves to the labors of harvesting. Those women who fail in this patriotic duty, shall be excluded from the assemblies, from the national festivals, while all good *citoyennes* are requested to repel them from their homes. All good citizens are requested to give to this rural festivity that *sentimental character* which befits it." And the programme is carried out, now in idyllic shape and now under compulsion. Around Avignon,[95] the commanding officer, the battalions of volunteers, and patriotic ladies, "the wives and daughters of patriots," inscribe themselves as harvesters. Around Arles, "the municipality drafts all the inhabitants; patrols are sent into the country to compel all who are engaged on other work to leave it and do the harvesting." The Convention, on its side, orders[96] the release, "provisionally, of all ploughmen, daylaborers, reapers, and professional artisans and brewers, in the coun-

---

the bread allowed to nonlaboring citizens because *muscadins* and *muscadines* have resources and, besides, lead an idle life."

94. AF., II., 111. (Letters of Ferry, Bourges, Messidor 23, to his "brethren in the popular club," and "to the *citoyennes* (women) of Indre-et-Cher.")

95. *Moniteur*, xxi., 171. (Letter from Avignon, Messidor 9, and letter of the Jacobins of Arles.)

96. *Moniteur*, xxi., 184. (Decree of Messidor 21.)

try and in the market-towns and communes, the population of which is not over twelve hundred inhabitants, and who are confined as 'suspects.'" In other terms, physical necessity has imposed silence on the inept theory; above all things, the crop must be harvested, and indispensable arms be restored to the field of labor. The governors of France are compelled to put on the brake, if only for an instant, at the last moment, at sight of the yawning abyss, of approaching and actual famine; France was then gliding into it, and, if not engulphed, it is simply a miracle.

Four fortunate circumstances, at the last hour, concur to keep her suspended on the hither brink of the precipice. The winter chances to be exceptionally mild.[97] The vegetables which make up for the absence of bread and meat provide food for April and May, while the remarkably fine harvest, almost spontaneous, is three weeks in advance. Another, and the second piece of good fortune, consists in the great convoy from America, one hundred and sixteen vessels loaded with grain, which reached Brest on the 8th of June, 1794, in spite of English cruisers, thanks to the sacrifice of the fleet that protected it and which, eight days previously, had succumbed in its behalf. The third stroke of fortune is the entry of a victorious army into the enemies' country and feeding itself through foreign requisitions, in Belgium, in the Palatinate and on the frontier provinces of Italy and Spain. Finally, most fortunate of all, Robespierre, Saint-Just, and Couthon, the Paris commune and the theorist Jacobins, are guillotined on the 23rd of July, and with them falls despotic socialism; henceforth, the Jacobin edifice crumbles, owing to great crevices in its walls. The *maximum*, in fact, is no longer maintained, while the Convention, at the end of December, 1794, legally abol-

---

97. Gouverneur Morris. (Correspondence with Washington. Letters of March 27 and April 10, 1794.) He says that there is no record of such an early spring. Rye has headed out and clover is in flower. It is astonishing to see apricots in April as large as pigeons' eggs. In the south, where the dearth is most severe, he has good reason to believe that the ground is supplying the inhabitants with food. A frost like that of the year before in the month of May (1793) would help the famine more than all the armies and fleets in Europe.

ishes it; the farmers now sell as they please and at two prices, according as they are paid in assignats or coin; their hope, confidence, and courage are restored; in October and November, 1794, they voluntarily do their own ploughing and planting, and still more gladly will they gather in their own crops in July, 1795. Nevertheless, we can judge by the discouragement into which they had been plunged by four months of the system, the utter prostration into which they would have fallen had the system lasted an indefinite time. It is very probable that cultivation at the end of one or two years would have proved unproductive or have ceased altogether. Already, subject to every sort of exhortation and threat, the peasant had remained inert, apparently deaf and insensible, like an overloaded beast of burden which, so often struck, grows obstinate or sinks down and refuses to move. It is evident that he would have never stirred again could Saint-Just, holding him by the throat, have bound him hand and foot, as he had done at Strasbourg, in the multiplied knots of his Spartan Utopia; we should have seen what labor and the stagnation it produces comes to, when managed through State manoeuvres by administrative mannikins and humanitarian automatons. This experiment had been tried in China, in the eleventh century, and according to principles, long and regularly, by a well-manipulated and omnipotent State, on the most industrious and soberest people in the world, and men died in myriads like flies. If the French, at the end of 1794 and during the following years did not die like flies, it was because the Jacobin system was relaxed too soon.

VI

But, if the Jacobin system, in spite of its surviving founders, gradually relaxes after Thermidor; if the main ligature tied around the man's neck, broke just as the man was strangling, the others that still bind him hold him tight, except as they are loosened in places; and, as it is, some of the straps, terribly stiffened, sink deeper and deeper into his flesh. In the first place, the requisitions continue:

there is no other way of provisioning the armies and the cities; the gendarme is always on the road, compelling each village to contribute its portion of grain, and at the legal rate. The refractory are subject to keepers, confiscations, fines, and imprisonment; they are confined and kept in the district lock-ups "at their own expense," men and women, twenty-two on Pluviose 17, year III., in the district of Bar-sur-Aube; forty-five, Germinal 7, in the district of Troyes; forty-five, the same day, in the district of Nogent-sur-Seine, and twenty others, eight days later, in the same district, in the commune of Traine alone.[98] The condition of the cultivator is certainly not an

---

98. Archives Nationales, AF., II., 73. (Letter by the Directory of Calvados, Prairial 26, year III.) "We have not a grain of wheat in store, and the prisons are full of cultivators."—Archives Nationales, D., § 1, file No. 3. (Warrants of arrest issued by Representative Albert, Pluviose 19, year III., Germinal 7 and 16.)—On the details of the difficulties and annoyances attending the requisitions, cf. this file and the five preceding or following files. (Letter of the National agent, district of Nogent-sur-Seine, Germinal 13.) "I have had summoned before the district court a great many cultivators and proprietors who are in arrears in furnishing the requisitions made on them by their respective municipalities. ... A large majority declared that they were unable to furnish in full even if their seed were taken. The court ordered the confiscation of the said grain with a fine equal to the value of the quantity demanded of those called upon. . . . It is now my duty to execute the sentence. But, I must observe to you, that if you do not reduce the fine, many of them will be reduced to despair. Hence I await your answer so that I may act accordingly."—(Another letter from the same agent, Germinal 9.) "It is impossible to supply the market of Villarceaux; seven communes under requisition prevented it through the district of Sozannes which constantly keeps an armed force there to carry grain away as soon as thrashed."—It is interesting to remark the inquisitorial sentimentality of the official agents and the low stage of culture. (Procès-verbal of the Magincourt municipality, Ventose 7.) Of course I am obliged to correct the spelling so as to render it intelligible. "The said Croiset, gendarme, went with the national agent into the houses of citizens in arrears, of whom, amongst those in arrears, nobody refused but Jean Mauchin, whom we could not keep from talking against him, seeing that he is wholly egoist and only wants for himself. He declared to us that, if, the day before his harvesting he had any left, he would share it with the citizens that needed it. . . . Alas, yes, how could one refrain from shutting up such an egoist who wants only for himself to the detriment of his fellow-citizens? A proof of the truth is that he feeds in his house three dogs, at least

easy one, while public authority, aided by the public force, extorts from him all it can at a rate of its own; moreover, it will soon exact from him one-half of his contributions in kind, and, it must be noted, that at this time, the direct contributions alone absorb twelve and thirteen sous on the franc of the revenue. Nevertheless, under this condition, which is that of laborers in a Mussulman country, the French peasant, like the Syrian or Tunisian peasant, can keep himself alive; for, through the abolition of the *maximum*, private transactions are now free, and, to indemnify himself on this side, he sells to private individuals and even to towns,[99] by agreement, on understood terms, and as dear as he pleases; all the dearer because through the legal requisitions the towns are half empty, and there are fewer sacks of grain for a larger number of purchasers; hence his losses by the government are more than made up by his gains on private parties; he gains in the end, and that is why he persists in farming.

The weight, however, of which he relieves himself falls upon the overburdened buyer, and this weight, already excessive, goes on increasing, through another effect of the revolutionary institution, until it becomes ten-fold and even a hundred-fold. The only money, in fact, which private individuals possess melts away in their hands, and, so to say, destroys itself. When the guillotine stops working, the assignat, losing its official value, falls to its real value. In August, 1794, the loss on it is sixty-six per cent., in October, seventy-two per cent., in December, seventy-eight per cent., in January, 1795, eighty-one per cent., and after that date the constant issues of enor-

---

one hundred and fifty chickens and even pigeons, which uses up a lot of grain, enough to hinder the satisfaction of all the requisitions. He might do without dogs, as his court is enclosed; he might likewise content himself with thirty chickens and then be able to satisfy the requisitions." This document is signed "Bertrand, agen." Mauchin, on the strength of it, is incarcerated at Troyes "at his own expense."

99. *Ibid.* Letter from the district of Bar-sur-Seine, Ventose 14, year III. Since the abolition of the *maximum*, "the inhabitants travel thirty and forty leagues to purchase wheat."—(Letter from the municipality of Troyes, Ventose 15.) "According to the price of grain, which we keep on buying, by agreement, bread will cost fifteen sous (the pound) next decade."

mous amounts, five hundred millions, then a billion, a billion and a half, and, finally, two billions a month, hastens its depreciation.[100] The greater the depreciation of the assignats the greater the amount the government is obliged to issue to provide for its expenses, and the more it issues the more it causes their depreciation, so that the decline which increases the issue increases the depreciation, until, finally, the assignat comes down to nothing. On March 11, 1795, the *louis d'or* brings two hundred and five francs in assignats, May 11, four hundred francs, June 12, one thousand francs, in the month of October, one thousand seven hundred francs, November 13, two thousand eight hundred and fifty francs, November 21, three thousand francs, and six months later, nineteen thousand francs. Accordingly, an assignat of one hundred francs is worth in June, 1795, four francs, in August three francs, in November fifteen sous, in December ten sous, and then five sous. Naturally, all provisions rise proportionately in price. A pound of bread in Paris, January 2, 1796, costs fifty francs, a pound of meat sixty francs, a pound of candles one hundred and eighty francs, a bushel of potatoes two hundred francs, a bottle of wine one hundred francs. The reader may imagine, if he can, the distress of people with small incomes, pensioners and employees, mechanics and artisans in the towns out of work,[101] in

100. Schmidt, "Parisir Zustande," 145–220. The reopening of the Bourse, April 25, 1795; *ibid.*, 322, ii., 105.—"Memoirs of Theobald Wolf," vol. i., p. 200 (February 3, 1796). At Havre, the *louis d'or* is then worth five thousand francs, and the *ecu* of six francs in proportion. At Paris (February 12), the *louis d' or* is worth six thousand five hundred: a dinner for two persons at the Palais Royal costs one thousand five hundred francs.—Mayer ("Frankreich in 1796.") He gives a dinner for ten persons which costs three hundred thousand francs in assignats. At this rate a cab ride costs one thousand francs, and by the hour six thousand francs.

101. "Correspondance de Mallet-Dupan avec la cour de Vienne," i., 253 (July 18, 1795). "It is not the same now as in the early days of the Revolution, which then bore heavily only on certain classes of society; now, everybody feels the scourge, hourly, in every department of civil life. Goods and provisions advance daily (in price) in much greater proportion than the decline in assignats. . . . Paris is really a city of furnishing shops. . . . The immense competition for these objects raises all goods twenty-five per cent. a week. . . . It is the same

brief, all who have nothing but a small package of assignats to live on, and who have nothing to do, whose indispensable wants are not directly supplied by the labor of their own hands in producing wine, candles, meat, potatoes, and bread.

Immediately after the abolition of the *maximum*,[102] the cry of hunger increases. From month to month its accents become more painful and vehement in proportion to the increased dearness of provisions, especially in the summer of 1795, as the harvesting draws near, when the granaries, filled by the crop of 1794, are getting empty. And these hungering cries go up by millions: for a good many of the departments in France do not produce sufficient grain for home consumption, this being the case in fertile wheat departments, and likewise in certain districts; cries also go up from the large and small towns, while in each village numbers of peasants fast because they have no land to provide them with food, or because they lack strength, health, employment, and wages. "For a fortnight past," writes a municipal body in Seine-et-Marne,[103] "at least two

---

with provisions. A sack of wheat weighing three quintals is now worth nine thousand francs, a pound of beef thirty-six francs, a pair of shoes one hundred francs. It is impossible for artisans to raise their wages proportionately with such a large and rapid increase."—Cf. "Diary of Lord Malmesbury," iii., 290 (October 27, 1796). After 1795, the gains of the peasants, land-owners, and producers are very large; from 1792 to 1796 they accumulate and hide away most of the current coin. They were courageous enough and smart enough to protect their hoard against the violence of the revolutionary government; "hence, at the time of the depreciation of assignats, they bought land extraordinarily cheap." In 1796 they cultivate and produce largely.

102. Archives Nationales, AF., II., 72. (Letter of the administrators of the district of Montpelier to the Convention, Messidor 26, year II.) "Your decree of Nivose 4 last, suppressed the *maximum*, which step, provoked by justice and the *maximum*, did not have the effect you anticipated." The dearth ceases, but there is a prodigious increase in prices, the farmer selling his wheat at from four hundred and seventy to six hundred and seventy francs the quintal.

103. Archives Nationales, AF., II., 71. (Deliberations of the commune of Champs, canton of Lagny, Prairial 22, year III. Letter of the *procureur-syndic* of Meaux, Messidor 3. Letter of the municipality of Rozoy, Seine-et-Marne, Messidor 4.)—*Ibid.*, AF., II., 74. (Letter of the municipality of Emérainville, endorsed by the Directory of Meaux, Messidor 14.) "The commune can procure

hundred citizens in our commune are without bread, grain, and flour; they have had no other food than bran and vegetables. We see with sorrow children deprived of nourishment, their nurses without milk, unable to suckle them; old men falling down through inanition, and young men in the fields too weak to stand up to their work." And other communes in the district "are about in the same condition." The same spectacle is visible throughout the Ile-de-France, Normandy, and in Picardy. Around Dieppe, in the country,[104] entire communes support themselves on herbs and bran. "Citizen representatives," write the administrators, "we can no longer maintain ourselves. Our fellow-citizens reproach us with having despoiled them of their grain in favor of the large communes." "All means of subsistence are exhausted," writes the district of Louviers,[105] "we are reduced here for a month past to eating bran bread and boiled herbs, and even this rude food is getting scarce. Bear in mind that we have seventy-one thousand people to govern, at this very time subject to all the horrors of famine, a large number of them having already perished, some with hunger and others with diseases engendered by the poor food they live on." In the Caen district,[106] "the unripe peas, horse-peas, beans, and green barley and rye are attacked"; mothers and children go after these in the fields in default

---

only oat-bread for its inhabitants, and, again, they have to go a long way to get this. This food, of so poor a quality, far from strengthening the citizen accustomed to agricultural labor, disheartens him and makes him ill, the result being that the hay cannot be got in in good time for lack of hands."—At Champs, "the crop of hay is ready for mowing, but, for want of food, the laborers cannot do the work."

104. *Ibid.*, AF., II., 73. (Letter from the Directory of the district of Dieppe, Prairial 22.)

105. *Ibid.* (Letter of the administrators of the district of Louviers, Prairial 26.)

106. *Ibid.* (Letter of the *procureur-syndic* of the Caen district, Caen, Messidor 23.—Letter of Representative Porcher to the Committee of Public Safety, Messidor 26.—Letter of the same, Prairial 24. "The condition of this department seemed to me frightful. . . . The privations of the department with respect to subsistence cannot be over-stated to you; the evil is at its height."

of other food; "other vegetables in the gardens are already consumed; furniture, the comforts of the well-to-do class, have become
the prey of the farming egoist; having nothing more to sell they
consequently have nothing with which to obtain a morsel of bread."
"It is impossible," writes the representative on mission, "to wait for
the crop without further aid. As long as bran lasted the people ate
that; none can now be found and despair is at its height. I have not
seen the sun since I came. The harvest will be a month behind.
What shall we do? What will become of us?" "In Picardy," writes
the Beauvais district, "the great majority of people in the rural communes overrun the woods" to find mushrooms, berries, and wild
fruits.[107] "They think themselves lucky," says the Bapaume district,
"if they can get a share of the food of animals." "In many communes," the district of Vervier reports, "the inhabitants are reduced
to living on herbage." "Many families, entire communes," reports
the Laon commissary, "have been without bread two or three months
and live on bran or herbs. . . . Mothers of families, children, old men,
pregnant women, come to the (members of the) Directory for bread
and often faint in their arms."

And yet, great as the famine is in the country it is worse in the
towns; and the proof of it is that the starving people flock into the
country to find whatever they can to live on, no matter how, and,
generally speaking, in vain. "Three-quarters of our fellow-citizens,"
writes the Rozoy municipality,[108] "are forced to quit work and overrun the country here and there, among the farmers, to obtain bread

107. Archives Nationales, AF., II., 74. (Letter of the Beauvais administrators, Prairial 15.—Letter of the Bapaume administrator, Prairial 24.—Letter of
the Vervier administrator, Messidor 7.—Letter of the commissary sent by the
district of Laon, Messidor.)—Cf., *ibid.*, letter from the Abbeville district, Prairial 11. "The quintal of wheat is sold at one thousand assignats, or rather, the
farmers will not take assignats any more, grain not to be had for anything but
coin, and, as most people have none to give they are hard-hearted enough to
demand of one his clothes, and of another his furniture, etc."

108. *Ibid.*, AF., II., 71. (Letter of the Rozoy municipality. Seine-et-Marne,
Messidor 4, year III.) A bushel of wheat in the vicinity of Rozoy brings three
hundred francs.

for specie, and with more entreaty than the poorest wretches; for the most part, they return with tears in their eyes at not being able to find, not merely a bushel of wheat, but a pound of bread." "Yesterday," writes the Montreuil-sur-Mer municipality,[109] "more than two hundred of our citizens set out to beg in the country," and, when they get nothing, they steal. "Bands of brigands[110] spread through the country and pillage all dwellings anywise remote. . . . Grain, flour, bread, cattle, poultry, stuffs, etc., all come in play; our terrified shepherds are no longer willing to sleep in their sheep-pens and are leaving us." The most timid dig carrots at night or, during the day, gather dandelions; but their town stomachs cannot digest this aliment. "Lately," writes the *procureur-syndic* of St. Germain,[111] "the corpse of a father of a family, found in the fields with his mouth still filled with the grass he had striven to chew, exasperates and arouses the spirit of the poor creatures awaiting a similar fate."

How, then, do people in the towns live? In small towns or scattered villages, each municipality, using what gendarmes it has, makes

109. *Ibid.*, AF., II., 74. (Letter of the Montreuil-sur-Mer municipality, Prairial 29.)

110. *Ibid.* (Letter of the Vervins administrators, Prairial 11, Letter of the commune of La Chapelle-sur-Somme, Prairial 24.)

111. *Ibid.*, AF., II., 70 (Letter of the *procureur-syndic* of the district of St. Germain, Thermidor 10.) This file, which depicts the situation of the communes around Paris, is specially heartrending and terrible. Among other instances of the misery of workmen the following petition of the men employed on the Marly water-works may be given, Messidor 28. "The workmen and employees on the machine at Marly beg leave to present to you the wretched state to which they are reduced by the dearness of provisions. Their moderate wages, which at the most have reached only five livres twelve sous, and again, for four months past, having received but two francs sixteen sous, no longer provide them with half-a-pound of bread, since it costs fifteen and sixteen francs per pound. We poor people have not been wanting in courage nor patience, hoping that times would mend. We have been reduced to selling most of our effects and to eating bread made of bran of which a sample is herewith sent, and which distresses us very much (nous *incommode* beaucoup); most of us are ill and those who are not so are in a very feeble state."—Schmidt, "Tableaux de Paris," Thermidor 9. "Peasants on the market square complain bitterly of being robbed in the fields and on the road, and even of having their sacks (of grain) plundered."

legal requisitions in its vicinity, and sometimes the commune obtains from the government a charitable gift of wheat, oats, rice, or assignats. But the quantity of grain it receives is so small, one asks how it is that, after two months, six months, or a year of such a system, one-half of its inhabitants are not in the grave-yard. I suppose that many of them live on what they raise in their gardens, or on their small farms; others are helped by their relations, neighbors, and companions; in any event, it is clear that the human machine is very resistant, and a few mouthfuls suffice to keep it going a long time. At Ervy,[112] in Aube, "not a grain of wheat has been brought in the last two market-days." "Tomorrow,[113] Prairial 25, in Bapaume, the chief town of the district, there will be only two bushels of flour left (for food of any sort)." "At Boulogne-sur-Mer, for the past ten days, there has been distributed to each person only three pounds of bad barley, or maslin, without knowing whether we can again distribute this miserable ration next decade." Out of sixteen hundred inhabitants in Brionne, "twelve hundred and sixty[114] are reduced to the small portion of wheat they receive at the market, and which, unfortunately, for too long a time, has been reduced from eight to three ounces of wheat for each person, every eight days." For three months past, in Seine-et-Marne,[115] in "the commune of Meaux, that

112. Archives Nationales, D., § 1, file 2. (Letter of the Ervy municipality, Floréal 17, year III.) "The indifference of the egoist farmers in the country is at its height; they pay no respect whatever to the laws, killing the poor by refusing to sell, or unwilling to sell their grain at a price they can pay."—(It would be necessary to copy the whole of this file to show the alimentary state of the departments.)

113. *Ibid.*, AF., II., 74. (Letter of the district administrators of Bapaume, Prairial 24.—Letter of the municipality of Boulogne-sur-Mer, Prairial 24.)

114. *Ibid.*, AF., II., 73. (Letter of the municipality of Brionne, district of Bernay, Prairial 7.) The farmers do not bring in their wheat because they sell it elsewhere at the rate of fifteen hundred and two thousand francs the sack of three hundred and thirty pounds.

115. *Ibid.*, AF., II., 71. (Letter of the *procureur-syndic* of the district of Meaux, Messidor 2.) "Their fate is shared by many of the rural communes" and the whole district has been reduced to this dearth "to increase the resources of Paris and the armies."

of Laferté, Lagny, Daumartin, and other principal towns of the canton, they have had only half-a-pound per head, for each day, of bad bread." In Seine-et-Oise, "citizens of the neighborhood of Paris and even of Versailles[116] state that they are reduced to four ounces of bread." At St. Denis,[117] with a population of six thousand, "a large part of the inhabitants, worn out with suffering, betake themselves to the charity depots. Workmen, especially, cannot do their work for lack of food. A good many women, mothers and nurses, have been found in their houses unconscious, without any sign of life in them, and many have died with their infants at their breasts." Even in a larger and less forsaken town, St. Germain,[118] the misery surpasses all that one can imagine. "Half-a-pound of flour for each inhabitant," not daily, but at long intervals; "bread at fifteen and sixteen francs the pound and all other provisions at the same rate; a people which is sinking, losing hope and perishing. Yesterday, for the fête of the 9th of Thermidor, not a sign of rejoicing; on the contrary, symptoms of general and profound depression, tottering spectres in the streets, mournful shrieks of ravaging hunger or shouts of rage, almost every one, driven to the last extremity of misery, welcoming death as a boon."

Such is the aspect of these huge artificial agglomerations, where the soil, made sterile by habitation, bears only stones, and where

---

116. Schmidt, "Tableaux de Paris." (Reports of the Police, Pluviose 6, year III.)—*Ibid.*, Germinal 16. "A letter from the department of Drome states that they are dying of hunger there, bread selling at three francs the pound."

117. Archives Nationales, AF., II., 70. (Deliberations of the Council-general of Franciade, Thermidor 9, year III.)

118. *Ibid.* (Letter of the *procureur-syndic* of the district of St. Germain, Thermidor 10.)—Delécluze, "Souvenirs de Soixante Années," p. 10. (The Delécluze family live in Mendon in 1794 and for most of 1795. M. Delécluze, senior, and his son go to Meaux and obtain of a farmer a bag of good flour weighing three hundred and twenty-five pounds for about ten *louis d'or* and fetch it home, taking the greatest pains to keep it concealed. Both father and son "after having covered the precious sack with hay and straw in the bottom of the cart, follow it on foot at some distance as the peasant drives along." Madame Delécluze kneads the bread herself and bakes it.

twenty, thirty, fifty, and a hundred thousand suffering stomachs have to obtain from ten, twenty, and thirty leagues off their first and last mouthful of food. Within these close pens long lines of human sheep huddle together every day bleating and trembling around almost empty troughs, and only through extraordinary efforts do the shepherds daily succeed in providing them with a little nourishment. The central government, strenuously appealed to, enlarges or defines the circle of their requisitions; it authorises them to borrow, to tax themselves; it lends or gives to them millions of assignats;[119] frequently,

---

119. Archives Nationales, AF., II., 74. The following shows some of the municipal expenditures. (Deliberations of the commune of Annecy, Thermidor 8, year III.) "Amount received by the commune from the government, one million two hundred thousand francs. Fraternal subscriptions, four hundred thousand francs. Forced loan, two million four hundred thousand francs. Amount arising from grain granted by the government, but not paid for, four hundred thousand francs." (Letter from the municipality of Lille, Fructidor 7.) "The deficit, at the time we took hold of the government, which, owing to the difference between the price of grain bought and the price obtained for bread distributed among the necessitous, had amounted to two million two hundred seventy thousand and twenty-three francs, so increased in Thermidor as to amount to eight million three hundred twelve thousand and nine hundred fifty-six francs." Consequently, the towns ruin themselves with indebtedness to an incredible extent.—Archives Nationales, AF., II., 72. (Letter of the municipality of Tours, Vendémiaire 19, year IV.) Tours has not sufficient money with which to buy oil for its street-lamps and which are no longer lit at night. A decree is passed to enable the agent for subsistences at Paris to supply its commissaries with twenty quintals of oil which, for three hundred and forty lamps, keeps one hundred agoing up to Germinal 1. The same at Toulouse. (Report of Destrene, *Moniteur*, June 24, 1798.) On November 26, 1794, Bordeaux is unable to pay seventy-two francs for thirty barrels of water to wash the guillotine. (Granier de Cassagnac, i., 13. Extract from the archives of Bordeaux.) Bordeaux is authorised to sell one thousand casks of wine which had formerly been taken on requisition by the government, the town to pay for them at the rate at which the Republic bought them and to sell them as dear as possible in the way of regular trade. The proceeds are to be employed in providing subsistence for its inhabitants. (Archives Nationales, AF., II., 72, orders of Vendémiaire 4, year IV.)—As to aid furnished by the assignats granted to towns and departments cf. the same files; four hundred thousand francs to Poitiers, Pluviose 18, four millions to Lyons, Pluviose 17, three millions a month to Nantes, after Ther-

in cases of extreme want, it allows them to take so much grain or rice from its storehouses, for a week's supply. But, in truth, this sort of life is not living, it is only not dying. For one half, and more than one half of the inhabitants simply subsist on rations of bread obtained by long waiting for it at the end of a string of people and delivered at a reduced price. What rations and what bread! "It seems," says the municipality of Troyes, "that[120] the country has anathematised the towns. Formerly, the finest grain was brought to market; the farmer kept the inferior quality and consumed it at home. Now it is the reverse, and this is carried still further, for, not only do we receive no wheat whatever, but the farmers give us sprouted barley and rye, which they reserve for our commune; the farmer who has none arranges with those who have, so as to buy it and deliver it in town, and sell his good wheat elsewhere. Half a pound per day and per head, in Pluviose, to the thirteen thousand or fourteen thousand indigent in Troyes; then a quarter of a pound, and, finally, two ounces with a little rice and some dried vegetables, "which feeble resource is going to fail us."[121] Half a pound in Pluviose, to the twenty thousand needy in Amiens, which ration is only nominal, for "it often happens that each individual gets only four ounces, while the distribution has repeatedly failed three days in

---

midor 14, ten millions to the department of Hérault in Frimaire and Pluviose, etc.

120. Archives Nationales, II., § 1, file 2. (Deliberations of the Commune of Troyes, Ventose 15, year III.)—"Un Séjour en France." (Amiens, May 9, 1795.) "As we had obtained a few six franc crowns and were able to get a small supply of wheat. . . . Mr. D—— and the servants eat bread made of three-fourths bran and one-fourth flour. . . . When we bake it we carefully close the doors, paying no attention to the door-bell, and allow no visitor to come in until every trace of the operation is gone. . . . The distribution now consists of a mixture of sprouted wheat, peas, rye, etc., which scarcely resembles bread." (April 12.) "The distribution of bread (then) was a quarter of a pound a day. Many of those who in other respects were well-off, got nothing at all."

121. *Ibid.* (Letters of the municipality of Troyes, Ventose 15, year III., and Germinal 6.) Letter of the three deputies, sent by the municipality to Paris, Pluviose, year III. (no date.)

succession," and this continues; six months later, Fructidor 7, Amiens has but sixty-nine quintals of flour in its market storehouse, "an insufficient quantity for distribution this very day; tomorrow, it will be impossible to make any distribution at all, and the day after tomorrow the needy population of this commune will be brought down to absolute famine." "Complete desperation!" There are already "many suicides."[122] At other times, rage predominates and there are riots. At Evreux,[123] Germinal 21, a riot breaks out, owing to the delivery of only two pounds of flour per head and per week, and because three days before, only a pound and a half was delivered. There is a riot at Deippe,[124] Prairial 14 and 15, because "the people are reduced here to three or four ounces of bread." There is another at Vervins, Prairial 9, because the municipality which obtains bread at a cost of seven and eight francs a pound, raises the price from twenty-five to fifty sous. At Lille, an insurrection breaks out Messidor 4, because the municipality, paying nine francs for bread, can give it to the poor only for about twenty and thirty sous. Lyons, in Nivose, remains without bread "for five full days."[125] At Chartres, Thermidor 15,[126] the distribution of bread for a month is only eight ounces a day, and there is not enough to keep this up

122. "Un Séjour en France" (Amiens, Jan. 30, 1795.) Archives Nationales, AF., II., 74. (Deliberation of the Commune of Amiens, Thermidor 8, and Fructidor 7, year III.)

123. "Souvenirs et Journal d'un Bourgeois d'Evreux," p. 97. (The women stop carts loaded with wheat, keep them all night, stone and wound Representative Bersusès, and succeed in getting, each, eight pounds of wheat.)

124. Archives Nationales, AF., II., 73. (Letter of the municipality of Dieppe, Prairial 22.)—AF., II., 74. (Letter of the municipality of Vervins, Messidor 7. Letter of the municipality of Lille, Fructidor 7.)

125. "Correspondence de Mallet-Dupan avec la Cour de Vienne," i., 90. *Ibid.*, 131. One month later a quintal of flour at Lyons is worth two hundred francs and a pound of bread forty-five sous.

126. Archives Nationales, AF., II., 13. (Letter of the deputies extraordinary of the three administrative bodies of Chartres, Thermidor 15: "In the name of this commune dying of hunger.")—"The inhabitants of Chartres have not even been allowed to receive their rents in grain; all has been poured into the government storehouses."

until the 20th of Thermidor. On the fifteenth of Fructidor, La Rochelle writes that "its public distributions, reduced to seven or eight ounces of bread, are on the point of failing entirely." For four months, at Painboeuf, the ration is but the quarter of a pound of bread.[127] And the same at Nantes, which has eighty-two thousand inhabitants and swarms with the wretched; "the distribution never exceeded four ounces a day," and that only for the past year. The same at Rouen, which contains sixty thousand inhabitants; and, in addition, within the past fortnight the distribution has failed three times; in other reports, those who are well-off suffer more than the indigent because they take no part in the communal distribution, "all resources for obtaining food being, so to say, interdicted to them." Five ounces of bread per diem for four months is the allowance to the forty thousand inhabitants of Caen and its district.[128] A great many in the town, as well as in the country, live on bran and wild herbs." At the end of Prairial, "there is not a bushel of grain in the town storehouses, while the requisitions, enforced in the most rigorous and imposing style, produce nothing or next to nothing." Misery augments from week to week: "it is impossible to form any idea of it; the people of Caen live on brown bread and the blood of cattle. . . . Every countenance bears traces of the famine. . . . Faces are of livid hue. . . . It is impossible to await the new crop, until the end of Fructidor." Such are the exclamations everywhere. The object now, indeed, is to cross the narrowest and most terrible defile; a fortnight more of absolute fasting and hundreds of thousands of

127. *Ibid.* (Petition of the commune of La Rochelle, Fructidor 25, that of Painboeuf, Fructidor 9, that of the municipality of Nantes, Thermidor 14, that of Rouen, Fructidor 1.)—*Ibid.*, AF., II., 72. (Letter of the commune of Bayonne, Fructidor 1.) "Penury of subsistences for more than two years. . . . The municipality, the past six months, is under the cruel necessity of reducing its subjects to half-a-pound of corn-bread per day . . . at the rate of twenty-five sous the pound, although the pound costs over five francs." After the suppression of the *maximum* it loses about twenty-five thousand francs per day.

128. *Ibid.* (Letter of Representative Porcher, Caen, Prairial 24, Messidor 3 and 26. Letter of the municipality of Caen, Messidor 3.)

lives would be sacrificed.[129] At this moment the government half opens the doors of its storehouses; it lends a few sacks of flour on condition of repayment—for example, at Cherbourg a few hundreds of quintals of oats; by means of oat bread, the poor can subsist until the coming harvest. But above all, it doubles its guard and shows its bayonets. At Nancy, a traveller sees[130] "more than three thousand persons soliciting in vain for a few pounds of flour." They are dispersed with the butt-ends of muskets. Thus are the peasantry taught patriotism and the townspeople patience. Physical constraint exercised on all in the name of all; this is the only procedure which an arbitrary socialism can resort to for the distribution of food and to discipline starvation.

VII

All that an absolute government can do for supplying the capital with food is undertaken and carried out by this one, for here is its seat, and one more degree of dearth in Paris would overthrow it. Each week, on reading the daily reports of its agents,[131] it finds itself on the verge of explosion; twice, in Germinal and Prairial, a popular outbreak does overthrow it for a few hours, and, if it maintains itself, it is on the condition of either giving the needy a piece of bread or the hope of getting it. Consequently, military posts are

129. *Ibid.* AF., II., 71. (Letter of the municipality of Auxerre, Messidor 19.) "We have kept alive thus far through all sorts of expedients as if by miracle. It has required incalculable efforts, great expenditure, and really supernatural means to accomplish it. But there is still one month between this and the end of Thermidor. How are we going to live! Our people, the majority of whom are farmers and artisans, are rationed at half-a-pound a day for each person and this will last but ten or twelve days at most."

130. Meissner, "Voyage à Paris," 339. "There was not a morsel of bread in our inn. I went myself to five or six bakeries and pastry shops and found them all stripped." He finds in the last one about a dozen of small Savoy biscuits for which he pays fifteen francs.—See, for the military proceedings of the government in relation to bread, the orders of the Committee of Public Safety, most of them by the hand of Lindet, AF., II., 68—74.

131. Schmidt, "Tableaux de Paris," vols. ii. and iii., *passim.*

established around Paris, eighteen leagues off, on all the highways—
permanent patrols in correspondence with each other to urge on the
wagoners and draft relays of horses on the spot; escorts despatched
from Paris to meet convoys;[132] requisitions of "all carts and all horses
whatever to effect transportation in preference to any other work or
service"; all communes traversed by a highway are ordered to put
rubbish and litter on the bad spots and spread dirt the whole way,
so that the horses may drag their loads in spite of the slippery road;
the national agents are ordered to draft the necessary number of
men to break the ice around the water-mills;[133] a requisition is made
for "all the barley throughout the length and breadth of the Republic"; this must be utilised by means of "the amalgam[134] for making
bread," while the brewers are forbidden to use barley in the manufacture of beer; the starchmakers are forbidden to convert potatoes
into starch, with penalty of death against all offenders "as destroyers
of alimentary produce"; the breweries and starch-factories[135] are to
be closed until further notice. Paris must have grain, no matter of
what kind, no matter how, and at any cost, not merely in the fol-

132. Archives Nationales, AF., II., 68. (Orders of Ventose 20, year III.;
Germinal 19 and 20; Messidor 8, etc.)

133. *Ibid.* Orders of Nivose 5 and 22.

134. Meal composed of every species of grain and bran.

135. *Ibid.* Orders of Pluviose 19, Ventose 5, Floréal 4 and 24. (The fourteen
brewers which the Republic keeps agoing for itself at Dunkirk are excepted.)—
The proceedings are the same in relation to other necessary articles—returns
demanded of nuts, rape-seed, and other seeds or fruits producing oil, also the
hoofs of cattle and sheep, with requisitions for every other article entering into
the manufacture of oil, and orders to keep oil-mills agoing. "All administrative
bodies will see that the butchers remove the fat from their meat before offering
it for sale, that they do not themselves make candles out of it, and that they do
not sell it to soap-factories, etc."—(Orders of Vendémiaire 28, year III.) "The
executive committee will collect eight hundred yoke of oxen and distribute them
among the dealers in hay in order to transport wood and coal from the woods
and collieries to the yards. They will distribute proportionately eight hundred
sets of wheels and harness. The wagoners will be paid and guarded the same
as military convoys, and drafted as required. To feed the oxen, the district
administrators will take by preemption the necessary fields and pasturages, etc."
(Orders of Pluviose 10, year III.)

lowing week, but tomorrow, this very day, because hunger chews and swallows everything, and it will not wait. Once the grain is obtained, a price must be fixed which people can pay. Now, the difference between the selling and cost price is enormous; it keeps on increasing as the assignat declines and it is the government which pays this. "You furnish bread at three sous," said Dubois-Crancé, Floréal 16,[136] "and it costs you four francs. Paris consumes eight thousand quintals of meal daily, which expenditure alone amounts to one billion two hundred millions per annum." Seven months later, when a bag of flour brings thirteen thousand francs, the same expenditure reaches five hundred and forty-six millions *per month*. Under the ancient régime, Paris, although overgrown, continued to be an useful organism; if it absorbed much, it elaborated more; its productiveness compensated for what it consumed, and, every year, instead of exhausting the public treasury it poured seventy-seven millions into it. The new régime has converted it into a monstrous canker in the very heart of France, a devouring parasite which, through its six hundred thousand leeches, drains its surroundings for a distance of forty leagues, consumes one-half the annual revenue of the State, and yet still remains emaciated in spite of the sacrifices made by the treasury it depletes and the exhaustion of the provinces which supply it with food.

Always the same alimentary system, the same long lines of people waiting at, and before, dawn in every quarter of Paris, in the dark, for a long time, and often to no purpose, subject to the brutalities of the strong and the outrages of the licentious! On the 9th of Thermidor, the daily trot of the multitude in quest of food has lasted uninterruptedly for seventeen months, accompanied with outrages of the worst kind because there is less terror and less submissiveness,

---

136. *Moniteur,* xxiv., 397.—Schmidt, "Tableaux de Paris." (Reports of Frimaire 16, year IV.) "Citizens in the departments wonder how it is that Paris costs them five hundred and forty six millions per month merely for bread when they are starving. This isolation of Paris, for which all the benefits of the Revolution are exclusively reserved, has the worst effect on the public mind."—Meissner, 345.

with more obstinacy because provisions at free sale are dearer, with greater privation because the ration distributed is smaller, and with more sombre despair because each household, having consumed its stores, has nothing of its own to make up for the insufficiencies of public charity. To cap the climax, the winter of 1794–1795 is so cold[137] that the Seine freezes and people cross the Loire on foot; rafts no longer arrive and, to obtain fire-wood, it is necessary "to cut down trees at Boulogne, Vincennes, Verrières, St. Cloud, Meudon and two other forests in the vicinity." Fuel costs "four hundred francs per cord of wood, forty sous for a bushel of charcoal, twenty sous for a small basket. The necessitous are seen in the streets sawing the wood of their bedsteads to cook with and to keep from freezing." On the resumption of transportation by water amongst the cakes of ice "rafts are sold as fast as the raftsmen can haul the wood out of the water, the people being obliged to pass three nights at the landing to get it, each in turn according to his number." There are "two thousand persons at least, Pluviose 3, at the Louviers landing," each with his card allowing him four sticks at fifteen sous each. Naturally, there is pulling, hauling, tumult, and a rush; "the dealers take to flight for fear, and the inspectors come near being murdered"; they get away along with the police commissioner and "the public helps itself." Likewise, the following day, there is "an abominable pillage;" the gendarmes and soldiers placed there to maintain order, "make a rush for the wood and carry it away the same as the crowd." Bear in mind that on this day the thermometer is sixteen degrees below zero, that one hundred, two hundred other lines of people likewise stand waiting at the doors of bakers and butchers, enduring the same cold, and that they have already endured it and will yet endure it a month and more. Words are wanting to describe the sufferings of these long lines of motionless beings, during the night, at daybreak,

137. Mercier, "Paris Pendant la Révolution," i., 355–357.—Schmidt, "Pariser Zustande," i., 224. (The Seine is frozen over on November 23 and January 23, the thermometer standing at sixteen degrees (Centigrade) below zero.)—Schmidt, "Tableaux de Paris." (Reports of the Police, Pluviose 2, 3, and 4.)

standing there five or six hours, with the blast driving through their rags and their feet freezing. Ventose is beginning, and the ration of bread is reduced to a pound and a half;[138] Ventose ends, and the ration of bread, kept at a pound and a half for the three hundred and twenty-four laborers, falls to one pound; in fact, a great many get none at all, many only a half and a quarter of a pound. Germinal follows and the Committee of Public Safety, finding that its magazines are giving out, limits all rations to a quarter of a pound. Thereupon, on the 12th of Germinal, an insurrection of workmen and women breaks out; the Convention is invaded and liberated by military force, Paris is declared in a state of siege and the government, again in the saddle, tightens the reins. Thenceforth, the ration of meat served out every four or five days, is a quarter of a pound; bread averages every day, sometimes five, sometimes six, and sometimes seven ounces, at long intervals eight ounces, often three, two, and one ounce and a half, or even none at all; while this bread, black and "making mischief," becomes more and more worthless and detestable.[139] People who are well-off live on potatoes, but only for them, for, in the middle of Germinal, these cost fifteen francs the bushel and, towards the end, twenty francs; towards the end of Messidor, forty-five francs; in the first month of the Directory, one hundred and eighty francs, and then two hundred and eighty-four

138. Schmidt, "Pariser Zustande," i., 228, and following pages. (February 25, the distribution of bread is reduced to one and one-half pounds per person; March 17, to one and one-half pounds for workmen and one pound for others. Final reduction to one-quarter of a pound, March 31.)—*Ibid.*, 251, for ulterior rates.—Dufort de Cheverney, (MS. Mémoires, August, 1795.) M. de Cheverney takes up his quarters at the old Louvre with his friend Sedaine. "I had assisted them with food all I could: they owned to me that, without this, they would have died of starvation notwithstanding their means."

139. Schmidt, "Tableaux de Paris." (Reports of Germinal 15 and 27, and Messidor 28, year III., Brumaire 14 and Frimaire 23, year IV.)—*Ibid.* (Germinal 15, year III.) Butter is at eight francs the pound, eggs seven francs for four ounces.—*Ibid.* (Messidor 19), bread is at sixteen francs the pound (Messidor 28), butter at fourteen francs the pound (Brumaire 29), flour at fourteen thousand francs the bag of three hundred and twenty-five pounds.

francs, whilst other produce goes up at the same rates. After the abolition of the *maximum* the evil springs not from a lack of provisions, but from their dearness. The shops are well-supplied. Whoever comes with a full purse gets what he wants.[140] Those who were once wealthy, all proprietors and large fundholders, may have a meal on handing over their bundles of assignats, on withdrawing their last *louis* from its hiding-place, on selling their jewelry, clocks, furniture, and clothes; but every tradesman and broker, the lucky, all experienced robbers who spend four hundred, one thousand, three thousand, then five thousand francs for their dinner, revel in the great eating establishments on fine wines and exquisite cheer; the burden of the scarcity is transferred to other shoulders. At present, the class which suffers, and which suffers beyond all bounds of patience, is that of employees and people with small incomes,[141] the

140. *Ibid.* (Report of Germinal 12, year III.) "The eating houses and pastrycooks are better supplied than ever."—"Mémoires (manuscript) of M. de Cheverney." "My sister-in-law, with more than forty thousand livres income, registered in the 'Grand Ledger,' was reduced to cultivating her garden, assisted by her two chambermaids. M. de Richebourg, formerly intendant-general of the Post-Office, had to sell at one time a clock and at another time a wardrobe to live on. 'My friends,' he said to us one day, 'I have been obliged to put my clock in the pot.'"—Schmidt. (Report of Frimaire 17, year IV.) "A frequenter of the Stock-Exchange sells a *louis* at five thousand francs. He dines for one thousand francs and loudly exclaims: 'I have dined at four francs ten sous. They are really superb, these assignats! I couldn't have dined so well formerly at twelve francs.'"

141. Schmidt. (Reports of Frimaire 9, year IV.) "The reports depict to us the sad condition of those who, with small incomes and having sold their clothes, are selling their furniture, being, so to say, at their last piece; and, soon without anything, are reduced to the last extremity by committing suicide."—*Ibid.*, Frimaire 2, "The *rentier* is ruined, not being able to buy food. Employees are all in the same situation."—Naturally, the condition of employees and *rentiers* grows worse with the depreciation of assignats. Here are house-keeping accounts at the end of 1795. (Letter of Beaumarchais' sister Julie to his wife, December, 1794. "Beaumarchais et son temps," by De Loménie, p. 486.) "When you gave me those four thousand francs (assignats), my dear friend, my heart went pit-a-pat. I thought that I should go crazy with such a fortune. I put them in my pocket at once and talked about other things so as to get the idea out of my mind. On returning to the house, get some wood and provisions as quick

crowd of workmen, the city plebeians, the low Parisian populace which lives from day to day, which is Jacobin at heart, which made the Revolution in order to better itself, which finds itself worse off, which gets up one insurrection more on the 1st of Prairial, which

---

as possible before prices go higher! Dupont (the old domestic) started off and did his best. But the scales fell from my eyes on seeing the cost of food for a month—four thousand two hundred and seventy-five francs!

1 load of wood	1460 francs
9 pounds of candles, from 8 to 100 francs per pound	900
4 pounds of sugar, at 100 francs per pound	400
3 measures of grain, at 40 francs	120
7 pounds oil, at 100 francs	700
12 wicks, at 5 francs	60
1½ bushels potatoes, at 200 francs per bushel	300
1 month's washing	215
1 pound ground powder	70
2 ounces pomatum (formerly 3 sous, now 25 francs)	50
	4,275 francs
There remains the month's supply of butter and eggs, as you know, 200 francs, meat 25 or 30 francs, and other articles in proportion	567
There was no bread for two days. . . . I have bought only four pounds the last two days, at 45 francs	180
	5,022 francs.

"When I think of this royal outlay, as you call it, which makes me spend from eighteen thousand to twenty thousand francs for nothing, I wish the devil had the system. . . . Ten thousand francs which I have scattered about the past fortnight, alarm and trouble me so much that I do not know how to calculate my income in this way. In three days the difference (in the value of assignats) has sent wood up from four thousand two hundred to six thousand five hundred francs, and extras in proportion, so that, as I wrote you, a load piled up and put away costs me seven thousand one hundred francs. Every week now, the *pot-au-feu* and other meats for ragouts, without any butter, eggs, and other details, cost from seven to eight hundred francs. Washing also goes up so fast that eight thousand francs do not suffice. All this puts me out of humor, while in all this expenditure I declare on my honor (*je jure par la sainte vérité de mon coeur*) that for two years I have indulged no fancy of my own or spent anything except on household expenses. Nevertheless, I have urgent need of some things for which I should require piles of assignats."—We see by Beaumarchais' cor-

forcibly enters the Tuileries yelling "Bread and the Constitution of '93," which installs itself as sovereign in the Convention, which murders the Representative Féraud, which decrees a return to Terror, but which, put down by the National Guard, disarmed, and forced back into lasting obedience, has only to submit to the consequences of its outrages, the socialism it has instituted and the economical system it has organised.

Owing to the workmen of Paris having been usurpers and tyrants they are now beggars. Owing to the ruin brought on proprietors and capitalists by them, individuals can no longer employ them. Owing to the ruin they have brought on the Treasury, the State can provide them with only the semblance of charity, and hence, while all are compelled to go hungry, a great many die, and many commit suicide. Germinal 6, "Section of the Observatory,"[142] at the distribution, "forty-one persons had been without bread; several pregnant women desired immediate confinement so as to destroy their infants; others asked for knives to stab themselves." Germinal 8, "a large number of persons who had passed the night at the doors of the bakeries were obliged to leave without getting any bread." Germinal 24, "the police commissioner of the Arsenal section states that many become ill for lack of food, and that he buries quite a number. . . . The same day, he has heard of five or six citizens, who, finding themselves without bread, and unable to get other food, throw themselves into the Seine." Germinal 27, "the women say that they feel so furious and are in such despair on account of hunger and want that they must inevitably commit some act of violence. . . . In the

---

respondence that one of his friends travels around in the environs of Paris to find bread. "It is said here (he writes from Soizy, June 5, 1795) that flour may be had at Briare. If this were so I would bargain with a reliable man there to carry it to you by water-carriage between Briare and Paris. . . . In the mean time I do not despair of finding a loaf."—Letter of a friend of Beaumarchais: "This letter costs you at least one hundred francs, including paper, pen, ink, and lamp-oil. For economy's sake I write it in your house."

142. Cf. Schmidt, "Tableaux de Paris," vols. ii. and iii. (Reports of the Police, at the dates designated.)

section of 'Les Amis de la Patrie,' one-half have no bread. . . . Three persons tumbled down through weakness on the Boulevard du Temple." Floréal 2, "most of the workmen in the 'République' section are leaving Paris on account of the scarcity of bread." Floréal 5, "eighteen out of twenty-four inspectors state that patience is exhausted and that things are coming to an end." Floréal 14, "the distribution is always unsatisfactory on account of the four-ounce ration; two thirds of the citizens do without it. One woman, on seeing the excitement of her husband and her four children who had been without bread for two days, trailed through the gutter tearing her hair and striking her head; she then got up in a state of fury and attempted to drown herself." Floréal 20, "all exclaim that they cannot live on three ounces of bread, and, again, of such bad quality. Mothers and pregnant women fall down with weakness." Floréal 21, "the inspectors state that they encounter many persons in the streets who have fallen through feebleness and inanition." Floréal 23, "a *citoyenne* who had no bread for her child tied it to her side and jumped into the river. Yesterday, an individual named Mottez, in despair through want, cut his throat." Floréal 25, "several persons, deprived of any means of existence, gave up in complete discouragement, and fell down with weakness and exhaustion. . . . In the 'Gravilliers' section, two men were found dead with inanition. . . . The peace officers report the decease of several citizens; one cut his throat, while another was found dead in his bed." Floréal 28, "numbers of people sink down for lack of something to eat; yesterday, a man was found dead and others exhausted through want." Prairial 24, "Inspector Laignier states that the indigent are compelled to seek nourishment in the piles of garbage on the corners." Messidor I,[143] "the said Picard fell through weakness at ten o'clock in the morning in the rue de la Loi, and was only brought to at seven o'clock in the evening; he was carried to the hospital on a hand-barrow." Messidor 11, "There is a report that the number of people trying to drown themselves is so great that the nets at St. Cloud scarcely

143. Dauban, "Paris en 1794," pp. 562, 568, 572.

suffice to drag them out of the water." Messidor 19, "A man was found on the corner of a street just dead with hunger." Messidor 27, "At four o'clock in the afternoon, Place Maubert, a man named Marcelin, employed in the Jardin des Plantes, fell down through starvation and died while assistance was being given to him." On the previous evening, the anniversary of the taking of the Bastille, a laborer on the Pont-au-Change, says: "I have eaten nothing all day"; another replies: "I have not been home because I have nothing to give to my wife and children, dying with hunger." About the same date, a friend of Mallet-Dupan writes to him "that he is daily witness to people amongst the lower classes dying of inanition in the streets; others, and principally women, have nothing but garbage to live on, scraps of refuse vegetables and the blood running out of the slaughter houses. Laborers, generally, work on short time on account of their lack of strength and of their exhaustion for want of food."[144] Thus ends the rule of the Convention. Well has it looked out for the interests of the poor! According to the reports of its own inspectors, "famished stomachs on all sides cry vengeance, beat to arms and sound the tocsin of alarm.[145] . . . Those who have to dwell daily on the sacrifices they make to keep themselves alive declare that there is no hope except in death."

Are they going to be relieved by the new government which the Convention imposes on them with thunders of artillery and in which it perpetuates itself?[146] Brumaire 28, "Most of the workmen in the 'Temple' and 'Gravilliers' sections have done no work for want of bread." Brumaire 24, "Citizens of all classes refuse to mount guard because they have nothing to eat." Brumaire 25, "In the 'Gravilliers' section the women say that they have sold all that they possessed, while others, in the 'Faubourg-Antoine' section, declare that it would be better to be shot down." Brumaire 30, "A woman beside

144. Mallet-Dupan, "Correspondance avec la cour de Vionne," i., 254. (July 18, 1795.)

145 Schmidt, *ibid*. (Report of Fructidor 3, year III.)

146. Schmidt, *ibid*., vols. ii, and iii. (Reports of the police at the dates designated.)

herself came and asked a baker to kill her children as she had nothing to give them to eat." Frimaire 1, 2, 3, and 4, "In many of the sections bread is given out only in the evening, in others at one o'clock in the morning, and of very poor quality. . . . Several sections yesterday had no bread." Frimaire 7, the inspectors declare that "the hospitals soon will not be vast enough to hold the sick and the wretched." Frimaire 14, "At the central market a woman nursing her child sunk down with inanition." A few days before this, "a man fell down from weakness, on his way to Bourg l'Abbé." "All our reports," say the district administrators, "resound with shrieks of despair." People are infatuated; "it seems to us that a crazy spirit prevails universally—we often encounter people in the street who, although alone, gesticulate and talk to themselves aloud." "How many times," writes a Swiss traveller,[147] who lived in Paris during the latter half of 1795, "how often have I chanced to encounter men sinking through starvation, scarcely able to stand up against a post, or else down on the ground and unable to get up for want of strength!" A journalist states that he saw "within ten minutes, along the street, seven poor creatures fall on account of hunger, a child die on its mother's breast which was dry of milk, and a woman struggling with a dog near a sewer to get a bone away from him."[148] Meissner never leaves his hotel without filling his pockets with pieces of the national bread. "This bread," he says, "which the poor would formerly have despised, I found accepted with the liveliest gratitude, and by well-educated persons"; the lady who contended with the

---

147. Meissner, "Voyage à Paris," 132. *Ibid.*, 104. "Bread is made with coarse, sticky black flour, because they put in potatoes, beans, Indian corn and millet, and moreover it is badly baked."—Granier de Cassagnac, "Histoire du Directoire," i., 51. (Letter of M. Andot to the author.) "There were three-quarter pound days, one-half pound, and one-quarter pound days and many at two ounces. I was a child of twelve and used to go and wait four hours in the morning in a line, rue de l'Ancienne Comédie. There was a fourth part of bran in the bread, which was very tender and very soft . . . and it contained one-fourth overplus of water. I brought back eight ounces of bread a day for the four persons in our household."

148. Dauban, 386.

dog for the bone was "a former nun, without either parents or friends and everywhere repulsed." "I still hear with a shudder," says Meissner, "the weak, melancholy voice of a well-dressed woman who stopped me in the rue du Bac, to tell me in accents indicative both of shame and despair: 'Ah, Sir, do help me! I am not an outcast. I have some talent—you may have seen some of my works in the *salon*. I have had nothing to eat for two days and I am crazy for want of food.'" Again, in June, 1796, the inspectors state that despair and despondency have reached the highest point, only one cry being heard—misery! ... Our reports all teem with groans and complaints. ... Pallor and suffering are stamped on all faces. ... Each day presents a sadder and more melancholy aspect." And repeatedly,[149] they sum up their scattered observations in a general statement: "A mournful silence, the deepest distress on every countenance; the most intense hatred of the government in general developed in all conversations; contempt for all existing authority; an insolent luxuriousness, insulting to the wretchedness of the poor *rentiers* who expire with hunger in their garrets, no longer possessing the courage to crawl to the Treasury and get the wherewithal to prolong their misery for a few days; the worthy father of a family daily deciding what article of furniture he will sell to make up for what is lacking in his wages that he may buy a half-pound of bread; every sort of provision increasing in price sixty times an hour; the smallest business dependent on the fall of assignats; intriguers of all parties overthrowing each other only to get offices; the intoxicated soldier boasting of the services he has rendered and is to render, and abandoning himself shamelessly to every sort of debauchery; commercial houses transformed into dens of thieves; rascals become traders and traders become rascals; the most sordid cupidity and a mortal egoism—such is the picture presented by Paris."[150]

149. Schmidt, *ibid*. (Reports of Brumaire 24, and Frimaire 13, year IV.)

150. This state of misery is prolonged far beyond this epoch in Paris and the provinces. Cf. Schmidt, "Tableaux de Paris," vol. iii.—Felix Rocquain, "L'Etat de la France au 18e Brumaire," p. 156. (Report by Fourcroy, Nivose 5, year IX.) Convoys of grain fail to reach Brest because the English are masters

One group is wanting in this picture, that of the governors who preside over this wretchedness, which group remains in the background; one might say that it was so designed and composed by some great artist, a lover of contrasts, an inexorable logician, whose invisible hand traces human character unvaryingly, and whose mournful irony unfailingly depicts side by side, in strong relief, the grotesqueness of folly and the seriousness of death. How many perished on account of this misery? Probably more than a million persons.[151] Try to take in at a glance the extraordinary spectacle

at sea, while the roads on land are impassable. "We are assured that the people of Brest have long been on half-rations and perhaps on quarter-rations."

151. It is difficult to arrive at even approximative figures, but the following statements will render the idea clear. 1. Wherever I have compared the mortality of the Revolution with that of the ancient régime I have found the former greater than the latter, even in those parts of France not devastated by the civil war; and the increase of this mortality is enormous, especially in years II. and III.—At Rheims, the average mortality from 1780 to 1789 is one thousand three hundred and fifty, which, for a population of thirty-two thousand five hundred and ninety-seven (1790), gives forty-one deaths per annum to every thousand inhabitants. In the year II., on thirty thousand seven hundred and three inhabitants there are one thousand eight hundred and fifty-six deaths, and in year III., one thousand eight hundred and thirty-six, which gives for each of the two years sixty-four deaths to every thousand persons; the increase is twenty-three deaths a year, that is to say more than one-half above the ordinary rate. (Statistics communicated by M. Jadart, archiviste at Rheims.)—At Limoges, the yearly average of mortality previous to 1789 was eight hundred and twenty-five to twenty thousand inhabitants, or at the rate of forty-one to a thousand. From January 1, 1792, to September 22, 1794, there are three thousand four hundred forty-nine deaths, that is to say, a yearly average of sixty-three deaths to one thousand inhabitants, that is to say, twenty-two extra per annum, while the mortality bears mostly on the poor, for out of two thousand and seventy-three persons who die between January 17, 1793, and September 22, 1794, over one-half, eleven hundred, die in the hospital.—(Louis Guibert, "Ancien registre des paroisses de Limoges," pp. 40, 45, 47.)—At Poitiers, in year IX., the population is eighteen thousand two hundred and twenty-three, and the average mortality of the past ten years was seven hundred and twenty-four per annum. But in year II., there are two thousand and ninety-four deaths, and in year III. two thousand and thirty-two, largely in the hospitals; thus, even on comparing the average mortality of the ten years of the Revolution with the mortality of

presented on twenty-six thousand square leagues of territory, the immense multitude of the starving in town and country, the long lines of women for three years waiting for bread in all the cities, this or that town of twenty-three thousand souls in which one-third of the population dies in the hospitals in three months, the crowds

---

years II. and III., it has almost trebled the average rate.—The same applies to Loudens, where the average death-rate being one hundred and fifty-one, in year II., it rises to four hundred and twenty-five. Instead of the triple for Chatellerault, it is double, where, the average rate being two hundred and sixty-two, the death-rate rises to four hundred and eighty-two, principally in the military hospitals. ("Statistique de la Vienne," by Cochan, préfet, year X.)—At Niort, population eleven thousand, the annual mortality of the ten years preceding 1793 averaged four hundred and twenty-three, or thirty-eight per thousand. In year II., there are one thousand eight hundred and seventy-two, or one hundred and seventy per thousand inhabitants, the number being more than quadrupled. In year III., there are eleven hundred and twenty-two deaths, or one hundred and two per thousand inhabitants, which is almost the triple. ("Statistique des Deux-Sèvres," by Dupin, préfet, 2d memorial Thermidor, year IX.)—At Strasbourg ("Recueil des Pièces Authentiques," etc., vol. i., p. 32. Declaration of the Municipality); "twice as many died last year (year II.) as during any of the preceding years."—According to these figures and the details we have read, the annual mortality during years II. and III. and most of year IV., may be estimated as having increased one-half extra. Now, previous to 1789, according to Moheau and Necker (Peuchet, "Statistique élémentaire de la France," 1805, p. 239), the yearly mortality in France was one person to every thirty, that is to say, eight hundred sixty-six thousand six hundred and sixty-six deaths to a population of twenty-six millions. One-half in addition to this for two and a half years gives, consequently, one million and eighty thousand deaths.

2. During the whole of the Directory episode, privation lasted and the rate of mortality rose very high, especially for sick children, the infirm and the aged, because the Convention had confiscated the possessions of the hospitals and public charity was almost null. For example, at Lyons, "The Asylums having been deprived of sisters of charity during years II., III., and IV., and most of year V., the children gathered into them could neither be fed nor suckled and the number that perished was frightful." ("Statistique du Rhone," by Vernier, préfet, year X.)—In Necker's time, there were about eight hundred asylums, hospitals, and charitable institutions, with one hundred thousand or one hundred and ten thousand inmates. (Peuchet, *ibid.*, 256.) For lack of care and food they die in myriads, especially foundlings, the number of which increases enormously: in 1790, the figures do not exceed twenty-three thousand; in year

of paupers at the poor-houses, the file of poor wretches entering and the file of coffins going out, the asylums deprived of their property, overcrowded with the sick, unable to feed the multitude of foundlings pining away in their cradles the very first week, their little faces in wrinkles like those of old men, the malady of want aggravating all other maladies, the long suffering of a persistent vitality amidst pain and which refuses to succumb, the final death-rattle in a garret or in a ditch—and contrast with this the small, powerful, triumphant group of Jacobins which, knowing where to make a good stand, is determined to stay there at any cost. About ten o'clock in

---

IX., the number surpasses sixty-two thousand (Peuchet, 260): "It is a 'perfect deluge,'" say the reports; in the department of Aisne, there are one thousand and ninety-seven instead of four hundred; in that of Lot-et-Garonne, fifteen hundred (Statistiques des préfets de l'Aisne, Gers, Lot-et-Garonne), and they are born only to die; in that of Eure, after a few months, it is six out of seven; at Lyons, seven hundred and ninety-two out of eight hundred and twenty (Statistique des Préfets du Rhone et de l'Eure). At Marseilles, it is six hundred out of six hundred and eighteen; at Toulon, one hundred and one out of one hundred and four; in the average, nineteen out of twenty. (Rocquain, "Etat de France au 18e Brumaire," p. 33. Report of François de Nantes.) At Troyes, out of one hundred and sixty-four brought in in year IV., one hundred and thirty-four die; out of one hundred and forty-seven received in year VII., one hundred and thirty-six die. (Albert Babeau, ii., 452.) At Paris, in year IV., out of three thousand one hundred and twenty-two infants received two thousand nine hundred and seven perish. (*Moniteur*, year V., No. 231.)—The sick perish the same. "At Toulon, only seven pounds of meat are given each day to eighty patients; I saw in the Civil Asylum," says François de Nantes, "a woman who had just undergone a surgical operation to whom they gave for a restorative a dozen beans on a wooden platter." (*Ibid.*, 16, 31, and *passim*, especially for Bordeaux, Caen, Alençon, St. Lô, etc.)—As to beggars, these are innumerable: in year IX., it is estimated that there are three or four thousand by department, at least three hundred thousand in France. "In the four Brittany departments one can truly say that a third of the population live at the expense of the other two-thirds, either by stealing from them or through compelling assistance." (Rocquain, preface, lxi., and "Report by Barbé-Marbois," p. 93.)

3. In year IX., the *Conseils-generaux* are called upon to ascertain whether the departments have increased or diminished in population since 1789. ("Analyse des procès-verbaux des Conseils-Generaux de l'an XI.") Out of fifty-eight which reply, thirty-seven state that the population with them has diminished;

the morning,[152] Cambacérès, president of the Committee of Public Safety, is seen entering its hall in the Pavillon de l'Egalité. That large, cautious and shrewd personage who, later on, is to become archchancellor of the Empire and famous for his epicurean inventions and other peculiar tastes revived from antiquity, is the man. Scarcely seated, he orders an ample *pot-au-feu* to be placed on the chimney hearth and, on the table, "fine wine and fine white bread; three articles," says a guest, "not to be found elsewhere in all Paris." Between twelve and two o'clock, his colleagues enter the room in turn, take a plate of soup and a slice of meat, swallow some wine, and then proceed, each to his bureau, to receive his coterie, giving this one an office and compelling another to pay up, looking all the time after his own special interests; at this moment, especially, towards the close of the Convention, there are no public interests, all interests being private and personal. In the mean time, the deputy in charge of subsistences, Roux de la Haute Marne, an unfrocked Benedictine, formerly a terrorist in the provinces, subsequently the protégé and employee of Fouché, with whom he is to be associated in the police department, keeps the throng of women in check which daily resorts to the Tuileries to beg for bread. He is well adapted for this duty, being tall, chubby, ornamental, and with vigorous

---

twelve, that it has increased; nine, that it remains stationary. Of the twenty-two others, thirteen attribute the maintenance or increase of population, at least for the most part, to the multiplication of early marriages in order to avoid conscription and to the large number of natural children.—Consequently, the average rate of population is kept up not through preserving life, but through the substitution of new lives for the old ones that are sacrificed. Bordeaux, nevertheless, lost one-tenth of its population, Angers one-eighth, Pau one-seventh, Chambéry one-fourth, Rennes one-third; in the departments where the war was carried on, Argenton-le-Chateau lost two-thirds of its population, Bressuire fell from three thousand to six hundred and thirty inhabitants; Lyons, after the siege, fell from a population of one hundred and forty thousand to eighty thousand. ("Analyse des procès-verbaux des Conseils-Generaux" and "Statistiques des Préfets.")

152. Lareveillère-Lepeaux, "Mémoires," i., 248. (He belongs to the Committee and is an eye-witness.)

lungs. He has taken his office in the right place, in the attic of the palace, at the top of long, narrow and steep stairs, so that the line of women stretching up between the two walls, piled one above the other, necessarily becomes immovable. With the exception of the two or three at the front, no one has her hands free to grab the haranguer by the throat and close the oratorical stop-cock. He can spout his tirades accordingly with impunity, and for an indefinite time. On one occasion, his sonorous jabber rattles away uninterruptedly from the top to the bottom of the staircase, from nine o'clock in the morning to five o'clock in the afternoon. Under such a voluble shower, his hearers become weary and end by going home. About nine or ten o'clock in the evening, the Committee of Public Safety reassembles, but not to discuss business. Danton and Larevellière preach in vain; each is too egoistic and too worn-out; they let the rein slacken on Cambacérès. As to him, he would rather keep quiet and drag the cart no longer; but there are two things necessary which he must provide for on pain of death. "It will not do," says he in plaintive tones, "to keep on printing the assignats at night which we want for the next day. If that lasts, *ma foi,* we run the risk of being strung up at a lantern. . . . Go and find Hourier-Eloi, as he has charge of the finances, and tell him that we entreat him to keep us a-going for a fortnight or eighteen days longer, when the executive Directory will come in and do what it pleases." "But food— shall we have enough for tomorrow?" "Aha, I don't know—I'll send for our colleague Roux, who will post us on that point." Roux enters, the official spokesman, the fat, jovial tamer of the popular dog. "Well, Roux, how do we stand about supplying Paris with food?" "The supply, citizen President, is just as abundant as ever, two ounces per head—at least for most of the sections." "Go to the devil with your abundant supply! You'll have our heads off!" All remain silent, for this possible dénouement sets them to thinking. Then, one of them exclaims: "President, are there any refreshments provided for us? After working so hard for so many days we need something to strengthen us!" "Why, yes; there is a good calf's-tongue, a large turbot, a large piece of pie and some other things."

They cheer up, begin to eat and drink champagne, and indulge in drolleries. About eleven or twelve o'clock the members of other Committees come in; signatures are affixed to their various decrees, on trust, without reading them over. They, in their turn, sit down at the table and the conclave of sovereign bellies digests without giving itself further trouble about the millions of stomachs that are empty.

BOOK IX

*The End of the
Revolutionary Government*

CHAPTER I

I. *The Convention after Thermidor 9—Reaction against the Terrorists—Aversion to the Constitutionalists—The danger they run if they lose power—* II. *Decrees for the reelection of the Two-thirds—Small number of Voters—Manoeuvres for preventing electors from voting on the decrees—Frauds in the returns of votes—Maintenance of the decrees by force—Recruiting of Roughs—The military employed—The 13th of Vendémiaire—* III. *The Directory chosen among the regicides—It selects agents of its own species—Leading Jacobins are deprived of their civic rights—The Terrorists are set free and restored to their civic rights—Example at Blois of these releases and of the new administrative staff—* IV. *Resistance of public opinion—Elections, year IV., at Paris and in the provinces—The Directory threatened by ultra Jacobins—Forced amelioration of the Jacobin administration—* V. *Elections of year V.—Character and sentiments of the elected—The new majority in the Corps Législatif—Its principles and programme—Danger and anxiety of the Jacobin minority—Indecision, division, scruples, and weakness of the moderate party—Decision, want of scruples, force, and modes of procedure of the Jacobin faction—The 18th of Fructidor—* VI. *Dictatorship of the Directory—Its new prerogatives—Purgation of the Corps Législatif—Purification of the administrative and judicial authorities—Military commissions in the provinces—Suppression of newspapers—The right of voting reserved to Jacobins alone—Despotism of the Directory—Revival of Terror—Transportation substituted for the guillotine—Treatment of the transported on the way, in Guyanna, and on the islands of Rhé and Oléron—Restoration of Jacobin feudalism—* VII. *Application and aggravation of the laws of the reign of Terror—Measures taken to impose civic religion—Arrest, transportation, and execution of Priests—Ostracism proposed against the entire anti-Jacobin class—The nobles or the ennobled, not émigrés, are declared foreigners—Decrees against émigrés of every class—Other steps taken against remaining proprie-*

I

NEVERTHELESS they too, these glutted sovereigns, are anxious, and seriously so, and we have just seen in what direction; their object is to keep in office, that they may preserve their lives, and henceforth this is their sole concern. A good Jacobin, up to the 9th of Thermidor, could, by shutting his eyes, still believe in his creed;[1] after the 9th of Thermidor, unless born blind, like Soubrany, Romme, and Goujon, a fanatic whose intellectual organs are as rigid as the limbs of a fakir, nobody in the Convention can longer believe in the *Contrat-Social*, in a despotic equalising socialism, in the merits of Terror, in the divine right of the pure. For, to escape the guillotine of the pure, the purest had to be guillotined, Saint-Just, Couthon, and Robespierre, the high-priest of the sect: that very day the *Montagnards*, in giving up their doctor, abandoned their principles, and there is no longer any principle or man to which the Convention could rally; in effect, before guillotining Robespierre and his asso-

---

1. Gaudin, Duc de Gaëte, "Mémoires," i., 28. Gaudin, commissioner of the Treasury, meets the president of the revolutionary committee of his quarter, an excellent Jacobin, who says to him: "Eh, well, what's all this? Robespierre proscribed! Is it possible? What is wanted—*everything was going on so well!*" (It is true that fifty or sixty heads fell daily.) "I replied, 'Just so, there are some folks that are never satisfied.'"

ciates as orthodox, it guillotined the Girondists, Hébert, and Danton, as heretics. Now, "the existence of popular idols and of head charlatans is irrevocably ended."[2] Ever the same conventional symbol before the empty sanctuary in the blood-stained temple, and ever the same loud-intoned anthem; but faith is gone, and only the acolytes remain to drone out the revolutionary litany, old train-bearers and swingers of incense, the subaltern butchers who, through a sudden stroke, have become pontiffs; in short, the valets of the church who have donned the mitres and croziers of their masters after having assassinated them.

From month to month, under the pressure of public opinion, they detach themselves from the worship at which they have officiated, for, however blunted or perverted their consciences, they cannot avoid admitting that Jacobinism, as they have practised it, was the religion of robbery and murder. Previous to Thermidor an official phraseology[3] drowned with its doctrinal roar the living truth, while each Conventional sacristan or beadle, confined to his own chapel, saw clearly only the human sacrifices in which he himself had taken part. After Thermidor, the friends and kindred of the dead, the oppressed, make their voices heard, and he is forced to see collectively and in detail all the crimes to which, nearly or remotely, he has contributed either through his assent or through his vote, the same as in Mexico, the priest of Huichilobos walks about in the midst of the six hundred thousand skulls amassed in the vaults of his temple. Blow after blow, during the whole of year III., the truth unintermittingly declares itself through the freedom of the press and the great public discussions. First, comes an account of the funereal journey of one hundred and thirty-two Nantese, dragged from

2. Mallet-Dupan, "Mémoires," ii., 16. (Letter of January 8, 1795.)—*Ibid.*, "Correspondance avec la cour de Vienne," i., 23, 25, 32, 34, (January 8, 1795, on the four parties composing the Convention).

3. Marshal Marmont: "Mémoires," i., 120. (Report of General Dugommier on the capture of Toulon.) "That memorable day avenged the general will of a partial and gangrened will, the delirium of which caused the greatest misfortunes."

Nantes to Paris,[4] and the solemn acquittal, received with transports, of the ninety-four who survive. After this, come the trials of the most prominent terrorists, that of Carrier and the Revolutionary Committee of Nantes, that of Fouquier-Tinville and the old revolutionary Tribunal of Paris, that of Joseph Lebon,[5] and, during thirty or forty consecutive sessions, hundreds of minute, verified depositions ending in the most complete and satisfactory testimony. In the mean time, revelations multiply at the tribune of the Convention; these consist of the letters of the new representatives on mission and the denunciations of the towns against their overthrown tyrants; against Maignet, Dartigoyte, Piochefer-Bernard, Levasseur, Crassous, Javogues, Lequinio, Lefiot, Piorry, Pinet, Monestier, Fouché, Laplanche, Lecarpentier, and many others; add to these the reports of commissions charged with examining into the conduct of old dictators, Collot d'Herbois, Billaud-Varennes, Barère, Amar, Vouland, Vadier and David; the reports of the representatives charged with investigating certain details of the abolished system, that of Grégoire on revolutionary vandalism, that of Cambon on revolutionary taxes, that of Courtois on Robespierre's papers. All these rays combine in a terrible illumination which imposes itself even on the eyes that turn away from it; it is now but too plain that France, for fourteen months, has been devastated by a gang of bandits; all that can be said in favor of the least perverted and the least vile is that they were born so, or had become crazy.[6] The growing majority

4. Memorial of the ninety-four survivors Thermidor 30, year II., acquitted Fructidor 28.

5. Carrier indicted Brumaire 21, year III. Decree of arrest passed by four hundred and ninety-eight out of five hundred votes, Frimaire 3; execution Frimaire 26. Fouquier-Tinville indicted Frimaire 28; execution Floréal 28, there being four hundred and nineteen witnesses heard. Joseph Lebon indicted Messidor 1, year III. Trial adjourned to the Somme court, Messidor 29; execution Vendémiaire 24, year IV.

6. Cf. chapters 4, 5 and 6 of the present volume. Numbers of printed documents of this epoch show what these local sovereigns were. The principal ones in the department of Ain were "Anselm, who had placed Marat's head in his shop. Duclos, a joiner, living before the 31st of May on his earnings; he became

of the Convention cannot evade this testimony and the *Montagnards* excite its horror; and all the more, because it bears them a grudge; the seventy-three put in confinement and the sixteen proscribed who have resumed their seats, with the four hundred mutes who have so long sat under the knife, remember the oppression to which they have been subject, and they turn first against the vilest wretches, and then against the members of the old committees. The "Mountain," upon this, as usual with it, launches forth its customary supporters in the riots of Germinal and Prairial, the greedy populace, the Jacobin rabble, and proclaims anew the reign of Terror; the Convention again sees the knife over its head. Saved by young men, by the National Guard, it becomes courageous through fear, and, in its turn, it terrorises the terrorists; the Faubourg St. Antoine is disarmed, ten thousand Jacobins are arrested,[7] and more than sixty

---

after that a gentleman living on his rents, owning national domains, sheep, horses and pocket-books filled with assignats. Laimant, a tailor, in debt, furnishing his apartment suddenly with all the luxuriousness of the ancient régime, such as beds at one hundred pistoles, etc. Alban, mayor, placing seals everywhere, was a blacksmith and father of a family which he supported by his labor; all at once he stops working, and passes from a state of dependence to one of splendor; he has diamonds and earrings, always wearing new clothes, fine linen shirts, muslin cravates, silk stockings, etc.; on removing the seals in the houses of those imprisoned and guillotined, little or nothing was found in them. Alban was denounced and incarcerated for having obliged a woman of Macon to give him four hundred francs on promising to interest himself in her husband. Such are the Ain patriots. Rollet, another, had so frightened the rural districts that the people ran away on his approach; on one occasion he had two of them harnessed to his carriage and drove them along for some time in this manner. . . . Another, Charcot (of Virieu), before the Revolution, was a highway assassin, and was banished for three years for an act of this description." (Bibliotheque Nationale. Lb. 41, No. 1318. "The truth in reply to calumnious charges against the department of Ain." Letter of Roux, Vendémiaire, year III.)

7. Decree of Germinal 12 for the transportation of Collot, Barère, Billaud-Varennes and Vadier. Eight *Montagnards* are put under arrest.—Decree of Germinal 14: the same against nine other *Montagnards*.—Decree of Germinal 29: the same against Maribon-Moutant.—Decree of Prairial 6: twenty-nine *Montagnards* are indicted.—Decree of Prairial 8, putting six *Montagnards* under arrest.—Decree of Prairial 9: the same against nine members of former com-

Montagnards are decreed under indictment; Collot, Billaud, Barère, and Vadier are to be transported; nine other members of former committees are to be imprisoned; the last of the veritable fanatics, Romme, Goujon, Soubrany, Duquesnoy, Bourbotte, and Duroy are condemned to death; immediately after the sentence five of them stab themselves on the stairs of the tribunal; two of the wounded who survive are borne, along with the sixth, to the scaffold and guillotined; two *Montagnards* of the same stamp, Rhul and Maure, kill themselves before their sentence. Henceforth the purged Convention regards itself as pure; its final rigor has expiated its former baseness, the guilty blood which it spills washing away the stains of the innocent blood it had shed before.

Unfortunately, in condemning the terrorists, it pronounced its own condemnation; for it has authorised and sanctioned all their crimes. On its benches, in its committees, often in the president's chair, at the head of the ruling coterie, still figure the members of the revolutionary government, many of the avowed terrorists like Bourdon de l'Oise, Bentabolle, Delmas, and Rewbell; presidents of the September commune like Marie Chénier; those who carried out "the 31st of May," like Legendre and Merlin de Douai, author of the decree which created six hundred thousand suspects in France; provincial executioners of the most brutal and most ferocious sort, the greatest and most cynical robbers like André Dumont, Fréron, Tallien, and Barras. Under Robespierre, the four hundred mutes "du ventre" were the reporters, the voters, the *claqueurs*, and the agents of the worst decrees against religion, property, and persons. The foundations of Terror were all laid by the seventy-three in confinement before they were imprisoned, and by the sixteen who were proscribed before their proscription. Excepting ten or a dozen who stayed away, the Convention, in a mass, pronounced judgment against the King and declared him guilty; more than one-half of the Convention, the Girondists at the head of them, voted his death.

---

mittees.—Decrees of Prairial 10 to Thermidor 22, condemning six *Montagnards* to death, one to transportation and twenty to arrest.

The hall does not contain fifty honorable men in whom character sustains conscience, and who had a right to carry their heads erect.[8] In no law they passed, good or bad, did the other seven hundred have in view the interests of their constituents; in all their laws, good or bad, they solely regarded their own interests. So long as the attacks of the "Mountain" and of the rabble affected the public only, they lauded them, decreed them, and had them executed; if they finally rebelled against the "Mountain," and against the rabble, it was at the last moment, and solely to save their lives. Before, as after the 9th of Thermidor, before, as after the 1st of Prairial, the mainsprings of the conduct of these pusillanimous oppressors or involuntary liberators were baseness and egoism. Hence, "the contempt and horror universally poured out against them; only Jacobins could be still more odious!"[9] If further support is given to these faithless mandatories, it is because they are soon to be put out. On the premature report that the Convention is going to break up, people accost each other in the street, exclaiming, "We are rid of these brigands, they are going at last. . . . People caper and dance about as if they could not repress their joy; they talk of nothing but the boy (Louis XVIII. confined in the Temple), and the new elections. Everybody agrees on excluding the present deputies. . . . There is less discussion on the crimes which each has committed than on the insignificance of the entire assemblage, while the epithets of *vicious*, *used up*, and *corrupt* have almost wholly given way to *thieves* and *scoundrels*."[10] Even in Paris, during the closing months of their rule, they hardly dare appear in public: "in the dirtiest and

8. Barbé-Marbois, "Mémoires," preface, p. viii. "Except about fifty men who are honest and intelligent, history presents no sovereign assembly containing so much vice, abjectness and ignorance."—Buchez et Roux, xxxvii., 7. (Speech by Legendre, Thermidor 17, year III.) "It is stated in print that, at most, there are but twenty pure men in this Assembly."—*Ibid.*, 27. Order of the Lepelletier section, Vendémiaire 10, year IV. "It is certain that we owe the dearth and all its accompanying evils to the incapacity and brigandage of the present government."

9. Mallet-Dupan, "Correspondance," etc., i., 211. (May 27, 1795.)

10. "Un Séjour en France," 267, 271. (Amiens, March 13, April 12, 1795.)

most careless costume which the tricolor scarf and gold fringe makes more apparent, they try to escape notice in the crowd[11] and, in spite of their modesty, do not always avoid insult and still less the maledictions of those who pass them." In the provinces, at home, it would be worse for them; their lives would be in danger; in any event, they would be dragged through the gutter, and this they know. Save about "twenty of them," all who are not to succeed in entering the new Corps Legislatif, will intrigue for offices in Paris and become "state messengers, employees in bureaux, and ushers to ministers"; in default of other places they would accept those of "hall-sweeps." Any refuge for them is good against the reprobation of the public, which is already rising and submerging them under its tide.

II

There is no other refuge for them except in supreme power, and no other means for maintaining this but in the excesses of despotism, dishonesty, mendacity, and violence. In the Constitution they manufacture, they desire to remain the sovereigns of France and they decree[12] at once that, willingly or not, France must select two-thirds of its new representatives from amongst them, and, that she may make a good selection, it is prudent to impose the selection upon her. There is a show, indeed, of consulting her in the special decrees which deprive her of two-thirds of her elective rights but, as in 1792 and in 1793, it is so contrived that she consents, or seems to consent, to this arrangement.[13] In the first place, they relied on the majority

11. Meissner, "Voyage à Paris," 123, 351. (The author arrives in Paris, September 22, 1795.)

12. Decrees of Fructidor 5 and 13, year III.

13. Mallet-Dupan ("Correspondance avec la cour de Vienne," i, 292, August 30, 1795).—*Moniteur,* xxv., 518, 551. (Session of Fructidor 3.) The first idea of the Commission of Eleven was to have the Convention itself choose the two-thirds. "Its opponents took advantage of the public outcry and broke off this plan . . . of the Girondist cabal." Louvet, Fructidor 3, mounted three times into the tribune to support this project, still more scandalous than the other. "Eh, what electoral assembly could be better than yours! You all know each other

of electors abstaining from a response. Experience indeed, had shown that, for a long time, the masses were disgusted with the *plebiscite* farces; moreover, terror has stifled in individuals all sentiment of a common interest;[14] each cares for himself alone. Since Thermidor, electors and mayors in the boroughs and in the rural districts are found with a good deal of difficulty, even electors of the second degree; people saw that it was useless and even dangerous to perform the duties of a citizen; they would have nothing to do with public functions. A foreigner writes,[15] after traversing France from Bourg-en-Bresse to Paris: "Ninety times out of a hundred that I have asked the question, '*Citizen, what was done in the primary meeting of your canton?*' the answer would be: '*Me, citizen, what have I to do with it? I' faith, they had hard work to agree!*' Or, '*What's the use? There were not many there! Honest folks stayed at home.*'" In effect, out of at least six million electors convoked, five millions do not come near the ballot-box, there being no embarrassment in this matter as they do not vote.[16]

In the second place, precautions have been taken to prevent those who come to vote on the Constitution from entertaining the idea of voting on the decrees. No article of the Constitution, nor in the decrees, calls upon them to do so; slight inducement is held out to them to come, in a vague style, through an oratorical interrogation, or in a tardy address.[17] In addition to this, on the printed blanks sent

---

well." Louvet adds this significant expression: "The armies also will vote the new Constitution. I have no fears of its fate."

14. *Moniteur*, xxii, 22. (Report of Lindet, 4th *sans-culottide*, year II.) "Each man confines himself to his family and calculates his resources."

15. Meissner, 58.

16. Decree of Fructidor 5. "All Frenchmen who voted at the last primary assemblies will be admitted to vote on the acceptance of the Constitution."— Archives Nationales, A. II. B. 638. (General recapitulation of the vote on the Constitution of the year III, and on the decrees of Fructidor 5 and 13 printed by order of the Convention Vendémiaire, year IV.) Number of voters on the Constitutional bill, one million one hundred and seven thousand three hundred and sixty-eight.

17. *Moniteur*, xxv., 637. (Address to Frenchmen by Lareveillère-Lepeaux, in the name of the Commission of Eleven, affixed to the decree of Fructidor 13.)

to them from Paris, they find but three columns, one for the number of votes accepting the Constitution, another for the number rejecting it, and the third for "written observations" in case there are any. There are no special columns for marking the number of votes accepting or rejecting the decrees. Thereupon, many illiterate or ill-informed electors might think that they were convoked to vote solely on the Constitution and not at all on the decrees, which is just what happened, and especially in the remote departments, and in the rural assemblies. Moreover, many assemblies, nearer Paris and in the towns, comprehend that if the Convention consults them it is only for form's sake; to give a negative answer is useless and perilous; it is better to keep silent; as soon as the decrees are mentioned they very prudently "unanimously" demand the order of the day.[18] Hence out of five primary assemblies on the average which vote for or against the Constitution, there is only one which votes for or against the decrees.[19] Such is the mode of getting at the voice of the nation. Apparently, it is induced to speak; practically, its silence is ensured.

"Let all opposition to the legitimacy of this measure cease! The only legitimate measure is that which saves the country! Besides, *if the majority of the primary assemblies of France approve of it, who dares say that the people would have renounced its sovereignty in thus expressing its will!*"—Cf. Sauzay, vii., 653 to 667, on the details and circumstances of the elections in one of the departments.

18. Archives Nationales, A. II. B., 688. (*Procès-verbaux* of the primary meetings of Seine-Inférieare, Dieppe, "Liberté" section, session of Fructidor 20.) The Constitution is unanimously accepted by forty-four voters, on a call of names. Then, "before proceeding to the nomination of electors the law was read, concerning the mode of electing the two-thirds of the National Convention. The President having asked if any one wished to speak on this law the order of the day was immediately called for on all sides." The electors are appointed forthwith and the assembly adjourns.—The clerk, who has to draw up the minutes, writes on the margin "forty-four voters unanimously accept the Constitution *as well as the decrees of Fructidor 5 and 13,*" which is false. It is clear that the scribe had been instructed to enlarge the number of votes accepting the decrees, which suggests doubts on the truth of the total furnished by the Convention.

19. *Ibid.,* A. II. B., 638 (General recapitulation). I have taken the number of primary assemblies in the twenty-two first departments on the alphabetical list, that is to say, one-quarter of the territory, which warrants a conclusion,

The last and most ingenious expedient of all: when a primary assembly speaks too loudly it is taken for granted that it kept silent. In Paris, where the electors are more clear-sighted and more decided than in the provinces, in eighteen well-known departments, and probably in many others, the electors who voted on the decrees almost all voted against them; in many cases, even their minutes state that the negative vote was "unanimous," but the minutes fail to state the exact number of the *noes*. On this, in the total of *noes* hostile to the decrees, these *noes* are not counted.[20] Through this

---

proportionately, on the whole country. In these twenty-two departments, one thousand five hundred and seventy assemblies vote on the Constitution and only three hundred and twenty-eight on the decrees. The figures are herewith given: in the Côtes-du-Nord, eighty-four primary assemblies; only one votes in favor of the decrees. Bouches du Rhone, ninety primary assemblies; four vote on the decrees, two for and two against. Aude, eighty-three primary assemblies; four vote on the decrees, three for and one against. Ariége, fifty-nine primary assemblies; two vote on the decrees. Basses-Alpes, forty-eight primary assemblies; two vote on the decrees. Maritime Alps, twenty-three primary assemblies; not one votes on the decrees.

20. *Ibid.* (*Procès-verbaux* of the primary assemblies of the department of the Seine, Popincourt section, Vendémiaire), 91. This section, on learning that its vote against the decrees "was put down as a cipher in the general count of votes," protested and declared that "when the vote was taken at the meeting of Fructidor 22, it was composed of eight hundred and forty-five citizens representing two thousand five hundred and ninety-four votes." Nevertheless, in the general recapitulation of Vendémiaire its vote counts for nothing.—The same remark for the "Fidélité" section. Its minutes state that the decrees are rejected "unanimously," and that it is composed of one thousand three hundred citizens; its vote, likewise, goes for nothing. The totals given by the recapitulation are as follows: Voters on the Constitution, one million one hundred and seven thousand three hundred and sixty-eight; for, one million fifty-seven thousand three hundred and ninety; against, forty-nine thousand nine hundred and seventy-eight.—Voters on the Decrees, three hundred and fourteen thousand three hundred and eighty-two; for, two hundred and five thousand four hundred and ninety-eight; against, one hundred and eight thousand seven hundred and ninety-four.—Mallet-Dupan (i., 313) estimates the number of electors, at Paris, who rejected the decrees, at eighty thousand. Fiévée, "Correspondance avec Bonaparte," introduction, p. 126.—(A few days before Vendémiaire 13, Fiévée, in the name of the Theatre-Français section, came, with two other commis-

trickery, the Convention, in Paris alone, reduced the number of negatives by fifty thousand and the same in the provinces, after the fashion of a dishonest steward who, obliged to hand in an account, falsifies the figures by substituting subtractions for additions. Such is the way, in relation to the decrees, in which, out of the three hundred thousand votes which it accepts, it is able to announce two hundred thousand *yeas* and one hundred thousand *noes* and thus proclaim that its master, the sovereign people, after giving it a general acquittance, a discharge in full, invests it anew with its confidence and expressly continues its mandate.

It now remains to keep by force this power usurped by fraud. Immediately after the suppression of the Jacobin riots the Convention, menaced on the right, turns over to the left; it requires allies, persons of executive ability; it takes them wherever it can find them, from the faction which decimated it before Thermidor and which, since Thermidor, it decimates. Consequently, its executive committee suspends all proceedings begun against the principal *Montagnards;* a number of terrorists, former presidents of the sections, "the matadors of the quarter," arrested after Prairial 1, are set free at the end of a month. They have good arms, are accustomed to vigorous striking without giving warning, especially when honest folks are to be knocked down or ripped open. The stronger public opinion is against the government the more does the government rely on men with bludgeons and pikes, on the strikers "turned out of the primary assemblies," on the heroes of September 2 and May 31, dangerous nomads, inmates of Bicêtre, paid assassins out of employment, and roughs of the *Quinze-Vingts* and Faubourg St. An-

----

sioners, to verify the returns announced by the Convention.) "We divided the returns into three parts; each commissioner undertook to check off one of these parts, pen in hand, and the conscientious result of our labor was to show that, although the Convention had voting done in a mass by all the regiments then in France, individually, the majority, incontestably was against its project. Thus, while trying to have the election law passed under the Constitution, both measures were rejected."

toine.[21] Finally on the 11th of Vendémiaire, it gathers together fifteen or eighteen hundred of them and arms them in battalions.[22] Such brigands are they, Menon, "major-general of the army of the interior and commandant of the armed force of Paris," comes the next day with several of his staff-officers and tells the Committee of Five that he "will not have such bandits in his army nor under his orders. I will not march with a lot of rascals and assassins organised in battalions" under the name of "patriots of '89." The true patriots, indeed, of '89 are on the other side, the constitutionalists of 1791, sincere liberals, "forty thousand proprietors and merchants," the élite and mass of the Parisian population,[23] "the majority of men really interested in public matters," and at this moment, the common welfare is all that concerns them. Republic or royalty is merely a secondary thought, an idea in the back-ground; nobody dreams of restoring the ancient régime; but very few are preoccupied with the restoration of a limited monarchy.[24] "On asking those most in ear-

21. Schmidt, "Tableaux de Paris pendant la Revolution." (Reports of Messidor 1 and 24, year III.) "Good citizens are alarmed at the numerous pardons granted to the members of the revolutionary committees." "The release of numerous terrorists is generally turned to account."—Mallet-Dupan, "Correspondance," etc., i., 259, 261, 321. "The vilest terrorists have been set free; a part of them confined in the château of Ham have been allowed to escape; they are summoned from all parts of the kingdom; they even send for them abroad, in Germany, in Belgium, in Savoy, in Geneva. On reaching Paris they are given leaders and organised. September 11 and 12 they began to meet publicly in groups and to use threats. I have proof of emissaries being engaged in recruiting them in the places I have mentioned and in paying their expenses to the capital." (Letter of September 26, 1795.)

22. Buchez et Roux, xxxvii., 36, 49. (Reports of Merlin de Douai and Barras on the 13th of Vendémiaire.)—Thibaudeau, "Histoire de la Convention et du Directoire," i., 209.—Fabre de l'Aude, "Histoire secrete du Directoire," i., p. 10. "The Convention opened the prison doors to fifteen or eighteen hundred Jacobin lunatics, *Seides* of the former members of the Committee of Public Safety."—Mallet-Dupan (*ibid.*, i., 332, 337, 361) estimates the numbers of terrorists enrolled at three thousand.

23. Barbé-Marbois, "Mémoires," i., p. ix.—Meissner, p. 246.

24. Mallet-Dupan, *ibid.*, i., 282. (Letter of August 16, 1795.) "At Paris, the

nest what government they would like in place of the Convention, they reply 'We want that no longer, we want nothing belonging to it; we want the Republic and honest people for our rulers.' "[25] That is all; their uprisal is not a political insurrection against the form of the government, but a moral insurrection against the criminals in office. Hence, on seeing the Convention arm their old executioners against them, "the tigers" of the Reign of Terror, admitted male-factors, they cannot contain themselves.[26] "That day," says a for-eigner, who visited many public places in Paris, "I saw everywhere the deepest despair, the greatest expression of rage and fury. . . . Without that unfortunate order the insurrection would probably not have broken out." If they take up arms it is because they are brought back under the pikes of the *Septembriseurs,* and under Robespierre's axe. But they are only national guards; most of them have no guns;[27] they are in want of gunpowder, those who have any having only five or six charges; "the great majority do not think of fighting"; they imagine that "their presence is merely needed to enforce a petition"; they have no artillery, no positive leader; it is simply excitement, precipitation, disorder, and mistaken manoeuvres.[28] On

---

patriots of 1789 have got the upper hand. The regicides have the greatest horror of this class because they regard it as a hundred times more dangerous than pronounced aristocrats." *Ibid.,* 316.—Meissner, p. 229. "The sectionists want neither a republic nor monarchy but simply intelligent and honest men for the places in the new Convention."

25. Lavalette, "Mémoires," i., 162, 170.

26. Meissner, p. 236.—Any number of details show the features and char-acters of the male and female Jacobins here referred to. For example, Carnot ("Mémoires," i., 581), says in his narrative of the foregoing riot (Prairial, i., year III.), "A creature with a horrible face put himself astride my bench and kept constantly repeating: "Today is the day we'll make you *passer le gout de pain?* and furies posted in the tribunes, made signs of the guillotine."

27. Meissner, p. 238.—Fiévée, p. 127, and following pages.

28. Mallet-Dupan, i., 333, and following pages. (Letter of October 24, 1795.) "Barras does not repeat the mistake made by the Court on the 10th of April, and shut himself up in the château and the Tuileries; he posts troops and artillery in all the avenues. . . . Fréron and two other representatives, supplied with coin

the contrary, on the side of the Convention, with Henriot's old bullies, there are eight or nine thousand regular troops, and Bonaparte; his cannon, which rake the rue St. Honoré and the Quai Voltaire, mow down five or six hundred sectionists; the rest disperse, and henceforth the check-mated Parisians are not to take up their guns against the Jacobin faction whatever it does.

III

Supreme authority is once more in the hands of the revolutionary coterie. In conformity with its decrees of Fructidor, it first obliges electors to take two-thirds of their new representatives from the Convention, and as, notwithstanding its decrees, the electoral assemblies have not reelected a sufficient number of the Conventionalists, it nominates itself the one hundred and four which are wanting, from a list prepared by its Committee of Public Safety; in this way, in the council of the Five Hundred, as in the Council of the Ancients, it secures a certain majority in both houses of the Corps Legislatif. In the executive branch, in the Directory, it assures itself of unanimity; for the Five Hundred, adroitly preparing the lists, impose their candidates on the Ancients, the five names being selected beforehand, Barras, Lareveillère-Lepeaux, Rewbell, Letourneur and Siéyès, and then, on Siéyès refusing, Carnot, all of them regicides and, under this terrible title, bound at the risk of their heads, to maintain

---

and assignats collected in the Faubourg St. Antoine, four or five hundred bandits which joined the terrorists; these formed the pretended battalions of the *loyal* section which had been pompously announced to the Convention. No section, excepting the "Quinze-Vingts," sent its battalion, this section having separated at the outset from the other forty-seven sections. . . . The gardens and court of the Tuileries resembled a feasting camp, where the Committees caused distributions of wine and all sorts of provisions; many of their defenders were intoxicated; the troops of the line were kept faithful with money and drink."— After Vendémiaire 13, the Convention brings further reinforcements of regular troops into Paris to keep the city under, amounting to eight or nine thousand men.

the regicide faction in power. Naturally the Directory chooses its agents from amongst those like itself,[29] ministers and the employees of their departments, ambassadors and consuls, officers of all ranks, collectors of taxes direct and indirect, administrators of the national domains, commissioners of civil and criminal courts, and the commissioners of the departmental and municipal administrations. Again, having the right to suspend and dismiss all elected administrative bodies, it exercises this right; if the local authorities of any town, canton, or department seem to be anti-Jacobin, it sets them aside and, either on its own authority, or with the assent of the Corps Legislatif, replaces them with Jacobins on the spot.[30] In other respects, the Convention has done its best to relieve its clients of their principal adversaries and most popular rivals; the night before its dissolution, it excluded from every "legislative, municipal, administrative, and judicial function,"[31] even that of juryman, not only the individuals who, rightly or wrongly, had been put on a list of *émigrés* and not yet stricken off, but likewise their fathers, sons and grandsons, brothers and brothers-in-law, their connections of the same degree, uncles and nephews, probably two or three hundred thousand Frenchmen, nearly the whole of the élite of the nation, and to this it adds the rest of this élite, all the honest and energetic who, in the late primary or electoral assemblies have "provoked or signed" any manifestation against its despotism; if still in office they are to resign within twenty-four hours, or be sent into perpetual exile. Through this legal incapacity of the anti-Jacobins, the field is free to the Jacobins; in many places, for lack of candidates that please them, most of the electors stay away from the polls; besides this, the terrorists resort to their old system, that is to say to brutal

29. Constitution of year III., Articles vi. and vii.

30. Albert Babeau, "Histoire de Troyes," ii., 367 and following pages. Sauzay, "His. de la Persécution Révolutionnaire dans le Doubs," viii., ch. 52 and 54.—Law of Pluviose 4, year IV., authorising the executive Directory to appoint the members who, up to Thermidor 1, year IV., shall compose the municipal bodies of Bordeaux, Lyons, Marseilles and Paris.

31. Decree of Brumaire 3, year IV.

violence.[32] On again obtaining the support of the government they have raised their heads and are now the titular favorites. The Convention has restored to them the civic rights of which they had deprived their adversaries: "every decree of indictment or arrest" rendered against them, "every warrant executed or not, all proceedings and suits" begun, every sentence bearing on their revolutionary acts, is cancelled.[33] The most "atrocious" *Montagnards,* the most sanguinary and foul proconsuls, Dartigoyte and Piochefer-Bernard, Darthé, Lebon's secretary, Rossignol the great September massacrer, the presidents of former revolutionary committees, "patriotic robbers, seal-breakers" and garroters, brazenly promenade the streets

---

32. Archives Nationales, AF., II., 65. (Letter of Gen. Kermorvan, to the Com. of Public Safety, Valenciennes, Fructidor 22, year III.) At Valenciennes, during the elections, "the leaders of the sections used their fists in driving out of the primary assemblies all the worthy men possessing the necessary qualities for election. . . . I knew that the "seal-breakers" (*brise-scellés*) were the promoters of these turbulent parties, the patriotic robbers, the men who have wasted public and private fortunes belonging to the commune, and who are revelling in the houses and on the estates of the *émigrés* which they have had awarded to them at a hundred times below their value. . . . All of them are appointed electors. . . . They have paid . . . and still pay agitators to intimidate honest folks by terror, in order to keep what they have seized, awaiting an opportunity to get more. . . . When the elections were over they sent daring men, undoubtedly paid, to insult people as they passed, calling them royalist *chouans.*" (He mentions the despatch of supporting affidavits.)—Mercier, "Le Nouveau Paris," ii., 315. "Peaceable people in Paris refuse to go to the polls," so as to "avoid being struck and knocked down."—Sauzay, viii., 9. At Besançon, Nov. 6, 1795, out of five thousand three hundred and nine registered voters, only one thousand three hundred and twenty-four vote and the elected are terrorists.—Archives Nationales, F[7], 7,090. (Documents on the Jacobin insurrection of Nivose 4 and 5, year IV., at Arles): "The exclusives, or amnestied, regarded the Constitution only as a means of arriving at a new state of anarchy by getting possession of all the offices. . . . Shouts and cries of *Vive Marat!* and *Robespierre to the Pantheon!* were often repeated. The principal band was composed of genuine Terrorists, of the men who under Robespierre's reign bore the guillotine about in triumph, imitating its cruel performances on every corner with a manikin expressly made for the occasion." "Domiciliary visits, rummaging everywhere, stealing jewelry, money, clothes, etc."

33. Decree of Brumaire 4, year IV.

of Paris.[34] Barère himself, who, condemned to transportation, universally execrated as he traverses France, and who, everywhere on his journey, at Orleans, Tours, Poitiers, Niort, comes near being torn to pieces by the people, Barère is not sent off to Guienne; he is allowed to escape, to conceal himself and live tranquilly at Bordeaux. Furthermore, Conventionalists of the worst species, like Monestier and Foussedoire return to their natal department to govern it as government commissioners.

Consider the effect of these releases and of these appointments in a town which, like Blois, has seen the assassins at work, and which, for two months, follows their trial.[35] Seven of them, members of the Revolutionary Committee, commanders of the armed force, members of the district or department, national agents in Indre-et-Loire, charged with conducting or receiving a column of eight hundred laborers, peasant women, priests and "suspects," cause nearly six hundred of them to be shot, sabred, drowned, or knocked down on the road, not in self-defence or to prevent escape, for these poor creatures tied two and two marched along like sheep without a murmur, but to set a good revolutionary example, so as to keep the people in proper subjection by terror and enable them to line their pockets.[36]

34. Mallet-Dupan, ii., 363.—Schmidt (Police report of Brumaire 26 and 27).

35. Dufort de Cheverney (manuscript memoirs communicated by Robert de Crêvecoeur).—Report of the public prosecutor, dated Thermidor 13, year III., according to documents handed in on Messidor 16, by the foreman of the jury of indictment and by the *juges de paix* of Chinon, Saumur, Tours, Amboise, Blois, Beaugency, etc., relating to the charges made by the administrators of the department of Loire-et-Cher, dated Frimaire 30, year II., concerning the fusillades at Blois, Frimaire 19, year II.

36. The line of this march from Saumur to Montsoreau could be traced by the blood along the road; the leaders shot those who faltered with fatigue.—On reaching Blois, Frimaire 18, Hézine says, before the town-hall, "Tomorrow morning they shall be straightened out and we'll show the *Blésois* how the thing is managed." The following day, Hézine and Gidouin, taking a walk with Lepetit, commander of the escort, in the court of the inn, say to him: "You'll shoot some of them for us. You must give the people an example by shooting some of those rascally priests." Lepetit orders out four peasants and placing them himself on the river bank, gives the command to fire and to throw them

A minute investigation has unfolded before the judges, jury, and public of Blois a long series of authentic facts and proofs, with eight days of pleading and the most complete and glaring evidence; the sentence is about to be pronounced. Suddenly, two weeks before Vendémiaire 13, a decree annuls the proceedings, which have already cost over six hundred thousand livres, and orders a new trial in another form. Next, after Vendémiaire 13, a representative arrives at Blois and his first care is to set the massacrers free. About thirty knaves ruled the town during the Reign of Terror, all strangers, save four or five, "all more or less befouled with crime"; at first, the principal slaughterers—Hézine, Gidouin, and their accomplices of the neighboring districts, Simon, and Bonneau the ex-mayor of Blois, Bézard, a former soldier, convicted of peculation and of robbing cellars which he had put under sequestration, Berger, an ex-monk, and then dragoon who, with pistol in hand, forced the superior of his old convent to give up the funds of the community, Giot, formerly a chief-butler of Monsieur (the King's brother), next, a judge in the September massacres and then a quartermaster in the Pyrenees army and a pillager in Spain, then secretary to the Melun tribunal of which he stole the cash, along with other nomads and outlaws of the same stamp, most of them sots and roysterers, one an ex-schoolmaster, another an ex-ladies hair-dresser, another an ex-chair-bearer; all of them a vile lot, chosen by the government for its agents, and, under new titles, resuming their old positions. At the head of the armed force is Gen. Bonnard, who is accompanied by a prostitute and who passes his time in orgies, pilfering wherever he can, and so shameless in his thievery as to be condemned, six months later, to three months in irons;[37] on arriving at Blois, he

---

in. Hézine and Gidouin shout *Vive la Nation!* Gidouin then says to Lepetit: "You don't mean to stop with those four peasants? won't you give us a few curés?" Five priests are shot.—At Beaugency, there is a fresh fusillade. The leaders take the best part of the spoil. Among other objects, Lepetit has a coffer sent into his chamber and takes the effects it contains and sells a bed and mattress beside.

37. *Ibid.*, (March, 1796). "Meanwhile, the young men who were recruited, hid themselves: Bonnard made them pay, and still made them set out. Baillon,

organises "a paid guard, composed of all the most abject Jacobins."
Elsewhere, as here,[38] it is the full staff of the Reign of Terror, the
petty potentates dethroned after Thermidor, the political Bohemians
restored to their functions; and, it seems, after Vendémiaire 13, that
the Jacobin band had made the conquest of France a second time.

IV

Not yet, however, for, if it has recovered its authority, it has not yet
recovered the dictatorship. In vain do Barras and Tallien, Dubois-
Crancé, Merlin de Douai, and Marie Chénier, Delmas, Louvet, Siéyès,
and their rotten, headlong crew, the *habitués* of power, the despotic,
unscrupulous theorists, try to postpone indefinitely the opening of
the Corps Legislatif, to annul the elections, to purge the Convention,
to reëstablish for their own advantage that total concentration of
powers which, under the title of revolutionary government, has converted France into a pachalic in the hands of the old Committee of
Public Safety:[39] the Convention has become alarmed for itself; at the
last moment the plot is exposed, the blow frustrated;[40] the Constitution, decreed, is put in operation, the system of the law has re-

---

quartermaster in the war, told me that he had paid Bonnard nine hundred
thousand livres in assignats in twelve days, and one million four hundred thousand in twenty days; there were thirty-five thousand livres in the memoir for
pens, penknives, ink, and paper."

38. Mallet-Dupan, "Correspondance, etc.," i., 383. (Letter of Dec. 13, 1795.)
"The Directory keeps on filling the offices with Terrorists. The government
agents in the departments arbitrarily set aside the constituted authorities and
replace them with Jacobins."

39. Thibaudeau, "Histoire de la Convention," i., 243. "Tallien, Barras, Chénier and Louvet talked of nothing but of annulling the elections. . . . Nothing
was heard at the bar and in the tribunals but the most revolutionary proposi-
tions. The "Mountain" showed incredible audacity. The public tribunes were
filled with confederates who applauded furiously. . . . Tallien and Barras ruled
and shared the dictatorship between them. . . . Since the 13th of Vendémiaire,
the deliberations of the Convention are carried on in a camp; the exterior, the
tribunes, the hall itself are invested by soldiers and terrorists."—Mallet-Dupan,
"Correspondence, etc.," i., 248. (Letter of Oct. 31, 1795.)

40. Thibaudeau, *ibid.*, i., 246, *et seq.*—Moniteur. (Session of Brumaire 1.)
Speech by Thibaudeau.

placed the system of arbitrariness. The Jacobin invasion, through that alone, is checked and then arrested; the nation is in a condition to defend itself and does defend itself; it gradually regains lost ground, even at the centre. At Paris, the electoral body,[41] which is obliged to take two-thirds of its deputies from the Convention, takes none of the regicide deputation representing Paris; all who are chosen, Lanjuinais, Larivière, Fermon, Saladin, Boissy d'Anglas, wished to save the King, and nearly all were proscribed after the 31st May. The departments show the same spirit. The members of the Convention for whom the provinces show a decided preference are the most prominent of the anti-Jacobins: Thibaudeau is reelected by thirty-two electoral colleges, Pelet de la Lozére by seventy-one, Boissy d'Anglas by seventy-two, Lanjuinais by seventy-three. As to the two hundred and fifty of the new third, these are liberals of 1789 or moderates of 1791,[42] most of them honorable men and many of them well-informed and of real merit, jurisconsults, officers, administrators, members of the Constitutional Assembly or Feuillants in the Legislative Assembly, Mathieu Dumas, Vaublanc, Dupont de Nemours, Siméon, Barbé-Marbois and Tronçon-Ducoudray. The capital, especially, chose Dambray, former general-advocate to the Paris parliament, and Pastoret, former minister of Louis XVI.; Versailles sends the two celebrated lawyers who defended the King before the Convention, Tronchet and De Séze. Now, previous to the 13th Vendémiaire, two hundred members of the Convention had

41. Mallet-Dupan, *ibid.*, i., 328. (Letter Oct. 4, 1795.) "Nearly all the electors nominated at Paris are former administrators, distinguished and sensible writers, persons recommendable through their position, fortune, and intelligence. They are the royalists of 1789, that is to say about in the sense of the constitution of 1791, essentially changed fundamentally. M. d'Ormesson, former comptroller-general of the Treasury, the Marquis of Gontant, M. de Vandeuil, former *maitre de requêtes*, M. Garnier, former *conseiller an Châtelet* of Paris and others of the same order, all electors. It is another world; in one month we have gone back five years."—*Ibid.*, 343, 350, 359, 373.

42. Barbé-Marbois, "Journal d'un Déporté," preface, p. xiv. "Outside of five or six men who might be regarded as 'suspects' of royalism the most animated were only really irritated against the despotic conduct and depredations of the directors and not against the republican system."

already heartily sided with the Parisian electors[43] against the terrorists. This makes a strong opposition minority in the Corps Legislatif
marching along protected by the Constitution; behind it and behind
them march the élite and the plurality of Frenchmen awaiting something better. The Directory is obliged to act cautiously with this
large group, so well supported by public opinion, and, accordingly,
not to govern à la Turk; to respect, if not the spirit, at least the letter
of the law, and not to exercise a too barefaced influence on local
elections. Hence most of the local elections remain free; in spite of
the decree excluding every relation of an émigré and every notorious
opponent of the government from present and future offices, in spite
of fear, lassitude, and disgust, in spite of the small number of votes,
the rarity of candidates and the frequent refusal of the elected to
serve,[44] the nation substantially exercises its privilege of electing its
administrators and judges according to its preferences. Consequently, the very large majority of new administrators in the departments, cantons, and municipalities, and the very large majority
of new civil and criminal judges and justices of the peace are, like
the new third of the Convention, highly esteemed or estimable men,
untainted with excesses, still preserving their hopes of 1789, but
preserved from the outset against, or soon cured of, the revolution-

43. Mallet-Dupan, *ibid.*, i., 369. (Letter of Nov. 22, 1795.) "Never would
the resistance of the sections have shown itself so unanimously and so perse-
veringly without the promptings of the two hundred monarchist members of
the Convention and the aid they promised. They had engaged to enter the
tribune and support the cause of Paris, to carry the majority and, in case they
did not succeed in revoking the decree respecting the two-thirds, to withdraw
from the Convention and come and take their seats with the sections; the pusillanimity of these two hundred members caused the failure of these promises.
... I guarantee the authenticity of this statement."

44. "Souvenirs et Journal d'un Bourgeois d'Evreux," pp. 103, 106. "The
Constitution has been adopted by a very small number of citizens, for, in the
section of the Nord only one hundred and fifty voters at most are found amongst
twelve hundred or fifteen hundred estimated." (September 6, 1795.)—On Tues-
day, November 10, "the section assemblies of Evreux completed their nomi-
nations of *juge de paix* and of its assessors and five municipal officers. It took
time, because there were a great many who declined."

ary fever. Every decree of spoliation or persecution loses some of its force in their hands. Supported by the steady and manifest will of their present constituents, we see them resisting the commissioners of the Directory, at least protesting against their exactions and brutality, gaining time in favor of the proscribed, dulling the point of, or turning aside, the Jacobin sword.

Again, on the other hand, the government which holds this sword dare not, like the Committee of Public Safety, thrust it in up to the hilt; if wielded as before it might slip from its grasp; the furious in its own camp are ready to wrest it away and turn the blade against it. It must defend itself against the reviving clubs, against Baboeuf and his accomplices, against the desperadoes who, through a nocturnal attempt, try to stir up the Grenelle camp: in Paris, there are four or five thousand now ready to undertake a "civic St. Bartholomew," with the old Conventionists who could not get themselves elected, at their head—Drouet, Amar, Vadier, Ricord, Laignelot, Chaudieu, Huguet, Cusset, Javogues; alongside of them, the friends of Chalier, Robespierre's and Marat's followers, and the disciples of Saint-Just, Bertrand de Lyon, Buonarotti, Antonelle, Rossignol and Baboeuf; behind them, the bandits of the street, those "who gutted houses during the Revolution," peculators or *Septembriseurs* out of employment, in short, the relics of the terrorist gang or of the revolutionary army. Their plan, in accordance with their precedents, character, and principles, consists not only in despatching "the rascals who keep coaches, the moneyed men and monopolisers," all the deputies and functionaries who do not resign at the first summons, but again, and especially, in killing "the General of the Interior, his staff, the seven ministers and the five 'cocked-hats' (*panachés*) of the Luxembourg," that is to say, the five Directors themselves. Such allies are troublesome. Undoubtedly, the government, which considers them as its forlorn hope, and that it may have need of them in a crisis, spares them as much as possible;[45] it allows Drouet to

---

45. Thibaudeau, "Mémoires sur le Convention et le Directoire," ii., 58.—Mallet-Dupan, ("Correspondence, etc.," ii., 281.) Dufort de Cheverney ("Mé-

escape, and lets the trial of the Babouvists drag along, only two of them being guillotined, Baboeuf and Darthé; most of the others are acquitted or escape. Nevertheless, for its own salvation, it is led to separate from the fiercest Jacobins and draw near to peaceable citizens. Through this internal discord of the ruling faction, honest people hold on the offices they occupy on the elections of the year IV.; no decree comes to deprive them of their legal arms, while, in the Corps Legislatif, as in the administrations and the tribunals, they count on carrying new positions in the elections of the year V.

V

"It was a long time," writes a small trader of Evreux, "since so many people were seen at the elections.[46] . . . The eight electors for the town obtained at the first ballot the absolute majority of suffrages. . . . Everybody went to the polls so as to prevent the nomination of any elector among the terrorists, who had declared that their reign was going to return." In the environs of Blois, a rural proprietor, the most circumspect and most peaceable of men, notes in his journal[47] that "now is the time to take a personal interest. . . . Every sound-thinking man has promised not to refuse any office tendered to him so as to keep out the Jacobins. . . . It is reasonably hoped that the largest number of the electors will not be terrorists and that the majority of the Corps Legislatif being all right, the minority of the furious, who have only one more year of office, will give way (in 1798) to men of probity not steeped in crime. . . . In the country, the Jacobins have tried in vain: people of means who employed a portion of the voters, obtained their suffrages, every proprietor wishing to have order. . . . The Moderates have agreed

---

moires" in manuscript). He is at Vendôme and attends the trial out of curiosity. "Germain, cheerful and witty, makes fun of the jurymen: they are really stupid, said he, not to see conspiracy when there was as complete a one as ever existed. . . . Besides, I conspired and always shall."

46. "Souvenir et Journal d'un Bourgeois d'Evreux," p. 118 (March 24, 1797).
47. Dufort de Cheverney, "Mémoires," (March, 1797).

to vote for no matter what candidate, provided he is not a Jacobin.
. . . Out of two hundred and thirty electors for the department, one
hundred and fifty are honest and upright people. . . . They adhered
to the last Constitution as to their sole palladium, only a very few
of them dreaming of reestablishing the ancient régime." Their object
is plain enough; they are for the Constitution against the Revolution,
for limited power against discretionary power, for property against
robbery, for upright men against thieves. "Would you prevent, say
the administrative authorities of Aube,[48] a return to the disastrous
laws of the *maximum,* of monopolies, to the resurrection of paper-
money? . . . Would you, as the price of a blameless life, be once
more humiliated, robbed, imprisoned, tortured by the vilest, most
repulsive, and most shameless of tyrants? You have only one re-
course: do not fail to go to your primary assemblies and remain
there." The electors, warned by their late personal and bloody souvenirs, rush to the polls in crowds and vote according to their consciences, although the government through the oaths it imposes, its
official candidatures, its special commissioners, its intimidation and
its money, bears down with all its weight on the resolutions they
have taken; although the Jacobins at Nevers, Macon, and elsewhere,
have forcibly expelled officers legally elected from their bureaux,
and stained the hall with their blood,[49] "out of eighty-four departments sixty-six elected a plurality of electors from among the anti-

48. Albert Babeau, ii., 408, *et seq.* (Address of the administrators of Aube
for the elections of year V.)—*Ibid.,* 414. (Speech by Herlinson, Librarian of the
Ecole Centrale at Troyes, Thermidor 10, year V. in the large hall of the Hôtel-
de-Ville, before the commissioners of the Directory, and received with unbounded applause.) "The patriots consisted of fools, madmen and knaves, the
first in their illusions, the second in their dreams and the third in their acts. . . .
Everywhere you would see two or three executioners, a dozen satellites, of
whom one-half trembled for their lives, and about a hundred witnesses, most
of them in spite of themselves, against thousands of victims. . . . Vengeance is
not necessary; never was special vengeance of any benefit to the public. Let
them rest in their slough, let them live as objects of contempt and horror."—
Cf. Sauzay, viii., p. 659 *et seq.*
49. Thibaudeau, ii., 152, 153.—Mallet-Dupan, ii., 262.

republicans, eight being neither good nor bad, while only ten remained loyal to the Jacobins."[50] Appointed by such electors, we can divine what the new Third will be. "Of the two hundred and fifty Conventionalists excluded by fate scarcely five or six have been reelected; there are but eight departments in which the Jacobins have had any success." Immediately after the arrival of the new representatives, the roll of the Corps Legislatif having been checked off, it is found that "the Government has seventy out of two hundred and fifty voices among the Ancients, and two hundred out of five hundred among the Council of the Young," and soon less than two hundred, one hundred and thirty[51] at most, who will certainly be excluded at the coming renewal of the chambers by more and more anti-Jacobin elections. One year more, as the rulers themselves admit, and not one Conventionalist, not one pure Jacobin, will sit in the Corps Legislatif and, therefore, according to the revolutionists, the counter-revolution will be effected in the year VI.

This means that the Revolution is to end in the year VI., and that the pacific reign of law will be substituted for the brutal reign of force. In fact, the great majority of the representatives and almost the entire French nation have no other end in view: they wish to rid themselves of the social and civil régime to which they have been subject since the 10th of August, 1792, and which, relaxed after Thermidor 9, but renewed by the 13th of Vendémiaire, has lasted up to the present time, through the enforcement of its most odious laws and the maintenance of its most disreputable agents. This is all. Not twenty avowed or decided royalists could be found in the two Councils;[52] there are scarcely more than five or six—Imbert-Colomès, Pichegru, Willot, Delarne—who may be in correspondence with Louis XVIII. and disposed to raise the white flag. For the other five hundred, the restoration of the legitimate King, or the

50. Mallet-Dupan, ii., 265, 268, 278.
51. Thibaudeau, ii., 244, 248.
52. Carnot, "Mémoires," ii., 108. "Not fifteen leaders."—Lacretelle, "Dix Années d'Epreuves," p. 308. "Twenty or thirty men devoted to monarchical opinions, but who did not dare state them openly."

establishment of any royalty whatever, is only in the background; they regard it only at a distance, as a possible accompaniment and remote consequence of their present undertaking. In any event, they would accept only "the mitigated monarchy,"[53] that which the Liberals of 1788 hoped for, that which Mounier demanded after the days of October 5 and 6, that advocated by Barnave after the return from Varennes, that which Malouet, Gouverneur Morris, Mallet-Dupan and all good observers and wise councillors of France, always recommended. None of them propose to proclaim divine right and return to aristocratic feudalism; each proposes to abrogate revolutionary right and destroy Jacobin feudalism. The principle condemned by them is that which sustains the theory of anarchy and despotism, the application of the *Contrat-Social*,[54] a dictatorship established by *coups d'état,* carried on arbitrarily and supported by terror, the systematic and dogmatic persistence of assaults on persons, property and consciences, the usurpation of a vicious, fanatical minority which has devastated France for five years and, under the pretext of everywhere setting up the rights of man, purposely maintaining a war to propagate its system abroad. That which they are really averse to is the Directory and its clique, Barras with his court of gorged contractors and kept women, Rewbell with his family of extortioners, stamp of a parvenu and ways of a tavern keeper, Larevellière-Lepaux with his hunchback vanity, philosophic pretensions, sectarian intolerance, and silly airs of a pedantic dupe. What they demand in the tribune,[55] is the purification of the administration,

---

53. Mallet-Dupan, ii., 267, 278, 331.

54. Mallet-Dupan, ii., 265. "Not only have they discarded (at Paris) the Republicans, but even those among the old Constituents, known or denounced for having taken too important a part in the first revolution. . . . Men have been chosen who aspired to a modified and not perverted monarchy. The suffrages have equally set aside the sectarian royalists of the ancient régime and violent antirevolutionists."

55. Mallet-Dupan, ii., 298. "The deputies never attack a revolutionary law, but they are mistrusted of some design of destroying the results of the Revolution, and every time they speak of regulating the Republic they are accused of ill-will to the Republic."

the suppression of jobbery, and an end to persecution; according as they are more or less excited or circumspect they demand legal sentences or simply the removal of Jacobins in office, the immediate and entire suppression or partial and careful reform of the laws against priests and worship, against *émigrés* and the nobles.[56] Nobody has any idea of innovation with respect to the distribution of public powers, or to the way of appointing central or local authorities. "I swear on my honor," writes Mathieu Dumas, "that it has always been my intention to maintain the Republican Constitution, persuaded as I am that, with a temperate and equitable administration, it might give repose to France, make liberty known and cherished, and repair in time the evils of the Revolution; I swear that no proposals, direct or indirect, have ever been made to me to serve, either by my actions, speech or silence, or cause to prevail in any near or remote manner, any other interest than that of the Republic and the Constitution." "Among the deputies," says Camille Jordan, "several might prefer royalty; but they did not conspire, regarding the Constitution as a deposit entrusted to their honor. . . . They kept their most cherished plans subordinate to the national will; they comprehended that royalty could not be reestablished without blows and through the development of this bill." "Between ourselves," says again Barbé-Marbois, "there were disagreements as to the way of getting along with the Directory, but none at all as to the maintenance of the Constitution."[57] Almost up to the last moment they confined themselves strictly to their legal rights, and when, towards the end, they were disposed to set these aside, it was simply to

56. Thibaudeau, ii., 171.—Carnot, ii., 106.—The programme of Barthélémy is contained in this simple phrase: "I would render the Republic administrative." On the foreign policy, his ideas, so temperate, pacific and really French, are received with derision by the other Directors. (André Lebon, "Angleterre et l'Emigration Française," p. 335.)

57. Mathieu Dumas, "Souvenirs," iii., 153.—Camille Jordan. (Letter to his constituents on the Revolution, Fructidor 18, p. 26.) "The Constitution, the Constitution alone, is the rallying word at Clichy."—Barbé-Marbois, "Souvenirs d'un Déporté," i., page 12 and preface. "The largest number wanted to disregard the future and forget the past."

defend themselves against the uplifted sabre above their heads.[58] It is incontestable that their leaders are "the most estimable and the ablest men in the Republic,"[59] the only representatives of free suffrage, mature opinions, and long experience, the only ones at least in whose hands the Republic, restored to order and justice, would have any chance of becoming viable, in fact, *the only liberals.* And this is the reason why the merely nominal Republicans were bound to crush them.

In effect, under a government which disavows attacks on persons and on public or private property, not only is the Jacobin theory impossible, but Jacobin wrongs are condemned. Now, the Jacobins, even if they have abjured their principles, remember their acts. They become alarmed on the arrival of the first Third, in October, 1795: "The Conventionalists," writes one of the new deputies,[60] "look upon us as men who will one day give them up to justice." After the entry of the second Third, in May, 1797, their fright increased;

58. Mallet-Dupan, ii., 336. "Eighty of the deputies who were menaced have slept elsewhere since the 30th of August, keeping together in one domicile for fear of being carried off at night."—Mathieu Dumas, iii., 10. "I could no longer occupy my house in Paris, rue Fosses-du-Temple, without risking an attack from the sbirri of the Directory, who proclaimed in the clubs that the people must be avenged in (our) houses."—Mallet-Dupan, ii., 343. "This pretended conspiracy imputed to the councils by the triumvirs, is a romance similar to those of Robespierre."—*Ibid.*, 346. "There has been no conspiracy, properly so-called, of the Corps Legislatif against the Directory."—Only, "every constitution in France kills the Revolution if it is not destroyed in time for the Revolutionary leaders. And this, because four-fifths of France being detached from the Revolution, the elections will put into the legislative and administrative offices men who were opposed to the Revolution."

59. Lord Malmesbury, "Diaries," ii., 544. (September 9, 1797.) The words of Mr. Colchen. "He went on to say that all the persons arrested are the most estimable and most able men in the Republic. It is for this reason and not from any principles of royalism (for such principles do not belong to them) that they are sentenced to transportation. They would have supported the Constitution, but in doing that they would have circumscribed the authority of the executive power and have taken from the Directory the means of acquiring and exercising undue authority."

60. Barbé-Marbois, "Journal d'un Déporté," preface, p. xvi.

the regicides, especially, feel that "their safety depends only on an exclusive and absolute dominion."[61] One day, Treilhard, one of their notables, alone with Mathieu Dumas, says to this old *Feuillant* and friend of Lafayette, of well known loyalty and moderation: "You are very honest and very able men, and I believe that you really desire to maintain the government as it is, because neither for you nor for us is there any sure way of substituting another for it. But we Conventionalists cannot allow you to go on; whether you mean it or not, you are gradually leading us to our certain ruin; there is nothing in common between us." "What guarantee do you then require?" "*But one. After that, we'll do all you want—we'll let you relax the springs—give us this guarantee and we'll follow you blindly!*" "Well, what do you mean by that?" "Enter the tribune and declare that if you had been a member of the Convention, you would have voted the death of Louis XVI. as we did!" "You demand an impossibility. You would not do this in our place. You sacrifice France to vain terrors." "No, the risk is not equal; *our heads are at stake!*" Perhaps their heads, but certainly their power, places, fortunes, comforts, and pleasures, all that in their eyes makes it worth while to live. Every morning, seventy Paris newspapers and as many local gazettes in the large towns of the provinces expose, with supporting documents, details and figures, not merely their former crimes, but, again, their actual corruption, their sudden opulence founded on prevarication and rapine, their bribes and peculations—one, rewarded with a sumptuously furnished mansion by a company of grateful contractors; another, son of a bailiwick attorney and a would-be Carthusian, now possessor of ecclesiastical property, restored by him at a great outlay for hunting-grounds; another also monopolises the finest land in Seine-et-Oise; another, the improvised owner of four châteaux; another, who has feathered his nest with fifteen or eighteen millions,[62] with their loose or arbitrary ways of

61. Mathieu Dumas, iii., 84, 86.
62. De Goncourt, "La Société Française pendant le Directoire," 298, 386. Cf. the *Thé,* the *Grondeur,* the *Censeur des journaux, Paris,* and innumerable

doing things, their habits as hoarders or spendthrifts, their display and effrontery, their dissipations, their courtiers, and their prostitutes. How can they renounce all this? And all the more because this is all they have. These jaded consciences are wholly indifferent to abstract principles, to popular sovereignty, to the common weal, to public security; the thin and brittle coating of sonorous phrases under which they formerly tried to hide the selfishness and perversity of their lusts, scales off and falls to the ground. They themselves confess that it is not the Republic for which they are concerned, but for themselves above everything else, and for themselves alone; so much the worse for it if its interest is opposed to their interest; as Siéyès will soon express it, the object is not to save the Revolution but the revolutionists. Thus disabused, unscrupulous, knowing that they are staking their all, and resolute, like their brethren of August 10, September 2, and May 31, like the Committee of Public Safety, they are determined to win, no matter at what cost or by what means, the same as their brethren of August 10, September 2, and May 31. For this time again, the Moderates cannot comprehend a declaration of war, and that it is war to the knife. They do not agree amongst themselves; they want to gain time, they hesitate and take refuge in constitutional forms—they do not act. The strong measures which the eighty decided and clear-sighted deputies propose, are weakened or suspended by the precautions of the three hundred others, short-sighted, unreliable, or timid.[63] They dare not even avail themselves

---

pamphlets.—In the provinces, the *Anti-Terrorist*, at Toulouse; the 9 *Thermidore*, at Besançon, the *Annales Troyennes* at Troyes, etc.

63. Mallet-Dupan, ii., 309, 316, 323, 324, 329, 333, 339, 347. "To defend themselves constitutionally, whilst the Directory attacks revolutionarily, is to condemn themselves to inevitable perdition." "Had it a hundred times more ability the Corps Legislatif without boldness is a lightning flash without thunder." "With greater resources than Louis XVI. had in 1792, the Corps Legislatif acts like this prince and will share his fate, unless it returns war for war, unless it declares that the first generals who dare send out the deliberations of their armies are traitors to the State." "It is owing to the temporising of the legislative councils, to the fatal postponement of the attack on the Luxembourg in the middle of August, on which Pichegru, Villot, General Miranda, and all the

of their legal arms, annul the military division of the interior, suppress Augereau's commission, and break the sword presented at their throats by the three conspiring Directors. In the Directory, they have only passive or neutral allies, Barthélémy, who had rather be assassinated than murder, Carnot, the servant of his legal pass-word, fearing to risk his Republic, and, moreover, calling to mind that he had voted for the King's death. Among the "Five Hundred" and the "Ancients," Thibaudeau and Tronçon-Ducoudray, the two leaders *"du ventre,"* arrest the arms of Pichegru and other energetic men, prevent them from striking, allow them only to ward off the blow, and always too late. Three days after the 10th of Fructidor, when, as everybody knew and saw, the final blow was to be struck, the eighty deputies, who change their quarters so as not to be seized in their beds, cannot yet make up their minds to take the offensive. On that day, an eye-witness[64] came to Mathieu Dumas and told him that, the evening before, in Barras' house, they discussed the slaughter or transportation to Cayenne of about forty members of the two Councils, and that the second measure was adopted; on which a commandant of the National Guard, having led Dumas at night into the Tuileries garden, showed him his men concealed behind the trees, armed and ready to march at the first signal; he is to possess himself at once of the Luxembourg (palace)[65] which is badly

clairvoyant deputies insisted on, . . . it is owing to foolishly insisting on confining themselves to constitutional defences, . . . it is owing to the necessity which the eighty firm and energetic deputies found of conciliating three hundred others who could not agree on the end as well as the means, which brought about the catastrophe of the Councils."

64. Carnot, "Mémoires," ii., 161. "The evil having reached its last stage, it was necessary to have a 10th of June instead of a 31st of May."—Mallet-Dupan, ii., 333, 334. The plan for cancelling the military division of the Interior under Augereau's command was to be carried out between the 15th and 20th of August. If the triumvirate should resist, Pichegru and Villot were to march on the Luxembourg. Carnot refused to accept the project "unless he might name the three new Directors."—De la Rue, "Histoire du 18 Fructidor." Carnot said to the Moderates who asked him to act with them: "Even if I had a pardon in my pocket, amply confirmed by the royal mouth, I should have no confidence."

65. Occupied by the members of the Directory.

guarded, and put an end to Barras and Rewbell on the spot: in war one kills so as not to be killed, and, when the enemy takes aim, you have the right to fire without waiting. "Only," says the commandant, "promise me that you will state in the tribune that you ordered this attack, and give me your word of honor."[66] Mathieu Dumas refuses, simply because he is a man of honor. "You were a fool," Napoleon afterwards said to him in this connection, "you know nothing about revolutions." In effect, honor, loyalty, horror of blood, respect for the law, such are the weak points of the party.

The opposite sentiments form the strong points of the other party. On the side of the triumvirs nobody knows twinges of conscience, neither Barras, a *condottiere* open to the highest bidder, and who understands the value of blows, nor Rewbell, a sort of bull, who, becoming excited, sees red, nor Merlin de Douai, the terrible legist, lay inquisitor, and executioner in private.[67] As usual with the Jacobins, these men have unsheathed the sword and brandished it. In contempt of the constitution, they provoked discussions in the army and let the Corps Legislatif see that, if it did not yield, it would be put out at the point of the bayonet. They let loose against it, "as in the good old times,"[68] their executive riff-raff, and line the avenues and tribunes with "their bandits of both sexes." They collect together their gangs of roughs, five or six thousand terrorists from Paris and the departments, and two thousand officers awaiting orders or on half-pay. In default of Hoche, whose unconstitutional approach was reported and then prevented, they have Augereau, arrived expressly from Italy, and who states publicly, "I am sent for

66. Mathieu Dumas, "Mémoires," iii., 113.

67. Mallet-Dupan, ii., 327. "Barras is the only one who plays squarely and who, taking the risk, wants Jacobinism to triumph *par fas et nefas.*"—*Ibid.*, 339. "The triumvirs hesitated up to Friday; Barras, the most furious of the three, and master of Augereau, decided his two colleagues."—*Ibid.*, 351. "Barras and Rewbell, by dint of exciting the imagination of that poor little philosophiser Larevellière, succeeded in converting him."—Thibaudeau, ii., 272. "It was Barras who bore off the honors of dictatorship that night. . . . Larevellière shut himself up in his house as in an impenetrable sanctuary. Rewbell, at this moment, his head somewhat affected, was watched in his apartment."

68. Mallet-Dupan, ii., 304, 305, 331.—Carnot, ii., 117.

to kill the royalists." It is impossible to find a more narrow-minded and greater military bully; Rewbell, himself, on seeing him, could not help but exclaim: "What a sturdy brigand!" On the 18th of Fructidor this official swordsman, with eight or ten thousand troops, surrounds and invades the Tuileries; the representatives are arrested in their committee-rooms or domiciles, or pursued, tracked, and hunted down, while the rest of their opponents, notables, officers, heads of bureaux, journalists, former ministers and directors, Barthélémy and Carnot, are treated in the same way. Barbé-Marbois, on demanding by virtue of what law they were arrested,[69] is told, "by the law of the sabre," while Sotin, Minister of the Police, adds with a smile, "You may be sure that after what I have taken on myself, it matters little whether one is more or less compromised." Thus purged, the two Councils complete their purgation; they cancel, in forty-nine departments, the election of their colleagues; through this decree and transportation, through forced and voluntary resignations, two hundred and fourteen representatives are withdrawn from the Corps Legislatif, while one hundred and eighty others, through fear or disgust, cease to attend its meetings.[70] Nothing remains of the two Councils, except, as in the English Parliament under Cromwell, a "rump," which rump does business under drawn swords. In the Council of the Ancients, which, on the 18th of Fructidor, discussed at midnight[71] the decree of transportation, "groups of grenadiers, with a haggard look, in brusque language, with threatening gestures" and fixed bayonets, surround the amphitheatre, and, mingled with the soldiers and civil cut-throats, shout out their orders. Such are the supporters of the scandalous stories got up by the Directory; voters who need this sort of argument to make them believe in the grand conspiracy which it denounces, to associate Barthélémy, Carnot, Siméon, Barbé-Marbois, Boissy d'Anglas, Mathieu Dumas, Pastoret, Tronçon-Ducoudray as accomplices with a

---

69. Barbé-Marbois, "Journal d'un Déporté," pp. 34 and 35.
70. Mallet-Dupan, ii., 343.
71. Barbé-Marbois, *ibid.*, p. 46.

knot of subordinate intriguers, contemptible "monkeys" (marmosets), dolts or spies, whose papers have been in the hands of the police for six months, and whom it forces to speak under lock and key.[72] All are enveloped in the same net, all are confounded together under the same title, all are condemned *en masse* without evidence or formality. "Proofs!" exclaims an orator, "none are necessary against the royalist faction. I have my own convictions."[73] "Formalities!" exclaims another, "the enemies of the country cannot invoke formalities which they would have despised had they triumphed." "The people are there," says a third, pointing to a dozen ill-looking men who are present; "the whole people ought to prevail against a few individuals!" "Hurry up!" shouts a soldier, who wants the discussion ended, "patriots, march, double-quick!" The debate, nevertheless, drags along, and the Government, growing impatient, is obliged to intervene with a message: "The people," says the message, "want to know what has become of the Republic, what you have done with it. . . . The conspirators have men who know something, even among yourselves." That is understood, and besides, the representatives comprehend that if they do not transport, they themselves will be transported. Therefore, "about fourteen or fifteen stand up for the decree, while seven are against it; the rest remain motionless": it is thus that the decree to save the Constitution is freely and legally passed. Four years before this a similar decree had passed to expel the Girondists, just in the same way, with this exception that, at that time, the Mountain made use of the populace, while now the army is employed; but save the difference in the *figurants,* the performance is simply a repetition of the same drama that was played on the 2d of June, and is now again played on the 18th of Fructidor.[74]

72. Mallet-Dupan, ii., 228, 342. "The use the triumvirs intended to make of D'Entraigues' portfolio was known two months ago."—Cf. Thibaudeau, ii., 279, on the vagueness, scanty proof and gross falsity of the charges made by the Directory.

73. Barbé-Marbois, *ibid.,* p. 46.

74. Lord Malmesbury, "Diary," iii., 559 (Sep. 17, 1797). At Lille, after the

VI

Thus is the system of 1793 revived, the concentration of all public powers in the hands of an oligarchy, a dictatorship exercised by about a hundred men grouped around five or six leaders. More independent, more despotic and less provisional than any Committee of Public Safety, the Directory has arrogated to itself the legal right of placing a commune in a state of siege, of introducing troops within the constitutional circle[75] in such a way that it may, at its discretion, violate Paris and the Corps Legislatif. In this body, mutilated by it and watched by its hireling assassins,[76] sit the passive mutes who feel themselves "morally proscribed and half-transported,"[77] who abandon debate, and vote with its stipendiaries and valets;[78] in fact, as formerly with the Convention, the two Councils have become chambers "of registry" of legislative mechanism charged with the duty of countersigning its orders. Its sway over the subordinate authorities is still more absolute. In forty-nine departments, specially designated by decree, all the administrators of departments, cantons and municipalities, all mayors, civil and criminal judges, all justices of the peace, all elected by popular suffrage,

news of the *coup d'état*, "it was a curious circumstance to see the horror that prevailed everywhere lest the system of Terror should be revived. People looked as if some exterminating spirit were approaching. The actors in the theatre partook of the sensation. The Director called Paris, said to Ross, on his paying him: 'Nous allons actuellement être vandalisés.'"

75. Decrees of Fructidor 18 and 19, year V., Article 39.

76. Thibaudeau, ii., 277. "I went to the meeting of Fructidor 20, the avenues of the Odéon were besieged with those subaltern agents of revolution who always show themselves after commotion, like vultures after battles. They insulted and threatened the vanquished and lauded the victors."

77. *Ibid.*, ii. 309.

78. *Ibid.*, ii., 277. "As soon as I entered the hall several deputies came with tears in their eyes to clasp me in their arms. The Assembly all had a lugubrious air, the same as the dimly lighted theatre in which they met; terror was depicted on all countenances; only a few members spoke and took part in the debates. The majority was impassible, seeming to be there only to assist at a funeral spectacle, its own."

are dismissed *en masse*,[79] while the cleaning out in the rest of France is almost as sweeping. We can judge by one example: in the department of Doubs, which is not put down among those to be weeded out, five hundred and thirty administrators or municipal magistrates are turned out in 1797, and, in addition, forty-nine others in 1798; the Directory puts its creatures in their places: suddenly, the departmental, cantonal, municipal, and judicial system, which was American, becomes Napoleonic; the local agents, instead of being delegates of the people, are government delegates. Note, especially, the most threatening of all usurpations, the way in which this government takes justice into its hands and attributes to itself the right of life and death over persons: not only does it break up common criminal courts and reorganise them as it pleases, not only does it renew and select among the purest Jacobins judges of the court of appeals, but again, in each military division, it institutes a special and expeditious court without appeal, composed of docile officers, subofficers, and soldiers, which is to condemn and execute within twenty-four hours, under pretext of emigration or priesthood, every man who is obnoxious to the ruling factions. As to the twenty-five millions of subjects it has just acquired, there is no refuge: even the right of complaint is interdicted. Forty-two opposition or "suspect" journals are silenced at one stroke, their stock plundered, or their presses broken up; three months after this, sixteen more take their turn, and, in a year, eleven others; the proprietors, editors, publishers and contributors, among whom are La Harpe, Fontanes, Fiévée, Michaud and Lacretelle, a large body of honorable or prominent writers, the four or five hundred men who compose the staff of the profession, all condemned without trial to transportation,[80] or to imprisonment, are arrested, take flight, conceal themselves, or

---

79. Decree of Fructidor 1, articles 4 and 5, 16 and 17, 28, 29 and 30, 35, and decree of Fructidor 22.—Sauzay, ix., 103. Three hundred communes of the department are thus purged after Fructidor.—*Ibid.*, 537, the same weeding-out of jurymen.

80. Lacretelle, "Dix ans d'Epreuves," p. 310.

keep silent. The only voice now heard in France is the speaking-trumpet of the government.

Naturally, the faculty of voting is as restricted as the faculty of writing, while the victors of Fructidor, who possess the right to speak, monopolise the right of electing. The government, on the first day, renewed the decree which the expiring Convention had rendered against allies or relations of *émigrés;* in addition to this, it excluded all relations or allies of the members of the primary assemblies, and forbade the primary assemblies to choose any of these for electors. Henceforth, all upright or even peaceful citizens consider themselves as warned and stay at home; voting is the act of a sovereign, and therefore a privilege of the new sovereigns, which is the view of it entertained by both sovereigns and subjects:[81] "a republican minority operating legally must prevail against a majority influenced by royalism."[82] They are to see the government on election days, launching forth "in each department its commission agents, and controlling votes by threats and all sorts of promises and se-

81. "Journal d'un Bourgeois d'Evreux," 143. (March 20, 1799.) "The next day the primary assemblies began; very few attended them; nobody seemed disposed to go out of his way to elect men whom they did not like."—Dufort de Cheverney, "Mémoires," March, 1799. "Persons who are not dupes think it of very little consequence whether they vote or not. The elections are already made or indicated by the Directory. The mass of the people show utter indifference." (March 24.) "In this town of twenty thousand souls (Blois) the primary assemblies are composed of the dregs of the people; but a very few honest people attend them; 'suspects,' the relations of *émigrés* and priests, all expelled, leave the field free to intriguers. Not one proprietor is summoned. The terrorists rule in three out of the four sections. . . . The Babouvists always employ the same tactics; they recruit voters in the streets who sell their sovereignty five or six times over for a bottle of wine." (April 12, according to an intelligent man coming from Paris.) "Generally, in Paris, nobody attends the primary assemblies, the largest not returning two hundred voters."—Sauzay, ix., ch. 83. (Notes on the election at Besançon, 1798, by an eye-witness.) "Jacobins were elected by most frightful brigandage, supported by the garrison to which wine had been distributed, their election being made at the point of the bayonet and under blows with sticks and swords. A good many Catholics were wounded."

82. Albert Babeau, ii., 444. (Declaration of the patriotic and secessionist minority of the canton of Riquy at the elections of the year VI.)

ductions,[83] arresting the electors and presidents of the primary assemblies," even pouncing on refractory Jacobins, invalidating the
returns of a majority when not satisfactory to them, and rendering
the choice of a minority valid, if it suited them, in short, constituting
itself the chief elector of all local and central authorities. Finally, all
institutions, laws, public and private rights, are down, and the nation,
body and soul, again becomes, as under Robespierre, the property
of its rulers, with this sole difference, that the kings of Terror, post-
poning their constitution, openly proclaim their omnipotence, whilst
the others hypocritically rule under a constitution which they have
themselves destroyed, and reign by virtue of a title which interdicts
royalty to them.

They, too, maintain themselves by Terror; only, like so many
Tartuffes, they are not disposed to act openly as executioners. The
Directory, heir to the Convention, affects to repudiate its inheritance: "Woe," says Boulay de la Meurthe, "to whoever would re-
establish scaffolds." There is to be no guillotine; its purveyors have
been too strongly denounced; they stand too near the red stream
and view with too great nervous horror those who fed it. It is better
to employ death at a distance, lingering and spontaneous, with no
effusion of human blood, "dry," less repulsive than the other sort,
but more painful and not less certain; this shall be imprisonment on
the marshes of Rochefort, and, better still, transportation to the
feverish coasts of Guyanna: there is no distinction between the mode
used by the Convention and that of the Directory, except the distinction between *to kill* and *to cause death*.[84] Moreover, every brutality that can be employed to repress the indignation of the proscribed

83. Mercure Britannique, No. for August 25, 1799. (Report read, July 15 and
August 5, before the Five Hundred on the conduct of the Directors Rewbell,
Larevellière-Lepaux, Merlin de Douai and Treilhard, and summary of the nine
articles of indictment.)—*Ibid.*, 3d article. "They have violated our constitution
by usurping legislative powers through acts which prescribe that a certain law
shall be executed, in all that is not modified to the present act, and by passing
acts which modify or render the present laws illusory."

84. Fiévée, "Correspondance avec Buonaparte," i., 147.

by fear is exhausted on the way. The first convoy which bears away, with thirteen others, Barthélémy, who negotiated the treaty of Basle, Pichegru, the conqueror of Holland, Lafond-Ladébat, president of the Council of the Five Hundred, Barbé-Marbois, president of the Council of the Ancients, was at first provided with carriages;[85] an order of the Directory substitutes for these the prison van, an iron car with one door bolted and padlocked, and, overhead, openings through which the rain poured in streams, and with common boards for seats; this lumbering machine without springs rolls along at a fast trot along the ruts in the road, each jolt sending the condemned inmates against the hard oak sides and roof; one of these, on reaching Blois, "shows his black-and-blue elbows." The man selected to command this escort is the vilest and most brutal reprobate in the army, Dutertre, a coppersmith foreman before the Revolution, next an officer and sentenced to be put in irons for stealing in the La Vendée war, and such a natural robber that he again robs his men of their pay on the road; he is evidently qualified for his work. On stopping at Blois, "he passes the night in an orgy with his brothers and friends," fellow-thieves and murderers as above described, cursing Madame Barbé-Marbois who comes to take leave of her husband, dismissing on the spot the commandant of the gendarmerie who supports her in a swoon, and, noticing the respect and attentions which all the inhabitants, even the functionaries, show to the prisoners, he cries out, "Well, what grimaces for people that will perhaps be dead in three or four days!" On the vessel which transports them, and still in sight of Rochelle, a boat is observed rowing vigorously to overtake them and they hear a shout of "I am Lafond-Ladébat's son! Allow me to embrace my father!" A speaking-trumpet from the vessel replies: "Keep away or you'll be fired on!" Their cabins, on the voyage, are mephitic; they are not allowed to be on deck more than four at a time, one hour in the morning and an hour in the evening; the sailors and soldiers are forbidden to speak to them;

85. Barbé-Marbois, i., 64, 91, 96, 133; ii., 18, 25, 83.—Dufort de Cheverney, "Mémoires." (September 14, 1797.)—Sauzay, ix., chapters 81 and 84.

their food consists of a sailor's ration, and this is spoilt; toward the end of the voyage they are starved. In Guyanna they are allowed one candle to a mess, and no table-linen; they lack water, or it is not drinkable; out of sixteen taken to Sinnamary only two survive.

Those who are transported the following year, priests, monks, deputies, journalists, and artisans accused of emigration, fare worse; on all the roads leading to Rochefort, sorrowful crowds are seen on carts or tramping along in files, on foot, the same as former chains of convicts. "An old man of eighty-two, Monsieur Dulaurent of Quimper, thus traverses four departments," in irons which strangle him. Following upon this, the poor creatures, between the decks of the "Décade" and "Bayonnaise," crammed in, suffocated through lack of air and by the torrid heat, badly treated and robbed, die of hunger or asphyxia, while Guyanna completes the work of the voyage: out of one hundred and ninety-three conveyed on board the "Décade," but thirty-nine remain at the end of twenty-two months, and of the one hundred and twenty brought by the "Bayonnaise," only one is left. Meanwhile, in France, in the casemates of the islands of Rhé and Oléron, over twelve hundred priests become stifled or rot away, while, on all sides, the military commissioners in the departments shoot down vigorously. At Paris, and in its environs, at Marseilles, Lyons, Bordeaux, Rennes, and in most of the large towns, sudden arrests and clandestine abductions go on multiplying.[86] "Nobody, on retiring to rest, is sure of awaking in freedom the next morning. . . . From Bayonne to Brussels, there is but one sentiment, that of unbounded consternation. No one dares either to speak to, encounter, look at or help one another. Everybody keeps aloof, trembles and hides away." In fine, through this third offensive reaction, the Jacobin Conquest is completed, and the conquering band, the new feudalism, becomes a fixed installation. "All who pass here," writes a Tours inhabitant, "state that there is no difference in the

---

86. Sauzay, vols. ix. and x.—Mallet-Dupan, ii., 375, 379, 382.—Schmidt, "Tableau de Paris Pendant la Revolution," iii., 290. (Report by the administrators of the Seine department.)

country between these times and Robespierre's.[87] . . . It is certain
that the soil is not tenable, and that the people are continually threatened with exactions as in a conquered country. . . . Proprietors are
crushed down with impositions to such an extent that they cannot
meet their daily expenses, nor pay the cost of cultivation. In some
of my old parishes the imposition takes about thirteen out of twenty
sous of an income. . . . The interest on money amounts to four per
cent. a month. . . . Tours, a prey to the terrorists who devour the
department and hold all the offices, is in the most deplorable state;
every family at all well-off, every merchant, every trader, is leaving
it." The veteran pillagers and murderers, the squireens (*hobereaux*),
of the Reign of Terror, again appear and resume their fiefs. At
Toulouse, it is Barrau, a shoemaker, famous up to 1792 for his fury
under Robespierre, and Desbarreaux, another madman of 1793, formerly an actor playing the parts of valet, compelled in 1795 to demand pardon of the audience on his knees on the stage, and, not
obtaining it, driven out of the house, and now filling the office of
cashier in the theatre and posing as department administrator. At
Blois, we find the ignoble or atrocious characters with whom we are
familiar, the assassins and robbers Hézine, Giot, Venaille, Bézard,
Berger, and Gidouin.[88] Immediately after Fructidor, they stirred up
their usual supporters against the first convoy of the transported,
"the idlers, the rabble of the harbor, and the dregs of the people,"
who overwhelmed them with insults. On this new demonstration of
patriotism the government restores to them their administrative or
judicial "satrapies," and, odious as they are, they are endured and
obeyed, with the mute and mournful obedience of despair. "The
soul sinks[89] on daily perusing the executions of conscripts and *émi-*

87. Dufort de Cheverney, "Mémoires," August, 1798, October, 1797 and
1799, *passim.*

88. Archives Nationales, F⁷, 3,219. (Letter of M. Alquier to the First Consul,
Pluviose 18, year III.) "I wanted to see the central administration; I found the
ideas and language of 1793."

89. Dufort de Cheverney, "Mémoires," (February 26, March 31 and September 6, 1797). "That poor theoristic imbecile, Larevellière-Lepaux, who, join-

grés, and on seeing those condemned to transportation constantly passing by. . . . All who displease the government are set down on these lists of the dead, people asserted to be *émigrés,* this or that curé who is notoriously known not to have left the department." It is impossible for honest people to vote at the primary assemblies; consequently, "the elections are frightful. Brothers and friends loudly proclaim that no more nobles, priests, proprietors, merchants, or justices are wanted; everything to be given up to pillage." Let France perish rather than their domination. "The wretches have announced that they will not give up their places without overthrowing all, destroying palaces, and setting Paris on fire." It is natural that with pure Jacobins pure Jacobinism should reappear, socialistic and anti-Christian equality, the programme of the funereal year; in short, the rigid, plain, exterminating ideas which the sect gathers together, like daggers encrusted with gore, from the cast-off robes of Robespierre, Billaud-Varennes, and Collot d'Herbois.[90]

VII

First of all comes the fixed and favorite idea of a senile philosophism, meaning by this a regular plan devised for the founding of a lay

---

ing Barras and Rewbell against Barthélémy and Carnot, made the 18th of Fructidor, and shut himself in his room so as not to witness it, himself avows the quality of his staff." ("Mémoires," ii., 164.) "The 18th of Fructidor necessitated numerous changes on the part of the Directory. Instead of putting republicans, but above all, honest, wise, and enlightened men in the place of the functionaries and employees dismissed or revoked, the selections dictated by the new Councils fell *for the most part on anarchists and men of blood and robbery.*"

90. Lacretelle, "Dix ans d'Epreuves," p. 317. A few days after Fructidor, Robert, an old Jacobin, exclaimed with great joy on the road to Brie-Comté, "All the royalists are going to be driven out or guillotined!" The series F[7] in the Archives Nationales, contains hundreds of files filled with reports "on the state of the public mind," in each department, town or canton between the years III. and VIII. I have given several months to their examination and, for lack of space, cannot copy any extracts. The real history of the last five years of the Revolution may be found in these files. Mallet-Dupan gives a correct impression of it in his "Correspondence avec la cour de Vienne," also in the "Mercure Britannique."

religion, and imposing on twenty-six millions of Frenchmen the observances and dogmas of the theory, and, consequently, the extirpation of Christianity, its forms of worship and its clergy. The inquisitors who hold office multiply, with extraordinary persistence and minuteness, proscriptions and vigorous measures for the forcible conversion of the nation with a view to substitute for the tender emotions nourished by the customs of eighteen centuries, the improvised rites of a logical abstraction mechanically elaborated in the closet. Never did the dull imagination of a third-rate litterateur and classic poetaster, never did the grotesque solemnity of a pedant fond of his phrases, never did the irritating hardness of the narrow and stubborn devotee display with greater sentimental bombast more administrative officiousness than in the decrees of the Corps Legislatif,[91] in the acts passed by the Directory and in the instructions issued by the ministers Sotin, Letourneur, Lambrechts, Duval, and François de Neufchateau. War on Sunday, on the old calendar and on fasting, obligatory rest on the *décadi* under penalty of fine and imprisonment,[92] obligatory fêtes on the anniversaries of January 21 and Fructidor 18, obligatory participation of all functionaries with their families in the new cult, obligatory attendance of public and private instructors with their pupils of both sexes at civic ceremonies, an obligatory liturgy with catechisms and programmes sent from Paris, rules for scenic display and for singings, readings, postures, acclamations, and imprecations; one might shrug his shoulders at these prescriptions of *cuistres* and these parades of puppets, if, behind the apostles who compose moral allegories, we did not detect the

91. Sauzay, x., chaps. 80 and 90.—Ludovic Sciout, iv., ch. 17. (See especially in Sauzay, x., pp. 170 and 281, the instructions given by Duval, December 16, 1796, and the circulars of François de Neufchateau from November 20, 1798, down to June 18, 1798, each of these pieces being a masterpiece in its way.)

92. "Journal d'un Bourgeois d'Evreux," p. 134. "June 7, 1798." "The day following the *décade,* the gardeners, who as usual came to show themselves off on the main street, were fined six livres for having treated with contempt and broken the *décade.*" January 21, 1799. "Those who were caught working on the *décade,* were fined three livres for the first offence; if they were caught more than once the fine was doubled and it was even followed by imprisonment."

persecutor who imprisons, tortures and murders. By the decree of Fructidor 19, not only were all the laws of the Reign of Terror against unsworn priests, their harborers and their followers, enforced again, but the Directory arrogated to itself the right of transporting, "through individual acts passed for cause," every ecclesiastic "who disturbed the public peace," that is to say who exercised his ministry and preached his faith;[93] and, moreover, the right of shooting down, within twenty-four hours, every priest who, banished by the laws of 1792 and 1793, has remained in or returned to France. Almost all the ecclesiastics, even those who are sworn, are comprised within the first category; the administration enumerates three hundred and sixty-six in the department of Doubs alone,[94] and five hundred and fifty-six in that of Hérault. Thousands of ecclesiastics are comprised in the second category; the administration enumerates over eight hundred who, returned from the frontier of Spain alone, still wander about the southern departments. On the strength of this the moralists in office proclaim a hunt for the black game in certain places, an universal destruction without exception or reprieve; for instance, in Belgium, recently incorporated with France, the whole of the regular and secular clergy is proscribed *en masse* and tracked for transportation; five hundred and sixty ecclesiastics in Ourbe and the forests, five hundred and thirty-nine in Escaut, eight hundred and eighty-three in Jemmapes, eight hundred and eighty-four in Sambre-et-Meuse, nine hundred and twenty-five in Lys, nine hundred and fifty-seven in Deux-Nèthes, one thousand and forty-three in Meuse-Inférieure, one thousand four hundred and sixty-nine in Dyle, in all six thousand five hundred and sixty-six, without counting the miss-

93. Ludovic Sciout, iv., 160. Examples of "individual motives" alleged to justify the sentence of transportation. One has refused to baptise an infant whose parents were only married civilly. Another has "declared to his audience that the Catholic marriage was the best." Another "has fanaticised." Another "has preached pernicious doctrines contrary to the constitution." Another "may, by his presence, incite disturbances," etc. Among the condemned we find septuagenarians, known priests and even married priests.—*Ibid.*, 634, 637.

94. Sauzay, ix., 715. (List of names.)

ing names.[95] A number of them escape abroad or hide away; but the rest are caught, and quite enough of them to load and fill the carts constantly. "Not a day passes," says an inhabitant of Blois,[96] "that from seven to twenty and more are not lodged at the Carmelites." The next day they set out for the casemates of Rhé and Oléron, or for the Sinnamary marshes, where it is known what becomes of them: after a few months, three-fourths of them lie in the cemetery. In the interior, from time to time, some are shot for the sake of example—seven at Besançon, one at Lyons, three in the Bouches-du-Rhone, while the opponents of fanaticism, the official philan-thropists, the enlightened deists of Fructidor, use all these disguised or declared murders as a basis on which to rear the cult of Reason.

It remains now to consolidate the worship of Reason with the reign of Equality, which is the second article in the Jacobin credo; the object now is to mow down all the heads which rise above the common level, and, this time, to mow them down, not one by one, but in large classes. Saint-Just himself had only covertly proposed so extensive and so sweeping an operation; Siéyès, Merlin de Douai, Rewbell, Chazal, Chénier, and Boulay de la Meurthe, more openly and decidedly insist on a radical amputation. According to them,[97] it is necessary "to regulate this ostracism," by transporting "all those whose prejudices, pretensions, even existence, in a word, are incom-patible with republican government"; that is to say, not alone priests, but likewise nobles and the ennobled, all parliamentarians, those who are well-off and distinguished among the bourgeoisie and former notables, about two hundred thousand property-holders, men and

95. Ludovic Sciout, iv., 656.

96. Dufort de Cheverney, "Mémoires," September 7, 1798. *Ibid.*, February 26, 1799. "In Belgium priests are lodged in the Carmelites (convent)." September 9, 1799. "Two more carts are sent full of priests for the islands of Rhé and Oléron."

97. Thibaudeau, ii., 318, 321.—Mallet-Dupan, ii., 357, 368. The plan went farther: "All children of emigrants," or of those falsely accused of being such, "left in France, shall be taken from their relatives and confided to republican tutors, and the republic shall administer their property."

women; in short, all who still remained among those oppressed and ruined by the Revolution. Forced back by the ex-noble Barras and by the public outcry "of merchants and workmen themselves," banishment is replaced by civic degradation. Henceforth,[98] every noble or ennobled person, even if he has not left the territory, even if he has constantly and punctually obeyed revolutionary laws, even if he be not related to, or allied with, any *émigré*, finds himself deprived of his quality as a Frenchman; the fact alone of his being ennobled or noble before 1789, obliged him to be naturalised according to legal forms and conditions. As to the one hundred and fifty thousand gentlemen, artisans, and farmers who have emigrated or who have been accused of emigration, if they have returned to, or remain in France, they are to leave Paris and all communes above twenty thousand souls within twenty-four hours, and France in fifteen days; otherwise, they are to be arrested, brought before the military commissions and shot on the spot;[99] in fact, in many places, at Paris, Besançon and Lyons, they are shot. Thereupon, a large number of pretended emigrants, who had never left France,[100] nor even their province, nor even their commune, and whose names have been put on the lists simply to strip them of their property, find that they are

---

98. Decree of Frimaire 9, year VI. (Exceptions in favor of the actual members of the Directory, ministers, military men on duty, and the members of the diverse National Assemblies, except those who in the Constituent Assembly protested against the abolition of nobility.) One of the speakers, a future Count of the Empire, proposed that every noble claiming his inscription on the civic registers should sign the following declaration: "As man and as republican, I equally detest the insolent superstition which pretends to distinctions of birth, and the cowardly and shameful superstition which believes in and maintains it."

99. Decree of Fructidor 19, year II.

100. Lally-Tollendal, "Défense des Emigrés" (Paris, 1797, 2d part, 49, 62, 74. Report of Portalis to the Council of Five Hundred, Feb. 18, 1796). "Regard that innumerable class of unfortunates who have never left the republican soil."—Speech by Dubreuil, Aug. 26, 1796. "The supplementary list in the department of Avignon bears one thousand and four or one thousand and five names. And yet I can attest to you that there are not six names on this enormous list justly put down as veritable emigrants."

no longer protected either by the constancy or the notoriety of their residence. The new law is no sooner read than they see the executive troops advancing; the natal soil is too warm for them and they speedily emigrate.[101] On the other hand, once the name is down on the list, rightly or wrongly, it is never removed; the government purposely refuses to strike it off, while two decrees are applied which render its removal impossible;[102] each name maintained on the list of spoliation and death relieves the Revolution of a probable adversary, and places one more domain at its disposal.

The Directory renews and aggravates the measures of the Convention against the remainder of the property-holders: there is no longer a disguised but a declared bankruptcy; three hundred and eighty-six thousand fund-holders and pensioners are deprived of two-thirds of their revenue and of their capital;[103] a forced loan of

101. Ludovic Sciout, iv., 619. (Report of the Yonne administration, Frimaire, year VI.) "The gendarmerie went to the houses, in Sens as well as Auxerre, of several of the citizens inscribed on the lists of *émigrés* who were known never to have left their commune since the Revolution began. As they have not been found it is probable that they have withdrawn into Switzerland, or that they are soliciting you to have their names stricken off."

102. Decrees of Vendémiaire 20 and Frimaire 9, year VI.—Decree of Messidor 10.

103. Dufort de Cheverney, "Mémoires." (Before the Revolution he enjoyed an income of fifty thousand livres, of which only five thousand remain.) "Madame Amelot likewise reduced, rents her hotel for a living. Through the same delicacy as our own she did not avail herself of the facility offered to her of indemnifying her creditors with assignats." Another lady, likewise ruined, seeks a place in some country house in order that herself and son may live."— "Statistique de la Moselle," by Colchen, préfet, year VI. "A great many people with incomes have perished through want and through payment of interest in paper-money and the reduction of Treasury bonds."—Dufort de Cheverney, *ibid.*, March, 1799. "The former noblesse and even citizens who are at all well-off need not depend on any amelioration. . . . They must expect a complete rescission of bodies and goods. . . . Pecuniary resources are diminishing more and more. . . . Impositions are starving the country."—Mallet-Dupan, "Mercure Britannique," January 25, 1799. "Thousands of *invalides* with wooden legs garrison the houses of the tax-payers who do not pay according to the humor of the collectors. The proportion of impositions as now laid in relation to those of the ancient régime in the towns generally is as eighty-eight to thirty-two."

one hundred millions is levied progressively, and wholly on "the well-off class"; finally, there is the law of hostages, this being atrocious, conceived in the spirit of September, 1792, suggested by the famous motions of Collot d'Herbois against those in confinement, and of Billaud-Varennes against the youth, Louis XVII., but extended, elaborated and drawn up with cool legal acumen, and enforced and applied with the foresight of an administrator. Remark that, without counting the Belgian departments, where an extensive insurrection is under way and spreading, more than one-half of the territory falls under the operation of this law; for, out of the eighty-six departments of France,[104] properly so-called, *forty-five* are at this moment, according to the terms of the decree,[105] "notoriously in a case of civil disturbance"; in effect, in these departments, according to official reports, armed mobs of conscripts are resisting the authorities charged with recruiting them; bands of two hundred, three hundred, and eight hundred men overrun the country; troops of brigands force open the prisons, assassinate the gendarmes and set their inmates free; the tax-collectors are robbed, killed, or maimed, municipal officers slain, proprietors ransomed, estates devastated, and diligences stopped on the highways." Now, in all these cases, in all the departments, cantons, or communes, three classes of persons, at first the relations and allies of the *émigrés,* next the former nobles and ennobled, and finally the "fathers, mothers, grandfathers, and grandmothers of persons who, without being ex-nobles or relations of *émigrés,*" nevertheless form a part of the bands or mobs, are declared "personally and civilly responsible" for the violent acts committed. Even when these acts are only "imminent," the administration of the department must, in its report, give a list of all the men and women who are responsible; these are to be taken as "hostages," and kept in confinement at their own expense in the local jail, and, if they escape, they must be put on the same footing as

104. De Tocqueville, "Oeuvres complètes," v., 65. (Extracts from secret reports on the state of the Republic, September 26, 1799.)

105. Decree of Messidor 24, year VI.

émigrés, that is to say punished with death; if any damage is sustained, they are to pay costs; if any murder is committed or abduction effected, four amongst them must be transported. Observe, moreover, that the local authorities are obliged, under severe penalties, to execute the law at once: that, at this date, they are ultra Jacobin; that, to inscribe on the list of hostages, not a noble or a bourgeois, but an honest peasant or respectable artisan, it suffices for these local sovereigns to designate his son or grandson, either absent, fugitive or dead, as "notoriously" insurgent or refractory; the fortunes, liberties, and lives of every individual in easy circumstances being thus legally surrendered to the despotism, cupidity, and hostility of the levellers in office. Contemporaries estimate that two hundred thousand persons were affected by this law;[106] the Directory, during the three months of its existence which yet remain to it, enforces it in seventeen departments; thousands of women and old men are arrested, put in confinement, and ruined, while several are sent off to Cayenne—and this is called respect for the rights of man.

VIII

According to the system which the Fructidoreans establish in France, we can judge of the system which they impose abroad—always the same contrast between the name and the thing, the same phrases covering the same misdeeds, and, under proclamations of liberty the institution of brigandage. Undoubtedly, in any invaded province which thus passes from an old to a new despotism, fine words cleverly spoken produce at first the intended effect; but, in a few weeks or months, the ransomed, enlisted, and forcibly "Frenchified" inhabitants, discover that the revolutionary right is much more oppressive, more harassing and more rapacious than divine right.

It is the right of the strongest. The reigning Jacobins know no other, abroad as well as at home, and, in the use they make of it, they are not restrained like ordinary statesmen, by a thorough com-

106. De Barante, "Histoire du Directoire," iii., 456.

prehension of the interests of the State, by experience and tradition, by far-sightedness, by an estimate of present and future strength. Being a sect, they subordinate France to their dogmas, and, with the narrow views, pride and arrogance of the sectary, they profess the same intolerance, the same need of domination and his instincts for propagandism and invasion. This belligerent and tyrannic spirit they had already displayed under the Legislative Assembly, and they are intoxicated with it under the Convention. After Thermidor,[107] and after Vendémiaire, they remained the same; they became rigid against "the faction of old boundaries," and against any moderate policy; at first, against the pacific minority, then against the pacific majority, against the entreaties of all France, against their own military director, "the organiser of victory" Carnot, who, as a good

107. A. Sorel, "Revue Historique," No. 1, for March and May, 1882. "Les Frontieres Constitutionelles en 1795." The treaties concluded in 1795 with Tuscany, Prussia, and Spain show that peace was easy and that the recognition of the Republic was effected even before the Republican government was organised. . . . That France, whether monarchical or republican, had a certain limit which French power was not to overstep, because this was not in proportion to the real strength of France, nor with the distribution of force among the other European governments. "On this capital point the Convention erred; it erred knowingly, through a long-meditated calculation, which calculation, however, was false, and France paid dearly for its consequences."—Mallet-Dupan, ii., 288, Aug. 23, 1795. "The monarchists and many of the deputies in the Convention sacrificed all the conquests to hasten on and obtain peace. But the fanatical Girondists and Siéyès' committee persisted in the tension system. They were governed by three motives: 1, the design of extending their doctrine along their territory; 2, the desire of successively federalising the States of Europe with the French Republic; and 3, that of prolonging a partial war which also prolongs extraordinary powers and revolutionary resources."—Carnot, "Mémoires," i., 476. (Report to the Committee of Public Safety, Messidor 28, year II.) "It seems much wiser to restrict our plans of aggrandisement to what is purely necessary in order to obtain the maximum security of our country."—*Ibid.*, ii., 132, 134, and 136. (Letters to Bonaparte, Oct. 28, 1796, and Jan. 1, 1797.) "It would be imprudent to fan the revolutionary flame in Italy too strongly. . . . They desired to have you work out the Revolution in Piedmont, Milan, Rome, and Naples; I thought it better to treat with these countries, draw subsidies from them, and make use of their own organisation to keep them under control."

Frenchman, is not desirous of gratuitously increasing the embarrassments of France nor of taking more than France could usefully and surely keep. If, before Fructidor, his three Jacobin colleagues, Rewbell, Barras, and Larevellière, broke with him, it was owing not merely to inside matters, but also to outside matters, as he opposed their boundless violent purposes. They were furious on learning the preliminary treaty of Leoben, so advantageous to France; they insulted Carnot, who had effected it;[108] when Barthélémy, the ablest and most deserving diplomatist in France, became their colleague, his recommendations, so sensible and so well-warranted, obtained from them no other welcome than derision.[109] They already desire, and obstinately, to get possession of Switzerland, lay hands on Hamburg, "humble England," and "persevere in the unlucky system of the Committee of Public Safety," that is to say, in the policy of war, conquest and propagandism. Now that the 18th Fructidor is accomplished, Barthélémy transported, and Carnot in flight, this policy is going to be displayed.

Never had peace been so near at hand;[110] they almost had it in their grasp; at the conference at Lille it was only necessary to take complete hold of it. England, the last and most tenacious of her enemies, was disarming; not only did she accept the aggrandisement of France, the acquisition of Belgium and the left bank of the Rhine, the avowed as well as the disguised annexations, the great Republic as patron and the smaller ones as clients, Holland, Genoa, and the

---

108. Carnot, *ibid.*, ii. 147. "Barras, addressing me like a madman, said, 'Yes, it is to you we owe that infamous treaty of Leoben!'"

109. André Lebon, "L'Angleterre et l'Emigration Française," p. 235. (Letter of Wickam, June 27, 1797, words of Barthélémy to M. d'Aubigny.)

110. Lord Malmesbury, "Diary," iii., 541. (September 9, 1797.) "The violent revolution which has taken place at Paris has overset all our hopes and defeated all our reasonings. I consider it the most unlucky event that could have happened." *Ibid.*, 593. (Letter from Canning, September 29, 1797.) "We were in a hair's breadth of it (peace). Nothing but that cursed revolution at Paris and the sanguinary, insolent, implacable and ignorant arrogance of the triumvirate could have prevented us. Had the moderate party triumphed all would have been well, not for us only but for France, for Europe and for all the world."

Cis-Alpine country, but, again, she restored all her own conquests, all the French colonies, all the Dutch colonies, except the Cape of Good Hope,[111] and all the Spanish colonies except Trinidad. All that *amour-propre* could demand was obtained, and they obtained more than could be prudently expected; there was not a competent and patriotic statesman in France who would not have signed the treaty with the greatest satisfaction. But the motives which, before Fructidor, animated Carnot and Barthélémy, the motives which, after Fructidor, animated Colchen and Maret, do not animate the Fructidoreans. France is of but little consequence to them; they are concerned only for their faction, for power, and for their own persons. Larevellière, president of the Directory, through vain-glory, "wanted to have his name go with the general peace"; but he is controlled by Barras, who needs war in order to fish in troubled waters,[112] and especially by Rewbell, a true Jacobin in temperament and intellect, "ignorant and vain, with the most vulgar prejudices of an uneducated and illiterate man," one of those coarse, violent, narrow sectarians anchored on a fixed idea and whose "principles consist in revolutionising everything with cannon-balls without examining wherefore."[113] There is no need of knowing the wherefore; the animal instinct of self-preservation suffices to impel the Jacobins onward, and, for a long time, their clear-sighted men, among them Siéyès, their thinker and oracle, have told them that "if they make peace they are lost."[114] To exercise their violence within they require

111. Carnot, ii., 152. "Do you suppose, replied Rewbell, that I want the Cape and Trinquemale restored for Holland? The first point is to take them, and to do that Holland must furnish the money and the vessels. After that I will make them see that these colonies belong to us."

112. Lord Malmesbury, "Diary," iii., 526. (Letter from Paris, Fructidor 17, year V.)—*Ibid.*, 483. (Conversation of Mr. Ellis with Mr. Pain.)

113. *Ibid.*, iii., 519, 544. (The words of Maret and Colchen.)—"Rewbell," says Carnot, "seems to be perfectly convinced that probity and civism are two absolutely incompatible things."

114. Mallet-Dupan, ii., 49. Words of Siéyès, March 27, 1797. *Ibid*, i., 258, 407; ii., 4, 49, 350, 361, 386. This is so true that this prevision actuates the concessions of the English ambassador. (Lord Malmesbury, "Diary," iii., 519.

peril without; lacking the pretext of public safety they cannot prolong their usurpation, their dictatorship, their despotism, their inquisition, their proscriptions, their exactions. Suppose that peace is
effected, will it be possible for the government, hated and despised
as it is, to maintain and elect its minions against public clamor at
the coming elections? Will so many retired generals consent to live
on half-pay, indolent and obedient? Will Hoche, so ardent and so
absolute, will Bonaparte, who already meditates his *coup-d'état*,[115] be
willing to stand sentry for four petty lawyers or litterateurs without
any titles and for Barras, a street-general, who never saw a regular
battle? Moreover on this skeleton of France, desiccated by five years
of spoliation, how can the armed swarm be fed even provisionally,
the swarm, which, for two years past, subsists only through devouring neighboring nations? Afterwards, how disband four hundred thousand hungry officers and soldiers? And how, with an empty
Treasury, supply the millions which, by a solemn decree, under the
title of a national recompense, have once more just been promised
to them.[116] Nothing but a prolonged war, or designedly begun again,
a war indefinitely and systematically extended, a war supported by
conquest and pillage can give armies food, keep generals busy, the

---

Letter to Canning. August 29, 1797.) "I am the more anxious for peace because,
in addition to all the commonplace reasons, I am convinced that peace will palsy
this country most completely, that all the violent means they have employed
for war will return upon them like an humour driven in and overset entirely
their weak and baseless constitution. This consequence of peace is so much
more to be pressed, as the very best conditions we could offer in the treaty."

115. Mathieu Dumas, iii., 256—Miot de Melito, i., 163, 191. (Conversations
with Bonaparte June and September, 1797.)

116. Mallet-Dupan, "Mercure Britannique," No. for November 10, 1798.
How support gigantic and exacting crimes on its own soil? How can it flatter
itself that it will extract from an impoverished people, without manufactures,
trade or credit, nearly a billion of direct and indirect subsidies? How renew
that immense fund of confiscations on which the French republic has lived for
the past eight years? By conquering every year a new nation and devastating
its treasuries, its character, its *monts-de-piété*, its owners of property. The Republic, for ten years past, would have laid down its arms had it been reduced
to its own capital.

nation resigned, the maintenance of power of the ruling faction, and secure to the Directors their places, their profits, their dinners and their mistresses. And this is why they, at first, break with England through repeated exactions, and then with Austria and the Emperor, through premeditated attacks, and again with Switzerland, Piedmont, Tuscany, Naples, Malta, Russia, and even the Porte.[117] At length, the veils fall and the character of the sect stands out nakedly. Defence of the country, deliverance of the people, all its grand phrases disappear in the realm of empty words. It reveals itself just as it is, an association of pirates on a cruise, who after ravaging their own coast, go further off and capture bodies and goods, men and things. Having eaten France, the Parisian band undertakes to eat all Europe, "leaf by leaf, like the head of an artichoke."[118]

Why recount the tragic comedy they play at home and which they repeat abroad? The piece abroad is the same as that played in Paris for the past eight years,[119] an absurd, hasty translation in Flemish, Dutch, German, and Italian, a local adaptation, just as it happens, with variations, elisions, and abbreviations, but always with the same ending, a shower of blows with gun and sword on all property-owners, communities, and individuals, compelling the surrender of their purses and valuables of every description, and which they gave up, even to remaining without a sou or even a shirt. As a rule, the nearest general, or resident titulary in every small state which has to be turned to account, stirs up malcontents against the established authorities, never lacking under the ancient régime, es-

117. Mallet-Dupan, "Mercure Britannique," Nos. for November 25, and December 25, 1798, and *passim*.

118. *Ibid.*, No. for January 25, 1799. "The French Republic is eating Europe leaf by leaf like the head of an artichoke." It revolutionises nations that it may despoil them, and it despoils them that it may subsist."

119. Letter of Mallet-Dupan to a deputy on a declaration of war against Venice and on the Revolution effected at Genoa. (The "Quotidienne," Nos. 410, 413, 414, 421.)—*Ibid.*, "Essai Historique sur la destruction de le Signe et de le Liberté Historique." (Nos. 1, 2, and 3 of the "Mercure Britannique.")— Carnot, ii., 153. (Words of Carnot in relation to the Swiss proceedings of the Directory.) "It is the fable of the Wolf and the Lamb."

pecially all social outcasts, adventurers, coffee-house ranters and young hot-heads, in short the Jacobins of the country; these, to the French representative, are henceforth the *people* of the country, if only a knot of the vilest sort. The legal authorities are forbidden to repress them, or punish them; they are inviolable. Employing threats or main force, he interferes in their support, or to sanction their assaults; he breaks up, or obliges them to break up, the vital organ of society; here, royalty or aristocracy, there, the senate and the magistracy, everywhere the old hierarchy, all cantonal, provincial, and municipal statutes and secular federation or constitutions. He then inaugurates on this cleared ground the government of Reason, that is to say, some artificial imitation of the French constitution; he himself, to this end, appoints the new magistrates. If he allows them to be elected, it is by his clients and under his bayonets; this constitutes a subject republic under the name of an ally, and which commissioners despatched from Paris manage to the beat of the drum. The revolutionary régime with anti-Christian despoiling and levelling laws, is despotically applied. The 18th of Fructidor is carried out over and over again; the constitution is revised according to the last Parisian pattern, while the Corps Legislatif and Directory are repeatedly purged in military fashion;[120] only valets are tolerated at the head of it: its army is added to the French army; twenty thousand Swiss are drafted in Switzerland and made to fight against the Swiss and the friends of Switzerland; Belgium, incorporated with France, is subjected to the conscription; national and religious sentiment is made the fulcrum of oppression and injury even to the provocation of mobs,[121] religious and national, five or six rural and

120. Overhauling of the Constitution, or purgation of the authorities in Holland by Delacroix. January 22, 1798, in Cisalpine by Berthier, February, 1798, by Trouve, August, 1798, by Brune, September, 1798, in Switzerland by Rapinat, June, 1798, etc.

121. Mallet-Dupan ("Mercure Britannique," numbers for November 26, December 25, 1798, March 10 and July 10, 1799). Details and documents relating to popular insurrections in Belgium, Switzerland, Suabia, Modena, the Roman States, Piedmont, and Upper Italy.—Letter of an officer in the French army

lasting Vendées in Belgium, Switzerland, Piedmont, Venetia, Lombardy, the Roman States and Naples, while fire, pillaging and shooting are employed to repress them. Any description of this would be feeble; statements in figures are necessary and I can give but two.

One of them is the list of robberies committed abroad,[122] and this comprises only the rapine executed according to order; it omits

---

dated at Turin and printed at Paris. "Wherever the civil commissioners pass the people rise in insurrection, and, although I have come near being a victim of these insurrections four times, I cannot blame the poor creatures; even the straw of their beds is taken. Most of Piedmont, as I wrote, has risen against the French *robbers*, as they call us. Will you be surprised when I tell you that, since the pretended revolution of this country, three or four months ago, we have devoured ten millions of coin, fifteen millions of paper money, with the diamonds, furniture, etc., of the Crown? The people judge us according to our actions and regard us with horror and execrations."

122. Mallet-Dupan, *Ibid.*, number for January, 1799. (List according to articles, with details, figures and dates.)—*Ibid.*, No. for May 25, 1799: details of the sack of Rome according to the "Journal" of M. Duppa, an eye witness.—*Ibid.*, Nos. for February 10 and 25, 1799: details of spoliation in Switzerland, Lombardy, Lucca, and Piedmont.—The following figures show the robberies committed by individuals: In Switzerland, "the Directorial commissary, Rapinat, the major-general, Schawembourg and the ordinance commissary, Rouhière, each carried away a million *tournois*." "Rouhière, besides this, levied 20 per cent. on each contract he issued, which was worth to him three hundred and fifty thousand livres. His first secretary Toussaint, stole in Berne alone, one hundred and fifty thousand livres. The secretary of Rapinat, Amberg, retired with three hundred thousand livres." General Lorge carried off one hundred and fifty thousand livres in specie, besides a lot of gold medals taken from the Hôtel-de-Ville at Berne; his two brigadier-generals, Rampon and Pijon, each appropriated two hundred and sixteen thousand livres. "Gen. Duheur, encamped in Brisgav, sent daily to the three villages at once the bills of fare for his meals and ordered requisitions for them; he demanded of one, articles in kind and, simultaneously, specie of another. He was content with one hundred florins a day, which he took in provisions and then in money."—"Massena, on entering Milan at eleven o'clock in the evening, had carried off in four hours, without giving any inventory or receipt, all the cash-boxes of the convents, hospitals and *monts-de-piété*, which were enormously rich, taking also, among others, the casket of diamonds belonging to Prince Belgioso. That night was worth to Massena one million two hundred thousand livres." (Mallet-Dupan, "Mercure Britannique," February 10, 1799, and "Journal," MS., March, 1797.)

private plunderings without any orders by officers, generals, soldiers, and commissaries; these are enormous, but cannot be estimated. The only approximative total which can be arrived at, is the authentic list of robberies which the Jacobin corsair, authorised by letters of marque, had already committed in December, 1798, outside of France, on public or on private parties; exactions in coin imposed in Belgium, Holland, Germany and Italy, amounting to six hundred and fifty-five millions; seizure and removal of gold and silver objects, plate, jewels, works of art, and other precious objects, three hundred and five millions; requisitions of provisions, three hundred and sixty-one millions; confiscations of the real and personal property of deposed sovereigns, that of the regular and secular clergy, that of corporations and associations even laic, of absent or fugitive proprietors, seven hundred millions; in all, in three years two billion livres. If we closely examine this monstrous sum, we find, as in the coffers of an Algerian pirate, a booty which up to this time, belligerent Christians, commanders of regular armies, would have shrunk from taking, and on which the Jacobin chiefs incontinently and preferably lay hands; the plate and furniture of churches in the Netherlands, in Liège, and in the Electoral sections of the Lower Rhine, twenty-five millions; the plate and furniture of churches in Lombardy, in the three Legations, in the State of Venice, in Modena, and the States of the Church, sixty-five millions; diamonds, plate, gold crosses and other depots of the *Monts-de-piété* at Milan, Bologna, Ravenna, Modena, Venice and Rome, fifty-six millions; furniture and works of art at Milan and in other towns, five millions; furniture and works of art in the Venetian towns and palaces of Brenta, six million five hundred thousand; the spoils of Rome sacked, as formerly by the mercenaries of the Duc de Bourbon, collections of

---

On the sentiments of the Italians, cf. the letter of Lieutenant Dupin, Prairial 27, year VIII.; (G. Sand, "Histoire de ma Vie," ii., 251) one account of the battle of Marengo, lost up to two o'clock in the afternoon; "I already saw that the Po, and the Tessin were to be crossed, a country to traverse *of which every inhabitant is our enemy.*"

antiques, pictures, bronzes, statues, the treasures of the Vatican and of palaces, jewels, even the pastoral ring of the Pope, which the Directorial commissary himself wrests from the Pope's finger, forty-three millions, and all this without counting analogous articles, and especially direct assessments levied on this or that individual as rich or a proprietor,[123] veritable ransoms, similar to those demanded by the bandits of Calabria and Greece, extorted from any traveller they surprise on the highway. Naturally operations of this kind cannot be carried on without instruments of constraint; the Parisian manipulators must have military automatons, "sabre hilts" in sufficient numbers. Now, through constant slashing, a good many hilts break, and the broken ones must be replaced; in October, 1798, two hundred thousand new ones are required, while the young men drafted for the purpose fail to answer the summons and fly, and even resist with arms, especially in Belgium,[124] by maintaining a revolt for many

123. Mallet-Dupan, *ibid.*, number for January 10, 1791. "December 31, 1796. Marquis Litta had already paid assessments amounting to five hundred thousand livres *milanais*. Marquis T., four hundred and twenty thousand, Count G., nine hundred thousand, and other proprietors in proportion." Ransom of the "*Decurioni* of Milan, and other hostages sent into France, one million five hundred thousand livres." This is in conformity with the Jacobin theory. In the old instructions of Carnot, we read the following sentence: "Assessments must be laid exclusively on the rich; the people must see that we are only liberators. . . . Enter as benefactors of the people, and at the same time as the scourge of the great, the rich and enemies of the French name." (Carnot, i., 433.)

124. Ludovic Sciout, iv., 776. (Reports of the year VII., Archives Nationales, F⁷, 7,701 and 7,718). "Out of one thousand four hundred men composing the first auxiliary battalion of conscripts, one thousand and eighty-seven cowardly deserted their flag (Haute-Loire), and out of nine hundred recently recruited at Puy, to form the nucleus of the second battalion, eight hundred again have imitated their example."—Dufort de Cheverney, "Mèmoires," September, 1799. "We learned that out of four hundred conscripts confined in the (Blois) château, who were to set out that night, one hundred had disappeared."—October 12, 1799. "The conscripts are in the château to the number of five hundred or six hundred. They say that they will not desert until out of the department and on the road, so as not to compromise their families."—October 14, "Two hundred have deserted, leaving about three hundred."—Archives Nationales, F⁷, 3,267. (Reports every ten days on refractory conscripts or deserters arrested by the

months, with this motto: "Better die here than elsewhere."[125] To compel their return, they are hunted down and brought to the depot with their hands tied; if they hide away, soldiers are stationed in their parents' houses; if the conscript or drafted man has sought refuge in a foreign country, even in an allied country as in Spain, he is officially inscribed on the list of *émigrés,* and therefore, in case of return, shot within twenty-four hours; meanwhile, his property is sequestrated and likewise that of "his father, mother, and grand-parents."[126] "Formerly," says a contemporary, "reason and philoso-phy thundered against the rigors of punishment inflicted on desert-ers; but, since French reason has perfected Liberty it is no longer the small class of regular soldiers whose evasion is punished with death, but an entire generation. An extreme penalty no longer suf-fices for these legislative philanthropists: they add confiscation, they despoil parents for the misdemeanors of their children, and render even women responsible for a military and personal offence." Such is the admirable calculation of the Directory—that, if it loses a soldier it gains a patrimony, and if the patrimony fails, it recovers the soldier: in any event, it fills its coffers and its ranks, while the faction, well-supplied with men, may continue turning all Europe to account, wasting, in the operation, as many French lives as it pleases; requiring more than one hundred thousand men per annum, which, including those which the Convention has squandered, makes nearly nine hundred thousand in eight years.[127] At this moment the

military police, year VIII. Department of Seine-et-Oise.) In this department alone, there are sixty-six arrests in Vendémiaire, one hundred and thirty-six in Brumaire, fifty-six in Frimaire and eighty-six in Pluviose.

125. Mallet-Dupan, No. for January 25, 1799. (Letter from Belgium.) "The revolt today is the United Provinces against the Duke of Alba. Never have the Belgians since Philip II. displayed similar motives for resistance and ven-geance."

126. Decrees of Fructidor 19, year VI. and Vendémiaire 27, year VII.— (Mallet-Dupan, No. for November 25, 1798.)

127. M. Léonce de Lavergne ("Economie rurale de la France since 1789," p. 38) estimates at a million the number of men sacrificed in the wars between 1792 and 1800.—Mallet-Dupan. (No. for December 10, 1798.)—*Ibid.* (No. for

five Directors and their minions are completing the mowing down of the virile, adult strength of the nation,[128] and we know through what motives and for what object. I do not believe that any civilised nation was ever sacrificed in the same way, for such a purpose and

---

March 20, 1799.) "Dumas stated, in the Corps Legislatif, that the National Guard had renewed the battalions of the defenders of the country three times. . . . The fact of the shameful administration of the hospitals is proved through the admissions of generals, commissaries and deputies, the soldiers dying for want of food and medicine. If we add to this the prodigality of lives by the leaders of the armies we can readily comprehend this triple renewal in the space of seven years."—("Histoire du Village de Croissy, Seine-et-Oise pendant la Révolution," by Campenon.) A village of four hundred and fifty inhabitants in 1789 furnished (1792 and 1793) fifty soldiers.—Meissner, "Voyage à Paris," p. 338, latter end of 1795): La Vendée was a bottomless pit, like Spain and Russia afterwards. A good republican, who had to supply the Vendée army with provisions for fifteen months, assured me that out of two hundred thousand men whom he had seen precipitated into this gulf there were not ten thousand that came of it."—The following figures ("Statistiques des Préfets" years IX. and X.) are exact. Eight departments (Doubs, Ain, Eure, Meurthe, Aisne, Aude, Drôme, Moselle) furnish the total number of their volunteers, recruits and conscripts, amounting to one hundred and ninety-one thousand three hundred and forty-three. These three departments (Arthur Young, "Voyage en France," ii., 31) had, in 1790, a population of two million four hundred and forty-six thousand souls; the proportion indicates that out of twenty-six million Frenchmen a little more than two millions went with the armies.—On the other hand, five departments (Doubs, Eure, Meurthe, Aisne, Moselle) gave, not only the number of their soldiers, one hundred and thirty-one thousand three hundred and twenty-two, but likewise that of their dead, fifty-six thousand nine hundred and seventy-six, that is to say, four hundred and thirty-five out of every thousand men furnished. This proportion shows eight hundred and seventy thousand dead out of two million soldiers.

128. The statistics of the prefects and reports of council-generals of the year IX. all agree in the statements of the notable diminution of the masculine adult population.—Lord Malmesbury had already made the same observation in 1796. ("Diary," October 21 and 23, 1796, from Calais to Paris.) "Children and women were working in the fields. Men evidently reduced in number. . . . Carts often drawn by women and most of them by old people or boys. It is plain that the male population has diminished; for the women we saw on the road surpassed the number of men in the proportion of four to one." Wherever the number of the population is filled up it is through the infantile and feminine increase.

by such rulers: the crippled remnant of a faction and sect, some hundreds of preachers no longer believing in their creed, usurpers as despised as they are detested, second-rate parvenus raised their heads not through their capacity or merit, but through the blind upheavals of a revolution, swimming on the surface for lack of weight, and, like foul scum, borne along to the crest of the wave— such are the wretches who strangle France under the pretence of setting her free, who bleed her under the pretence of making her strong, who conquer populations under the pretence of emancipating them, who despoil people under the pretence of regenerating them, and who, from Brest to Lucerne, from Amsterdam to Naples, slay and rob wholesale, systematically, to strengthen the incoherent dictatorship of their brutality, folly and corruption.

IX

Once again has triumphant Jacobinism shown its antisocial nature, its capacity for destruction, its impotence to reconstruct. The nation, vanquished and discouraged, no longer resists, but, if it submits it is as to a pestilence, while its transportations, its administrative purifications, its decrees placing towns in a state of siege, its daily violence, only exasperate the mute antipathy. "Everything has been done," says an honest Jacobin,[129] "to alienate the immense majority of citizens from the Revolution and the Republic, even those who had contributed to the downfall of the monarchy. . . . Instead of seeing the friends of the Revolution increase as we have advanced on the revolutionary path . . . we see our ranks thinning out and the early defenders of liberty deserting our cause." It is impossible for the Jacobins to rally France and reconcile her to their ways and dogmas, and on this point their own agents leave no illusion. "Here,"

Nearly all the prefects and council-generals state that precocious marriages have multiplied to excess through conscription.—Dufort de Cheverney, "Mémoires," September 1, 1800. "The conscription having spared the married, all the young men married at the age of sixteen. The number of children in the commune is double and triple what it was formerly."

129. Sauzay, x., 471. (Speech by Representative Biot, Aug. 29, 1799.)

writes the Troyes agent,[130] "public spirit not only needs to be revived, but it needs to be re-created. Scarcely one-fifth of the citizens side with the government, and this fifth is hated and despised by the majority. . . . Who attend upon and celebrate the national fêtes? Public functionaries whom the law summons to them, and many of these fêtes often dispense with them. It is the same public spirit which does not allow honest folks to take part in them and in the addresses made at them, and which keeps the women away who ought to be their principal ornament. . . . The same public spirit looks only with indifference and contempt on the republican, heroic actions given on the stage, and welcomes with transport all that bears any allusion to royalty and the ancient régime. The parvenus themselves of the Revolution, the generals, the deputies, dislike Jacobin institutions;[131] they place their children in the chapel schools and send them to the confessional, while the deputies who, in '92 and '93, showed the most animosity to priests, do not consider their daughter well-brought up unless she has made her first communion." The little are still more hostile than the great. "A fact unfortunately too true," writes the commissary of a rural canton,[132] "is that the people *en masse* seem not to want any of our institutions. . . . It is considered well-bred, even among country folks, to show disdain for everything characteristic of republican usages. . . . Our rich farmers, who have profited most by the Revolution, are the bitterest enemies of its forms: any citizen who depended on them for the slightest favor and thought it well to address them as *citizen*, would be turned out of their houses. Citizen is an insult, and *patriot* a still

130. Albert Babeau, ii., 466. (Letter of Milany, July 1, 1798, and report by Pout, Messidor, year VI.)

131. Schmidt, iii., 374. (Reports on the situation of the department of the Seine, Ventose, year VII.)—Dufort de Cheverney, "Mémoires," October 22, 1799. "The column of militia sets out today; there are no more than thirty persons in it, and these again are all paid or not paid clerks, attachés of the Republic, all these belonging to the department, to the director of domains, in fine, all the bureaux."

132. Schmidt, iii., 313. (Report of Guyel, Commissary of the Directory in the canton of Pierrefitte, Seine, Germinal, year VI.)

greater one; for this term signifies Jacobin, partisan, murderer, robber[133] and, as they were then styled, "man-eaters." What is worse
is that a falsification of the word has brought discredit on the thing."
Nobody, say the reports, troubles himself about the general interest;[134] nobody will serve as national guard or mayor. "Public spirit
has fallen into such a lethargic slumber as to make one fear its
complete collapse. Our successes or our failures excite neither un-
easiness nor pleasure.[135] It seems, on reading the accounts of battles,
as if it were the history of another people. The changes that take
place within our borders no longer excite any emotion; one asks out
of curiosity, one is answered without any interest, one learns with
indifference." "The pleasures of Paris[136] are not disturbed a moment
by any of the crises which succeed each other, nor by those which
are feared. Never were the theatres and public entertainments more
frequented. At the 'Tivoli,' it is said that it is going to be worse
than ever; the country (*patrie*) is called *la patraque,* and dancing
goes on." This is intelligible; how can one interest one's self in the
public weal when there is none, when the common patrimony of all
has become the private property of a band, when this band is devouring or wasting all in the interior and outside the frontier, where
it is playing pitch and toss? The Jacobins, through their final victory,
have dried patriotism up, that is to say, the deep inward spring which

133. M. de Lafayette, "Mémoires," ii., 162. (Letter of July 22, 1799.) "The
other day, at the mass in St. Roch, a man by the side of our dear Grammont,
said fervently: "My God, have mercy on us, exterminate the nation!" This,
indeed, simply meant: "My God, deliver us from the Convention system!"

134. Schmidt, 298, 352, 377, 451, etc. (Ventose, Frimaire and Fructidor,
year VII.)

135. *Ibid.,* iii. (Reports of Prairial, year III., department of the Seine.)

136. M. de Lafayette, "Mémoires," ii., 164. (Letter of July 14, 1799.)—De
Tocqueville, "Oeuvres complètes," v., 270. (Testimony of a contemporary.)—
Sauzay, x., 470, 471. (Speeches by Briot and de Chasseriaux.) "I cannot understand the frightful state of torpor into which minds have fallen; people have
come to believing nothing, to feeling nothing, to doing nothing. . . . The great
nation which had overcome all and created everything around her, seems to
exist only in the armies and in a few generous souls."

supplies the substance, the vitality and the force of the State. In vain
do they multiply rigorous decrees and imperious prescriptions; each
energetic blow is half deadened against the general and mute resistance of voluntary inertia and of insurmountable disgust; they do
not obtain from their subjects any of that mechanical obedience, that
degree of passive coöperation, without which the law remains a dead
letter.[137] Their Republic, so young, "is attacked by that nameless
malady which commonly attacks only old governments, a species of
senile consumption to which one can give no other definition than
that of the *difficulty of living;* nobody strives to overthrow it, although it seems to have lost the power of standing erect."[138]

Not only does their domination paralyse instead of animating the
State, but, with their own hands, they undermine the order they
themselves have established; whether legal or extra-legal, it makes
no difference: although they reign, no constitution, made and re-
made, no government, not even that of their chief, can subsist. Once
masters of France, they quarrel over it amongst themselves, each
claiming for himself the whole of the prey. Those who are in office
want to stay there; those who are out want to get in. Thus is formed

137. Lord Malmesbury's "Diary," (November 5, 1796). "At Randonneau's,
who published all the acts and laws. . . . Very talkative, but clever. . . . Ten
thousand laws published since 1789, but only seventy enforced."—Ludovic
Sciout, iv., 770. (Reports of year VII.) In Puy de Dome: "Out of two hundred
and eighty-six communes there are two hundred in which the agents have
committed every species of forgery on the registers of the *Etat-Civil,* and in
the copying of its acts, to clear individuals of military service. Here, young men
of twenty and twenty-five are married to women of seventy-two and eighty
years of age, and even to those who have long been dead; then, an extract from
the death register clears a man who is alive and well." "Forged contracts are
presented to avoid military service, young soldiers are married to women of
eighty; one woman, thanks to a series of forgeries, is found married to eight or
ten conscripts." (Letter of an officer of the Gendarmerie to Roanne, Ventose 9,
year VIII.)

138. Words of De Tocqueville.—"Le Duc de Broglie," by M. Guizot, p.
16. (Words of the Duc de Broglie.) "Those who were not living at this time
could form no idea of the profound discouragement into which France had
fallen in the interval between Fructidor 18 and Brumaire 18."

two factions, while each repeats against the other the *coup d'état* which both have together carried out against the nation. According to the ruling coterie, its adversaries are simply "anarchists," former *Septembriseurs,* Robespierre's confederates, the accomplices of Baboeuf, eternal conspirators. Now, as in the year VI., the five agents still keep the sabre-hilt firm in their grasp, and they can oblige the Corps Legislatif to vote as they please; on the 22d of Floréal, the government cancels, in whole or in part, in forty-five departments, the new elections, not alone those of representatives, but again those of judges, public prosecutors, and the grand-jurymen; then, it dismisses the terrorist administrations in the departments and towns.[139] According to the governing coterie, the Directory and its agents are false patriots, usurpers, oppressors, contemners of the law, dilapidators, and stupid politicians; as all this is true, and as the Directory, in the year VIII., used up through its twenty-one months of omnipotence, out of credit on account of its reverses, despised by its generals, hated by the beaten and unpaid army, dares no longer and can no longer raise the sabre, the ultra Jacobins resume the offensive, have themselves elected through their kith and kin, reconquer the majority in the Corps Legislatif, and, in their turn, purge the Directory on the 30 of Prairial. Treilhard, Merlin de Douai, and Larevellière-Lepaux are driven out; narrow fanatics replace them, Gohier, Moulins, and Roger Ducos; terrorist spirits install themselves in the Ministries, Robert Lindet in the Treasury, Fouché in the Police; after that, in the departments, they give office to, or restore "the exclusives," that is to say, the resolute scoundrels who have proved their capacity.[140] The Jacobins reopen their club under

139. Buchez et Roux, xxxviii., 480. (Message of the Directory, Floréal 13, year IV., and report of Bailleul, Floréal 18.) "When an election of deputies presented a *bad result* to us we thought it our duty to propose setting it aside. . . . It will be said that your project is a veritable proscription." "Not more so than the 19 of Fructidor."—Cf. for dismissals in the provinces, Sauzay, v., ch. 86.—Albert Babeau, ii., 486. During the four years the Directory lasted the municipal council of Troyes was renewed seven times, in whole or in part.

140. Buchez et Roux, xxxix., 61. (Session of Prairial 30, year VII.)—Sauzay,

its old name in the hall of the Manège; two directors and one hundred and fifty members of the Corps Legislatif fraternise with "all that the dregs of the people provide that is vilest and most disgusting." Eulogies are here pronounced on Robespierre and on Baboeuf himself; they demand the levy *en masse* and the disarming of "suspects." Jourdan exclaims in a toast, "Here's to the resurrection of pikes! May they in the people's hands crush out all its enemies!" In the Council of the Five Hundred, the same Jourdan proposes in the tribune to declare the "country in danger," while the gang of shouting politicians, the bull-dogs of the streets and tribunes, gather around the hesitating representatives and howl and threaten as in 1793.

Is it, then, the régime of 1793 which is about to be set up in France? Not even that one. Immediately after the victory, the victors of Prairial 30 separated and formed two camps of enemies, watching each other with arms in hand, intrenched and making sorties on each other; on one side are the simple bandits and the lowest of the populace, the tail (*queue*) of Marat, incorrigible monomaniacs, headstrong, conceited spirits proud of their crimes and disposed to repeat them rather than admit their guilt, the dogmatic simpletons who go ahead with their eyes shut and who have forgotten everything and learnt nothing; on the other side, men still possessing common sense, and who have profited somewhat by experience, who know what a

---

x., ch. 87.—Léouzon-Leduc, "Correspondence Diplomatique avec la cour de Suede," p. 293. (Letters of July 1, 7, 11, 19; August 4; September 23, 1799.) "The purification of functionaries, so much talked about now, has absolutely no other end in view but the removal of the partisans of one faction in order to substitute those of another faction without any regard to moral character. ... It is this choice of persons without probity, justice or any principles of honesty whatever for the most important offices which makes one tremble, and especially, at this moment, all who are really attached to their country." "The opening of the clubs must, in every relation, be deemed a disastrous circumstance. ... All classes of society are panic-stricken at the faintest probability of the reestablishment of a republican government copied after that of 1793. ... The party of political incendiaries in France is the only one which carries out such designs energetically and directly."

government of clubs and pikes leads to, who fear for themselves and are unwilling to begin again, step by step, the mad course on which at each stage, they have come near perishing; on one side two members of the Directory, the minority of the Ancients, the majority of the Five Hundred, and the vilest of the Parisian rabble; on the other, the majority of the Ancients, the minority of the Five Hundred, and three members of the Directory, the latter supported by their executive staff.[141] Which of the two troops will crush the other? Nobody knows; for most of them are ready to pass from one to the other camp according as the chances for succeeding become more or less great, and, from day to day, any defection amongst the Five Hundred, amongst the Ancients, or in the Directory, foreseen or not, may change a minority into a majority. Where will the majority be tomorrow? From which side is the next *coup d' état* to come? Who will make it? Will it be the ultra Jacobins, and, through another 9th of Thermidor, will they declare the mitigated Jacobins "outlaws"? Will it be the mitigated Jacobins, and, through another 18th of Fructidor, will they put the ultras under lock and key? If one or the other of these blows is struck, will it succeed? And if it succeeds will a stable government be at last established? Siéyès well knows that it will not; he is far seeing in his acts, although chimerical in his theories. In power himself, titular Director, counsellor and guardian of the intelligent republic against the stupid republic, he well knows that all of them, so long as they are republicans of both bands, take a road without an issue.[142] Barras is of the same opinion,

141. Léouzon-Leduc, *ibid.*, 328, 329. (Despatches of September 19 and 23.)—Mallet-Dupan, "Mercure Britannique." (No. for October 25, 1799. Letter from Paris, September 15. Exposition of the situation and tableau of the parties.) "I will add that the war waged with success by the Directory against the Jacobins (for, although the Directory is itself a Jacobin production, it wants no more of its masters), that this war, I say, has rallied people somewhat to the government without having converted anyone to the Revolution or really frightened the Jacobins who will pay them back if they have time to do it."

142. Gohier, "Mémoires," conversation with Siéyès on his entry into the Directory. "Here we are," says Siéyès to him, "members of a government

and taking time by the forelock, turns around and promises Louis XVIII. his coöperation in restoring the legitimate monarchy; in exchange he receives letters patent granting him full pardon, exemption from all future prosecution and a promise of twelve millions. Siéyès, more sagacious, seeks force where it exists, in the army; he prepares Joubert, sounds Moreau, thinks of Jourdan, of Bernadotte and of Macdonald, before surrendering himself to Bonaparte; "he requires a sword." Boulay de la Meurthe, comparing in a pamphlet the English revolution with the French revolution, announces and brings on the establishment of a military protectorate. "The Constitution of the year III. will not work," said Baudin, one of the Five Hundred, to Cornet, one of the Ancients, "only I do not see when to find *the executive arm*." The Jacobin republic still lives, and its servants, its doctors, already speak aloud of its interment the same as strangers and heirs in the room of a dying man who has become unconscious, like Tiberius when sinking in his palace at Misene.[143] If the expiring man does not go fast enough some one will help him. The old monster, borne down with crimes and rotten with vices, rattles in his throat on his purple cushions; his eyes are closed, his pulse is feeble, and he gasps for breath. Here and there, around his bed, stand groups of those who minister to his debauches at Capri and his murders at Rome, his minions and executioners who publicly take part in the new reign; the old one is finished; one need no longer be circumspect and mute before a corpse. Suddenly the dying man opens his eyes, speaks and asks for food. The military tribune, "the executive arm," boldly clears the apartment; he throws a pile of bedclothes over the old man's head and quickens the last sigh. Such is the final blow; an hour later and breathing stops.

---

which, as we cannot conceal from ourselves, is threatened with a coming fall. But when the ice melts skilful pilots can escape in the breaking up. A falling government does not always imperil those at the head of it."

143. Tacitus, "Annales," book vi., § 50. "Macro, intrepidus, opprimi senem injectu multae vestis discedique a limine."

X

If the Jacobin Republic dies, it is not merely on account of decrepitude, nor because of its murders, but, and above all, because it is not born viable: at the outset it harbored within itself a principle of dissolution, an innate mortal poison, not alone for others but for itself. That which maintains a political society is the *mutual respect of its members*, especially the respect of the governed for its rulers and of the rulers for the governed, and, therefore, habits of mutual trust and confidence; on the part of the governed, a well-grounded certainty that the rulers will not attack private rights, and, on the part of the rulers, a well-founded certainty that the governed will not attack public powers; both inwardly recognising that these rights, more or less broad or restricted, are inviolable; that these powers, more or less ample or limited, are legitimate; in fine, each being convinced that, in case of conflict, the trial will be conducted according to forms which law or custom provide; that pending the discussion, the strongest will not abuse his strength, and that, when the discussion is over, the successful party will not wholly sacrifice the loser. Only on this condition can there be concord between governors and the governed, the concurrence of all in the common work, internal tranquillity, and, accordingly, stability, security, wellbeing, and force. Without this deep and persistent disposition of minds and hearts, the bond of union among men is wanting. It constitutes the brightest of social sentiments; it may be said that this is the soul of which the State is the body. Now, in the Jacobin State, this soul has perished; it has not died out through unforeseen accidents, but through a forced result of the system, through a practical effect of the speculative theory, which, converting each man into an absolute sovereign, sets every man warring against other men, and which, under the pretence of regenerating the human species, lets loose, authorises and consecrates the worst instincts of human nature, all the lusts of license, tyranny and domination. In the name of the ideal people whom it declares sovereign, and which has no existence, the Jacobins have violently usurped all public powers, brutally abolished all private rights, regarding the actual living people as a beast of burden, and yet worse, as an automation, subjecting their human automation to the cruellest restraints in order to mechanically maintain it in the antinormal, rigid posture, which, according to principles, they inflict upon it. Thenceforth, all ties are sundered between them and the nation; to prey upon, bleed and starve this nation, to reconquer it after it had escaped them, to repeatedly enchain and gag it—all this they could well do; but to reconcile it to their government, never! Between them, and for the same reason, through another consequence of the same theory, and another effect of the same lusts, no bond between them would hold. Each faction inside of the party, having forged its ideal people according to its own logical process and necessities, exercised the orthodox privilege of claiming the monopoly of sovereignty;[144] to secure the benefits of omnipotence, it has combated its rivals with falsified, annulled, or constrained elections, with plots and mendacity, with ambushes and sudden assaults, with the pikes of the rabble and with the bayonets of soldiers; it has then massacred, guillotined, shot, and transported the vanquished as tyrants, traitors, or rebels, and the survivors do not forget this. They have learnt what their so called eternal constitutions amount to; they know how to estimate their proclamations and oaths, their respect for law, their justice,

144. Mallet-Dupan, "Mercure Britannique." (Nos. for December 25, 1798 and December 10, 1799.) "From the very beginning of the Revolution, there never was, in the uproar of patriotic protestations, amidst so many popular effusions of devotion to the popular cause and to Liberty in the different parties, but one fundamental conception, that of grasping power after having instituted it, of using every means of strengthening themselves, and of excluding the largest number from it, in order to centre themselves in a privileged committee. As soon as they had hurried through the articles of their constitution and seized the reins of government, the dominant party conjured the nation to trust to it, notwithstanding that the farce of their reasoning would not bring about obedience. . . . Power and money and money and power, all projects for guaranteeing their own heads and disposing of those of their competitors, end in that. From the agitators of 1789 to the tyrants of 1798, from Mirabeau to Barras, each labors only to forcibly open the gates of riches and authority and to close them behind them."

their humanity; they understand them and know that they are all so many fraternal Cains,[145] all more or less debased, dangerous, soiled and depraved by their work; distrust with such men is irremediable. They can still turn out manifests, decrees and cabals, and get up revolutions, but they can no longer agree amongst themselves and heartily defer to the justified ascendency and recognised authority of any one or more among their own body. After ten years of mutual assault there is not one among the three thousand legislators who have sat in the sovereign assemblies that can count on the deference and loyalty of a hundred Frenchmen. The social body is disintegrated; amongst the millions of disconnected atoms not a nucleus of spontaneous cohesion and stable coördination remains. It is impossible for civil France to reconstruct itself; as impossible as it would be to build a Notre Dame of Paris, or a St. Peter's of Rome out of the slime of the streets or the dust of the highways.

With military France it is otherwise. Here, men have made trial of each other, and are devoted to each other, subordinates to their leaders, and all to one great work. The sentiments are strong and healthy which bind human wills with one fasces of mutual sympathy, trust, esteem, and admiration, and all these superabound, while the free companionship which still subsists between inferior and superior,[146] that gay unrestrained familiarity so dear to the French, draws the knot still closer. In this world unsullied by political defilements and ennobled by habits of abnegation,[147] there is all that constitutes

145. Mallet-Dupan, *ibid.*, No. for April 10, 1799. On the Jacobins. "The sources of their enmities, the prime motive of their fury, their *coup-d'état* lay in their constant mistrust of each other. . . . Systematic, immoral factionists, cruel through necessity and treacherous through prudence, will always attribute perverse intentions. Carnot admits that there were not ten men in the Convention that were conscious of probity."

146. See in this respect "Histoire de ma Vie," by George Sand, volumes 2, 3, and 4, the correspondence of her father enlisted as a volunteer in 1798 and a lieutenant at Marengo.—Cf. Marshal Marmont, "Mémoires," i., 186, 282, 296, 304. "Our ambition, at this moment, was wholly secondary; we were occupied solely with our duties or pleasures. The most cordial and frankest union prevailed amongst us all."

147. "Journal de Marche du sergent Fracasse."—"Les Cahiers du Capitaine

an organised and visible society, a hierarchy, not external and ve-
neered, but moral and deep-seated, with uncontested titles, recognised superiorities, an accepted subordination, rights and duties
stamped on all consciences, in brief, what has always been wanting
in revolutionary institutions, the discipline of sentiments and emotions. Give to these men a countersign and they do not discuss;
provided it is legal, or seems so, they act accordingly, not merely
against strangers, but against Frenchmen: thus, already on the 13th
Vendémiaire they mowed down the Parisians, and on the the 18th
of Fructidor they purged the Corps Legislatif. Let a famous general
appear, and provided he respects formalities, they will follow him
and once more repeat the operation. One does appear, one who for
three years has thought of nothing else, but who on this occasion
will repeat the operation only for his own advantage; he is the most
illustrious of all, and precisely the conductor or promoter of the two
previous ones, the very same who personally brought about the 13th
of Vendémiaire, and likewise, at the hands of his lieutenant, Augereau, the 18th of Fructidor. Let him be authorised by the semblance
of a decree, let him be appointed major-general of the armed force
by a minority of one of the Councils, and the army will march
behind him. Let him issue the usual proclamations, let him summon
"his comrades" to save the Republic and clear the hall of the Five
Hundred; his grenadiers will enter with fixed bayonets and even
laugh at the sight of the deputies, dressed as for the opera, scram-
bling off precipitately out of the windows.[148] Let him manage the
transitions, let him avoid the ill-sounding name of dictator, let him
assume a modest and yet classic revolutionary Roman title, let him
along with two others be simple consuls; the soldiers, who have
neither time nor leisure to be publicists and who are only skin-deep

---

Coignet."—Correspondence of Maurice Dupin in "Histoire de ma Vie," by
George Sand.

148. "Les Cahiers du Capitaine Coignet," p. 76. "And then we saw the big
gentlemen getting out of the windows. Mantles, caps and feathers lay on the
floor and the grenadiers ripped off the lace." *Ibid.*, 78, Narration by the gren-
adier Chome: "The pigeons all flew out of the window and we had the hall to
ourselves."

republicans, will ask nothing more; they regard their system as a very good one for the French people, the despotic system without which there can be no army, that which places the absolute command in the hands of one individual. Let him put down other Jacobins, let him revoke their late decrees on hostages and the forced loan, let him restore safety and security to persons, property, and consciences; let him bring back order, economy, and efficiency to the administrations; let him provide for public services, hospitals, roads and schools, the whole of civil France will welcome its liberator, protector, and restorer.[149] In his own words, the system he brings

149. Dufort de Cheverney, "Mémoires," September 1, 1800. "Bonaparte, being fortunately placed at the head of the government, advanced the Revolution more than fifty years; the cup of crimes was full and overflowing. He cut off the seven hundred and fifty heads of the hydra, concentrated power in his own hands, and prevented the primary assemblies from sending us another third of fresh scoundrels in the place of those about to take themselves off. . . . Since I stopped writing things are so changed as to make revolutionary events appear as if they had transpired more than twenty years ago. . . . The people are no longer tormented on account of the decade, which is no longer observed except by the authorities. . . . One can travel about the country without a passport. . . . Subordination is established among the troops; all the conscripts are coming back. . . . The government knows no party; a royalist is placed along with a determined republican, each being, so to say, neutralised by the other. The First Consul, more a King than Louis XIV., has called the ablest men to his councils without caring what they were."—Anne Plumptre, "A Narrative of Three Years' Residence in France from 1802 to 1805," i., 326, 329. "The class denominated the people is most certainly, taking it in the aggregate, favorably disposed to Bonaparte. Any tale of distress from the Revolution was among this class always ended with this, 'but now, we are quiet, thanks to God and to Bonaparte.'"—Mallet-Dupan, with his accustomed perspicacity ("Mercure Britainnique," Nos. for November 25 and December 10, 1799), at once comprehended the character and harmony of this last revolution. "The possible domination of the Jacobins chilled all ages and most conditions . . . Is that nothing, to be preserved, even for one year, against the ravages of a faction, under whose empire nobody can sleep tranquilly, and find that faction driven from all places of authority just at a time when everybody feared its second outburst, with its torches, its assassins, its taxers, and its agrarian laws, over the whole French territory? . . . That Revolution, of an entirely new species, appeared to us as fundamental as that of 1789."

is that of "the alliance of Philosophy with the Sword," philosophy meaning, as it was then understood, the application of abstract principles to politics, the logical construction of a State according to general and simple notices with a social plan, uniform, and rectilinear. Now as we have seen,[150] two of these plans square with this theory, one anarchical and the other despotic; naturally, the master adopts the latter, and, like a practical man, he builds according to that theory a substantial edifice, with sand and lime, habitable and well-suited to its purposes. All the masses of the great work—civil code, university, Concordat, prefectoral and centralised administration—all the details of its arrangement and distribution of places, tend to one general effect, which is the omnipotence of the State, the omnipresence of the government, the abolition of local and private initiative, the suppression of voluntary free association, the gradual dispersion of small spontaneous groupings, the preventive interdiction of prolonged hereditary works, the extinction of sentiments by which the individual lives beyond himself in the past or in the future. Never were finer barracks constructed, more symmetrical and more decorative in aspect, more satisfactory to superficial views, more acceptable to vulgar good sense, more suited to narrow egoism, better kept and cleaner, better adapted to the discipline of the average and low elements of human nature, and better adapted to etiolating or perverting the superior elements of human nature. In this philosophical barracks we have lived for eighty years.

150. The Ancient Régime, p. 144.

INDEX

Roman-numeral page numbers are in Volume I.

The typeface in which this book has been set is Monotype Fournier, a digitized version of the 1925 hot-metal release. It was based on Pierre Simon Fournier's "St. Augustin Ordinaire," cut in Paris in the 1740s. Fournier, one of the great innovators in the history of typography, devised a system of measurements, or points, to relate the size of type bodies to each other. His work built upon that of a committee established in 1692 by King Louis XIV to create a new series of types for the exclusive use of the Imprimerie Royale. This committee, supervised by the Academie des Sciences, moved to "rationalize" type. The transitional nature of the Romain du Roi, and later, Fournier, was, according to Stanley Morison, its own revolution: it marked the move away from humanistic, calligraphic traditions of typography to a more mechanized, disciplined art of engraving and punchcutting.

This book is printed on paper that is acid-free and meets the requirements of the American National Standard for Permanence of Paper for Printed Library Materials, Z39.48-1992. ⊗

Book design by Barbara E. Williams, Durham, North Carolina.

Typography by Impressions Book and Journal Services, Inc., Madison, Wisconsin.

Printed and bound by Edwards Brothers, Inc., Ann Arbor, Michigan.